INTRODUCTION TO BEHAVIORAL ECONOMICS

INTRODUCTION TO BEHAVIORAL ECONOMICS

NONECONOMIC FACTORS THAT SHAPE ECONOMIC DECISIONS

David R. Just
Cornell University

Vice President & Executive Publisher	George Hoffman
Executive Editor	Joel Hollenbeck
Content Editor	Jennifer Manias
Assistant Editor	Courtney Luzzi
Senior Editorial Assistant	Erica Horowitz
Director of Marketing	Amy Scholz
Assistant Marketing Manager	Puja Katariwala
Marketing Assistant	Mia Brady
Photo Editor	Felicia Ruocco
Senior Production Manager	Janis Soo
Associate Production Manager	Joel Balbin
Production Editor	Yee Lyn Song
Cover Designer	Kenji Ngieng
Cover Photo Credit	Alan Shortall/The Image Bank/Getty Images

This book was set in Times Regular by MPS Limited and printed and bound by Edwards Brothers Malloy. The cover was printed by Edwards Brothers Malloy.

This book is printed on acid-free paper.

Founded in 1807, John Wiley & Sons, Inc., has been a valued source of knowledge and understanding for more than 200 years, helping people around the world meet their needs and fulfill their aspirations. Our company is built on a foundation of principles that include responsibility to the communities we serve and where we live and work. In 2008, we launched a Corporate Citizenship Initiative, a global effort to address the environmental, social, economic, and ethical challenges we face in our business. Among the issues we are addressing are carbon impact, paper specifications and procurement, ethical conduct within our business and among our vendors, and community and charitable support. For more information, please visit our website: www.wiley.com/go/citizenship.

Library of Congress Cataloging-in-Publication Data

Just, David R.
    Introduction to behavioral economics: noneconomic factors that shape economic decisions /
David R. Just, Cornell University.
        pages   cm
    Includes bibliographical references and index.
    ISBN 978-0-470-59622-7 (pbk.)
        1. Economics–Psychological aspects.   2. Human behavior–Economic aspects.   I. Title.
HB74.P8J87 2014
330.01'9—dc23
                                                                                            2013019192

Printed in the United States of America
10 9 8 7 6 5 4 3 2 1

*To Vibeka, Liam, Alex and Caden for the inspiration
and education they have lovingly provided me.*

BRIEF CONTENTS

CONTENTS

ix

PART 2 INFORMATION AND UNCERTAINTY

6 BRACKETING DECISIONS   125

7 REPRESENTATIVENESS AND AVAILABILITY   156

PART 4   SOCIAL PREFERENCES

PREFACE

With the popularity of books such as *Nudge* or *Predictably Irrational*, we have seen a corresponding increase in interest among undergraduate students and professional students in behavioral economics. These concepts have great appeal to interested students because they are presented in the popular media as—at once—both novel and rooted in common sense or intuition. In my experience teaching behavioral economics I find that with each new irrational behavior I introduce, students are drawn in by the puzzle: why would someone would behave in such a way. This suspense makes them all the more engaged when it is time for the reveal— the behavioral explanation that makes the behavior intuitive. Over the first years of instructing I came to enjoy the in class response of the students to each of the anomalies, and especially those I could demonstrate with their own behavior in an in-class experiment. It wasn't until later that I realized just how important this class was. An alumnus of my class then employed gainfully on Wall Street, sought me out while visiting campus to tell me how the principles I had taught changed his career and how he viewed his life. He cited how several of the behavioral models in the class were now very important in determining a winning strategy, and encouraged me to drive this message home with the current crop of students. This was the first of many interactions with students having similar stories.

Who Should Use this Book

The primary audience for this book is juniors and seniors in economics and business programs who want to know how the theories of economics stack up against reality. The book may also be appropriate for some graduate programs. The book assumes that students have had a course in intermediate microeconomics. Most students of behavioral economics are not primarily seeking training as experimental economists or academic researchers in general. Rather they are lead by a desire to (1) learn to avoid the common pitfalls of irrational behavior, and (2) increase the profitability of employers by learning to take advantage of consumer behavior or (3) more accurately model or predict market outcomes. The current set of textbooks exploring areas of behavioral economics focus primarily on the research experiments that have fueled the discipline. These experiments hold an important place in training any behavioral economist. However, the proper audience for this book is interested in experiments more as a set of examples of the broader principles of behavior. This is a basic textbook on behavioral economics focusing on the broader principles of behavior. Behavioral economic principles are illustrated using real world examples, examples from the experimental literature as well as experiential examples in the form of laboratory exercises. While presenting experimental and real world examples are useful, a key to helping students understand behavioral economics is to put them in a position to experience the effects themselves. Thus, the instructions provided with the instructor's edition provides a set of classical classroom experiments that complement the material in this text.

Some pieces of the text require a calculus background. However, an attempt has been made to isolate these sections within Advanced Concept Boxes so that they may be easily skipped if necessary. Exercises related to these advanced sections are marked with a ¤. The overwhelming majority of behavioral economics can be described in simple language, graphs, examples and a few simple equations. Thus I have attempted to create a text that is flexible enough to be useful for a wide variety of audiences. Economics instructors, for example, may desire a more rigorous treatment of the mathematical models than many business instructors. Separate sections of each chapter focus on the modeling of behavior from an individual choice perspective, and on the implications of behavior from a profit-maximizing firm perspective. Economics training tends to focus attention on the individual choice model and implications for public policy and markets. Business teaching tends to focus on how firms profit motives can best be met given the behavior of individuals.

In addition to discussion of applications, significant space is devoted to management and policy implications. Behavioral economics has only recently begun to take seriously the potential impacts of behavioral theory on welfare economics and policy. Yet the contributions of Matthew Rabin and others have been substantial and influential. One important point of debate includes the role of government in helping individuals avoid mistakes in judgment. This has lead to heated debate about whether we can determine what is a mistake and what is simply an expression of preferences. Further, ethical issues can be raised when firms seek to take advantage of behavioral anomalies. Is it ethical to use auction mechanisms that are known to elicit winning bids that exceed the winner's willingness to pay? Should the government step in to regulate firms that take advantage of behavioral anomalies? These issues will be touched upon throughout the book, while the final chapter focuses attention of these issues in a much more thorough and rigorous discussion.

Philosophy

Behavioral economics seeks to explain common and systematic deviations from the behavior implied by rational economic models. These deviations are called behavioral anomalies. In order to appreciate what is and is not an anomaly, the student needs to have some basic understanding of the rational economic model taught in core economics classes. Indeed, I have found my own course in behavioral economics to be very useful in cementing a student's understanding of the basics of consumer, producer and elementary game theory concepts. In order to underscore the contrast between rational and irrational, each chapter contains sections that describe the standard economic model that is relevant to the behavior being explored. Advanced economics students who already appreciate these concepts will be able to make quick work of these sections and focus more attention on the deviations described. These deviations are called behavioral anomalies, and can often be explained or understood through the marriage of rational economic models with basic psychological principles.

Currently, most who teach behavioral economics have either resorted to using collections of academic papers (published anthologies or their own selections), or popular books written for a lay audience as text books. This creates two very distinct problems. The first is an issue of level. Using a collection of papers often requires students to have a deeper understanding than can be expected of an advanced undergraduate while using books for a lay audience can leave the reader with only a superficial understanding. An organized text can help bridge this gap, building a deeper treatment on a foundation of basic principles. The second issue is organization into topics. Many behavioral and experimental economics books are organized by topics, and present many diverse experiments with conflicting results together. While this is a reasonable approach for a reference text, it can be confusing for the first-time reader. While anomalies and experiments are very diverse, the behavioral principles that have been used to explain the anomalies can be categorized into a few over-arching behavioral principles (e.g., status quo bias, overconfidence, representativeness, loss aversion, etc.). This book is organized by behavioral principles. My approach more closely mirrors the approach of typical undergraduate microeconomics textbooks. By focusing on over-arching principles, students will more easily see how to apply the principles in new contexts. I have intentionally chosen the most simple of anomalies for presentation within the first few chapters of the book allowing students to ease into the world of behavioral models through somewhat familiar concepts like the sunk cost fallacy. These are followed by some of the more difficult or confusing concepts that require greater effort to master intuitively.

A Short Word on Experiments

Behavioral economics has long been tied to experimental economics due to the direct evidence experimental techniques have provided of decision heuristics and other non-rational decision-making. For this reason, many outside of the field of experimental economics or the field of behavioral economics believe the two are one in the same. Rather, experimental economics is a tool that is extremely useful in ferreting out behavioral phenomena. While experimental and experiential evidence is important in learning behavioral economic concepts, experimental techniques are not. An intricate understanding of experimental concepts (e.g., payoff dominance or internal validity) is no more central to learning behavioral economics than econometric techniques are to understanding intermediate microeconomics.

Acknowledgments

Special thanks to Julia Hastings-Black for her able assistance in preparing the manuscript for this book.

Rationality, Irrationality, and Rationalization

1

If economics is the study of how scarce resources are allocated given unlimited wants, **behavioral economics** may be said to focus more specifically on how scarce decision resources are allocated. Standard microeconomic modeling supposes that people make decisions with the sole purpose of making themselves better off. Behavioral economics often focuses on how people systematically deviate from the best possible decisions and what it will mean for the allocation of scarce resources. Behavioral economics is the study of how *observed* human behavior affects the allocation of scarce resources. Although the majority of microeconomic theory has focused on developing a unifying theory of behavior based on how one can logically obtain one's goal (e.g., through utility maximization) or the market forces one is likely to encounter, behavioral economics may more rightly be termed the odds and ends of economic theory. We often refer to the standard model of an economic decision maker as the **rational choice model** or simply **rational model**.

To the extent that people are observed to behave according to the rational model, behavioral economics does not deviate from standard microeconomic analysis. Were this all that was ever observed, behavioral economics would not have any use as a subdiscipline (and this would be a very short book indeed). Fortunately for us, economists have often noted a set of systematic deviations from the rational model that are either difficult to explain or model through an appeal to economic theory or that outright violate the standard economic model. We call any such deviations a **behavioral anomaly** or simply an **anomaly**. In such a situation, economic models might not be appropriate by themselves. In this case, behavioral economists seek to explain behavior by augmenting the rational choice model with principles developed in the fields of psychology, sociology, or, to a lesser extent, anthropology. Unfortunately, because behavioral economics draws from a disparate set of disciplines, there is no unifying theory of behavioral economics. Rather, the tools of behavioral economics are an eclectic and diverse set of principles that must be applied with care. Some theories are appropriate for some circumstances, but none apply generally to all decisions. This presents a challenge for the student first embarking on the journey to becoming a behavioral economist. Unlike the rest of economics, there is no single key to understanding behavioral economics. Rather, the student is responsible for learning to use a number of diverse tools that may be loosely grouped by the particular failings in rational choice theory they seek to address.

Because behavioral economics focuses so much on how people deviate from the rational choice model, it is important that the beginning student first have a clear understanding of this model and its roots. Rightly, this is the first theory that a behavioral economist seeks to apply when describing individual behavior. It is only when using a rational model becomes impractical or inaccurate that behavioral economists seek alternative explanations. Nonetheless, these alternative explanations may be very important depending on the purpose of the modeling exercise. For example, if, as an individual, you discover that you systematically make decisions that are not in your best interest, you may be able to learn to obtain a better outcome. In this way, behavioral economics tools may be employed therapeutically to improve personal behavior and outcomes. Alternatively, if a retailer discovers that customers do not fully understand all relevant product information, the retailer might improve profits by altering the types and availability of product information. In this case, behavioral economics tools may be employed strategically to take advantage of the behavior of others. An economics researcher might also be interested in finding general theories of decision making that can be applied and tested more broadly. In this case, behavioral economics tools may be applied academically. The motivation for employing behavioral economics, be it therapeutic, strategic, or academic, in large part determines the types of models and phenomena that are important to the interested student. To this end, we employ three types of economic models: rational, behavioral, and procedurally rational. Throughout this book, we use these distinctions in discussing the uses and applications for behavioral economic modeling.

Finally, the roots and history of behavioral economics are inextricably linked to experimental economics. Although this text tries to avoid becoming one on experimental methods, it is important to discuss some of the basics of experimental economics, why it is so useful in behavioral economics, and what this might mean for the wider use of behavioral economic concepts.

Rational Choice Theory and Rational Modeling

Behind every rational model is the notion that people are making optimal decisions given their access to information or the other constraints that they might face in their decisions. The most common rational models used in economics are the utility-maximization model and the profit-maximization model. The utility-maximization model assumes that the person has preferences over choices that can be expressed as a utility function. This function represents the level of enjoyment or welfare the person receives for a set of choices, often thought of as a bundle of goods that can be consumed. For example, a typical model presented in a course on microeconomics might suppose that one can consume two goods measured by the quantities x_1 and x_2. The person's decision problem could then be represented as

$$\max_{x_1, x_2} U(x_1, x_2) \tag{1.1}$$

subject to a budget constraint

$$p_1 x_1 + p_2 x_2 \leq y, \tag{1.2}$$

where $U(x_1, x_2)$ is the utility obtained from consuming amounts x_1 and x_2, p_1 is the price of good 1, p_2 is the price of good 2, and y is the total budget that can be spent. The consumer's problem in equations 1.1 and 1.2 is to find the consumption bundle (x_1, x_2) that maximizes his utility without exceeding his budget constraint. It is generally assumed that utility increases as either x_1 or x_2 increases. Further, the underlying preferences are assumed to be **complete** and **transitive**. By complete, we mean that given any two possible consumption bundles, $(\hat{x}_1, \hat{x}_2)$ and $(\tilde{x}_1, \tilde{x}_2)$, the consumer prefers bundle 1, $(\hat{x}_1, \hat{x}_2)$, prefers bundle two, $(\tilde{x}_1, \tilde{x}_2)$, or is indifferent between the two. No possible pair of bundles exists for which the consumer has no preference. By transitive, we mean that given any three bundles, if the consumer prefers $(\hat{x}_1, \hat{x}_2)$ to $(\tilde{x}_1, \tilde{x}_2)$, and the consumer prefers $(\tilde{x}_1, \tilde{x}_2)$ to $(\overline{x}_1, \overline{x}_2)$, then the consumer cannot prefer $(\overline{x}_1, \overline{x}_2)$ to $(\hat{x}_1, \hat{x}_2)$. Information about the consumer's preferences over consumption bundles is coded in the utility function by assigning a higher utility number to any bundle that is preferred or by assigning an equal number to any bundles to which the consumer is indifferent.

The decision problem can be represented as in Figure 1.1. The consumer can only consume any point in the triangle with sides formed by the x_1 axis, the x_2 axis, and the budget constraint, which is the straight downward-sloping line found by solving the budget constraint for the quantity of good 2 as a function of the amount of good 1, $x_2 = (y - p_1 x_1)/p_2$. Preferences are represented in Figure 1.1 by indifference curves, a collection of consumption bundles such that each point in the set results in the same level of utility. Figure 1.1 depicts three indifference curves, each curving to the southeast as one moves down the x_2 axis. Indifference curves that are farther to the northeast of the figure represent higher levels of consumption of both goods and thus represent a higher level of utility. The assumption of complete and transitive preferences implies that these indifference curves cannot intersect one another. The intersection of two different indifference curves would require the intersection point to result in two different levels of utility.

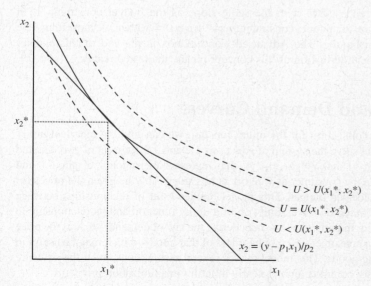

$U > U(x_1{}^*, x_2{}^*)$

$U = U(x_1{}^*, x_2{}^*)$

$U < U(x_1{}^*, x_2{}^*)$

$x_2 = (y - p_1 x_1)/p_2$

FIGURE 1.1
Utility Maximization

For a full discussion of the utility maximization model, the reader is referred to Nicholson and Snyder or Varian. The consumer problem is to maximize utility by finding the northeastern-most indifference curve that has at least one point that satisfies the budget constraint. This can occur at the intersection of the budget constraint with the x_1 axis (where $x_1 = y/p_1$ and $x_2 = 0$), where the budget constraint intersects the x_2 axis (where $x_1 = 0$ and $x_2 = y/p_2$), or at a point such as (x_1^*, x_2^*) in Figure 1.1, where the indifference curve is tangent to the budget constraint. We call this third potential solution an internal solution, and the first two are referred to as corner solutions. Internal solutions are the most commonly modeled solutions given the mathematical convenience of determining a tangency point and the triviality of modeling single-good consumption. The set of tangency points that are traced out by finding the optimal bundle while varying the total budget is called the **income expansion path**. It generally reflects increasing consumption as income increases for any normal good, and it reflects decreasing consumption for any inferior good.

To find the solution to the utility-maximization problem, we must define the concept of marginal utility. The marginal utility of x_1, which we denote $\partial U(x_1, x_2)/\partial x_1$, is the amount of utility gained by increasing consumption of x_1, or the slope of the utility curve with respect to x_1. The marginal utility of x_2, denoted $\partial U(x_1, x_2)/\partial x_2$, is the utility gained from increasing consumption of x_2, or the slope of the utility curve with respect to x_2. An internal solution to the utility maximization problem occurs where the ratio of the marginal utilities is equal to the ratio of prices:

$$\frac{\frac{\partial}{\partial x_1} U(x_1^*, x_2^*)}{\frac{\partial}{\partial x_2} U(x_1^*, x_2^*)} = \frac{p_1}{p_2}. \tag{1.3}$$

Note that $-p_1/p_2$ is the slope of the budget constraint. The slope of an indifference curve is equal to $-\frac{\partial U(x_1, x_2)}{\partial x_1} \Big/ \frac{\partial U(x_1, x_2)}{\partial x_2}$. Thus, any point solving equation 1.3 yields a point on the indifference curve with the same slope as the budget constraint. If in addition that point is on the budget constraint, $p_1 x_1^* + p_2 x_2^* = y$, then we have found the optimal consumption bundle. The Advanced Concept box at the end of this chapter presents a mathematical derivation of this concept for the interested reader.

Rationality and Demand Curves

If we know the functional form for the utility function we can find the marginal utility function. Then we can solve the system of equations 1.2 and 1.3 for a set of two demand functions, $x_1^*(p_1, p_2, y)$ and $x_2^*(p_1, p_2, y)$, that represent the amount of good 1 and good 2 that will make the consumer as well off as he can possibly be given the prices for the goods and the allocated budget. This model implies a set of relationships between prices and quantities based on the assumption of a utility function and its relationship to the quantity consumed. In particular, one may derive the law of demand—that as the price of a good increases, a consumer will purchase less of that good—which may be useful in pricing and marketing goods. This model makes several assumptions about the structure of the problem that are common among nearly all utility-maximization problems.

Foremost among these assumptions is the notion that the consumer has a set of well-understood and stable preferences over the two goods. However, simple introspection can lead us to question even the most basic of these assumptions. If consumers have a well-defined and stable set of preferences over goods, then what role can advertising serve other than to inform the customer about the availability or characteristics of a product? Were this the case, advertisements for well-known products should not be terribly effective. However, marketers for well-known products continue to buy advertising, often providing ads that yield no new information to the consumer. Further, consumers are often faced with goods with which they are unfamiliar or have not considered purchasing, and thus they might have incomplete preferences.

The utility-maximization model assumes that consumers know how their choice will result in a particular outcome. It seems reasonable that consumers choosing to buy four apples would know that the result would be their consuming four apples at some point in the future; but they might not know how many contain worms or have irregularities in taste or texture. In fact, consumers seldom face decisions with completely certain outcomes even for the simplest actions. In some cases, the consumer might not even be certain of the possible choices available. In an unfamiliar restaurant, diners might not fully read the menu to know the full range of possible choices. Even if they do, they might not be aware of the menu of the neighboring ice cream parlor and consider only the dessert possibilities at the restaurant.

Finally, the model assumes that consumers have the ability to determine what will make them better off than any other choice and that they have the ability to choose this option. The notion that the consumer can identify the best outcome before making a choice seems counter to human experience. Students might believe they should have studied more or at a different time in the semester, and people often feel that they have overeaten. Where exams and food consumption are repeated experiences, it seems strange that a person would not be able to eventually identify the correct strategy—or lack the ability to choose that strategy. Nonetheless, it happens. Perhaps this is due to an inability to execute the correct strategy. Maybe the spirit is willing but the flesh is weak. Rational models of consumer choice rely heavily on complete and transitive preferences, as well as on the ability of the consumer to identify and execute those preferences. If any of these assumptions were violated, the rational model of consumer choice would struggle to describe the motivation for individual behavior.

Even so, these violations of the underlying assumptions might not matter, depending on how we wish to use the model. There are two primary lines of argument for why we might not care about violations. First, if these assumptions are violated, we may be able to augment the model to account for the discrepancy resulting in a new model that meets the conditions of rationality. For example, if the consumer is uncertain of the outcomes, we may be able to use another rational-based model that accounts for this uncertainty. This would involve assuming preferences over the experience of uncertainty and modeling the level of uncertainty experienced with each good, such as the expected utility model discussed in later chapters, and supposing again that consumers optimize given their constraints and preferences. A second argument notes that a model is designed to be an abstraction from the real world. The whole point of a model is to simplify the real-world relationships to a point that we can make sense or use of it. Thus, even if the assumptions of our model are violated, consumers might behave as if they are maximizing some utility function. Paul Samuelson once compared this as-if approach to a billiards player who, although he does not carry out the mathematical calculations, behaves as if he can employ the physics formulas necessary to calculate how to direct the desired ball into the desired hole. This as-if utility function, once estimated, may be useful for predicting behavior under different prices or budgets or for measuring the effects of price changes. Even if it is only an approximation, the results may be close enough for our purposes.

In truth, the adequacy of the model we choose depends tremendously on the application we have in mind. If we wish primarily to approximate behavioral outcomes, and the variation from the behavior described by the model is not substantial for our purpose, the rational model we have proposed may be our best option. Our reference to a deviation from rational behavior as an anomaly suggests that substantial deviations are rare, and thus rational theory is probably adequate for most applications. If the variations are substantial, then we might need to consider another approach. It is true that many of the applications of behavioral economics could be modeled as some sort of rational process. For example, a consumer might use a rule of thumb to make some decisions because of the costs involved in making a more-deliberate and calculated choice. In this case, the consumer's cognitive effort might enter the utility function leading to the observed heuristic. The consumer, though not at the best consumption choice given unlimited cognitive resources, is still the best off he or she can be given the cognitive costs of coming upon a better consumption choice. On occasion this is a successful strategy for dealing with an observed behavior. More often than not, however, it leads to an unwieldy model that, although more general, is difficult to use in practice. Occam's razor, the law of research that states that we should use as few mechanisms as possible to explain a relationship, might compel us to use a nonrational approach to modeling some economic behavior.

If instead, we are interested in the motivation of the decision maker, rather than simply approximating behavior under a narrow set of circumstances, the as-if approach might not be useful. For example, using mathematical physics to describe a pool player's shots might yield relatively accurate descriptions of the players' strategy until the pool table is tilted 15 degrees. At this point, the pool player is dealing with an unfamiliar circumstance and could take some significant time learning to deal with the new playing surface before our model might work again.

The need for a simple model drove classical economists to abstract from real behavior by assuming that all decision makers act as if they are interested only in their own well-being, with full understanding of the world they live in, the cognitive ability to identify the best possible choices given their complete and logical preferences, and the complete ability to execute their intended actions. Such omniscience might seem more befitting a god than a human being. Nineteenth-century economists dubbed this ultrarational being *Homo economicus*, noting that it was a severe but useful abstraction from the real-world behavior of humans. Although no one ever supposed that individual people actually possessed these qualities, nearly the whole of economic thought was developed based on these useful abstractions. As theory has developed to generalize away from any one of the superhuman qualities of *Homo economicus*, the term has become more of a derisive parody of traditional economic thought. Nonetheless, there is tremendous use in this, absurd though it is, starting point for describing human behavior.

In addition to the utility model, microeconomic theory also hinges very heavily on the notion that firms make decisions that will maximize their profit, defined as revenues minus costs. This is actually a somewhat stronger assumption than utility maximization because it generally specifies a relationship between a choice variable and the assignment of profit, which is generally observable. Alternatively, utility is not observable, and thus it can have an arbitrary relationship to choice variables. For example, a common profit-maximization model may be written as

$$\max_{x} pf(x) - rx - C, \tag{1.4}$$

where x is the level of input used in the production process, p is the price the firm receives for output, $f(x)$ is a production function representing the level of output as a function of input, r is the input price, and C is the fixed cost of operation. To find the solution to equation 1.4, we must define the marginal revenue and the marginal cost functions. Revenue in equation 1.4 is given by $pf(x)$. Marginal revenue, denoted $\partial(pf(x))/\partial x = p \times \partial f(x)/\partial x$, is the additional amount of revenue (price times quantity sold) that is received by increasing the input, or the slope of the revenue function. Here, $\partial f(x)/\partial x$ is the slope of the production function. The marginal cost is the additional cost of increasing the amount of input used, r. The profit-maximization problem is generally solved where the marginal revenue from adding an additional input is equal to the marginal cost of production so long as rent, $pf(x) - rx$, is great enough to cover the fixed cost of operation. Otherwise the firm will not produce because they would lose money by doing so. Marginal cost is equal to marginal revenue where $p\,\partial f(x^*)/\partial x = r$, or in other words at the point where a line tangent to the production function has a slope of r/p. This is the point depicted in Figure 1.2, where φ is an arbitrary constant required to satisfy tangency.

The profit-maximization model generally employs assumptions that are similar to *Homo economicus* assumptions in scope and scale. However, unlike people, firms face

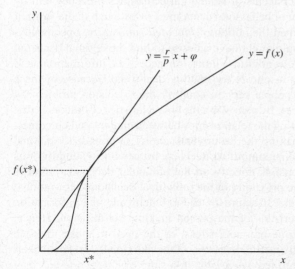

FIGURE 1.2
Profit Maximization

competitive pressures from others such that they disappear or cease to operate if they continually make bad decisions while their competitors make better decisions. A systematic error in judgment may be considered as an added cost to production or a competitive disadvantage. Because of this, in the context of a competitive industry, many have argued that behavioral economics has no place because firms that fail to maximize profit will be driven from the marketplace by smarter firms. Moreover, many behaviors that are rational under the utility-maximization model are not admissible under profit maximization. The models allow for differences in taste but not for differences in the measurement of profit. Thus those whose preferences get in the way of profit maximization may also be pushed out of the market by competitive pressures. This places a heavier burden on behavioral economists to prove the existence of behavior that is inconsistent with profit maximization by firms in cases where they believe profit is not truly the only motive.

Importantly, analysis using a rational model limits the scope of benevolent policy. By assuming that people have made the best choice possible, only policies that deal in interpersonal effects of economic behavior may improve an individual's well-being. Thus, a person who decides to smoke cigarettes, or, in a more extreme case, jump off of a bridge, cannot be made better off by a government that wishes to stop them. The rational model assumes these people knowingly chose the outcome that would make them the best off they could be. However, a secondhand smoker, who unwillingly inhales the smoke of nearby smokers, may be made better off if a policymaker limits the ability of others to smoke. In general, the rational model cannot suggest ways to abridge the choice of an individual to make that individual better off. In this sense, the rational model is not therapeutic.

Bounded Rationality and Model Types

Although many of the important concepts in behavioral economics precedes him by many years, the current incarnation of behavioral economics owes much to the work of Herbert Simon. Simon first described the notion of *bounded rationality*. Specifically, this is the notion that whereas people might have a desire to find the optimal decision, they have limits on their cognitive abilities, limits on access to information, and perhaps limits on other necessary resources for making decisions. Because of these limitations, rather than optimize, people seek to simplify their decision problem by narrowing the set of possible choices, by narrowing the characteristics of outcomes that they might consider, or by simplifying the relationships between choices and outcomes. Thus, instead of optimizing by making the best overall choice, a boundedly rational person instead optimizes using some simplified decision framework. Naturally, this simplified decision framework depends directly on the particular decision resources available to that person. Hence, the proximity of the individual decision to the rational optimum depends not only on the structure of the problem and the information available but also on the characteristics of the person making the decision. Hence, education, experience, emotion, time pressure, stress, or the need to make multiple decisions at once might play directly into the accuracy of the individual decision maker. The decision mechanism may be termed a *heuristic*, or a simple general rule that may be used to approximate the solution to the utility or profit-maximization problem. The heuristic most likely results in a close approximation of the true optimum under most circumstances. It is this ability to approximate the optimal choice that makes it useful to the decision maker. However, there may be some circumstances under which the differences are substantial and observable.

Economists have taken several approaches to modeling boundedly rational behavior. Two primary approaches are of particular importance. The first approach is a **behavioral model**. A behavioral model seeks to simply describe observed behavior. In some cases, it augments a rational model of behavior with some function or appendage that describes the observed deviations from rational decision making. One advantage of such a model is that it is based in empirical observations, and it is thus extremely accurate in the context in which observations were made. Additionally, behavioral models can be used to describe *any* type of behavior, because they are not based on any particular assumptions about the underlying motivations of the individual. For this same reason, however, behavioral models might not be the best tool for many jobs. Because the model is observation based, it is only as accurate as the observations taken. Thus, if we changed the decision context substantially, the model might no longer be appropriate. For example, we might repeatedly observe someone with two food objects placed in front of him: an apple on the left and a lemon on the right. Suppose each time we observe a choice, the person chooses the apple. One behavioral model might suggest the person always chooses the object on the left. If we then used this model to predict what would happen if a lemon were placed on the left and an apple on the right, we would be disappointed if the individual were actually choosing the object that delivered a preferred taste.

The downfall of the behavioral model is that it does not tell us *why*, only *what*. Thus, we cannot generalize the behavioral model to various contexts and decisions. To do this, we would need to understand the actual decision mechanism underlying the decision. Additionally, because the behavioral model does not yield the individual motivation for decisions, it provides an inappropriate instrument for trying to help someone to make better decisions. By simply describing the types of behavior observed, a behavioral model does not provide any rationale for how someone may be made better off. Thus again, our model might describe what behaviors or conditions are associated with deciding to smoke. However, this alone does not tell us if the person would be better off if the choice to smoke were removed by some policymaker. Alternatively, a behavioral model may be very appropriate for making predictions in highly similar contexts. For example, a firm marketing a product may derive and estimate a behavioral model of consumer purchases for the product. So long as the underlying decision problems of the consumers remain the same, the behavioral model may be very accurate and appropriate for their particular marketing efforts.

An alternative approach is to attempt to model the motivation for the decision mechanism. We call this a *procedurally rational model*. A person is procedurally rational if his or her decision is the result of logical deliberation. This deliberation might include misperceptions or other constraints, but the process by which the decision is arrived at itself is reasoned. Thus, a procedural rational model attempts to provide a reasoned decision mechanism that might not always arrive at the correct choice owing to misperceptions, limits on cognitive ability, or other constraints on decision resources. Given the decision motivations are properly modeled, a procedurally rational model may be highly predictive of general behavior over vastly different contexts. Additionally, given the model of motivations is accurate, the model naturally suggests a set of normative behaviors. For example, if a particular demographic of people typically begin smoking because they overestimate the benefits of belonging to the particular social group that smokes, a policy limiting the availability of cigarettes to this demographic might be justified.

Special Relationship between Behavioral Economics and Experimental Economics

Many of the most prominent behavioral economics concepts have their roots in experimental economics research. Although this book focuses more exclusively on behavioral economics theory, it is useful to note why a particular theory would have such a close relationship to a particular methodology. This has much to do with the assumption of rationality in general economics.

Throughout the history of economics, the vast majority of empirical research has employed secondary data sets to explore the relationships implied by theory. A secondary data set records the transactions that have occurred in the past and potentially some data on the demographic and economic qualities of the persons making the decisions. These transactions occur naturally without any opportunity for the researcher to manipulate conditions or parameters that could affect the decisions. To use such data to understand the underlying relationships, one must use a mathematical model to interpret the behavior. Thus, to estimate the way consumption will change with a change in price, you must have a theory that allows you to derive a demand curve that may then be estimated. Referring to the two-good consumption problem we explored earlier in the chapter, the demand curve in this case tells us that the quantity of good 1 demanded depends negatively on the price of good 1, positively on the price of good 2, and in some unspecified way on income. Our ability to test our model is somewhat limited by the particular data on hand. Often between any pair of observations all three of these variables will change depending on other conditions that face decision makers and that the researcher might not directly care about (e.g., supply conditions), leaving no clear prediction of the direction of change in demand. Nonetheless, we can use our models of supply and demand to interpret estimates of the relationships between the prices and income derived from these secondary data.

Alternatively, economics experiments offer the researcher tremendous control to alter the variables that independently influence decisions. Typically, an experiment brings a large number of participants into a laboratory where they make decisions that will be rewarded monetarily or substantially, with the reward structure designed by the researcher. This reward system is changed between various treatment groups in order to test some underlying theory of behavior. Thus, a researcher could run experiments on a random sample of participants and determine if they were willing to purchase good 1 with $p_1 = \$1$, $p_2 = \$1$ after having endowed the participants with $10. A second treatment could increase p_1 while holding the budget and the price of good 2 constant. If consumption of good 1 increased, we would have a rejection of our rational model. Alternatively, if consumption decreased we would fail to reject the rational model. Failing to reject does not mean that the rational model (or any other model we fail to reject) is the true underlying model. Rather, we only find that the behavior in our particular experiment is consistent with this assumed model. Other experiments using other variable values may be found to reject the model. This ability to discern a causal link between some decision variable and observed behavior is called **internal validity**.

Although there are circumstances that allow us to test rational models using secondary data, these are certainly rare and more difficult than when using an experimental approach. The experimental approach allows us the direct control to set up choices where an obvious violation of rational choice is possible. Real-world observations have so many variables—many of them unobservable—that such clear violations are usually not discernable. For this reason, behavioral economics is closely associated with experimental economics. On the other hand, we must recognize that an economics experiment cannot control all important decision parameters. For example, in this experiment we suggest endowing each participant with $10. However, some participants may be wealthier than others and thus have a different sensitivity to price changes. It would be difficult to control wealth except perhaps by targeting a particular wealth cohort. This is difficult in practice. Alternatively, preferences might differ among participants in a way that influences the outcome of our result. For example, if good 1 were pork, and some subjects rejected pork on religious grounds, we might find no relationship to price. However, this is not a rejection of our model. Rather, the participants simply have extremely low utility for pork.

It would be difficult to take behavioral relationships estimated in an experiment and directly apply them to policy in a market. Suppose for example, we find some set of conditions under which the rational model fails in the laboratory. Before this anomaly could be of use to a policy maker, we would need to know first how likely it would be that these conditions would ever occur in a natural market. It could be that the necessary conditions are extremely rare or even impossible in a natural market setting. Second, we would need to know whether the magnitude of the effect was sufficiently important in a broader context. For example, we might find a violation of the law of demand for some range of prices. But if the violation is a relatively small effect or over a very small range of prices, it might not be possible for a producer to determine if increasing price in this range truly increases sales.

Empirical estimates from field data are usually much more readily generalized to other conditions so long as the underlying model being estimated is correct. This ability to apply an estimated relationship more broadly is called **external validity**. Internal validity is necessary in order to find evidence of a behavioral economics result, but we desire external validity before we can begin to apply the model in a forecasting, managerial, marketing, or policymaking exercise. Without having both pieces of the puzzle, we cannot move ahead with confidence in our results. Thus, although behavioral economics has been associated closely with experimental economics, there have been strong movements both to extend experiments to more natural settings and to use secondary data to estimate the behavioral relationships implied by behavioral economics theory.

Experiments can be useful to behavioral researchers in establishing a causal relationship. They may also be useful to informed participants in providing an educational experience in which they can learn to avoid unwanted behaviors. This book is accompanied by several simple guides to classroom exercises for instructors' use that allow the student to participate in some of the canonical behavioral experiments. Several researchers have found that with some experience and training, it is possible for people to make decisions that appear to be more like the rational model. However, this is by no means a panacea. Often what learning can accomplish in a specific experiment is undone by making only slight changes in the conditions of the experiment. Potentially more important to applied decision makers is the ability to learn that they have a problem. Notably, people are generally unaware of their own behavioral anomalies, even when they are aware of the behavior in the general population. We will not focus on experimental economics directly, but will make heavy use of experimental results.

Biographical Note

© Bettmann/CORBIS

Herbert A. Simon (1916–2001)

B.A., University of Chicago, 1936; Ph.D., University of Chicago, 1943; held faculty positions at the Illinois Institute of Technology and Carnegie Mellon University

Educated first as an engineer, Herbert Simon stated that his lifelong goals were a "hardening" of the social sciences and the development of stronger ties between the natural and social sciences. He considered his efforts to describe and model human limitations in decision making central to this task. Simon believed that mathematical modeling was key to creating a more-rigorous behavioral science. His work, however, ran against the grain of other theorists of his time looking for greater rigor in economics, which he thought was too cavalier in assuming away human qualities. Though recognized most by economists for his contributions to decision science, he had publications in many other fields, including cognitive psychology, artificial intelligence, and classical mechanics. He is considered one of the founding fathers of artificial intelligence, and he won prestigious awards for his work in economics, computer science, psychology, automation, and public administration. He believed that economics had much to learn from other social sciences. His work questioned the usefulness of purely rational models of choice, citing the need to test these assumptions rigorously. Simon famously argued that equilibrium concepts used in economics might not be useful in empirical work owing to the ever-shifting nature of reality. Equilibrium might never actually be achieved, and we might not know how far from equilibrium our observations lie. Simon won the Nobel Prize in economics in 1978 for his work on bounded rationality.

THOUGHT QUESTIONS

1. Many economists consider behavioral economics to be an affront to the field of economics for its focus on irrational behavior. Others consider anomalies to be so rare as to make the study of behavioral anomalies irrelevant. Do rational and behavioral economics work against each other? What role might each play in describing economic decisions? What does Occam's razor have to say about the relationship between rational and behavioral economics?

2. Describe a behavior either you or a friend has engaged in that you would describe as irrational. Why would you consider this behavior irrational? What was the motivation for engaging in this behavior?

3. Why has behavioral economics come to be so heavily associated with experimental economics? Why might econometric approaches to behavioral economics be so challenging?

4. Describe the difference among rational, procedural rational, and behavioral models of economic decisions.

REFERENCES

Conlisk, J. "Why Bounded Rationality?" *Journal of Economic Literature* 34(1996): 669–700.

Nicholson, W., and C.F. Snyder. *Microeconomic Theory: Basic Principles and Extensions*. Eagan, Minn.: South Western College Publishers, 2008.

Simon, H.A. "Theories of Decision-Making in Economics and Behavioral Science." *American Economic Review* 49(1959): 253–283.

Simon, H.A. "Rationality as Process and as Product of Thought." *American Economic Review* 68(1978): 1–16.

Simon, C.P., and L.E. Blume. *Mathematics for Economists*. New York: W.W. Norton, 1994.

Varian, H.R. *Microeconomic Analysis*. New York: W.W. Norton, 1992.

Advanced Concept

Deriving Demand Curves

At times in this book it is useful to solve for consumer demand relationships explicitly. This is done by setting up the LaGrangian for the constrained optimization problem. A LaGrangian can be considered a simple trick to remember the first-order conditions for a constrained optimization problem. In this case, we can write the LaGrangian as

$$L = U(x_1, x_2) + \lambda(y - p_1 x_1 - p_2 x_2),$$

where λ is the LaGrangian multiplier, representing the marginal utility gained from relaxing the constraint (in this case increasing y). For a full discussion of optimization theory and the conditions required for an internal solution the reader is referred to Simon and Blume. The LaGrangian is solved by the point at which the derivative of the LaGrangian with respect to each decision variable and the LaGrangian multiplier is equal to 0, or $(x_1^*, x_2^*, \lambda^*)$ such that

$$\frac{\partial L}{\partial x_1} = \frac{\partial}{\partial x_1} U(x_1^*, x_2^*) - \lambda^* p_1 = 0, \tag{1.A}$$

$$\frac{\partial L}{\partial x_2} = \frac{\partial}{\partial x_2} U(x_1{}^*, x_2{}^*) - \lambda{}^* p_2 = 0, \tag{1.B}$$

and

$$y - p_1 x_1{}^* - p_2 x_2{}^* = 0. \tag{1.C}$$

The demand curve can be found by solving this system for $x_1{}^*(p_1, p_2, y)$ and $x_2{}^*(p_1, p_2, y)$. Substituting (1.B) into (1.A) results in the optimal consumption relationship

$$\frac{\frac{\partial}{\partial x_1} U(x_1{}^*, x_2{}^*)}{\frac{\partial}{\partial x_2} U(x_1{}^*, x_2{}^*)} = \frac{p_1}{p_2}. \tag{1.D}$$

Here, the left side represents the slope of the indifference curve at the optimal consumption point, and the right side represents the slope of the budget constraint. By solving (1.C) for the proper consumption quantity and substituting into (1.D), we may derive the demand function for either good.

CONSUMER PURCHASING DECISIONS

People make hundreds of consumption decisions each day. With so many decisions, it can be very difficult for them to muster the level of attention, focus, and thought necessary to deliberate each one. Thus, consumer purchasing behavior is a field ripe for investigating behavioral economics. Given the importance of consumer behavior and consumer psychology in the field of marketing, this should not be surprising. This section outlines many of the consistent behavioral patterns that have been identified in the literature. These patterns are important to the economics of markets because they can influence consumer demand and potentially affect quantities and prices through aggregation of individual behavior. Patterns of consumer behavior may be important to a policymaker if they represent judgment errors that lead consumers to purchase goods they don't want or to pay more than they should be willing to for a good. In this case, a policymaker may be interested in creating greater transparency in the market to facilitate a more convenient and accurate decision process on the part of consumers. Finally, marketers are interested in behavioral patterns in consumer purchasing for the ability it can give them to inflate the sale or the perceived value of their product in the eyes of consumers.

Transaction Utility and Consumer Pricing

Suppose you were in an upscale, yet unfamiliar, restaurant and while perusing the menu you come across your favorite dish. It sounds delicious, but it is very expensive. You convince yourself that it will be worth the price given the reputation of the restaurant: This will be something special. When the food arrives, it looks different from what you had expected. You taste it and are disappointed. The sauce that is integral to your preference for the food is all wrong. In fact, it is so bitter that it makes eating the food somewhat unpleasant. Nevertheless, you convince yourself to eat because you paid so much for the meal. Why should you let all that money go to waste?

The consumer is constantly faced with deciding what to buy and how much to buy. To make these decisions, they must take into account the potential gain or loss from the purchase. Cost–benefit analysis is a staple of economic policy analysis and business planning. This analysis requires one to tally all potential income or benefit from a project and potential cost to engage in the project. The idea is that if the planned benefit of a venture exceeds the cost, it may be a worthwhile venture to engage in. More to the point, if a set of choices are mutually exclusive (i.e., one cannot choose more than one option), then an individual or firm should choose the option with the highest net benefit, defined as total benefit minus total cost. Inasmuch as the price of a good, as well as the atmosphere, can signal quality, price can perhaps influence the expectations of the consumer. This could in turn influence the consumer's willingness to pay for the good.

Questions of how much to consume should follow the simple economic rule of equating marginal cost and marginal benefit. So long as initial consumption produces more benefits than costs, one should consume until the cost of the marginal good increases and/or the benefit of the marginal good decreases to the point that there is zero net benefit for consumption of the next unit. If one reaches a constraint on consuming (such as finishing the entire dish one has been served) before net benefits are reduced to zero, then the consumer should consume all that is possible.

In many of our experiences we take price or atmosphere as a signal of the quality of a good. As well, we might order items in a restaurant that leave us wanting more when we have finished eating. This does not imply that price always signals quality differences, nor does it mean we should always complete a meal at a restaurant whether we like what we are eating or not. Nonetheless, in many cases people seem to react in curious ways to the pricing of goods. Often we hear of the need to "get your money's worth" for a transaction. Such a notion can take on a life of its own, so that rather than simply losing some money, we lose the money and have an unpleasant meal to boot. In this chapter we discuss Richard Thaler's notion of **transaction utility** and resulting behavioral anomalies. Transaction utility can be defined as the utility one receives for feeling one has received greater value in a transaction than one has given away in paying for the good. This leads to three prominent anomalies: the sunk cost fallacy, flat-rate bias, and reference-dependent preferences.

Rational Choice with Fixed and Marginal Costs

Economists are often taught about the impact of fixed costs on choice through the profit-maximization model. As we saw in Chapter 1, the firm generally faces the following problem:

$$\max_{x} pf(x) - rx - C \qquad (2.1)$$

which is solved by x^*, where price times the slope of the production function is equal to the cost of inputs, $p\, \partial f(x)/\partial x = r$. In this case, the **fixed cost** C does not enter into the solution condition. Thus, whether fixed costs increase or decrease, so long as the firm chooses positive production levels, the level of production remains the same. The fixed cost does affect the amount of profit, but it does not affect the amount of inputs required to maximize profits.

The same need not be the case under utility maximization. Consider a rational consumer who could consume two goods, where consuming one of the goods requires that the consumer pay a fixed amount for access to a good, plus some amount for each piece consumed. This is generally referred to as a **two-part tariff**. One example might be a phone plan that charges a fixed amount per month, plus a fee for each text message sent. **Linear pricing**, or charging a fixed amount for each unit of the good, can be thought of as a special case of the two-part tariff where the fixed amount is set to zero. We will assume that the second good is priced linearly. **Flat-rate pricing**, where consumers are allowed to consume as much as they like for a fixed fee, can be considered a special case of the two-part tariff where the per-piece rate has been set to zero. The consumer's problem can be written as

$$\max_{x_1, x_2} U(x_1, x_2) \qquad (2.2)$$

subject to the budget constraint

$$p_0 \hat{x}_1 + p_1 x_1 + p_2 x_2 \le y, \qquad (2.3)$$

where $x_1 \ge 0$ is the amount of the two-part tariff good, $x_2 \ge 0$ is the amount of the linearly priced good, $U(x_1, x_2)$ is the consumer's utility of consumption as a function of the amount consumed, p_0 is the fixed cost of access, p_1 is the per-unit price of consumption for the two-part tariff good, p_2 is the per-unit cost of the linearly priced good, and y is the total available budget for consumption. Finally, $\hat{x}_1$ is an indicator of whether the consumer has decided to consume any of the two-part tariff good, with $\hat{x}_1 = 1$ if x_1 is positive and zero otherwise. We assume for now that the consumer always gains positive utility for consuming additional amounts of good 2.

If the flat fee p_0 is set equal to zero, this problem becomes the standard two-good consumption problem found in any standard microeconomics textbook. The solution in this case requires that the consumer optimize by consuming at the point of tangency between the highest utility level indifference curve that intersects at least one point of the budget constraint as presented in Chapter 1.

If both the flat fee and the linear price are positive, consumers will only purchase good 1 if doing so allows them to obtain a higher level of utility. If the first good is not purchased, then the budget constraint implies that consumers will consume as much of good 2 as they can afford, $\bar{x}_2 = y/p_2$, with a corresponding level of utility $U(0, \bar{x}_2)$. If the consumer purchases at least some of the two-part tariff good, the consumer decision problem functions much like the standard utility-maximization problem, where the budget constraint has been shifted in reflecting a loss in budget of p_0. This problem is represented in Figure 2.1. In Figure 2.1, the consumer can choose not to consume good 1 and instead consume at $\bar{x}_2$ on the outermost budget constraint (solid line representing $y = p_1 x_1 + p_2 x_2$, or equivalently $x_2 = (y - p_1 x_1)/p_1$) and obtain utility $U(0, \bar{x}_2)$, or she can find the greatest utility possible along the innermost budget constraint (dashed line representing $y = p_0 + p_1 x_1 + p_2 x_2$, or equivalently $x_2 = (y - p_0 - p_1 x_1)/p_1$) and obtain utility $U(x_1^*, x_2^*)$. If the indifference curve that passes through the point $U(x_1^*, x_2^*)$ intersects the x_2 axis below the point $\bar{x}_2$, then the consumer is better off not purchasing any of good 1 and avoiding the fixed cost. In this case, pictured in Figure 2.1, increasing the fixed fee cannot alter consumption because the good associated with the fee is not purchased. Decreasing the fee shifts the dashed budget curve out, potentially reaching a point where it is optimal to consume both goods.

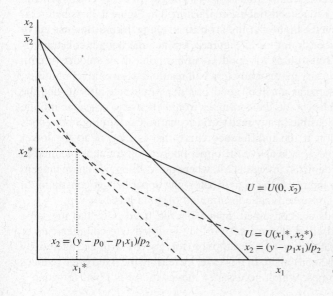

FIGURE 2.1
Utility Maximization with a Two-Part
Tariff: A Corner Solution

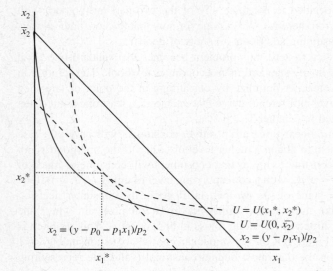

FIGURE 2.2
Utility Maximization
with a Two-Part Tar-
iff: An Internal
Solution

Alternatively, in Figure 2.2, the indifference curve that passes through the point $U(x_1^*, x_2^*)$ does not intersect the x_2 axis below the point $\bar{x}_2$, and thus a greater level of utility can be obtained by consuming both goods and paying the fixed access fee. Increasing or decreasing the fee can alter the consumption of both goods as the tangency points forming the income expansion path shift either northwest or southeast along the budget curve. However, if both goods are normal, more of each good should be purchased as the fixed fee is decreased.

Finally, if the per-unit price for good 1 is zero, as would be the case at an all-you-can-eat buffet, the budget constraint can be written as $p_2 x_2 \leq y$ if good 1 is not consumed and as $p_2 x_2 \leq y - p_0$ if it is. These budget constraints are illustrated in Figure 2.3. As before, if both goods are consumed, then the highest utility is obtained along the indifference curve that is tangent to the budget constraint, as in Figure 2.3. Since the budget constraint is flat, this can only occur at a **bliss point** for good 1. A bliss point is an amount of consumption such that consuming any more or any less will result in a lower level of utility. Given that a person can consume as much of good 1 as she would like after paying the fixed price, if there were no bliss point, the consumer would choose to consume infinite amounts, a solution that is infeasible in any real-world scenario. Consuming both goods is always the optimal solution if the indifference curve that is tangent to the lower budget constraint intersects the x_2 axis above the upper budget constraint as pictured in Figure 2.3. The alternative is depicted in Figure 2.4, where the indifference curve tangent to the lower budget constrain intersects the x_2 axis below the upper budget constraint. In this case, none of good 1 is consumed and consumption of good 2 is $x_2 = y/p$.

In the case that both goods are consumed, increasing the fixed price has the same impact as reducing the total budget (Figure 2.3). If the two goods are complements or substitutes, then the marginal utility of consumption for good 1 will be altered by adjusting the amount of good 2 consumed. In this case, increasing the fixed price reduces the amount of good 2 consumed, which necessarily moves the bliss point for good 1

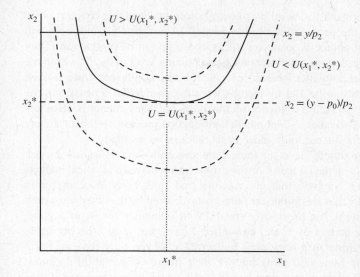

FIGURE 2.3
Utility Maximization with Flat-Rate
Pricing: An Internal Solution

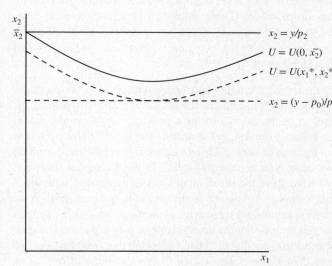

FIGURE 2.4
Utility Maximization with Flat-Rate
Pricing: A Corner Solution

through the change in marginal utility for good 1. Alternatively, if the two goods are neither substitutes nor complements but are independent, then increasing or decreasing consumption of good 2 should have no impact on the marginal utility for good 1. In this case, no matter what the level of the fixed price is, the amount of good 1 consumed should be the same so long as it is positive.

Fixed versus Sunk Costs

A concept that is related to, though distinct from, fixed costs is **sunk costs** (Figure 2.4). At the time of a decision, a fixed cost may be avoided either by not choosing the good associated with it (e.g., good 1 in the utility-maximization model in this chapter) or by not producing it (as in the profit-maximization model). Alternatively, sunk costs are incurred no matter what choice is made regarding consumption or production. They are unavoidable. Sunk costs do not alter the profit-maximizing level of inputs within the rational production model no matter what their level. The firm could shut down if fixed costs of production might not be met by income from the production process, but the level of sunk costs should have no influence on this decision: They cannot be avoided. Hence, when considering whether to continue in a production process, the costs already incurred should not be considered, only those costs that can be avoided.

Similarly, sunk costs should have no impact on the utility-maximization model, except through the impact on the budget. Consider two consumers with identical budgets and identical preferences. Suppose that one has incurred sunk costs associated with obtaining access to good 1 that are double the sunk costs incurred by the other consumer. In other words, consumer 1 has previously spent $2S$ on obtaining access to a good, resulting in a remaining budget of y, and consumer 2 has spent only S on obtaining access to the good, resulting in a remaining budget of y. Given they have identical preferences and have the same remaining budget, their future consumption decisions should likewise be identical no matter what level of sunk cost has been incurred if they both conform to the rational-choice model. Those interested in a mathematical demonstration of this are referred to the Advanced Concept box at the end of the chapter.

The Sunk Cost Fallacy

The **sunk cost fallacy** is often described as chasing bad money with good. A person might expend effort or money on a project, only to find that the project is unlikely to pay off. At the point where there appears to be no possibility of a positive return on any future investment, a rational person ceases to invest and abandons the project. The sunk cost fallacy occurs when one tries to recover sunk costs by continuing an activity for which there is a negative return. We often hear arguments such as "I can't abandon this now, I have worked too hard" or "I have spent too much money not to go through with this." Such arguments belie rational thought. As argued in the previous sections, sunk costs should not influence one's decision to continue an activity. Rational arguments to continue must consider the future costs and returns, not the unavoidable or past expenses. Rational counterparts to the sunk cost arguments might be, "I can't abandon this now, I will get so much more out of continuing than I would put in," or "I have so little effort left to complete the project relative to the benefits, that I will be better off completing it."

Richard Thaler gave the following two hypothetical examples of the sunk cost fallacy:

> A family pays $40 for tickets to a basketball game to be played 60 miles from their home. On the day of the game there is a snowstorm. They decide to go anyway, but note in passing that had the tickets been given to them, they would have stayed home.
>
> A man joins a tennis club and pays a $300 yearly membership fee. After two weeks of playing he develops a tennis elbow. He continues to play (in pain) saying "I don't want to waste the $300!"[1]

---

[1] Reprinted from Journal of Economic Behavior & Organization, Vol. 1(1), Thaler, R., "Toward a positive theory of consumer choice," pp. 39–60, Copyright (1980), with permission from Elsevier.

In both of these cases, the consumers base their decisions about current and future activities on the amount that had been paid in unrecoverable costs. Clearly, if being given a ticket would not result in attending a game in a snowstorm, then it cannot be worth it to attend the game if one has paid for the tickets. Further, after an injury one would likely not want to play tennis and will not recover the value of a yearly membership by undergoing pain and difficulty to play. Nonetheless, there is some ring of truth to the reasoning offered in each of the hypothetical stories. We probably have known people who made such arguments, and we can most likely recall making similar arguments ourselves. Why would such an argument be convincing on occasion if there is no merit to it? Do people really behave in this way? More importantly, if people do behave this way, would they necessarily be better off by avoiding the behavior? What implications might there be for manufacturers and retailers of goods?

For example, people attending an amusement park and purchasing an all-day pass may be influenced by the purchase price. Someone who purchases an all-day pass to an amusement park for $10 might get tired and uncomfortable and want to go home by 1 P.M. The same person paying $30 for the pass might feel just as tired at 1 P.M. but might also feel that she has not sufficiently realized the value of her purchase. Thus, she might stay for several more hours trying to have fun despite her desire to go home. Detecting such an effect may be difficult. For example, those who are likely to go home at 1 P.M. may be less willing to purchase a pass in the first place and thus more likely to show up when the pass price is only $10. In this case, simply finding that people stay later when the prices are higher might not be very good evidence of the sunk cost fallacy; it might simply be evidence that higher prices drive lower-value customers away. The sunk cost fallacy is generally related to the notion that a fixed access fee influences the extent of an activity. Thus, even if the return on the project does not necessarily turn negative, the people paying a larger fixed fee may be expected to consume more. This observation has led to several experiments examining the impact of fixed fees on use.

EXAMPLE 2.1   Theater Tickets and Pricing Programs

Theater ticket subscriptions are designed so that the subscriber pays a fixed fee for a package of tickets to several plays or productions. Theatergoers receive their tickets in a bundle before the first show. The subscriber may subsequently decide to attend a show, to give away the tickets to that show, or to simply discard the tickets.

Hal Arkes and Catherine Blumer worked with the Ohio University Theater to randomly offer different prices to the first 60 people to order tickets. Some paid full price, $15, some received a $2 (roughly 13%) discount, and some received a $7 (roughly 47%) discount. Over the first five plays of the 10-play season, the full-price group attended significantly more of the plays than either of the discount groups. Thus, it appears that at least some of the theatergoers were led to attend more plays because they had paid too much for the tickets to miss the plays. Their results are very suggestive of sunk cost fallacy–style reasoning. They also observed that over the last five plays of the season there were no real differences in attendance. They suggest that their results show that the effects of sunk cost persist over a substantial period of time, though not indefinitely. Following their reasoning, eventually people forget the pain they associate with the cost of the tickets and begin to decide attendance based on the enjoyment the play would offer.

EXAMPLE 2.2   The Concorde Paradox and Public Policy

The sunk cost fallacy is also sometimes called the *Concorde paradox* in honor of the late supersonic jet. The Concorde, the supersonic plane that was once used for cross-Atlantic traffic, was originally a joint venture between the British and French governments. The governments drew wide publicity in 1962 for their plans to develop a commercially viable passenger plane that could travel faster than the speed of sound. Each government had agreed to contribute $224 million to the project for a total of $448 million. Early into the design phase of the project, expenses began to run over budget. By 1964 the projected cost was more than $900 million. By completion, the plane had cost more than six times the original projected cost to develop. In the later stages of development, around 1973, both governments began to realize that the plane would not generate enough money to cover future costs of development and production.

Because there were only 100 passengers per plane and a substantially increased cost of operation with respect to conventional aircraft, few airlines were willing to take the chance of purchasing a Concorde. Despite the dismal prospects, the project continued to completion at considerable cost. Only 14 of the planes were ever used commercially, with most purchased with a substantial subsidy from either the British or French governments to induce operation. The planes were in service from 1976 until 2003. A crash in 2000, caused by a small piece of debris, killing all 100 passengers, led to a brief grounding of the planes. Later, with rising oil prices and decreased interest in flight following the 2001 terror attacks in the United States, the planes were permanently decommissioned. Other governments with similar projects (notably the Soviet Union and the United States) abandoned similar programs owing to concerns over costs and viability.

Of course, political decisions are made by politicians who might have very different motives than profit maximization. It may be that politicians believed that public opinion would turn on them if they abandoned the project when it was known to be a money loser. In this case, it may be perfectly rational for the politicians to continue a project, using constituent money for projects that will help ensure their own political gain. It may truly be the constituents who fall for the sunk cost fallacy.

Sunk cost reasoning is commonplace in politics. For example, when asked about the need for a NASA mission to Mars and Florida's role in this mission, presidential candidate John McCain said "There's too much invested there. There's infrastructure that's very expensive and very extensive." Regarding the possibility of the United States withdrawing from the lengthy engagement in Iraq, Cal Thomas, a conservative columnist, argued in *USA Today* that "We have too much invested to quit now," echoing earlier sentiments expressed by President George W. Bush. Similar arguments have been heard when discussing the termination of a missile shield defense or other defense projects. Arkes and Blumer cite two senators from the early 1980s lamenting the termination of a waterway project given the level of prior investment. Although it must be acknowledged that these are not the only reasons given for continuing these projects, the fact that sunk cost rhetoric is used by those whose profession is primarily to argue is a de facto statement on how effective this (il)logic is perceived to be.

Theory and Reactions to Sunk Cost

When making decisions on extent of consumption given a fixed price for access, or after some unrecoverable sunk cost, the consumer should have a demand for the activity, $x_1^*(y)$, that depends entirely on her remaining budget, or on her ability to purchase other goods that may be a complement or substitute for good 1. If all other goods can be considered independent of consumption of good 1, then the optimal consumption level is independent of even wealth, x_1^*. A behavioral model of reacting to fixed or sunk costs could simply insert the level of costs as an argument in the function $x_1^*(y, p_0)$, or $x_1^*(p_0)$, with the assumption that the consumer will increase consumption when the fixed cost is increased, $dx_1^*/dp_0 > 0$. Such a model could then be used by a retailer to determine the profit-maximizing price for access based on the quantity their customers would consume as a result of price.

On the other hand, if we were interested in *why* consumers may be influenced by fixed costs, we would need to employ and test a procedurally rational model. There are two primary explanations for why one might display the sunk cost fallacy or more generally adjust quantity decisions to fixed costs. The first supposes that consumers derive some value from believing they have gotten a good deal, called **transaction utility** as opposed to just utility derived from consumption, as is modeled in the rational model of consumption (Thaler refers to this utility of consumption as **acquisition utility**). Paying $10 for four hours at an amusement park might sound like an extremely good deal, whereas paying $30 for the same experience might not. Thus, someone who paid $30 for entry into the amusement park might consider going home and receiving some utility from not being in the park anymore, but also receiving some disutility for knowing she paid a lot for the experience at the park. If this feeling of disutility is strong enough, she might consider lengthening her stay to increase her transaction utility. For example, $30 for six hours at the park might sound like a much better deal than $30 for four hours.

In this case, the consumer problem may be more generally written as

$$\max_{x_1, x_2} U(x_1, x_2, z(x_1, p_0)) \qquad (2.4)$$

subject to the budget constraint

$$p_0 \hat{x}_1 + p_2 x_2 \leq y, \qquad (2.5)$$

where z represents the consumer's perception of how good a deal she has received as a function of the level of consumption and the fixed price paid for the good. Really, this is just a generalization of the previous model where the bliss point for good 1 now depends upon the fixed price charged for consumption of good 1. Thaler further supposes that transaction utility is additively separable from consumption utility. In this case, we could write the utility function as $U(x_1, x_2, z(x_1, p_0)) = u(x_1, x_2) + z(x_1, p_0)$. The bliss point for x_1 occurs where the sum of marginal consumption utility and marginal transaction utility is zero, $\partial u(x_1, x_2)/\partial x_1 + \partial z(x_1, p_0)/\partial x_1 = 0$. If this utility function accurately describes preferences, then the bliss point would potentially increase as p_0 increases. This would happen if marginal transaction utility increases as p_0 increases, requiring marginal consumption utility to become more negative in order to reach a bliss point.

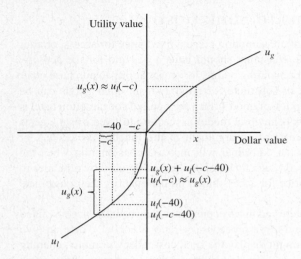

FIGURE 2.5
Sunk Costs in
Prospect Theory

A more-common second explanation for why consumers would allow fixed or sunk costs to influence consumption is that people might not evaluate all events using the same utility function. Rather, Daniel Kahneman and Amos Tversky propose that people classify each event as either a gain or a loss. Gains are evaluated with respect to a utility function over gains, which we will call $u_g(x)$, that displays diminishing marginal utility of consumption. Thus, utility over gains displays the familiar diminishing marginal utility shape, depicted in the upper right quadrant of Figure 2.5. We refer to a curve with this shape as *concave*. Alternatively, losses are evaluated with respect to a utility function over losses, $u_l(x)$, where the utility function over losses is somewhat steeper than the utility function over gains and displays increasing marginal utility of consumption, as displayed in the lower left quadrant of Figure 2.5. We call a curve with this shape *convex*. This shape is motivated by the notion that consumers feel diminishing marginal pain from losses, called **loss aversion**. Loss is negative consumption, and thus diminishing marginal utility of loss is identical to increasing marginal utility of consumption. This model, called **prospect theory**, is developed and discussed in greater detail throughout the book.

Thaler theorizes that if goods are consumed long after purchase, then their costs are classified as losses and considered alongside the value of consumption rather than all being lumped into a single transaction and evaluated using a single utility function. In other words, when paying for the good, a consumer takes note, opening a mental account. This account is closed and evaluated once a consumption decision has been realized. Thus, if attending the basketball game in the snowstorm with tickets that were given to them, consumers obtain utility $u_g(x) + u_l(-c) < 0$, where x is the value of viewing the game and c is the cost of driving 60 miles in a blizzard. Not attending in this case will yield $u_g(0) + u_l(0) = 0$. The value of attending must be negative if the consumer would decide not to attend. Figure 2.5 displays a hypothetical example showing how one might perceive a gain by attending the game. If the people paid $40 for the tickets, the utility from attending would be considered $u_g(x) + u_l(-c - 40)$. If the consumers decided not to attend after paying, they would continue to feel the pain of the $40 loss without any consumption gain, obtaining $u_l(-40)$. If the value of viewing the game is approximately equal to the cost of driving, then $u_g(x) + u_l(-c-40) > u_l(-40)$, owing to the convexity of the utility of loss function. Thus, one feels less pain from loss by realizing some benefit and closing out one's mental account with a smaller negative balance than if one had forgone the game.

Note that both of these explanations require that the consumer evaluate the sunk cost as an object of current value. The transaction cost explanation supposes that sunk cost is used to generate a feeling of obtaining a good deal, whereas loss aversion supposes sunk cost is compared against other costs and gains from consumption.

The manager of a pizza restaurant may be motivated to offer all-you-can-eat pricing if it allows her to employ fewer servers, potentially cutting costs by more than the increase in pizza consumed. However, these results suggest it will be important to determine how price affects consumption to make the greatest profit. Charging smaller amounts might increase profits if it reduces pizza consumption and thus reduces the production costs of the restaurant. Thus transaction utility could play a significant role in determining the best pricing strategy from the point of view of a pizza seller.

EXAMPLE 2.3   Pizza Buffets and Pricing

Upon entering an all-you-can-eat pizza buffet, diners pay a fixed fee for consumption and then must choose how much of any pizza offered to consume. Thaler conjectured that owing to transaction utility, the price of the pizza buffet would have an influence on the amount of pizza consumed. If the pizza is independent of any other good, then the rational model would predict no impact of price paid on pizza consumption. To test this hypothesis, David Just and Brian Wansink convinced an all-you-can-eat pizza restaurant to allow them to experiment on their customers. Upon entering the establishment, each of 66 diners were given either a coupon for a free drink or a coupon for 50% off the price of their meal and a free drink. They observed the number of slices taken by each diner in the study and measured the weight of the food left on each plate after tables were bused. Further, they administered surveys to try to determine the diners' motivation for their consumption decisions.

Their results showed that diners who had paid half price for their meal tended to eat one fewer slice of pizza than their full-price counterparts, or about 25% less. This was true even when controlling for sex, height, weight, or other potentially important consumption factors. Thus, buffet goers might eat to get their money's worth, falling prey to the sunk cost fallacy. An additional and interesting result found that within either treatment, diners who rated the pizza as being less tasty ate significantly more pizza than those who professed to like the taste. They take this as support for the notion of transaction utility. Clearly it takes more bad pizza than good to get your money's worth.

This example also shows how we might use our behavioral model therapeutically to advise consumers on how to make themselves better off. If we were to use the rational consumer model as a normative description of how people should behave, we would advise individual consumers to consume solely to enjoy the pizza and forget about how much they paid. Once the pizza is purchased, there is no longer a reason to consider the costs involved. In general, every project should be evaluated based on its future costs and future contribution to utility or profit rather than on any prior considerations.

History and Notes

It is difficult to pin down exactly when the sunk cost fallacy was discovered or named. Economists generally recognized the irrelevance of sunk costs before 1900, and the topic was covered briefly in the classic text *Economics* by Paul Samuelson and William Nordhaus in 1948. Nineteenth-century works on agriculture and railroad management make mention of the concept of sunk costs and often argue the concept as if the sunk cost fallacy were pervasive, though it was not yet named.

Rational Explanations for the Sunk Cost Fallacy

As alluded to previously, there are some reasons sunk costs might truly matter in future decisions. As with examples in politics, discontinuing a project often induces a future cost by publicly signaling a failure. A business might negatively influence future investment, or a politician might negatively influence public opinion of her ability, with such a public signal. Further, sometimes ending a project involves substantial fixed costs in terms of disposal of equipment or waste. In this case, marginal costs of production can exceed marginal benefits at the optimum given the fixed costs that may be incurred if production were stopped short.

In consumer choice, we have already noted that sunk costs can influence choice if they create an income effect (as displayed in Figure 2.3). In this case, higher sunk costs reduce the amount of wealth that can be allocated, leading to substitution between goods as consumers move along their income expansion path (or in this case, down toward the x_1 axis). Agnar Sandmo provides an argument as to why fixed costs can also influence the production of a firm. If the firm must make decisions about the amount of production before they know what price they will receive for their output, they might wish to reduce production as a means of reducing risk. This will occur if the firm maximizes the expected utility of profit rather than expected profit, topics that are covered in Chapter 9. In this model, aversion to risk is represented by the shape of a utility of profit function, $u(\pi)$. Suppose $\pi = py - c(y) - FC$, where p is the random price, y is the output chosen by the firm, $c(y)$ is the variable cost of production, and FC is the fixed cost. In this case, the fixed cost shifts the distribution of profits and thus alters the shape of the utility curve at any particular price. The firm will alter production in response to changes in fixed costs because the change in the shape of the utility function at any given price necessarily alters their preferences regarding risk.

Finally, people might derive some (fixed) added joy from finishing a project that is unaccounted for in the marginal calculations. Thus, the marathon runner might obtain positive enjoyment from running the first 13 miles and negative marginal enjoyment for the next 13. In fact, the overall enjoyment for the race may be negative between mile 20 and mile 26 if the race is not finished. But if the joy of crossing the finish line itself is enough to wipe out all negative utility realized between mile 13 and mile 26, it is rational to continue running until the end. In this case, even if a project begins to be a loser, a management team might consider the joy of completing the project more important than the monetary loss incurred. Such a decision may be rational, but it is far from the profit-maximizing assumption that is most often used in economic theory.

Transaction Utility and Flat-Rate Bias

A phenomenon that is related to the sunk cost fallacy is **flat-rate bias**. Many services can be purchased on a per-use basis or with a fixed fee for access. For example, a consumer can buy issues of a magazine at the newsstand or purchase a subscription to that magazine. A subscription usually offers a substantial discount over the newsstand price, but it would only truly be worth the cost if the subscriber reads the magazines she has ordered. If the subscription reduces the price per magazine by 50%, that may be a good deal, but only if you read at least half of the magazines that are delivered to your door. Similarly, a monthly bus pass often provides a substantial discount over paying for individual trips if the rider makes enough trips; but a consumer would need to determine that her level of ridership would lead to a discount rather than an added expense. The flat-rate bias occurs when consumers choose to use the fixed-fee option when they would have been better off choosing the per-use option. For example, telephone services can be purchased by the minute using a pay-as-you-go plan or can be based on a monthly fee for unlimited access. Suppose the consumer can choose either a fixed rate p_0 for unlimited consumption of a good or a linear price p_1 per unit consumed. Then, we can modify the consumer problem

$$\max_{x_1, x_2, \delta \in \{0,1\}} U(x_1, x_2) \tag{2.6}$$

subject to the budget constraint

$$\delta p_0 + (1 - \delta)p_1 x_1 + p_2 x_2 \leq y, \tag{2.7}$$

where δ is equal to 1 if the fixed-price plan is chosen and 0 if the linear-pricing plan is chosen, x_1 is the number of minutes used, and x_2 is consumption of other goods. The notation in equation 2.6 indicates that the consumer must choose δ, which can either equal 1 or 0, in addition to x_1 and x_2, to maximize her utility of consumption.

There are two possible solutions to this problem. If the consumer chooses the fixed-price plan, she will consume good 1 until she reaches her bliss point as in Figure 2.3. Otherwise, she will consume until she reaches the budget constraint, as in the standard consumer model presented in Chapter 1. Importantly, two potential behaviors are ruled out by the rational model. The two choices have equal cost at the level of consumption defined by $p_0 = p_1 \bar{x}_1$, for $\bar{x}_1 = p_0/p_1$. If one consumes more than $\bar{x}_1$, it will always be cheaper to use the fixed-price plan. Thus, no one should be observed to consume more than $\bar{x}_1$ under the linear-pricing plan. Alternatively, below $\bar{x}_1$ it is always cheaper to use the linear-pricing plan. Thus, no one should be observed to consume less than $\bar{x}_1$ under the fee-for-unlimited-service plan.

In actuality this does not appear to be the case. Rather, in most cases, it appears that consumers prefer flat-rate pricing even if their usage will not justify it.

EXAMPLE 2.4   Telecommunications

Telephone and cell phone plans are often offered in both flat-rate and pay-as-you-go options. In the late 1980s, Southwestern Bell Telephone introduced extended area service (EAS), which offered unlimited calling to the Dallas area for a set of customers in a nearby community who would normally have to pay relatively high per-minute long-distance fees. The cost of EAS was $19.85 per month. Donald Kridel, Dale Lehman, and Dennis Weisman examined a sample of 2,200 EAS customers and found that only 24% of the customers had placed enough calls to the Dallas calling area to exceed the $19.85 cost of service had they instead been charged the per-minute fee. Thus, 76% had chosen the flat rate when they should have chosen a linear-pricing option, displaying the flat-rate bias. Similar results (though perhaps not as strong) were found when examining behavior when selecting more general long-distance usage. Thus the telephone company might have been able to increase their profits by inducing customers to pay for services that 76% never used. Analogously, consumers today need to be wary of relatively expensive flat fees for unlimited phone, text, or data plans. Many of us may be lining the pockets of the phone companies without enjoying any greater benefits.

EXAMPLE 2.5   Gym Memberships

Another context in which the consumer can choose between flat-rate and linear pricing is in attending a gym. Members usually pay a monthly fee that allows them to attend the gym whenever they like. Alternatively, some gyms offer a fee for use or a pass that is good for a small number of uses. Gyms regularly lament that a large number of customers join the gym when they resolve to finally get in shape but, soon after, their resolve fades and they stop coming. Stefano Della Vigna and Ulrike Malmendier analyzed the membership decisions and attendance records for close to 8,000 gym members over a three-year period. These members could pay a monthly fee of $70 or could purchase a 10-visit pass for $100. The average gym member attended the gym just 4.3 times per month. At that rate, a person could use a 10-visit pass for an entire year and pay just $600. Instead, using the monthly membership option costs $840 per year. Over the course of membership, an average person pays about $600 more than necessary ($1,400 total) for the level of gym attendance, making the flat-rate bias rather costly.

Procedural Explanations for Flat-Rate Bias

The notion of transaction utility seems to suggest that using a flat rate would encourage the consumer to use more of the product in order to reduce the average price per unit of consumption. Though consumers displaying the flat-rate bias are clearly not getting a good deal, this thought process might still take place. Nonetheless, before purchasing, consumers might think very differently about transaction utility and their future potential use of a consumption good. Several motivations for the flat-rate bias have been proposed. The most central to the topic of this chapter are based on the notion of transaction utility.

A consumer considering a gym membership might believe that $10 for a single visit to the gym sounds like a high average cost resulting in a low level of transaction utility. Alternatively, paying $70 for the opportunity to go to the gym as many times as you like for a month might sound like a much better deal. The consumer might either neglect to consider, or fail to accurately project, the number of times she will attend. The monthly option is not stated in a way that allows the consumer to easily compare the average cost. Thus instead of choosing the minimum cost option for the level of use the consumer is intent upon, she might simply consider the transaction utility associated with each option, where perception of transaction utility might depend heavily on the way the problem is stated.

This is closely related to the notion of **framing**, which is covered more thoroughly in later chapters. The wording or phrasing of a choice can have serious implications for how consumers perceive the tradeoffs. In this case, consumers may be influenced by the comparison of potential (though not actual) use between a single trip to the gym versus a month's worth of attendance. The decision may be written by modifying equations 2.6 and 2.7 as follows:

$$\max_{x_1, x_2, \delta \in \{0,1\}} U(x_1, x_2, \delta z_0 + (1-\delta)z_1) \tag{2.8}$$

subject to the budget constraint

$$\delta p_0 + (1-\delta)p_1 x_1 + p_2 x_2 \leq y, \tag{2.9}$$

where z_0 and z_1 are the anticipated transaction utility associated with fixed and linear-pricing options, respectively. For the purpose of making a managerial decision, it would be important to model the factors that can affect the transaction utility under each option.

Flat-rate pricing can allow the consumer to disassociate the payment from the actual consumption. Drazen Prelec and George Loewenstein refer to this as the effect of **payment decoupling**. When we pay for a good at the time of consumption, we link the price and consumption directly to each other. When payment and consumption are separated substantially in time, price and consumption might not be as closely linked. For example, some consumers might save substantial money by using public transportation or taxis rather than owning a car. However, when one already owns a car, one has the luxury of considering a trivial trip to the convenience store for a forgotten toiletry to be a "free" trip—or at least this trip to the store comes at zero marginal cost. On the other hand, the person without the car would be confronted by the cost of this simple trip, potentially paying $2.50 for a trip to the store to purchase a $2-tube of toothpaste. The potential negative transaction utility from trivial uses such as this can lead to choosing the fixed-price option even if the linear price produces a lower cost. Payment decoupling may be of particular importance in examining credit card behavior, which can allow the consumer to ignore the direct cost of some items both because of the time delay in receiving the bill and because the bill will include potentially dozens of purchases all lumped together under a single total amount due.

A consumer might also simply have a distaste for linear pricing. Using a service, like a cell phone, on a pay-as-you-go plan requires the rational consumer to evaluate before each use (or each minute of use) whether the use really justifies the cost. For example, Verizon Wireless currently offers a pay-as-you-go plan that charges you $3.99 for your first call on any day. Before you make your first call of the day, you must determine that it will be a relatively valuable call. Alternatively, with a flat-rate price, you would not need to evaluate this because the call will not add to the bill on the margin. Thus, even if you do not use the service enough to justify the flat rate, you might use the flat rate to eliminate the nagging feeling that can accompany a linear-pricing plan. Such an effect could be modeled by introducing an added utility cost to the consumer for consuming under linear pricing, replacing the utility function with $U(x_1, x_2) - (1 - \delta)kx_1$. Here k is the marginal cognitive cost of using the service under a linear price. If this cost is great enough, it can lead the individual to choose flat-rate pricing despite a monetary cost disadvantage.

A final potential motivation is the notion that the consumer might have problems with self-control. This topic is covered more thoroughly in later chapters. In essence, if you believe that going to the gym is good for you, you might worry that a marginal fee for service could discourage future use, whereas a fixed fee for service can introduce, through transaction utility, an incentive for higher levels of use. In this case, you might try to induce gym attendance by purchasing the monthly membership, so that you will feel guilty for not attending because it keeps your average price for use high and your transaction utility low. Our data on gym usage may simply be the evidence of how ineffective this strategy is.

A manager who is considering offering a flat rate for services could potentially benefit from the flat-rate bias. If consumers have a bias for purchasing using a flat-rate pricing plan even when their use does not justify it, there is the potential to increase profits from those who do not increase use above the threshold where the flat rate is actually cheaper. However, there is also the potential of increased use by those who would pay more under the linear-pricing plan. Hence, this is not always a profit-maximizing strategy. The actual benefit to the firm depends on how sensitive consumers are to the price of the flat-rate program and on how many adjust their consumption above the break-even level of consumption.

From a normative perspective, some consumers could be better off by consuming the same amount under the linear-pricing plan. However, to determine which pricing plan is better requires the effort of examining one's usage and comparing the cost under different plans. One should at times analyze the use of flat-rate services (such as cell phones) and determine if cheaper pricing alternatives exist given one's own historical usage behavior.

Rational Explanations for Flat-Rate Bias

Two primary rational explanations have been given for the flat-rate bias. The first supposes that consumers might not actually know the amount of use they are projected to have. Given this uncertainty about use, they might opt for the fixed-price plan to avoid the uncertain cost of consumption. For example, it may be that one occasionally uses a cell phone extensively, whereas in a normal month one might only use a few minutes. Expected utility theory suggests that a consumer may be willing to reduce the average payout of a gamble in return for eliminating the uncertainty. The flat-rate bias could be explained by the same phenomenon where consumers are willing to pay a larger amount on average to ensure that they are certain of the eventual total cost. In this case, although future use is a decision variable rather than an externally determined random variable, the value of the calls may be random. Thus, one might buy the fixed-price option because of the value of the option to place more calls without facing a penalty. Kridel, Lehman, and Weisman find that this appears to be a good explanation for many of the apparent mistakes in pricing choices.

Eugenio Miravete claims that there is little evidence of incorrect choices to begin with. He uses a survey of telephone customers' anticipated and actual use of services in Kentucky to determine the extent of such errors. In fact, he finds that customers' anticipated use was consistent with the pricing scheme they chose. Further, he finds evidence that customers respond to charges in a way that suggests they are trying to minimize their bill given their level of use. Thus, those who incorrectly predicted their use usually shifted to the correct service plan after discovering the error. He finds that less than 6% of customers commit the error of subscribing to a flat-rate service when they would have benefited by using another system. His explanation for the observed errors is that consumers are in transition and still discovering which is the best plan for them. He concludes that the rational model of pricing choice is the best model to describe behavior. Miravete finds that among those who choose the flat rate pricing, a majority overestimate their eventual use of the phone service. However, even if the phone-use data contain no direct or incontrovertible evidence of the anomaly, the data are consistent with the underlying behavioral tendencies that could lead to the anomalous behavior. Even if the anomalous behavior is not evident, a behavioral economist would find the consumer's formation of use forecasts important in discerning the motivations for behavior.

History and Notes

Although there was ample evidence and discussion before his observation, Kenneth Train is credited with coining the term *flat-rate bias* in discussing telephone pricing plans in 1994. In coining this term he cited evidence from his own work from the 1980s. This bias has been noted in Internet subscriptions, software licensing, electricity use, and gym memberships. Not only is there evidence of the flat-rate bias, but there is also evidence that those subscribing through a flat rate are much less likely to abandon service. Thus, the service provider not only gets more money for the level of service, but it is also more likely to retain the customer. Thus there is substantial incentive for service providers to offer a flat-rate option for premium levels of use.

Transaction Utility and Consumer Preferences in Reference

Often our perception of how good a deal we have achieved depends not only on the amount we are able to consume and the quality of the good itself but also on the context within which we make our purchase. In some contexts, items are expected to be more expensive than in other contexts. This leads consumers to display very different demand behavior depending upon the purchase context. Someone might refuse to purchase a good in one venue because it is too expensive, but the same person might purchase the good at an identical price when in a context where the price seems justified. Consumers might use cues from the environment or memory of previous transactions in similar contexts to form an idea of what is a fair price. A comparison used to aid in making a decision is called a **reference point**. For example, your reference point may be the price you have paid in the past at a particular establishment. If a hamburger has always cost $5 at a particular restaurant, that hamburger might feel like a particularly good deal if you could purchase it for $3. It might feel like a terrible deal if the price rose to $6. Thus the reference point can play an important role in determining the consumer's transaction utility. The reference point may be influenced by the context. An identical hamburger at another restaurant might always be priced at $2. Here it might feel like you have been ripped off if they were to suddenly increase the price to $3.

EXAMPLE 2.6   Beverage Demand and References

Richard Thaler surveyed consumers about their intended behavior under a couple of different hypothetical scenarios. Each respondent saw only one scenario. The first asks you to consider that you are at the beach on a hot day and want to buy a bottle of your favorite beer. A companion offers to get you one from a run-down grocery store. Your friend asks how much you are willing to pay for the beer, saying she will buy it if the price is less than or equal to your stated willingness to pay. The second scenario is identical except that instead of a run-down grocery store, your friend is going to a fancy resort hotel. Note that both scenarios suggest that the respondent will receive their favorite beer, and thus the item itself is identical in both choices. Respondents were willing to pay much more for the beer from the resort than from the grocery store (median value of $2.65 versus $1.50). Moreover, because both scenarios involve consuming the beer on the beach with the friend after she returns, there is no chance that environmental factors could influence the utility the consumer derives from the beer. Thus, the willingness to pay for the experience was influenced by the context in which the purchase takes place.

EXAMPLE 2.7 Internet Auctions

Internet auctions often offer either a minimum bid or a price at which the potential buyer could forgo the auction altogether and buy the item outright—sometimes called a *buy now* price. Anna Dodonova and Yuri Khoroshilov examined how the listed buy now price affected bids on a jewelry auction website. They found several mass-marketed items that come up for auction regularly on the site that could offer valid comparisons of behavior. This allowed them to compare items that are identical in design and content and thus in market value. However, the buy now price varied among the auctions. When items were posted with higher buy now prices, bidders placed higher bids, signaling that they valued the item more highly than when they saw the identical item with a low buy now price. Somehow, the buy now price had influenced the bidders' valuations, perhaps by creating a reference point.

Theory and Reference-Dependent Preferences

The response of consumers to context in forming consumption decisions tells us a lot about how transaction utility works. To use the notion of transaction utility in predicting behavior, we need to know the potential reference points that drive the decision behavior. Thus, a behavioral theory of reference points might suppose that the consumer considering the purchase of a good will be influenced by her transaction utility for the purchase given the context of the purchase, $z(x, p|\xi)$, where ξ represents the reference point in the given context. The consumer will also be influenced by the utility of consumption, as in equation 2.8. This particular theory contains very little predictive power because it does not tell us how the reference point was created or how we could determine it.

We could create a procedural rational model of reference point selection. For example, the reference price may be the average price the consumer had previously observed in a particular context (e.g., a resort hotel). This would tell us that the consumer considered previous observed prices in determining if the price was reasonable or not. If the price was higher than at previous resorts, the consumer would think it was a bad deal and have a lower transaction utility. If the price was lower than at previous resorts, the consumer would feel she had gotten a good deal. There is substantial evidence of the use of reference points in decision making. This concept is examined in several of the chapters in this book.

A pervasive problem with using reference-based behavioral theories is that we seldom have a theory describing why a consumer selects a particular reference point. One of the reasons for a lack of clarity in theory is that it can be difficult to test for differences in reference points empirically. In purchasing behavior, the formation of reference points may be particularly difficult to isolate. What is it that quintessentially separates a resort hotel from a run-down grocery store? How can we classify different purchasing locations or experiences into different categories? Does the presence of luxury items nearby signal that higher prices are to be expected?

Alternatively, some have found success in manipulating reference points. For example, the buy now price creates a very simple reference point. In this case, the bidder will purchase or not purchase the item but will judge the transaction utility of a potential purchase based on what price she pays relative to the buy now price. In this case, transaction utility may be written as $z(p|p_{bn})$, where p_{bn} is the buy now price and where transaction utility is decreasing in p and increasing in p_{bn}. By raising the buy now price, the consumer is more likely to be willing to purchase at a higher price because she will receive a greater transaction utility in addition to the same level of consumption utility.

For the manager trying to set prices within her store, the implication is that one can manipulate the reference point of the consumer and potentially receive higher prices and greater profit. Stores can list comparison prices for items that they are selling in order to induce customers to feel they are obtaining a good deal. We often hear of stores that perpetually mark items as on sale in order to induce this type of feeling. For example, consumers are more likely to buy an item marked "On sale for $2 regularly $4" than they are to buy the same item marked simply $2. The item may be the same price, but consumers feel they are getting a better deal in comparison to the regular price. Stores often manipulate regular and sale prices to take advantage of this behavior. Some stores that offer everyday low prices instead advertise their own price in relation to their competitors' regular price to the same effect.

From a normative standpoint, transaction utility can lead consumers to make two types of mistakes. First, consumers might purchase items that they otherwise would not want, simply because they think they are getting a good deal. Second, consumers might fail to purchase things that would make them better off because the context suggests a lower reference price to them. In this case, a consumer might not purchase the $3 hamburger at a relatively cheap restaurant even though she would be willing to pay $5 for the same sandwich at a relatively more expensive restaurant. Normatively, consumers would receive higher consumption utility if they did not consider the transaction utility and made purchase decisions based on price irrespective of context. The difficulty in offering our consumers prescriptive advice is that we do not know which context represents true consumption preferences. Nevertheless, we are often given advice designed to combat such context-dependent preferences. For example, one should never use the snacks provided in your room at a high-end hotel: The markup is enormous.

Rational Explanations for Context-Dependent Preferences

Two primary alternative explanations exist for reference-dependent preferences. First, it may be that the context itself conveys information. For example, bidders might not have substantial knowledge about the prices of jewelry and might look to the buy now price to learn something regarding the overall value of the item. Although this might not be the best way to research the price of a good, other ways may be prohibitively costly in terms of effort or time. In this case, it might not be the reference point that was manipulated but simply the bidder's expectation of prices she may be able to obtain if she looked elsewhere for a similar item. In this case, shifting bids may be perfectly rational given the costs of alternative forms of learning.

Alternatively, it could be that some contexts truly add value to goods. Whereas the beach example is carefully constructed to try to avoid this issue, in practice it may be hard to isolate the reference-point effect from the effect of context on value in a more-general consumption setting. I may be willing to pay more for a hot dog at a Chicago Cubs baseball game because I have fond memories of consuming a hot dog at another game in the past. Or I may be willing to pay more for a beverage at a resort because I like the atmosphere in the resort more than that of a run-down grocery store. If the atmosphere is a complement for consumption of a particular good, then willingness to pay for that good should increase in context.

Biographical Note

© Benschop/Hollandse Hoogte/Redux

Richard H. Thaler (1945–)

B.A., Case Western Reserve University, 1967; M.S., University of Rochester, 1970; PhD, University of Rochester, 1974; held faculty positions at the University of Rochester, Cornell University, and the University of Chicago

Though all his degrees were in economics, Thaler is famous for incorporating concepts from cognitive psychology into models of economic decision making. Many consider him to be the founder of behavioral economics. From his early work on, he has asserted that consumers suffer from biases in perception as well as emotions that influence decisions. Much of his work has been in the development of the field of behavioral finance, focusing on how behavioral biases can influence financial markets. He laid the foundation for nearly every behavioral economics contribution to date. From 1987 to 1991 (and occasionally thereafter) he produced a series of review articles for the *Journal of Economic Perspectives* entitled "Anomalies." In it he wrote of phenomena that appeared to defy rational economic modeling. For many academic economists, this was their first serious exposure to the field of behavioral economics and helped to codify and define the field. His fingerprints can be found throughout the field of behavioral economics. More recently, he has become an advocate for the notion of using behavioral economics to create policies that do not restrict choice but that have a tendency to lead the consumer to a desired decision. The case for such policies is made in his book *Nudge* with Cass Sunstein. Daniel Kahneman praised Thaler for his direct contributions in incorporating psychology and economics and for the contributions of the many students who have flocked to work with him.

THOUGHT QUESTIONS

1. This chapter has presented some evidence that consumers derive utility from getting a good deal. Have you observed evidence that people purchase goods when it is not necessarily in their best interest just so they can get a good deal?

2. If retailers and manufacturers are aware that consumers derive utility from "getting a good deal," they may be able to take advantage of this to increase their own profits. Can you find evidence that retailers take steps to manipulate the perception of the deals they offer?

3. Policy makers concerned with the increasing number of overweight consumers have long complained about the pricing of sodas at fast food restaurants. In most cases, a small soda (usually around 16 ounces) sells for a couple dollars. For just a few cents more, one could purchase a drink that was double that size and obtain a much better deal. Why would fast food chains offer such steep discounts on larger sodas? In one extreme case, a major fast food chain has offered all sizes of drinks for the same price. How could this be profitable? Policymakers have suggested requiring linear pricing (eliminating discounts for larger amounts) to fight obesity. New York also attempted to ban the sale of large soft drinks. Are these policies likely to be effective?

4. Suppose a telephone company had two kinds of customers. One had a utility function that could be represented as $u_1(x) = 5x - x^2 - k(x)$, where x is the total amount of time spent on the phone and k is the total cost to the customer for service. This results in a marginal utility curve $\partial u_1(x)/\partial x = 5 - 2x - \partial k/\partial x$. The other type of consumer possesses a utility function that can be written as $u_2(x) = 5x - x^2 - k(x) - x/k(x)$, resulting in a marginal utility curve $\partial u_2(x)/\partial x = 5 - 2x - \partial k/\partial x - \frac{\left[k(x) - x\frac{\partial k(x)}{\partial x}\right]}{[k(x)]^2}$. Suppose that each faces no budget constraint (so that they will purchase until marginal utility declines to zero). Suppose the firm charges a linear price so that $k(x) = px$, and marginal cost is given by $\partial k(x)/\partial x = p$. What is the demand curve for each customer type? (*Hint:* Simply solve each case for the amount of line use, x, that results in zero marginal utility). Are these demand curves downward sloping? Alternatively, suppose that the firm charges a flat fee, so that $k(x) = p$, and $\partial k(x)/\partial x = 0$. What is the demand curve for each consumer type given this pricing structure? Are these demand curves downward sloping? Which consumer displays a desire for transaction utility? How does this influence demand under each pricing scheme? What does demand look like if consumers face a two-part tariff so that $k(x) = p_0 + p_1 x$, so that $\partial k(x)/\partial x = p_1$? (Do not solve for the demand curve, but give some intuition as to how it will behave.)

5. Further, suppose that the cost function for providing minutes on the phone is given by $c(x) = x^2$. The profit function is given by $\pi = k(x^*) - C(x^*)$, where x^* is the optimal consumption given the pricing scheme solved in the previous exercise. What are the optimal price choices for the firm under linear or flat-fee pricing if all customers were of type 1? Write down the profit function for each pricing scheme. Use a spreadsheet application (like Microsoft Excel) to solve for the price that maximizes the profit by trying various prices until you find the price yielding the highest profits. Which pricing scheme provides greater profits? Now try the same exercise assuming all customers are of type 2. Which pricing scheme now provides the greatest profits? How do you think the answer would change if the phone company believed they would have customers of both types?

REFERENCES

Arkes, H.R., and C. Blumer. "The Psychology of Sunk Cost." *Organizational Behavior and Human Decision Processes* 35(1985): 124–140.

Della Vigna, S., and U. Malmendier. "Paying Not to Go to the Gym." *American Economic Review* 96(2006):694–719.

Dodonova, A., and Y. Khoroshilov. "Anchoring and the Transaction Utility: Evidence from On-Line Auctions." *Applied Economics Letters* 11(2004): 307–310.

Just, D.R., and B. Wansink. "The Flat-Rate Pricing Paradox: Conflicting Effects of 'All-You-Can-Eat' Buffet Pricing." *Review of Economics and Statistics* 93(2011): 193–200.

Kridel, D.J., D.E. Lehman, and D.L. Weisman. "Option Value, Telecommunications Demand, and Policy." *Information Economics and Policy* 5(1993): 125–144.

Miravete, E.J. "Choosing the Wrong Calling Plan? Ignorance and Learning." *American Economic Review* 93(2003): 297–310.

Prelec, D., and G.F. Loewenstein. "The Red and the Black: Mental Accounting of Savings and Debt." *Marketing Science* 17(1998): 4–28.

Samuelson, P.A., and W.D. Nordhaus. *Economics*. New York: McGraw-Hill, 1948.

Sandmo, A. "On the Theory of the Competitive Firm under Price Uncertainty." *American Economic Review* 61(1971): 65–73.

Thaler, R. "Toward a Positive Theory of Consumer Choice." *Journal of Economic Behavior and Organization* 1(1980): 39–60.

Thaler, R. "Mental Accounting and Consumer Choice." *Marketing Science* 4(1985): 199–214.

Train, K.E. *Optimal Regulation*. Cambridge, Mass.: MIT Press, 1994.

Advanced Concept

Fixed Costs and Rational Choice

More explicitly, we can consider the LaGrangian associated with equations 2.1 and 2.2:

$$L = U(x_1, x_2) + \lambda(y - p_0 - p_1 x_1 - p_2 x_2) \tag{2.A}$$

with first-order conditions for an internal solution given by

$$\frac{\partial L}{\partial x_1} = \frac{\partial}{\partial x_1} U(x_1^*, x_2^*) - \lambda^* p_1 = 0 \tag{2.B}$$

$$\frac{\partial L}{\partial x_1} = \frac{\partial}{\partial x_2} U(x_1^*, x_2^*) - \lambda^* p_2 = 0 \tag{2.C}$$

$$y - p_0 - p_1 x_1 - p_2 x_2 = 0. \tag{2.D}$$

As in Chapter 1, equations 2.B and 2.C imply that

$$\frac{1}{p_2} \frac{\partial}{\partial x_2} U(x_1^*, x_2^*) = \frac{1}{p_1} \frac{\partial}{\partial x_1} U(x_1^*, x_2^*). \tag{2.E}$$

We can solve the budget constraint for x_2 and substitute into equation 2.E to find

$$\frac{p_1}{p_2} = \frac{\frac{\partial}{\partial x_1} U\left(x_1^*, \frac{y - p_0 - p_1 x_1^*}{p_2}\right)}{\frac{\partial}{\partial x_2} U\left(x_1^*, \frac{y - p_0 - p_1 x_1^*}{p_2}\right)}, \tag{2.F}$$

which implicitly defines the demand function for good 1. Altering p_0 in this equation will almost certainly alter the consumption of good 1. To see this, note that as p_0 increases, if x_1^* were to remain the same, x_2^* must increase through the budget constraint. If there is diminishing marginal utility of consuming good 2, the denominator of the right side must decline, requiring a proportional decline in the numerator—the marginal utility of good 1. This is an unlikely occurrence if we are holding $x_1{}^*$ constant. Alternatively, good 1 may remain the same if the two goods are independent and if good 2 displays constant marginal utility.

Were we to assume $p_1 = 0$, then equation 2.B is replaced by

$$\frac{\partial L}{\partial x_1} = \frac{\partial}{\partial x_1} U(x_1{}^*, x_2{}^*) = 0, \qquad (2.G)$$

or, after substituting the budget constraint

$$\frac{\partial}{\partial x_1} U\left(x_1{}^*, \frac{y - p_0}{p_2}\right) = 0, \qquad (2.H)$$

which implicitly defines the demand function. Totally differentiating equation 2.H with respect to $x_1{}^*$ and p_0 yields the relationship between fixed costs and demand for good 1

$$\frac{\partial^2}{\partial x_1^2} U\left(x_1{}^*, \frac{y - p_0}{p_2}\right) dx_1 - \frac{1}{p_2} \frac{\partial^2}{\partial x_2 \partial x_1} U\left(x_1{}^*, \frac{y - p_0}{p_2}\right) dp_0 = 0, \qquad (2.I)$$

or,

$$\frac{dx_1}{dp_0} = \frac{\frac{1}{p_2} \frac{\partial^2}{\partial x_2 \partial x_1} U\left(x_1{}^*, \frac{y - p_0}{p_2}\right)}{\frac{\partial^2}{\partial x_1^2} U\left(x_1{}^*, \frac{y - p_0}{p_2}\right)}. \qquad (2.J)$$

The two goods are independent (neither compliments or substitutes) if $\partial^2 U(x_1, x_2)/\partial x_2 \partial x_1 = 0$, in which case the derivative in equation 2.J is equal to zero, implying that consumption of good 1 will not change with a marginal change in the fixed price of consumption.

Mental Accounting

3

Suppose you had a coupon for a free ice cream cone from a local ice cream parlor. While walking by the store on a particularly hot day, you decide to redeem your coupon. Leaving the store, you stroll down the street and accidently drop the cone on the ground, rendering the ice cream inedible. You are disappointed at first, but you achieve some comfort by reminding yourself that it was free to begin with. You reason that if you didn't have to pay for it, it was no real loss.

Alternatively, suppose you had been wanting to buy a new video game system. You had contemplated saving for the system, but knew you really needed to save your money for a new pair of eyeglasses. Your prescription had changed substantially and it was beginning to be difficult to do everyday things. One afternoon you check your mail and find that your grandmother has written you a check. It is just enough to purchase either the game system or the new glasses. After thinking about it for a minute or two you decide to purchase the video game system. What kind of a gift would glasses make, anyway?

Consumers must deal with new income from varied sources and new expenses on a variety of items on a regular basis. Additionally, people face changes in the state of the world (often referred to as *shocks*) that can render prior investments useless or make them even more valuable. The sheer volume of decisions one must make can lead people to use simple rules of thumb to make decisions rather than to optimize in the way that economic theory suggests. In particular, people can use a system called **mental accounting** to make decisions as well as to rationalize previous decisions. Mental accounting is a procedure of keeping accounts of income and expenses, similar to that used by corporations, except in this case, each person is his or her own bookkeeper and the books are kept in the ledgers of one's mind.

In the previous chapter, we detailed how people can be motivated by transaction utility—the desire to get a good deal on an item. In a sense, when a sunk cost is incurred, it is entered into the mental ledger as an expense in a particular account. To balance the books, the person then seeks a gain of equal or greater value that allows him to close the mental account. Thus, for example, you might open a mental account when you enter an all-you-can-eat restaurant and pay the admission fee. This account could only be closed by consuming enough food for you to feel you have received a value that exceeds the cost of entry. In this case, you would choose to consume more when the price is higher. Decision making based on mental accounting can lead directly to the transaction utility–based behavior described in the previous chapter, though many other anomalous types of behavior are implicated.

This chapter discusses the full theory of mental accounting and describes several types of behavior that apparently result from this decision heuristic. In particular, we discuss how income source can determine the types of spending, how individual consumers can rationalize bad investments, and how consumers can group events in their mind to obtain a balanced account. Mental accounting is a procedural rational model of consumer choice in that it tells us what is motivating the consumer to make these choices. Although mental accounting can lead to many and varied anomalous decisions, the model itself is surprisingly similar to the accounting methods used by large firms for exactly the same purposes.

Rational Choice with Income from Varying Sources

Many people take income from a wide variety of sources. Some work several jobs; others operate a business in addition to their regular job. Even if only working one job, people can receive money in the form of gifts or refunds that may be considered a separate source of income. Consider the consumer who faces the consumption problem

$$\max_{x_1,\, x_2} U(x_1, x_2) \tag{3.1}$$

subject to a budget constraint

$$p_1 x_1 + p_2 x_2 \leq y_1 + y_2, \tag{3.2}$$

where y_1 is income from source 1 and y_2 is income from source 2. The solution to equations 3.1 and 3.2 can be represented by an *indirect utility function*. An indirect utility function is defined as $V(k, p_1, p_2) \equiv \{\max_{x_1,\, x_2} U(x_1, x_2) | p_1 x_1 + p_2 x_2 \leq k\}$, or the most utility that can be obtained given the prices and the budget $k = y_1 + y_2$.

Because utility is only derived from consumption of goods 1 and 2, the particular source of income should not alter the level of utility so long as we remain at the same overall level of income k. Figure 3.1 displays the budget constraints and tangent utility curves under two potential income totals, k_1 and k_2, such that $k_1 < k_2$. The figure shows the optimal consumption bundles under each scenario. Notably, the figure is agnostic about the source of the increase in income. For example, suppose $k_1 = 100$. The particular source of income does not affect the indifference curve. Rather, the shape of the indifference curve is entirely determined by the shape of the utility function, which, as seen in Figure 3.1, is not a function of income source. Increasing y_1 by 100 shifts the budget constraint out, so that total income equals 200, resulting in $k_2 = 200$. At this point the consumer will consume more of any normal good and less of any inferior good (the figure displays two normal goods). If, instead, y_1 remains at its original level and we add 100 to y_2, then we still have a total income of 200, and we remain on the budget constraint given by k_2. Thus, although adding 100 to income does alter consumption, it does not matter from which source the added income is derived. All points along the line described by $y_1 + y_2 = k_2$ will result in an identical budget constraint and result in the same consumption decision. This implies that the indirect utility function increases as income increases. Further, the indirect utility function increases by the same amount, no matter where the additional income comes from.

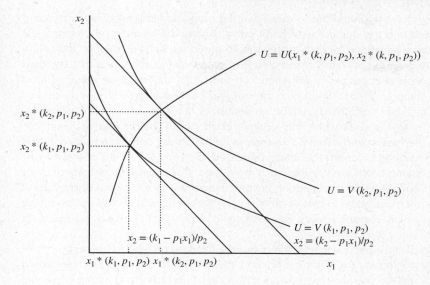

FIGURE 3.1
Income Effects on Consumption

The expansion path (the set of points representing the optimal bundle for all possible budget levels) is represented by the curve stretching from the southwest corner to the northeast corner of Figure 3.1 and passing through the tangency points of the indifference curves and the various possible budget constraints. Because utility is independent of the source of income, the expansion path is a single curve that does not depend upon which source of income we may assume the expansion of income is derived from.

Thus, if a consumer behaves according to the standard rational model, any time the consumer receives an amount of money from one source, the additional money results in some change in the consumption bundle the consumer chooses to purchase. If you receive an identical amount of money from any other source (or any combination of other sources), you should alter your purchasing behavior in exactly the same way. By this account, no matter if you receive gift money, hard-earned wages from a job, or a tax refund, you should spend your marginal dollars on the same items. Money is money and should not be treated as a differentiated good.

EXAMPLE 3.1   Food Stamps versus a Cash Payment

The U.S. Supplemental Nutrition Assistance Program (SNAP) was originally introduced as the Food Stamp Program in 1939. The purpose of this program was to provide low-income individuals or families with money to purchase food. Over the course of its history, the program has altered the way benefits were delivered to recipients. Originally, recipients received books of stamps that could be exchanged for food. Currently, recipients are given a card—much like a debit card—that can be used at a supermarket to purchase food.

Historically, most food stamp recipients spent their entire allotment each benefit period and also spent some substantial additional amount from other cash on food.

Economists have interpreted this to mean that the program, though income enhancing, was not distorting the purchases of participants. If they are spending more than just the food stamp benefit on food, then they should spend the same amount on food if the benefit were given in cash rather than a card that can only be used for food. The standard theory suggests that recipients will spend on food until the marginal utility of food divided by the price of food is equal to the marginal utility of other activities divided by their price (as seen from the discussion on consumer demand in Chapter 1). The only exception to this is seen when this optimal point occurs before the recipient has exhausted the food stamp benefit. Food stamp spending can only include food, and if this point is reached before the benefit is exhausted, then one should still spend the rest of the food stamp benefit, obtaining much more food. If spending the entirety of one's food stamp budget led to consumption beyond the point where marginal utility of food divided by price was equal to that of other goods, then recipients should not be willing to spend any of their cash on food. This cash could return higher utility by spending on other items.

If people did not spend at least some of their own money on food as well as the SNAP benefit, this would indicate that the program had led them to buy food that they would not have purchased had they been given cash instead. Because food stamp recipients historically spent more than the amount of the benefit that was restricted to food pur- chases, economists had assumed that this indicated that the food stamp benefit was not leading people to behave differently than they would were we to give them cash, a condition that is important in determining whether there is dead-weight loss from the policy. The notion that cash would be spent the same as a food stamp benefit was tested at one point when the U.S. Department of Agriculture experimented with giving a cash benefit instead of a restrictive benefit card. The original intent of this move was to eliminate the potential stigma associated with participation in the food stamp program. If the program provided cash, no one could tell the difference between someone buying food with food stamp money and someone using money from some other source. Sur- prisingly, recipients spent substantially less on food when they were given cash instead of a food stamp benefit. Thus, income in cash was being treated differently from income designated as food stamp cash, even though the purchasing power was the same. Clearly, recipients were not finding the point where the marginal utility gained from spending the marginal dollar was equal across activities (in this case, food and all other activities).

EXAMPLE 3.2   Buying Tickets to a Play

Consumers often create a system of budgets for various activities when deciding on consumption activities. Once these budgets are created, they can create artificial barriers in consumption such that the marginal utility gained for the marginal dollar spent on some activities with an excessive budget may be much lower than activities with a less- substantial budget. This implies that the indifference curve is not tangent to the budget constraint, as the rational model implies. In this case, consumers could make themselves better off by reallocating money from one budget to the other and approximating the optimal decision rule embodied by the indifference curve having the same local slope as the budget constraint.

An example of how these budgets can affect behavior was described by Chip Heath and Jack Soll. They asked some participants in an experiment if, given they had spent $50 on a ticket to an athletic event, they would be willing to purchase a $25 theater ticket. Others were asked if they would purchase the theater ticket if they had been given the ticket to an athletic event. A third group was asked if they would pay for the play if they had spent $50 to be inoculated against the flu. Rational decision making should be forward thinking, considering the costs and benefits of the play and not the past spending activities. Interestingly, participants were more likely to turn down the opportunity to attend the play if they had already spent money on the sporting event than if the sporting event were free or if they had spent money on a flu inoculation. Here it appears that having spent money on other entertainment events in the recent past (controlling for any income effects) reduces spending on this category in the future. Alternatively, when the previous entertainment is free, no effect is found. Several other examples are given by Heath and Soll. If consumers consider money to be **fungible**— easily transferred between uses—then such previous spending should not affect current spending because previous spending is sunk cost. Here we see a very different sunk-cost effect, one that is contingent on budget category.

The Theory of Mental Accounting

At a gross level, mental accounting is a theory of grouping and categorizing money and transactions so that the consumer can systematically evaluate the potential tradeoffs. Spending is categorized into separate budgets for various types of items, such as food in the food stamp example. People can deposit money into separate physical accounts, such as a savings or checking account, and they also treat these as physically different types of money. Income is classified by type (e.g., regular income, bonus, gift). The real work-horse of the theory of mental accounting is that people classify items to allow them to segment decisions. Segmenting decisions allows them to simplify the decision process. Clearly it would be difficult to consider all income, wealth, and transactions at once. By narrowing the items that must be considered when making a decision, people create a manageable problem that can allow better control.

Rather than considering all transactions together to determine the optimal consumption bundle, the theory of mental accounting supposes that people keep a mental ledger of income and expenses by category in their mind in order to keep track of and make spending decisions. Thus decisions may be made either on a categorical basis or on a transaction-by-transaction basis. This ledger can be thought of as a series of accounts with a traditional double-entry accounting system for each account. The **double-entry accounting** system requires that each transaction be recorded twice: once as a debit and once as a credit. Typically, a business acquires an item; suppose it is a computer costing $1,000. The business needs to keep track of the amount spent as well as the item. The business keeps track of the transaction in books called ledgers, which contain two columns. The left column is for recording debits and the right column is for recording credits. The computer is entered in a ledger detailing acquisitions in the left column as a debit of $1,000. The transaction is also written in the right hand of another ledger detailing inventory as a credit of $1,000 worth of equipment. Thus, the process of accounting identifies the gains and losses from each transaction and then records them.

Mental accounting supposes that people open a ledger for each transaction or transaction category, classify each event associated with the transaction as a gain or loss, and seek to have a positive or zero balance by the close of the transaction. Because each transaction is entered in a ledger by itself, decisions are not made on a comprehensive basis but on a piecemeal basis. Thus, food stamp recipients do not determine the optimal overall bundle to consume given their wealth, prices of alternatives, and the amount of food stamps. Instead they might consider the food stamps as a positive entry in their ledger for food purchases, and thus increase their consumption of food by a corresponding amount irrespective of what other alternative uses for the money may be possible.

Because items are evaluated piecemeal based on the category of the transaction, people might behave very differently depending on the source of income or depending on the category of item they consider purchasing. Essentially, a person creates budget categories and evaluates these separately from other budget categories in considering a transaction. Because each income source is categorized, the person fails to treat separate accounts or income sources as completely *fungible*. Thus money in a savings account is not treated the same as money in a checking account. One may consider one to be more appropriate for a particular type of transaction. For example, one may consider a checking account to be more useful for day-to-day expenses, whereas a savings account is more useful for longer-term holding of money and thus only for more expensive items. Thus, you might regularly spend down the amount in your checking account but loathe to transfer money from your savings account to your checking account, making day-to-day purchasing decisions as if the savings account did not exist.

Mental accounting combines this notion of a budget and double-entry accounting with the prospect theory notion of valuing outcomes described in the previous chapter. Each event must be classified as a gain or a loss. Then, the amount is evaluated based on the prospect theory value function as pictured in Figure 3.2. The value function is generally made up of two utility functions: one for gains, $u_g(x)$, and one for losses, $u_l(x)$. The value function is concave over potential gains; thus it displays diminishing marginal utility from gains. Thus, the first dollar of gain results in greater pleasure on the margin than the hundredth dollar of gain. As well, the value function is convex over losses, displaying diminishing marginal pain from losses. Thus, the first dollar of loss is more painful on the margin than the hundredth dollar of loss. Additionally, the value function demonstrates loss aversion. This can be seen near the origin as the slope of the utility curve is kinked right at the point between gains and losses, with a much steeper slope for losses than gains. In other words, the consumer considers a marginal loss much more painful than a marginal gain. We typically measure the physical outcomes that make up the argument of the value function, x, either in dollar amounts or in dollar equivalents. Therefore, if you lose $20, then $x = -20$. If instead you lose basketball tickets that were worth $20 to you, then $x = -20$ also.

Whether an outcome is considered a gain or a loss is measured with respect to a reference point. This might seem like a trivial task to begin with. For example, if an

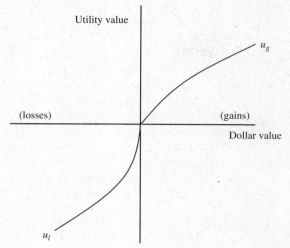

FIGURE 3.2
The Prospect Theory Value Function

employee is paid a salary of $70,000, this might form his reference point. Thus, a bonus of $5,000 for a total of $75,000 would be considered a gain. Alternatively, a deduction of $5,000 from the annual pay would be considered a loss. This process is complicated when there are several events to be evaluated at once. Different outcomes may be suggested depending on how items are grouped. For example, a $20 gain and a $10 loss may be coded either as $u_g(10) + u_l(-20)$ or as $u_l(10 - 20)$, depending on whether the events are **integrated** or **segregated**. This is discussed in greater detail later in the chapter. If we define our reference point as k, we can define the value function as

$$v(x|k) \equiv \begin{cases} u_g(x-k) & \text{if} \quad x \geq k \\ u_l(x-k) & \text{if} \quad x < k. \end{cases} \tag{3.3}$$

We often suppress the reference point in our notation by using the form $v(z) = v(x - k|0)$, in which case any negative value is a loss and any positive value is a gain.

The extent to which outcomes are integrated or segregated can be very important in determining the value of a particular transaction or consumption episode. First, consider a man who, after eating dinner at an expensive restaurant, finds that the bill is about $30 more than he was expecting to pay. In addition, suppose he leaves the restaurant and picks his car up at the nearby parking garage and finds that he is charged $4 more than he had expected to pay for parking for the dinner. Here, the amount the man expected to pay serves as the reference point. In each case, the man spent more than he expected, resulting in a loss relative to the reference point. If these expenses are segregated, then he would experience $v(-30) + v(-4)$. Alternatively, if he integrated these expenses, he would experience $v(-34)$. He might reason that they were both added expenses of going out to eat and thus treat them all as one loss. He might reason, "I had to pay way too much to go out tonight." Alternatively, he might separate the experiences because they occurred at different times and in different places. He might reason, "First I was charged

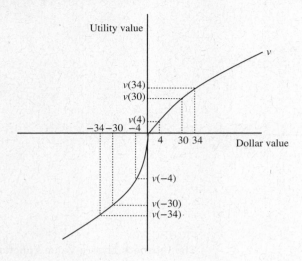

FIGURE 3.3
Integrating or Segre-
gating Events

way too much for dinner, and then later I was charged too much to park." Figure 3.3 depicts the two possible scenarios. Because the value function over losses is convex, the $4 loss evaluated on its own is associated with a much greater loss in utility than when added to the original $30 loss. This means that the person who integrates the two losses is much better off than the person who segregates the two losses. When they are integrated, we may say that they are entered into the same mental account.

The same thing happens in reverse for gains. If instead the man had been charged $30 less than he expected for dinner and $4 less than he expected for parking, he would be much better off for segregating the gains. Again, Figure 3.3 shows that because the value function is concave over gains, the pleasure experienced for saving $4 in parking when evaluated on its own is slightly greater than the pleasure for adding $4 in savings to the $30 savings experienced when paying for dinner. Thus, the person who segregates the experiences in this case feels better off than the person who integrates them.

Finally, if a person experiences some gains and some losses, we can make some further generalizations. For example, suppose the man paid $30 less than he expected for dinner but found a $30 parking ticket on his car when he left the restaurant. If he integrated these experiences, he would experience utility of $v(30 - 30) = v(0)$. Alternatively, if he segregates these experiences, he obtains $v(-30) + v(30)$. Because of loss aversion, the pain from the loss of $30 is greater than the pleasure for the gain of $30. In this case, the man might feel better off if he integrates the events. This might lead the reader to believe that a person will strategically choose either to integrate or segregate events in order to obtain the greatest utility. This possibility is discussed later in the chapter.

The final component of mental accounting incorporates the notion of transaction utility. People use a value function to assess their consumption experience relative to their expectations—their consumption utility—but they also use a value function to assess their enjoyment of the particular deal they were able to obtain—their transaction utility. Again, this raises the specter of whether a person will integrate or segregate transaction and consumption events. Generally, this outcome has been modeled as the person maximizing the sum of consumption and transaction value functions.

Mental accounting is a collection of several theoretical concepts: budgets, accounts, reference points, value functions, consumption utility, and transaction utility. As with many behavioral models, the model makes no clear a priori predictions of behavior in many cases. Because the theory itself provides no particular guidance on how budgets or accounts are formed, in many cases, virtually any behavior could be reconciled with the general mental accounting framework. Indeed, one of the primary criticisms of behavioral economics is that by failing to make clear predictions, it might not be possible to test the proposed theory. Although it might not be possible to create a grand test of mental accounting, it is possible to test various components of the model and to discover where the particular pieces are most likely important and applicable.

Budgeting and Consumption Bundles

The use of budgeting categories creates isolated choice problems. The standard rational model supposes that all goods are considered together, implying that an overall optimum can be achieved. If a person does not have the cognitive resources to conduct the types of complicated optimization this might imply, he or she might reduce the problem into various budgets by category. So, for example, a person might have one budget for food, another for clothing, another for utilities, and so forth. In the past, people often kept separate envelopes of money for each of these budgets. More recently, people tend to use software to keep track of spending in each category.

The consumer decision problem could now be written as

$$\max_{x_1, \ldots, x_n} v(x_1, \ldots, x_n | k) \tag{3.4}$$

subject to a set of budget constraints

$$\begin{aligned}
p_1 x_1 + \cdots + p_i x_i &< y_1, \\
p_{i+1} x_{i+1} + \cdots + p_j x_j &< y_2, \\
&\vdots \\
p_k x_k + \cdots + p_n x_n &< y_l,
\end{aligned} \tag{3.5}$$

where x_s is the amount of good s the person chooses to consume, p_s is the price the person pays per unit of good s, and y_m is the allotted budget for category m, and where the consumer has allotted budgets to l categories over n goods.

In any budget, m, the problem functions much like the standard consumer choice problem. In the category there is a budget constraint. If this constraint is binding, then the consumer chooses to consume at the point of tangency between the budget constraint and an indifference curve, given the consumption level of all other goods as pictured in Figure 3.4. Note that all of the consumption choices now depend on the reference point. We will ignore this reference point for now; however, later discussions develop this point further.

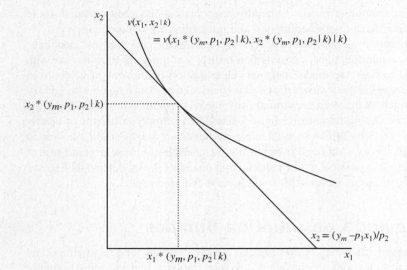

FIGURE 3.4
The Consumption
Problem within a
Single Budget
Category (Holding
Consumption of All
Other Goods
Constant)

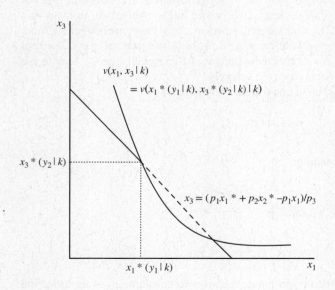

FIGURE 3.5
Nonoptimality
between Budgets

If instead we compared across budgets, we would see that the overall optimum consumption bundle is not necessarily achieved, because the budget process imposes artificial constraints. Suppose we plot two goods from separate budgets, good 1 from budget 1 and good 3 from budget 2 as pictured in Figure 3.5. With the same level of expenditure between these two goods, $p_1 x_1^*(y_1|k) + p_2 x_2^*(y_2|k)$, the consumer could purchase any bundle such that $p_1 x_1 + p_3 x_3 < p_1 x_1^*(y_1|k) + p_3 x_3^*(y_2|k)$, where we now suppress the prices of all goods in the arguments of the consumption functions. However, the consumer did not compare these possible bundles because of the artificial budget category. Instead, the consumer found the tangency of the indifference curve to budget 1 for all items in budget 1 and then found the tangency to the indifference curve for all items in budget 3. The budget may be set such that the rational optimum is excluded. For example, the consumer might allocate less money to budget 1 than would be required to purchase the unconditional optimal bundle suggested by the standard choice problem depicted in equations 3.1 and 3.2. Further, the consumer might allocate more to budget 2 than would be suggested by the unconditional optimal bundle. In this case, the consumer will purchase less of good 1 than would be optimal and more of good 3 than would be optimal. This is the condition displayed in Figure 3.5. The indifference curve crosses the budget curve so that there are many points along the budget curve that lie to the northeast of the indifference curve, constituting the dashed portion of the budget constraint. The consumer would be better off by choosing any of these consumption points. Each of these points consists of consuming more of good 1 and less of good 3.

Thus, budgeting leads to misallocation of wealth so that the consumer could be made better off without having access to any more resources. Except in the case where the budget allocations happen to line up exactly with the amount that would be spent in the unconditional optimum, this will be the case. If particular income sources are connected with particular budgets, any variability in income leads to a further shifting of funds. For example, if money that is received as a gift is only budgeted for entertainment or for items that are considered fun, a particularly large influx of gift money will lead to overconsumption of entertainment and fun, relative to all other items. The consumer who optimizes unconditionally could instead spend much of this money on more practical items for which he or she will receive a higher marginal utility.

The consumer problem in equations 3.4 and 3.5 is solved much the same way as the standard consumer problem from Chapter 1. Now, in each budget, the consumer will consume each good until marginal utility divided by the price for each good in a budget is equal. Where $\partial v(x_1, \ldots, x_n|k)/\partial x_i$ is the marginal utility of good i, this requires

$$\frac{1}{p_s} \frac{\partial}{\partial x_s} v(x_1{}^*, \ldots, x_n{}^*|k) = \frac{1}{p_r} \frac{\partial}{\partial x_r} v(x_1{}^*, \ldots, x_n{}^*|k), \qquad (3.6)$$

which is the standard condition for tangency of the budget constraint with the indifference curve. Additionally, we can use the budget constraint for this particular budget to determine the amount of each good in the budget. However, the solution does not imply equality of the marginal utility divided by price for goods appearing in different budgets because they are associated with a different budget constraint. This necessarily implies that the indifference curve will cross the *overall* budget constraint except in the rare case that the budget is set so that the unconditional optimum described is attainable.

EXAMPLE 3.3   Income Source and Spending

Since 2000, the U.S. government has cut individual income taxes several times, generally with the goal of increasing consumer spending. In each case, lowering taxes was seen as a way of combatting a sluggish economy. With lower taxes, people have more money in their pocket and thus might be willing to spend more. Nicholas Eply, Dennis Mak, and Lorraine Idson conducted an experiment whereby shoppers were intercepted in a mall and asked to recall how they had spent their rebate. The interviewer sometimes referred to the rebate as a return of "withheld income" and with other participants described it as "bonus income." When the rebate was described as bonus income, 87 percent said they had spent it, whereas only 25 percent said they had spent it when it was described as a refund of withheld income. Further experiments confirmed that labeling income as a bonus led to greater spending than labeling it as a return of income that the participant was due.

Until 2008, the tax rebates were embodied in a one-time refund check that was sent to the taxpayer in the amount of the tax cut. For example, people who paid income tax in 2007 received a check for between $300 and $600 beginning in May 2008. A similar program in 2009 cut taxes by $400 per taxpayer. However, this cut was implemented by reducing the amount withheld from paychecks rather than in a single check. This reduction increased take-home pay by an average of $7.70 per week. Valrie Chambers and Marilyn Spencer used survey methods to determine which method of returning the money might be more effective in inducing spending. Using a sample of university students, they found that students are more likely to spend when given the money on a per-paycheck basis than when given the money as a lump sum. Students indicated that they would save around 80 percent of a lump-sum payment, whereas they would only save about 35 percent of the per-paycheck payments. This example shows how timing and the amount of the payment can influence mental accounting. Perhaps a smaller amount per week is not large enough to enter on the ledger at all and is thus more likely to be spent instead of saved.

Accounts, Integrating, or Segregating

The shape of the value function suggests that people who are experiencing multiple events will be better off when their gains are segregated and their losses are integrated (see Figure 3.3). In truth there are four possibilities for multiple events:

- If a person experiences multiple gains, $x > 0$ and $y > 0$, then concavity of the value function over gains implies that $v(x) + v(y) > v(x+y)$ (as in Figure 3.3). In this case, the person is better off if the events are segregated and evaluated separately.

- If a person experiences multiple losses, $x < 0$ and $y < 0$, then convexity of the value function over losses implies $v(x) + v(y) < v(x+y)$ (as in Figure 3.3). In this case, the person is better off if the events are integrated and evaluated jointly.

- If a person experiences a loss and a gain, $x > 0$ and $y < 0$ with $x + y > 0$, so that the gain overwhelms the loss, the shape of the value function implies that $v(x) + v(y) < v(x+y)$ if we assume a strong form of loss aversion (Figure 3.6). A value function conforms to **strong loss aversion** if for any two positive numbers

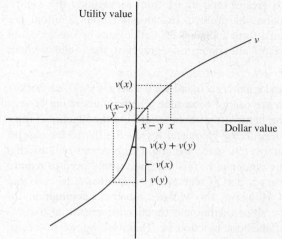

FIGURE 3.6
Integrating an Overall Gain

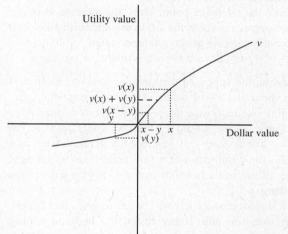

FIGURE 3.7
Integrating an Overall Gain without Strong Loss
Aversion

z_1 and z_2 with $z_1 < z_2$ it is always the case that $v_g(z_2) - v_g(z_1) < v_l(z_2) - v_l(z_1)$. This requires that a loss function always has a greater slope than the gain function a given distance from the reference point. The slope over losses near the reference point is always assumed to be steeper than the slope for gains. Further, the slope over gains is decreasing owing to diminishing marginal utility over gains. Then the decrease in utility when moving from x to $x-y$, given that $x-y$ is still in the gain domain, must be less than the loss when moving from the reference point to y given strong loss aversion. In this case, the person is better off integrating the events. Without strong loss aversion, although the slope of the value function over losses is greater than for gains near the reference point, if the marginal pain from losses diminishes quickly relative to equivalent gains (shown in Figure 3.7), then the pain from the loss of y may be smaller starting from the reference point than starting from x, leading to greater total utility from segregating the events. Thus, without strong loss aversion, the problem has an ambiguous solution. We would need to specify a functional form and sizes for both events before we could determine whether one is better off integrating or segregating the events without strong loss aversion.

• If a person experiences a loss and a gain, $x > 0$ and $y < 0$ with $x + y < 0$, so that the loss overwhelms the gain, then we cannot determine whether integrating or segregating losses makes the person better off without specifying the functional form for the value function and the size of the gains and losses. Similar to the case of mixed outcomes leading to an overall gain, we could impose restrictions that would allow us to determine the outcome. In this case, we would need to require that for any two positive numbers z_1 and z_2 with $z_1 < z_2$ it is always the case that $v_g(z_2) - v_g(z_1) > v_l(z_2) - v_l(z_1)$. However, this violates the basic assumptions of loss aversion, requiring that the slope of the gain function be greater at the reference point than the slope of the loss function is. Thus, we ignore this case. However, as a rule, if gains are very small relative to the losses, they should be segregated. Again this results because the slope of the value function over losses is relatively small farther away from the reference point. Thus, the increase in utility from a small gain starting from a point very far to the left of the reference point will be small relative to the same gain beginning at the reference point.

The early literature on mental accounting supposed that people would be motivated to group events in order to make themselves feel better off. If this were the case, people who had faced multiple gains would choose to segregate them to maximize their utility. Someone facing multiple losses would choose to integrate them to maximize utility. Further, people who lose an item that was recently given to them as a gift will be better off considering this the elimination of a gain rather than an outright loss. This is due to the steeper slope of the value function over losses than gains. This theory has been called **hedonic editing**.

However, initial research by Eric Johnson and Richard Thaler suggests that people do not engage in hedonic editing. Johnson and Thaler tested the hedonic editing hypothesis by offering subjects the choice between gains and losses spaced over different time periods. The idea was that offering a pair of losses or gains spaced farther apart in time might make it easier for the subject to segregate the outcomes. Johnson and Thaler found that subjects preferred gains to be spread out and they also preferred losses to be spread over time. Thus, people prefer to spread all changes over time, whether positive or negative.

Prior research by Richard Thaler had asked subjects several questions regarding outcomes that were described in ways that were intentionally worded to integrate or separate outcomes. For example, one question asked whether a man who received notice that he owed an unexpected additional $150 on his federal income taxes would feel better or worse than a man who received notice that he owed $100 in federal income taxes and another notice that he owed $50 in state income taxes. Among this set of questions, participants showed a clear preference for segregating gains and integrating losses. When the wording of a question, independent of the actual outcomes, influences preferences, we call this a **framing effect**. In this case, people show a preference for having losses framed in an integrated way and gains framed in a segregated way. We call this a preference for **hedonic framing**. Although people show a preference for hedonic framing, it appears they either do not have the ability to conduct or a preference for hedonic editing. Thus, they experience integration or segregation based on how the events are presented to them and do not necessarily control this presentation.

Up until now, we have treated the value function much like a standard utility function. More generally, however, the literature on mental accounting acknowledges that people feel some degree of loss or pain for the money traded away in a transaction, and this pain should enter into the value function. Thus, if purchasing a good, one obtains the value of consuming the good and feels the pain of losing the money associated with the price. Together the gain from consumption and loss from paying is the **acquisition utility**. The person will also experience any transaction utility. If the pain of paying the price is integrated with the consumption value, then acquisition utility may be written as $v_a(x - p)$, where v_a is the acquisition value function, x is the monetary equivalent value of consuming the good, and p is the price paid. We may consider x to be the amount one would be required to pay for the experience of consumption that would leave one indifferent between consuming and not consuming. If one segregated the pain of payment from the joy of consumption we could write acquisition utility as $v_a(x) + v_a(-p)$.

One's transaction utility could be written as $v_t(-p + p_r)$, where v_t is the transaction utility value function and p_r is the reference price, or the price one feels is a fair price to pay for the object. It is generally assumed that people integrate consumption and payment, so that the value of purchase can be written as $v_a(x - p) + v_t(-p + p_r)$. Alternatively, if sufficient time passes between purchase and consumption, it may be that at the time of consumption the consumer disregards the payment altogether when consuming, called **payment decoupling**. Such payment decoupling might explain why people feel more indulgent when using credit cards than when using cash for payment. If a person integrates the price and consumption, he or she should purchase the good so long as $v_a(x - p) + v_t(-p - p_r)$ is greater than the value obtained for the best alternative use of the money. If one disregarded price through payment decoupling, one need only find that $v_a(x)$ is greater than the best alternative.

Payment Decoupling, Prepurchase, and Credit Card Purchases

According to the theory of mental accounting, when an item is purchased, a person figuratively opens a mental account that may be closed when the good is consumed. This account is evaluated through the value functions to determine if the account has a positive or negative balance. Drazen Prelec and George Loewenstein propose that transaction and consumption activities often bring these accounts to mind, causing additional pleasure when the account balance is positive or additional pain when the account balance is negative. Thus, someone who has taken out a loan for a car might recall the outstanding balance on the loan when he drives. Because the loan has not been paid, the framing of the loan and driving events forces him to integrate the debt and the driving, making the experience of driving unpleasant. Alternatively, someone who has paid for the car outright does not consider the expense of the car when driving. Rather, he only considers the consumption experience, making driving a much more pleasant experience. Payment decoupling leads one to write off past payment at the time of consumption, while recognizing the weight of future payments. Prelec and Loewenstein speculate that items that provide repeated consumption (such as a clothes washer) allow one to stomach future payments, whereas single-use items (e.g., a vacation) do not. They propose that people **prorate** future payments over future expected consumption experiences. In other words, consumers consider the number and quality of the anticipated future consumption episodes when considering the number and size of the future payments. Thus, a consumer facing future payments on a durable good might consider the value of the account

$$v\left(\sum_{t=0}^{\infty}\delta^t(x-p)\right),\tag{3.7}$$

where x is the value of consumption in any time period, p is the payment on debt for the good in any period, δ is a discount factor, and the index t represents time. If instead the good is consumed once but paid for over time, then after consumption has already taken place, the account is evaluated as

$$v\left(\sum_{t=0}^{\infty}\delta^t(-p)\right).\tag{3.8}$$

If the consumer anticipates this future dread of payment when consumption no longer occurs, then prorating payment can lead consumers to prefer to prepay for goods that can be consumed only once but potentially prefer to buy durable goods on credit.

By prorating, the consumer considers the future payment and the future consumption when evaluating the account. Thus, if the future consumption is expected to be at least as good as the forgone money, consumers evaluate the account as having a positive balance even if there is outstanding debt. Alternatively, if there is no future consumption, the consumer considers only the future payment, ignoring (or at least discounting) the prior consumption when evaluating the account, which thus has a negative balance. Prelec and Loewenstein asked participants whether they would prefer to prepay for a vacation at $200 a month for six months or to pay upon returning at $200 a month for six months. Additionally they asked participants whether they would prefer to prepay for delivery of a washing machine at $200 a month for six months or pay after delivery $200 a month for six months. On average participants preferred to prepay for the vacation and preferred to buy the washing machine on credit. Thus, Prelec and Loewenstein find support for the notion of payment decoupling together with prorating.

Similar motives can drive credit card spending. Intuitively, credit cards are often used for purchases of single-use goods, which seems counter to the principles outlined by Prelec and Loewenstein. Some evidence suggests that credit cards allow consumers to ignore the cost of purchase while consuming, much like the prepayment option described above. Perhaps, by aggregating a large number of insignificant purchases in one bill, the credit card serves to effectively decouple payment from consumption, despite the knowledge of future payment. In effect, the bill obscures the costs of each individual purchase, thus eliminating payment from the account. Thus, one may enjoy one's impulse purchase without the dread of future payment.

Investments and Opening and Closing Accounts

One of the primary suppositions of the mental accounting model is that consumers have a desire to close accounts only when they have a positive or zero balance. Consider a person who makes an investment. The initial cost of the investment sets a natural reference point for the decision maker. Any return above the reference point may be considered a gain, and any return below the reference point may be considered a loss. If people are motivated to close accounts that have a positive or zero balance, they are more likely to sell an investment that has made a gain than one that has made a loss. For example, selling a house that has declined in value forces the seller to realize the money loss he incurred. Alternatively, holding onto the house and waiting for the price to come back up above the purchase price can allow the seller to forgo (for a time) the pain of the loss in investment. Selling the investment would instead close the mental account, solidifying the reality of the losses.

This effect is potentially one of the causes of the sunk-cost fallacy, causing people to continue with investments or activities that are losers in hopes of obtaining a balanced mental account. Were these sunk costs to persist in one's memory forever, the accounts may be at a loss in perpetuity, and the person would continue with bad investments forever, hoping to eventually balance the account. Luckily, this does not appear to be the case. Rather, people depreciate the cost of investments over time in a process called **payment depreciation**. Over time, the pain of payment diminishes, and they feel less and less motivated by the initial payment. They get over it. Recall the example from Hal Arkes and Catherine Blumer where subjects were charged different prices for theater ticket subscriptions. Although there was substantial difference in attendance in the first half of the theater season, there was no real difference in the second half of the season. By this time, the additional money spent on tickets had been fully depreciated, and both sets of participants were equally motivated to attend. Suppose a person paid p at time $t = 0$ for purchase of a durable good (e.g., shoes). Suppose further that value of a consumption incident for the durable good is equal to x. Then, at any point in time, consuming the good would yield utility that may be written as $v_a(x - p\delta^t)$, where δ is a discount factor that is positive and less than 1. Thus, as time passes, the price paid plays less and less of a role in acquisition utility gained from consumption as δ^t gets smaller and smaller. Further, the price is depreciated in transaction utility as $v_t((-p + p_r)\delta^t)$, so that eventually accounts may be closed at a minimal mental loss. This can create a motivation for hanging onto more-expensive items as they age, whereas comparably functional items that were cheaper would be thrown away or sold.

EXAMPLE 3.4   Investment and Divestment

Suppose you hold a portfolio of stock investments. Over time, some of the stocks drop in price and are worth less than you purchased them for, and others increase in price and are worth more. Traditional economic tools suggest that you should make decisions to sell based on the expected future return on investment, not on the history of price. Further, future stock prices are often modeled as a random walk. If stock prices follow a random walk, then the expected future price should be equal to the current price. In this scenario, there may be no particular reason to prefer to sell either stocks that have lost or stocks that have gained value. The past change in value should provide no information about the future performance. Further, tax laws in the United States allow people to reduce tax payments once losses are realized on the stock market. In this case, we might expect people to be motivated to sell losing stocks more often than winning stocks. Mental accounting predicts the opposite. A person behaving according to the theory of mental accounting will hold the stocks that have lost value in the hope of balancing the account. Thus, mental accounting supposes that stocks that have gained in value will be sold more often than those that have lost.

Terrance Odean used transaction data for 10,000 customers of a discount brokerage firm to examine this prediction. He found that customers were much more likely to sell investments that had increased in value rather than those that had decreased in value. Over the course of the year, customers would sell and realize close to 15 percent of the gains in their portfolio. On the other hand, they would sell and realize only 10 percent of the losses in their portfolio. This tendency to realize gains and avoid realizing losses is called the **disposition effect**. Here, customers selling a stock value the sale as $v(p_s - p_p)$, where p_s is the price at sale, and p_p is the price a purchase. Clearly, this value is larger for a gaining stock than for a losing stock. Thus the customer, hoping to avoid realizing a loss, favors selling the gaining stocks.

Customers who sold the gaining stocks tended not to reinvest their gains, suggesting that they were not simply rebalancing their portfolio after a gain so as to reduce the percentage of value in the particular gaining stock and return to the original mix of investments. It is difficult to discern the customer's expectations of future returns. However, Odean compared the actual returns of the stocks that were sold after gains against those that were held after losses. The average return on the winning stocks that were sold was about 2.4% over the next 252 trading days after sale. The return over the same period for the losing stocks that were not sold was about −1%. Thus, if individual beliefs mirrored reality, customers should have sold the losers. Interestingly, the trend reverses in the month of December. In December, customers might have been motivated to realize their losses to take advantage of tax deductions for the sale of stock at a loss. The reversal in December, however, is not strong enough to outweigh the strong disposition effect throughout the rest of the year.

EXAMPLE 3.5   More on Paying for Gym Memberships and Attendance

John Gourville and Dilip Soman proposed and tested the notion of payment depreciation—that the price paid for an item has a diminishing effect on consumption behavior as time goes on. They provide several hypothetical and experimental examples of payment depreciation, and the most compelling is a study of the attendance behavior at a gym in Colorado. Membership in the gym was purchased on an annual basis, but payments were made once every six months from the time of enrollment. Thus, a member joining in January would pay in January and June each year. Interestingly, no matter when the month of payment occurred, there was a substantial spike in attendance following payment. Approximately 35 percent of attendance in any six-month window occurs in the month of payment. Alternatively, less than 10 percent of attendance occurs in the fourth or fifth month after payment. First-time members of the gym were excluded from their study so that initial excitement for a gym membership would not bias results.

Imagine a member considering a trip to the gym. He has attended $n-1$ times since the last time he paid to renew his membership, and he can attend and obtain a value of $v_a(x_n - p\delta^t/n) + v_t(-p\delta^t + p_r(n))$, where x_n is the monetary value to the member of experiencing the n th single attendance event at the gym, p is the price paid once every six months, δ is the monthly rate of depreciation, t is the number of months since the last payment was made, n is the number of times the member has attended the gym since paying (including the attendance event under consideration), and $p_r(n)$ is the price the individual considers fair for attending the gym n times. In the acquisition value function, the price paid is divided by n to indicate amortization of costs over the number of times attended. In the first month after paying, the price looms large, being multiplied in both instances by $\delta^0 = 1$. Right after payment, the member has not yet attended and $n = 1$, and thus the value of attending for the first time since paying in the first month after paying is $v_a(x_1 - p) + v_t(-p + p_r(1))$. Almost certainly the fair price of attending one time, $p_r(1)$, is much less than the rate for six months of membership. Thus the transaction utility is heavily negative. As well, the value of the experience of attending once is certainly much less than the cost of a six-month membership. Thus, acquisition utility is also heavily negative. Thus, the account is considered a loss at the time of payment and must remain open while the member pursues a balanced account. Still, although attending the first time has a negative value, the value is more than not attending the first time in that month, $v_a(-p) + v_t(-p)$, because at least the member obtains the value of the single instance of attendance.

Over time, the number of times attended and the number of months increases. Suppose the rate of depreciation is $\delta = .75$. In the fourth month, if the member has attended 11 times, the value of additional attendance is $v_a(x_{12} - 0.002p) + v_t(-0.316p + p_r(12))$. If the fair price for attending 12 times is more than 0.316 times the price of a six-month membership, then the transaction utility is clearly positive. At this point, the member is no longer motivated to keep the account open by a negative transaction utility. Suppose for now that attending the gym for the twelfth time in four months is actually considered to be of negative value (I feel like I am spending all my time in the gym), $x_{12} < 0$. At this point, the member can choose to close the account and cease attending. If instead, the fair price for attending 12 times was much less than 0.316 times the price of a six-month membership, the member could continue to attend for the potential gain in transaction utility. Note that not attending would result in $v_a(-0.002p) + v_t(-0.316p + p_r(11))$. This is less than the value of additional attendance if x_{12} is small in absolute value relative to the change in the fair price $p_r(12) - p_r(11)$. In this case, the member is reluctant to close the account and could continue to consume simply for the increase in transaction utility, thus demonstrating the sunk cost fallacy.

Reference Points and Indifference Curves

Up until now, we have represented all indifference curves using the familiar concave shapes found commonly in the economics literature (e.g., those depicted in Figures 3.4 and 3.5). However, prospect theory suggests that this shape does not hold universally. This topic is covered more thoroughly in Chapter 4, but for completeness in presenting the theory of mental accounting, it is important to have some understanding of how reference points affect indifference curves.

We have commonly written the prospect theory value function in terms of monetary outcomes and a reference point as a monetary amount. This type of analysis suffices when considering a single consumption activity or good. However, if we are considering multiple consumption activities, it may be that the consumer faces a reference point that includes a consumption level of each activity. Thus, someone who consumes two eggs and a piece of toast every morning for breakfast might consider two eggs and two pieces of toast a gain. Additionally he might consider three eggs and one piece of toast a gain. Further, reducing the number of eggs or eliminating the toast may be considered a loss. But suppose we considered consuming just one egg and two pieces of toast. This is a loss in the number of eggs but a gain in the number of pieces of toast. If the person is loss averse, consuming less than the reference point in any dimension reduces utility by much more than increasing consumption above the reference point in the same dimension.

This has implications for the shape of indifference curves. If I lose one egg (i.e., consume one less than the reference amount) this has a sharply negative impact on utility relative to gaining eggs. To compensate this loss and place me back on my indifference curve, I must be given more toast. But, gaining toast has a small impact on my utility relative to losing toast. Thus, I need to be compensated with a lot more toast for a loss of one egg than I would be willing to give up in order to gain another egg (beyond the reference level). This implies a kink in indifference curves around the reference point, as depicted in Figure 3.8.

In Figure 3.8, the reference amount of good 1 is given by x_1^r and the reference amount of good 2 is given by x_2^r. Anything to the southwest of (x_1^r, x_2^r) is considered a loss in both domains, and thus utility drops quickly in this direction. Anything to the northeast of (x_1^r, x_2^r) is considered a gain in both domains, and thus utility increases more slowly in this direction. Alternatively, anything to the southeast of the reference point is a gain (slow ascent) in terms of good 1 but a loss (rapid decline) in terms of good 2. The indifference curve must be relatively flat in this region so that larger quantities of good 1 compensate for losses in good 2. Anything to the northwest of the reference point is a gain (slow ascent) in terms of good 2 but a loss (rapid decline) in terms of good 1. The

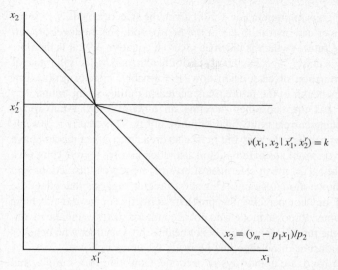

FIGURE 3.8
Indifference Curves with a Reference Point

indifference curve must be relatively steep in this quadrant so that large quantities of good 2 compensate for losses in good 1. The fact that these slopes change abruptly at the reference point leads to the kink in the indifference curve at the reference point.

Kinks in curves cause problems with the conditions for maximizing utility subject to a budget constraint. In particular, there may not be any point on some indifference curves that have the same slope as the budget constraint. No point of tangency exists for some indifference curves. If the optimum occurs on a curve without a tangency point, the conditions for optimization are rather different from the standard conditions. This is the case presented in Figure 3.8. Here, the slope of the budget constraint is between the slope of the upper portion of the indifference curve as you approach the reference point and the slope of the lower portion of the indifference curve as you approach the reference point. If the kink of an indifference curve lies on the budget constraint and satisfies this condition, then the consumption bundle depicted at the point of the kink is optimal. Chapter 4 discusses more of what happens in the southwest and northeast quadrants, as well as the shape of indifference curves that do not pass directly through the reference point.

Rational Choice, Temptation and Gifts versus Cash

Rational choice models have a difficult time explaining the notion of temptation. Inherent in the problem of temptation is the idea that consumers want something but don't think they should have that thing. Traditional economics uses the utility function to capture both what consumers want and what they think they should have, eliminating the possibility of temptation. One way that has been proposed to model cases in which a decision maker feels temptation is to differentiate between the short-term and long-term impacts of items. Thus, a good can generate an immediate positive utility (say, the taste of a particularly desirable dessert), but a negative long-term impact on utility (e.g., additional unattractive pounds). Then, the consumer problem could be written as

$$\max_{x} u(x|h_0) + \delta u(z|h_1(x)),$$ (3.9)

where $u(\cdot|\cdot)$ is the utility of consumption in any period given the state of health, h_t, x is the amount of cake the consumer can choose to eat in the first period, z is the level of consumption that occurs in the future (which is taken as given in equation 3.9), δ is the time discounting applied to future utility, h_0 is the initial state of health, and $h_1(x)$ is the state of health in the future as a function of cake eaten now. Presumably, increasing the consumption of cake decreases health in the future, thus decreasing utility in the future.

The traditional model has the consumer selecting an amount x^* that maximizes intertemporal utility, balancing current utility against future utility. This clearly represents the notion that the diner desires the cake now but must also dread the impact it could have on his future utility. However, problems of temptation also often involve regret. Thus, on a regular basis, a diner might eat so much cake that afterwards he regrets his actions and believes he should have shown more restraint. This sort of regret suggests that either the individual decision maker did not perceive the problem correctly, or he did not have complete control of his actions. Rational models do not account for such systematic regret. Although the consumer in the future might desire better health, the consumer who behaves according to equation 3.9 must acknowledge that he made the correct choice.

Gift givers, on the other hand, are not always so accurate. Consider, for example, that your grandmother sends you a sweater she purchases for $75. The sweater is nice, but had you been given the $75, you would have purchased a new MP3 player instead. In this case, you must prefer the MP3 player to the sweater. Further, you would have been better off if your grandmother had given you the $75 directly. Under the assumptions of rationality, so long as consumers are aware of all the possible options they could spend their money on, they will always be at least as well off receiving cash as receiving a gift that cost the same amount. But if money always makes people better off, why would one give anything else?

Budgets, Accounts, Temptation, and Gifts

Because budgets are treated as nonfungible, consumers can use accounts as a means of limiting temptation. Consumers often view their checking account as being much more easily accessed than their savings account. In essence, they place in this account money that they are comfortable spending. Alternatively, they place money in their savings account partially to limit the temptation to use it. Hersh Shefrin and Richard Thaler propose that consumers classify each physical monetary account into one of three categories: current income, current wealth, and future wealth. Current income consists of accounts intended to be spent in the immediate term. Current wealth consists of money accumulated to purchase items too expensive for paycheck-to-paycheck purchases. Finally, future wealth is money that is intended for future consumption, such as retirement savings.

Corresponding to the three different orientations of these accounts, each type provides a different level of temptation to spend. Money in the current income account is very tempting because it is intended to spend in the near term. Money in the current wealth account is less tempting, and one needs to find some substantial justification for spending from this account. Finally, future wealth accounts may be treated as nearly untouchable. People might place money into these accounts to restrict their temptation to spend. Thus, one might want a portion of one's paycheck to be placed in each of these three accounts to ensure that one doesn't spend the entire paycheck. Shefrin and Thaler suggest that the propensity to spend from each account differs. People code income into differing categories based on their intention to spend it, and they place the money in the appropriate account.

The theory predicts that people are able, to some extent, to overcome temptation by viewing different accounts as nonfungible and setting the amount in the more-tempting accounts artificially lower than the amount they are tempted to spend. Similar behavior is possible in limiting specific consumption temptations. Richard Thaler gives the example of a couple who are tempted to purchase and consume expensive wine. To limit their expenditures on and consumption of expensive wine, they might limit themselves to purchasing only bottles of wine that cost less than $20. They set their budget as an artificial mechanism to prevent giving in to temptation. This artificial rule might not always lead to optimal behavior. It might save them from overspending, but it might prevent them from consuming more-expensive wine on an occasion when such a purchase may be justified by the utility it would yield. Thaler points out that this budget constraint necessarily implies that the couple might, on such an occasion, be made better off by receiving a gift of a $50 bottle of wine than they would by receiving $50 in cash. The $50 in cash would be artificially budgeted away from the wine that would make them better off. Alternatively, a gift of wine would not fall under such a restriction and would be consumed, making the person better off than the equivalent cash. Thus, if a budget is set arbitrarily too low owing to an aversion to some temptation, the person might at times be made better off by a gift. This increase in well-being by receiving a gift rather than cash can only take place if the budget is set to arbitrarily eliminate the optimal consumption bundle. If the couple truly preferred $20 bottles of wine to $50 bottles of wine, a gift of $50 would clearly be preferred.

EXAMPLE 3.6   Limiting Temptation

Some consumer items are considered tempting or sinful if they are pleasurable to consume but cause negative long-term effects. Other items are not considered tempting but rather are considered virtuous because they have very positive long-term benefits relative to the immediate consumption experience. Some people use consumption budgets to limit the temptation from sinful items. A consumption budget is a limit on how much one will consume under any circumstance. If people use strict budgets to limit consumption quantities of tempting items, then we would expect people to be less prone to purchasing more of the tempting item if offered a larger quantity at a per-unit discount. When virtuous items (carrots) are buy one get one free, people are likely to take advantage of the offer and the transaction utility that comes with it. Alternatively, when a tempting item (cheesecake) is offered on special as buy one get one free, people might not buy because they have set a limit on their consumption of the item.

Klaus Wertenbroch set out to test this theory performing an experiment. Subjects were presented six-ounce bags of potato chips and told they could purchase one bag or could purchase three bags at a discount. The amount of the discount was varied among subjects. Some of the subjects were told the potato chips were 75 percent fat free, framing the potato chips as being relatively healthy. Others were told the chips were

25 percent fat, framing the potato chips as being relatively unhealthy. By increasing the discount on the three-bag deal for the 75 percent fat-free potato chips, the percentage of participants purchasing the three-bag deal increased by more than 40 percent. Decreasing the price of the deal for the 25 percent fat chips increased the percentage of participants taking the three-bag deal by only about 10 percent. Thus, those viewing the potato chips as a more-virtuous item were more price sensitive than those viewing it as more of a tempting item. This may be explained by people setting a limit on the number of bags of fatty potato chips they will take given the temptation to consume them once they are purchased. On the other hand, the more-virtuous chips might not be considered a temptation because people don't believe they will have the same negative future consequences. Thus, they do not face the same budget constraint.

Rational Choice over Time

Some of the important predictions of mental accounting deal with how people trade off consumption choices over time. Temptation and self-control issues are just one example. Rational models of consumption over time assume that people are forward looking and try to smooth consumption over time. For example, a typical model of consumer choice over time may be written as

$$\max_{\{c_t\}_{t=1}^{T}} \sum_{t=1}^{T} \delta^t u(c_t) \tag{3.10}$$

subject to

$$\sum_{t=1}^{T} c_t < w + \sum_{t=1}^{T} y_t, \tag{3.11}$$

where u represents the instantaneous utility of consumption in any period, δ represents the discount factor applied to future consumption and compounded each period, c_t represents consumption in period t, y_t represents income in period t, w represents some initial endowment of wealth, and T represents the end of the planning horizon—when the person expects to die. Equation 3.11 requires that consumers cannot spend more than their wealth plus the amount they can borrow against future earnings in any period. This model can be used to model how a windfall gain in wealth should be spent. Generally, the model shows that people should smooth consumption over time. Thus, if you suddenly come into some unexpected money, this money is incorporated into your income wealth equation (3.11) and will be distributed relatively evenly across consumption in future periods (though declining over time owing to the discount on future consumption).

As a simple example, consider a two-period model, $T = 2$, with no time discounting, $\delta = 1$. As with all consumer problems, the consumer optimizes by setting the marginal utility divided by the cost of consumption equal across activities. In this case, the two activities are consumption in period 1 and consumption in period 2. Because the utility

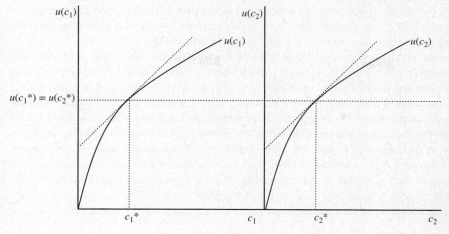

FIGURE 3.9
Two-Period Consumption
Model without Discounting

derived from each activity is described by the same curve, $u(\cdot)$, and because the cost of consumption is assumed to be equal across periods, this occurs where $c_1 = c_2$. Figure 3.9 depicts the cost of consumption using the two tangent lines with slope of 1. Thus, any amount received unanticipated would be divided between the two periods equally. Similarly, any anticipated income is distributed equally throughout the future consumption periods. Discounting modifies only slightly, with the marginal utility in the second period multiplied by the discount factor being equal to the marginal utility in the first period. So long as δ is relatively close to 1, the income should be distributed very near equality.

The optimum occurs where $\delta^i \partial u(c_i)/\partial c_i = \delta^j \partial u(c_j)/\partial c_j$ for every period j and i. Thus marginal utility should increase by a factor of $1/\delta$ each period, and as marginal utility increases, consumption declines owing to diminishing marginal utility. An unexpected gain in wealth should be distributed just as an expected gain: nearly evenly among all future consumption periods but at a rate that declines over time.

EXAMPLE 3.7   Windfall Gains

Whether money is anticipated or comes as a surprise, traditional theory suggests that people should optimize by spending their marginal dollar on the activity with the highest return. Behavioral economists have studied the impact of unanticipated money, or windfall gains, on spending behavior. Experimental evidence suggests that people might have a greater propensity to spend money that comes as a surprise than money that is anticipated.

Hal Arkes and a team of other researchers recruited 66 undergraduate men to participate in the experiment. Participants were asked to fill out a questionnaire, go to an indoor stadium to watch a varsity basketball game, and then return to fill out a second questionnaire. All of the participants were given $5 before they attended the basketball game. Some were told that they would receive the money, and others were not. Participants were asked to report how much money they had spent at the concession stands during the game. Those who had anticipated being paid spent less than half as much at the basketball game on average. Thus those who had known they would receive the money were much less likely to spend the money impulsively.

Mental accounting provides one possible explanation for this activity. For example, anticipated income may be placed in a mental account designated for certain purchases and budgeted already when received. Unanticipated money may be entered into a separate account specifically for unanticipated income and designated for more frivolous or impulsive purchases. Thus, whether the money is anticipated or not determines which budget the money enters, and it thus determines the level of marginal utility necessary to justify a purchase, as in Figure 3.4. Presumably in this case, people have allocated more than the overall optimal amount to their impulse budget and less than the overall optimal amount to their planned spending budget. Thus, the propensity to spend out of the impulse budget is much higher than out of the planned-spending budget.

Rational Explanations for Source-Based Consumption and Application

Little work has been done to reconcile mental accounting–based behavior with the rational choice model. However, the mental accounting model is based on the methods of accounting employed by major corporations. These corporations have many resources and many activities. It is relatively difficult for central decision makers in these organizations to keep track of all the various activities in order to make informed decisions. The method of accounting, including the keeping of separate accounts and budgets for various activities, has been developed as a method of keeping track of expenses and capital. This may be thought of as a response to mental costs of trying to optimize generally. Instead of considering all possible activities and income sources at once, breaking it down into components might simplify the problem and allow manageable decisions. People might face similar problems in managing their own purchasing and income decisions. Hundreds of decisions are made each day. To optimize generally would be too costly. Perhaps the loss in well-being for using mental accounts is less than the cost of carrying out general optimization over all decisions.

With respect to marketing, mental accounting suggests that how you categorize your product and how you frame purchasing decisions does matter. In selling products that require repeated expenditure, you may be able to increase sales of the item by framing these continued expenses so as to aggregate them in the minds of consumers. Additionally, segregating the gains can induce greater sales. This could explain the late-night infomercials that meticulously describe each item they are selling in a single package, asking after each new item, "Now how much would you pay?" The use of prepayment for single-consumption items might induce greater sales than offering consumer financing alone. Additionally, goods that receive repeated use may be more easily sold with financing that amortizes the costs over the life of the product. Clever use of mental accounting principles can induce sales without significant cost to a producer.

To the extent that people suffer from self-control problems, using budget mechanisms may be an effective tool. If self-control is not an explicit issue, budgets should be set to maximize the enjoyment from consumption over time. More generally, people who behave according to mental accounting heuristics can potentially improve their well-being by reevaluating their spending budgets regularly, cutting budgets for categories for which the marginal utility is low relative to others.

Much like the rest of behavioral economics, mental accounting can seem to be a loose collection of heuristics. By spurning the systematic overarching model of behavior embodied by traditional economics, behavioral economics often provides a less-than-systematic alternative. In particular, mental accounting combines elements of prospect theory, double-entry accounting, and mental budgets to describe a wide set of behaviors. To the extent that these behaviors are widespread and predictable, this collection is useful in modeling and predicting economic behavior. One of the most pervasive and systematic sets of behaviors documented by behavioral economists is loss aversion.

Behavioral economics is eclectic and somewhat piecemeal. Loss aversion is the closest thing to a unifying theory proposed by behavioral economics. The notion that people experience diminishing marginal utility of gains and diminishing marginal pain from losses, as well as greater marginal pain from loss than marginal pleasure from gain, can be used to explain a wide variety of behaviors. In the framework of mental accounting, loss aversion provides much of the punch. Loss aversion is discussed further in many subsequent chapters.

Biographical Note

Courtesy of George Loewenstein

George F. Loewenstein (1955–)

B.A., Brandeis University, 1977; Ph.D. Yale University, 1985; held faculty positions at the University of Chicago and Carnegie Mellon University

George Loewenstein received his bachelor's degree and Ph.D. in economics. He helped lay the foundation for incorporating psychological effects in the economics literature on intertemporal choice. He has also made contributions to mental accounting, inconsistent preferences, predictions of preferences, and neuroeconomics. His foundational work recognizes that the state of the person can affect how the person perceives an event. Further, people have a difficult time anticipating how changes in their state might affect decision making. For example, a person who is not hungry might not be able to anticipate a lower level of resistance to temptation in some future hungry state. Such changes in visceral factors can lead people to expose themselves to overwhelming temptation, potentially leading to risky choices regarding drinking, drug use, or sexual behavior. More recently, his work on neuroeconomics, a field using brain imaging to map decision processes, has found support for the notion that people use separate processes to evaluate decisions using cash or a credit card. This work may be seen as validating at least a portion of the mental accounting framework. His groundbreaking work has resulted in his being named a fellow of the American Psychological Society and a member of the American Academy of Arts and Sciences.

THOUGHT QUESTIONS

1. Consider a high school student who is given $3 every school day by her parents as "lunch money." The student works a part time job after school, earning a small amount of "spending cash." In addition to her lunch money, the student spends $5 from her own earnings each week on lunch. Suppose her parents reduced her lunch money by $2 per day but that she simultaneously receives a $10-per-week raise at her job, requiring no extra effort on her part. What would the rational choice model suggest should happen to her spending on lunch? Alternatively, what does the mental accounting framework predict?

2. Suppose you manage a team of employees who manufacture widgets. You know that profits depend heavily on the number of widgets produced and on the quality of those widgets. You decide to induce better performance in your team members by providing a system of pay bonuses for good behavior and pay penalties for bad behavior. How might hedonic framing be used to make the system of rewards and penalties more effective? How does this framing differ from the type of segregation and integration suggested by hedonic editing?

3. Suppose you are a government regulator who is concerned with the disposition effect and its potential impact on wealth creation. What types of policies could be implemented to reduce the sale of winning stocks and increase the sale of losing stocks? The government currently provides a tax break for the sale of stocks at a loss. This tax break tends to encourage the sale of losing stocks only in December. What sorts of policies could encourage more regular sales of losing stocks?

4. You are considering buying gifts for a pair of friends. Both truly enjoy video gaming. However, both have reduced their budget on these items because of the temptation that they can cause. Dana is tempted to buy expensive games when they are first on the market rather than waiting to purchase the games once prices are lower. Thus, Dana has limited himself only to purchase games that cost less than $35. Alternatively, Avery is tempted to play video games for long periods of time, neglecting other important responsibilities. Thus, Avery has limited herself to playing video games only when at other people's homes. Would Dana be better off receiving a new game that costs $70 or a gift of $70 cash? Would Avery be better off receiving a video game or an equivalent amount of cash? Why might these answers differ?

5. Suppose Akira has two sources of income. Anticipated income, y_1 is spent on healthy food, represented by x_1, and clothing, x_2. Unanticipated income, y_2 is spent on dessert items, x_3. Suppose the value function is given by $v(x_1, x_2, x_3) = (x_1 x_2 x_3)^{\frac{1}{3}}$, so that marginal utility of good 1 is given by $\frac{\partial v(x_1, x_2, x_3)}{\partial x_1} = \frac{1}{3}x_1^{-\frac{2}{3}}(x_2 x_3)^{\frac{1}{3}}$, marginal utility for good 2 is $\frac{\partial v(x_1, x_2, x_3)}{\partial x_2} = \frac{1}{3}x_2^{-\frac{2}{3}}(x_1 x_3)^{\frac{1}{3}}$, and marginal utility of good 3 is given by $\frac{\partial v(x_1, x_2, x_3)}{\partial x_3} = \frac{1}{3}x_3^{-\frac{2}{3}}(x_1 x_2)^{\frac{1}{3}}$. Suppose $y_1 = 8$ and $y_2 = 2$, and that the price of the goods is given by $p_1 = 1$, $p_2 = 1$, $p_3 = 2$. What is the consumption level observed given the budgets? To find this, set the marginal utility of consumption to be equal for all goods in the same budget, and impose that the cost of all goods in that budget be equal to the budget constraint. Suppose Akira receives an extra $4 in anticipated income, $y_1 = 12$ and $y_2 = 2$; how does consumption change? Suppose alternatively that Akira receives the extra $4 as unanticipated income, $y_1 = 8$ and $y_2 = 6$; how does consumption change? What consumption bundle would maximize utility? Which budget is set too low?

6. Consider the problem of gym attendance as presented in this chapter, where Jamie perceives the value of attending the gym to be $v_a(x_n - p\delta^t/n) + v_t(-p\delta^t + p_r(n))$, where x_n is the monetary value to Jamie of experiencing the n th single attendance event at the gym, p is the price paid once every six months, δ is the monthly rate of depreciation, t is the number of months since the last payment was made, n is the number of times Jamie has attended the gym since paying, including the attendance event under consideration, and $p_r(n)$ is the price Jamie considers fair for attending the gym n times. Suppose that the cost of gym membership is $25. Further, suppose Jamie considered the value of attending the gym n times in a six-month window to be $v_a(n) = 5n - n^2 - \delta^t 25/n$. Also, suppose that Jamie considers the fair price for a visit to be $4, so the transaction utility is equal to $v_t(n) = -25\delta^t + 4n$. Payments depreciate at a rate of $\delta = .5$. Determine the number of visits necessary in each of the six months in order to obtain a positive account. How much time would have to pass before only a single visit could close the account in the black?

REFERENCES

Arkes, H.R., and C. Blumer. "The Psychology of Sunk Cost." *Organizational Behavior and Human Decision Processes* 35 (1985): 124–140.

Arkes, H.R., C.A. Joyner, M.V. Pezzo, J. Nash, K. Siegel Jacobs, and E. Stone. "The Psychology of Windfall Gains." *Organizational Behavior and Human Decision Processes* 59(1994): 331–347.

Chambers, V., and M. Spencer. "Does Changing the Timing of a Yearly Individual Tax Refund Change the Amount Spent vs. Saved?" *Journal of Economic Psychology* 29(2008): 856–862.

Eply, N., D. Mak, and L.C. Idson. "Bonus or Rebate? The Impact of Income Framing on Spending and Saving." *Journal of Behavioral Decision Making* 19(2006): 213–227.

Gourville, J.T., and D. Soman. "Payment Depreciation: The Behavioral Effects of Temporarily Separating Payments from Consumption." *Journal of Consumer Research* 25(1998): 160–174.

Heath, C., and J.B. Soll. "Mental Budgeting and Consumer Decision." *Journal of Consumer Research* 23(1996): 40–52.

Odean, T. "Are Investors Reluctant to Realize their Losses?" *Journal of Finance* 53(1998): 1775–1798.

Prelec, D., and G. Loewenstein. "The Red and the Black: Mental Accounting of Savings and Debt." *Marketing Science* 17(1998): 4–28.

Shefrin, H.M., and R.H. Thaler. "The Behavioral Life Cycle Hypothesis." *Economic Inquiry* 26(1988): 609–643.

Thaler, R.H. "Mental Accounting and Consumer Choice." *Marketing Science* 4(1985): 199–214.

Thaler, R.H., and E. Johnson. "Gambling with the House Money and Trying to Break Even: The Effects of Prior Outcomes on Risky Choice." *Management Science* 36(1990): 643–660.

Wertenbroch, K. "Consumption Self-Control by Rationing Purchase Quantities of Virtue and Vice." *Marketing Science* 17(1998): 317–337.

4 Status Quo Bias and Default Options

Jill is a transfer student who arrived on campus several months ago, deciding to live off campus. When she was hungry on her first day after arriving, she walked around the street near her apartment, where dozens of restaurants were located. Each of the restaurants looked good, and eventually she decided simply to walk in the next one she came across. Since that time, she has tried some of the other restaurants nearby, and some are very good, but she most often eats at that same restaurant. It is not the nearest to her apartment, but nonetheless she considers it worth the walk.

Consider also a person who is buying auto insurance for the first time, meeting with the insurance agent. The policies are rather complicated and involve making decisions regarding several different parameters (e.g., collision coverage, deductibles). The purchaser desires a good price on the insurance policy, but she finds it difficult to determine how likely it is that she will need each type of coverage, to determine the level of coverage she would need, and to decide how often she would need to pay the deductible. After describing all of the potential parameters and options, the agent says, "Here is our standard policy," pushing across the desk a packet of paper describing the types of coverage included in the standard policy. "It is possible to add any of the extras or subtract many of the options from this, but this is the policy we recommend." After considering for a couple of minutes, the purchaser decides to purchase the standard policy. Later, when she has the chance to reexamine her policy upon renewal, she opts to continue with the standard package.

A single decision—or even a chance event—can set up habitual behavior that continues for long periods of time relatively unexamined. The fact that one has always walked a particular way to work might lead one to continue to walk that way to work even if one discovers other routes are more scenic or shorter. Further, when other, potentially more desirable, options are presented, people might resist change altogether. People often shape their view of the correct choice by the actions that seem to be suggested by the situation. In many cases, a default option is available. A **default option** is one that is automatically selected when the decision maker expresses no explicit choice. For example, many brands of computer arrive with the Windows operating system installed unless the consumer requests some other operating system.

This chapter further develops the prospect theory foundation to explain why people might favor the status quo, as well as why they might value items in their possession more than identical items not in their possession. Further, we discuss the use of default options to shape consumer choice in policy and in business applications. In many respects, the use of default options can be considered the most successful contribution of behavioral economics to public policy at the present writing.

Rational Choice and Default Options

Standard models of economic choice consider that people evaluate every option based upon the utility they will derive from the choice and then select the option with the highest utility. Thus, default options should hold no special place in the mind of the individual decision maker. For example, someone choosing between two possible choices x and y simply chooses x if the utility derived from consuming x is greater than the utility derived from consuming y, $u(x) > u(y)$. If more utility is derived from consuming y, then y will be chosen.

Suppose x represents choosing a car with an automatic transmission, and choosing y represents an identical car with a manual transmission. Cars often have an automatic transmission by default unless the consumer requests a manual transmission. Consumers might decide to request manual transmission, for example, if they live in a snowy area where the manual transmission could add to their ability to control their car on slippery surfaces. Unless the customer explicitly enjoys choosing whatever item is named the default, the naming of a default should not change the preference for either choice x or choice y. Thus, naming a default option should have no impact on choice so long as making the choice is free and so long as the customer is not indifferent between the two options. So, if suddenly auto manufacturers named manual transmission the default, we would expect most consumers to persist in choosing the automatic transmission if it were not costly to do so. In this case, we might expect the default option to affect choice only when the options are not very different in terms of outcome or when the cost to switching to the nondefault option is large. In other cases where the decision is relatively costless and where outcomes are relatively dissimilar, we should expect very little impact from switching the default option.

EXAMPLE 4.1   Organ Donors

The lack of suitable organ donors creates a constant problem in the United States and in many other countries. Those who have failing kidneys, livers, or other organs can extend their life significantly if their failing organs can be replaced with healthy organs harvested from those who have recently died. Thousands of people die each year as a result of the dearth of suitable organs. One of the primary reasons for the scarcity of suitable organs is that a majority of Americans have chosen not to donate their organs upon death. Only 28 percent of U.S. citizens sign the donor card necessary to become an organ donor.

Eric Johnson and Daniel Goldstein found that the level of organ donations across countries is very closely related to the default option specified. In the United States, Denmark, the Netherlands, the United Kingdom, and Germany, people are not considered for organ donation upon death unless they explicitly specify their willingness to be an organ donor. In each of these countries the rate of organ donors is less than 28 percent, and in the case of Denmark it is only around 5 percent. Alternatively, Austria, Belgium, France,

Hungary, Poland, Portugal, and Sweden all consider people to be organ donors unless they have explicitly stated their objection. Aside from Sweden, the rate of those selecting organ donation is greater than 98 percent; the rate in Sweden is about 85 percent.

To determine how much of this effect may be due to the cost of choosing, Johnson and Goldstein ran an online experiment asking subjects to make a hypothetical choice. Some subjects were asked to imagine that they had just moved to a new location where one was not considered on organ donor unless one stated one's preference to donate. Others were given the same scenario but were told that one was considered an organ donor unless otherwise stated. Finally, a third group was asked to state their preference when no default was designated. Donation rates for those who were required to opt in were 42 percent, compared to 82 percent and 79 percent in the opt-out and no-default conditions. We call a preference for the default option the **default option bias**.

EXAMPLE 4.2   Journal Subscriptions

Members of professional societies often receive research journals as part of their membership. For example, the American Economic Association for many years included subscriptions to three journals in the price of membership: *American Economic Review*, *Journal of Economic Literature*, and *Journal of Economic Perspectives*. With the increasing printing costs of journals, some associations sought to save money by offering members a discount for eliminating their subscription to some journals. This brings up the question of what the default option would be. Apparently, at one point the American Economic Association considered offering a discount for subscribing to only two of the three journals and receiving the third only electronically. Daniel Kahneman, Jack Knetsch, and Richard Thaler report that many prominent economists involved in this decision believed that more members would subscribe to all three journals if that was presented as the default option, with a discount for eliminating one, rather than a default to receive two of the journals with an optional extra fee for receiving the third.

Preference Formation, Framing, and the Default Option

The rational model of choice supposes that people have well-formed and consistent preferences. It is conceivable, or even probable, that people have not formed preferences over many of the choices they face. If this is the case, people may be unduly influenced by the framing of the question or other subtle cues that help to determine the value. Johnson and Goldstein propose that default options shape choice by providing an anchor for subsequent decision making. Essentially, in the absence of preferences, a person looks for suggestions. The default option fills the void of preferences.

This is not the only realm where preferences appear to respond to suggestions. For example, Dan Ariely, George Loewenstein, and Drazen Prelec conducted an experiment in which many M.B.A. students were presented with various items with an average retail price of around $70. Each student was first asked whether he or she would be willing to pay the amount given by the last two digits of their Social Security number for the items. They recorded a yes or no response. Afterwards, they were asked the maximum amount they would be willing to pay for each item. A random device then determined a sale price, and those who had stated a willingness to pay above that price were given the item in exchange for the selected price. Interestingly, the subjects' stated willingness to pay for the items was substantially correlated with the last two digits of the subjects' Social Security number. Thus, those with a Social Security number ending in "99" were willing to pay more for the items than those with a Social Security number ending in "01." It is clearly unlikely that one's Social Security number truly determines the enjoyment received from consumption of a selected group of items. Nor is it likely that Social Security numbers are complements or substitutes for various items. Rather, it appears that the subjects are behaving according to an **anchoring and adjusting** mechanism.

Anchoring and adjustment supposes that when forming a belief, especially when the belief is expressed as a number, people anchor on numbers that are conveniently available and that their eventual stated belief is the result of adjusting from this anchor. Thus, people might anchor on the last two digits of their Social Security number when asked if they would be willing to pay that amount. Then, when asked what their maximum will-ingness to pay would be, they start from the anchor and adjust up or down to approximate their preference. The resulting belief contains the fingerprints of the anchor that was originally used to formulate an answer because it was used to form the preference. Thus, those who have a high Social Security number state a relatively high willingness to pay. Those with a low Social Security number state a relatively low willingness to pay. In this case, the Social Security number becomes a simple tool to help create a set of preferences. Similar experiments have shown evidence of this effect in other contexts.

As applied to the default option problem, it may be that the default option functions much like an anchor, in that it is given special **salience**, or prominence, in decision making. Thus, because it is the default, although people might form varying preferences for all options, they anchor their preferences on the default option, giving it particular salience. Additionally, the naming of a default can have the effect of framing the decision. In this sense, an anchor in preferences can perform much like a reference point. When organ donation is the default, one might consider the notion of retaining one's organs after death to be a relatively small gain given the loss in benefits to others. Alternatively, when not donating is the default, one might feel that losing one's organs after death is adding insult to injury. In this way, preferences for default options can result in setting a reference point, thus determining preferences.

To see this more clearly, if the default option and the alternative contain tradeoffs, then moving from one option to the other involves losing something and gaining something else. For example, choosing the two-journal option results in the loss of a journal and the gain of some cash. Figure 4.1 displays indifference curves resulting from two possible reference points. Suppose the person is considering either (x_1^r, y_1^r) or (x_2^r, y_2^r). As discussed in Chapter 3, the selection of a reference point alters the shape of indifference curves. At a reference point, reducing the amount of one good is considered a loss, requiring a substantial increase in the amount of the other good to compensate. This creates a kink in the indifference curve at the reference point.

The curve in Figure 4.1 with a value of k_1 represents the indifference curve that intersects the point (x_1^r, y_1^r), given that (x_1^r, y_1^r) is the reference point. Clearly, the point

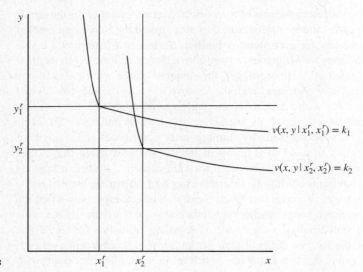

FIGURE 4.1
Considering Trade-
offs from
Two Reference Points

(x_2^r, y_2^r) results in a lower utility value because it falls below the indifference curve in question. In essence, (x_2^r, y_2^r) does not provide enough of good x to compensate for the loss of y given the reference point (x_1^r, y_1^r). If the reference point is (x_2^r, y_2^r), the indifference curve with value of k_2 represents the indifference curve intersecting the point (x_2^r, y_2^r). When using (x_2^r, y_2^r) as the reference point, clearly (x_1^r, y_1^r) is inferior because it lies to the left of the indifference curve in question. In essence, (x_1^r, y_1^r) does not provide enough of good x to compensate for the loss of good y. Notably, these indifference curves cross, contrary to the requirements for rational transitive preferences. Selection of a reference point changes the shape of the indifference curves with respect to the reference point selected, leading to the potential for nontransitive preferences and the reversal of preferences between two options. If selecting a default option essentially designates the reference point, this might explain the strength of defaults in shaping choices. People emphasize the losses associated with alternatives to the default rather than the gains, leading many to select the default. In this way, a clever marketer or policymaker can shape the preferences of their target audience.

Interestingly, people appear to make consistent choices when choices are made simultaneously under the same reference point. Thus, once the reference point or anchor is set for a group of decisions, the person reacts to tradeoffs in a way that mimics rational decision making. However, if choices are made in isolation, reference points can change between choices, resulting in choices that cannot be reconciled with a consistent set of preferences. For example, Ariely, Loewenstein, and Prelec provided an arbitrary anchor (a number) and then asked a set of participants how much they would need to be compensated to listen to varying lengths of unpleasant noise. Although the responses were consistent with standard choice theory in that longer lengths of unpleasant noise required greater compensation, the anchor appeared to influence the first elicited compensation measure. Those who were asked first about short durations required more compensation than those asked first about longer durations. In fact, the compensation required for the longest duration when the longest was asked first was about the same as the compensation required for the shortest duration when the shortest was asked first. Although preferences appear coherent in many circumstances, they can result from arbitrary anchoring.

EXAMPLE 4.3   Retirement Savings and Default Options

The use of defaults to shape behavior has often been discussed in the context of retirement savings. There is a documented need to increase the propensity of workers to save more for retirement, preventing future public expenditures. Nearly 50 percent of Americans exhaust their retirement savings before they die. Brigitte Madrian and Dennis Shea examined the enrollment of employees at a particular firm in 401(k) retirement programs. These programs generally require some minimum level of contribution by employees from their regular paycheck. The employer then contributes some additional amount to the retirement account. The money is allowed to accumulate and earn a return on investment that will not be taxed until it is withdrawn from the account after retirement. Before April 1998, this firm had allowed employees to opt into the 401(k) if they wished. After that date, employees were automatically enrolled unless the employee decided to opt out. Controlling for age disparities, they compared enrollment rates of those hired before and after the change in the default, finding the default option increased participation by about 50 percent. Thus, policymakers interested in reducing the number of elderly with inadequate retirement savings may be able to induce savings without eliminating the employee's participation choice by simply setting up a default option.

EXAMPLE 4.4   Insurance and the Right to Sue

States often set guidelines for the types of auto insurance policies offered in its borders. At one point, many states considered limiting the types of lawsuits that one could pursue following an accident. In particular, they debated allowing one insurance policy that allowed full rights to sue for any damages and another policy that cost somewhat less that limited the amount the policyholder could seek in certain types of lawsuits. Again, this leads to the question of which policy would be considered the default option. A team of researchers led by Eric Johnson conducted an experiment asking subjects to imagine they had moved to a new state and that they needed to decide on the type of coverage. One group was presented the full-rights insurance policy as the default, a second was given the limited-rights policy as the default, and a third group was presented the two policies without any default specified. In each group, a set of fixed prices was associated with both choices. Of those presented the full rights as the default, 53 percent retained these rights, whereas only 28 percent retained these rights when the limited policy was the default. Of the neutral group, 48 percent decided to choose the full-rights policy. Thus, the amount one is willing to pay for the right to sue depends on how the choice is framed. If the default includes this right, giving it up requires more money in compensation than if the default excludes this right.

EXAMPLE 4.5   Status Quo Bias and Health Insurance

Default option bias is a special case of the status quo bias. The status quo bias is a general preference for things to remain as is. If people have been in a particular state for a long time, they might take this state as the reference point. As in the default option bias, if the status quo is the reference point, a person requires substantial compensation for a loss in any dimension. In essence, the default option in most circumstances is to do nothing, thus remaining at the status quo.

William Samuelson and Richard Zeckhauser provide numerous illustrations of the status quo bias. One of the more compelling illustrations is their analysis of health insurance plan choices among employees at Harvard University. Over time, Harvard University had expanded the plan options available to staff. Of those who were continuing staff members, only a very small portion, about 3 percent, changed their plan in any given year. Yet, newer employees disproportionately selected options that had not been previously available. Samuelson and Zeckhauser found large disparities in enrollment rates in newer plans between newer employees and older employees. Those with longer tenure were more likely to remain with older health insurance options than the newer employees.

Rational Explanations of the Status Quo Bias

Some care must be given when invoking the status quo bias. In some cases, true and substantive switching costs exist. For example, switching health plans can result in needing to find a new primary care physician. In this case, the investment of time and resources in developing a working relationship with the previous physician would be lost. Indeed, the Harvard University employees were more likely to switch between plans that preserved their ability to continue with their current physician. The status quo bias is not always a result of switching costs. Samuelson and Zeckhauser mention one person who buys the same chicken salad sandwich for lunch every day. This may be an example of being unwilling to explore one's preferences for other options owing to the status quo bias. It might also be due to a strong and observed rational preference for that particular sandwich. If preferences are stable over time, the rational model would predict continuing with the same choices repeatedly when faced with the same decision.

History and Notes

The status quo bias was discovered and named by Samuelson and Zeckhauser in the late 1980s. More recently, since Eric Johnson's work, there has been tremendous excitement among policymakers about the possibility of using default options to shape public well-being. However, some caution is necessary. Although default options are effective in shaping behavior, they also appear to be effective in shaping preferences. In this case, there is a serious question regarding the proper role of the policymaker. Is it reasonable for the policymaker to be taking action to shape the people's preferences about rather mundane issues? Additionally, whereas defaults as presented here offer relatively costless ways to shape choice without limiting the choices available to the individual, this would not be the case if the default options were relatively onerous, if there were some hassle involved in switching options, or if the use of defaults was so pervasive as to become an annoyance. For example, you might become annoyed if, by default, your account was debited $10 and you were delivered a chicken salad sandwich every day at noon if you did not call by 7:00 A.M. to express your wish for a different item (though Samuelson and Zeckhauser found at least one person who might be happy with the arrangement). Further, defaults are primarily effective where there is no strong preference between the options, or more especially where no preference has been formed. This could limit the usefulness of defaults in more well-developed policy spheres where people have given thought to preferences and outcomes. For example, recent efforts to require grade school students to take a fruit or vegetable with their school lunch have resulted in a sharp increase in the amount of fruits and vegetables tossed in the garbage.

Reference Points, Indifference Curves, and the Consumer Problem

In earlier chapters, we originally defined loss aversion in terms of a value of wealth function. We also made use of loss aversion in the creation of indifference curves, but we never formally identified the meaning of loss aversion in the context of trading off consumption of various goods. Consider that a person must choose among a set of consumption bundles. Standard economic theory assumes a preference relation exists that represents the person's motivation for choice. We can represent preferences using the relation $\succ$, where $x \succ y$ means that consumption bundle x is preferred to consumption bundle y. Similarly, $x \succeq y$ means that bundle x is at least as good as y, and $x \sim y$ means that the person is indifferent between x and y. Rationality assumes that the preference relation is complete and transitive. Completeness requires simply that given any two bundles, the person will be able to assign a preference relationship between the two. Transitivity requires that for any three bundles x, y, z, with $y \succ x$, $z \succ y$ it cannot be the case that $x \succ z$.

If people have a set of preferences that satisfy completeness and transitivity, it is possible to represent their preferences in the form of a utility function, $u(x)$, over consumption bundles, with the person behaving so as to maximize this utility function. Violations of transitivity are often called **preference reversals**. The simplest case of a preference reversal occurs when we observe that a person strictly prefers one bundle in one case, $x \succ y$, but in another strictly prefers the other, $y \succ x$. This appears to be the case we observe with the status quo bias or the default option bias. Utility maximization is predicated on a set of stable rational preferences. Thus, without these basic relations, we lose the ability to use standard utility maximization to describe the behavior.

Amos Tversky and Daniel Kahneman propose overcoming this problem by supposing that people have reference-dependent preferences. Here we define a reference state (not a reference point) as some outside set of conditions that cause preferences to change. Thus, given a reference state, the person has a set of rational preferences. However, the preferences are not necessarily rational when the reference is allowed to change between choices. A **reference structure** is a collection of preference relations indexed by a reference state, $\succ_r$. Consider two different reference states, r_1 and r_2, in the same reference structure. The preference relation $\succ_{r_1}$ must be complete and transitive given any reference state r_1. However, it could be the case that $x \succ_{r_1} y$ and $y \succ_{r_2} x$. If people behave according to a reference structure, then it is possible to find a set of utility functions indexed by the reference state representing the person's preferences as a function of the consumption bundle and the reference state, $v_r(x)$. Further, the person will behave as if she maximizes the utility function given the observed reference state. Standard utility theory is a special case of the reference-dependent model, where the reference state has no impact on preferences.

As we have employed this model thus far, we will assume that the reference state is embodied by a single consumption bundle, called a **reference point**. Suppose that a consumption bundle consists of a collection of n goods in various nonnegative amounts and that the consumption bundle can be written as $x = (x_1, \ldots, x_n)$, where x_1 represents the amount of good 1 consumed (and so on). Then, given a reference point, we can define **loss aversion in consumption space**.

Let x and y be any two consumption bundles, with $x_i > y_i$ and $y_j > x_j$. Further, let r and s be any two reference points in consumption space, with $x_i \geq r_i > s_i$, $s_i = y_i$, and $r_j = s_j$. A reference structure displays loss aversion if for any consumption bundles and reference points satisfying these conditions, $x \succ_r y$ whenever $x \sim_s y$.

An example of this condition for the two-good case is shown in Figure 4.2. When the reference point is either r or s, consumption bundle x is considered a gain in terms of good i but a loss in terms of good j. Consumption bundle y is considered a gain in good j for either reference point. However, when the reference point is s, consumption bundle y is considered neither a gain nor a loss in good i, whereas from the point of view of reference point r, consumption bundle y is clearly a loss in good i. Because y is a loss in good i when considering reference point r, it requires a greater amount of good j to compensate the loss in i than if the reduction in i were simply considered the reduction of a gain. Thus, r implies a steeper indifference curve through bundle x than does s because s implies the removal of a gain rather than a loss. This notion of loss aversion generalizes the principles we have thus far used to represent loss-averse indifference curves. However, this simple version permits a wide variety of behavior, reducing the clarity of behavioral prediction as well as allowing behaviors that seem to be contradicted in observation. Thus, further restrictions on the shape of the indifference curves seem necessary.

Prospect theory generally proposes both loss aversion and that people experience diminishing marginal utility of gains and diminishing marginal pain from losses, commonly resulting in the convex shape of the value function over losses and the concave shape over gains. This notion of **diminishing sensitivity** to distance from the reference point can also be translated into consumption space.

Let x and y be any two consumption bundles, with $x_i > y_i$ and $y_j > x_j$. Further, let r and s be any two reference points, with $r_j = s_j$ and either $y_i > s_i > r_i$ or $r_i > s_i \geq x_i$. A

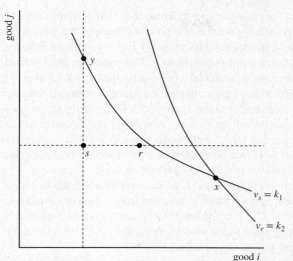

FIGURE 4.2
Loss Aversion in Consumption Space

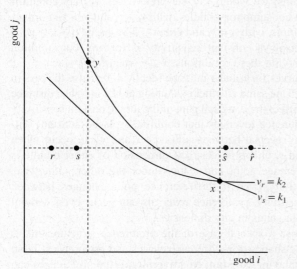

FIGURE 4.3
Diminishing Sensitivity in Consumption Space

loss-averse reference structure displays diminishing sensitivity if for any consumption bundles and reference points satisfying these conditions, $x \succ_r y$ whenever $x \sim_s y$.

A reference-dependent structure satisfying diminishing sensitivity for two different sets of reference points is displayed in Figure 4.3. Here, when considering from the point of view of either reference point r or s, both x and y are considered gains in terms of good i, y is considered a gain in terms of good j, and x is considered a loss in terms of good j. The difference is that the consumption bundles are a greater distance from r than from s in the dimension of good i. When moving from y to x one gains $x_i - y_i$ of good i. Owing to diminishing marginal utility of gains, this gain should provide a greater impact on utility when it is realized closer to the reference point. Thus, this gain is more valuable when evaluating from reference point s than reference point r. Because the gain from $x_i - y_i$ is smaller evaluating from r, it requires less of good j to compensate a move from x_i to y_i evaluating from reference point r than from s. This leads the indifference curve for $v_r(x)$ to have a shallower slope than that of $v_s(x)$. Such effects may be why the bait-and-switch approach is so effective. This common marketing technique usually advertises some good at a price well below some (potentially never truly employed) regular price. However, when the customer arrives, the advertised good is sold out or otherwise not available, but some similar (potentially better quality) good at a modestly higher price is available. Setting the reference point at regular price and the original good makes the customer less sensitive to changes in other aspects of the deal.

If instead we evaluate from reference points $\hat{r}$ and $\hat{s}$, we can find the same relationship. Here, the loss of $x_i - y_i$ has a greater impact when evaluating from $\hat{s}$ than at $\hat{r}$ owing to diminishing marginal pain from loss. Thus, it requires greater compensation for the loss when moving from x_i to y_i evaluating from $\hat{s}$ than evaluating from $\hat{r}$. This again leads the indifference curve for $v_{\hat{s}}(x)$ to have a greater slope than that for $v_{\hat{r}}(x)$.

Alternatively, if the decision maker displays constant marginal pain from loss and constant marginal utility from gains, we would say the preferences display **constant sensitivity**. Let x and y be any two consumption bundles, with $x_i > y_i$ and $y_j > x_j$. Further, let r and s be any two reference points, with $r_j = s_j$ and either $y_i > s_i \geq r_i$ or $r_i > s_i \geq x_i$. A loss-averse reference structure displays constant sensitivity if for any consumption bundles and reference points satisfying these conditions, $x \sim_r y$ whenever $x \sim_s y$.

In this case, the indifference curves for r and s must be identical, because the loss in value for a reduction from x_i to y_i is the same whether evaluating at r or at s. The distance from the reference point does not affect the marginal pain of the loss. Constant sensitivity places limits on the types of preference reversals that could take place. Constant sensitivity implies that no preference reversal between a bundle x and y can occur when considering reference points r and s, unless at least one dimension of either bundle is considered a gain under one reference point and a loss under the other. Otherwise, preferences would satisfy transitivity even if the reference point changes between decisions. Under diminishing sensitivity, preference reversals can occur even without bundles changing their loss or gain status in any dimension.

Tversky and Kahneman propose a special case of the preference structure that is particularly useful in exploring the shapes of indifference curves and preferences. First, define a reference structure as displaying **constant loss aversion** if the preferences can be represented as a utility function of the form $v_r(x) = U(R_1(x_1), \ldots, R_n(x_n))$, with

$$R_i(x_i) = \begin{cases} u_i(x_i) - u_i(r_i) & \text{if} \quad x_i \geq r_i \\ (u_i(x_i) - u_i(r_i))\lambda_i & \text{if} \quad x_i < r_i. \end{cases} \qquad (4.1)$$

Here $u_i(\cdot)$ is an increasing function, and λ_i is a positive constant representing the degree of loss aversion; thus each argument of the value function is akin to a prospect theory value function in good i. Without loss of generality, suppose that $u_i(r_i) = 0$. Given a reference point, when in the gain domain for any good, the $u_i(\cdot)$ function represents the value of the gain. In the loss domain, this function is multiplied by the added factor

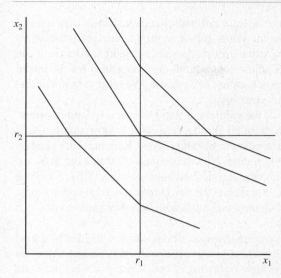

FIGURE 4.4
Indifference Curves with Constant Loss Aversion

$\lambda_i > 1$, exaggerating the impact of losses, and creating a kink in the value function at the reference point in each dimension. We refer to the reference structure as displaying

constant additive loss aversion if we can write the utility function as $v_r(x) = \sum_{i=1}^{n} R_i(x_i)$.

This is consistent with assuming that someone displays preferences that are loss averse over each good and that goods are not substitutes or complements.

If the reference structure displays constant loss aversion, the indifference curves take on a relatively intuitive shape as displayed in Figure 4.4. In each quadrant, the indifference curves are parallel. However, each indifference curve is kinked as it crosses the reference line in any dimension. Indifference curves become steeper in the northwest quadrant because more of good 2 is needed to compensate for the loss of good 1. Indifference curves become flatter in the southeast quadrant because it requires more of good 1 to compensate for losses of good 2. Indifference curves in the northeast and southwest quadrants have an intermediate slope because here both goods have the same loss or gain status. A derivation of the indifference curves under constant loss aversion is presented in the Advanced Concept box found at the end of this chapter for the interested reader. Indifference curves with flat portions create a possibility that the point of tangency with a budget constraint is not particularly sensitive to price changes. In other words, as the slope of the budget constraint changes, over a relatively wide range of prices the same kink point will likely be the optimum, leading to a sort of status quo bias in consumption bundles.

An Evolutionary Explanation for Loss Aversion

Although it seems intuitive why people would want to maximize their utility, it is a little more difficult to understand why their utility might be reference dependent. It seems that one would be better off on average if one behaved according to standard utility maximization, and thus one potentially has a greater chance to survive and procreate, passing one's genes down to future generations. Instead, our bodies appear to have evolved and adapted to perceive changes and ignore the status quo. You might experience this when someone turns on the light in an otherwise dark room. As soon as the light goes on, it can be painful and annoying. After a brief adjustment period, the eyes adjust for the added light and the light becomes pleasant, or at least not of any note. We react to temperature, pain, or background noise in much the same way.

A good illustration is given in one of the exhibits in San Francisco's Exploratorium. When you first approach this exhibit, a small plastic card with a light shining on it appears. When you inspect the card, it appears to be white. Then, a second card appears directly next to the first, only it is much brighter. Now it becomes clear that the first card was not white at all, but slightly gray, and the second card appears white. This process of cards appearing continues until, at last, you realize the first card was actually pitch black. Only because it appeared with a light shining on it and with no other cards to use as a reference did it appear to be white.

We are hard wired to use references and changes in our decisions. This may be useful on an evolutionary basis. Imagine the world if you experienced every sensation just as keenly at every instant whether changes were occurring or not. When you were bitten by an unseen snake or burned by some unexpectedly hot item, you might not react quickly enough because it would not draw your attention significantly. If you tend not to notice anything until a change occurs, the snake or burn draws immediate attention, providing you time to react before serious damage is done.

Evidence of loss aversion as a hard-wired trait comes from the work of Keith Chen, Venkat Lakshminarayanan, and Laurie Santos. They studied a colony of capuchin monkeys. By introducing a currency among the monkeys, they could observe trades and run economic experiments. In their study they found that monkeys tend to display loss aversion under many of the same circumstances in which it is found in human behavior. Because these monkeys lack the type of social communication found among humans, the researchers conclude that the behavior is inherited rather than learned. Thus, loss aversion may be an adaptation driven by evolutionary pressures rather than a skill learned from social interactions or from training as a child.

EXAMPLE 4.6   The Endowment Effect

Suppose you have just purchased a new car. You ordered the car online choosing all of the options you wanted and then picked the vehicle up from the dealer several days later. After driving the car home, you park it in your garage and spend a few minutes admiring the new vehicle. Upon entering your home, you discover a phone message from the dealer. Apparently someone else had ordered a car that was identical in every respect, except the sound system was not quite as powerful as you had wanted. The dealership accidentally sent you home with the wrong car. They inform you that you can drive back and exchange the vehicle for the one you ordered. You consider exchanging for a moment, but then decide to let the other person have the car you ordered. Driving the other car would not quite be the same as the car you have already come to know. Several weeks later you upgrade the sound system as you had originally desired.

Rational Choice and Getting and Giving Up Goods

The rational model of choice supposes that the change in utility upon receiving a good is identical to the amount that would be lost if the good is taken away. Consider the case where someone who is consuming none of good 1 and some amount of good 2, given by x_2. Her utility can be written as $u(0, x_2)$. If she is given an amount of good 1, x_1, her utility increases by the amount $u(x_1, x_2) - u(0, x_2)$. If the amount of good 1 is subsequently taken away, she loses utility $u(x_1, x_2) - u(0, x_2)$, resulting in the original level of utility, $u(0, x_2)$.

Consider also the problem of determining the maximum amount one is willing to pay to acquire a good. Consider someone who currently only has good 2 available to her. She thus solves

$$\max_{x_2} u(0, x_2), \tag{4.2}$$

subject to the budget constraint

$$p_2 x_2 \leq w, \tag{4.3}$$

where w is wealth and p_2 represents the price of good 2. If the utility function is strictly increasing in the consumption of good 2 (i.e., more of good 2 is always better), then she solves the decision problem by consuming $x_2^* = w/p_2$ and obtaining utility $u(0, x_2^*)$. Now consider this person is offered one unit of good 1. She would not be willing to buy if the purchase reduced her overall utility level. Further, if she could purchase the item and receive a greater level of utility, she could clearly pay more and still be better off. Thus, to solve for the maximum amount the decision maker is willing to pay, we must find the price for the unit of good 1 that keeps the person on the same indifference curve. Given that she purchases the unit of good 1 at a price p_1, the remaining wealth is given by $w - p_1$, which must be spent on good 2. This results in a new optimal amount of good 2 given by $\hat{x}_2^* = (w - p_1)/p_2 = x_2^* - p_1/p_2$. Thus, the maximum willingness to pay (WTP) for x_1 can be written as p_1^{WTP} such that

$$u\left(1, x_2^* - p_1^{\text{WTP}}/p_2\right) = u(0, x_2^*). \tag{4.4}$$

Now instead, let us find the minimum amount one would be willing to accept to part with the same good. Consider that someone was originally endowed with one unit of good 1, and we wished to determine how much she would be willing to sell the item for. In this case, her original consumption can be described by

$$\max_{x_2} u(1, x_2), \tag{4.5}$$

subject to the budget constraint

$$p_2 x_2 \leq w. \tag{4.6}$$

This problem is solved by $x_2^* = w/p_2$ and results in a utility of $u(1, x_2^*)$. Because x_2^* is clearly greater than $\hat{x}_2^*$, it is clear that the level of utility obtained when the person is endowed with good 1 is greater than when the person is charged the maximum willingness to pay, $u(1, \hat{x}_2^*)$. If the person sold the unit of good 1 for p_1, her budget constraint is then given by $w + p_1$. Thus, she would choose $\tilde{x}_2^* = (w + p_1)/p_2 = x_2^* + p_1/p_2$. The minimum amount she is willing to take in place of the unit of good 1, or the willingness to accept (WTA), can now be written as p_1^{WTA} such that

$$u\left(0, x_2^* + p_1^{\text{WTA}}/p_2\right) = u(1, x_2^*). \tag{4.7}$$

It is noteworthy that equation 4.7 is not equivalent to equation 4.4 and that rational decision makers in general display a minimum WTA, p_1^{WTA}, that is larger than their maximum WTP, p_1^{WTP}.

To see this, consider the special case of additive utility, $u(x_1, x_2) = u_1(x_1) + u_2(x_2)$. In this case, equation 4.4 implies

$$u_2\left(x_2^* - p_1^{\text{WTP}}/p_2\right) = u_2(x_2^*) + u_1(0) - u_1(1), \tag{4.8}$$

meaning that if the person had x_2^* of good 2, and lost p_1^{WTP}/p_2 of it, it would reduce their utility from good 2 by the quantity $\Delta u_1 \equiv [u_1(1) - u_1(0)]$, as pictured in Figure 4.5. Equation 4.7 implies

$$u_2\left(x_2^* + p_1^{\text{WTA}}/p_2\right) = u_2(x_2^*) + u_1(1) - u_1(0) = u_2(x_2^*) + \Delta u_1. \tag{4.9}$$

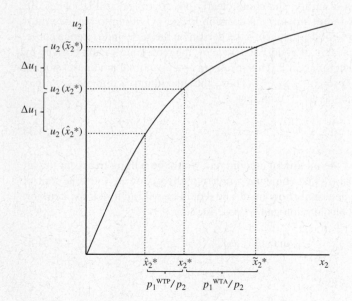

FIGURE 4.5
Disparity between
Willingness to
Pay (WTP) and
Willingness to
Accept (WTA)

Thus, if the person had x_2^* of good 2, and was given p_1^{WTA}/p_2 more of good 2, his utility from good 2 would be increased by the quantity Δu_1. If the utility for good 2 displays diminishing marginal utility, it must require a larger increase in the amount of good 2 to increase utility by Δu_1 than a loss to reduce utility by Δu_1. Thus, diminishing marginal utility of good 2 would imply that $p_1^{\mathrm{WTP}}/p_2 < p_1^{\mathrm{WTA}}/p_2$, or $p_1^{\mathrm{WTP}} < p_1^{\mathrm{WTA}}$. This is due to the wealth effect. Endowing the person with a unit of good 1 increases the person's overall resources, changing the marginal utility of each good and thus the worth of the good. However, if the value of good 1 is small relative to overall wealth, we would expect this wealth effect to be small. Over smaller changes in wealth, the effect of diminishing marginal utility must also be small, and the utility function could be approximated by a straight line. One of the foundational notions behind the development of calculus is that continuous and smooth functions can be approximated by a line over small changes in the domain. If the utility for good 2 in this example were a straight line, then $p_1^{\mathrm{WTP}}/p_2 = p_1^{\mathrm{WTA}}/p_2$. Thus, if the value of good 1 is small, we may suppose that $p_1^{\mathrm{WTP}} \approx p_1^{\mathrm{WTA}}$. For example, we would expect virtually no wealth effect from a small gift such as a coffee mug, which should then feature almost identical values for WTP and WTA.

Loss Aversion and the Endowment Effect

Because a gain of a particular value results in a smaller change in utility than a corresponding loss, loss aversion predicts that a good will take on a different value before and after it is incorporated into the reference point. Thus, a good that might be purchased may be evaluated as a potential gain, whereas a good that has been purchased will eventually be incorporated into the reference point. Once the good is incorporated into the reference point, parting with the good would be considered a loss. Hence, loss aversion predicts that the amount one is willing to pay to acquire a good should be substantially less than the amount the person is willing to accept to part with the good once it is incorporated into the reference point. This effect is called the **endowment effect**.

As noted previously, measures of willingness to pay and willingness to accept should always be the same if the utility of consumption for both can be represented by a straight line. Further, the measures should be similar if the utility function can be approximated by a line over the change in wealth induced by endowing the person with a good. Loss aversion suggests that no matter how small the change in wealth, we cannot approximate the utility function using a line. This is because the function is kinked at the reference point, x_2^*, with a steeper slope below this point and a shallower slope above, as pictured in Figure 4.6. Figure 4.6 depicts both a kinked and a standard utility function that are equal at the reference point. Note that under this condition, the WTP is necessarily smaller with the kinked curve, and WTA is necessarily larger under the kinked curve. This means that even for small changes in wealth, the utility function will behave as if it is concave. Thus, even for very small changes in wealth, we should observe $p_1^{\mathrm{WTP}} < p_1^{\mathrm{WTA}}$, suggesting substantial differences between willingness to accept and willingness to pay.

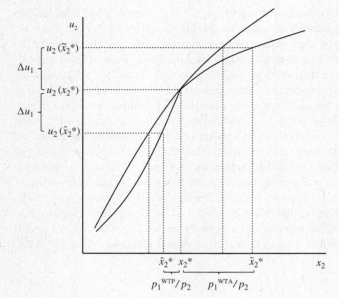

FIGURE 4.6
Loss Aversion and
the Disparity
between Willingness
to Pay (WTP)
and Willingness to
Accept (WTA)

EXAMPLE 4.7   Loss Aversion and the Endowment Effect

Daniel Kahneman, Jack Knetsch, and Richard Thaler designed a series of experiments to test for the endowment effect predicted by loss aversion. To test this, they needed to use an item of relatively small value so that willingness to pay and willingness to accept would be similar for any rational decision maker. In one of these experiments, several participants were brought to a room. Half of them were given a mug, and the other half were not. The participants were told that they would have the opportunity to buy or sell mugs in a market. Those who had been given a mug were asked for the minimum amount of money they would be willing to take in return for the mug. This information was used to determine a supply schedule for mugs. Those who had not been given a mug were asked to report the maximum amount they would be willing to pay for the mug. This information was used to determine a demand schedule for mugs. A price was determined by the intersection of the supply and demand schedules derived from the participants.

All those willing to pay more than the price determined by the market received a mug in exchange for that price, and all those willing to accept less than that price sold their mug for that price. The median willingness to accept was $5.25, and the median willingness to pay was only around $2.25. Referring again to Figure 4.5, this would require that the marginal utility above x_2^* be roughly half of the marginal utility below. Further, this requires that over the course of a change in wealth of $2.25 + $5.25 = $7.50, the marginal utility of wealth must decline by more than 50 percent! Similar responses were obtained when using pens, a good with even smaller value.

This suggests that the utility function truly is kinked near the reference point, as proposed by prospect theory. Further, this experiment seems to suggest that goods are incorporated immediately upon receipt into the reference point. Thus, individual preferences can change very rapidly in response to gifts or other similar changes in endowment. Finally, these experiments were performed several times with the same participants with very similar results in each round. This suggests that such behavior is likely to persist in a marketplace, unlike many less-than-rational behaviors. The effect in a market should be to reduce the number of transactions that can take place because those who own value a good more highly than those who don't.

EXAMPLE 4.8 Money-Back Guarantees and Free Trials

Many stores in the United States offer money-back guarantees for their products. These guarantees allow a consumer to return an item to the store for a refund if they discover they do not like the good as much as they thought they would. Many stores require that the good must be returned in 30 days, but some stores even offer lifetime money-back guarantees. Why might a store be willing to offer a money-back guarantee? First, consumers might face some uncertainty about the product they are buying. For example, consumers might feel that a clothing item fits and seems to complement their existing wardrobe while they are in the store, but they worry that they will feel differently at home. Or, they may be uncertain whether an electronics item is compatible with their other equipment. The money-back guarantee offers the consumer some insurance, limiting the risk from purchase. Thus, the money-back guarantee adds value to the good before purchase and experience with the good, encouraging sales. Second, once the good is purchased it takes on additional value owing to the endowment effect. Thus, before the purchase customers might believe that they would return an incompatible piece of electronic equipment, but once they purchase it they would consider a return a loss. Thus, they might keep the item and potentially purchase other items to make their original purchase more useful. The money-back guarantee lowers the threshold of value the consumer must expect the good to hold in order to purchase, and it raises the threshold of value the consumer must have for the good in order to return the item. Thus, the money-back guarantee is likely to improve the profits of the retailer.

A related marketing technique is the free trial. Much like the money-back guarantee, the free trial offers the customer the opportunity to own the good for a time at no expense. After the period of the free trial, the customer must decide whether to pay for the good or return it. The endowment effect suggests that once customers own the good, they will be less willing to part with it. Thus, the marketer will be able to demand a higher price than if the good were purchased before a trial.

Rational Explanations for the Endowment Effect

Several potential rational explanations have been given for the endowment effect. One explanation is that people face uncertainty about the value of the good before obtaining the item. Thus, when deciding on a willingness to pay, I might believe the item is worth as much as $7 or as little as $2, but on average I feel it is worth $4. In this case, I might only be willing to pay $3, less than what I feel the average guess at the price would be, owing to my uncertainty. On the other hand, if I were given an item and became certain of its value,

I would be willing to accept that value in return. Thus, if the value is $4, my willingness to pay is greater than my willingness to accept for the good. However, many have pointed out that mugs and pens are relatively known quantities. Thus it may be difficult to imagine that there is substantial uncertainty regarding the value of these items.

Further, there are questions as to whether the endowment effect really persists. John List ran a set of experiments by setting up markets for trading candy bars and mugs at a sports trading card exhibition. He found evidence of the endowment effect when market participants were amateur sports card collectors, but the endowment effect disappeared when the market participants were sports card dealers. He suggests that the sports card dealers have intense experience with trading markets owing to their trade in sports cards. Thus, it may be that the endowment effect is eliminated when the participant is familiar enough with markets and trading environments. Interestingly, this experience is not exclusive to the market the person usually participates in. Presumably the sports card dealers had little experience in selling and trading mugs or candy bars.

History and Notes

The term "endowment effect" was coined by Thaler in his 1980 paper describing various anomalies in consumer behavior. This effect soon drew the attention of environmental and resource economists. Economists studying issues involving environmental policy often need to find a value for goods that cannot be traded in the market. Thus, they might need to determine the value to local consumers of a new mall in order to determine if it is worth the environmental costs. Potential consumers could be asked their willingness to pay for the new mall. Alternatively, those who own homes very near the site might lose a spectacular view when the mall goes up, as well as needing to deal with added traffic, noise, and bright lights at all hours of the night. These people may be asked their willingness to accept these inconveniences. Then the economist could determine whether the mall would improve or decrease welfare by examining whether those who want the mall could potentially pay those who do not want it enough to compensate them. Early on it had been noted that willingness-to-accept responses seemed to be inflated relative to willingness-to-pay measures. This led Jack Knetsch, a trained environmental and resource economist, to begin investigating the endowment effect on an experimental basis in a series of papers culminating in his work with Daniel Kahneman and Richard Thaler. Knetsch's work confirmed that indifference curves appear to cross in experiments and that differences in willingness to pay and willingness to accept seem disproportionate to the changes in wealth that are taking place. The endowment effect calls into question many of the techniques that have been used to determine the value of environmental goods—a fruitful field for application of behavioral economic models.

Biographical Note

© Barbara Tversky

Amos N. Tversky (1937–1996)
B.A., Hebrew University, 1961; Ph.D. University of Michigan, 1965; held faculty positions at the Hebrew University and Stanford University

Trained as a cognitive psychologist, Amos Tversky pioneered the examination of systematic bias in reasoning. His works include studies of how people misjudge the probabilities of random outcomes, the valuation of gains versus losses, the impacts of framing on decision making, and dealing with ambiguous choices. Much of his best work was conducted in collaboration with Daniel Kahneman, who, after Tversky's death, won the Nobel Prize for economics primarily for their joint work. Tverky's work developed the notions of decision heuristics as an alternative to the rational choice model, with the implication that people may be making mistakes in judgment owing to their inability to carry out the necessary calculations. The biases were not limited to uneducated people but could be found even in articles in peer-reviewed physics journals. He helped to found the Stanford Center for Conflict Resolution and Negotiation, an interdisciplinary research center. In the course of his career he was honored with a MacArthur Fellowship, was elected to the American Academy of Arts and Sciences and the National Academy of Science, and was awarded numerous honorary doctorates. In addition to his academic contributions, Tversky was a war hero in Israel, serving in three wars. At one point, he saved the life of a fellow soldier who had fallen on an explosive about to detonate, throwing him to safety while risking his own life and sustaining some injuries in the blast. Tversky died from cancer at the age of 59.

THOUGHT QUESTIONS

1. Default options have proved to be effective in guiding public behavior, possibly by helping to shape individual preferences where none existed. Suppose, in an attempt to increase calcium intake by children, a school decided to include a small carton of plain skim milk with each school lunch purchased. The children are very familiar with milk and have well-formed preferences. Alternatively, children could request milk with higher fat content, chocolate milk, or no milk, if they desired, at no extra cost. How might this default function differently from the default examples given in this chapter?

2. It is generally found that those who are willing to change jobs earn greater amounts of money. Essentially, these people apply for alternative jobs on a regular basis and change jobs when they receive better offers than their current employment. However, a relatively small percentage of employed workers ever seek other jobs unless they are informed they might lose their job. Using the terminology and models of behavioral economics, explain why such a small percentage of employees would actively look for alternative jobs when they are secure in their employment. Additionally, consider employees who are informed

that they might lose their job shortly. Considering that the potential job loss is not based on performance but is based rather on the structural conditions of the firm, they might expect to earn more upon finding a new job. What does the endowment effect have to say regarding how the employee values the outcome of the job hunt before and after finding their new job?

3. A novelty store is worried that customers may be unfamiliar with the items they sell and thus reluctant to purchase. The owner is considering either using in-store demonstrations of the objects they are selling or providing some sort of money-back guarantee. Use diagrams representing the value function of the consumer to describe the tradeoffs in profit for each option. What impact should each policy have on the pricing of the items in the store?

4. Consider again the problem of determining the maximum amount one is willing to pay to obtain a good versus the amount willing to accept to part with a good.

Consider Terry, who behaves according to the model presented in equations 4.4 and 4.7. Let the utility function be given by $u(x_1, x_2) = x_1^{.5} + x_2^{.5}$, wealth is given by $w = 100$, and $p_2 = 1$, so that $x_2^* = 100$. Derive the maximum willingness to pay and the minimum willingness to accept for 100 units of good 1. Which measure of value is larger? How do you answers change if instead we considered only 1 unit of good 1? Under which scenario are the measures of value more nearly the same? Why? How do these answers change if $u(x_1, x_2) = x_1^{.5} x_2^{.5}$?

5. Now suppose Terry displays constant additive loss aversion, with $v_r(x_1, x_2) = R(x_1) + R(x_2)$, with

$$ R(x_i) = \begin{cases} x_i - r_i & \text{if} \quad x_i \geq r_i \\ 2(x_i - r_i) & \text{if} \quad x_i < r_i. \end{cases} $$

Complete the same exercise as in question 4. How do these answers differ from those in question 4? Why?

REFERENCES

Ariely, D., G. Loewenstein, and D. Prelec. "'Coherent Arbitrariness': Stable Demand Curves without Stable Preferences." *Quarterly Journal of Economics* 118(2003): 73–105.

Chen, K., V. Lakshminarayanan, and L. Santos. "The Evolution of Our Preferences: Evidence from Capuchin Monkey Trading Behavior." Cowles Foundation Discussion Behavior No. 1524, Yale University, 2006.

Johnson, E.J., and D. Goldstein. "Do Defaults Save Lives?" *Science* 302(2003): 1338–1339.

Johnson, E.J., J. Hershey, J. Meszaros, and H. Kunreuther. "Framing, Probability Distortions, and Insurance Decisions." *Journal of Risk and Uncertainty* 7(1993): 35–51.

Kahneman, D., J.L. Knetsch, and R.H. Thaler. "Experimental Tests of the Endowment Effect and the Coase Theorem." *Journal of Political Economy* 98(1990): 1325–1348.

Kahneman, D., J.L. Knetsch, and R.H. Thaler. "The Endowment Effect, Loss Aversion, and Status Quo Bias." *Journal of Economic Perspectives* 5(1991): 193–206.

Knetsch, J.L., and J.A. Sinden. "Willingness to Pay and Compensation Demanded: Experimental Evidence of an Unexpected Disparity in Measures of Value." *Quarterly Journal of Economics* 99 (1984): 507–521.

List, J.A. "Neoclassical Theory versus Prospect Theory: Evidence from the Marketplace." *Econometrica* 72(2004): 615–625.

Samuelson, W., and R. Zeckhauser. "Status Quo Bias and Decision Making." *Journal of Risk and Uncertainty* 1(1988): 7–59.

Thaler, R. "Toward a Positive Theory of Consumer Choice." *Journal of Economic Behavior and Organization* 1(1980): 39–60.

Tversky, A., and D. Kahneman. "Loss Aversion in Riskless Choice: A Reference Dependent Model." *Quarterly Journal of Economics* 106(1991): 1039–1061.

Advanced Concept

The Shape of Indifference Curves with Constant Loss Aversion

To derive the shape of the indifference curve under constant loss aversion, we must find all points that satisfy

$$v_r(x) = U(R_1(x_1), R_2(x_2)) = k, \tag{4.A}$$

where k is an arbitrary constant and where we now limit ourselves to the two-good case. So long as we do not evaluate at a reference point, the function in equation (4.A) is differentiable, and thus we can totally differentiate (4.A) to find

$$\frac{\partial}{\partial R_1} U(R_1(x_1), R_2(x_2)) \frac{\partial}{\partial x_1} R_1(x_1) dx_1$$
$$+ \frac{\partial}{\partial R_2} U(R_1(x_1), R_2(x_2)) \frac{\partial}{\partial x_2} R_2(x_2) dx_2 = 0, \tag{4.B}$$

or

$$\frac{dx_2}{dx_1} = - \frac{\frac{\partial}{\partial R_1} U(R_1(x_1), R_2(x_2)) \frac{\partial}{\partial x_1} R_1(x_1)}{\frac{\partial}{\partial R_2} U(R_1(x_1), R_2(x_2)) \frac{\partial}{\partial x_2} R_2(x_2)}. \tag{4.C}$$

By differentiating (4.1), we obtain

$$\frac{\partial R_i(x_i)}{\partial x_i} = \begin{cases} \partial u_i(x_i)/\partial x_i & \text{if} \quad x_i > r_i \\ \lambda_i \partial u_i(x_i)/\partial x_i & \text{if} \quad x_i < r_i. \end{cases} \tag{4.D}$$

Thus, we can rewrite (4.C) as

$$\frac{dx_2}{dx_1} = - \frac{\frac{\partial}{\partial R_1} U(R_1(x_1), R_2(x_2)) \frac{\partial}{\partial x_1} u_1(x_1)}{\frac{\partial}{\partial R_2} U(R_1(x_1), R_2(x_2)) \frac{\partial}{\partial x_2} u_2(x_2)} z, \tag{4.E}$$

where

$$z = \begin{cases} 1 & \text{if} \quad x_1 > r_1, x_2 > r_2 \\ \lambda_1/\lambda_2 & \text{if} \quad x_1 < r_1, x_2 < r_2 \\ \lambda_1 & \text{if} \quad x_1 < r_1, x_2 > r_2 \\ 1/\lambda_2 & \text{if} \quad x_1 > r_1, x_2 < r_2. \end{cases} \tag{4.F}$$

When crossing the reference point along any dimension, the derivative changes discontinuously according to z. In the northern half of Figure 4.2, as the indifference curve crosses r_1, the slope of the indifference curve is λ_1 times steeper to the left of the reference line than on the right. In the southern hemisphere, the slope of the indifference curve is also λ_1 times steeper to the left of the reference line than to the right. Similarly, as one moves from the northern half of the figure to the southern half, the slope of the indifference curve is divided by a factor of λ_2, leading to a shallower slope.

In the special case of constant additive risk aversion, (4.E) can be rewritten simply as

$$\frac{dx_2}{dx_1} = -\frac{\frac{\partial}{\partial x_1} u_1(x_1)}{\frac{\partial}{\partial x_2} u_2(x_2)} z, \qquad (4.\text{G})$$

which appears much like the standard indifference curve multiplied by the loss aversion factor, z.

The Winner's Curse and Auction Behavior

5

Consider Rick, who found a rare coin listed on an online auction website. The auction is to last two weeks. Rick is very familiar with coin collecting and has a very good idea of the coin's value. He places a bid based upon the value he believes the coin holds when he discovers the auction, and is satisfied because his bid is the highest thus far. He then waits, checking the auction site daily to see if his bid is still the top. One day before the auction is to close, he notices that someone has outbid him by at least $10. Rick quickly responds by upping his bid by $20, only to discover that he is still being outbid. Thus he follows up with another increase of $30, obtaining the top bid and winning the coin. Rick is very satisfied to have won the auction, and he doesn't seem to be bothered by paying almost $50 more for the coin than he thought it was worth.

With the advent of online auctions, personal experience with bidding and auction behavior is much more prevalent than it once was. Most who have participated in online auctions can attest to a certain level of gaming and scheming by auction participants. Students have suggested what they consider to be optimal strategies. For example, one suggests not to bid until the very end of the auction so that it is difficult for your competitors to react to your bid and thereby win the object of the auction. In almost all cases, the strategies suggested the importance of tricking or taking other bidders by surprise with your own actions or strategy. How should one best respond to the actions of others in an auction? What sorts of psychological biases govern individual behavior in an auction setting? This chapter describes the regular behaviors found in auctions and their implications for strategy, marketing, and procurement. When the behavior of one person can affect the outcomes of others and vice versa, we say that the people are engaged in a **game**. Economists generally use a game-theory model to predict or describe behavior in games. This chapter builds on the basic elements of game theory, incorporating behavioral heuristics to describe deviations from the predictions of game-theory approaches.

Rational Bidding in Auctions

The most common type of auction found online is a **second-price auction**. A second-price auction awards the object of the auction to the highest bidder, with the price being determined by the second-highest bid. An auction with n participants can be described as a game among n players. Each player might value the object of the auction differently. Let v_i represent the monetary value of the auction object to player i. Each participant's behavior must depend on the payoffs that he or she will receive for each possible strategy. More formally, a game is a collection of available actions for all players and a set of payoffs, with one payoff value corresponding to each possible collection of actions by all players. Thus to specify a game, we must list the players, the actions available to each player, and the payoffs for every result. First, let's examine the case of a second-price sealed-bid auction, often referred to as a **Vickrey auction**. A sealed-bid auction means that no bidder is aware of other bidders' bids at the time they place their own bid. Because players cannot observe the bids of others, a player cannot condition his actions on the actions of other players. In this case, bidder i's payoffs can be characterized as

$$\pi_i = \begin{cases} v_i - p & \text{if} \quad x_i > p \\ 0 & \text{if} \quad x_i \leq p, \end{cases} \tag{5.1}$$

where p is the second-highest bid and thus the realized price for the object, and x_i is bidder i's bid. First, consider a bid with $x_i < v_i$. In this case, if the bidder wins the auction, $x_i > p$, then the bidder obtains the value from the good but loses the auction price, resulting in a net gain of $v_i - p > 0$. Because this value is positive, the bidder could only benefit from wining the auction in this case.

Alternatively, suppose the bidder lost the auction, $x_i < p$. In this case, the bidder obtains zero benefit. If the price is above his bid, but below his valuation, $v_i > p > x_i$, then increasing his bid to any value above p will result in winning the item and obtaining $v_i - p > 0$, which is strictly better than if he had bid below p. Thus, the bidder might fail to purchase the item when it is in his best interest to obtain it if he bid below his valuation and the realized price is also below his valuation of the object.

Suppose instead that the bidder bid above his value, $x_i > v_i$. If his bid is above the price, then he wins the item, obtaining a value of $v_i - p$. This is positive if $v_i > p$, but nonpositive otherwise. Thus, if the price realized is over the bidder's value but below his bid, $x_i > p > v_i$, the bidder is strictly worse off than if he had bid below p. Thus, if the bidder bids above his valuation of the object, any realized price above his valuation could result in his obtaining the item at more than it is worth, resulting in a loss.

Finally, suppose the bidder bids exactly his valuation, $x_i = v_i$. In this case, if the realized price is below his bid, he will obtain $v_i - p > 0$, which is the most he could receive under any possible bid. Alternatively, if the realized price is above his bid, then he obtains 0. Increasing his bid could obtain the item, but it would necessarily result in a loss because he would pay more than it was worth to him. Thus, in this case, 0 is the best outcome that could be obtained under any bid. Bidding one's value results in obtaining the highest payout of any strategy, no matter what price results from the combination of all participants' bids. When a strategy produces the highest payout to the individual of any possible strategy under all possible outcomes, the strategy is called a **dominant strategy**. In this case, each player in the Vickrey auction has a dominant strategy to bid his or her valuation of the object no matter what anyone else does. Thus a rational model would predict that people bid their valuation no matter what. In this scenario, the bidder who values the good the most wins the auction and pays the second-highest valuation for the item.

Suppose instead that people could observe others' bids and could sequentially increase their bid if they decided. In this case, whenever all other bids were below the bidder's valuation, the bidder should bid above all others. If he subsequently saw further bids from others above his previous bid but below his valuation, he should increase his bid again. However, if any bid occurs above his value, he should cease to bid. This will lead to an outcome where the bidder who values the good the most will eventually outbid all others and will pay the second-highest bid, which will be given by the second-highest valuation, just as in the sealed-bid auction. Thus, there is no advantage to gaming a second-price auction. One could just as easily bid one's valuation of the item at the onset of the auction and wait to see if others valued the item more or less.

Finally, consider a first-price auction. A **first-price auction** is an auction mechanism where the top bidder wins the item but must pay his own bid for the item. In this case, the winner's payout can be described as

$$\pi_i = \begin{cases} v - x_i & \text{if} \quad x_i = p \\ 0 & \text{if} \quad x_i < p, \end{cases} \tag{5.2}$$

so that the winner obtains the value of the item, minus his bid if his bid is the realized price, and obtains zero if his bid is less than the realized price. If this were a first-price open-bid auction, then the bidder could observe the bids of others. If there were any bids above his valuation, he would choose to bid at a lower value, lose the item, and gain zero. Alternatively, if the highest bid by any other player were below his valuation, he would choose to bid just slightly higher than the next highest bid, so as to obtain the item, gaining the difference between his valuation and his bid—essentially the next-highest bid. Thus, the first-price open-bid auction results in outcomes that are much like the second-price auction. Everyone should bid up to their assessed value except the bidder with this highest valuation, who bids as high as the second-highest value and obtains the item. Thus, in a wide range of auction types, the bidder valuing the object the most should win and should pay an amount equal to the second-highest valuation.

In more-general sets of games it is not always possible to find a dominant strategy. The primary tool to make predictions when the player's outcome depends on the actions of others is the concept of the **Nash equilibrium**. To define the Nash equilibrium, we need first to define a few useful terms.

Define a **node** as any point in the game where a decision can be made by player i and the information available to the player at that point. For example, in playing a game of tic-tac-toe, the beginning of the game places player 1 at a node where she can choose to place her mark in any of nine squares, with no knowledge of where player 2 will choose to respond. If player 1 places her mark in the center square, this places player 2 at a node where player 1 has placed a mark in the center square; he now knows where player 1 placed her mark and can choose to place his mark on any of the remaining eight squares. Had player 1 placed her mark in the upper left square, we would have arrived at a different node where eight squares were available, but now the upper left square is taken, and the center square is available.

A **strategy** is a collection of the decisions a player intends to make at each possible node of the game should that node be reached. It is important to differentiate between a strategy and an action. One action might be "place an X on the center square." A strategy would be a long list of actions, one for each node, such as "if player 1's first move is to place an O in the top left corner, then my first move will be to place an X in the center square; if player 1's first move is to place an O in the upper middle square, then my first move . . . ," and so on, describing every action in response to every action or history of actions in the game. Let $\pi_i(s_i|\mathbf{S}_{-i})$ be the payoff received by player i for playing strategy s_i, when all other players are playing strategies represented by the symbol $\mathbf{S}_{-i}$.

The Nash equilibrium is a collection of strategies $\mathbf{S} = \{s_1, \ldots, s_n\}$, such that for each player i, $\pi_i(s_i|\mathbf{S}_{-i}) \geq \pi_i(s_i'|\mathbf{S}_{-i})$, where $\mathbf{S} = s_i \cup \mathbf{S}_{-i}$. Intuitively, the Nash equilibrium is a set of strategies, one for each player, such that each player is maximizing his or her payoff given the strategies of all others involved. Thus, given the strategies of all others, any single player should not be better off for choosing a different strategy. In the second-price auction, a Nash equilibrium is given by each bidder bidding his or her valuation. In the open-bid first-price auction, a Nash equilibrium is given by each bidder choosing to bid his own valuation unless he is the top bidder, in which case he bids just above the second-highest bidder. In general, if any player has a dominant strategy, all Nash equilibriums must require this player to play his dominant strategy. The Nash equilibrium is widely considered the basic requirement for rationality in a game.

EXAMPLE 5.1   Second-Price Auctions

John Kagel, Ronald Harstad, and Dan Levin conducted a set of experiments to test the predicted Nash equilibrium under several types of auctions. Among these, they tested the Vickrey auction mechanism. Participants were randomly assigned a private valuation for winning the auction—in other words, each was assigned a value they would receive if they won the auction and each participant's value was different. This valuation took the form of an amount of money they would receive if they happened to win the auction. Participants were informed of the auction mechanism and they engaged in several rounds of Vickrey auctions. In each round, the participant was assigned a new private valuation for winning. The Nash equilibrium strategy is to bid one's private value for the auction, but the bids were, on average, substantially above the private valuation assigned. On average, the bids were between 12 percent and 20 percent above the private value, with larger percentages when the private value was lower. Participants experienced dozens of Vickrey auctions, with no evidence that their bids were converging to the dominant strategy of bidding one's valuation. This led to the curious condition that in 80 percent of the auctions, the price (determined by the second-highest bidder) was above the second-highest valuation in the auction, with 36 percent of the auction winners paying a price that was above their own private valuation. These 36 percent were winners only in the nominal sense of the word, as they were the only participants in these auctions to lose money.

Procedural Explanations for Overbidding

Although little research has directly addressed why people overbid in Vickrey auctions, Kagel, Harstad, and Levin posit a procedural explanation. The Vickrey mechanism itself is not transparent because bidders cannot directly see the tradeoffs of their actions at the time they place their bid. Bidders might consider that there is no direct cost to increasing their bid, because they will never be called upon to pay the bid price—only the second-highest bid price—should they win. If they treat the second-highest bid price as fixed and below their valuation, they will not recognize any cost to increasing their bid. On the other hand, increasing their bid increases their chance of winning the auction. Without recognizing the cost of increasing their bid, they overvalue their ability to win. Unfortunately, the only auctions that may be won by bidding above one's valuation and that cannot be won by bidding one's valuation are auctions you don't want to win. In any case where it is necessary to bid above your valuation to win, you lose value by winning the auction. One useful way to think about this behavior is as a result of anchoring and adjusting. Just as in the case where bidders created a willingness to pay for items based on an arbitrary anchor, now bidders are forming bids based on an anchor. In this case, bidders anchor on the private valuation they are given. Then, falsely believing they can increase their bid from the anchor without penalty, they adjust upward, a procedure that is likely to make a loser of the highest bidder.

EXAMPLE 5.2   Timing of Bids and Online Auctions

The online auction site eBay employs a second-price auction, but the current price (or current second-highest bid) is always visible throughout the duration of the auction. Participants are able to revise their bids at any time before the auction closes, yet at the time specified for the end of the auction, all bids are final. Amazon.com offers a very similar auction mechanism. The primary difference is that whereas there is a specified time for the bidding to end, if a bid is placed in the last 10 minutes, an additional 10 minutes is given for bidding. This addition of time can happen several times. Thus, the auction does not end until the time for regular bidding has elapsed and at least 10 minutes has passed without an additional bid. Amazon introduced this feature to eliminate the prevalence of sniping. Sniping occurs when a bidder observes bidding behavior by others and then at the last minute places a bid in an attempt to prevent others from responding to that bid. Online sites offer software that is specifically designed to allow sniping in eBay auctions.

If all bidders understood the rules of the game and knew their certain private valuation of the object, their dominant strategy would be to bid their value and wait for the end of the auction. If a last-minute bid exceeded their own, they should be happy to lose to ensure they do not spend more than their valuation. However, this is not what is observed. Rather, Alvin Roth and Axel Ockenfels found rapid run-ups in bidding in the final moments of auctions on eBay, suggesting a sniping strategy is employed by many users. Alternatively, the auctions on Amazon.com more nearly represent the laid-back, once-and-for-all bidding behavior commonly modeled by economists. If rationality suggests once-and-for-all bidding that is independent of the behavior of others, why should anyone care about sniping?

Levels of Rationality

There are several reasons why people engage in sniping. If all others are following the strategy of bidding their value once and for all, then it is rational to bid your valuation once and for all as well. This would constitute a Nash equilibrium. But suppose others did not follow the Nash equilibrium strategy. For example, suppose you knew there were others who would engage in bidding wars by always bidding just a little bit higher if your bid exceeds theirs. Then, bidding your value early in the game will ensure that they bid higher and take the auction with no possibility of benefit for you. Alternatively, if you waited for the last instant to place your bid and bid your value, they might have no time to respond and you could obtain the item with a potential net gain.

Another possibility is that others might mistakenly ignore the auction mechanism and believe that this is a sequential first-price auction. Suppose some players naïvely bid below their valuation, waiting for higher bids from competitors before increasing their bid. We call this **incremental bidding behavior**. In this case, it is again optimal to put off bidding until the last minute so that other bidders do not have the chance to respond. By doing so, the second-highest bid is minimized and bidders can maximize their net benefits from having won the auction.

Finally, people might increase their attachment to the item through the process of bidding on the object. For example, bidders might begin to incorporate the item in their reference point and thereby increase their valuation via the endowment effect, leading to higher bids toward the end of the auction. For example, if they know they have the highest bid for a time, they might begin to regard the item as theirs and increase their valuation. Then when the bids increase above their prior bid, they now feel they need to bid higher.

A follow-up study by Dan Ariely, Axel Ockenfels, and Alvin Roth used an experimental setting to determine the reasons behind sniping behavior. Essentially, they had participants engage in experimental auctions designed to mimic the properties of the eBay and Amazon auctions, except that bidding took place in well-defined bidding periods, and the object of the auctions were induced values. **Induced values** means each participant was randomly assigned a value for winning the auction, as in the other experiments described previously. They found some evidence that bidders engage in sniping behavior as a rational response to incremental bidding by others. This creates an interesting situation whereby people might respond rationally to behavior that appears to be less than rational. This has led to a literature hypothesizing several different types of players who differ in their level of sophistication or rationality.

For example, Dale Stahl and Paul Wilson posit one type of player that does not think strategically at all, rather just randomly choosing actions with equal probabilities assigned to each. A second type (which may be thought of as a first-level rational model) thinks about their own payoffs, considering that all others simply choose their actions at random; in other words, this type believes they are the only strategic players. One can imagine further types who consider the mix of strategic and nonstrategic players and formulates a strategy based on the anticipated behaviors. Thus, in games, we must differentiate between irrational behavior and behavior that is rationally motivated by the irrational behavior of others.

EXAMPLE 5.3   English Auctions and Magic

In an English auction, an auctioneer calls out an initial price. All those willing to pay this price indicate their willingness to buy at the initial price. Then the auctioneer raises the price by some small increment. At each increment, bidders must again indicate that they are willing to purchase at that price. The auction ends when there is only one bidder who is still willing to purchase. Variants on the English auction are used to sell rare antiques at large auction houses. The English auction can be called a first-price open-bid auction because the highest bid wins, and all are aware of all other bids at all times. The dominant strategy in this case would be for a bidder to continue to indicate willingness to purchase until the price is raised above his or her valuation of the good. Because the auction stops when only one bidder is left, the price is exactly one increment above the second-highest bidder's valuation of the item. Thus, the English and Vickrey auctions should produce the same result both in terms of price and winner.

David Lucking-Reiley used a field experiment to test the equivalence of these two auctions. He auctioned off sets of trading cards that are part of the role-playing game *Magic: The Gathering*. In the game, each card represents a spell that can be cast, providing the owner with a more interesting gaming experience. Lucking-Reiley auctioned off 184 of the trading cards using a Vickrey auction, and he auctioned off another 184 cards using an English auction. Participants were solicited in online chat communities that regularly trade and auction these cards. Hence, one might consider these to be experienced traders. The cards used for the auctions were selected to have a similar value and quality. The results were somewhat mixed. In an auction with a large number of bidders, the Vickrey auction bids were substantially higher than the English auction bids. However, there was some evidence that the relationship was reversed with a smaller number of bidders.

Previous laboratory experiments using randomly assigned individual values by Kagel, Harstad, and Levin found that Vickrey auction bids were predictably and regularly higher than English auction bids. Whereas the Vickrey auction bids were persistently above valuation, the majority of English auction bids were below valuation, though by a very small amount. Further, participants in the English auction appeared to adjust their strategy after each session, eventually converging on bidding their valuation. Thus, experience with the English auction mechanism tended to lead bidders to eventually recognize and use their dominant strategy.

Bidding Heuristics and Transparency

Why the potential difference between Vickrey and English bidding? Previously, we reasoned that in the Vickrey auction, people anchored on their value and then adjusted up for the apparent gain in probability of winning without apparent cost. In the English auction, the price is **transparent**. This means that at the time of bidding, the bidder knows what the price will be if his bid wins. Further, the English mechanism draws full attention to this price. Thus, little reasoning effort is required in the English auction for bidders to determine their dominant strategy. If the price exceeds their value, they won't bid. Determining the dominant strategy in the Vickrey auction can require some significant level of cognitive effort, leading bidders to give up on determining the optimal bid in favor of a rule of thumb such as that suggested by anchoring and adjusting. The transparency of the English mechanism not only facilitates reasoning out the dominant strategy bid, it also facilitates learning over time. Even if one had a difficult time discerning one's optimal bid in the first few rounds of an English auction, after watching the announced price rise, seeing the final bidder still standing, and then seeing the announced price, it would be difficult to persist in the notion that one should bid above their valuation of the object.

Although people have a strong tendency to overbid in Vickrey auctions, they display a somewhat weaker tendency to underbid in the English auction. This deserves some additional analysis. In the Vickrey auction, people appear to anchor on their valuation and adjust upward. In the Vickrey auctions conducted in the laboratory, bidders are given no numbers to anchor on except their randomly assigned valuation. As was seen in the previous chapter, having any number presented in the process of eliciting a willingness to pay from the participants can influence the final bids. Without anything else to anchor on, the randomly assigned valuation becomes the anchor for bidding. In the English auction, the bidding process invariably starts with a minimum bid and slowly works its way up until the final bidder is the only one left. This initial bid might serve as an anchor to those who, for whatever reason, do not take advantage of the transparency to determine the dominant strategy bid. Thus, those who use this initial bid as an anchor will adjust upward toward their optimal bid but not quite reach the dominant strategy bid, leading to nominal underbidding behavior. In fact, Patrick Bajari and Ali Hortaçsu found that increasing the minimum bid increases the revenue for rare coins auctioned on eBay, using their second-price auction mechanism. This suggests that minimum bid levels can influence the bidding behavior in Vickrey and English auctions.

Finally, the lack of clear evidence of higher bids in the Vickrey auction for *Magic* cards deserves some mention. The Vickrey auction has produced clearly higher bidding than the English auction in dozens of published laboratory experiments. The result in the online field experiment calls these results into question. However, this experiment was conducted in a very experienced community and one with an active trading market for all cards involved. It could be that such a market context draws only bidders who have substantial experience with auctions and bid formation. The laboratory experiments show no evidence of improved bidding behavior with experience, but the laboratory presents a very special sample. Over the course of obtaining experience, no bidders are allowed to drop out of the auctions in the laboratory. On the other hand, public auctions such as those conducted for *Magic* cards might draw only those who prefer to obtain their cards through an auction. Those who have gotten burned by an auction in the past might simply drop out and never bid in an auction again. Thus, whereas a bidder might display no particular effects of learning in a Vickrey auction, experienced bidders might behave more like the dominant strategy because poor bidders are weeded out of the market.

Rational Bidding under Dutch and First-Price Auctions

Some auction mechanisms do not present the bidder with a clear dominant strategy. One such auction is a first-price sealed-bid auction. In this case, the bidder with the highest bid wins the auction and must pay the amount he bid. Further, because it is a sealed-bid auction, bidders cannot observe the bids of other players before determining their own bid. If bidders are not allowed to observe the bids of others before placing their bids, there is not one single bid that clearly yields a higher payout no matter what all other bidders choose to do.

Bidders who bid their value are guaranteed a zero return in all cases. If their bid is not the highest, then they neither pay nor receive any payoff. If their bid is the high bid, they would pay exactly their valuation and receive the value from the object of the auction exactly offsetting the amount paid. The only way to receive a positive return from this auction is to bid something below the valuation of the object. Suppose bidder i places a bid of $x_i = v_i - k$, where k is a positive constant. In this case, if some other bidder bids $x_j = v_i - k/2$ and wins the auction, player i receives a payoff of zero, neither receiving the object of the auction or paying any money. Player i could clearly have done better. By bidding something above x_j and something below v_i, player i could have won the auction and made a positive gain upon paying that bid. Thus, players face a tradeoff in placing bids. By increasing the bid up to the level of their valuation, players increase their probability of winning the auction and obtaining some positive value. However, as players increase their bid, they also reduce the eventual payoff for having won by increasing their eventual price paid. To discuss the optimal strategy for bidding, we need to use the tools of elementary probability and some discussion of decision under uncertainty.

Consider a random variable z that can take on real number values. We call the set of values the variable can take on the **support** of z. Thus, if z were the roll of a single six-sided game die, the support is given by $\{1, 2, 3, 4, 5, 6\}$. Let us suppose that the random variable displays predictable properties that allow us to discuss how likely some outcomes are relative to others. For example, when a fair, evenly weighted die is rolled hundreds of times, each number is rolled in approximately 1/6 of the rolls. The **probability** of an outcome is the proportion of times that outcome would occur if the random variable could be drawn a large number of times (approaching infinity). Thus, probability is a number between 0 and 1 representing the likelihood of a particular outcome. Further, the probability of a draw of the random variable being contained in the support of that random variable (obtained by adding the probability of each individual outcome in the support) must be 1. Thus the probability of rolling some integer between and including 1 to 6 is 1. The probability of any outcome outside of the support must be zero—the probability of rolling a 7 is 0.

The **expectation**, or mean, of a random variable can be defined as $E(z) = \sum_{i=1}^{n} p_i z_i$, where p_i is the probability of outcome z_i, and $E(\cdot)$ is the expectation operator. The expectation is simply a sum of all outcomes weighted by their relative frequency in a large sample, thus representing the average or mean outcome of a draw from the distribution. When an individual decision will result in a randomly distributed payoff, we refer to this as a decision under **uncertainty**. Often, economists suppose that when facing uncertainty, people seek to maximize the expectation of their payout, $\max_x E(\pi(x))$. Thus, in the first-price sealed-bid auction, the bidder tries to solve

$$\max_x E(\pi_i),\qquad(5.3)$$

where

$$\pi_i = \begin{cases} v - x_i & \text{if} \quad x_i = p \\ 0 & \text{if} \quad x_i < p. \end{cases}\qquad(5.4)$$

Here, the uncertainty arises because the price depends on the bidding strategies of all others in the auction. In particular, if everyone formulates their bid as a function of their own valuation, v_i, then the underlying uncertainty arises from the distribution of probability over valuations in the bidding pool. Thus, bidders face uncertainty because they do not know how much other people value the good being auctioned. If one could somehow observe the individual valuation of each person participating in the auction, one could easily bid the valuation of the bidder directly below one's valuation, producing the familiar rational prediction from the Vickrey auction. In the absence of this, the bidder must form a bid based upon his own valuation, the number of bidders participating in the auction, and his belief as to what others' valuations may be.

Suppose that valuations are independent observations from a random variable with the probability of any single outcome given by $p(v)$. Then suppose that all bidders will choose a bid as a particular function of their own valuation, $x(v_j)$, with presumably higher bids resulting from higher valuations, so that each bidder employs the same bid function. Then these bids become random variables with a distribution such that the probability of a bid $x(v)$ is $p(v)$. The probability that bidder i will win by bidding $x(v_i)$ is equal to the probability that $n-1$ draws of the valuation will yield a bid lower than $x(v_i)$, where n is the number of bidders. Suppose we relabeled the valuations in order, such that $v_i > v_j$ whenever $i > j$. Then the probability that bidder j produces a bid that is lower than $x(v_i)$ is just $\sum_{j=1}^{i} p(v_j)$. If individual valuations are independent draws from this same distribution, then the probability of all $n-1$ bidders having a lower bid than $x(v_i)$ can be found by multiplying the probability of each individual having a lower value, or, $\left[\sum_{j=1}^{i} p(v_j)\right]^{n-1}$. Thus, the expected payout for bidding amount $x(v_i)$ can be written as $E(\pi_i) = (v_i - x_i)\left[\sum_{j=1}^{i} p(v_j)\right]^{n-1}$, the probability that all other bidders submit lower bids multiplied by the value obtained if all other bids are lower. Maximizing the expected payout involves increasing x_i until the marginal expected payout becomes zero. Bidding less than this means that bidders could increase the expected benefit of their bid, and bidding more than this would mean that they could receive a higher benefit by lowering their bid.

Finding the Nash equilibrium for such a game is difficult. As an example, let us suppose that valuations are drawn from a uniform distribution over all integers 0 to 100. The uniform distribution assigns the same probability to every individual outcome. Thus the probability that any particular bidder has a valuation of 10 is equal to 0.01, and the probability that any particular bidder has a valuation of 100 is also equal to 0.01. Let us first examine the possibility that everyone bids their own valuation. If player i believes that everyone will bid their own valuation, then the payout for a bid x_i is $v_i - x_i$ if $x_i > x_j$ for all $j \neq i$. The probability of this occurring when player i bids his own value is $x_i = v_i$, is $\left[\sum_{j=1}^{i} p(v_j) \right]^{n-1} = [0.01 v_i]^{n-1}$. Thus, the expected payout is $E(\pi_i) = (v_i - x)[0.01 v_i]^{n-1}$. If one bids exactly one's value, then $x = v_i$, meaning the expected payout is 0. If instead the bidder bids slightly more than his value but not enough to surpass the next highest valuation, the probability of winning remains the same. So long as the probability of winning remains positive, the expected payout is negative if his bid exceeds his valuation. Thus, given that others' bid their value, it is not in the interest of any bidders to bid above their value. Alternatively, if the a player bids slightly below his value, then $v_i - x > 0$, and so long as the probability of winning remains positive, the expected payout is positive. Thus, if all others bid their value, an individual bidder has an incentive to bid below his value, making him better off. Thus it cannot be a Nash equilibrium for everyone to bid their value because any individual player could be better off trying a different strategy given that others bid their value. So the first-price sealed-bid auction should result in a different outcome than either the English or Vickrey auctions.

Suppose instead that all other players bid a fraction α of their valuation. Thus, if my valuation were 50 and $\alpha = 0.5$, I would bid 25. Then, if player i bids αv_i, the probability of winning x is $\left[\sum_{j=1}^{i} p(v_j) \right]^{n-1} = [0.01 v_i]^{n-1}$, the probability that player i's drawn value is above all others. The expected payoff from winning in this case is $E(\pi_i) = (v_i - \alpha v_i)[0.01 v_i]^{n-1} = (1 - \alpha) v_i^n [0.01]^{n-1}$. Given that others are bidding α times their value, and the next highest value is $v_i + 1$, increasing their bid by less than α will not increase the probability of winning. Thus, bidding less than α above αv_i decreases the expected payoff by decreasing the payoff in the event of a win, and the probability of winning remains the same. Increasing the bid by α results in a payoff of $E(\pi_i) = (v_i - \alpha v_i - \alpha)[0.01(v_i + 1)]^{n-1}$, with the probability increased by raising the bid above those with a valuation just 1 unit higher. Alternatively, decreasing the bid immediately decreases the probability by $[0.01]\left(v_i^{n-1} - (v_i - 1)^{n-1} \right) \geq [0.01]$ because the bid will potentially fall below others with value v_i who are bidding αv_i. But once bidders have lowered their bid, they do not further reduce the probability of winning until the bid has been lowered by α, and they continue to increase the payoff for winning. The Nash equilibrium occurs where α is such that bidding an amount either α less or α more would result in a lower expected value, or

$$E(\pi_i | x = \alpha v_i + \alpha) = (v_i - \alpha v_i - \alpha)[0.01(v_i + 1)]^{n-1} < (1 - \alpha) v_i^n [0.01]^{n-1}, \quad (5.5)$$

and

$$E(\pi_i | x = \alpha v_i - \alpha) = (v_i - \alpha v_i + \alpha)[0.01(v_i - 1)]^{n-1} < (1 - \alpha) v_i^n [0.01]^{n-1}. \quad (5.6)$$

Solving equation 5.5 for α yields

$$\alpha > \frac{v_i(v_i + 1)^{n-1} - v_i^n}{(v_i + 1)^n - v_i^n} \quad (5.7)$$

and equation 5.6 yields

$$\alpha < \frac{v_i(v_i-1)^{n-1} - v_i^n}{(v_i-1)^n - v_i^n}.$$ (5.8)

With any number of players, and for any value v_i, these two conditions will always be met where $\alpha = (n-1)/n$. In a more-general first-price auction, if values are drawn from a uniform distribution over all real numbers between $[0, \bar{v}]$, the Nash equilibrium bid is

$$x_i^* = v_i(n-1)/n.$$ (5.9)

Thus, the appropriate strategy depends on the number of players in the game, with the bid increasing toward the valuation as n gets large. The interested reader can find the derivation of this more general case in the Advanced Concept box at the end of this chapter.

Another common form of auction is the Dutch auction. In this auction, the auctioneer begins by calling out a very high price. The auctioneer then lowers the price by small increments until a bidder indicates he or she is willing to pay the price. This form of auction is common in the sale of large batches of flowers, as well as corporate and public bonds. Because the auction stops when the first bidder indicates his willingness to buy, no bidder has any information on others' valuations or intended bids before the auction concludes. Thus, despite the difference in mechanism, the Dutch auction acts exactly like a first-price sealed-bid auction. The highest bidder wins and pays his own bid price, but this bid must be determined before any observed actions by others.

EXAMPLE 5.4   Dutch Auctions

James C. Cox, Bruce Roberson, and Vernon L. Smith conducted early experimental comparisons of Dutch and first-price sealed-bid auctions. The rational economic model of bidding suggests that both auction mechanisms should yield the same bids and that these bids should be somewhat below the individual valuation of the object. They found that the Dutch auction bids are regularly below the bids of those in identical first-price auctions. The bidder assigned the highest valuation wins the auction approximately 88 percent of the time in the first-price auction, compared to only 80 percent in the Dutch auction. Thus, lower-valuation bidders have a greater tendency to outbid the top-value bidder in the Dutch auction. Further, they found that both the first-price and Dutch auction bids are above the bids in the second-price auctions. The anchoring and adjustment model might suggest that bidders in a Dutch auction should overbid, as appears to be the case, by anchoring on the opening amount called and failing to adjust down sufficiently. The Dutch auction starts with the highest possible price, providing a high anchor, which should lead to higher overall bids. The first-price sealed-bid auction provides no clear anchor but the induced value of the bidder: The amount the bidder will receive should he win the auction. Hence, the anchoring and adjustment model suggests lower overall bids for the first-price than the Dutch auction, a prediction that is not borne out in laboratory experiments. In fact, both appear to be higher than the bids predicted by theory by a substantial amount.

When David Lucking-Reiley conducted a set of experiments by auctioning off *Magic: The Gathering* trading cards in a series of Internet auctions (see Example 5.3), he also auctioned off 175 cards each in Dutch and first-price auctions. In the end he found substantially higher bids in the Dutch than in the first-price auctions, in line with the anchoring and adjustment prediction. In fact, the bid price per card increased by about $0.30 when using the Dutch versus the first-price auction on cards that are valued at about $3 apiece. It is difficult to say why laboratory experiments have produced such different results from the field experiment. One possible reason is that real-life auctions draw a particular type of person who might differ from those likely to participate in a laboratory experiment. In this case, however, those choosing to participate in the real-world auctions fall prey to an errant anchor.

History and Notes

Auctions have long been used to determine prices for rare objects or objects that are difficult to price as a commodity. The Dutch auction became famous as a mechanism for flower auctions in Holland in the early seventeenth century. At the time, tulips had recently been introduced into Europe. Their vibrant colors and novelty created a fervent interest in the new flower. Because there were very few tulip bulbs relative to the number who wanted to buy, it became a practice to sell the bulbs at auction to the highest bidder, giving rise to the Dutch auction. From about 1634 to 1637 the auction prices for bulbs soared by several hundred percent, with the top prices for a single bulb of 5,200 Guilder, the equivalent of several hundred thousand dollars today. This steep and seemingly unrealistic rise in the price of tulip bulbs was dubbed "tulipomania." Investors purchased the bulbs expecting to resell them for a quick profit. In 1637, participants in a Haarlem auction failed to bid at the levels investors had come to expect. News spread quickly and spooked those holding bulbs. The price quickly dropped nearly 100 percent, and the Dutch government suspended trade in all tulips. Although it seems unlikely to be a primary factor, perhaps the Dutch auction mechanism itself played a role in setting initially high prices where the steady stream of new and inexperienced bidders might have anchored on high starting auction prices, resulting in overly high bids and thus increasing prices.

Rational Prices in English, Dutch, and First-Price Auctions

Although there are no good reasons why bids in the first-price and Dutch auctions should differ, or why anyone would ever bid above their valuation, there are some rational explanations for why the Dutch and first-price auctions might produce realized prices that are above those in second-price auctions. In the derivation of the optimal bids in this chapter we have assumed that people maximize the expected payout. This assumption eliminates the possibility that people might value less-risky choices over riskier choices, called **risk aversion**. For example, a strategy that has a 50 percent chance of resulting in a payoff of five cents and a 50 percent chance of resulting in a loss of five cents has an expected payout of $0. Suppose an alternative strategy were available that offered a 50 percent chance of obtaining $1,000,000 and a 50 percent chance of losing $1,000,000. This also has an expected payout of $0, but many might be more inclined to choose the lower-stakes strategy because it offers less risk. More generally, risk preferences are often represented by a utility of money function, $u(\pi)$, so that people maximize the expected utility of their payout rather than the expected payout itself. If the utility function is increasing and displays diminishing marginal utility of payout (in other words, it is a concave function), then the consumer prefers lower levels of risk given the same expected payout (this is discussed in greater detail in Chapter 6).

In the Vickrey and English auctions, the dominant strategy still prevails if bidders maximize their expected utility. In these auctions, bidding your valuation is always the optimal bid no matter what the behavior of others, and it thus involves no uncertainty. Alternatively, in the Dutch and first-price auctions, there is no dominant strategy and each possible bid involves some level of uncertainty. Although both the Dutch and English auctions should result in the same behavior, risk aversion might lead to higher bids. In essence, higher bids reduce the payout in the event of winning the auction, while increasing the probability of a win, making the bid safer. On the other hand, no matter what the bid, the payout in the event of a loss is 0. Thus, bidding higher than the risk-neutral (or expected payout-maximizing) bid can reduce the risk involved in bidding at a cost of some reduction in expected payout. Aversion to risk can induce bids that are somewhat higher than the bids in the Nash equilibrium we have discussed. Further, the risk-neutral bids in the first-price and Dutch auctions generally result in the same expected price for the item being auctioned as in the Vickrey and English auctions. Thus, risk aversion can lead to higher prices in the Dutch and first-price sealed-bid auctions in general, as has been observed. Despite this, many properties of the observed bids are inconsistent with risk aversion or any sort of Nash equilibrium strategy.

Auction with Uncertainty

Consider a different type of uncertainty in auctions. Suppose, for example, that the bidder wishes to bid on an object so that he can sell it to a third party at a later date. He may be uncertain of the price he will be able to obtain for the item in the future. Thus, it may be that the bidder is uncertain about his own valuation of the item. In addition, some objects have some intrinsic value that is common to all involved. For example, when bidding on an oil well, generally all bidders may be uncertain regarding the actual amount of oil in the well, but all are agreed that it is the value of the oil in the market that determines the value of the well. In this case, valuation is not subjective because the object will not be consumed by the bidder but will be used to derive some monetary value (e.g., through sale on a market). This is called a **common-value auction**. In a common-value auction, different bidders might have differing estimates or beliefs regarding the eventual value of the item they are bidding on and must form a bid without knowing for certain the value they will obtain. In this case, the estimate of the value plays a significant role. Auctions that are commonly thought of as common-value auctions include oil lease contracts, bidding for free agents in professional sports, or bidding for the rights to publish highly anticipated books (e.g., biographies of recent presidents or their counselors).

Rational Bidding under Uncertainty

Suppose n bidders are engaged in a first-price auction for an item of common value v that is unknown to each individual bidder. Further, suppose that each bidder i obtains a different estimate of v, which we will label $\hat{v}_i$. For example, the general manager of a major league baseball team might use prior performance to guess the value of a baseball player approaching free agency. The true valuation is not known, but let us suppose that each estimated valuation is drawn at random from a distribution that can be described by a probability function $p(\hat{v})$, where $\hat{v}$ must be in the set $\{v-k/2, \ldots, v+k/2\}$, k is some positive even integer, and the average value of the estimates is $E(\hat{v})=v$. Then each bidder must formulate a bid to solve

$$\max_{x} E(\pi), \tag{5.10}$$

where

$$\pi_i = \begin{cases} v-p & \text{if} \quad x_i=p \\ 0 & \text{if} \quad x_i<p, \end{cases} \tag{5.11}$$

subject to the strategy of all other bidders.

The problem here is that bidders need to know how to use their imperfect signal of the underlying value in compiling the optimal bid. Given that one has received the signal $\hat{v}_i$, this value could be as much as $k/2$ above the true valuation or as much as $k/2$ below the true value. The probability that $\hat{v}_i$ is $k/2$ above v is $p(v+k/2)$, and the probability that $\hat{v}_i$ is $k/2-1$ greater than v is $p(v+k/2-1)$, and so on. Thus, the bidder receiving the signal $\hat{v}_i$, might view the probability function as representing their beliefs regarding the placement of the true value of winning the auction. If the probability that $\hat{v}_i$ is $k/2$ above v is $p(v+k/2)$, then to the bidder, the probability that $v=\hat{v}_i-k/2$ is equal to $p(v+k/2)$. Thus, the signal produces a probability distribution over possible valuations.

This distribution also tells the bidder about the possible estimates received by others in the auction. For example, if bidder i receives estimate $\hat{v}_i$, then the probability that bidder j receives valuation $\hat{v}_j=v_i-k$ is equal to $p(v+k/2) \cdot p(v-k/2)$. To see this, note that given the probability function specified, the only way $\hat{v}_j$ could fall k below $\hat{v}_i$ is if $\hat{v}_i=v+k/2$ and $\hat{v}_j=v-k/2$. If we assume that each estimate is an independent draw from the distribution, then the probability of drawing $\hat{v}_i=v+k/2$ and $\hat{v}_j=v-k/2$ is just the product of the probabilities of each individual draw. On the other hand, the probability that $\hat{v}_j=v_i-k+1$ is $p(v+k/2) \cdot p(v-k/2+1)+p(v+k/2-1) \cdot p(v-k/2)$. In this case, there are two possible ways to obtain a difference of $k-1$ between the estimates. Either $\hat{v}_i$ is the highest possible estimate and $\hat{v}_j$ is one above the lowest possible estimate (with a probability of $p(v+k/2) \cdot p(v-k/2+1))$, or $\hat{v}_i$ is one below the highest possible estimate and $\hat{v}_j$ is the lowest $p(v+k/2-1) \cdot p(v-k/2)$. The probability that either one of these events happens is the sum of the probability of each event.

As a simple example, suppose that there are three possible estimates, $\{v-1, v, v+1\}$, with a uniform probability distribution, so that $p(\hat{v}) = 1/3$ that $\hat{v}$ takes on any of these three values, and that $n = 2$. Suppose bidder 1 draws an estimate of the value of the good, $\hat{v}_1 = 10$. Then, the true value is either 9, 10, or 11, with the probability of each outcome being 1/3. Further, the possible estimates that could be drawn by bidder 2 are 8, 9, 10, 11, or 12. To find the Nash equilibrium, suppose that bidder 1 believes that the other bidder will form his bid according to some rule $x_2 = b(\hat{v}_2)$. Given a true valuation of v, the probability that a particular bid of x is higher than bidder 2's bid is $\sum_{j=v-1}^{b^{-1}(x)} p(j) = \sum_{j=v-1}^{b^{-1}(x)} 1/3$, where $v-1$ is the lowest possible estimate an opponent could draw given v, and $b^{-1}(x)$ is the valuation of an opponent that would result in a bid of x. In this event, the expected payout from bidding x is given by

$$E(\pi) = (1/3)(9-x)\left[\sum_{t=8}^{t=\max\{b^{-1}(x),\, 10\}} 1/3\right] + (1/3)(10-x)\left[\sum_{t=9}^{t=\max\{b^{-1}(x),\, 11\}} 1/3\right]$$

$$+ (1/3)(11-x)\left[\sum_{t=10}^{t=\max\{b^{-1}(x),\, 12\}} 1/3\right],$$

$$(5.12)$$

where the first term on the right side of the equation is the benefit to the bidder given the possible true value, $v = 9$, multiplied by the probability that $v = 9$, (1/3), and the probability that the bid x will win. The second and third terms are constructed similarly for the case where $v = 10$ and $v = 11$, respectively. Suppose that $b(\hat{v}_2) = \hat{v}_2 - 1$, so that $b^{-1}(x) = x + 1 = \hat{v}$. Then, bidding 9 in this case would yield $E(\pi) = 1/9$, bidding 10 would yield $E(\pi) = -1/9$, and bidding 11 would yield $E(\pi) = -1$. Further, bidding slightly less than 9 yields a lower expected payout by eliminating the possibility of winning if $v > 9$, and resulting in only a small (less than 1) payout in the event of $v = 9$. Thus, the expected value for bidding less than 9 would be smaller than 1/9. Bidding slightly above 9 increases the potential price of winning without increasing the possibility of a win and thus results in a lower expected payout. Thus, the optimal bid when faced with an opponent who bids according to $b(\hat{v}_j) = \hat{v}_j - 1$ is to bid $b(\hat{v}_1) = \hat{v}_1 - 1$. The same can be shown for any possible $\hat{v}_i$, and thus bidding one below the estimated value constitutes a Nash equilibrium in this case.

This strategy eliminates the possibility of overbidding. By subtracting one from the received estimate, the bid is below the estimate by the maximum possible error in the bid. By receiving an estimate of 10, one immediately knows that the lowest possible valuation is 9. Thus, one guarantees oneself a nonnegative payoff by bidding 9. If both bidders bid 1 below their valuation, the bidder who draws the higher valuation wins the auction.

Suppose that the true value of the object, v, is drawn from a uniform distribution over the set $[\underline{v}, \overline{v}]$ and that the estimates of valuation are drawn from a continuous uniform distribution, with the support of $\hat{v}$ being given by $[v - \varepsilon, v + \varepsilon]$. With n bidders participating in the auction, the Nash equilibrium bid in the common-value auction is given by[1]

$$b(\hat{v}) = \hat{v} - \varepsilon + \frac{2\varepsilon}{N+1} e^{-(N/2\varepsilon)\left[\hat{v} - (\underline{v} + \varepsilon)\right]}. \tag{5.13}$$

Thus, the rational model predicts that people bid their value, minus a correction term that reduces the probability of overbidding, plus another correction term that adjusts the bid up if the estimated valuation is improbably low. The second correction term becomes very small as the valuation estimate moves above $\underline{v} + \varepsilon$. Because this term is likely to be very small for the bidder obtaining the highest estimate of value, the highest bidder's expected payoff is $v - b(\hat{v}) = v - v - \varepsilon + \varepsilon - \frac{2\varepsilon}{N+1} e^{-\left(\frac{N}{2\varepsilon}\right)\left[\bar{v} - (\underline{v} + \varepsilon)\right]} \approx 2\varepsilon/n$, which must be positive. Also, both correction terms become smaller as the number of bidders increases, thus raising bids closer to the estimated valuation. The work of Robert Wilson has shown that if the information about the valuation of the good is drawn independently by each bidder from the same distribution and that this distribution is actually a nontrivial function of the true value of the good, the highest bid is very close to the true value of the item. Each bidder must expect nonnegative profits on average in the Nash equilibrium, otherwise it would be in their best interest to place a lower bid. In fact, the highest bid that conforms to equation 5.13 occurs when the highest valuation estimate is drawn, $\hat{v} = v + \varepsilon$, and the number of bidders, N, tends toward infinity. In this case the bid converges to v. Thus, no one should ever bid above the true underlying value under this framework.

EXAMPLE 5.5   Oil Lease Contracts

The right to drill for oil offshore is typically auctioned off by the government using either first-price or second-price sealed-bid auctions. Oil companies bid for the right to drill, basing their bids on estimates of the amount of oil in the particular region. These estimates are produced by geologists working for the individual company considering a bid.

In 1971, three physicists who had been working in the petroleum industry noted the extremely low profitability of oil lease contracts in the Gulf of Mexico. They noted that the returns from 1950 to the late 1960s were about that of a credit union—extremely low. They thought this occurred because in an auction for a good with an uncertain value, the highest bidder is the bidder with the highest probability of having overestimated the value of the good. Thus, this highest bidder is the one most likely to have overbid and to be turning a loss on the lease. In fact, Capen, Clapp, and Campbell found that often the highest bid is more than four times the second-highest bid, suggesting that the highest bidder was in fact overestimating the value of the oil in the well.

---

[1] This formula must be modified somewhat if the signal is in ε of $\underline{v}$ or $\bar{v}$. I ignore these special cases in the text. See John Kagel and Jean-Francois Richard for more details.

Walter Mead, Asbjorn Moseidjord, and Philip Sorensen found that over the same period, an oil lease yielded an average net present value of −$192,128. In fact, 78 percent of all oil leases resulted in either no oil (the vast majority) or not enough oil to offset the costs of exploration and lease. However, the small number that did produce profits had high returns, leading to overall returns that were about average for all industries in the United States. Further research has suggested that the high-returning leases have resulted from firms placing bids on adjacent lands that they might have had additional information regarding. Those bidding on single leases not adjacent to their own land tend to have much smaller average returns on the lease, suggesting that they might not be realizing the expected return. This means those bidding on oil leases do not appear to be following a Nash equilibrium strategy.

EXAMPLE 5.6   Free Agents in Sports

Bidding wars often erupt in professional sports over the biggest and most recognizable names. In Major League Baseball, any player who has played for at least six years in the league at the time his current contract expires becomes a free agent. This means that he has the opportunity to negotiate a contract with any team he likes. Eligible players declare their free agency on October 15, and subsequently interested teams begin the bidding process. Because the bids of any particular team are generally secret, and the commodity is valued primarily for his playing ability, this can function somewhat like the common-value first-price auction with uncertainty.

James Cassing and Richard Douglas examined the resulting pay for free agents, finding that they are substantially overpaid. They first estimated the marginal revenue product of a point of overall team slugging average (total number of bases on hits divided by total at bats) as well as the ratio of strikeouts to walks. They then compared the free agent's pay to productivity of slugging and ratio of strikeouts to walks. Of the 44 free agents they examined, 28 were overpaid. Those overpaid were paid an average of 20 percent more than their value to the team. Because the overpayments are so astoundingly high, free agents as a whole are paid more than they are worth on average.

Similar results have been found in auctions for the rights to publish books. When a famous person is intent on writing a book, book publishers sometimes bid on the rights to publish the book, offering money in advance of publication in return for the right to publish the work. In a large number of cases, the books never make enough money to cover the advances. Other examples occur in the initial public offerings of stocks, where prices systematically rise in dramatic fashion in the first day of trading.

The Winner's Curse and Anchoring and Adjusting

If a bidder fails to take account of the uncertainty in his information or the number of bidders he is bidding against, he might overbid relative to the Nash equilibrium strategy.

Further, when his estimate of the value is high, the expected profit for bidding might become low relative to the Nash equilibrium expected return, or it might even become negative. This phenomenon is called the **winner's curse**. Because the highest bidder is the most likely to have overbid the true underlying valuation of the good, if he fails to account for the intricacies of optimal bidding in a Nash equilibrium he is highly likely to lose money for having won the auction.

In describing behavioral theories of why this might happen, two points are important. First, although market prices are the result of the behavior of many market participants, auction prices tend to be the result of just a couple of bidders—and in the case of the first-price auction one bidder. Thus, in an auction with 100 participants, one irrational bidder who happens to draw a high estimate of the valuation could lead to the behavioral anomaly. Anomalous market prices would require irrational behavior by nearly all participants—an unlikely event. Thus, markets are very stable and robust. Auctions are very volatile, with the outcome depending on each individual participant. Second, the Nash equilibrium under the common-value first-price auction is highly complex. Even in the very simplified version under which I have derived the Nash equilibrium in this chapter, I would guess (from previous experience in teaching) that whereas students understand the concept that bids should be below the estimated valuation, many students of economic theory fail to fully understand how the strategy is derived. I have omitted the derivation of the more complicated general Nash strategy for bidding because it is lengthy enough to be omitted from nearly all game-theory texts, as well as academic papers discussing optimal bidding in the common-value auction. It is then a very strange idea that people who have good training in mathematics and theory have trouble understanding this strategy even when they are concentrating significant cognitive effort on it, yet somehow this same strategy comes naturally to untrained persons who are participating in auctions.

The typical behavioral model of bidding under uncertainty is based on the anchoring and adjustment model. Bidders recognize the error in their estimate and the need to make profit. Thus, they anchor on their estimated value and adjust downward to obtain a bid that is closer to the Nash equilibrium bid. However, because their anchor is high, they fail to adjust downward fully, and thus the bid is too close to the anchor. One result of this model is that the larger the number of bidders, the greater the probability of the winner's curse. When each participant has an independently drawn estimate of the underlying value, the higher the number of draws, the higher the probability that the highest estimate of value is significantly over the true value. Suppose the estimate of value that is required in order to estimate at or above the true value is $\bar{v}$, and the probability of drawing $\hat{v} > \bar{v}$ is p. Then the probability that no one draws an estimate greater than $\bar{v}$ with n bidders is $(1 - p)^n$, which is clearly decreasing as n increases. Thus, we would expect to see many more cases of the winner's curse with many auction participants rather than with fewer auction participants.

An alternative behavioral model supposes that people underappreciate the impact of information differences between bidders regarding individual bidding behavior. Thus, whereas bidders might correctly anticipate the bids of their competitors, they might not fully attribute the differences in bids to the differences in estimates of the underlying value. Rather they might believe the difference is due to poor strategy on the part of others. This possibility has been implicitly used to explain both the winner's curse and several other anomalies in the trade of goods with common yet unknown values.

Most notably, Erik Eyster and Matthew Rabin propose an alternative to the Nash equilibrium in such games. In the Nash equilibrium, people are assumed to know the distribution of estimates of value and to employ the strategy that anticipates the strategies of other players based on this distribution. Alternatively, Eyster and Rabin suppose that people know the true distribution of actions taken by others, but they suppose that these actions have no particular relationship to the underlying estimates of values. Thus, the distribution of actions by others is seen as not representing strategic behavior but just as some static environmental variables. Then the **fully cursed equilibrium** is given where each player is maximizing the expected payout given the distribution of actions by other players. More generally, the **χ-cursed equilibrium** assumes that each player assigns probability χ to the event that all other players' actions are not related to their underlying estimate of valuation (or type), and the remaining $(1-\chi)$ probability is assigned to the event that players are fully strategic in responding to their estimate of valuation.

Let us consider the fully cursed equilibrium of the simple first-price auction considered in the previous section. There are three possible values of the estimate $\hat{v}$, $\{v-1,\ v,\ v+1\}$, with a uniform probability distribution, so that $p(\hat{v})=1/3$ for each possible value of $\hat{v}$, and $n=2$. Suppose again that player 1 draws $\hat{v}_1=10$. As derived previously, the probability distribution of the other player's estimate of valuation is given by

$$p(\hat{v}_2) = \begin{cases} 1/9 & \text{if} \quad \hat{v}_2 = 8 \\ 2/9 & \text{if} \quad \hat{v}_2 = 9 \\ 1/3 & \text{if} \quad \hat{v}_2 = 10 \\ 2/9 & \text{if} \quad \hat{v}_2 = 11 \\ 1/9 & \text{if} \quad \hat{v}_2 = 12. \end{cases} \tag{5.14}$$

This would result in the probability distribution of the other player's action z given by

$$p(z) = \begin{cases} 1/9 & \text{if} \quad z = b(8) \\ 2/9 & \text{if} \quad z = b(9) \\ 1/3 & \text{if} \quad z = b(10) \\ 2/9 & \text{if} \quad z = b(11) \\ 1/9 & \text{if} \quad z = b(12). \end{cases} \tag{5.15}$$

Further, let $\mu = E(v) = \sum_v p(v)v$ be the expected value of the item being auctioned given the signal received by the player in question. This expected value in the auctions we have described is just the value of the signal itself. In this case $\mu = \hat{v}_1 = 10$. Given this distribution, player 1 must solve

$$\max_x E_\chi(\pi) = (\mu - x) \sum_{b(\hat{v}_2)<x} p(b(\hat{v}_2)) = (10-x) \sum_{b(\hat{v}_2)<x} p(b(\hat{v}_2)), \tag{5.16}$$

where E_χ denotes expectation given cursed beliefs, and the probabilities $p(b(\hat{v}_2))$ are drawn from equation 5.15. The key difference between the Nash and the cursed equilibrium is in how the player evaluates the potential payout from a bid. Here, the player multiplies the overall expected benefit should he win the auction, $10-x$, by the probability of winning should he bid, x. However, the player treats winning the auction and the payout he receives as if they are unrelated. He doesn't recognize that he has a higher probability of winning when he has overbid. When the player does not consider the strategic nature of others' bids, the relationship between the possible true value and the bids of other players is not considered.

Compare this to the equation 5.12, where the player considers the impact of the true underlying valuation on the impact of others' bids. For example, if the true valuation is low (in this case, 9), the probability of the other player drawing an 8 increases from 0 to 1/3. Equation 5.12 takes this possibility into account when determining the expected payout, whereas the fully cursed equilibrium does not. Here the player only considers the average value given the signal he received and then considers his chances of winning based on that value. The player behaves as if winning the auction is independent of the underlying value.

Recall that the Nash equilibrium strategy was to bid one below the estimated valuation. If player 2 plays $b(\hat{v}) = \hat{v} - 1$, then consider the payout for bidding 9 when your drawn estimate is 10:

$$E_\chi(\pi) = 1 \times \left(\frac{1}{9} + \frac{2}{9}\right) = \frac{1}{3}. \tag{5.17}$$

Alternatively, bidding just slightly more than 9, say 9.1, would yield

$$E_\chi(\pi) = \frac{9}{10} \times \left(\frac{1}{9} + \frac{2}{9} + \frac{1}{3}\right) = \frac{3}{5}, \tag{5.18}$$

which is much greater than 1/3. Thus, bidding 1 less than your estimated value cannot be the fully cursed equilibrium strategy. In fact, the only strategy that will produce a probability distribution such that the player is not tempted to increase his bid is $b(\hat{v}) = \hat{v}$, yielding $E_\chi(\pi) = 0$. Further, the true expected payout is found by multiplying the probability of winning given a particular true underlying value by the value of winning in that instance. For simplicity, assume that the bidder in question loses if there is a tie bid. Thus, the probability that the underlying value is 9 is 1/3, and the probability of winning when bidding 10 if the value is 8 is 2/3 (the probability of the other player drawing a 8 or a 9). The value of winning in this case is -1. The probability that the value is 10 is 1/3, and the probability of winning in this case is 1/3 (the probability the other player draws a 9). The value of winning in this case would be 0. The probability that the true value is 11 is 1/3. The probability of winning in this case is 0. Thus, the true expected profit from winning the auction with a bid of 10 given $\hat{v} = 10$ is

$$E(\pi) = (-1) \times \frac{1}{3} \times \frac{2}{3} + 0 \times \frac{1}{3} \times \frac{1}{3} + 0 = -\frac{2}{9}. \tag{5.19}$$

Thus, the winner would on average lose money. Hence, a rational bidder would never choose to follow this strategy.

More generally, Eyster and Rabin show that in Vickrey auctions with large numbers of bidders, the true expected payout of bidders will be negative, whereas with smaller numbers this might not be the case. They show evidence of such behavior in several experiments involving a wide variety of games with uncertainty. The cursed equilibrium is closely related to the previously mentioned literature on the level of rationality, or degree to which people anticipate the actions of others. In the cursed equilibrium, the player does not believe the others are reacting to his or her private information rather, the player just takes their actions as given.

EXAMPLE 5.7   Experimental Evidence

John Kagel and Dan Levin (and others at the University of Houston) have run several sets of economics experiments to test for the winner's curse in a well-controlled setting. Subjects were placed in a series of common-value sealed-bid first-price auctions. In each auction, the true value, v, of the item was drawn at random from a uniform distribution on a known interval, $[\underline{v}, \bar{v}]$, that was unknown to the bidders. Each bidder was given a private estimate of the value, $\hat{v}$, drawn from a uniform distribution on an interval of known width $[v - \varepsilon, v + \varepsilon]$. The support of the true value ranged from as low as \$12 in some auctions to as high as \$500 in others. Additionally, they varied the number of bidders in the auctions from as low as three to as many as seven. In all auctions with more than five bidders, the average realized profits were negative, providing substantial evidence of the winner's curse. In nearly all treatments the winner took away strictly less than the amount implied by Nash-equilibrium bidding. Perhaps more puzzling, the winner was often not the participant given the highest estimate of value. In fact, this phenomenon was more prevalent when there were more bidders. This might suggest that some people respond to the competitiveness of the situation with larger bids in excess of their estimated valuation. Over the course of many rounds of auctions, bidders who had won previous auctions eventually showed some learning and convergence toward the Nash equilibrium behavior.

William Samuelson and Max Bazerman used M.B.A. students to conduct a hypothetical choice experiment describing a mergers and acquisitions problem. With some regularity, it has been shown that when one company decides to purchase another, the purchasing company pays more than the acquired company is worth and receives a negative return on the investment. Many have linked this to the winner's curse, where the private company might be using their private information and ignoring the publicly available information regarding the company's value embodied in publicly traded stock prices. For example:

> Place yourself in the position of a CEO of a major pharmaceuticals firm who is considering the purchase of a smaller firm in the same field. Should you decide to acquire the smaller firm, your firm will pay cash and purchase all of the firms outstanding stock. The smaller firm is heavily invested in a project that could produce a cure for common form of cancer. In the best case

scenario, if the project pays off, the company will be worth $100/share. If the project does not yield such a cure, the company could be worth as little as $0/share. You consider all share values between $0 and $100 to be equally likely to occur. Because the companies perform similar tasks, there are some potential cost savings should you decide to acquire the smaller firm. Thus, the smaller firm is worth approximately 1.5 times as much to your firm as it would be worth on the market generally. The smaller firm already knows whether their project will pay off or not, and will only accept an offer that exceeds the anticipated fair price per share of their firm. What would you bid?

The correct answer to this question would consider the amount of value obtained if the bid is accepted. Samuelson and Bazerman conducted an experiment asking participants to make a similar decision. If any bid of x per share is accepted, then the fair value can be at most x per share, otherwise this bid would be rejected. With a uniform distribution of possible values between $0 and x per share, the expected value per share given the bid is accepted is $E(x) = \$x/2$. In this case, the expected value of purchasing the smaller firm per share is $\$1.5E(x) - \$x = \$3x/4 - \$x = -\$x/4$. Thus, if the firm is willing to accept your bid, you do not want the company. The optimal bid is zero. However, if, as in the cursed equilibrium, the bidder does not consider the strategic action of the firm but only the expected gain, then the bidder will use the expected value of the smaller firm, not conditioned on whether the bid is accepted, to calculate the potential gain. This expected value is $50 per share. The expected benefit of acquiring the smaller firm would be 1.5 times this expected value, $75, and thus the bidder would choose some value between $50 and $75.

Samuelson and Bazerman's experiment provided monetary incentives to some participants by paying them a fraction of the value of the acquisition. In fact, bidders who were given monetary incentives, as well as those who were not, all bid positive amounts for the firm, contrary to the optimal strategy. In both cases, more than half of the bids fell between $50 and $75, demonstrating something that closely resembles cursed equilibrium behavior.

EXAMPLE 5.8   **Building Contractors**

Construction firms are often required to bid on larger projects that could be worth substantial amounts in terms of revenue and profits. However, in this case, the firm bids their payment for construction, and then they must construct the building project for some unknown cost. The uncertainties involved in construction projects lead costs to be substantially volatile. Given this need to participate in regular auctions, one might expect construction firms to face the winner's curse, leading to eroding profits and potential failure. In laboratory experiments, building contractors, in fact, fall prey to the winner's curse. But there is much less evidence of the winner's curse in real-life construction bidding. Douglas Dyer and John Kagel used interviews with building contractors as well as some publicly available bidding data to learn why there might be a difference between the laboratory outcomes and the real-world outcomes. In essence, they found three real reasons why the winner's curse is rare in construction bidding.

First, contractors monitor the difference between their bid and the bids of others on any particular project. They monitor closely enough that they have a good feel for the average difference between the top and second bid for various types of jobs. When the differences between the lowest (winning) and the next lowest bid were greater than about 7 percent, they often inquired of other bidders to determine the reason for the difference, a clear sign that they were aware of and worried about the winner's curse. Contractors also clearly understand the need to mark up bids in anticipation of random costs that might occur unforeseen in the construction process.

The second mechanism that allows a contractor to avoid the winner's curse is the ability to withdraw an apparent winning bid once all bids have been announced if there has been any arithmetic error in calculating the bid. In this case, winning the bid with a significant distance between the top and second bid might lead a contractor to reevaluate the bid and search for reasons for the difference. If the difference is due to an error, he may withdraw the bid.

Finally, the contractor has the ability to adjust costs. For example, in the course of construction some of the plans might change, allowing the bidder to renegotiate for higher pay in midstream. The lesson from this study appears to be that the winner's curse is a real threat, but industries with experience in bidding might find heuristics and other mechanisms to reduce or eliminate the threat.

History and Notes

The term *winner's curse* was first coined by Capen, Clapp, and Campbell in their description of the oil lease contracts of the 1950s and 1960s. The early study of the winner's curse was driven first by field data from various industries. The notion has become quite popular in describing many different phenomena where parallels can be drawn. The winner's curse has inspired research-based books by Richard Thaler and by John Kagel and Dan Levin and a score of popular books by various authors. For participants in bidding, the implication is clear. One must scrutinize one's bid with the goal that the bid should likely be below the lowest possible value one would consider for the good. This is especially important when there are large numbers of bidders or when the person formulating the bid is inexperienced. Although this might result in losing the auction even when it might have been profitable, this is a much better outcome than winning the auction when it is unprofitable. From the point of view of sellers, it may be better to employ auctions with large numbers of inexperienced bidders, because this is the most likely way to generate bids well in excess of the true value of the object being auctioned.

Rational Explanations for the Winner's Curse

Most of the rational explanations for the winner's curse deal with identifying imperfections in the field data used to demonstrate the effect. Unfortunately, it is not generally possible to observe individual information about the value of an object in a field setting. As well, it is impossible to determine the expected profit for an object or endeavor with any degree of accuracy.

For example, in studying the oil lease contracts, it is necessary to assume specific discount factors for future consumption in order to determine if the net present value of returns is negative or positive. Assuming less discounting for the future provides a larger return. Further, there were tremendous increases in the price of oil over the period generally studied that are unlikely to have been anticipated. Similarly, estimating the overpayment of baseball players relies heavily on the underlying assumptions of that player's value. Certainly there may be factors other than slugging, strikeouts, and walks. Finally, risk aversion alters the optimal bid and generally leads to higher bids. Thus, if winning bidders are risk averse, we would expect them to display profits that are below the expected payout-maximizing amount on average, though these profits should not be negative on average.

All of these factors make it difficult to say with certainty that the winner's curse has been observed in the wild. Thus, many have suggested that the winner's curse is simply an illusion. However, this phenomenon appears to have had tremendous impacts on the way several industries respond to unknown values. The simple presence of mechanisms such as those found in the construction industry is tangible evidence that people develop heuristics to deal with the problem of the winner's curse, while not fully understanding the mathematics behind the problem itself. These heuristics develop out of systematic experience, providing a key point of evidence that the curse exists in some contexts and is strong enough to lead to long-term changes in institutions.

Biographical Note

© KENDRA LUCK/San Francisco Chronicle/Corbis

Matthew Rabin (1963–)

B.A., University of Wisconsin at Madison, 1984; Ph.D., Massachusetts Institute of Technology, 1989; held faculty positions at the University of California at Berkeley

Matthew Rabin conducted his undergraduate study in economics and mathematics. His training has led to an approach that is behavioral, yet based on rigorous mathematical modeling of the underlying phenomena. Much of this work employs behavioral concepts in a game-theory setting. His earliest work posits that people consider the motivations of others when deciding how to behave. For example, one might wish to help someone who has been nice to one in the past and might wish to harm those who have harmed one in the past. His works have contributed to behavioral theory of auctions, risk and uncertainty, the impacts of cheap talk (nonbinding talks) in games, the discounting and anticipation of future events, probability judgment bias, and welfare analysis. His colleagues describe him as a voracious reader, approaching new research by first pulling all related literature from any discipline that may be connected to it. In 2001, he won the John Bates Clark Medal, which is generally awarded to the economist younger than 40 years who has contributed the most to the field. He has won the MacArthur fellowship (often called the "Genius" fellowship). Personally, Matthew Rabin is known as an engaging teacher and presenter, endowed with more than his fair share of humor. As an example of the humor inherent in his personality, his personal résumé lists his first professional honor as being voted "Most Likely to Express His Opinion," by the Springbrook High School class of 1981.

THOUGHT QUESTIONS

1. Consider that you are preparing to sell some antique items at auction. How might you design the auction so as to receive the highest possible sale price? What sorts of behavioral anomalies will be important to consider? What role will the number and experience of the bidders play in the auction?

2. Consider now that you are preparing to purchase an item at auction for your personal use. What factors should you consider in forming your bid? What behavioral tendencies should you try to avoid? What if you were purchasing the item for resale at a later date instead?

3. Building contractors bidding on a building project often calculate their anticipated costs, add some percentage for profit, and then double this number and submit it as a bid. Similar rules of thumb have been reported in other auction arenas. Why do you think such rules of thumb developed? What purpose do they serve? In what ways might the contractors be worse off for using this rule of thumb?

4. Suppose that two people are engaged in a Vickrey auction for a good with two possible values: $10 or $20. Further, suppose each bidder receives a signal of the value, x_n, where x_n is equal to the true value with probability 0.8, and equal to the other possible value with probability 0.2. No information other than this signal is available. Each player must select a bid based on his own signal. What bidding strategy would be suggested by the fully cursed equilibrium (e.g., what should you bid if you receive a signal of $10 and what should you bid if you receive a signal of $20)? Suppose that players can only bid integer amounts, and follow the example given in the text. Thus, if player 1 draws $x_1 = 10$, the mean value of winning the auction is $\mu = 0.8 \times 10 + 0.2 \times 20 = 12$, the probability of signals that player 2 might receive is (similar to equation 5.14)

$$p(\hat{x}_2) = \begin{cases} 0.8 \times 0.8 + 0.2 \times 0.2 = 0.68 & \text{if} \quad \hat{x}_2 = 10 \\ 0.8 \times 0.2 + 0.2 \times 0.8 = 0.32 & \text{if} \quad \hat{x}_2 = 20. \end{cases}$$

If player 1 draws $x_1 = 20$, the expected value of winning the auction is $\mu = 0.8 \times 20 + 0.2 \times 10 = 18$, and the probability distribution of signals that player 2 might receive is

$$p(\hat{x}_2) = \begin{cases} 0.8 \times 0.8 + 0.2 \times 0.2 = 0.68 & \text{if} \quad \hat{x}_2 = 20 \\ 0.8 \times 0.2 + 0.2 \times 0.8 = 0.32 & \text{if} \quad \hat{x}_2 = 10 \end{cases}$$

Suppose that in the event of a tie, both players receive the value of the object. First try the strategy in which each player bids the expected value of the gamble given the signal each has received. Show that this constitutes a cursed equilibrium. What is the expected profit in this case (the actual, not perceived)? Do these strategies constitute a Bayesian Nash equilibrium? If not, can you find the Bayesian Nash equilibrium?

REFERENCES

Ariely, D., A. Ockenfels, and A.E. Roth. "An Experimental Analysis of Ending Rules in Internet Auctions." *RAND Journal of Economics* 36(2005): 890–907.

Baraji, P., and A. Hortaçsu. "The Winner's Curse, Reserve Prices and Endogenous Entry: Empirical Insights from eBay Auctions." *RAND Journal of Economics* 34(2003): 329–355.

Capen, E.C., R.V. Clapp, and W.M. Campbell. "Competitive Bidding in High-Risk Situations." *Journal of Petroleum Technology* 23(1971): 641–653.

Cassing, J., and R.W. Douglas. "Implications of the Auction Mechanism in Baseball's Free Agent Draft." *Southern Economic Journal* 47(1980): 110–121.

Cox, J.C., B. Roberson, and V.L. Smith. "Theory and Behavior of Single Object Auctions." *Research in Experimental Economics* 2(1982): 1–43.

Dyer, D., and J.H. Kagel. "Bidding in Common Value Auctions: How the Commercial Construction Industry Corrects for the Winner's Curse." *Management Science* 42(1996): 1437–1475.

Eyster, E., and M. Rabin. "Cursed Equilibrium." *Econometrica* 73(2005): 1623–1672.

Kagel, J.H., R.M. Harstad, and D. Levin. "Information Impact and Allocation Rules in Auctions with Affiliated Private Values: A Laboratory Study." *Econometrica* 55(1987): 1275–1304.

Kagel, J.H., and D. Levin. "The Winner's Curse and Public Information in Common Value Auctions." *American Economic Review* 76(1986): 894–920.

Kagel, J.H., and J.-F. Richard. "Super-Experienced Bidders in First-Price Common Value Auctions: Rules of Thumb, Nash Equilibrium Bidding, and the Winner's Curse." *Review of Economics and Statistics* 83(2001): 408–419.

Lucking-Reiley, D. "Using Field Experiments to Test Equivalence between Auction Formats: Magic on the Internet." *American Economic Review* 89(1999): 1063–1080.

Mead, W.J., A. Moseidjord, and P.E. Sorensen. "The Rate of Return Earned by Lessees under Cash Bonus Bidding of OCS Oil and Gas Leases." *Energy Journal* 4(1983): 37–52.

Roth, A.E., and A. Ockenfels. "Last-Minute Bidding and the Rules for Ending Second Price Auctions: Evidence from eBay and Amazon Auctions on the Internet." *American Economic Review* 92(2002): 1093–1103.

Samuelson, W.F., and M.H. Bazerman. "The Winner's Curse in Bilateral Negotiations." *Research in Experimental Economics* 3(1985): 105–137.

Stahl, D.O., and P.W. Wilson. "On Players' Models of Other Players: Theory and Experimental Evidence." *Games and Economic Behavior* 10(1995): 218–254.

Wilson, R. "A Bidding Model of Perfect Competition." *Review of Economic Studies* 44(1977): 511–518.

Advanced Concept

Bayesian Nash Equilibrium and Bidding under Uncertainty

When dealing with a continuum of possible valuations, we use a **probability density function** to represent the likelihood of any particular draw falling in any particular range of values. Let z be a random variable with support given by $[\underline{z}, \overline{z}]$. Then, the probability density function is a function $f(z)$ such that the probability of z falling in any interval (z_1, z_2) is given by $\int_{z_1}^{z_2} f(z)dz$. Thus, $\int_{\underline{z}}^{\overline{z}} f(z)dz = 1$, and if the probability density is continuous, the probability of any single outcome is given by $\int_{z_1}^{z_1} f(z)dz = 0$. We now define the expectation function as $E(z) = \int_{\underline{z}}^{\overline{z}} zf(z)dz$. Let $F(z) = \int_{\underline{z}}^{z} f(z)dz$. Thus, $F(z)$ is the probability of any particular draw from the distribution falling below z. In this context, given a probability density $g(v)$ of valuations, if the bidder believes others will bid according to the bid function $x_j = b(v_j)$, his expected payoff for bidding x is given by $E(\pi_i) = (v_i - x)[G(b^{-1}(x))]^{n-1}$. Here, $b^{-1}(x)$ is the valuation that will result in a bid of x. Hence, $G(b^{-1}(x))$ is the probability of a single draw from the distribution of valuations falling below the valuation that would bid x. To find the probability that all other players bid less than x, we need only multiply this probability together $n - 1$, times, or $[G(b^{-1}(x))]^{n-1}$. This is thus the probability of wining the auction given a bid of x. If we differentiate the expected payout with respect to v_i, we obtain

$$\frac{d}{dv_i} E(\pi_i) = [G(b^{-1}(x))]^{n-1} - (v_i - x)(n-1)[G(b^{-1}(x))]^{n-2}$$

$$\times \frac{d}{dv} G(b^{-1}(x)) \frac{d}{dx} b^{-1}(x) \frac{dx}{dv}(v_i) \qquad (5.A)$$

$$= [G(b^{-1}(x))]^{n-1} + \frac{d}{dx} E(\pi_i) \frac{d}{dv_i} b(x).$$

When evaluated at the optimal bid, $dE(\pi_i)/dx = 0$ so that the second term of equation 5.A is zero. Thus,

$$\frac{dE(\pi_i)}{dv_i} = [G(b^{-1}(x))]^{n-1}, \qquad (5.B)$$

in Nash equilibrium. Further, note that no bidder should ever bid lower than the lowest possible valuation. Each bidder knows that all other bidders have a minimum valuation of $\underline{v}$, and that bidding below this value will ensure losing the auction. Further, no one will ever bid above their valuation. Thus, we know that whatever the optimal rule, the bidder who has drawn the lowest possible valuation must bid his own valuation, $b(\underline{v}) = \underline{v}$. We can then solve for the optimal bidding strategy by solving the differential equation given by equation 5.B and the condition that $b(\underline{v}) = \underline{v}$. Solving equation 5.B obtains

$$E(\pi_i) = k + \int_{\underline{v}}^{v_i} [G(b^{-1}(x(v)))]^{n-1} dv = k + \int_{\underline{v}}^{v_i} [G(v)]^{n-1} dv, \qquad (5.C)$$

where k is an arbitrary constant and the second equality holds by assuming that $x(v) = b(v)$; in other words, all bidders with the same value make the same bid. The definition of the expected payout function (assuming again that all bidders with the same valuation submit the same bid) is given by

$$E(\pi_i) = (v_i - x)[G(v_i)]^{n-1}, \qquad (5.D)$$

or substituting equation 5.C we find

$$k + \int_{\underline{v}}^{v_i} [G(v)]^{n-1} dv = (v_i - x^*)[G(v_i)]^{n-1}. \qquad (5.E)$$

Solving equation 5.E for the optimal bid yields

$$x^* = v_i - \frac{k + \int_{\underline{v}}^{v_i} [G(v)]^{n-1} dv}{[G(v_i)]^{n-1}}. \tag{5.F}$$

The condition requiring the lowest valuation to result in $b(\underline{v}) = \underline{v}$ allows us to solve for the constant, $k = 0$. Hence, the optimal bid is given by

$$x^* = v_i - \frac{\int_{\underline{v}}^{v_i} [G(v)]^{n-1} dv}{[G(v_i)]^{n-1}}. \tag{5.G}$$

In the special case when the distribution of v is uniformly distributed on support $[0, \bar{v}]$, the probability density is given by $g(v) = 1/\bar{v}$ over the support and zero elsewhere. Thus, $G(v) = \int_0^v 1/\bar{v} dv = v/\bar{v}$. Also, $\int_0^{v_i} [G(v)]^{n-1} dv = \int_0^{v_i} [v/\bar{v}]^{n-1} dv = v_i{}^n / (\bar{v}^{n-1} n)$. Thus,

$$x^* = v_i - \frac{\bar{v}^{n-1} v_i^n}{n \bar{v}^{n-1} v_i^{n-1}} = v_i - \frac{v_i}{n} = v_i \frac{(n-1)}{n}, \tag{5.H}$$

which is the result reported in equation 5.9. When we employ a Nash equilibrium in a game of uncertainty such as this we refer to it as a **Bayesian Nash equilibrium**. This is in reference to the requirement that each player must have beliefs regarding the strategies and payoffs of all other players that is consistent with their strategies in the equilibrium. Thus, in this game we require that each player has the same prior beliefs regarding the distribution of valuations and that each anticipates the correct strategy of others given their valuation.

INFORMATION AND UNCERTAINTY

Many decisions involve outcomes that are unknown at the time of making a decision. For example, homebuyers may opt to purchase flood or earthquake insurance but must decide to do so before it becomes obvious whether or not a flood or earthquake will inflict damage on their home. Investment, education, family planning, production, and other decisions all require decision makers to leap before they can look. Economics has proposed a well-developed and intuitively satisfying theory for how people make decisions when facing uncertainty; this theory is built on the work of John von Neumann and Oscar Morgenstern in proposing a rational decision framework.

However, there has been evidence from early on of behavioral anomalies in decision under risk. Such decisions are particularly prone to behavioral anomalies because of the random nature of the outcomes. For example, consider the case where a homebuyer insures her house against flooding when it would be in her best interest not to. Perhaps she overestimated the relative frequency of floods. In other words, given her tolerance for risk, she would be better off not purchasing insurance and facing the risk of catastrophic loss from a flood given the relative rarity of flooding near her home. Given that flooding is relatively rare, she might not particularly notice or revise her beliefs regarding the frequency of floods over the course of many years without an observed flood.

With any event that happens with relative rarity, people can have a very hard time distinguishing between events with vastly different relative frequency. Behavioral economists have noted several behavioral anomalies that are relatively predictable, and they have proposed alternative theories as to why these anomalies occur. This section of the book presents many of these theories, which can be divided into three general categories: theories of learning, theories of decision under uncertainty, and choice bracketing. I begin with choice bracketing because it makes a relatively easy transition from consumer theories to the theory of decision under risk.

Bracketing Decisions

6

Consider your friend who has a final paper due in a relatively important class. The paper will be worth about half of his grade in the class. It is Friday at 7:00 P.M., and he must complete the paper by Monday morning at 9:00 A.M. He believes that the paper will take about six hours of hard work to complete. However, he is in the middle of a role-playing video game and is really itching to play the game for at least another 20 minutes before diving into his paper. Upon considering his options, he believes the 20 minutes will not set him back too far because it is such a small amount of time. Further, the 20 minutes would not allow him to make very much progress at all on his paper relative to the amount of progress he might be able to make on the game. Thus, he decides to play. About 20 minutes later, he faces the same decision. But 20 minutes still seems like such a short period compared to the amount of time he has left to finish the paper. So, he continues to play. At about 3:00 A.M., after playing for eight hours, he decides to go to bed and work on the paper the next day. He regrets the amount of time he spent playing video games, and realizes that he could have made significant progress on the paper and could perhaps have completed it by then. He laments, "How could I have played video games for eight hours instead of working on my paper?"

Consider, alternatively, a company headed by two people: a CEO and a president of operations. The CEO has ultimate responsibility for the company, and the president directly oversees the eight team leaders who make up the senior management. Each of the team leaders has some autonomy and can decide on the particular projects that they will undertake. The CEO is worried that although the company is profitable, profits are smaller than she would like. Wondering the root cause of the problem, she calls on the president to consider the problem. The president meets one by one with each team leader, asking for detailed accounts of their decision-making process. He finds that each has engaged in relatively safe projects. As well, each has turned down some risky projects. For example, a typical risky project would return $20 million with about 50 percent probability and lose $10 million with 50 percent probability. Considering the overall budget of this individual team is only around $20 million, the president considers the decision to scuttle such risky projects sound. He compiles his report detailing the similar decision processes and abandoned opportunities from each of the eight teams to the CEO. The CEO, upon reading about the potential for eight projects, each returning about $20 million with 50 percent probability, and losing $10 million with 50 percent probability, calculates the expected value to be $40 million, with less than a 15 percent chance of losing *any* money. She immediately fires the president of the company.

Much like the framing effects discussed in previous chapters, how decisions are grouped together can have a tremendous impact on which outcomes look most attractive. Although few in the position of needing to work on a substantial class project in the next 48 hours would choose to play video games for several hours straight before beginning the project, many might make several individual decisions to play for 20 minutes at a time. Further, whereas a single investment choice might sound prohibitively risky, a group of many choices each bearing the same risk might sound very attractive. **Bracketing** or *choice bracketing* refers to how choices are grouped together. Often choices are grouped naturally by their placement in time. For example, one generally decides on what to have for breakfast before deciding on what to have for lunch or dinner. Nonetheless, decisions regarding the size and content of breakfast can severely affect what may practically be eaten for lunch. Once you have had an especially large lunch, you might feel uncomfortable having a particularly heavy dinner in addition.

Decision bracketing is closely related to hedonic editing or framing. However, hedonic editing and framing deal only with how people evaluate events (valuing them more or less), whereas choice bracketing deals directly with how the decisions themselves are made (which tradeoffs or variables are considered when making the choice). Choice bracketing has implications both for risky and riskless choice. However, discussing risky choice requires some review of rational choice under uncertainty, hence the placement of this chapter in the Information and Uncertainty section of the book. We review rational models of multiple decisions as well as the most widely accepted rational model of decision under risk: expected utility theory. This model is covered in greater detail in Chapter 9, including its axiomatic foundation (i.e., why we consider it rational).

Multiple Rational Choice with Certainty and Uncertainty

Rational choice theory generally supposes that a person makes a single decision to purchase a consumption bundle rather than making a series of individual purchase decisions for each item in the bundle. This abstraction is considered necessary in order to allow the theory to address the wide variety of purchasing decisions that people make. Truly, very few purchasing decisions are made simultaneously. Consider, for example, that we wish to model food consumption for lunch and dinner of a particular day. For simplicity, suppose that there are only two items that can be purchased for lunch: either one peanut butter sandwich, x_1, or one ham sandwich, x_2. Also, suppose there are only two items that can be purchased for dinner, either one steak, y_1, or one plate of pasta, y_2. Further, assume that the person must eat both lunch and dinner (so not consuming is not an option) and that both lunch options and both dinner options cost exactly the same amount. If the person were to make a single decision at lunchtime regarding consumption of both lunch and dinner, we may model the individual problem as

$$\max_{x \in \{x_1, x_2\},\, y \in \{y_1, y_2\}} U(x, y). \tag{6.1}$$

In this case there are four possible consumption bundles of lunch and dinner. Suppose that the diner's preferences could be represented as $U(x_1, y_1) > U(x_2, y_2) > U(x_2, y_1) > U(x_1, y_2)$, so that the diner most enjoys eating a peanut butter sandwich for lunch and a steak for dinner and least enjoys eating a peanut butter sandwich for lunch with a plate of pasta for dinner. If taken all together, this diner will always choose the most-preferred bundle.

Suppose instead the diner made the choices sequentially, so that lunch is determined around noon and dinner is determined in the evening. If the diner is certain of the options that will be available at the time of the dinner decision when making the lunch decision, then iterating these decisions should have no impact on the chosen consumption bundle. At lunchtime, the diner would still consider which lunch would give her the greatest utility in combination with the two possible dinners and would decide on the peanut butter sandwich, intending on having the steak. When dinnertime arrives, given the previous consumption of the peanut butter sandwich, the steak will seem more attractive and thus the diner will fulfill her plan. We can write this iterated decision as

$$\max_{x \in \{x_1, x_2\}} \left\{ \max_{y \in \{y_1, y_2\}} U(x, y) \right\}, \tag{6.2}$$

which will always yield mathematical results that are identical to equation 6.1. To see this, consider solving equation 6.2 sequentially beginning with the expression in the braces (like backward induction from game theory). In this case, one will choose y to maximize utility given x and thus will choose y_1 if $x = x_1$ and y_2 if $x = x_2$. After solving for y as a function of x, we must evaluate the maximization over x. In this case, the diner is choosing between (x_1, y_1) and (x_2, y_2), which results in a choice of (x_1, y_1). Thus, in the rational model, if the diner knows all the choices she will face in the future at each point, segmenting or sequencing decisions should not have any impact on the final decision. This result is called **segmentation independence**. Under all rational models, the division or segmenting of decisions should not affect the final decision so long as the availability of decisions is known and certain beforehand.

A version of segmentation independence holds if the outcomes from choices are unknown when employing a rational model of choice under risk. The commonly accepted rational model of decision under risk is the **expected utility model**. For now we introduce the expected utility model briefly. In later chapters, we describe the foundation for expected utility and why it is considered a rational model.

The expected utility model supposes that a person maximizes the expectation (or mean) of utility. For example, consider a gamble that yields $100 with probability 1/2 and $-$100 with probability 1/2. Probability gives us the percentage of times an event will happen if we could repeat the experiment an infinite number of times. In this case, the expected value of the gamble is found by summing each outcome multiplied by the percentage of times that outcome would occur if we repeat the experiment a large number of times, $E(\pi) = 0.5 \cdot 100 - 0.5 \cdot 100 = 0$. This is essentially the average value we would expect given a large sample of observed outcomes from this gamble. Thus on average, one gains and loses nothing by taking this gamble. Alternatively, suppose that the person has a utility of money function $u(\pi)$, with $u(100) = 1$, $u(-100) = -2$, and that $u(0) = 0$. Then the expectation of the utility function is found by multiplying the probability of each outcome by the utility of that outcome, $E(u(\pi)) = 0.5 \cdot u(100) + 0.5 \cdot u(-100) = 0.5 \cdot 1 - 0.5 \cdot 2 = -0.5$. The expected utility of the gamble is below zero in this case (because the loss of utility from losing \$100 is greater than the gain in utility from gaining \$100), and thus the person would prefer to refuse the gamble and obtain the utility of no change in wealth, $u(0) = 0$. If instead each dollar yielded a constant rate of utility, say $u(1) = 1$, then $u(-100) = -100$, $u(100) = 100$, $u(0) = 0$. In this case, the expected utility is given by $E(u(\pi)) = 0.5 \cdot 100 - 0.5 \cdot 100 = 0$. Thus, the person would be indifferent between taking the gamble or not.

Consider Figure 6.1, which depicts a person's evaluation of a gamble with probability of 0.5 that the person obtains x_1 and probability 0.5 that the person obtains x_2, where x_1 and x_2 are amounts of money. The expected payoff from this gamble, $E(x) = 0.5x_1 + 0.5x_2$, is represented by the location on the x axis that is exactly equidistant from x_1 and x_2. If the person could obtain the expected value of the gamble with certainty, she would obtain $u(E(x))$, as depicted on the y axis. Instead, she values the gamble according to its expected utility, given by $E(u(x)) = 0.5u(x_1) + 0.5u(x_2)$, which is the location on the y axis that is exactly equidistant from $u(x_1)$ and $u(x_2)$. Note the shape of the utility function in Figure 6.1 is concave, displaying diminishing marginal utility of wealth. This means that the slope of the utility function between $E(x)$ and x_2 is smaller than between x_1 and $E(x)$, leading the midway point between $u(x_1)$ and $u(x_2)$ to fall below $u(E(x))$. Thus, the gambler would prefer to have the expected value of the gamble with certainty than to take the gamble and obtain the resulting expected utility.

Further, we can define the **certainty equivalent** as the amount of money with certainty that yields the same level of utility as the expected utility of the gamble, or $u(x_{CE}) = 0.5u(x_1) + 0.5u(x_2)$, where x_{CE} is the certainty equivalent. In Figure 6.1, the certainty equivalent falls below the expected value of the gamble, reflecting that the person is willing to give up some amount of money on average in return for certainty. In general, if a person is willing to take a reduced expected value to obtain certainty, we call the person **risk averse**.

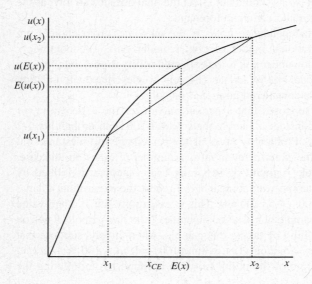

FIGURE 6.1
Risk Aversion under
Expected Utility
Theory

Under the expected utility model, diminishing marginal utility of wealth, as displayed by a concave utility function, implies risk aversion. Diminishing marginal utility of wealth simply requires that the next dollar provides less utility to a wealthy person than to a poor one. Consider a more general gamble with α probability of obtaining x_1 and $(1 - \alpha)$ probability of obtaining x_2. The person displays risk aversion if for any two amounts of money x_1 and x_2, the utility function is such that

$$u(\alpha x_1 + (1 - \alpha)x_2) > \alpha u(x_1) + (1 - \alpha)u(x_2), \tag{6.3}$$

or if the expected utility from the gamble is lower than the utility of the expected value. This necessarily implies that the certainty equivalent is less than the expected value of the gamble (because it yields lower utility). Because $0 < \alpha < 1$,

$$u(\alpha x_1 + (1 - \alpha)x_2) = \alpha u(\alpha x_1 + (1 - \alpha)x_2) + (1 - \alpha)u(\alpha x_1 + (1 - \alpha)x_2). \tag{6.4}$$

Substituting equation 6.4 into equation 6.3 yields

$$\alpha[u(\alpha x_1 + (1 - \alpha)x_2) - u(x_1)] > (1 - \alpha)[u(x_2) - u(\alpha x_1 + (1 - \alpha)x_2)]. \tag{6.5}$$

If we suppose that $x_2 > x_1$, then dividing both sides of (6.4) by $\alpha(1 - \alpha)(x_2 - x_1)$, obtains

$$\frac{u(\alpha x_1 + (1 - \alpha)x_2) - u(x_1)}{(1 - \alpha)(x_2 - x_1)} > \frac{u(x_2) - u(\alpha x_1 + (1 - \alpha)x_2)}{\alpha(x_2 - x_1)} \tag{6.6}$$

or adding and subtracting x_2 from the denominator of the right side and rearranging the denominator of both sides yields

$$\frac{u(\alpha x_1 + (1 - \alpha)x_2) - u(x_1)}{(\alpha x_1 + (1 - \alpha)x_2) - x_1} > \frac{u(x_2) - u(\alpha x_1 + (1 - \alpha)x_2)}{x_2 - (\alpha x_1 + (1 - \alpha)x_2)}. \tag{6.7}$$

Note that the terms on both sides of the equation are analogues of the slope or derivative of the utility function, having the familiar form of rise over run. The left side term is the slope of the utility function between x_1 and $\alpha x_1 + (1 - \alpha)x_2$, and the slope of the right side term is the slope of the utility function between x_2 and $\alpha x_1 + (1 - \alpha)x_2$. Thus, equation 6.7 simply says that the slope over the upper portion of the curve is smaller than the one over the lower portion of the curve. Reflecting on equation 6.3, the condition in this equation is the general condition for concavity of a function or diminishing marginal utility of payouts. Thus in general, a concave utility function implies risk aversion under expected utility theory.

If instead the utility function is linear, $u(x) = \phi x$, where ϕ is a scalar constant, the utility function implies that risk itself does not matter. This case is depicted in Figure 6.2. In this case, the slope of the utility function is constant everywhere. Thus, a dollar means as much to the person no matter what her starting wealth. In this case, the analogue to equation 6.7 requires that

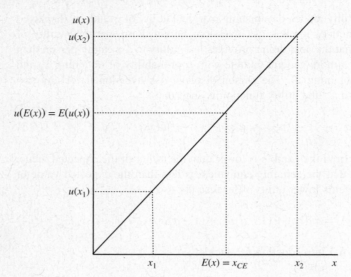

FIGURE 6.2
Risk Neutrality under
Expected Utility
Theory

$$\frac{u(\alpha x_1 + (1-\alpha)x_2) - u(x_1)}{(\alpha x_1 + (1-\alpha)x_2) - x_1} = \frac{u(x_2) - u(\alpha x_1 + (1-\alpha)x_2)}{x_2 - (\alpha x_1 + (1-\alpha)x_2)} = \phi. \tag{6.8}$$

Also, the expected utility can be calculated as

$$E(u(x)) = \alpha\phi x_1 + (1-\alpha)\phi x_2 = \phi[\alpha x_1 + (1-\alpha)x_2] = u(E(x)). \tag{6.9}$$

Thus, no matter how much risk is involved, the expected utility of the gamble equals the utility of the expected value of the gamble if the utility function is linear. If the person is **risk neutral**, the expected value of the gamble always equals the certainty equivalent. In the expected utility model, a risk-neutral decision maker is always represented by a linear utility function.

Finally, consider the case of a convex utility function. In this case, the person is **risk loving**, meaning she prefers a gamble to its expected value. Thus, in this case we reverse the relationship in equation 6.3,

$$u(\alpha x_1 + (1-\alpha)x_2) < \alpha u(x_1) + (1-\alpha)u(x_2), \tag{6.10}$$

which, after following the same steps as before, yields

$$\frac{u(\alpha x_1 + (1-\alpha)x_2) - u(x_1)}{(\alpha x_1 + (1-\alpha)x_2) - x_1} < \frac{u(x_2) - u(\alpha x_1 + (1-\alpha)x_2)}{x_2 - (\alpha x_1 + (1-\alpha)x_2)}. \tag{6.11}$$

Thus, the slope above the expected payout from the gamble must be larger than the slope below the expected payout of the gamble. This possibility is displayed in Figure 6.3. Here, the certainty equivalent is above the expected value of the gamble. As well, the

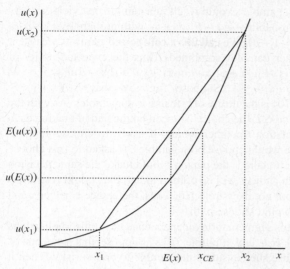

FIGURE 6.3
Risk Loving under Expected Utility Theory

expected utility of the gamble is above the utility of the expected value of the gamble. In general, a convex utility function implies risk-loving behavior.

Part of the long love affair between economists and the expected utility model is due to the model's simplicity. All risk preferences are completely captured in the curvature of the utility function, which represents how money is valued over various levels of wealth. If one has a concave utility function, one is willing to pay less than the expected value of winning the lottery (a truly small number) for a lottery ticket, because the value of the ten millionth dollar (and every dollar above the initial outlay) one could possibly win is much smaller than the value of the dollar one must pay to buy it. Alternatively, if one has a convex utility function, one would be willing to pay more than the expected value of the lottery ticket, because the value of every dollar one could win above the amount one must pay for the ticket is worth more to one than the dollar one would pay to buy it.

Risk aversion is commonly measured using coefficients of absolute or relative risk aversion. The coefficient of absolute risk aversion is given by $R_A = -u''(w)/u'(w)$, where $u'(w)$ is the marginal utility of wealth and $u''(w)$ is the slope of the marginal utility of wealth curve evaluated at w. The coefficient R_A is a simple measure of concavity of the utility function: the more concave, the larger the value R_A. The higher the level of **absolute risk aversion**, the less willing to take any particular gamble the decision maker will be. A closely related measure of risk aversion is **relative risk aversion**, given by $R_R = wR_A$, where w is wealth. The higher the degree of relative risk aversion, the less willing to risk a particular portion of her wealth the decision maker will be. Generally, economists suppose that relative risk aversion falls between 1 and 3.

Now, with the basic tools of expected utility theory, consider the person who must decide whether to take either or both of two gambles. One gamble yields x_1 with probability α and x_2 with probability $(1-\alpha)$. The second gamble yields y_1 with probability β and y_2 with probability $(1-\beta)$. For simplicity, let us suppose that the gambles are independent, so that the outcome of one gamble does not depend upon the outcome of another. In this case, taking both gambles would result in a gamble that yields $x_1 + y_1$ with probability $\alpha\beta$, $x_1 + y_2$ with probability $\alpha(1 - \beta)$, $x_2 + y_1$ with probability $(1 - \alpha)\beta$, and $x_2 + y_2$ with probability $(1 - \alpha)(1 - \beta)$. We call this a **compound gamble** because it is a gamble composed of two other gambles combined. Thus the expected utility of taking both gambles together is $E[u(x + y)] = \alpha\beta u(x_1 + y_1) + \alpha(1 - \beta)u(x_1 + y_2) + (1 - \alpha)\beta u(x_2 + y_1) + (1 - \alpha)(1 - \beta)u(x_2 + y_2)$. Suppose for now that $E(u(x + y)) > u(0) > E(u(y)) > E(u(x))$, where $u(0)$ is the utility of refusing both gambles. As with the choice problems in equations 6.1 and 6.2, the choice between taking and not taking each gamble is independent of segmentation. In other words, if asked to choose simultaneously, the person in this example would choose both gambles. If asked to first choose whether to take x, and then whether to take y, the person should make the same decision so long as she understands that both choices will be offered to her. She would consider y to be beneficial given x is chosen but not if x is rejected. Thus, the choice is either x and y or no gambles. In this case she would choose both.

Paul Samuelson observed that this segmentation independence has some implications for choice between an individual risk and multiple risks. Suppose that someone is unwilling to take a gamble x because she considers the gamble to be too risky. Then it is very unlikely that she would be willing to take two identical gambles x. In particular, suppose that the maximum she could gain or lose by taking gamble x is $\$k$. Because risk preferences are determined by a utility of money function, a person's behavior depends on her level of wealth. Suppose the person has initial wealth w. If her risk preferences are such that she is unwilling to take the bet given any wealth level in the range of wealth $[w - (n - 1)k, \ w + (n - 1)k]$, where n is some positive integer, then she will be unwilling to take a combination of n identical gambles x.[1] The segmenting works just as before. If someone is unwilling to take the gamble x over a range of wealth $[w - k, \ w + k]$, then suppose she somehow was given the one gamble x against her will. She would still be unwilling to take the second bet no matter the outcome of the first gamble because wealth still falls within the relevant range. If the person would reject each individually given sequential decision, then she would reject both jointly by segmentation independence. Thus, if you are unwilling to take a 50 percent chance of winning $200 and a 50 percent chance of losing $100, and this preference would persist if your wealth shifted by $2,000, you should be unwilling to take 10 such chances together.

EXAMPLE 6.1 Paul Samuelson and His Colleague

Out at lunch with his colleagues one day, Paul Samuelson proposed a bet to each person at the table. He would pay them $200 if they could predict the result of a single coin toss, and if not they would pay him $100. One of his colleagues, whom Samuelson describes as a distinguished scholar with no claim to advanced mathematical skills, answered, "I won't bet because I would feel the $100 loss more than the $200 gain. But I will take

---

[1] Actually, the required range of wealth is much smaller and could be rather negligible. However, the intuition is easiest to explain with the given range. In truth, the range need only cover the loss between current wealth and the certainty equivalent of the gamble multiplied by n.

you on if you promise to let me make 100 such bets." The willingness to take on 100 such bets but not one suggests that the colleague's preferences are not independent of segmentation. Rather, he appears willing to take on many undesirable bets in violation of the basic rational choice model.

It is notable that the colleague cites the pain of loss from $100 dollars dominating the gain of $200, suggesting that loss aversion plays some role. Moreover, it is clear that the desirability of each individual gamble depends on whether the decision is made independently or jointly with the decision to take on many other similar gambles. Samuelson saw this as potential evidence that behavior did not conform to expected utility or that people have difficulty in understanding how concepts such as diversifying risk really works. In this case, the probability of loss is much smaller with 100 gambles (less than 1 percent) than with 1 gamble (50 percent), but the potential magnitude of the losses is much larger ($10,000 vs. $100). The increase in potential losses must dominate the reduced probability of losses under the expected utility model.

Thus, diversifying investments can reduce the probability of a loss, but if the investments are not desirable to begin with, diversification cannot magically make a bad gamble good. Consider a group of two of Samuelson's gambles. In this case, the colleague faces a 0.25 probability of losing $200, a 0.50 probability of gaining $100, and a 0.25 probability of gaining $400. I suspect that many readers at this point might consider this gamble much more attractive than the original gamble. Nonetheless, in almost all reasonable cases, turning down the original gamble should lead a rational decision maker to reject this latter gamble under expected utility theory. Why then does grouping the gambles together seem to make them more attractive?

The Portfolio Problem

Often we might want to consider something similar to the stock portfolio problem, where a person might decide how much to invest in several activities at once. For example, suppose that an investor can divide her wealth between two assets. One is a safe asset that returns exactly the amount invested with certainty. Thus, if an investor invests x in the safe asset, she will be able to obtain x at the time she sells this asset. The second is a risky asset, such that every dollar invested in the asset will be worth z at the time of sale, where z is a random variable. Suppose that the expected value of z is $\mu > 1$. Then, the investor with wealth w who wishes to maximize her expected utility of investing in the safe and risky assets will solve

$$\max_{w_z} E[u((w - w_z) + w_z z)] \tag{6.12}$$

where w is wealth to be invested and w_z is the amount of wealth invested in the risky asset. The solution to this problem is approximated by:

$$w_z = \frac{(\mu - 1)}{\sigma^2 R_A}, \tag{6.13}$$

where R_A is the coefficient of absolute risk aversion and the value $\sigma^2 = E[(x - \mu)^2]$ is commonly called the **variance** of z. The variance measures how dispersed the values of z

are—how far away from the mean we believe the value of z may be. The higher the value of σ^2, the riskier the investment. Thus, the higher is the aversion to risk, the lower the investment in the risky asset. Similarly, the riskier the asset (the higher the variance), the lower the investment in the risky asset. As well, increasing the expected payout of the risky asset relative to the safe asset increases investment in the risky asset. (The interested reader can see the derivation in the Advanced Concept box, The Portfolio Problem.)

EXAMPLE 6.2   The Equity Premium Puzzle

The return from investing in stocks has historically been far superior to the return from investing in bonds. For example, from 1871 until 1990 the return on stocks was about 6.5 percent per year, whereas the return on bonds was around 1 percent. Over any long-term investment horizon (more than 30 years), stocks overwhelmingly outperform bonds—often by more than seven times—leading one to wonder why anyone would ever invest in bonds. Bonds are often used as a relatively risk-free investment, though they still contain significant risk. Bonds pay a fixed nominal rate of return so long as the issuing body remains obligated. This issuing body may be a firm or a government. Thus, if the issuing body goes bankrupt it might default. As well, inflation can erode the rate of return over the life of the bond. Nonetheless, if we were to think about this problem in terms of the portfolio problem presented above, the rate of return, μ, would be about 7. Further, the commonly assumed range for the level of relative risk aversion is about 1 to 3. Thus, absolute risk aversion is between 1 and 3 divided by the total amount of wealth, a truly small number. If we assume 3, then we could rewrite the formula (equation 6.13) as

$$w_z = \frac{3w}{\sigma^2}, \tag{6.14}$$

where w_z is the optimal amount of money to invest in stocks, σ^2 is the variance in return of the stock portfolio, and w is the total amount of wealth.

The variance of the stock portfolio depends on the time horizon. If we consider the long horizon on a representative portfolio of stocks, this variance is actually quite low, well below 3. In this case, the optimal investment is greater than the total wealth to be invested, leaving no room for bonds. More generally, economists estimate that the level of relative risk aversion necessary to induce one to purchase *any* bonds must be about 30, ten times the reasonable upper bound used by economists. To put this in perspective, consider a gamble with 0.50 probability of ending with $100,000 of wealth and a 0.50 probability of ending with $50,000 of wealth. The investor must be willing to pay at least $50,000 for this gamble, because this is the lowest possible outcome. An investor with relative risk aversion of 30 would have a certainty equivalent for this gamble of just $51,209 despite the expected value of $75,000. Thus, a 50 percent chance of winning an extra $50,000 is worth only $1,209 to her. This is an astounding and unreasonable level of risk aversion. Thus, one might reasonably conclude that stock prices reflect a violation of the rational model of decision under uncertainty.

Narrow versus Broad Bracketing

One could explain both examples 1 and 2 through a combination of loss aversion and a model of decision bracketing. **Bracketing** refers to the grouping of decisions. If a set of choices are made so as to take account of the impact of each individual choice in the set on all other choices, we say they are bracketed together. As a simple example, if I choose to have a light breakfast, I might prefer to have a larger lunch. If when I decide to have a light breakfast I anticipate the need for a larger lunch, my breakfast and lunch decisions are bracketed together. If I ignore the impact of my breakfast on lunch, these decisions are bracketed separately. A decision is narrowly bracketed if it is bracketed together with only a small set of decisions. A decision is broadly bracketed if it is bracketed with a larger set of decisions. Generally a person brackets decisions based upon how they are framed. Thus, if the diner is presented several decisions at once (e.g., which entrée and side dishes she would like at dinner), they may be bracketed together. Alternatively, if decisions are presented sequentially (e.g., what she will eat for breakfast, lunch, and dinner), they will most likely not be bracketed together.

Shlomo Benartzi and Richard Thaler note that one could easily explain the behavior of Samuelson's colleague through an appeal to loss aversion and bracketing. Suppose for example, that the person has a value of money function that is given by

$$v(x) = \begin{cases} x & \text{if} \quad x \geq 0 \\ 2.5x & \text{if} \quad x < 0. \end{cases} \tag{6.15}$$

Then, replacing the utility of wealth with the value function, the expected utility of the gamble in example 1 is $E(v(x)) = 0.5 \cdot v(200) + 0.5 \cdot v(-100) = 100 - 125 = -25$. Thus, the person would turn down the gamble because it would result in a negative value. Also, if the person were forced to take one gamble and then asked if she would take a second, the calculation would be the same. This is because even if the person had experienced seven gains of $200 in a row, she would evaluate a loss on the eighth gamble as a loss, thus resulting in a much more severe penalty than the reduction of a gain. From whatever the starting point, the potential loss of $100 looms larger than the potential gain of $200, just as Paul Samuelson's colleague speculated, resulting in negative expected utility. Instead, suppose the person were offered to play two of the gambles jointly, thus leading to a more broadly bracketed choice. In this case, the expected value is $E(v(2x)) = 0.25 \cdot v(400) + 0.5 \cdot v(100) + 0.25 v(-200) = 100 + 50 - 125 = 25$. Thus, the person would choose to take two gambles together, although she would not choose to take any single gamble individually. The same would hold true for 100 of these gambles.

Note that one of the reasons the value function can explain this choice is that the value function in equation 6.15 violates the condition required by Samuelson. Because the value function is linear both above and below, the individual gamble would be accepted if the gambler were to interpret all outcomes as gains or all outcomes as losses. For example, if all were interpreted as gains, all values would be treated as if $x > 0$ and $v(x) = x$. The expected value would be $E(v(x)) = 0.5 \cdot 200 + 0.5 \cdot (-100) = 50$. The same thing would be found if all values were considered losses. Thus, the range over which the gamble would be rejected is small, encompassing just the gambles that span the kink in the value function.

Alternatively, consider a commonly used utility function under the rational model, $u(x) = 1 - \exp\{-R_A x\}$. This is commonly referred to as the constant absolute risk aversion utility function because this function displays absolute risk aversion of R_A for all values of x. No matter what parameter of absolute risk aversion we choose, $u(0) = 0$, so the gambler would take the gamble if and only if expected utility is positive. If we choose the parameter $R_A = 0.1$, the expected utility of the single gamble is negative, $E(u(x)) = -11012.23$, as is the expected utility of two of the gambles, $E(u(2x)) = -1.2 \times 10^8$. If we were to arbitrarily add \$200, the maximum change in wealth resulting from one gamble, to the gambler's wealth before taking the gamble, the new utility function would be given by $u(x + 200) = 1 - \exp\{-R_A(x + 200)\}$, with the utility resulting from rejecting any gamble equal to approximately 1. In this case, expected utility of a single gamble is slightly less than 1, so that the gamble would still be rejected. We can infer that the single gamble would be rejected over any starting level of wealth between 0 and 200.

It is possible to find parameters that lead to accepting multiple gambles and rejecting the initial gamble. However, these parameters violate Samuelson's conditions that the single gamble would be rejected in a region of wealth $\lfloor w - 200, w + 200 \rfloor$. If instead, we chose $R_A = 0.00481211825$, the expected utility of the single gamble is $E(u(x)) = -1.1 \times 10^{-10}$, suggesting rejection of the single gamble. The expected utility of two of the gambles is $E(u(2x)) = 2.1 \times 10^{-10}$, suggesting acceptance of the joint gamble. However, the single gamble would be accepted if we were to arbitrarily add \$200 to the initial wealth, $E(u(x + 200)) > u(200)$, and thus Samuelson's condition does not hold.

Benartzi and Thaler propose that the equity premium puzzle might also be due to a combination of loss aversion and narrowly bracketed investment decisions. The length of the planning horizon in investment affects the variance or variation in the return of the portfolio. Although bonds have a slow and stable return with relatively constant variation, stocks have high return but relatively high variation in the near term. Thus, on any given day the return from a diverse bundle of stocks can range from −10 percent to +10 percent, and the variance of returns for the same stocks over a 30-year investment period is quite small. This is somewhat like gambling on one coin flip versus gambling on the average outcome of a series of 100 coin flips. Although the average return is the same, the variance is substantially reduced. Thus, with a long planning horizon, the difference in returns for stocks and bonds should lead one to invest all of one's assets in stocks.

If the planning horizon is short, the variance is much larger relative to the average return, thus the right side of equation 6.14 may be smaller than the total amount of wealth to be invested, leading one to hold bonds as well. Benartzi and Thaler hypothesize that people narrowly bracket their investment decisions relative to their planning horizon. Thus, although an investor may be investing for a 30-year period, she might evaluate her portfolio much more often and invest as if her planning horizon was much shorter. Using simulations based on stock and bond return data, they find that the returns on stocks relative to bonds are consistent with loss-averse investors evaluating (or bracketing) their decisions on an annual basis. Because they behave as if they are maximizing their expected utility of investing over a one-year period, rather than the longer period they may be investing in, they could potentially be made better off by reducing their holding of bonds and increasing their holding of stocks. Nonetheless, each year when they evaluate the return, the variation and losses lead them to purchase bonds and ignore their longer planning horizon.

Richard Thaler, and a group of distinguished colleagues, conducted a series of experiments to test for time bracketing in investments. The theory of bracketing suggests that if people evaluate their investments regularly they will bracket narrowly, and they will tend toward less-risky investments no matter what the planning horizon. Thus, people are willing to take on larger risks over long periods of time if they are not allowed to evaluate the outcomes throughout the duration. When not allowed to evaluate, the investor is essentially facing a compound gamble consisting of n groups of the single-period gamble, where n is the number of periods before they can evaluate. When allowed to evaluate, it is like facing n individual gambles sequentially. Broad bracketing can lead to a more favorable view of the gamble.

A group of 80 participants were asked to allocate 100 units of a portfolio between two investments, fund A and fund B. They were told that the returns per period for a unit of fund A would be drawn from a distribution with a mean of 0.25 percent and a standard deviation (defined as the square root of the variance) of 0.177 percent. Fund B returns per period were drawn from a distribution with a mean return of 1.00 percent and a standard deviation of 3.54 percent. Thus B was much riskier, yet it had a mean return of about four times that of A.

Participants were randomly placed into treatments. Participants in the first treatment were asked to make 200 decisions, with one decision following each period and after being able to observe the returns for that period. The second treatment required participants to make 25 decisions, with each decision binding for eight periods. The third treatment required participants to make five decisions, which would be binding for 40 periods. No matter which treatment was applied, the same set of random draws for A and B were used, so that all subjects in all treatments were viewing the same return history in any decision period. Subjects would only observe returns when they were allowed to make a decision. Those in the condition that required a decision every period placed more than 50 percent of their portfolio in A, the lower-risk option, over the course of the experiment. Those making fewer decisions placed less than 50 percent of their portfolio in the safer option, between 30 percent and 40 percent on average. Thus, by simply manipulating the frequency of evaluation, the researchers found that subjects become more sensitive to risk.

The notion that people would choose long-term investments based on short-term priorities is closely related to the notion of **melioration**. Melioration is a concept from experimental psychology whereby someone chooses the option that yields the highest utility in the current period, ignoring the impacts of their decision on choices and experiences available in future periods. Melioration has been explained using many different behavioral models. Decision bracketing provides one explanation, whereby the person is given a choice framed in such a way that future consequences are altogether ignored. For example, in the case of investment decisions, the investor makes investments that are attractive in the near term, ignoring the properties of the potential investments in the longer term. Alternative models of melioration are presented in Part III of this book examining time discounting.

Thus far we have discussed the possibility that bracketing decisions by time sequence can affect investment decisions. But it is also possible to bracket decisions by individual investments in the portfolio. If an investor uses broad bracketing in this context, she might solve

$$\max_{\{x_1,\ldots,x_n\}} E\left[C + v\left(\sum_{i=1}^{n} x_i z_i\right)\right], \tag{6.16}$$

subject to the constraint

$$C = w - \sum_{i=1}^{n} x_i, \tag{6.17}$$

where x_i represents the investment in asset i, z_i is the random variable that represents the return from asset i, $v(\cdot)$ is a loss-averse value function with a reference point of $\sum_{i=1}^{n} x_i$ (in other words, the reference point is the amount invested), C represents money spent in current consumption (the utility of consuming C is equal to C), and w is the total amount of wealth. Here I have suppressed the intertemporal nature of investment for simplicity.

In this case, the investor will experience an overall loss if the total return is less than $\sum_{i=1}^{n} x_i$. The kinked shape of the value function leads the investor to display risk aversion by choosing an investment portfolio that displays a lower level of risk but also possibly a lower return. Nonetheless, it is possible that several of the stocks in the optimal portfolio will be quite risky because their risk will be averaged with the other n investments. The probability of an overall loss becomes quite small if n is large, the returns are all positive on average, and the investment returns are independent of one another. This result is similar to the reduction in the probability of loss obtained in Samuelson's gamble when n is increased. If the portfolio decisions are narrowly bracketed, however, we may write the problem as

$$\max_{\{x_1,\ldots,x_n\}} E\left[C + \sum_{i=1}^{n} v(x_i z_i)\right] \tag{6.18}$$

with the same budget constraint. The difference is that now each investment is evaluated by itself in the value function with a reference point of x_i. In this case, the investor becomes severely averse to loss in any single investment. Here each investment is evaluated based on gains or losses in the investment. Thus, the investor would feel severe pain for a \$1 loss in investment i even if the overall return of the portfolio is positive. This focus on the individual stock return means the investor cannot fully take advantage of diversification but rather seeks that all investments will have minimal risk of losses.

Nicholas Barberis and Ming Huang find that this alternative form of narrow bracketing is quite consistent with the patterns of investment decisions in the market, leading to the highly inflated returns on stocks that are necessary to justify the purchase of relatively risky investments among the loss averse when relatively safe investments are available. Clearly, one can obtain better returns by broad bracketing than by narrow bracketing. Barberis and Huang suppose that equation 6.18 might prevail because people take a loss on a stock personally. One might feel the individual loss as an indication of one's investing ability and a failure of one's own decision making.

Bracketing the Portfolio Problem

By substituting equation 6.17 into equation 6.16, we can rewrite the broad bracketing optimization problem as

$$\max_{\{x_1, \ldots, x_n\}} E\left[w - \sum_{i=1}^{n} x_i + v\left(\sum_{i=1}^{n} x_i z_i\right)\right],$$ (6.19)

If we ignore the kink in the value function (in other words, use a single smooth function to represent gains and losses), the solution can be written as

$$x_i = \frac{\mu_i}{R_A \sigma_{ii}} + \frac{\frac{1}{v''} - \left(\sum_{j \neq i} x_j \sigma_{ij}\right)}{\sigma_{ii}}.$$ (6.20)

Where v'' is the slope of the marginal utility function (negative over gains, positive over losses). Here, $\sigma_{ij} = E\left[(z_i - \mu_i)(z_j - \mu_j)\right]$ is the variance of investment i when $i = j$ and the covariance of investment i and j when they are unequal. The covariance is a measure of how random variables are related. A positive covariance indicates that the random variables are positively related (when one is higher, the other is likely to be higher, like height and weight), and a negative covariance indicates a negative relationship, like speed and weight. The interested reader can turn to the Advanced Concept box, Bracketing the Portfolio Problem, to read the derivation of this solution.

If instead, we suppose that decisions are narrowly bracketed, then substituting equation 6.17 into equation 6.18 yields

$$\max_{\{x_1, \ldots, x_n\}} E\left[w - \sum_{i=1}^{n} x_i + \sum_{i=1}^{n} v(x_i z_i)\right],$$ (6.21)

which has a solution given by

$$x_i = \frac{\mu_i}{R_A \sigma_{ii}} + \frac{\left(\frac{1}{v''}\right)}{\sigma_{ii}}.$$ (6.22)

Notably, this is very similar to equation 6.20, except that all of the covariance terms are omitted. This means that the investor will fail to recognize when the return of investment options are related, allowing diversification to reduce the risk. In particular, negatively correlated investments allow one to create portfolios that should reduce the variance of the outcome. If risks are negatively correlated, equation 6.20 suggests that a broad-bracket decision maker will increase her level of investment in that given asset. Alternatively, if risks are positively correlated, this too will be ignored, leading the investor to take a much larger risk than she might otherwise by overinvesting in stocks that all move together. Loss aversion can amplify this effect.

More than the Sum of Its Parts

By nature, narrow bracketing leaves the person worse off than broad bracketing if one decision will affect the choices available in other decisions. An example of how this might happen is if there are properties of groups of decisions that are not apparent or present in single decisions. For example, it is not possible to diversify a portfolio of investments with only a single stock. To diversify, one must be able to make assessments about the covariance of returns among stocks, a property that would not be assessed when examining a single stock by itself. Whenever an attractive property is present in groups of choices but not individual choices, narrow bracketing leads the decision maker to make suboptimal choices.

The Utility Function and Risk Aversion

Expected utility theory supposes that all risk behavior is due to changes in the marginal utility of wealth or the concavity or convexity of the utility function. Whenever the function is concave, the decision maker behaves so as to avoid risks. Whenever it is convex, the decision maker seeks risk. Typically, economists assume that people are risk averse, displaying diminishing marginal utility of wealth. Matthew Rabin made an important observation regarding the curvature of utility of wealth functions. One of the basic principles upon which calculus is based is that any continuous and smooth function is approximately a line over very small ranges of the input variable. Thus, even though the sine function, $\sin(x)$, wiggles up and down when plotted over $\lfloor 0, 2\pi \rfloor$, it is closely approximated by a straight line if we plot it over $\lfloor 0, 0.0001 \rfloor$. Thus, a standard concave utility function is also approximated by a straight line over small changes in wealth. Utility functions that are straight lines display risk neutrality, leading to choices that maximize expected payouts without regard for variance of the gamble. Thus, when gambles involve very small amounts of money, people who maximize expected utility should behave approximately as if they are risk neutral.

Matthew Rabin turns this principle on its head. If people are risk averse over small gambles, this tells us something of how concave their utility function must be for somewhat larger gambles. More explicitly, suppose someone was offered a gamble that yielded $x_1 < 0$ with 0.50 probability and $x_2 > 0$ with 0.50 probability. Further, suppose that the gamble had a positive expected value but that we observed the person reject the gamble. This possibility is depicted in Figure 6.4. In this case, we know that $u(0) > E(u(x))$. Then we know that $u(0) > 0.5u(x_1) + 0.5u(x_2)$. This means that the utility function must be at least as concave as the bolded line segments in Figure 6.4. Knowing this, we can use these line segments to find other gambles for larger amounts that must also be turned down.

Therefore, suppose that for all w, $U(w)$ is strictly increasing and weakly concave. Suppose there exists $g > l > 0$, such that for all w, the person would reject a 0.50 probability of receiving g and a 0.50 probability of losing l. Then, the person would also turn down a bet with 0.50 probability of gaining mg and a 0.50 probability of losing $2kl$, where k is any positive integer, and $m < m(k)$, where

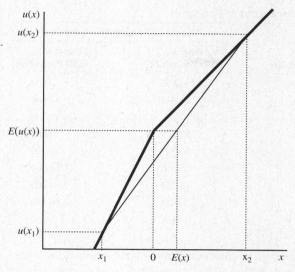

$u(x)$

$u(x_2)$

$E(u(x))$

$u(x_1)$

x_1 0 $E(x)$ x_2 x

FIGURE 6.4
Calibration of a Utility Function

$$
m(k) = \begin{cases} \dfrac{\ln\left(1 - \left(1 - \dfrac{l}{g}\right) 2 \sum_{i=0}^{k-1} \left(\dfrac{g}{l}\right)^i\right)}{\ln(l/g)} & \text{if} \quad 1 - \left(1 - \dfrac{l}{g}\right) 2 \sum_{i=0}^{k-1} \left(\dfrac{g}{l}\right)^i > 0 \\[2em] \infty & \text{if} \quad 1 - \left(1 - \dfrac{l}{g}\right) 2 \sum_{i=0}^{k-1} \left(\dfrac{g}{l}\right)^i \le 0. \end{cases}
$$

$$(6.23)$$

This is a rather complicated statement, but a few examples can help illustrate why this is important. For example, suppose that a person is unwilling to take on a 0.50 probability of winning $110 and a 0.50 probability of losing $100. Then, the person must also turn down a 0.50 probability of winning $990 and a 0.50 probability of losing $600. If the person would turn down a 0.50 probability of gaining $120 and a 0.50 probability of losing $100, then the person would also turn down any bet that had a 0.50 probability of losing $600, no matter how large the possible gain. Although it seems reasonable that people might want to turn down the smaller gamble, it seems unreasonable that virtually anyone would turn down such a cheap bet for 50 percent probability of winning an infinite amount of money. Further results are displayed in Table 6.1.

Rabin takes this as further evidence that people combine loss aversion with narrow bracketing. First, note that we relied on the smoothness and concavity of our function to obtain equation 6.23. Loss aversion does away with smoothness, allowing a kink in the function at the reference point. Thus, no matter how small the gamble, no single line will approximate the value function. Further, the function is convex over losses, limiting the ability to use arguments such as that presented in Figure 6.4.

Table 6.1 Examples Applying Rabin's Theorem

If You Would Turn Down		Then You Should Also Turn Down	
Winning with 0.50 Probability	Losing with 0.50 Probability	Winning with 0.50 Probability	Losing with 0.50 Probability
$110	$100	$555	$400
		$1,062	$600
		$∞	$1,000
$550	$500	$2,775	$2,000
		$5,313	$3,000
		$∞	$5,000
$1,100	$1,000	$5,551	$4,000
		$10,628	$6,000
		$∞	$10,000

This result can be extended to continuous choices and continuous distributions, where the results become even more bizarre. Note that continuous choices necessarily involve very small tradeoffs in risk at the margin. Hence, a lot of information about the shape of the utility function is contained in these continuous decisions. Interestingly, calibration results like this can be made in the context of loss aversion (and other behavioral models of decision under risk). Perhaps the failure of these models under broad bracketing to explain such anomalies points to the necessity of modeling the bracketing of decisions.

EXAMPLE 6.3 An Experimental Example of Bracketing

A clear example of how bracketing can influence decisions was given by Amos Tversky and Daniel Kahneman by way of a hypothetical experiment. Participants were first asked to make two choices:

> Imagine that you face the following pair of concurrent decisions. First, examine both decisions, then indicate the options you prefer.

Decision 1. Choose between:
A. A sure gain of $240
B. A 25 percent chance to gain $1000 and a 75 percent chance to gain nothing
Decision 2. Choose between:
C. A sure loss of $750
D. A 75 percent chance to lose $1000 and a 25 percent chance to lose nothing[2]

Of 150 participants, the overwhelming majority chose both A and D.

First, note that choice A is a risk-averse choice, whereas choice D is a risk-loving choice. Choice A takes place over the domain of gains, and choice D takes place over the domain of losses. Thus, this pattern of choices suggests that the utility function is concave over gains and convex over losses. This result supports the notion of loss aversion with a concave value function over gains and a convex value function over losses. Second, note

---

[2] Tversky, A., and D. Kahneman. "Rational Choice and the Framing of Decisions." *Journal of Business* 59, Issue 4 (1986): S251–S278, University of Chicago Press.

that participants were instructed to treat the decisions concurrently. Thus, choosing A and D is choosing a compound gamble A and D over every other combination of gamble. The compound gamble A and D yields a 75 percent chance of losing $760 and a 25 percent chance of gaining $240.

Consider the alternative choice (chosen by less than 13 percent of participants) of the compound gamble B and C. This gamble yields a 75 percent chance to lose $750, and a 25 percent chance to win $250. The compound gamble B and C clearly dominates A and D, yielding more money for the same probability. Clearly, if the gambles had been presented as combined, people would have chosen B and C instead of A and D.

Narrow bracketing was perhaps induced by the difficulty in calculating the compound gambles from the separate gambles, thus leading to a suboptimal decision. In this case, the lack of transparency in the choice led to narrow bracketing.

EXAMPLE 6.4   A Taste for Diversity—or Not

Suppose it was Halloween and you were trick-or-treating. You visit three houses that happen to offer exactly the same three types of candy bars. At the first house, you are allowed to take one candy bar, and you choose your favorite. At the second house, you are also allowed to choose only one, and you decide to take your favorite. At the third house, you are allowed to choose two, and you decide to choose one of your favorite and one of the others. Daniel Read and George Loewenstein set up three such houses on Halloween and observed the choices by individual trick-or-treaters. At the houses allowing only one choice, people tended to choose the same candy. At the house allowing children to take two, trick-or-treaters overwhelmingly chose two different treats.

A majority of the time, we make decisions in a sequence, one at a time. For example, someone might purchase her lunch each day, deciding each day what to eat independently. Sometimes, however, we make a single decision that determines our consumption over several periods. For example, someone who brings a bag lunch might buy the materials for her lunches only once a week or even less often. In this case, it is natural to think that the sequential choices will be narrowly bracketed and the single choice will be broadly bracketed.

Itamar Simonson asked students in his class to choose among six possible snacks: peanuts, tortilla chips, milk chocolate with almonds, a Snickers bar, Oreo cookies, or crackers and cheese. They were to receive these snacks once a week at the end of class for three consecutive weeks. Students in some of his classes were asked to choose in class on the day they would receive the snacks. Students in other classes were asked to choose before the first distribution of snacks what they would receive all three weeks. A total of 362 students participated in either the sequential or the joint choice conditions. In the sequential choice condition, 9 percent of students chose a different snack each week. In the joint choice condition, 45 percent chose a different snack each week. Read and Loewenstein replicated this experiment, but they asked the students in the simultaneous choice condition if they wanted to change their mind on the days they were to receive their second and third snacks. A little less than half of the participants in these sessions wanted to revise their choices, and those who wanted to change desired *less* diversity in their selection.

Bracketing and Variety

It appears that when people bracket broadly, the person values variety much more than when bracketing narrowly. This might not be too surprising, because one has a much more difficult time identifying variety in a single item. This is a property that only emerges when choices are grouped together. The question then arises: Who is better off? Generally we regard people who have made broadly bracketed decisions as better off because they are able to account for how one decision influences the other. But it is possible that it works the other way. In this case, it may be that the broadly bracketed decisions anticipate valuing variety much more than they truly will. Remember that these food choices were made a week apart. If one were eating the same thing every day, monotony might lead you away from your favorite food after a short period. But if you chose to eat the same thing every Friday, there is plenty of room for variety in the intervening six days. Thus, people might display a **diversification bias**.

This has been evident in many different contexts. For example, people tend to spread their retirement investments equally among all possible options in a retirement program, even if some are relatively unattractive. In this case, people seek variety when broadly bracketing choices, even if it might make them worse off when consumption takes place. The type of diversity sought might have much to do with the framing of the decision. For example, suppose a tourist is visiting a new city for a week and is deciding where to eat that week. If presented with a list of restaurants divided into categories by the type of food they serve, the diner may be led to choose one traditional American restaurant, one Chinese restaurant, one Italian, and so on. Alternatively, if she is presented a list divided into regions in the city, she might choose to eat in a different location each day.

Rational Bracketing for Variety

Simonson explains the results of his study by suggesting that people might simply be uncertain of their future preferences for individual snacks, and thus they seek variety as a means of diversifying the outcome and maximizing expected utility. Read and Loewenstein sought to test this hypothesis. If one is unsure of one's preferences, then one should not be able to predict one's subsequent choices with accuracy. In fact, when students were asked to predict what they would choose in sequential choice, they were highly accurate, with virtually no difference. Further, those in the simultaneous choice condition predicted that they would seek less variety if they were to choose sequentially. It appears that at some level people are aware of how bracketing influences variety seeking. Nonetheless, the degree of accuracy of predictions seems contrary to the notion that people are uncertain of their future preferences for the items.

EXAMPLE 6.5   Cigarette Addiction

Cigarettes, and other items containing powerful drugs, are extremely addicting. These items provide some immediate pleasure or high, making them highly attractive at any one point in time. However, the drugs in the cigarettes have a diminishing effect on the body as the smoker builds up a resistance to the drug. Thus, someone who has been smoking for years does not get the same high or pleasure from the nicotine in a single cigarette that a new smoker receives. How then can it be addicting? Generally, we believe that diminishing marginal utility of use leads to cessation of consumption. For example, pizza displays diminishing marginal utility of use. Thus, I receive less enjoyment from the third slice than from the first slice. When the enjoyment is low enough, it is no longer worth the effort to eat it, and I stop eating. Suppose I tried eating pizza for every meal. Eventually, I would grow tired of the monotony as my marginal utility of pizza diminished, and I would start eating some other food instead. How are cigarettes different?

Consider the alternative activities that one could engage in. Suppose, for example, the only other alternatives to smoking were to play sports. Smoking may reduce the pleasure from playing sports. It becomes more difficult to breathe or run when one smokes on a regular basis. More generally, doing anything for long periods that is incompatible with smoking may be made unpleasant if feelings of withdrawal kick in. If, in fact, smoking reduces the pleasure from alternative activities more than it decreases the pleasure from smoking, the smoker might face an ever-increasing urge to smoke because everything else looks less attractive by comparison. In fact, smoking and other drug use has been shown to have strongly negative effects on the pleasure one derives from other activities. If this were true, why would one then choose to smoke if it reduces future pleasure from all activities?

Bracketing may play a role. At any one time, a smoker might consider the high of smoking and perhaps other immediate social advantages. But narrowly bracketing the choice to the single cigarette ignores the future impact of the cigarette on the utility of all future activities. Thus, narrow bracketing could lead to melioration: a focus on the now at the expense of long-term goals. Many smokers when asked would like to quit being smokers. Nonetheless, very few would turn down their next cigarette.

Changing Preferences, Adding Up, and Choice Bracketing

Richard Hernstein and several colleagues propose a simple model of melioration in this context. Suppose that the consumer may choose between two consumption items in each of two decision periods: cigarettes, x, and other consumption goods, y. Suppose that consumption of cigarettes influences the utility of consuming either cigarettes or other goods in the second period, but doing other activities has no impact on future utility. The consumer's rational decision problem can be written as

$$\max_{x_1,x_2,y_1y_2} u_1(x_1, y_1) + u_2(x_2, y_2, x_1), \tag{6.24}$$

subject to the budget constraint

$$p_x(x_1 + x_2) + p_y(y_1 + y_2) \le w. \tag{6.25}$$

Here, $u_1(x_1, y_1)$ is the utility of consumption in the first period as a function of cigarette consumption and other activities in that period, $u_2(x_2, y_2, x_1)$ is the utility of consumption in the second period as a function of cigarettes consumed in both periods and other consumption in the second period, w is the total budget for consumption in both periods, and p_1 and p_2 are the prices of cigarette and other consumption, respectively. But, under melioration, the consumer does not consider the impact of the first period consumption of cigarettes on the second period consumption of either cigarettes or other goods. Thus, the consumer would bracket narrowly and behave as if she were to solve

$$\left(\max_{x_1,\, y_1} u_1(x_1,\, y_1) \right) + \left(\max_{x_2,\, y_2} u_2(x_2,\, y_2,\, x_1) \right) \tag{6.26}$$

subject to the budget constraint in equation 6.25. A decision maker solving equation 6.26 will ignore all future consequences of her consumption in period 1 and pay the price for her naïveté in period 2.

The condition for the solution to equation 6.26 finds the point where marginal utility of consumption divided by the price of consumption is equal for cigarettes and other consumption in the first period. But this ignores the added cost that cigarettes impose on future consumption. If cigarettes reduce the utility of consumption in the future, then this cost should also be considered. Thus, the proper solution to equation 6.24 equates the marginal utility of cigarette consumption in period 1 plus the marginal impact of period 1 consumption of cigarettes on period 2 utility, all divided by the price of consumption with the marginal utility of consumption of other items divided by their price. By ignoring this cost in terms of future utility, the smoker consumes more cigarettes in the first period than would be optimal. Further, if cigarettes make consumption of cigarettes relatively more attractive in the second period than other goods, it leads to greater-than-optimal consumption of cigarettes in the second period also.

Suppose that both goods had the same price. Then, the smoker displaying melioration would equate marginal utility across cigarettes and other consumption in the first period. Let us further suppose that utility in the first period is additive and that the smoker receives constant marginal utility from consumption of other goods, $u_1(x_1,\, y_1) = u_{x1}(x_1) + ky_1$. Then we can represent the problem as in Figure 6.5. Here, if the smoker displays melioration, she will set the marginal utility of cigarettes in period 1, u'_{x1}, equal to marginal utility of other goods in period 1, $k = u'_{y1}$, obtaining x_1^M. Optimally, she should set the sum of marginal utilities from cigarettes over both periods equal to the marginal utility of other goods. That is, the marginal utility of cigarettes in period 1, u'_{x1} plus the marginal utility in period 2 of cigarettes consumed in period 1, u'_{x2} should be set equal to k. If the marginal utility in the second period is negative, then the optimal consumption of cigarettes will be above the melioration optimum. If on the other hand the marginal utility in the second period is positive, then the melioration optimum will be below the true optimum. In this case, narrow bracketing could lead to addictive behaviors where one does not consider the future costs of one's actions.

Addiction and Melioration

One can imagine a series of choices between action x and action y. In the first period, choosing x returns a utility of 10, and choosing y returns a utility of 7. But playing x reduces the utility of playing x in the next period by 1 and reduces the utility of playing y in the following period by 2. Thus, if one chooses x in the first period, in the second

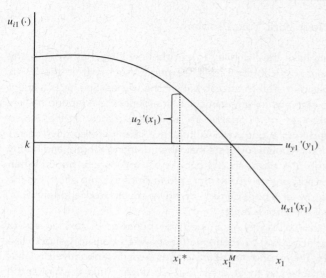

FIGURE 6.5
Melioration in the Cigarette Problem

period one could choose x and obtain 9 or could choose y and obtain 5. Someone who does not discount future periods playing any more than 7 periods of this choice should choose to play y in the first period, and continue playing y until she reaches the seventh period from the end of the game, when the reduction in future utility ceases to be important. On the other hand, once one has played x, y becomes less and less attractive. Thus, a narrowly bracketed decision to play x on a repeated basis could lead to a state in which broadly bracketed decisions also lead to choosing x. This paints the picture of addiction as a slippery slope, where unsuspecting and perhaps naïve people fall prey to a few bad decisions. However, those decisions recreate the incentives in such a way as to alter the desired path even if one begins to fully understand the consequences of one's actions. Hence, over time a person with the most pernicious of addictions might rationally choose to continue in her potentially destructive behavior.

EXAMPLE 6.6   Experimental Evidence

Richard Hernstein and several colleagues conducted a set of trial experiments to see if people could discern the impact of one choice on future available choices. Participants played a simple computer game in which they were presented a screen with two "money machines." In each of 400 periods, the machines would be labeled with the amount of money they would dispense if chosen for that period. The participants could choose either the left or right machine in each period. The payoffs were set up to mirror the cigarette problem discussed earlier in that the percentages of times one of the machines was chosen affected the payoff from that activity in the future, and the percentage of times the other was chosen had no effect. They then compared the subjects' behavior to see if it was closer to the meliorating optimum or the true optimum payout. In fact, almost all subjects received payouts that fell somewhere in between, suggesting that behavior might not be quite so simple as the narrow-bracketing story.

EXAMPLE 6.7   The New York Taxi Problem

Cab drivers in New York City have the flexibility to decide how long they work in any given day. The cab driver rents the cab for a fixed fee per 12-hour shift (in the 1990s it was about $80), and can decide to return the cab early if she wishes. She faces a fine if the cab is returned late. The earnings for any particular time period can depend heavily on the particular day. For example, more people are likely to take a cab in the rain so they can avoid getting soaked from a long walk. Cultural events might also drive spikes in demand. Traditional economic theory suggests that when demand is high, and hourly wages are thus relatively high, the driver should choose to work longer hours. When wages are high over brief periods, one can make more money for the same effort. On the other hand, when wages are low for a brief period, the driver should work shorter hours, because the marginal benefit for labor is lower.

Colin Camerer and several colleagues examined the behavior of taxi drivers to determine if they responded according to economic theory when transitory shocks like weather affected their wages. They found that hourly wages are in fact negatively related to the hours worked in a particular day for an individual cab driver. Thus, the higher the marginal revenue of an hour of labor for the day, the less the driver decides to work. Moreover, the supply elasticity of labor among the less-experienced cab drivers is close to −1; thus for every 1 percent increase in revenue per hour, there is a 1 percent decrease in hours worked. This is consistent with the cab drivers targeting a particular amount of revenue each day and then quitting. If the driver is loss averse, she might set the rental rate for the cab (plus living expenses) as a reference point and feel a substantial loss below this level. In fact, some drivers who drive a company car without paying for the lease do not display the same bias. However, the target-income explanation only makes sense if the driver brackets labor supply choices by day. If considering over several days, one could take advantage of the effect of averaging wages over many days and decide to quit early when there is little business and decide to work later when there is lots of business. On average, cab drivers could have increased their income by 8 percent without increasing the number of hours worked in total by responding rationally to wage incentives. This might also explain why it is so difficult to find a cab on a rainy day.

EXAMPLE 6.8   For Only a Dollar a Day

Narrow bracketing can potentially lead to people ignoring the consequence of small transactions. For example, transactions for only a dollar or less might not seem like enough to care about on their own when failing to account for the sheer number of transactions one makes for such small amounts. This is called the **peanuts effect**. Often, financial advice columns suggest that people who are seeking to cut back on their spending look first at the smallest of transactions. For example, one might not consider a cup of coffee at a local coffee house to be a big expense and thus not consequential. Nonetheless, the amount of money spent each day on small items can add up quickly. Such an effect is often used to advertise lease agreements for cars, appliances, or furniture. For example, auto dealers often emphasize the amount of the monthly payment rather than the total cost. It sounds much cheaper to buy a car for "only $450 a month" than for "only $37,000." Old commercials for charitable organizations often suggested that for just the cost of a cup of coffee each day, one could help others in need. Read, Loewenstein, and Rabin mused, "Imagine the response to the plea that your donation will cost 'only $350 per year, no more than the cost of a small refrigerator.'"

Narrow Bracketing and Motivation

There is evidence of yet another way narrow bracketing can lead to higher overall utility. In some cases, narrow bracketing may be used as a self-control device. On the surface, this seems counterintuitive after a lengthy discussion on how narrow bracketing can lead to addiction and poor behavior. However, we often observe people intentionally using narrow bracketing to achieve very large goals. For example, many addicts try to avoid the object of their addiction "one day at a time." Similarly the common adage states that great journeys begin with a single step. In both of these examples, the object is to break down a difficult and apparently insurmountable task into very small and doable tasks. It might sound very difficult for addicts to cease their addictive behavior for the next 40 years. Stopping for a day is much more achievable. As well, bracketing too broadly can make it difficult to verify progress on a goal. If one's goal is to save $5,000 in a year, it may be easier to splurge in the interim because there is so much time left until the goal must be reached. Alternatively, if the goal is to save $210 from every paycheck, one quickly knows if one is on track and whether there is room to splurge and still meet the goal.

Behavioral Bracketing

Read, Loewenstein, and Rabin suggest several potential causes of bracketing and factors that can affect bracketing behavior. Among these are social heuristics, the timing of decisions, limits on cognitive capacity, and motivation. It is easy to see how joint decisions can quickly become so complex as to require someone to narrowly bracket decisions to create any reasoned response. Food consumption is a convenient example. Optimizing would require that a diner take into account all the food decisions she will make together. But, in a day one person makes an average of 200 to 300 food decisions (what to eat, when, where, etc.). It would take too much time and energy to consider these problems together. Thus, it is not particularly clear that one would be better off for having done it.

The rational model does not consider the cognitive costs of such an optimization problem. The timing of decisions makes sequential bracketing natural. We are somewhat forced to think through a decision when it is placed in front of us. Thus, we often make decisions as they arise, bracketing decisions by sequence. Returning to our food example, we would decide on breakfast in the morning, not considering our later meals. Around noon we would be forced to decide what to eat for lunch. Here our decision on breakfast might influence our decision because we are more or less hungry or feel more or less guilty about our level of consumption that morning. But we do not consider dinner at the time we decide on lunch. If the sequence of decisions is one of the primary drivers of bracketing, then our decisions are much more backward looking than forward looking.

Social heuristics clearly play a role as well. Social heuristics include cases in which society has, by convention, bracketed certain decisions or items together. Thus, we have conventions on the number and timing of meals throughout the day. Such conventions can influence the types of choices we make. For example, Read, Loewenstein, and Rabin find that people indicate a desire to consume more bread pudding when asked separately how much they would eat each weekday and each weekend day than if they were simply asked how much they would eat on each day in a week. Bracketing the weekend separately might induce people to think of this as an opportunity to make some exceptions to their normal routine and consume more of those things they normally try to limit.

History and Notes

The issue of bracketing has lurked in the economics and marketing literatures for quite some time, but the question of bracketing was first raised in a serious fashion by Itamar Simonson regarding the sequencing of choices. Issues such as the peanuts effect and segmenting of decisions were raised in passing by Richard Thaler, Daniel Kahneman, and Dan Lovallo, among others, in proposing mental accounting and other behavioral economic phenomena. Later these concepts were formalized by Daniel Read, George Loewenstein, and Matthew Rabin, whose work much of this chapter is based upon. These models have been very valuable in solving a puzzle in the addiction literature. Addicts display compulsive and binging behavior, but there is also evidence that they respond to monetary incentives to stop the addictive behavior. This is inconsistent with most other psychology-based models of addiction because these models suppose that the behavior ignores the monetary consequences of their actions. Alternatively, financial incentives might allow the narrowly bracketed decision to lead away from addictive substances, thus bringing the melioration optimum in line with the overall optimum.

The general rule would guide the consumer to use broader brackets when it is feasible. This leads to better decisions in nearly all cases. However, there are some clear exceptions, such as when using narrow bracketing to motivate behavior (like quitting an addiction) or if the cognitive decision costs of broad bracketing are overwhelming. The types of bracketing you as a marketer might want to induce depends substantially on the types of products you are selling. Goods that cost substantial amounts up front, but that provide delayed benefits, are more likely to be purchased using broad bracketing. Thus, universities often tout the long-term benefits of being an alumnus and the strength of their alumni organizations. Alternatively, goods that provide substantial benefits now (potentially with greater costs in the future) are better sold using narrow bracketing. Thus, automobiles are sold for their visual appeal, the feel of driving, and other things that can be experienced now.

Rational Explanations for Bracketing Behavior

A quick note is necessary regarding addictive behavior and rational models. Gary Becker and Kevin Murphy proposed a rational model of addiction in the late 1980s that is often used to inform policy regarding addictive and compulsive behaviors. Their model supposes that addictive goods provide greater and greater utility as one consumes them. Thus, the person who becomes strongly addicted may be optimizing over time by developing their addiction. Such a model, however, requires that addicted people on average would not regret their addiction or change their consumption pattern. This does not appear to be the case. Rather, many addicts wish to end the addiction and lament their having started in the first place. Such regret is consistent with irrational addiction. We have presented one model of addiction in this chapter whereby the addictive substance reduces the value of all activities while increasing the relative utility of the addictive activity. In Part III of this book, another model of irrational addiction is discussed.

Biographical Note

Courtesy of Drazen Prelec

Drazen Prelec (1955–)
B.A., Harvard College, 1978; Ph.D. Harvard University, 1983; held faculty positions at Massachusetts Institute of Technology and Harvard University

Drazen Prelec was trained as an experimental psychologist and an applied mathematician. Combining these skills, his work encompasses mathematical models of human irrationality and the neuroscience of decision. He has made substantial contributions in the behavioral economics of consumer decision making, risky choice, self-control, and time discounting. His work on neuroscience uses magnetic resonance imaging to map the location of brain activity as people are faced with various types of choices. Experimental work has examined questions such as whether the payment mechanism (cash or credit) influences how much one is willing to spend. His work on self-control has contributed to the science of bracketing and to time discounting. More recent work examines how people may be motivated to obtain indicators of success even if the indicators are not causally related to success. Prelec has published in many of the top economic, business, and psychology journals, holding appointments in all three disciplines. He is the recipient of a prestigious John Simon Guggenheim Fellowship.

THOUGHT QUESTIONS

1. Financial planners and investment advisors often instruct their clients to hold a broad portfolio of investments to reduce the overall risk. Having a large number of uncorrelated or negatively correlated investments in one's portfolio reduces the variance of the return on investment. At first blush, it might appear that the advisor is suggesting that investments are more attractive when grouped together. Contrast this with the risk aggregation bias discussed in this chapter. Is this diversification a good idea? If the investor were not allowed to diversify, should she still be willing to buy any single investment in the portfolio?

2. Expected utility theory suggests that all risk preferences are due to diminishing marginal utility of wealth. We have briefly discussed some reasons for doubting this hypothesis. Why might diminishing marginal utility of wealth be related to risk preferences? What other explanations for risk behavior can you think of? How would these alternative motives suggest behavior that is different from diminishing marginal utility of wealth?

3. Many small farms sell their vegetable crops through cooperative arrangements. A subscriber pays in advance for a certain portion of the crop. When the crop is harvested, the subscriber receives (usually weekly) deliveries of produce. The produce is composed of the particular crops the farmer has decided to grow that year. Consider yourself as a potential subscriber to this system. You can subscribe for a fixed fee or you can purchase your vegetables as needed throughout the year. Suppose someone considering subscribing before the season starts brackets broadly, and someone purchasing vegetables throughout the season brackets narrowly. How will bracketing affect the number and types of vegetables purchased? If you were marketing such a subscription, how could you use bracketing to encourage purchases?

4. (a) Suppose that Schuyler faces the choice of whether to take a gamble that results in $120 with probability 0.50, and −$100 with 0.50 probability. Suppose that Schuyler's preferences can be represented by the value function in (6.15). Would she take the gamble? Would she be willing to take four of these gambles?

(b) Suppose that Sydney would turn down a single case of this gamble. Consider a gamble that results in a loss of $600 with probability 0.5 and a gain of x with the remaining probability. If we knew Sydney behaved according to expected utility, how much would x need to be before he could possibly be willing to take the new gamble? Use equation 6.23 to produce your answer.

5. Suppose Rosario faces a two-period time-allocation problem. Rosario can allocate 10 hours of time in each period between two activities: work and family. The utility function for the first time period is $u_1(x_1, 10-x_1) = x_1^{0.5}(10-x_1)^{0.5}$, where x is the amount of time spent at work, $10-x$ is the amount of time spent with family, and the subscript refers to time period. Thus the marginal utility of time at work in the first period is $\partial u_1/\partial x_1 = 0.5x_1^{-0.5}(10-x_1)^{0.5} - 0.5x_1^{0.5}(10-x_1)^{-0.5}$. In the second period, the utility function is given by $u_2(x_2, 10-x_2, x_1, 10-x_1) = x_1x_2^{0.5} + (10-x_1)(10-x_2)^{0.5}$. Marginal utility of time at work in the second period is given by $\frac{\partial u_2}{\partial x_2} = 0.5x_1x_2^{-0.5} - 0.5(10-x_1)(10-x_2)^{-0.5}$. Thus, total utility for both periods is given by $u_1 + u_2 = x_1^{0.5}(10-x_1)^{0.5} + x_1x_2^{0.5} + (10-x_1)(10-x_2)^{0.5}$, resulting in total marginal utility of work in period 1 of $\partial u_1/\partial x_1 = 0.5x_1^{-0.5}(10-x_1)^{0.5} - 0.5x_1^{0.5}(10-x_1)^{-0.5} + x_2^{0.5} - (10-x_2)^{0.5}$, and total marginal utility of work in period 2 of $\frac{\partial u_2}{\partial x_2} = 0.5x_1x_2^{-0.5} - 0.5(10-x_1)(10-x_2)^{-0.5}$. The optimal allocation can be found by setting marginal utility of time at work in each period to zero. If Rosario brackets broadly, what will be the optimal allocation of time between work and family in both time periods? How will Rosario allocate her time if she displays melioration? What is the level of utility in each solution?

REFERENCES

Barberis, N., and M. Huang. "Mental Accounting, Loss Aversion, and Individual Stock Returns." *Journal of Finance* 56(2001): 1247–1292.

Benartzi, S., and R.H. Thaler. "Myopic Loss Aversion and the Equity Premium Puzzle." *Quarterly Journal of Economics* 110(1995): 73–92.

Camerer, C., L. Babcock, G. Loewenstein, and R. Thaler. "Labor Supply of New York City Cabdrivers: One Day at a Time." *Quarterly Journal of Economics* 112(1997): 407–441.

Hernstein, R.J., G.F. Loewenstein, D. Prelec, and W. Vaughan, Jr. "Utility Maximization and Melioration: Internalities in Individual Choice." *Journal of Behavioral Decision Making* 6(1993): 149–185.

Rabin, M. "Risk Aversion and Expected-Utility Theory: A Calibration Theorem." *Econometrica* 68(2000): 1281–1292.

Read, D., and G. Loewenstein. "Diversification Bias: Explaining the Discrepancy in Variety Seeking Between Combined and Separated Choices." *Journal of Experimental Psychology: Applied* 1 (1995): 34–49.

Read, D., G. Loewenstein, and M. Rabin. "Choice Bracketing." *Journal of Risk and Uncertainty* 19(1999): 171–197.

Samuelson, P.A. "Risk and Uncertainty: A Fallacy of Large Numbers." *Scientia* 98(1963): 108–113.

Simonson, I. "The Effect of Purchase Quantity and Timing on Variety Seeking Behavior." *Journal of Marketing Research* 32(1990): 150–162.

Thaler, R.H., A. Tversky, D. Kahneman, and A. Schwartz. "The Effect of Myopia and Loss Aversion on Risk: An Experimental Test." *Quarterly Journal of Economics* 112(1997): 647–661.

Tversky, A., and D. Kahneman. "Rational Choice and the Framing of Decisions." *Journal of Business* 59(1986): S251–S278.

Advanced Concept

The Portfolio Problem

The portfolio problem can be written as in equation 6.12:

$$\max_{w_x} E[u((w - w_z) + w_z z)] = \int_{-\infty}^{\infty} u((w - w_z) + w_z z)f(z)dz, \qquad (6.A)$$

where w_z is the amount to be invested in the risky asset, w is the total amount of wealth to be allocated between the two assets, and $f(z)$ is the probability density function. The first-order condition can be written as

$$E[u'(w - w_z) + w_z z(z - 1)] = \int_{-\infty}^{\infty} u'((w - w_z) + w_z z)(z - 1)f(z)dz = 0. \qquad (6.B)$$

It is often useful to use Taylor series approximations to derive results when using expected utility theory. In this case, we can generate a Taylor series approximation around the expected value of the investment portfolio, $E((w - w_z) + w_z z) = (w - w_z) + w_z \mu = \overline{w}$. A first-order Taylor series expansion of the marginal utility function results in

$$u'(w_z + (w - w_z)z) \approx u'(\overline{w}) + u''(\overline{w})w_z(z - \mu). \qquad (6.C)$$

Using the utility approximation from (6.C), the first-order condition from (6.B) can be written as

$$\begin{aligned} E[u'((w - w_z) + w_z z)(z - 1)] &\approx E[u'(\overline{w})(z - 1) \\ &+ u''(\overline{w})w_z(z - \mu)(z - 1)] = 0, \end{aligned} \qquad (6.D)$$

or, completing the square in the second term,

$$u'(\overline{w})(\mu - 1) + u''(\overline{w})w_z E\left[(z - \mu)^2 + \mu(z - \mu) - (z - \mu)\right]$$

$$= u'(\overline{w})(\mu - 1) + u''(\overline{w})w_z \sigma^2 = 0 \tag{6.E}$$

where $\sigma^2 = E\left[(z - \mu)^2\right]$. The value σ^2 is commonly called the *variance* of z, and it measures how dispersed the values of z are. Thus the higher the value of σ^2, the more risky is the investment. The result in (6.E) follows because $E(z - \mu) = \mu - \mu = 0$. Thus, the first-order condition results in

$$w_z = \frac{(\mu - 1)}{\sigma^2 R_A}, \tag{6.F}$$

where $R_A = -u''/u'$, is the coefficient of absolute risk aversion.

Advanced Concept

Bracketing the Portfolio Problem

For now, let us suppose that v in equations 6.16 and 6.18 is continuously differentiable. This will allow us to again use a Taylor series expansion to approximate the decision rule and compare behavior with broad and narrow bracketing. Thus, we are omitting the possibility of loss aversion, which involves a function that is kinked at the reference point. equation 6.19 yields first-order conditions given by

$$E\left[-1 + v'\left(\sum_{i=1}^{n} x_i z_i\right) z_i\right] = 0. \tag{6.G}$$

As before, we will approximate the marginal value function using a first-order Taylor series expansion around the mean. This yields

$$v'(y) \approx v'(E(y)) + v''(E(y))(y - E(y)). \tag{6.H}$$

In the case of the portfolio value $y = \sum_{i=1}^{n} x_i z_i$, the expectation of the return is $E(y) = \sum_{i=1}^{n} x_i \mu_i$, where μ_i is the mean return of investment i. We will use $\overline{w} = E(y)$ in the argument of the value function to signify that this value is held constant. Thus, we can rewrite the first-order condition in equation (6.G) as

$$E\left[-1 + v'(\overline{w})z_i + v''(\overline{w})\left(\sum_{j=1}^{n} x_j z_j - \sum_{j=1}^{n} x_j \mu_j\right)z_i\right] = 0, \tag{6.I}$$

which can be rewritten as

$$-1 + v'(\overline{w})\mu_i + v''(\overline{w})E\left[\sum\nolimits_{j=1}^{n} x_j(z_j - \mu_j)(z_i - \mu_i) + \sum\nolimits_{j=1}^{n}(z_j - \mu_j)\mu_i\right]$$
$$= -1 + v'(\overline{w})\mu_i + v''(\overline{w})\left(\sum\nolimits_{j=1}^{n} x_j\sigma_{ij}\right) = 0. \tag{6.J}$$

Here, $\sigma_{ij} = E\left[(z_i - \mu_i)(z_j - \mu_j)\right]$ is the variance of investment i, when $i=j$, and the covariance of investment i and j when they are unequal. Thus, solving (6.I) yields

$$x_i = \frac{\mu_i}{R_A\sigma_{ii}} + \frac{\frac{1}{v''} - \left(\sum_{j\neq i} x_j\sigma_{ij}\right)}{\sigma_{ii}}. \tag{6.K}$$

If instead, we suppose that decisions are narrowly bracketed, equation 6.21 has first-order conditions

$$E\left[-1 + v'(x_iz_i)z_i\right] = 0. \tag{6.L}$$

Again we can use the Taylor series approximation from equation 6.H, only now $y = x_iz_i$, and $E(y) = x_i\mu_i$. Thus, we can rewrite equation 6.K as

$$E\left[-1 + v'(\overline{w})z_i + v''(\overline{w})x_i(z_i - \mu_i)z_i\right] = 0. \tag{6.M}$$

Completing the square, we obtain

$$-1 + v'(\overline{w})\mu_i + v''(\overline{w})x_i\sigma_{ii} = 0, \tag{6.N}$$

or,

$$x_i = \frac{\mu_i}{R_A\sigma_{ii}} + \frac{\left(\frac{1}{v''}\right)}{\sigma_{ii}}. \tag{6.O}$$

7

Representativeness and Availability

Cornell University's basketball team won the Ivy League championship in 2008, 2009, and 2010. Along the way the team set several team records for three-point shooting. In conversation, the basketball coach was asked about how he decides which players he will use in any particular game. He listed several key factors such as the particular matchups with the opposing team's players, but he also mentioned the importance of putting in the guy who has been on a shooting streak in the last several games. When pressed, he admitted that there were several factors that could contribute to such a streak but felt that if in a single game a regularly good shooter was cold, he would sit him on the bench in favor of a player with lower average percentage shooting. In fact, many coaches, players, and fans feel they can quickly discern when a player is either on a streak or in a slump in terms of shooting.

In dealing with risky decisions, one must first come to grips with the underlying uncertainty. In other words, before one can make a decision between two choices that involve uncertain outcomes, one must first develop a perception of how uncertain each of the choices is. Thus, a coach deciding which basketball players to put on the court wants to determine how reliable his shooters are and how likely each of his players are to stop key players on the other team from scoring. The coach cannot know before placing a player in a game how that player will perform. But the coach can use previous performance to form beliefs about how the players will perform, thus helping to decide which will play and for how long.

Scientists often find themselves in a similar situation in trying to decide which of several hypotheses may be true. Before conducting experiments, they cannot know with certainty which hypothesis performs best. Often, scientific data are relatively weak, providing little information about the true underlying relationship. In this case it can be difficult to determine the causal effects that might have generated the data. Nonetheless, in order to publish the results, it is necessary to draw some conclusions even from weak data. This chapter deals with how people use available information to form beliefs when facing uncertainty. These beliefs are the basis for decisions regarding investment, hiring, strategy, and virtually every aspect of business management. In reality, we face uncertainty on a constant basis, and given our cognitive limits, we have developed heuristics and other tools to simplify the process of learning and forming perceptions when facing uncertain outcomes. To appreciate the impact of these heuristics on decision outcomes, it is first important to review some basic statistical theory.

Statistical Inference and Information

The basic statistical problem assumes that we observe several independent draws of a random variable in which we may be interested. We might not know the underlying distribution for this random variable, but we hope to use the few observations we have in order to learn about that distribution. More often than not, we might know (or assume we know) the functional form for the probability density function of the random variable, but we need to use the data to estimate the parameters of that function.

For example, consider a coin that will be used in a coin toss. We might believe that there is a fixed probability, p, that the coin will come up heads each time that we toss the coin. But, we might not know exactly what p is, and wish to find out. One way we can try to do this is to toss the coin several times and see how often it lands on heads versus tails. Suppose we toss the coin 20 times, and it comes up heads eight times. Then we might estimate the probability of a heads to be $\hat{p} = 8/20 = 0.4$. But how certain are we that this is the answer? This point estimate communicates nothing but our best guess. It does not tell us how sure we are of that guess.

To think about this, we might wish to consider the probability that we might have drawn eight heads given some other probability that a heads would be drawn. Suppose the probability of a heads is p. Then the probability of drawing k heads in n tries is just the probability of k heads and $n - k$ tails, times the number of different orders in which k heads and $n - k$ tails could be flipped. This is commonly called the binomial probability function:

$$f(k) = \frac{n!}{k!(n-k)!} p^k (1-p)^{n-k}. \tag{7.1}$$

Thus, the probability of eight heads in 20 tries is just $125970 \times p^8 (1-p)^{12}$.

Suppose we wanted to know if it was likely that the coin was actually fair (i.e., $p = 0.5$). One common way to determine this is to use a statistical test. Formally, suppose we want to test the initial hypothesis $p = 0.5$ against the alternative hypothesis that $p < 0.5$. We will fail to reject our initial hypothesis when our estimate $\hat{p}$ is large, and we will reject our initial hypothesis in favor of the alternative hypothesis when $\hat{p}$ is small. We will start out by specifying the probability at which we will reject. As is common in scientific journals, let us reject the initial hypothesis if there is less than $\alpha = 0.05$ probability of observing eight heads or fewer under the initial hypothesis of $p = 0.5$. The probability of observing eight heads under $p = 0.5$ can be found as $f(8) \approx 0.12$. The probability of observing eight or fewer heads under $p = 0.5$ is $\sum_{k=0}^{8} f(k) \approx 0.25$. Thus, because this probability is greater than 0.05, we fail to reject the initial hypothesis that $p = 0.5$. Alternatively, if our initial hypothesis was that $p = 0.65$, we find the corresponding probability $\sum_{k=0}^{8} f(k) \approx 0.02$, which is less than 0.05. In this case we would reject the initial hypothesis in favor of the hypothesis $p < 0.65$. This is called a **one-tailed test** because the alternative hypothesis is given by an inequality, and thus we only reject the hypothesis if the observations are on one side (in this case less than) the hypothesized amount.

Instead, suppose our initial hypothesis were $p = 0.7$, and our alternative hypothesis were $p \neq 0.7$. In this case we reject for values that are too large or too small, and we reject symmetrically. Thus, if the probability at which we will reject is $\alpha = 0.05$, we will reject if the probability that the number of heads observed is less than or equal to eight is less than $\alpha/2 = 0.025$, or if the probability of observed values greater than or equal to eight is less than $\alpha/2 = 0.025$. If either of these two conditions is true, we will reject our initial hypothesis. This is called a **two-tailed test**. Given our initial hypothesis that $p = 0.7$, the probability that eight or more heads are drawn is $\sum_{k=8}^{20} f(k) \approx 0.99$, and the probability that eight or fewer heads are drawn is $\sum_{k=0}^{8} f(k) \approx 0.01$. Because the probability that eight or fewer heads are drawn is less than $\alpha/2 = 0.025$, we reject the initial hypothesis that $p = 0.7$.

We might also be interested in stating an interval on which we believe the true value falls given our observed draws. This would be called a **confidence interval**. For example, a 95 percent confidence interval gives the maximum and minimum values of initial hypotheses p for which we can reject the initial hypothesis using a two-tailed test with $\alpha = 1 - .95 = 0.05$. In this case, the 95 percent confidence interval is $[0.19, 0.64]$. To see this, if we assume $p = 0.19$, then $\sum_{k=8}^{20} f(k) \approx 0.025$, which is equal to $\alpha/2$. If p were any less, we would reject the initial hypothesis at the $\alpha = 0.05$ level of significance. As well, if we assume $p = 0.64$, then $\sum_{k=0}^{8} f(k) \approx 0.025$. If p were any greater, we would reject the initial hypothesis at the $\alpha = 0.05$ level of significance.

Confidence intervals and statistical tests like those discussed here form the primary basis for all scientific **inference**. Inference here refers to the information we discern from the data we are able to observe. In most problems, scientists assume a **normal distribution** for the random variable. Where the binomial distribution has one parameter, in our example the probability of a heads, the normal distribution has two parameters: the mean and the variance. We commonly represent the mean, or expectation, of a random variable as μ, and we represent the variance as σ^2. In general, if the sequence $\{x_i\}_{i=1}^{n}$ are each drawn from the same normal distribution with mean μ and variance σ^2, then the average of the n draws from this distribution, $\hat{\mu} = \sum_{i=1}^{n} x/n$, will be distributed normally with mean μ and variance σ^2/n. Moreover, we could define a variable z such that

$$z = \frac{\hat{\mu} - \mu}{\sqrt{\frac{\sigma^2}{n}}}, \tag{7.2}$$

which will always have a normal distribution with mean 0 and variance 1, called a **standard normal distribution**. When we perform the transformation implied by equation 7.2, we call this *standardization*.

Although it is difficult to calculate probabilities using a normal distribution (and hence we have left this information out) the standard normal distribution is well known. Virtually all books on statistics, spreadsheet software, and statistical software have tools that allow you to determine the probability that z is above or below some threshold. Thus, the standard normal distribution is very convenient to use for hypothesis testing. The 95 percent confidence interval for a standard normal random variable is approximately $[-1.96, 1.96]$. Often, we do not know the variance or have a hypothesis regarding it. However, equation 7.2 is approximately standard normally distributed if we replace σ^2 with an estimate of the variance, $\hat{\sigma}^2 = \sum_{i=1}^{n} (x_i - \hat{\mu})^2/(n-1)$, if n is large enough. Thus, considering equation 7.2, if we replace $\hat{\mu}$ with our observed average, replace μ with our initial hypothesized value, replace n with the number of observations, and replace σ^2 with our estimate of the variance, we can use the resulting value to test the initial hypothesis. If the resulting z is either larger than 1.96 or smaller than -1.96, we would reject the initial hypothesis that the mean equals μ in favor of the alternative that it does not equal μ at the $\alpha = 0.05$ level. By rejecting this test, we would say that the mean of the distribution is **significantly different** from μ.

Much of statistics relies on the use of large samples of data. Having more observations makes estimates more reliable and less variable. The embodiment of this statement is the oft-misunderstood **law of large numbers**. There are many versions of the law of large numbers.

The weak law of large numbers can be stated as follows:

Law of Large Numbers

Let $\{x_i\}_{i=1}^{n}$ be a sequence of independent random variables, each identically distributed with mean μ and variance σ^2. Then for any $\varepsilon > 0$, $\lim_{n \to \infty} P(|\hat{\mu} - \mu| < \varepsilon) = 1$, where P represents the probability function.

Thus, as the number of observations increases to infinity, the average of a sample of observations converges to the true mean in probability. For example, if we had a fair coin and tossed it a large number of times, the fraction of times it came up heads would approach 0.50 as the number of tosses went to infinity. But suppose we tossed it 10 times and it happened to come up with nine heads and one tail. The law of large numbers does not state that future tosses will result in a surplus of tails to balance out the previous tosses. Rather, the law of large numbers states that on average the next n draws will come up about half heads. Then, as n goes to infinity, eventually the surplus of heads in the first ten tosses becomes small relative to the sample size. Thus,

$$\lim_{n \to \infty} \frac{9 + 0.5n}{10 + n} = 0.5. \tag{7.3}$$

In determining how much we learn from observing several draws from a distribution, it is important to understand the concept of statistical **independence**. Two random variables are independent if knowing the realized value of one provides no information about the value of the other. For example, if I toss a coin and it comes up heads, this has not changed the probability that the next time I toss the coin it will come up heads. Alternatively, we could consider cases where random variables are related. For example, if we know the price of corn is high, this increases the probability that the price of bourbon (made from corn) is also high. More formally, we say that two events A and B are independent if $P(A \cup B) = P(A)P(B)$, where P is the probability function. If two random variables x and y are independent, then $E(xy) = E(x)E(y)$. When a high realization of one random variable increases the probability of a high outcome of another, we say that they are **positively correlated**. If a high outcome of one leads to a higher probability of a low outcome of the other, we say that they are **negatively correlated**. More formally, we can define the correlation coefficient as

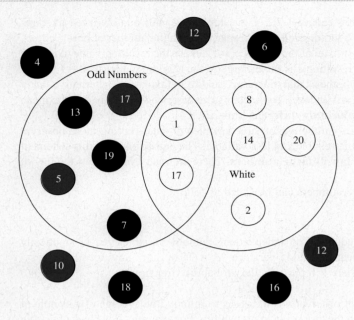

FIGURE 7.1
Venn Diagram of
Colored and Num-
bered Bingo Balls

$$\rho(x,\,y) = \frac{E(xy) - E(x)E(y)}{\sqrt{\sigma_x^2\sigma_y^2}}. \tag{7.4}$$

The correlation coefficient is positive, but less than one, if x and y are positively correlated. It is negative and greater than -1 if x and y are negatively correlated. If x and y are independent, then the correlation coefficient is zero.

Finally, we need to make use of Bayes' rule. Consider Figure 7.1, which displays a Venn diagram of bingo balls that are both colored and numbered. If we consider the diagram displays the entire population of bingo balls, then there are exactly 18 balls total, with six being white and seven being odd-numbered balls. Bayes used statistical theory to determine the optimal rule for learning when combining two different pieces of information. Suppose the bingo balls in the diagram are placed in a bingo cage at the front of a large lecture hall and are drawn at random by a professor. You are seated in the back of the large lecture hall and can see the color of the ball drawn, but because you are too far away, you cannot see the number on the ball. Let us suppose that we want to know if event $A = \{$an odd numbered ball was drawn$\}$ occurred or not. We don't know whether A occurred and cannot observe it even if it did. But we can observe event $B = \{$a white ball was drawn$\}$, and event A and B are statistically dependent—in this case the probability of drawing an odd ball from a bingo cage containing all the balls is different from the probability of drawing an odd ball from a bingo cage containing only the white balls.

Suppose further that we have some beliefs about how likely it is that A occurred irrespective of whether B occurred. In this case, we know that seven of 18 balls are odd, resulting in $P(A) = \frac{7}{18}$. We want to know what our observation of B tells us about A. Bayes' rule tells us how to combine the information about underlying probabilities and the observable information about a draw to update our beliefs about the unobservable events. Let our prior beliefs regarding the probability of A be represented by $P(A) = \frac{7}{18}$. This function is commonly called a **prior**, representing the probability with which we believe A will occur if we did not have the chance to observe B. We also know that there are only two balls that are both white and odd numbered. So we know the probability of A and B occurring together is $P(A \cap B) = \frac{2}{18}$. Then the probability of B occurring when A has occurred is given by $P(B|A)$, the **conditional probability function**, which is defined as

$$P(B|A) = \frac{P(A \cap B)}{P(A)} = \frac{2/18}{7/18} = \frac{2}{7}. \tag{7.5}$$

In other words, the probability of B given that A has occurred is just the probability of both occurring (the fraction of times that both occur together) divided by the probability that A occurs (the fraction of times that A occurs regardless of B). This conditional probability density is often referred to as the **likelihood function**, and it tells us the probability of a ball being white given that it is odd numbered.

What we really want to know, however, is $P(A|B)$, the probability of the ball being odd given that the ball drawn was white. Rearranging equation 7.5, we find that

$$P(B|A)P(A) = P(A \cap B) = \frac{2}{18}. \tag{7.6}$$

The same calculations can be used to show that

$$P(A|B)P(B) = P(A \cap B) = \frac{2}{18}. \tag{7.7}$$

By combining equations 7.6 and 7.7, we find Bayes' rule

$$P(A|B) = \frac{P(B|A)P(A)}{P(B)} = \frac{\left(\frac{2}{7}\right)\left(\frac{7}{18}\right)}{\frac{6}{18}} = \frac{1}{3}. \tag{7.8}$$

Here, the value $P(B) = \frac{6}{18}$ results from there being a total of six white balls. Thus, if we observe a white ball being drawn, there is a $\frac{1}{3}$ probability that the ball is odd numbered.

An additional illustration of how this may be used is helpful. Suppose you knew that there were two urns full of red and white balls. Urn 1 contains 80 red balls and 20 white balls, and urn 2 contains 50 red balls and 50 white balls. Without you being able to observe, I roll a die and select an urn. If the die roll is 3 or higher, I select urn 2, and I select urn 1 otherwise. Then, I draw one ball out of the selected urn and allow you to observe its color. Suppose the ball is red. What is the probability that I have drawn from urn 1? We can rewrite equation 7.8 thus:

$$P(\text{Urn } 1|\text{Red}) = \frac{P(\text{Red}|\text{Urn } 1)P(\text{Urn } 1)}{P(\text{Red})}. \tag{7.9}$$

The unconditional probability that I have drawn from urn 1 is just the probability of rolling a 1 or a 2 on a six-sided die, $P(\text{Urn } 1) = 1/3$. The probability of drawing a red ball given urn 1 is selected is just the fraction of red balls in urn 1, $P(\text{Red}|\text{Urn }) = 4/5$. Finally, the unconditional probability of drawing a red ball can be calculated as the sum of the probability of drawing red from each urn, multiplied by the probability of drawing that urn, $P(\text{Red}) = P(\text{Red}|\text{Urn } 1)P(\text{Urn } 1) + P(\text{Red}|\text{Urn } 2)P(\text{Urn } 2)$, or $P(\text{Red}) = 4/5 \times 1/3 + 1/2 \times 2/3 = 3/5$. Thus, by equation 7.9, we can find the probability that I am drawing from urn 1, $P(\text{Urn } 1|\text{Red}) = (4/5 \times 1/3)/(3/5) = 4/9$. Thus it is more likely that I have drawn from urn 2. Economists often use Bayes' rule as a model of learning in a market setting. It can be used as a model of price expectations or as a model of learning about competitor preferences in a game.

Calibration Exercises

As anyone who has ever taught statistics can tell you, people have a hard time reasoning through questions of probability. At a very basic level, people appear to have difficulty in making accurate probabilistic predictions. An example of a probabilistic prediction is found in most weather forecasts. The meteorologist predicts, for example, a 60 percent chance of rain. There are two important components of accuracy. First, it would be nice if the probabilities associated with the prediction were either near 1 or 0. In other words, a forecast of 99 percent chance of rain is probably more useful in planning activities than a 50 percent chance of rain. We refer to this component of accuracy as **precision**. Second, to be accurate, the probabilistic prediction must occur with the frequency suggested by the associated probability. In other words, it should rain about half the time when the meteorologist forecasts a 50 percent chance of rain. We will refer to this component of accuracy as **calibration**.

There is a fundamental tradeoff in accuracy and precision. Suppose you lived in an area where it rained about one of every five days. Then, without any special knowledge of the particular weather patterns at the time, the meteorologist could simply say there was a 20 percent chance of rain each day when called on for the forecast. The forecast would be well calibrated because it would truly rain about 20 percent of the time. However, most people would be frustrated by the lack of informational content in the forecast. With greater understanding of the underlying patterns, the meteorologist can begin to forecast higher probabilities on some days and lower probabilities on other days. In fact, forecasts are very well calibrated in the short run. Thus, you can rely on the forecasts, though there are limits to their precision based on the state of meteorological science.

Economists are generally well calibrated (though again not very precise) when predicting changes in the economy in the short run. However, their calibration is significantly poorer when predicting several months ahead. They tend to overstate the probability that the economy will continue on its current course. It is generally not the case that people are well calibrated. Much of this chapter and the next deals with how individual probabilistic forecasts are biased by subtle cues in the decision process or by the process used to determine the probability of a specific event.

EXAMPLE 7.1 Of Taxicabs and Colors

Consider the following problem proposed by Daniel Kahneman and Amos Tversky:

A cab was involved in a hit and run accident at night. Two cab companies operate in the city: a Blue Cab company, and a Green Cab company. You are given the following data: 85 percent of the cabs in the city are Green and 15 percent are Blue, and a witness at the scene identified the cab involved in the accident as a Blue Cab. This witness was tested under similar visibility conditions and made correct color identifications in 80 percent of the trial instances. What is the probability that the cab involved in the accident was a Blue Cab rather than a Green one?

This question was given to participants in several experiments. Overwhelmingly, the majority believed the probability that the cab involved in the accident was a Blue Cab was 80 percent, that being the probability that the witness identifies the correct color of the cab under similar conditions. However, this ignores the underlying probability that the cab was either Blue or Green. Bayes' rule in this case states that the probability that the cab was Blue given that the witness identified it as Blue is given by

$$P(\text{Blue}|\text{Witness says Blue}) = \frac{P(\text{Witness says Blue}|\text{Blue})P(\text{Blue})}{P(\text{Witness says Blue})}. \quad (7.10)$$

Here, the prior probability that the cab was Blue is $P(\text{Blue})=0.15$. The probability that the witness identifies Blue given that the cab is Blue is $P(\text{Witness says Blue}|\text{Blue})=0.80$. Finally, the probability that the witness identifies Blue can be found by adding the probability that the cab is Blue times the probability that the witness identifies it as Blue given it truly is Blue to the probability that the cab is Green times the probability that the witness identifies it as Blue given that it is truly Green. Or, $P(\text{Witness says Blue}) = P(\text{Witness says Blue}|\text{Blue})P(\text{Blue}) + P(\text{Witness says Blue}|\text{Green})P(\text{Green}) = 0.80 \times 0.15 + 0.20 \times 0.85 = 0.29$. Substituting these values obtains

$$P(\text{Blue}|\text{Witness says Blue}) = \frac{0.80 \times 0.15}{0.29} \approx 0.41. \quad (7.11)$$

Thus, when you include the baseline probability of observing a Blue Cab, it is actually more likely that the cab was Green even if the witness identified the cab as Blue.

EXAMPLE 7.2 Bingo

David Grether conducted a set of experiments in which 341 participants were asked to guess which cage a series of bingo balls was drawn from. Three bingo cages were involved. The first cage contained six balls numbered 1 to 6. A second cage contained six balls, with four marked N and two marked G. The third cage contained six balls, with three marked N and three marked G. The experiment proceeded much like the example of Bayes' rule given earlier. Participants were put through several trials. In each trial, participants were placed so they could not see the bingo cages. They were told that a ball would be chosen from cage 1. If a certain set of numbers came up, then a series of six balls would be drawn from cage 2. If the number drawn from cage 1 did not belong to that set, then cage 3 would be used. With each draw, the letter on the ball was announced, and then the ball was replaced into the cage so that a single ball could potentially be drawn several times. The participants were then asked to record the cage they believed the series of six drawn balls came from. In many cases, the participants received a reward for correct choices.

Participants responded to the prior probability of each cage being chosen. However, their response was very muted relative to what Bayes' rule would predict. Consider for example the case where the sample included four balls marked N and two marked G. In this case, the sample exactly resembles the distribution of balls in cage 2. Nonetheless, the probability that we are drawing from cage 2 depends heavily on the initial conditions for the draw from cage 1. If, for example, we draw from cage 3 if the initial draw is equal to or smaller than 2, and we draw from cage 2 otherwise, Bayes' rule yields

$$
\begin{aligned}
P(\text{Cage 2}|4N2G) &= \frac{P(4N2G|\text{Cage 2})P(\text{Cage 2})}{P(4N2G|\text{Cage 2})P(\text{Cage 2}) + P(4N2G|\text{Cage 3})P(\text{Cage 3})} \\
&= \frac{(2/3)^4(1/3)^2(1/3)}{(2/3)^4(1/3)^2(1/3) + (1/2)^4(1/2)^2(2/3)} \approx 0.41.
\end{aligned}
\tag{7.12}
$$

However, in situations like this, the majority of people would choose cage 2 rather than cage 3. Thus, the participants appear to have looked more closely at the distribution of balls drawn than to the underlying probability of drawing from cage 2. In nearly all cases, people seemed to be swayed by how closely the draw resembled the two possible cages when making their choice than they were by the probability of drawing from either cage determined by the initial draw from cage 1.

If we were to take equation 7.12 and remove the unconditional probabilities, we would find

$$
\frac{P(4N2G|\text{Cage 2})}{P(4N2G|\text{Cage 2}) + P(4N2G|\text{Cage 3})} = \frac{(2/3)^4(1/3)^2}{(2/3)^4(1/3)^2 + (1/2)^4(1/2)^2} \approx 0.58,
\tag{7.13}
$$

which more closely approximates how people predicted which cage was being used. Like the cab example, the base rates seem to be ignored. However, Grether found other evidence suggesting that base rates are not altogether ignored. If the initial probability of drawing from cage 2 is $1/2$, then $P(\text{Cage 2}|4N2G) \approx 0.58$. Finally, if the initial probability of drawing from cage 2 is $2/3$ then $P(\text{Cage 2}|4N2G) \approx 0.73$. Thus, as the base rate shifts around, the resulting probability of drawing from cage 2 shifts around. Although people tended to favor the draw to the base rate when determining which cage to choose, the answers of some subjects did respond to the base rate. Uniformly, when the base probability of drawing from cage 2 was smaller, a smaller proportion of participants chose cage 2. This effect, however, was not large enough to bring the majority of participants into line with Bayes' rule.

Representativeness

The behavior in both of these examples shows what has become known as the **representativeness heuristic**. According to Daniel Kahneman and Amos Tversky, people who display the representativeness heuristic determine the probability of an event by the degree to which the event is similar in essential characteristics to its parent population and reflects the salient features of the process by which it is generated. In a framework of Bayesian updating, this leads to a situation in which base rates are either discounted or ignored altogether.

In Grether's experiment this is relatively easy to see. The draw of bingo balls from either cage could end up having distributions that are either identical to or close to the distributions of balls in one or the other cages. With an even distribution of N and G balls as in cage 3, it is not that unlikely to draw a sample of four N balls and two G balls. But if we did not know the probability associated with the draw from cage 1, a sample of balls with four N balls and two G balls would more probably have originated with cage 2. Given a relatively low probability of selecting cage 2 from the initial draw, it very quickly becomes less probable that the given sample was from cage 2. Nonetheless, the sample looks like cage 2. In this sense, the sample is more representative of cage 2 than of cage 3. Thus, it becomes easier to convince oneself that the draw was more probably from cage 2.

In the taxicab example, the witness identifies the taxicab as being Blue. At that point, either the taxicab is Blue and the witness is correct or the taxicab is Green and the witness is wrong. We are told the witness is 80 percent accurate. Thus, the case of the witness identifying the taxicab as being Blue is much more representative of the case in which the taxicab is actually Blue. In both cases, the information in the prior is ignored. This form of representativeness is often called **base rate neglect**.

Grether formalizes a model of base rate neglect based on the generalized Bayes rule. Because he found that people did not ignore base rates altogether, but appeared simply to discount them, he was interested in determining how large a role the base rate, or prior, played in forming beliefs. The generalized Bayes rule can be written as

$$P(A|B) = \frac{[P(B|A)]^{\beta_L}[P(A)]^{\beta_P}}{[P(B|A)]^{\beta_L}[P(A)]^{\beta_P} + [P(B|-A)]^{\beta_L}[P(-A)]^{\beta_P}}, \qquad (7.14)$$

where $-A$ is the set of all possible events that exclude A, β_L is a parameter representing the weight placed on the likelihood information, and β_P is a parameter representing the weight placed on the prior or base rate information. The generalized Bayes rule simplifies to the standard Bayes rule in the case when $\beta_L = \beta_P = 1$. Grether used the data from his experiment to estimate the weighting parameters, finding that $\beta_P = 1.82$ and $\beta_L = 2.25$. Thus, variation in the likelihood has a substantially larger influence on decisions than the variation in the prior, but the prior is not entirely ignored. Participants initially favored the likelihood just slightly more than those who had been through several trials of the experiment and thus had developed some experience. Thus, the data seem to confirm the notion of base rate neglect.

Base rate neglect can lead to biased decision making. For example, a short streak of declines in the stock indices often leads quickly to talk of a recession or a bear market. Nonetheless, bear markets are relatively rare and thus have a relatively low base rate. More often than not, a string of down days is simply a short-term chance event. Nonetheless, a string of down days is more representative of a bear market than a bull market. Here, base rate neglect could potentially drive investment decisions, leading people to jump to conclusions too early.

Base rate bias is only one example of how a representativeness heuristic can affect beliefs. In general, representativeness leads people to inflate their belief regarding the probability of events that resemble the data available. This can lead to several biases that are similar in nature to base rate neglect but that might not involve base rates at all. Several examples will be helpful in developing an understanding of how representativeness can affect beliefs and eventual decision making.

EXAMPLE 7.3   Linda

Consider the following question from Amos Tversky and Daniel Kahneman.

Linda is 31 years old, single, outspoken, and very bright. She majored in philosophy. As a student she was deeply concerned with issues of discrimination and social justice, and she also participated in antinuclear demonstrations.

Please rank the following statements by their probability, using 1 for the most probable and 8 for the least probable:

(a) Linda is a teacher in an elementary school.
(b) Linda works in a bookstore and takes yoga classes.
(c) Linda is active in the feminist movement.
(d) Linda is a psychiatric social worker.
(e) Linda is a member of the League of Women Voters.
(f) Linda is a bank teller.
(g) Linda sells insurance.
(h) Linda is a bank teller and is active in the feminist movement.

When participants in a psychological experiment responded to this question, the average rank of item (c) was 2.1; thus people believed it was very probable that Linda would be active in the feminist movement. The average rank of item (f) was 6.2 and was considered to be a relatively improbable event. But the rank of item (h) was 4.1, somewhere in between. Note that item (h) is the intersection of (c) and (f). Clearly, it must be less probable that Linda is both a bank teller *and* active in the feminist movement than that she is a bank teller at all. If it were not possible to be a bank teller and avoid being active in the feminist movement, these events should have equal probability and would thus be tied. If it is possible that she could be one and not the other, then the probability of being both must be smaller. In fact, around 90 percent of participants—even among those who have had several advanced courses in probability and statistics—ranked (h) as being more probable than (f).

Conjunction Bias

As participants rank these possibilities in their mind, they are drawn to the description of Linda and tend to rank the items in order of how representative of each item that description is. Thus, participants might have felt that relatively few bank tellers are deeply concerned with social justice, and thus this outcome is thought to be improbable. But if we think about feminist bank tellers, this group is probably much more concerned about social justice, and thus people consider this event to be more likely. This is called the **conjunction effect**. By intersecting relatively unrepresentative events (bank teller) with very representative events (feminist), the conjunction of the two is considered more probable than the unrepresentative event because the description is more representative of the combined events. Such effects may be related to the heuristics and biases that lead to stereotyping, bigotry, or other potentially undesirable phenomena. This possibility is discussed later in the chapter.

EXAMPLE 7.4   Calling the Election Early

The 2000 presidential election was notable for how difficult it was to determine the winner. In fact, it took more than a month and several legal actions before the Supreme Court finally declared George W. Bush to be the winner of the election. The confusion all centered around the vote count in Florida. Should Florida be called for Bush, Bush would have the necessary electoral votes to become president. If instead Florida were called for Albert Gore, Gore would have enough electoral votes to become president.

Election night was particularly interesting. In most modern elections, news media cooperated under the banner of Voter News Service (VNS) to compile exit polls to determine a winner. Voters were interviewed as they left the polls and asked how they voted. These numbers were then reported to the news media, and usually the news networks would project a winner of the election when they had determined they had enough data to make a prediction. News programs are very careful not to call a state for one particular candidate until they are certain they know the outcome. Their reputation as a reliable news source depends on this accuracy. From years of experience, television viewers had come to expect a declaration of a winner before they went to bed on election night. Come election night 2000, almost every state fell to the expected candidate—the candidate who had polled better in each state—but something strange happened in Florida.

Early in the counting, 7:50 P.M., the news networks predicted Gore was a lock to win Florida. Later, at 9:54 P.M., the networks retracted that lock and called the outcome ambiguous. Later, at 2:17 A.M. the next day, they stated that Bush was a lock to win Florida and the election. At this point Gore decided to concede the election to his rival. He called George W. Bush and congratulated him on the outcome. A short time later, Gore called to retract his concession in what must have been a truly awkward exchange. At 3:58 A.M., the networks retracted their projection of Florida and said the outcome of the election was ambiguous. Similar reversals happened in a couple other states as well, but neither of these was important to the outcome of the election. In response to this debacle, VNS was terminated, and news agencies began holding their projections until vote totals were certified by election officials. What led to these historic and misleading reversals? How could the prognosticators from the major networks get their statistics so incredibly wrong?

The final official vote count was 2,912,790 to 2,912,253 in favor of Bush, with 138,067 votes for other candidates. Vote totals for the moment when the election was called for Gore are not available. However, when the election was called for Bush, he had a 50,000 vote lead. So, at what point do you gain confidence enough in a trend to make a prediction? The true distribution of legal votes (ignoring votes that could not be verified) was 48.85 percent for Bush, 48.84 percent for Gore, and 2.31 percent for other candidates. When making such a forecast, we should make our prediction when we can say that the vote total we currently observe is improbable if the true vote total were to be a tie.

Let's suppose we had 6,000,000 colored balls in a jar. For simplicity let's suppose some are red and some are white (so no other candidates). We start pulling these balls out of a jar, and at some point, when we have drawn $n > 50,000$, we observe 50,000 more red than white. What is the probability of a tie given our observation? The formula for calculating such a thing is actually quite complicated. Let n_r be the number of red balls drawn, n_w the number of white balls drawn, n be the total number of balls drawn, and N be the total number of balls in the jar. Suppose that there are equal numbers of red and white balls in the jar (a tie). We can write the probability that there are k more red balls that have been drawn than white balls as

$$P(n_r - n_w > k \mid n) = \sum_{n_r = \frac{1}{2}(n+k)}^{\min\{n, \frac{N}{2}\}} \left[\frac{\binom{n}{n_r}\binom{N-n}{\frac{N}{2} - n_r}}{\binom{N}{\frac{N}{2}}} \right], \qquad (7.15)$$

where

$$\binom{x}{y} = \frac{x!}{x!(y-x)!} \qquad (7.16)$$

is the number of orderings in which x objects can be drawn from a total of y objects. This formula is somewhat difficult to calculate with large numbers. To simulate, let us suppose there are only 600 voters, with 300 voting for Bush and 300 voting for Gore. Here, a difference of 50,000 is equivalent to a difference of just five votes. Table 7.1 displays the probability of observing a five-vote difference in favor of red for various total numbers of balls drawn.

From Table 7.1, the probability of observing a five-vote difference does not drop below 20 percent until one has drawn and counted at least 550 of the 600 balls in the jar. If we scale these numbers back up to our original voting problem, it appears that probability of observing a difference of 50,000 would not drop significantly until you have counted the equivalent of 5,500,000 of the ballots. This is a poor approximation of the probabilities for 6 million ballots, but it will do for our purposes. The news networks

Table 7.1 The Probability of a Five-Vote Difference
for Various Sample Sizes

n =	Probability
595	0.031
550	0.230
500	0.292
400	0.333
300	0.342
200	0.333
100	0.292
50	0.230
5	0.031

were making projections based on precinct-by-precinct data. They only received the data as the precinct polls closed and local votes were tallied. The problem they ran into was taking account of the order of the reports.

They first received reports from suburban precincts in the east that voted mostly for Gore. Thus, if they anticipated early data to arrive from Gore precincts, they should have expected an early large lead for Gore. When the rural (Bush) districts in the west began reporting, suddenly Bush erased Gore's lead and built a 50,000-vote lead. But results still had not been reported from the urban (Gore) centers in Miami and other cities where voting totals take longer to count. The networks used a projection trigger that must have well overstated the probability that the observed trends would hold. At the time the vote was called for Bush they should have known that a 50,000 vote lead with large and heavy Gore territory still to come was not good enough for prediction. In fact, there was less than a 70 percent chance that the lead would hold. Simply put, this decision was made way too early, but despite knowing and using statistical models, they made this call.

The Law of Small Numbers

In general, psychologists and economists have found that people tend to believe that small samples from a distribution will be very similar in all respects to the population from which they are drawn. The law of large numbers tells us that when we have large numbers of observations, the sample mean of our observations will converge to the true mean. In this way, when we have a large sample of observations, it is very likely that the properties of this sample will resemble the population from which it is drawn. However, small samples do not provide the same guarantee. If we were to toss a fair coin four times, it is more likely that we should observe an outcome with either zero, one, three, or four heads than one with exactly two heads. Nonetheless, people believe that the outcome with two heads, which is most representative of a fair coin toss, is more likely than it truly is.

This tendency to exaggerate the probability that a small sample is representative of the underlying process that generated it has been facetiously named the **law of small numbers** by Amos Tversky and Daniel Kahneman. As the name suggests, people treat small samples of data as if they were dealing with much larger samples of data. Thus, for example, one might rely too heavily on trends in early voting when predicting the outcome of an election. Similarly, one might rely too heavily on performance data over a short period of time. For example, each year a list of mutual funds that had the highest return in the last year is widely circulated in the financial press. Many people select which mutual funds to purchase based upon this list. However, it is very seldom that the results for any year are good predictors of performance in the future. For example, only three of the top 10 mutual fund families for 2008 were also in the top 10 for 2007. Even when we consider the top performer over five years, only four of the top 10 remained on the list in both 2007 and 2008. Such a high level of volatility suggests that performance may be almost entirely random. Nonetheless, people behave as if the differences are systematic because the small sample is taken to be representative of the true underlying differences in mutual fund performance.

Matthew Rabin has proposed a behavioral model of learning according to the law of small numbers. It will be helpful to first describe his model intuitively. Suppose we are considering the repeated flipping of a fair coin. We know the probability of a heads is 0.5 for any flip, and we know that this probability does not depend on whether heads or tails was drawn previously. We can represent the beliefs of someone regarding what will be drawn as a distribution of balls in an urn containing N balls. I will refer to this as the *mental urn* to emphasize that it is merely a concept used in modeling and does not truly exist. Half of the balls are labeled "heads," representing the probability that a heads would be tossed, and half of the balls are labeled "tails." This person believes that a sequence of tosses should be representative of the true underlying probability and thus should display about half heads. Each toss draws one of the balls from the urn.

Suppose the mental urn originally contained six balls, with three labeled "heads" and three labeled "tails." The original beliefs are thus that the probability of a heads is $3/6 = 0.5$. Suppose then that the first coin is tossed and it comes up heads. This removes one of the balls labeled heads from the mental urn, so that the beliefs for the next toss are that the probability of a heads is $2/6 \approx 0.3$. Thus, when a heads is tossed, this observer feels that it is more likely that a tails will be tossed to balance out the sequence, making it more representative of the overall probability.

Further, Rabin supposes that the mental urn is refreshed periodically, for example after every two tosses. In this process, the number of balls in the mental urn determines how biased the observer may be. For example, if we had considered a mental urn with 1,000 balls, the bias would be very small. In this case, after tossing one heads the believed probability of a heads moves from 0.5 to 0.499. On the other hand, if the number of balls in the mental urn were two, the believed probability would move from 0.5 to 0. This process results in a belief that draws are negatively correlated when in actuality they are independent. Thus, the observer believes heads are more likely following tails than following heads. In actuality the probability is always 0.5 regardless of whether a heads or tails has recently been tossed. Refreshing the balls in the mental urn has the effect that the law of small numbers is applied locally to a series of draws rather than to the overall process. This can be considered the sample window for the law of small numbers.

Rabin's model can be used to describe the process of inference. For example, suppose that Freddie[1] faces the problem of deciding on whether a mutual fund is a good investment or not. In this case, suppose that there are only two types of mutual funds: good and bad. A good mutual fund receives a good return 2/3 of the time and a bad return 1/3 of the time; a bad mutual fund receives a good return 1/2 of the time and a bad return 1/2 of the time. Freddie believes that only 1/3 of mutual funds are good. In examining the previous returns, he finds that a mutual fund had the following performance over the past five years: good, good, bad, bad, good. A rational person could use Bayes' rule to find

$$P(\text{Good Fund}|3\,\text{Good}\,2\,\text{Bad})$$
$$=\frac{P(3\,\text{Good}\,2\,\text{Bad}|\text{Good Fund})P(\text{Good Fund})}{P(3\,\text{Good}\,2\,\text{Bad}|\text{Good Fund})P(\text{Good Fund})+P(3\,\text{Good}\,2\,\text{Bad}|\text{Bad Fund})P(\text{Bad Fund})}$$
$$=\frac{(2/3)^3(1/3)^2(2/3)}{(2/3)^3(1/3)^2(2/3)+(1/2)^3(1/2)^2(1/3)}\approx0.68.$$

$$(7.17)$$

Alternatively, suppose Freddie believes in the law of small numbers and has two mental urns. One mental urn represents the probability of drawing good or bad returns if the mutual fund is good. The other mental urn represents the probability of good or bad returns if the mutual fund is bad. This problem is rather similar to Grether's exercise. Suppose further that the "good" mental urn has three balls: two labeled "good return" and one labeled "bad return." Also suppose that the "bad" mental urn has four balls: two labeled "good return" and two labeled "bad return." Finally, let us suppose that after every two draws the balls in each urn are refilled and refreshed. Then the probability of observing the draw given that the mutual fund is good now depends on the order in which we observe good and bad returns. For example, given that we are drawing from the "good" urn, the probability that the first ball drawn is labeled "good return" is 2/3. The subsequent probability that the second ball drawn is labeled "good return" is then 1/2 (because the first ball has been removed). After the second ball is drawn, the urn is refreshed and now the probability that the third ball is good is 2/3 again. Calculating this way, the probability of observing this sequence of draws from a good fund is

$$P(\text{Good Good Bad Bad Good}|\text{Good Fund})=(2/3)(1/2)(1/3)(0)(2/3)=0. \quad (7.18)$$

The same sequence from the bad fund would yield

$$P(\text{Good Good Bad Bad Good}|\text{Bad Fund})=(1/2)(1/3)(1/2)(1/3)(1/2)=1/72.$$

$$(7.19)$$

---

[1] Rabin refers to all believers in the law of small numbers as Freddie.

Thus, applying Bayes' rule as a believer in the law of small numbers yields

$$P(\text{Good Fund}|\text{Good Good Bad Bad Good}) = \frac{0 \times (2/3)}{0 \times (2/3) + (1/72) \times (1/3)} = 0.$$

(7.20)

In this case, Freddie feels it is too improbable that a good fund would have two bad years in a row. Once the second bad year in a row is realized, Freddie immediately believes there is no chance that he could be observing a good fund. He thus would choose not to invest, when in fact there is a higher probability that he is dealing with a good fund than a bad fund. Adjusting the size of the mental urns so that they are larger brings the result more closely in line with Bayes' rule. Further, refreshing the urns less often (while holding the number of balls constant) leads to a greater expectation of correlated draws before refreshing the urn. Thus, Freddie will infer more and more information from the second, third, or fourth draw before the mental urns are refreshed. Note in this example that the "good fund" was excluded on a second draw for exactly this reason.

In general, the law of small numbers leads people to jump to conclusions from very little information. Early counts from a sample will be taken as overly representative of the whole, leading to snap judgments. When making judgments based on data, it is important to consider the true variability and the amount of information contained in any sample of data. Early judgments may be based on an odd or nonrepresentative sample. Further, one must be aware that others are likely to judge their efforts based on small and potentially unrepresentative samples of their output. Thus, a newly hired worker might do well to put in extra hours early on when initial judgments are being formed.

EXAMPLE 7.5   Standards of Replication

In scientific inquiry, replication forms the standard by which a research discovery is validated. Thus, one scientist tests a hypothesis using an experiment and publishes the results. Others who may be interested validate these results by running identical experiments and trying to replicate the outcome. But what constitutes replication?

Earlier in this chapter we reviewed the mechanics of a statistical test. Nearly all experimental results are reported in terms of a statistical test. For example, a scientist may be interested in the effect of a treatment (say, the presence of chemical A) on a particular population (say, bacteria B). Thus, he would take several samples of bacteria B and apply chemical A under controlled conditions. He would also take additional samples of bacteria B and keep them in identical controlled conditions without introducing chemical A. He would then measure the object of his hypothesis in each sample. For example, he may be interested in measuring the number of living bacteria cells remaining after the experiment. He would measure this number from each sample and then use statistics to test the initial hypothesis that the means were equal across the treatment and control samples.

Typically, scientists reject this hypothesis if there is less than a 5 percent chance of observed difference in means, given the true means were equal. This is generally tested using a test statistic of the following form

$$t = \frac{\hat{\mu}_1 - \hat{\mu}_2}{\sqrt{\frac{n_1 S_1^2 + n_2 S_2^2}{n_1 + n_2 - 2} \left(\frac{1}{n_1} + \frac{1}{n_2} \right)}}, \tag{7.21}$$

where $\hat{\mu}_i$ is the sample mean for treatment i, n_i is the sample size for treatment i, and S_i^2 is the sample variance for treatment i. We generally test the null hypothesis that $\mu_1 = \mu_2$ against the alternative hypothesis that $\mu_1 \neq \mu_2$. With larger samples, this test statistic is approximately distributed as a standard normal. If the two means are equal, then t should be close to 0. If the two means are different, then t should be farther away from zero. The generally accepted statistical theory suggests that given reasonable numbers of observations, if $t > 2.00$ or $t < -2.00$, then there is less than a 5 percent chance that the two means are equal. In this case we would call the difference statistically significant. However, if we obtain a weaker result, we might want to obtain a larger sample to confirm the difference. Note that if the means and sample variances remain the same, increasing the sample sizes makes t larger.

Amos Tversky and Daniel Kahneman wanted to see if the law of small numbers played a role in scientists' understanding of how replication works. They asked 75 Ph.D. psychologists with substantial statistical training to consider a result reported by a colleague that seems implausible. The result was obtained by running 15 subjects through an experiment yielding a test statistic of $t = 2.46$ that rejects the initial hypothesis of equal means between the two treatments at the $\alpha = 0.0275$ level (in other words, the 97.25 percent confidence interval does not contain the possibility that both treatment and control have the same mean). Another investigator attempts to replicate the result with another 15 subjects, finding the same direction of difference in means, but the difference in means in this case is not large enough to reject the initial hypothesis of equal means at the industry standard $\alpha = 0.05$ level. The psychologists were then asked to consider how strong the difference in means would need to be in order to consider the replication successful. The majority of respondents thought that if the replication resulted in a test statistic that was any lower than $t = 1.70$, then we fail to reproduce the result, calling the initial result into question. Hence they would look at any study that produced $t < 1.70$ as contradicting the previous study.

Let's look at our test statistic again. In the first study, we obtain

$$t^1 = \frac{\hat{\mu}_1^1 - \hat{\mu}_2^1}{\sqrt{\frac{15 S_1^2 + 15 S_2^2}{28} \left(\frac{2}{15} \right)}} = 2.46, \tag{7.22}$$

where the superscript 1 indicates that the result is from the initial sample. With 15 new observations, the replication results in

$$t^2 = \frac{\hat{\mu}_1^2 - \hat{\mu}_2^2}{\sqrt{\frac{15 S_1^2 + 15 S_2^2}{28} \left(\frac{2}{15} \right)}} = 1.70. \tag{7.23}$$

Now suppose instead that we combined the data from the first and second studies. Supposing that the sample variances were identical, we would find

$$\hat{\mu}_1 - \hat{\mu}_2 = \frac{2.46 + 1.70}{2}\sqrt{\frac{15S_1^2 + 15S_2^2}{28}\left(\frac{2}{15}\right)} = 2.08\sqrt{\frac{15S_1^2 + 15S_2^2}{28}\left(\frac{2}{15}\right)} \qquad (7.24)$$

and thus,

$$t = \frac{2.08\sqrt{\frac{15S_1^2 + 15S_2^2}{28}\left(\frac{2}{15}\right)}}{\sqrt{\frac{30S_1^2 + 30S_2^2}{58}\left(\frac{2}{30}\right)}} = 2.99 > 2.46. \qquad (7.25)$$

In truth, if we conducted a new study and found $t = 1.70$, this should strengthen our confidence in the results of the previous study, now being able to reject the initial hypothesis at the $\alpha = 0.0056$ level. Instead, the psychologists believed the second study contradicts the first. Owing to belief in the law of small numbers, they believe that if the first study were true, the second study should have an extremely high probability of producing a test statistic that is very close to the statistic in the first study. In fact, they exaggerate this probability. In other words, they believe the data should be more representative of the underlying process than it truly is given the small sample sizes.

Similar questions asked the psychologists to consider a student who had run an experiment with 40 animals in each of two treatments, finding a test statistic of 2.70. The result was very important theoretically. The psychologists were asked to consider whether a replication was needed before publication, and if so, how many observations would be needed. Most of the psychologists recommended a replication, with the median number of recommended subjects being 20. When asked what to do if the resulting replication produced a test statistic of only 1.24 (which cannot reject the initial hypothesis of equal means) a third of the psychologists suggested trying to find an explanation for the difference between the initial study subjects and the subjects included in the replication. Tversky and Kahneman note that the statistical difference between the initial group and the replication group was incredibly small. The treatment effects in the replication are about 2/3 of the treatment effects in the initial sample. Trying to explain this difference is like trying to explain why a penny came up heads on one toss and tails on another. The differences are almost certainly due to random error. Nonetheless, believers in the law of small numbers can attribute even small differences in very small samples to systematic causes. In the pursuit of scientific progress and publications, this can have disastrous consequences. There are numerous examples of early medical studies where failure to understand the statistics of replication has done real harm to people.

EXAMPLE 7.6   Punishments and Rewards

The representativeness heuristic can lead people to believe in causal effects that are nonexistent. For example, suppose you managed a flight school. Psychologists have generally suggested that positive reinforcement, or rewarding good behavior, is an effective tool in teaching. Hence, you decide to reward trainees after a particularly good flight. After several months of this policy, you begin to notice that after each pilot has been rewarded for a good flight, their next flight tends to be worse—sometimes much worse. In fact, almost no rewarded pilot has ever improved in the next following flight. Seeing this, you begin to question the psychologists and revamp your policy. Now, instead of rewarding good flights, you decide to punish bad flights. Again several months pass and you begin to evaluate the results. This time you are satisfied to learn that students almost always improve after receiving punishment. Clearly this must be a very effective policy.

In fact, Daniel Kahneman and Amos Tversky put a similar question to a sample of graduate students and found that all agreed with the logic of this story. This example arose out of Daniel Kahneman's experience in the military in which flight instructors had concluded that reward leads to worse performance and punishment leads to better performance. Yet, in flight training one is very unlikely to make much improvement from one flight to the next. Progress takes a long time. Thus, big changes in performance are most likely due to random variation in conditions (e.g., weather, task, individual rest or alertness) rather than changes in skill. Thus, a particularly good flight is almost certainly due to a very lucky draw. Suppose the probability of an especially good flight was 0.10. If rewards and punishment had no effect on pilots' performance, following any good flight there would be a 0.90 chance of doing worse on the next flight. As well, if there was a 0.10 chance of a particularly bad flight, then there would be a 0.90 chance of improving on the next flight. This is called **reversion to mean**. Performance near the mean or average is the most probable outcome. Thus, high performance is most likely to be followed by low performance, and low performance is most likely to be followed by high performance. However, people have a hard time perceiving reversion to the mean as a possible cause in this case.

In a more general context, reversion to the mean can appear to be some mysterious but systematic cause of apparently random events. For example, suppose you observed a slot machine over time. Because of reversion to the mean, you would notice that after a large payout, the machine is likely to return a smaller payout on the next pull. Further, if you observed a zero payout (which is most common), there is a higher probability of a higher payout on the next pull. This could lead you to reason that you should play slot machines that haven't given a prize recently, and switch machines if you win anything. This, of course, is statistical fallacy. In truth, the probability of each possible payout is the same on each pull. It is not the probability of an $x payout that has increased or decreased; this remains the same with each pull; rather, it is the probability of a higher or lower payout than the previous pull. Because the previous pull is a random event, it is the threshold that determines what is higher or lower that is moving. If you feel that playing a slot machine after a zero payout pull is a reasonable gamble, you should also be willing to pull after a large payout on the same machine.

Rabin's model of beliefs can be used to model this anomaly. Suppose the gambler has a mental urn with 10 balls, one labeled "win" and nine labeled "lose." With each play, a ball is drawn from the mental urn, adjusting the perceived probability of a win on the next pull. After a series of zero-dollar payouts (lose), the probability of a win increases. After a single win, the gambler might perceive that there is a zero probability of a second win, and thus stop. Thus, the law of small numbers can lead people to misinterpret a series of random numbers, leading them to believe they are systematic.

EXAMPLE 7.7   The Hot Hand

In watching a basketball game, it is hard not to be amazed by the long streaks of shots made by the best players. Often sportscasters keep track of how many shots a particular player has made in a row without missing. In fact, 91 percent of basketball fans believe that after a player has made one shot, he has a higher probability of making the next shot. This leads 84 percent of basketball fans believe that it is important to get the ball into the hands of a player who has made several shots in a row.

Thomas Gilovich, Robert Vallone, and Amos Tversky used videotapes of basketball games as well as records to test for shooting streaks. Their analysis focused primarily on the Philadelphia 76ers; however, similar results were found with the New Jersey Nets and the New York Knicks. In interviewing the 76ers themselves, they found that the players believed in systematic shooting streaks. Players said that once they have made a few shots in a row, they felt they could not miss. Gilovich, Vallone, and Tversky then used data collected over an entire season to calculate the percentage of shots hit given the previous performance. If the player had just missed one shot, he hit 54 percent of his next shots. If the player had just hit one shot, he hit 51 percent of his next shots. After hitting two shots, his probability was 50 percent. Basketball fans, when surveyed, had expected a 50 percent shooter to have a 61 percent chance of making a second shot once the first was made. The estimated correlation coefficient between the outcome of one shot and the next was −0.039. This value is small enough that it is not statistically different from zero, suggesting that streaks are an illusion. Each shot is essentially independent of the previous shot. They are unrelated draws from the same distribution. Gilovich, Vallone, and Tversky also analyzed game-by-game shooting percentages to see if a player's performance in a single game could be distinguished from any other game. Similarly, they found no evidence that players have hot and cold shooting nights. They also found no evidence that free-throw shooting follows streaks. For example, Larry Bird, in the 1980–81 season, made 91 percent of his free throws that followed a missed free throw, and he only made 88 percent when following a hit free throw.

The Cornell University basketball team was enlisted to test the **hot hand** theory that players go on hot or cold streaks. Players were paired up. One would shoot and the other would observe the shooter. Each was allowed to bet either a high or low amount on each shot. If they bet the low amount they would win 2 cents for a made shot and lose 1 cent for a missed shot. If they bet high, they would win 5 cents for a made shot and lose 4 cents for a missed shot. The bets of both the shooters and the observers were highly correlated with the outcome of the previous shot. Thus, they bet high more often when the previous shot was made. However, predictions were relatively unrelated to the outcome of the shot being predicted. Several analyses have found that the perception of the hot hand affects the betting markets for teams that are on winning streaks. The point spread necessary for a win widens as the team lengthens it streak. Yet the wider the point spread, the higher the probability that the team loses.

Clearly, both players and fans misperceive the relationship between shots taken. In fact, after publication of this study there was a fair amount of outrage on the part of coaches. Several prominent coaches from both the pro and college ranks criticized the findings heavily. For example, Bobby Knight was prominently quoted in the newspapers suggesting that the researchers did not understand the game. Alternatively, we might consider these coaches to be operating with a mental urn that is too small. People infer too much information from the streak of hits that are entirely consistent with shooting averages. Rather, they believe they are drawing from a more favorable mental urn—an urn representing an event that does not actually exist.

The Gambler's Fallacy

When playing the roulette wheel at a casino, a wheel with red and black sections is spun, and gamblers place bets on the color of the section that will come to rest under a pointer. Clearly, each spin is an independent random event, and state gambling commissions verify the fairness of the equipment on a regular basis.

Rachel Croson and James Sundali observed casino gamblers placing bets on a roulette wheel. They found that, for example, if red had been spun on the previous spin, or even up to the previous three spins, people tended to bet about 50 percent of the time on red and about 50 percent of the time on black. However, when the number of spins has reached four in a row, people start betting against the streak. After four in a row of black, about 58 percent bet red. After five in a row of black, about 65 percent bet red. After six or more in a row of black, 85 percent bet red. Nonetheless, a black or red draw is just as likely after six black spins in a row as it is after one black spin in a row. This phenomenon is called the **gambler's fallacy**. In this case, people know the probability of each outcome, and they believe (according the law of small numbers) that the draws should even out to the correct proportions over time. Thus, they begin to bet more and more heavily on the outcome that has appeared least.

At first glance, this might appear to be the exact opposite of the hot hand bias. In the hot hand, a streak leads one to bet on continuing the streak. In the gambler's fallacy, a streak leads one to bet against the streak. The key difference is that in the hot hand bias, there is not a known probability. Thus, the gambler is trying to infer the probability from the performance. Hence, according to Rabin's model, the gambler is trying to figure out which mental urn best represents the data. The particular mental urn chosen might change as the result of a streak if the mental urns are small. Alternatively, under the gambler's fallacy the probability of each outcome is transparent. For example, a standard roulette wheel has 18 red sections, 18 black sections, and two green sections. Each section is of identical size, resulting in a probability of red of about 47 percent. In this case, the gambler knows what mental urn he is drawing from but uses the remaining contents of the urn to predict the future outcomes. Thus, the more red draws, the fewer red balls in the mental urn and the higher the probability of a black on the next draw. The same pattern can be observed in the play of state lotteries. After a winning number is drawn, the number of people choosing that number in the next day's lottery falls by roughly one third, and it remains below normal for close to a month (or until the number is drawn again).

Another interesting and potentially related anomaly has been found in lottery play. People ascribe more value to a ticket when they are allowed to choose the numbers than when the numbers are chosen for them. Ellen Langer conducted a study in which she sold lottery tickets to about 50 people under the guise of a Super Bowl–themed lottery. Each lottery ticket had the picture of a professional football player on it and a corresponding number. Half of the participants were allowed to choose their ticket, and the other half were assigned tickets. On the day of the drawing, participants were approached by one of the experimenters and asked how much they would be willing to sell their ticket for. Those who were assigned the ticket were willing to sell for about $1.96, but those who had chosen would not part with the ticket unless given $8.67. This and similar experiments have shown that people believe that they might somehow control random events. For example, the **illusion of control** leads people to throw dice harder when they want to roll higher numbers when playing craps. Further, people are willing to bet more on the unknown outcome of a random event when they are told the event will happen in the future than when they are told it happened in the past. In many cases, people might convince themselves that they have the ability to influence things that are well beyond their own control.

Conservatism versus Representativeness

Representativeness, or learning too much from the given information, appears to be pervasive in its influence on learning and decision making. Nonetheless, people do not always jump to conclusions. In fact, Ward Edwards conducted a series of experiments in the 1960s that found what he termed **conservatism**. If representativeness is learning too fast, conservatism can be thought of as learning too slowly. He conducted a series of experiments that look very similar to the later work of David Grether except that there were hundreds of balls in each container and still only a small number of draws. In his experiments he finds that the base rate, or prior information about which ball is drawn, receives more weight than would be implied by Bayes' rule. Thus, the subjects stick to their initial beliefs regardless of the information presented. What accounts for the difference?

The work of Robin Hogarth and Hillel Einhorn has tried to answer exactly this question by presenting participants various types and series of information to see how it influences beliefs. When the information is less complicated and easier to understand, people seem to update their beliefs too quickly, displaying a **recency** effect. Recency is consistent with the representativeness heuristic. When the information is very complicated and requires real cognitive effort to discern, they found that initial beliefs persist—a **primacy** effect. Primacy is consistent with Edwards's conservatism. Thus, in Edwards's experiment, it may be that drawing a small number of balls from distributions with hundreds of balls provides information that is too difficult to process, leading to conservatism. The implication is that simple messages are much more likely to change people's minds. A well-reasoned, though complex, argument might not have a chance to succeed.

EXAMPLE 7.9   Diseases and Accidental Death

Among the decisions most closely associated with risk and risk perceptions are the precautions we take to prolong our lives. There are many different ways one might die and many different actions we might take to prevent each particular mode of death. For example, one who has a family history of stroke could alter one's diet to reduce the possibility of a stroke. Which actions are worth taking depends heavily on how likely we believe a particular mode of death is. For example, the overwhelming majority (around

80 percent) feel that accidental death (e.g., car accident, accidental fall) is much more likely than death by stroke. This should lead people to worry more about their driving habits or their proximity to cliffs than they would about diet. However, in truth, you are about twice as likely to die from a stroke as you are from all accidental sources combined. In fact you are more than 15 times more likely to die from some disease than you are to die from some accident. Only 57 percent believe that death by disease is more likely than death by accident. About 70 percent believe that there are more victims of homicide than suicide. In actuality there are close to 1.5 suicides for every homicide.

Although there are many potential explanations for why people might so poorly predict the possible sources of death, Sarah Lichtenstein and a team of researchers propose that news coverage may be partially to blame. They compared the amount of newspaper coverage for 41 various causes of death to the estimates of 61 participants of the prevalence of the various causes, and they found a very high correlation. Participants believed that causes like homicide, which are covered much more frequently by the press than stroke, were much more prevalent. Importantly, the newspaper coverage was not very related to actual prevalence of the various causes of death.

Consistent with representativeness, Lichtenstein also found evidence that people ignore base rates in their data. For example, participants felt that death due to smallpox was much more likely than death due to complications arising from smallpox vaccination. In fact, partially owing to smallpox vaccinations, cases of smallpox are very rare and thus death by smallpox is very rare. Alternatively, nearly all school-age children have been vaccinated for smallpox. Although the probability death from being vaccinated for smallpox is very small, the sheer number of vaccinations leads to a much higher prevalence of death by vaccination than death by the disease itself.

EXAMPLE 7.10 **Begins with R**

If we were to take a Standard English dictionary and tabulate the number of words contained therein, do you believe we would find more words that begin with the letter R or that have R in the third position? Amos Tversky and Daniel Kahneman asked 152 participants this question, as well as identical questions for the letters K, L, N, and V. If you were to write down as many words as you know that begin with the letter R, you would likely fill the list rather easily. This is because we tend to classify words by their first letter. We often list words alphabetically. Further, these words would all have the same initial sound. Alternatively, if you were asked to construct a list of all the words you knew that had R as the third letter, the list would likely be considerably shorter. We tend not to classify words with the same third letter together. This is an unfamiliar task and so we might fail to produce much of a list. In fact, English has more words that have R in the third letter than in the first. For example, in this paragraph so far, 16 words have R in the third letter, but only one begins with R. Participants believed that words beginning with the letter R would be about twice as numerous as those with R as the third letter. Similar results were achieved for each of the other letters, though each appears more often as a third letter than as a first letter.

Availability Heuristic

As illustrated in the previous two examples, people tend to assess the probability of an event based on how easily an instance of the event may be recalled. This tendency to judge probability based on the difficulty one has in recalling an event has been termed the **availability heuristic**. The availability heuristic naturally leads people to exaggerate the probability of events that are easily recalled and underestimate the probability of events that are difficult to recall. Thus, newspaper coverage of violent deaths could lead one to believe that such deaths are common. At the same time, the lack of news coverage for deaths by disease could lead one to judge these deaths to be uncommon in comparison, despite their statistical prevalence. Such results could influence the actions of people worried about their eventual demise. The availability bias may be a useful tool for a policymaker or marketer. It is no surprise that smokers tend to view smoking as less of a threat of death than nonsmokers. However, it might surprise you that both groups significantly overestimate the probability of death from smoking. By highly publicizing the health risks from smoking, information campaigns have biased public opinion, causing people to believe that cigarettes are more lethal than they truly are. Nonetheless, such a view almost certainly reduces the risk to others from secondhand smoke as well as the true risks from smoking to the people who might have smoked otherwise.

The availability heuristic depends heavily on exposure to the possible events and on the cognitive process that is necessary to recall events. Newspapers and public information campaigns can affect exposure, making the events that are discussed or viewed seem more prevalent. Alternatively, the word-construction task illustrates how cognitive processes can bias probability judgment. Tasks that are unfamiliar, such as constructing words with a specific third letter, results in underestimating the probability of the associated outcome.

As another example, consider a bus route with 10 potential bus stops. How many possible routes could be constructed that stop at exactly two of the 10 bus stops? Is this more or fewer than the number of routes that could be constructed that stop at eight of the 10 bus stops? In fact the number is identical. Nonetheless, the first task seems easier given the apparent large number of potential stopping places relative to the number of stops. The task of producing the eight stop possibilities is more difficult. Thus, most people intuitively predict that there are more possible two-stop routes than eight-stop routes. Similar results have been found in consumer evaluations of the risk of product failures. If the failures have occurred with brands that have interesting or distinctive names, people are much more likely to assess the probability of failure as being high. The distinctive name enables them to remember the failure.

One phenomenon related to the availability heuristic is the **false consensus**. People have the tendency to believe that others hold the same opinions and preferences that they themselves hold. Thus, people might exaggerate the extent to which their views and actions are normal or are similar to those of others in the general population.

EXAMPLE 7.11   Earthquake Insurance

The availability heuristic can lead to some strange behavior when dealing with risk and uncertainty. Roger Shelor, Dwight Anderson, and Mark Cross note a prominent example. On October 17, 1989, at 5:04 P.M. (just before game 3 of a World Series matchup between the Oakland Athletics and the San Francisco Giants) a major earthquake struck the San Francisco Bay area. The earthquake registered 7.1 on the Richter scale, causing buildings and highways to collapse in San Francisco and Oakland. The quake killed dozens of people and caused several billions of dollars in damage.

One might think that such an event would have severe and negative implications for the insurance industry. After such an event, the insurance industry is responsible for restoring all damaged property that was covered by earthquake insurance. Unintuitively, stock prices for insurance companies rose significantly following the 1989 earthquake. Those who follow the market for earthquake insurance have noted that following a major earthquake, the demand for earthquake insurance spikes. The prevalence of news coverage and the visions of the damage leads people to temporarily consider earthquakes more probable and thus to seek insurance against the possible damage. Along the fault where the quake has occurred, the risk actually declines, with the earthquake itself relieving some of the pressure on the fault line. Thus, people insure just as the probability of an event decreases. In fact, the increase in demand for earthquake insurance observed following the 1989 earthquake more than offset the billions of dollars in losses the earthquake generated. Further, the increase in demand was not just limited to the San Francisco Bay area. Rather, earthquake insurance demand increased substantially all across the country—even in areas where earthquakes are truly rare.

Bias, Bigotry, and Availability

Hiring an employee often represents a substantial and risky investment. Once the person is hired, usually a substantial amount of time must be invested in training the new employee to fill that particular position. It could take several months to discover if the new hire is a poor fit, is undereducated for that particular job, or might have a less-than-desirable work ethic. Even once a poor fit is identified, it can cost substantial resources to fire an employee in a way that minimizes the chance of a lawsuit or other undesirable situations. Once a want ad is placed, interested parties often apply for the job by sending a résumé and perhaps filling out a form. At that point, a manager or human resources specialist examines the résumés and identifies the most-promising candidates. These candidates are called in for interviews, after which the winning candidate is identified. At each step of the process, the employer must evaluate candidates based on imperfect information and assess the probability that the candidate will be a good fit for the job. With so little information to work with, there is substantial room for behavioral heuristics to step in.

In the past few decades, government and private employers have been under tremendous pressure to eliminate racial bias in hiring practices. Many have argued that competitive markets should eliminate racial discrimination. Intuitively, any firm willing to hire the most productive workers at the going wage will make a larger profit and drive discriminating firms out of business. Thus (absent any racial preference by customers) employers should be interested in hiring in a way that ignores race. Employers prominently advertise that they are equal opportunity employers, implying that they have systems in place to ensure a fair evaluation of people who belong to a race that has been historically discriminated against. Further, federal and other government offices must adhere to guidelines governing the evaluation of minority candidates. With the tremendous changes in the evaluation process, one would expect evaluation of résumés and candidates to be fair and evenhanded.

Marianne Bertrand and Sendhil Mullainathan sought to test just how fair the employment market was. They conducted an experiment in which they fabricated résumés for a large number of fictitious people. They randomly assigned names to résumés, with some names intentionally chosen to signal racial background. For example, some résumés bore the names Todd or Brad, and others bore the names Jamal or Darnell. This latter group was selected to suggest that the applicant was black. Because the names were randomly assigned to résumés, the quality of the résumés was held constant across racial soundingness of the names. After sending the résumés in response to job advertisements, the researchers recorded the number of callbacks they received for each resume. White-sounding names had about a 9.5 percent chance of receiving a callback for an interview. Alternatively, black-sounding names received callbacks only 6.5 percent of the time—about one third less. This pattern held true in government job openings as well as private-sector jobs. If employers are actively trying to even the playing field, why would they discriminate against minority applicants with identical credentials? In fact, many employers included in this study were surprised by the findings and contacted the authors of the study for information on how to improve. Although some employers purposely discriminate against minorities, there appears also to be a group that unintentionally discriminates. Why might this happen?

There are many candidate causes. However, the availability heuristic might provide a clue. Myron Rothbart and a team of researchers conducted several psychology experiments examining the formation of stereotypes. In one experiment, people were shown a series of statements about hypothetical people belonging to a hypothetical group, such as "John is lazy." The same statement may be shown several times in the sequence. Rothbart found that when dealing with a smaller population of people (16), participants are able to correctly predict the proportion of people in a group displaying particular traits. However, when the number of people is larger (64), the predicted proportion displaying a trait depends on how often the phrases including that trait were repeated. Thus, if "John is lazy" was displayed four times in the sequence, the participant would begin to think that more of the people in the group were lazy. In other words, the frequency of a message might influence the availability of the message, leading to stereotyping. Thus, when large numbers of news articles talk about racial difference in academic performance and achievement, crime rates, or other potential indicators of the desirability of a potential job candidate, they might inadvertently alter the treatment of people belonging to a particular race.

A separate experiment sought to determine how extreme traits in a small portion of a population might influence availability and thus stereotyping. Participants were told the height of 50 men, one at a time, and later asked to guess the number of them who were taller than 6 feet. In both treatments, exactly 10 of the men were taller than 6 feet, and the mean height was 5 feet 10 inches. In the extreme condition, the tallest man was 6 feet 11 inches, and in the control condition the tallest man was 6 feet 4 inches. In the control, people believed there had been about 10 men taller than 6 feet, and in the extreme condition they believed it was 15 men. Thus, because the same number were much taller than 6 feet, people thought more of them were taller than 6 feet. The extremeness of the height led to greater availability of the trait when evaluating the group. Similarly, examples of extreme behavior by even a small number in a group can lead to unfair stereotyping of the whole. Such biases would be difficult to eliminate when making subjective judgments of résumés with very little information about individual character or ability. Firms may be able to overcome such biases by using more-objective measures to make a first pass at résumés (e.g., highest degree completed, years of experience). If subjective decisions are held off until the number of candidates is small, and the decision maker has been able to interview each candidate, the effects of such stereotyping may be minimized.

History and Notes

Psychologist Ward Edwards began to examine Bayes' rule as a behavioral model in the late 1950s. His interest was primarily to discover the cognitive processes behind information processing and the factors that could affect that process. His early work on conservatism was highly influential in the later work of David Grether, Daniel Kahneman, Amos Tversky, and others. Related work by Edwards examined how people misperceive probabilities in general, finding generally that people overestimate small probabilities and underestimate large probabilities. As you will see in later chapters, this finding became foundational in the study of behavioral decision under uncertainty. Edwards advised and mentored Amos Tversky. Edwards's work fed directly into Tversky and Kahneman's first study introducing the representativeness heuristic and later related work developing the concept of the law of small numbers. Ongoing work by economists has sought to incorporate these concepts into mathematical models and explore applications to economic decision making. The availability heuristic is a related concept whereby the small representative samples are the events that are most easily recalled. Although it is clearly an important determinant of economic behavior (see the earthquake example), less work has been done to formalize the availability heuristic in economic modeling.

Biographical Note

Ziv Koren/Polaris/Newscom

Daniel Kahneman (1934–)

B.A., Hebrew University of Jerusalem, 1954; Ph.D., University of California at Berkeley, 1961; held faculty positions at Hebrew University in Jerusalem, University of British Columbia, University of California at Berkeley, and Princeton University

Daniel Kahneman received his undergraduate training in psychology and mathematics and his Ph.D. in psychology. Following this undergraduate training, he served in the Israeli military, where he was assigned to evaluate the character of new recruits to determine whether they were fit for officer training. He noted after some experience that their methods had very little predictive ability, yet that they were still used to determine admission to the officer ranks. He dubbed this puzzle the *illusion of validity*, and he later used this concept in his research. He credits many of the tasks he performed in the military as leading directly to the lines of research for which he has become so well known. He describes his early career as "humdrum," consisting of rather tame research. When Amos Tversky by chance discussed the conservatism work of Edwards in one of Kahneman's classes, a debate ensued regarding whether people jump to conclusions or fail to react to new information. From this debate, the collaborative effort of the two was born. Kahneman's contributions to the psychology of judgment and decision making, primarily coauthored with Tversky, provided the foundation for much of behavioral economics. His later collaborations with Richard Thaler formally introduced heuristics and biases into economic models of decision making. More-recent work has focused on what makes an experience pleasant or unpleasant and how we recall experiences. This work has the potential to redefine our notions of utility and enjoyment. For his contributions to the development of behavioral economics, Kahneman won the 2002 Nobel Prize for economics. In addition he has won numerous prizes and honorary degrees. Kahneman attributes much of his curiosity about psychological phenomena to his upbringing. Though born in Palestine before the founding of Israel, he lived much of his boyhood in France. During World War II, as Jews in occupied France, his family moved often to avoid internment in prison camps. His father was at one point interned for six weeks, though he was later released through action by his employer. In this climate, his mother's gossip—short stories about human behavior—served as his primary entertainment and curiosity.

THOUGHT QUESTIONS

1. In this chapter, brief mention was made of the false consensus as a form of the availability heuristic. Consider an entrepreneur who has developed a product that she finds very useful in her own life. What might the false consensus have to say regarding her beliefs that the product is marketable to a more general audience? How might these beliefs affect her decision to invest in a new business venture distributing the product, and what impact will this have on the riskiness of her investment? Suppose we were to examine a large sample of entrepreneurs who each had developed products around their own needs. Given the false consensus, what types of entrepreneurs are most likely to succeed?

2. In 2003 Andy Pettitte pitched for the New York Yankees baseball team, a team that won the American League pennant and qualified for the World Series. In the postseason, the Yankees played a series of games with each of three teams: Minnesota, Boston, and Florida. In each series, Pettitte pitched the second game and won. A prominent sportswriter noticed this and wrote an article touting this notable streak of wins when pitching the second game of a series. Over the season, Pettitte had pitched in 29 games and won 21 of them. Is this a streak? Why might the sportswriter believe this is a streak? How could you profit from this perception? Model the sportswriter's beliefs supposing that the individual has two mental urns. One urn (average) has three balls, with two marked "win" and one marked "lose." Suppose the other urn (streak) also has three balls but all are marked "win." Suppose that the urns are never refreshed. What is the lowest probability of a streak that would lead the sportswriter to interpret this series of wins as a streak? Suppose

instead that the urns are refreshed after every two games. Now what must the unconditional probability of a streak be before one would believe one was observing a streak?

3. Suppose there is an unconditional probability of a bull market of 0.8, and a 0.2 probability of a bear market. In a bull market, there is a 0.7 probability of a rise in stock prices over a one-week period and 0.3 probability of a fall in stock prices over the same period. Alternatively, in a bear market there is a 0.4 probability of a rise in stock prices in a one-week period and a 0.6 probability of a decline in stock prices in a one-week period. Suppose, for simplicity, that stock price movements over a week are independent draws. In the last 10 weeks, we have observed four weeks with rising prices and six weeks with declining prices. What is the probability that you are observing a bear market? Suppose a cable news analyst behaves according to Grether's generalized Bayes' model of belief updating, with $\beta_P = 1.82$ and $\beta_L = 2.25$. What probability would the news analyst assign to a bear market? Finally, suppose a competing news analyst behaves according to Rabin's mental urn model, refreshing after every two weeks of data. Suppose further that this analyst has 10 balls in each urn with distributions of balls labeled "rise" and "fall" corresponding to the true probabilities. What probability will he assign to a bear market? What if the analyst had 100 balls in each urn?

4. Many lotteries divide the winnings evenly among all those selecting the winning number. Knowing this, how could one use the gambler's fallacy to increase the expected earnings from playing the lottery? Under what conditions would it be profitable to do so?

REFERENCES

Bertrand, M., and S. Mullainathan. "Are Emily and Greg More Employable than Lakisha and Jamal? A Field Experiment on Labor Market Discrimination." *American Economic Review* 94 (2004): 991–1013.

Clotfelter, C.T., and P. J. Cook. "The 'Gambler's Fallacy' in Lottery Play." *Management Science* 39(1993): 1521–1525.

Croson, R., and J. Sundali. "The Gambler's Fallacy and the Hot Hand: Empirical Data from Casinos." *Journal of Risk and Uncertainty* 30(2005): 195–209.

Edwards, W. "Conservatism in Human Information Processing." In D. Kahneman, P. Slovic, and A. Tversky (eds.). *Judgment under Uncertainty: Heuristics and Biases.* New York: Cambridge University Press, 1982, pp. 359–369.

Folkes, V.S. "The Availability Heuristic and Perceived Risk." *Journal of Consumer Research* 15(1988): 13–23.

Gilovich, T., R. Vallone, and A. Tversky. "The Hot Hand in Basketball: On the Misperception of Random Sequences." *Cognitive Psychology* 17(1985): 295–314.

Grether, D.M. "Bayes Rule as a Descriptive Model: The Representativeness Heuristic." *Quarterly Journal of Economics* 95(1980): 537–557.

Hogarth, R.M., and H.J. Einhorn. "Order Effects in Belief Updating: The Belief-Adjustment Model." *Cognitive Psychology* 24(1992): 1–55.

Kahneman, D., and A. Tversky. "On Prediction and Judgment." *Oregon Research Institute Research Bulletin* 12(1972).

Kahneman, D., and A. Tversky. "On the Psychology of Prediction." *Psychological Review* 80(1973): 237–251.

Langer, E.J. "The Illusion of Control." In D. Kahneman, P. Slovic, and A. Tversky (eds.) *Judgment under Uncertainty: Heuristics and Biases*. New York: Cambridge University Press, 1982, pp. 231–238.

Lichtenstein, S., P. Slovic, B. Fischoff, M. Layman, and B. Combs. "Judged Frequency of Lethal Events." *Journal of Experimental Psychology: Human Learning and Memory* 4(1978): 551–578.

Rabin, M. "Inference by Believers in the Law of Small Numbers." *Quarterly Journal of Economics* 117(2002): 775–816.

Rothbart, M., S. Fulero, C. Jensen, J. Howard, and P. Birrel. "From Individual to Group Impressions: Availability Heuristics in Stereotype Formation." *Journal of Experimental Social Psychology* 14(1978): 237–255.

Shelor, R.M., D.C. Anderson, and M.L. Cross. "Gaining from Loss: Property-Liability Insurer Stock Values in the Aftermath of the 1989 California Earthquake." *Journal of Risk and Insurance* 59(1992): 476–488.

Tversky, A., and D. Kahneman. "Belief in the Law of Small Numbers." *Psychological Bulletin* 76(1971): 105–110.

Tversky, A., and D. Kahneman. "Availability: A Heuristic for Judging Frequency and Probability." *Cognitive Psychology* 4(1973): 207–232.

Tversky, A., and D. Kahneman. "Judgments of and by Representativeness." In D. Kahneman, P. Slovic, and A. Tversky (eds.) *Judgment under Uncertainty: Heuristics and Biases*. New York: Cambridge University Press, 1982, pp. 84–100.

Confirmation and Overconfidence

8

Throughout the last several years, the cry of political bias has been directed at the news media from nearly all quarters. Interestingly, though, one hears very different accusations from each quarter. In particular, when asked, a majority of political conservatives accuse the network news and major newspapers of a deep liberal bias. However, when one questions the most politically liberal, they claim that the same media display a conservative bias. If we consider both groups of people to be sincere, it appears that they have come to exactly opposite conclusions while viewing the exact same information. In fact, because of the supposed bias, many have chosen to obtain their news primarily from cable news outlets that seem much more open about their bent. Thus, more-conservative people tend to view more-conservative networks, and more-liberal people tend to view more-liberal networks. Here they may view news that generally confirms their already-held beliefs and are unlikely to encounter news that would cause them to question or abandon these beliefs. What drives people to these havens of safe information?

Other interesting behavior can be seen on the part of entrepreneurs. Entrepreneurs take great financial risks on the bet that their business idea will produce a successful venture. More often than not, however, these ventures fail, leaving in their wake lost dreams, lost money, and often lost marriages. Even those founding successful businesses tend to put in greater amounts of work for less money than they would make in alternative employment. Given the overwhelming prevalence of failure, why would any rational person take such risks? Moreover, among well-established firms, we often see waves of mergers. One firm buys another, hoping that the two pieces together will provide a greater profit than they do separately. If the firms perform some set of overlapping functions, it is possible to eliminate the redundant portions, thus reducing costs, and obtain the same revenues. However, this is not how it generally works out. In fact, the overwhelming majority of mergers lead to lower profits for the purchasing firm. What would lead firms to systematically misjudge the benefits of such mergers?

This chapter builds on the previous chapter in exploring the ways people seek new information and how this systematically affects beliefs and subsequent actions. In searching for new information, we often have a choice as to what type of information we will see. For example, we can choose to consume news with a conservative spin or with a liberal spin. One might have a greater tendency to confirm our currently held beliefs, and others might tend to disconfirm our currently held beliefs. In making decisions under uncertainty, we often must grapple with conflicting information and choices between information sources. Our choice affects the accuracy of our perceptions and the success of our decisions.

Rational Information Search

For the first-time student, models of information search can be difficult to understand. This is because information search involves two levels of uncertainty. The first level of uncertainty is regarding the economic phenomenon that the individual wants to learn about (e.g., future stock market prices). The second level of uncertainty is regarding what signal the resulting information will yield (e.g., whether the signal will indicate rising or falling prices, and whether this signal will accurately reflect future events). Information signals are most often modeled as random variables that have distributions that are conditional on the underlying uncertainty.

For a simple example, consider a farmer who is making a production decision. She must decide, before she knows what weather will come, how much seed to plant, x. If the weather is good, then planting x will result in $\alpha_g x$ bushels of wheat being harvested. If the weather is bad, then planting x will result in $\alpha_b x$ bushels of wheat, where $\alpha_g > \alpha_b > 0$. The cost of purchasing and planting seed is given by the cost function $C(x)$, and the resulting wheat can be sold for price p. Suppose the farmer initially believes (accurately) that there is a P_g probability of good weather. Then, without any further information, a risk-neutral farmer would solve

$$\max_x P_g p \alpha_g x + (1 - P_g) p \alpha_b x - C(x). \tag{8.1}$$

We write the solution to this problem as $x^*(P_g)$.

Now, suppose that two different weather forecasts are available that can further inform the farmer of the future weather. Each forecast predicts either GOOD or BAD weather. Let y represent the choice of weather forecast. When forecast y predicts GOOD, good weather results with probability $P(good|GOOD, y)$. Similarly, we can write the probability that bad weather will occur when forecast y predicts BAD as $P(bad|BAD, y)$. Here let us suppose that both of these probabilities are a result of Bayesian updating. Suppose further that the farmer is aware of these conditional probabilities and is only allowed to choose one forecast. The farmer will be able to observe the forecast before making the input decision. Thus, the input decision is based upon the forecast she receives. Given that forecast y predicts STATE, where STATE can be either GOOD or BAD, the farmer will solve

$$\max_x P(state|STATE, y) p \alpha_g x + (1 - P(state|STATE, y)) p \alpha_b x - C(x). \tag{8.2}$$

In general, we will write the solution to (8.2) as $x^*(STATE, y)$.

Further, we can determine the probability of receiving a GOOD forecast versus a BAD forecast given the chosen forecast. Let $P(STATE, y)$ be the unconditional probability of receiving a forecast of STATE given the chosen forecast. Then, to be consistent, it must be that

$$P(GOOD, y) = P_g P(good|GOOD, y) + (1 - P_g)P(bad|GOOD, y) \qquad (8.3)$$

and

$$P(BAD, y) = P_g P(good|BAD, y) + (1 - P_g)P(bad|BAD, y). \qquad (8.4)$$

These equations must hold given that the unconditional probability of good weather is P_g. Table 8.1 summarizes the possible outcomes given forecast y and the resulting probabilities.

Let us suppose that $P_g = 0.7$. Suppose that of the two possible forecasts, one predicted the weather with absolute certainty, and the other tended to confirm the initial belief that good weather was on the way. Suppose that forecast $y = 1$ is perfectly accurate. Thus, $P(good|GOOD, 1) = 1$ and $P(bad|BAD, 1) = 1$, so that after receiving the signal, the farmer had a perfect knowledge of what weather would come. Further, suppose that forecast $y = 2$ is such that $P(good|GOOD, 1) = 0.7$ and $P(bad|BAD, 1) = 0.3$, so that no matter what the signal, the farmer continued to believe that there was a 0.70 probability of good weather. By choosing the second signal, the farmer receives no new information no matter what signal is realized. In this case, $x^*(GOOD, 2) = x^*(BAD, 2) = x^*(P_g)$. Because the farmer chooses the same input no matter what the forecast, the farmer will receive the same profits when receiving forecast 2 as when no signal is received, as in equation 8.1. Thus, signal 2 is worth nothing to the farmer, and she will not be willing to pay anything for this forecast. Alternatively, with signal 1, the farmer can perfectly discern what weather will come and can choose the input level that maximizes the profit in each state. Thus, it is as if the farmer is solving

$$P_g \max_{x_g} \left(p\alpha_g x_g - C(x)\right) + (1 - P_g) \max_{x_g} \left(p\alpha_b x_b - C(x)\right), \qquad (8.5)$$

where x_g is the planned input when in a good-weather state and x_b is the planned input when in a bad-weather state. In this case, the farmer can make input dependent on state and obtain the greatest possible profit in each state. Clearly the realized profit of equation 8.5 is larger than the realized profit in equation 8.1, where the farmer must choose one level of input for both possible states. Thus, this signal must be valuable to the farmer and be worth paying the difference in expected profits with and without the forecast.

In general, information increases in value as it increases in resolution or accuracy. In other words, if the probability of all possible states of the world near either 1 or 0

Table 8.1   Probabilities States and Forecasts

	Weather		Unconditional Probability
Forecast	Good	Bad	
GOOD	$P(good|GOOD, y)$	$P(bad|GOOD, y)$	$P(GOOD, y)$
BAD	$P(good|BAD, y)$	$P(bad|BAD, y)$	$P(BAD, y)$
Unconditional Probability	P_g	$1 - P_g$	

increases once a forecast signal is received, the signal will have high value. The more extreme the probability of various states, the greater the person's ability to plan and avoid the reduced average profits that come with uncertainty. If a forecast signal almost always results in beliefs that are similar to the currently held beliefs, we call it a **confirming forecast**. A confirming forecast has little value for planning purposes. Because it does not change beliefs, it cannot change the planned choice. Thus, in this sense, confirming information has no value.

Alternatively, we could think of information as confirming if it strengthens your current belief in a particular state, for example, a forecast that can lead to belief that the probability of good weather is greater than the initial belief of 0.7. This signal has value in that it leads to a better ability to discern between the possible states of the world and thus allows better decisions. However, such a forecast also necessarily allows you to more accurately predict a bad state. In other words, if $P(good|GOOD, y) > P_g$, then $P(bad|BAD, y) > (1 - P_g)$. Thus, this information can potentially disconfirm current beliefs also. A rational economic agent always weakly prefers a more accurate set of beliefs whether the more-accurate beliefs resemble their current beliefs or not.

EXAMPLE 8.1   On the Objectivity of Grades

Many students have had the experience of receiving a grade they feel is unfair. One often hears the claim from students who have been unpleasantly surprised by their grades that the teacher or professor is biased in some way against the student.

Here is some ammunition that may be helpful the next time you face such a dispute. John Darley and Paget Gross conducted a series of experiments where subjects watched a video tape of a fourth grade girl and were asked to assess her academic capability. A control group viewed only a tape of the girl answering questions from an achievement test. On average this group believed that she performed very near grade level in reading and liberal arts but just slightly below grade level in math. An additional group was shown a video of the girl playing and was not allowed to view the answers to the achievement test. Half of the participants in this group were shown the girl playing in an upper-class suburban neighborhood, and half of the participants viewed the girl in a low-income urban setting. Those viewing the girl in the upper-class neighborhood rated her as being somewhat above grade level in reading and in arts and sciences and on grade level in math. Those viewing her in the urban setting rated her as being slightly below grade level in all three. Of course neither of these groups had any chance to really observe her ability in any of the subjects, and thus these ratings might simply represent their prior beliefs.

A third group was first shown the video of the girl playing and then her answers to the achievement test, and the group was asked to rate her performance. In this case, the viewers had the chance to form initial beliefs about the girl while watching her play, and then they used the test answers to update their beliefs. In this case, those watching her play in the upper-class neighborhood rated her well above grade level in reading and in arts and sciences and somewhat above grade level in math. Those who initially viewed her playing in a low-income neighborhood rated her well below grade level in all three.

Thus, no matter what their initial beliefs were regarding the girl's ability, all participants saw her performance on the achievement test as reinforcing their original view. If they initially believed she was above grade level, their views after seeing the test was that she was well above grade level. If they initially believed she was below grade level, after seeing the test they thought she was well below grade level. This is after seeing the exact same video of her performance on the test. Apparently, evidence is in the eye of the beholder.

EXAMPLE 8.2   Flipping Cards and the Contrapositive

Causal links between events can be very difficult to establish in practice. Often a decision maker is searching for information that will help to establish a decision-rule. For example, we might hypothesize that expected stock prices decline on days when it rains in New York City. One way to test such a hypothesis is to examine stock price data on the days when it rained in New York City and to test whether the average change in price on these days was negative. Alternatively, we could obtain weather data for only days when stock prices increased, and test if the average rainfall was greater than 0. This might seem like a less-obvious route to testing the hypothesis, but it is just as powerful. Obtaining data concerning the change in stock prices on sunny days, however, cannot be used to test or support this hypothesis. In fact the original hypothesis said nothing regarding sunny days. It could be that prices rise on average both on sunny and rainy days (for example if weather has nothing to do with stock returns). Nonetheless, if I were to state that stock prices increase on average on sunny days, many might increase their confidence in the original hypothesis regarding rainy days, believing that this somehow makes it more likely that prices decline on rainy days. This mistake is relatively common when dealing with **contrapositive statements**. Statements of the form "if P then Q" and "if not P then not Q" are contrapositive statements, and people often make the mistake of looking for evidence to support the contrapositive as a means of confirming their original hypothesis.

P. C. Wason conducted several experiments to examine how such confusion can influence the search for information. Participants in one experiment were shown four cards placed in random order. They were told that each card had a number on one side and a letter on the reverse side. For example, in one treatment they were shown four cards with the faces showing respectively "D", "3", "B", "7," as displayed in Figure 8.1. Then participants were asked which of the cards they would need to flip over to test the hypothesis that "If there is a D on one side of any card, then there is a 3 on its other side." Clearly in order to test this hypothesis one would need to flip the "D" card, as every participant could identify. However, one would also need to flip over the "7." If the letter on the opposite side of the "7" were "D," then the hypothesis would be false. The need

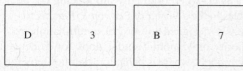

FIGURE 8.1
Visible Cards in the Wason Experiment

to flip over "7" was identified by only 20 percent of participants. Alternatively, 74 percent of participants thought it would be necessary to flip over the "3" to test the hypothesis. This is, of course, false. If we were to flip over the "3" and find a "K" written on the other side, we succeed only in finding that the rule could not be applied for the card because the rule only states what will appear opposite a "D." Alternatively, if we find a "D" on the other side of the "3," this does not confirm or rule out the hypothesis. Thus, no new information could possibly be obtained by flipping over the "3."

Later studies by Wason and others have shown similar biases by scientists and students attempting to apply scientific principles. When one has a working hypothesis, the tendency is to run tests that display the hypothesized relationship but that have no ability to reject the hypothesis (e.g., flipping over the "3" card). We refer to such information as **confirmatory**, because it can display the hypothesized relationship, providing some confirmation, although it has no power to reject the relationship. Alternatively, we refer to information such as flipping over the "7" as **disconfirmatory**. Disconfirmatory evidence cannot potentially display the hypothesized relationship (by flipping the "7" we will never see a card with a "3" on one side and a "D" on the other) but can reject the hypothesis. Clifford Mynatt, Michael Doherty, and Ryan Tweney found that whether participants in experiments are instructed to find confirming evidence or to find disconfirming evidence, they tend to choose confirming evidence about 70 percent of the time. Thus, decision makers, even after having some instruction on the differences between confirming and disconfirming information, have a difficult time discerning between the two. Further, decision makers have an apparent tendency to seek confirmatory information rather than disconfirmatory information.

Confirmation Bias

People have a strong tendency to seek information that is likely to confirm their currently held beliefs rather than information that might cause them to reconsider. Further, people have a tendency to interpret new information as supporting their currently held beliefs. This pair of tendencies is called **confirmation bias**. By seeking information that can only confirm currently held beliefs, new information cannot change one's mind; thus, the person flips over the "3" instead of the "7," looking for confirming information. Further, people tend to discount, question, and scrutinize information that contradicts their own currently held beliefs, whereas information that is consistent with their current beliefs is generally taken at face value, thus strengthening currently held beliefs. Thus, one is much more likely to see vague information as confirming a currently held belief than disconfirming it. Given a random stream of information, one who displays a confirmation bias thus interprets the information as largely supporting one's already-held beliefs. As an illustration of this principle, Thaler, when originally introducing the field of behavioral economics in his series of articles in the *Journal of Economic Perspectives,* suggested that behavioral economics is largely designed to combat confirmation bias among economists. The overwhelming majority of economic studies look for evidence that can possibly confirm classical economic models, whereas behavioral studies look for evidence that classical models could fail.

We refer to seeking after confirmatory information or selectively scrutinizing disconfirming information as **hypothesis-based filtering**. Matthew Rabin and Joel Schrag point out that although it is reasonable and rational to use current hypotheses to inform one's search and interpretation of information, it is unreasonable to then use this interpretation or resulting information as further evidence for the hypothesis. The example they use to drive home this result is of a teacher grading a test. When the teacher comes upon a vague or odd answer, she might use her knowledge of the student to interpret the meaning of the answer and decide on the student's mastery of the subject and thus assign the grade on the question. This is all quite reasonable. However, once the answer is graded based on the working understanding the teacher has of how well the student understands the material, it is thereafter invalid to use the resulting grade as further proof of how well the student understands the material. The grade at that point contains no information beyond the initial hypothesis used to filter the information contained in the student's test response.

Two other conditions commonly lead to confirmation bias. First, when information is ambiguous and requires interpretation, people often interpret the information according to their initially held beliefs, engaging in hypothesis-based filtering. This leads to a case where vague information is almost always viewed as confirming and strengthening the currently held belief. Thus, for example, an essay is likely to be graded in a way that displays a confirmation bias resulting from the level of judgment necessary in completing this task, whereas a multiple-choice question is not. Second, people have a difficult time detecting the correlation of random events. Thus, when their beliefs center around the correlation between some event that is potentially causal and the event that it potentially causes, people tend to see confirmation where none exists. For example, without employing rigorous statistical analysis, sports fans might watch several basketball games and feel they have seen confirmation of the hot hand if they initially believed in the phenomenon. Believing that shots are positively correlated often leads one to view a string of shots taken as being correlated, even if no correlation exists.

Rabin and Schrag propose a model of confirmation bias based on the possibility of two states of the world. Consider again our farmer who wishes to know whether there will be *good* weather or *bad* weather for the season. Suppose that each week before the planting season, the farmer receives a different forecast of the weather, predicting either GOOD or BAD. Each of these forecasts is considered independent from each of the other forecasts, with the probability of a GOOD forecast given good weather indicated by $P(GOOD|good) > 0.5$ and the probability of a BAD forecast given bad weather indicated by $P(BAD|bad) > 0.5$. Initially, suppose that the farmer believes there is a 0.5 probability of good weather. Suppose now that the forecast is communicated in some way that is ambiguous, leading to confirmation filtering. Then, over the course of the preplanting season, the farmer *receives* a series of forecasts (e.g., GOOD, GOOD, BAD, . . .), but the farmer *perceives* a potentially different series of forecasts. Let a perceived forecast of GOOD be denoted by $\widetilde{GOOD}$ and a perceived forecast of BAD be denoted by $\widetilde{BAD}$. At any point in time, if the farmer believes that either good or bad weather is more probable, then she has a probability of $q > 0$ of misperceiving disconfirming information while correctly perceiving confirming information with probability 1. The farmer then updates her beliefs according to Bayes rule, as if her perception were reality. Thus, if she perceives the signals $\widehat{GOOD}$, $\widehat{GOOD}$, $\widehat{BAD}$, her perceived beliefs could then be written as

$$\widehat{P}\left(good | \widehat{GOOD}, \widehat{GOOD}, \widehat{BAD}\right)$$

$$= \frac{0.5 \times (P(GOOD|good))^2 (1 - P(GOOD|good))}{0.5 \times (P(GOOD|good))^2 (1 - P(GOOD|good)) + 0.5 \times (1 - P(BAD|bad))^2 (P(BAD|bad))}.$$

(8.6)

Here, the 0.5 in the numerator is the Bayesian prior belief that good weather will prevail, which is multiplied by the probability of a GOOD forecast given that good weather is actually on the way raised to the power of the number of good forecasts received (in this case 2), multiplied by the probability of a BAD forecast given that good weather is on the way raised again to the power equaling the number of bad forecasts (in this case 1). The denominator contains the term from the numerator, plus a similar term using the probabilities given that bad weather is on the way. Note that the perceived beliefs are independent of the order of the perceived forecasts. Thus, if the farmer had perceived the sequence $\widehat{BAD}$, $\widehat{GOOD}$, $\widehat{GOOD}$, she would have maintained the same beliefs. This should be the case if the perceived forecasts were independent of one another, as the true forecasts are. However, the order of perception actually does affect the true probability of the events in this case because the perceived signals depend on one another.

The prior belief was that there was a 0.5 probability of good weather. If one first perceives the signal $\widehat{GOOD}$, one's initial beliefs do not favor either good or bad weather, so this perception must be accurate. However, once one perceives the first $\widehat{GOOD}$, one's beliefs become

$$\widehat{P}\left(good | \widehat{GOOD}\right)$$

$$= \frac{0.5 \times (P(GOOD|good))^1 (1 - P(GOOD|good))^0}{0.5 \times (P(GOOD|good))^1 (1 - P(GOOD|good))^0 + 0.5 \times (1 - P(BAD|bad))^1 (P(BAD|bad))^0}$$

$$= \frac{P(GOOD|good)}{P(GOOD|good) + (1 - P(BAD|bad))} > 0.5.$$

(8.7)

Here the last inequality follows because $P(GOOD|good) > 0.5$ and $P(BAD|bad) > 0.5$. At this point, if the next signal is GOOD, it will be accurately perceived as $\widehat{GOOD}$. However, if the next signal is BAD, there is a probability of q that $\widehat{GOOD}$ will be perceived. Thus, the second perceived $\widehat{GOOD}$ should not move beliefs as much given the possibility that this was a misperceived signal. In this case, the probability of perceiving the second $\widehat{GOOD}$ is

$$P\left(\widehat{GOOD} | GOOD, good\right) = [P(GOOD|good) + q(1 - P(GOOD|good))], \quad (8.8)$$

given that the weather will truly be good, and

$$P\left(\widehat{GOOD}|GOOD, bad\right) = [qP(BAD|bad) + (1 - P(BAD|bad))]. \qquad (8.9)$$

In fact, this is the true probability of perceiving $\widehat{GOOD}$ in any period in which the farmer believes that good weather is more probable. Thus, a true Bayesian who understands her tendency to misperceive signals would believe (compare to equation 8.6)

$$P\left(good|\widehat{GOOD}, \widehat{GOOD}, \widehat{BAD}\right)$$

$$= \left\{0.5 \times P(GOOD|good)P\left(\widehat{GOOD}|GOOD, good\right)\left(1 - P\left(\widehat{GOOD}|GOOD, good\right)\right)\right\}$$

$$\div \left\{ \begin{array}{l} 0.5 \times P(GOOD|good)P\left(\widehat{GOOD}|GOOD, good\right)\left(1 - P\left(\widehat{GOOD}|GOOD, good\right)\right) \\ + 0.5 \times (1 - P(BAD|bad))P\left(\widehat{GOOD}|GOOD, bad\right)\left(1 - P\left(\widehat{GOOD}|GOOD, bad\right)\right) \end{array} \right\}.$$

$$(8.10)$$

As an example, suppose that $P(GOOD|good) = 0.75$ and $P(BAD|bad) = 0.6$, and $q = 0.5$. Then, the perceived probability of the sequence $\widehat{GOOD}, \widehat{GOOD}, \widehat{BAD}$ is

$$\widehat{P}\left(good|\widehat{GOOD}, \widehat{GOOD}, \widehat{BAD}\right) = \frac{0.5 \times (0.75)^2 \times (1 - 0.75)}{0.5 \times (0.75)^2 \times (1 - 0.75) + 0.5 \times (1 - 0.6)^2 \times (0.6)}$$

$$\approx 0.59.$$

$$(8.11)$$

However, the true probability that good weather is on the way is

$$P\left(good|\widehat{GOOD}, \widehat{GOOD}, \widehat{BAD}\right)$$

$$= \{0.5 \times 0.75 \times [0.75 + 0.5 \times (1 - 0.75)] \times [1 - 0.75 - 0.5 \times (1 - 0.75)]\}$$

$$\div \left\{ \begin{array}{l} 0.5 \times 0.75 \times [0.75 + 0.5 \times (1 - 0.75)] \times [1 - 0.75 - 0.5 \times (1 - 0.75)] \\ + 0.5 \times (1 - 0.6) \times [0.5 \times 0.6 + (1 - 0.6)] \times [1 - 0.5 \times 0.6 - (1 - 0.6)] \end{array} \right\}$$

$$\approx 0.49.$$

$$(8.12)$$

Thus, the farmer would objectively hold the wrong beliefs, believing that good weather is more likely, when in fact bad weather was more likely. In general, the perceived probability of the state that the farmer perceives to be more likely is greater than the objective probability of that state. This will continue to be true no matter how many forecasts are received.

Figure 8.2 displays results from two runs of a simulation of the Rabin–Schrag model of hypothesis filtering. For both runs, the prior belief that good weather would prevail was set so $P(good) = 0.5$. The probability of receiving a signal of good weather given good weather was the true state was $P(GOOD|good) = 0.8$. The probability of receiving a signal of bad weather given bad weather was the true state was $P(BAD|bad) = 0.8$. Finally, the probability of misperceiving a signal if the signal was disconfirming was $q = 0.25$. A random-number generator was used to generate the weather and the weather

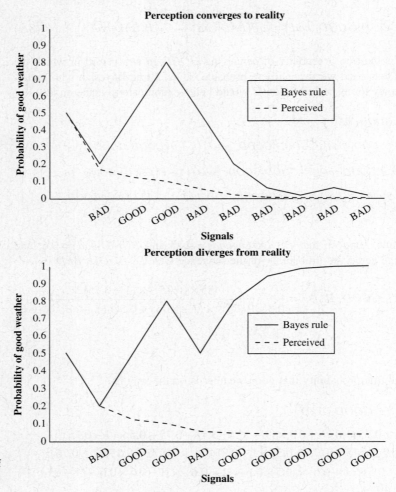

FIGURE 8.2
Simulations of Rabin
and Schrag's Model of
Hypothesis Filtering

signals for nine periods in each simulation. Panel 1 of Figure 8.2 displays a case in which perceived probability converges to the Bayesian beliefs (and the truth). In this case, the weather was bad. The first weather forecast was BAD, and the Bayesian probability of good weather quickly declines to 0.20. Then two GOOD forecasts are received, leading Bayesian beliefs in the probability of good weather to increase to 0.80. After that, a string of BAD forecasts eventually lead the Bayesian probability of good weather to converge to 0. The hypothesis-filtering model converges more quickly to a probability of 0 because it discounts the information in any good-weather signals after the first BAD is received. That initial information tilts the playing field in favor of bad weather, leading to a faster convergence to the truth.

But it is not always the case that initial information is accurate. The lower graph of Figure 8.2 shows a case in which the perceptions resulting from hypothesis filtering diverge from the Bayesian probabilities (and from the truth). In this simulation, weather is *good*, but the first signal is BAD. This again tilts perceptions toward a bad state and leads the hypothesis-filtering simulation to discount the next two GOOD signals, remaining flat while the Bayesian beliefs increase to 0.8. The next BAD signal locks in the belief that weather will be bad and leads to a point where additional GOOD signals will not noticeably sway perceptions.

When a person predicts that a state is the most probable and assesses the probability of that state as higher than objective measures of that probability would warrant, we call the person **overconfident**. Most studies of confirmation bias suggest that overconfidence is a natural result of hypothesis-based filtering.

Given confirmation bias, people fail to learn as much from new information as they really should. This is very closely related to the phenomenon of conservatism outlined in Chapter 7. Thus, the phenomenon of confirmation bias can be seen in some respects as an opposing force to representativeness.

EXAMPLE 8.3   Business Executives and Mergers

Firms often acquire or merge with other firms in the hope of reducing costs. If firms perform overlapping functions, the merged firm could ostensibly cut expenses on capital and labor in one of the redundant operations and perform the same function for both previous ventures at a lower cost, obtaining higher profits. Thus, if you were a business executive considering the acquisition of another firm, significant effort would be made to assess the cost of acquisition, the potential for cutting costs after merging, and the potential net benefit of the merger. If firms make these assessments in a reasonable way, it seems likely that mergers would on average increase firm profits.

In fact, the opposite is true. Fewer than half of all mergers add value to the acquiring company, and only 30 percent of mergers result in a profit increase that meets the stated objective of the merger. Regarding this poor rate of success, Ulrike Malmendier and Geoffrey Tate suggest that CEOs who engage in mergers overestimate their own ability to generate returns from the acquired company. Further, they link this to general over-confidence in the success of their own company. CEOs are often given stock options, the option to buy company stock at a fixed price any time before the expiration date of the option. In general, if the current price of the stock is above the price specified in the option, we say that the option is "in the money." The CEO at this point could exercise the in-the-money options by buying the stock at the specified price and then could sell the stock for the much higher market price. In general, when one holds in-the-money options, one only continues to hold the options if one believes the stock price will go *much* higher. Holding, rather than exercising, in-the-money options is a high-risk bet that the company will increase in value. Malmendier and Tate use the holding of in-the-money options as a measure of how overconfident a CEO is regarding the future of their company. They find that those who are more overconfident are also substantially more likely to engage in merger behavior. Thus, it appears that overconfidence about the future of the merger explains some merger activity.

Vicki Bogan and David Just show that such overconfidence might develop as a result of confirmation bias when firms are gathering information about a potential merger. They ran an economics experiment in which participants were placed in the position of a CEO at a firm considering the acquisition of another firm. The participants used a Web browser to access Web pages containing information about the potential costs, benefits, legal issues, and marketing issues regarding the merger. The computer recorded the

number of visits and the amount of time each participant spent for each type of information. The participants in the end were asked to make a decision whether to bid on the
target company and at what level to bid. The participants were then paid a proportion of
the expected profits from their actions. Enough information was available on the separate Web pages that one could calculate the expected profits under each scenario.

Two different groups of participants were used in the experiment. One group consisted of college students in business classes, and the other consisted primarily of
executive officers of Fortune 500 companies. The executives were about 1/3 less likely to
visit pages presenting information regarding the costs of the merger—information that
could potentially disconfirm the belief that the merger was profitable. More than half of
the executives never examined the costs, but only about 18 percent of other participants
did not view information about costs. Thus, they were looking primarily for information
about the potential benefits—confirming information. Participants were asked to indicate
their likely decision after each page of information was viewed. Executives were also less
likely to change their mind about the profitability of the merger. Thus, executives appear
to display a substantial confirmation bias in the exercise. This confirmation bias could be
the source of overconfidence that drives bad merger behavior.

EXAMPLE 8.4   Political Bias and Information

A growing chorus of voices have accused the news media of being biased in their
reporting of political events. The Pew Research Center conducts periodic studies of bias
in the media, including several opinion polls. In 2000, they found that 48 percent of survey
respondents claimed that there was no particular bias in the news media and 32 percent
thought there was some bias. In 2004 the number perceiving no bias was down to 38
percent, with 39 percent now claiming bias based on political party affiliation. If we restrict
ourselves to just those identifying themselves either as a politically conservative Republican or a politically liberal Democrat, a plurality of those polled believe there is media
bias. Both liberals and conservatives can agree on media bias but not on the direction of
the bias. Of conservative Republicans, 47 percent believe the media display a Democratic
bias and only 8 percent believe the media coverage favors Republicans. Among liberal
Democrats, 36 percent believe that coverage favors Republicans, and only 11 percent
believe the news coverage favors Democrats. One may argue that perhaps they see
things differently because they view different media. For example, twice as many
Republicans get their news from Fox News as Democrats. Viewers of major network
newscasts are more often Democrats than Republicans, also by a ratio of 2 to 1. But if one
follows the accusations of bias, Fox is more often charged with favoring the Republican
party, and the major networks are more often charged with favoring the Democratic party.
Thus, viewers tend to discount most news coverage as biased against their own views,
and they elect to watch news that skews somewhat toward their own views.[1]

Charles Lord, Lee Ross, and Mark Lepper sought to study how political views might
influence how people process information. They asked 151 participants to complete a

---

[1] Pew Research Center for the People and the Press. "Perceptions of Partisan Bias Seen as Growing—Especially by
Democrats." News Release, January 11, 2004.

questionnaire identifying themselves as either in favor of capital punishment (the death penalty) or against capital punishment. A few weeks later, 48 of the participants were called back and asked to participate in an exercise. Of the 48, half indicated that they believed capital punishment was an effective deterrent against crime and that they believed the research supported their position. The other half believed that capital punishment was an ineffective deterrent and that the research supported their position. The participants were asked to read two index cards that contained a short summary of a research paper. For example

> Kroner and Phillips (1977) compared murder rates for the year before and the year after adoption of the capital punishment in 14 states. In 11 of the 14 states, murder rates were *lower after* adoption of the death penalty. This research supports the deterrent effect of the death penalty.

or,

> Palmer and Crandall (1977) compared murder rates in 10 pairs of neighboring states with different capital punishment laws. In 8 of the 10 pairs, murder rates were *higher* in the state *with* capital punishment. This research opposes the deterrent effect of the death penalty.

After reading these short summaries, participants were then allowed to read some critiques of the particular study, then asked to rate how convincing the research result was. Proponents of capital punishment saw the pro-deterrence research as much more convincing than the anti-deterrence research. As well, opponents of capital punishment saw the anti-deterrence research as much more convincing. After viewing the same information, proponents of capital punishment reported they were more in favor of capital punishment, and opponents considered themselves more against capital punishment. Perhaps more information once a political view is formed only serves to polarize viewpoints via confirmation bias.

EXAMPLE 8.5 Harvard Students are Overconfident

Recall that an x percent confidence interval for an unknown parameter is an interval based on a sample of data such that if we could repeat the experiment that caused the sample of data an infinite number of times, *x percent* of the resulting intervals would contain the unknown parameter value. One intuitive way to think about it is that there is an $x/2$ probability that the parameter is above the upper bound of the confidence interval and an $x/2$ probability that the parameter falls below the lower bound of the interval. If we have very little information upon which to base our decision about the endpoints, the confidence interval should be very wide. Alternatively, if we have a lot of information about the parameter value, our interval should be very narrow. Instead of producing a confidence interval based on statistical data, it should be possible to ask people to create confidence intervals intuitively based on their own understanding of the world. If the respondents are well calibrated, then it seems reasonable that they would be able to arrive at two values such that, for example, the number of foreign automobiles imported into the United States last year exceeds the upper value with probability 0.01 and is smaller than the lower value with probability 0.01. If we could then run this same experiment on various pieces of trivia, we could measure whether respondents were correctly calibrated. After asking hundreds of questions, if we knew the true values, we could determine the percentage that exceed or fall below the respondent's interval estimates.

This is the experiment first performed by Marc Alpert and Howard Raiffa on more than 1,000 Harvard University students in the late 1960s. The original set of students were asked to form 50 percent and 98 percent confidence intervals (thus the values such that the true value will fall below them with probability 0.01, 0.25, 0.75, and 0.99), as well as determine the value such that the probability of a higher value is 0.50 and the probability of a lower value is 0.50. They were to determine these intervals for 10 unknown values. Several examples are

"1. The percentage of first-year students responding, excluding those who never drink, who prefer bourbon to scotch."
"4. The percentage of respondents expressing an opinion to a July, 1968 Gallup Poll surveying a representative sample of adult Americans who felt that if a full-scale war were to start in the Middle East, the U.S. should send troops to help Israel."
"6. The number of "Physicians and Surgeons" listed in the 1968 Yellow Pages of the phone directory for Boston and vicinity."
"8. The total egg production in millions in the U.S. in 1965."
"9. The number of foreign automobiles imported into the U.S. in 1967 in thousands."

The initial set of 800 M.B.A. students responded with values for each of these and the remaining questions. Table 8.2 compares the true value to the confidence interval responses for the Harvard students. By way of example, consider the first question, which asks students about the percentage of other students who prefer bourbon to scotch. In reality, 42.5 percent of students prefer bourbon. None of the students knew that for certain, though they probably had some idea of what others drink at parties or other social gatherings. If asked for a number such that there was only a 0.01 probability that a smaller percentage preferred bourbon, one might start by guessing at the true

Table 8.2   Accuracy of Harvard Students' Confidence Intervals

		Percentage with the True Value Falling:						
Number	Title	Below 0.01	Below 0.25	Below 0.50	Above 0.50	Above 0.75	Above 0.99	True Value
1	Bourbon	3	19	39	61	21	10	42.5
4	Israel	51	92	98	2	1	0	10.4
6	Doctors	24	38	50	50	37	27	2,600
8	Eggs	9	11	24	76	66	58	64.588
9	Cars	25	40	58	42	33	26	697

percentage, and then lowering the number until one felt there was only a very small probability (0.01 to be exact) the number could be below that point. Students who did not have much knowledge of what others drank (e.g., if they didn't attend such gatherings), they should guess an extremely low number to reflect their lack of knowledge—perhaps a number like 2 percent. If they had a lot of knowledge regarding the actual percentage (perhaps they had conducted a survey previously) they should choose a number much closer to the truth—perhaps 40 percent. When each student conducts this exercise, if all are correctly calibrated, only one out of a hundred on average should choose a number above the true value. Table 8.2, however, shows that three out of 100 chose a number that was higher than the truth. This indicates that students were not successful in assessing how little knowledge they truly held regarding other students' drinking preferences.

First examine the column labeled "Below 0.01." If the students were correctly calibrated, the percentage falling below 0.01 should be 1 for each of the questions. In fact the closest to this number were the responses to question 1, with only 3 percent falling below, three times the amount that should have fallen below. In fact, of all 10 questions they were asked, the correct number fell below the 0.01 mark for only two of the questions. On average, 15.8 percent of the true values fell below the 0.01 values given by the students.

One may argue that the questions are esoteric, and thus the students might have had very little knowledge upon which to base their answers. If their knowledge is lacking, the correct response would be to lower their guess at the 0.01 value to reflect their lack of knowledge. For example, one could be certain there were more than 10 doctors in the phone book. Similarly, the column labeled "Above 0.99" contains values that exceed the 0.01 that should appear were the students well calibrated. Here, among all 10 questions, 26.8 percent of the 0.99 values fell below the true value, where only 1 percent should have fallen below. On average, the 75 percent confidence intervals contained the true value about 33 percent of the time. The 98 percent confidence intervals contained the truth about 57 percent of the time. Clearly these confidence intervals were too narrow, a form of overconfidence. Harvard students thought they knew more about the answers than they truly did, creating confidence intervals that did not contain the truth with as high a probability as they had thought.

Alpert and Raiffa thought it should be possible to train people to avoid overconfidence. Thus, following the first round of questions, students were given feedback as to how they and other students had performed on the task, emphasizing how narrow the confidence intervals had been relative to the proper size of the confidence interval. After this training, students were asked another 10 similar questions. After the training, the 50 percent confidence intervals contained the truth about 43 percent of the time. The 98 percent confidence intervals contained the truth only 77 percent of the time. This is an improvement. However, even after training and awareness of the overconfidence problem, students could not widen their confidence intervals enough to account for their lack of knowledge. This was a particular problem for the extreme values. In other similar experiments participants were asked to find 99.8 percent and 99.98 percent confidence intervals with results that only contained the true value about 45 percent of the time. Thus, overconfidence may be persistent even when we are aware of our overconfidence.

EXAMPLE 8.6   Entrepreneurship and Risk

Starting a new business venture involves substantial risk. Four of 10 new businesses fail in their first year of operation, and nearly nine in 10 fail in the first several years of operation. On top of this, new business owners generally make substantially less money over the first few years of operation than they could have earned by sticking to more-conventional employment. Given the huge risks and the investment of time, money, and resources, what would drive someone to be an entrepreneur? One might think that entrepreneurs are simply less risk averse than the rest of the population and are more willing to tolerate the large risks they face.

Robert Brockhaus (among others) compared the responses of entrepreneurs and nonentrepreneurs to a series of questions intended to gauge their propensity to take on risk. Essentially, he asked them for their willingness to take on a series of simple lotteries. He found no particular difference between entrepreneurs and nonentrepreneurs in their willingness to take on financial risk. If one takes on greater risks, but does not prefer more risk, what would drive the behavior?

One possibility is that entrepreneurs do not perceive the risks they face as well as others. For example, Lowell Busenitz and Jay Barney administered a test of overconfidence to a set of entrepreneurs and a set of managers in large companies. This test asked participants a set of questions with two possible answers. Participants were required to state their guess as to which answer was right and their assessment of the probability that they were correct (they were allowed to choose 0.5, 0.6, 0.7, 0.8, 0.9 or 1). Aside from when specifying a probability of 0.5, entrepreneurs were right substantially less often than would be implied by perfect calibration. For example, when they specified that they were 90 percent certain that they had selected the right answer, they were right about 70 percent of the time. Moreover, aside from at the 0.8 probability of being correct (where managers and entrepreneurs were tied) entrepreneurs were more overconfident than managers at every level of confidence. Thus, entrepreneurs simply might not recognize the level of risk that they will face in their venture.

Colin Camerer and Dan Lovallo used economic experiments to test for a link between overconfidence and entrepreneurial activity. Participants were placed in groups and asked to decide whether to enter a market or not. All players had to make their decision without communicating with other participants. If a participant decided not to enter the market, they would receive K. If they decided to enter, they would be assigned a rank. For each round, a number of participants, c, was specified as the market capacity. The top c ranked players would receive K plus some reward based on rank (totaling to $50 across all c of those in this group). Those ranked below c would receive K minus $10. Some participants were assigned a rank based on their ability to answer a set of trivia questions (after all rounds of the experiment concluded), and others were simply randomly assigned a rank. However, participants were told whether skill or chance would determine rank prior to deciding on whether to enter. When rank is determined by skill, people enter based on their own belief regarding their ability relative to others. Alternatively, when rank is determined by a random device, individual ability does not play into their decision. Of subjects participating in both random and skill-based versions of the game, 77 percent had higher profit per round in the random-rank game. On average, participants earned $1.31 more when playing the random-rank game. In fact, only 52 of 111 participants achieved a positive profit when playing the skill-based game. Thus, it appears participants were likely to overestimate the probability that their skill would exceed that of other participants.

Risk Aversion and Production

Under the rational—expected utility—model, someone facing a decision of whether to engage in a venture or not will decide to continue with the venture if the expected utility of engaging in the venture is greater than the utility of other options, or if

$$E[U(\pi)] > U(\overline{\pi}),\qquad(8.13)$$

where π is the random profit potentially generated by the new venture and $\overline{\pi}$ is the certain income generated by the opportunities forgone if the venture is started. To see the competing impacts of risk aversion and overconfidence on entry, consider the Taylor series expansion of the utility function about the mean of profits, μ_π. This approximation is given by

$$U(\pi) \approx U(\mu_\pi) + U'(\mu_\pi)(\pi - \mu) + \frac{1}{2}U''(\mu_\pi)(\pi - \mu)^2.\qquad(8.14)$$

Substituting equation 8.14 into equation 8.13 obtains

$$E\left[U(\mu_\pi) + U'(\mu_\pi)(\pi - \mu) + \frac{1}{2}U''(\mu_\pi)(\pi - \mu)^2\right] > U(\mu_\pi)$$
$$+ U'(\mu_\pi)(\overline{\pi} - \mu) + \frac{1}{2}U''(\mu_\pi)(\overline{\pi} - \mu)^2\qquad(8.15)$$

which is equivalent to

$$U(\mu_\pi) + \frac{1}{2}U''(\mu_\pi)\sigma_\pi^2 > U(\mu_\pi) + U'(\mu_\pi)(\overline{\pi} - \mu) + \frac{1}{2}U''(\mu_\pi)(\overline{\pi} - \mu)^2.\qquad(8.16)$$

Here, σ_π^2 is the variance of π. Subtracting $U(\mu_\pi) - \mu_\pi$ from both sides of the inequality and dividing both sides of equation 8.16 by $U'(\mu_\pi) > 0$ yields

$$\mu_\pi - \frac{1}{2}R_A\sigma_\pi^2 > \overline{\pi} - \frac{1}{2}R_A(\overline{\pi} - \mu_\pi)^2,\qquad(8.17)$$

where R_A is the coefficient of absolute risk aversion, usually thought to be greater than zero. Thus, the greater the variance of the profit resulting from the new venture, the less likely the person is to start up the new venture. Alternatively, the higher the mean profit, the more likely it is that the person will start the venture. If people misperceive the variance or the mean of the distribution of profits from the new venture, this can cause them to decide to engage in the venture when in fact they should abstain.

Overconfidence

Overconfidence can fall into one of two categories. Thus far we have talked about overconfidence as a general inflation of the probability that the person holds the correct view. This is the type of overconfidence most often referred to in the psychology literature, and it is the type that generally results from a pattern of confirmation bias. This type of overconfidence necessarily results in believing that the person faces less uncertainty (e.g., a lower variance of profit) than is truly the case. For clarity, we refer to this as **overconfidence of one's own knowledge**. Alternatively, many use the term overconfidence to refer to a bias of beliefs in favor of whatever outcomes may be more favorable for the person. Thus, for example, entrepreneurs might not only fail to perceive the potential variance of the distribution of profits for their new venture, they might believe the profits that would be realized on average are much higher than truth would dictate. We refer to a biasing of beliefs in favor of one's own welfare as **optimistic overconfidence**.

Interestingly, it can be very difficult to disentangle these two types of overconfidence in many situations. Entrepreneurship creates an interesting example. In this case, overestimating the profits one will achieve has the same impact on entry as underestimating the amount of risk one faces. Camerer and Lovallo's experiment is clearly designed to examine how people evaluate their own abilities—primarily a function of optimistic overconfidence. People face risk in both treatment arms of the experiment, and they could potentially display overconfidence of one's own knowledge in both treatments. Only the skill-based treatment directly inserts an assessment of one's own ability. Unfortunately, nearly all direct tests of overconfidence muddle these two types of overconfidence. For example, Busenitz and Barney conducted tests of whether probabilistic judgments are well calibrated, ostensibly seeking to find overconfidence of one's own knowledge. Unfortunately, the probabilities were elicited by asking participants to assess their ability to make a correct guess to a series of questions. Thus, the probability judgments would also be affected by optimistic overconfidence. Similarly, when asked to guess confidence interval values, one might not widen the confidence interval enough because one overestimates one's own ability to guess the correct answer.

In general, overconfidence (of either type) leads to decisions that might seem rash or ill informed to an objective observer. Potential entrepreneurs start a business failing to recognize the risks involved or overestimating the probability of profits. Stock traders might not diversify as much as they should, believing that there is much less risk in the particular investments they have chosen than will actually be realized. As a rule, people tend to be overconfident. However, they become more overconfident when they face a more difficult question. Thus, questions about which they have little information will inspire overconfidence, and questions that they know with certainty might actually induce underconfidence. On average, when people say that something will occur with certainty, it occurs about 80 percent of the time—thus the impossible happens about one fifth of the time!

EXAMPLE 8.7   Gender Differences and Trading

Rational models of stock trading suggest people should seldom trade stocks. Intuitively, if everyone has access to the same information, then everyone must have identical expectations about the future value of a stock. Thus, if all are rational and none have private information, trading stock in any company is unnecessary unless the person selling is seeking to cash out, say, to provide income in retirement. In reality, however, a majority of stocks in the New York Stock Exchange change hands every year (for example, 76 percent of stock shares changed hands in 1998). This seems to entirely defy the rational model of trading. A risk-averse person should be willing to buy a share of a stock if $E(p_{t+1}) - (R_A/2)\sigma^2 > p_t$, where p_{t+1} is the future value of the stock and p_t is the current trading price, R_A is the level of absolute risk aversion, and σ^2 is the perceived variance of the future value of the stock. The term $(R_A/2)\sigma^2$ can be called the **risk premium**, or the penalty for the level of risk involved in investing in the stock. Further, anyone holding the stock would be willing to sell only if $E(p_{t+1}) - (R_A/2)\sigma^2 < p_t$. If everyone has the same beliefs regarding the future value of the stock, and if all have the same aversion to risk, then no seller would sell below and no buyer would buy above $p_t = E(p_{t+1}) - (R_A/2)\sigma^2$. Thus, this would determine the market price and no one would have any particular motivation to sell or buy.

Given this model, people should normally take the current price as a signal of the future value of the stock. Thus, those who learn rationally will modify their beliefs to fit in with the market view. Alternatively, those who are overconfident might fail to take the market price as a signal of the true value of the stock. Rather, they might see any difference between their own beliefs and the market price as an opportunity. For example, suppose a trader believes that value of a stock is above the market price. If she were rational she might learn from the price that she overvalues the item and revise her beliefs downward. Alternatively, if she is overconfident, she believes the probability she is right is higher than it is in truth. Thus, she will fail to revise her beliefs downward enough and will decide to buy more of the stock. In this way, overconfidence leads to the execution of more trades than truthful perceptions about the market. Moreover, if she buys the stock and her perceptions about future value are wrong, she will be surprised by earning a smaller amount on average than if she had not purchased the stock. A similar story would lead to selling and earning less than expected if the initial beliefs were that the stock was worth less than the market price.

Brad Barber and Terrance Odean argue that although both men and women are overconfident, men tend to be more overconfident than women. Further, men are particularly overconfident in their ability to engage in "masculine" tasks. They asserted that stock trading is perceived generally as a masculine task and set out to find the fingerprints of gender-based overconfidence on trading patterns. They examined investment data from nearly 40,000 households over the years 1991 through 1996. Single women bought or sold an average of about 4 percent of their stock portfolio each month, and single men bought or sold about 7 percent of their portfolio each month. Thus the turnover for men is much higher. However, both men and women display a relatively high rate of turnover compared to the near 0 percent predicted by rational theory. Further, these trades reduce the returns of the portfolio. The average single man earns 0.24 percent less per month than he would have without trading, about 3 percent less per year. The average single woman earns about 0.12 percent less per month than she would without trading, about 1.5 percent per year.

Men and women also have different attitudes toward risk generally. Men are usually less risk averse than women and should thus be willing to pay more for risky stocks. Being less risk averse than the rest of the market can also lead to excess trading. People who are less risk averse than the market average will be willing to pay more for the stock because they do not care about the risk and face a lower-than-average risk premium. As an extreme case, consider someone who is risk neutral, $R_A = 0$. The risk-neutral person is willing to purchase any stock at a price at or below expected future value. Thus any stock with a risk premium built into the current market price should be purchased by the risk-neutral investor. At the same time, the risk-neutral investor behaves so as to maximize the expected value of the investment, finding the maximum average return. Thus, if differences in trading were driven solely on differences in risk aversion, those who trade more (less averse to risk) should display a higher return on average. Differences in risk aversion cannot explain the trading patterns of men because the men earn *lower* average returns owing to the trades. This must be due to misperception of risk rather than differing attitudes toward the risk faced.

EXAMPLE 8.8   Amateurs and Professionals

It is to be expected that professional experience will help to hone one's skills in whatever task is common in a profession. Stuart Oskamp sought to examine how amateur and professional psychologists differ in their ability to recognize or predict behavioral patterns in a clinical setting. Thus, Oskamp wanted to simulate the way information would unravel or develop in a series of meetings with a psychologist. Participants were presented a series of background stories and information about a client. The information consisted of four stages in all, each covering a different chronological piece of the client's life. After each stage of the information was presented, each participant was asked the same series of 25 multiple-choice questions about the client's behavior that was related to, but not directly addressed by, the information that had been presented. For example, one question asks how the client acted in social situations in college (e.g., "stayed aloof and withdrawn," or "acted the clown"). Further, participants were to rate their degree of confidence in their answer by assessing the probability that their answer is correct. Participants consisted of professional psychologists, graduate students in psychology, and undergraduate students in psychology.

Table 8.3 presents the average accuracy and confidence of all participants by stage in Oskamp's experiment. The accuracy of the predicted behaviors does increase slightly as a participant obtains more information about the client (from 26 percent to about 28 percent). However, the improvement in true accuracy is minuscule compared to the increase in confidence (from 33 percent to 53 percent). Not only are the participants overconfident in every stage, their level of overconfidence increases as they obtain more information. This is a pattern that is highly consistent with confirmation bias, whereby people increasingly believe in their conclusion as they receive *any* information. Although

Table 8.3   Average Accuracy and Confidence by Stage

	Stage 1	Stage 2	Stage 3	Stage 4
Percent Accurate	26.0	23.0	28.4	27.8
Confidence	33.2	39.2	46.0	52.8

this pattern of behavior was observed among all participants, it was most pronounced among the less-experienced undergraduate students. The experienced and inexperienced participants all displayed similar levels of accuracy in prediction, but the less-experienced were substantially more confident in their answers, particularly in stage 4. Thus, the value of consulting experts might not be the diagnosis they provide. Rather, the true value of experts might just be their ability to recognize the inherent level of uncertainty displayed in the diagnosis they provide.

EXAMPLE 8.9   Better than Average

Many of us fancy ourselves to be rather good drivers. Just how good? Ola Svenson asked 161 participants in the United States and Sweden to rate their overall driving skill. Of the Swedes, roughly 69 percent believed they drove better than 50 percent of all drivers, and 93 percent of U.S. drivers believed they drove better than 50 percent of all drivers. Clearly people overestimate their own ability to drive. Similar results have been shown for a variety of other skills (for example, achievement on standardized tests or grade point averages). In a similar vein, Michael Ross and Fiore Sicoly interviewed dozens of married couples, asking each spouse individually to assess their percentage contribution to various household chores. Of 20 different activities, there were 16 in which the husband's and wife's contributions added to more than 100 percent. Thus, at least one member of the household was overestimating his or her contribution to the household as a whole. Similar results have been found in basketball teams or on class projects. People seem to take too much credit for their work and believe they perform it at a level that not many others can achieve.

Self-Serving Bias

In close connection with optimistic overconfidence, people tend to bias information in self-serving ways. Thus, one overestimates one's ability to perform a specific task. One overestimates the importance of one's contribution to specific tasks. Finally, one interprets ambiguous information in a way that exaggerates one's value or worth. Such mistakes in judgment are collectively called **self-serving bias**. Such an effect appears to be pervasive in many various contexts. Psychologists have argued that a self-serving bias can be useful in helping someone to be self-assured and confident. However, such biases do not come without consequences. For example, those who wrongly believe that they are gifted in their ability to pick winners and losers on the stock market can end up paying the price for their bias. As well, people who inflate their previous accomplishments on a résumé or job application can be ousted from any position obtained on the false pretext. More interestingly, self-serving bias can negatively affect people and any organization that engages in a contract with them. For example, a contractor could overestimate her ability to perform on a construction job. This leads her to place bids for the job that claim a cost savings or a time savings over other contractors. Once on the job, the contractor's optimistic bias is exposed by reality. As costs or time mount beyond the bid, her employer will begin to feel the pinch.

EXAMPLE 8.10 Paying an Honest Tithe

Many churches ask for parishioners to donate to support church charity or other services, though some provide stricter guidelines than others. Members of the Church of Jesus Christ of Latter-day Saints (LDS) believe in scripture that commands them to donate 10 percent of their income. However, the church avoids providing unambiguous direction about what should be considered income. For example, one LDS member receiving an inheritance from a relative who had regularly paid tithing on her income when alive might not consider it necessary to pay tithing on the inheritance.

Gordon Dahl and Michael Ransom administered a survey of members of the LDS church, asking their opinions on what sorts of income parishioners should pay tithing on. Further, they asked the same respondents about their own previous income history. They found mild evidence of the self-serving bias in terms of financial gain. For example, parishioners who own a home were much less likely to believe that income earned by selling a home for more than it was originally purchased was subject to tithing (43 percent versus 34 percent). Alternatively, there was relative agreement on the need to pay tithing on inheritances, income earned from stock investments, or income from public benefits. In contrast, those who attend church less frequently were much more willing to say that it was not necessary to pay tithing on nearly any income source. For example, about nine in 10 of those who attend church weekly say it is necessary to pay tithing on inherited income. For those attending once or twice a month it was only about 65 percent. Similar differences were seen for stock value gains, housing gains, or public benefits. In this case, people with less of an attachment to the LDS church appear to be willing to alter the interpretation of a commandment of God in a self-serving way. Moreover, they find that the majority of respondents do not seek advice on what income is subject to tithing. By seeking such advice, they might find that they need to pay more tithing in order to meet their ideal of morality. Thus, self-serving bias can affect information search much like confirmation bias, leading one to avoid information that is potentially damaging to one's well-being.

Is Bad Information Bad?

It is worth noting that information only derives its value from how it might change the actions of a person. Consider again the farming example. In this case, the farmer was interested to learn whether the weather conditions would be good or bad. But this information is only valuable if the farmer can do something to respond to these whether conditions. Thus, learning that there would be little rain could be of use if it leads the farmer to invest in water conservation or reduce the investment in seed or fertilizer. Taking these actions allows the farmer to make a greater profit (or a smaller loss) given the conditions. Once all production input decisions are made and are irreversible, information is no longer valuable. Profits may be different if weather is good rather than bad, but if the farmer would not do anything to change her strategy in either state, the information does not increase expected profit. In this vein it is important to realize that misleading information does not always reduce the utility or profit of the information user. Watching and believing the reports from a news channel that skews all the news toward conservative views—even to the point of dishonesty—might not be damaging to the person's utility if the person would have responded with the same actions (e.g., voting, political donations, or activism) anyway. It is only damaging if it persuades the person to action that would not be taken if more-accurate information had been absorbed.

Obviously this argument would also apply to erroneous beliefs such as overconfidence. Thus overconfidence does no damage to people if it does not change their actions. However, in the case of overconfidence a stronger statement can be made. In fact, many psychologists have found that there are substantial benefits to overconfidence in some circumstances. This can occur, for example, if being overconfident about one's ability leads to a better or more-relaxed performance. For example, someone who is giving a presentation and who feels she is a poor speaker when underprepared and nervous might speak more haltingly or speak with less volume or emphasis. The person who feels she is a great public speaker may be able to perform better with the same level of preparation simply for lack of nerves. Oliver Compte and Andrew Postlewaite show that when performance depends on the level of confidence, overconfidence could actually improve utility or well-being. In this case, bad beliefs or information can improve well-being even if acted upon.

EXAMPLE 8.11   Self-Serving Bias and Negotiation Impasse

When modeling the negotiating process, economists typically assume that both parties face a significant cost if there is an impasse. For example, if labor negotiations fail, labor union members face significant loss of income in the course of a strike, and employers face significant losses in profits for either shutting down or using less-skilled replacements. Similarly, when a plaintiff sues a defendant, both face steep costs in court costs, and attorneys' fees. Thus, it is usually in their best interest to seek an out-of-court settlement. If this is the case, why do any cases go to court? Why are labor strikes as common as they are?

Linda Babcock and George Loewenstein suggest that self-serving bias may be the answer to both of these questions. They conducted two studies to see if self-serving bias played a role in the breakdown of negotiations. In the first study, an experiment, participants were asked to read the evidence and proceedings of an actual court case resulting from a traffic accident in Texas. Participants were asked to estimate the award given by the judge in the case. After being assigned as either defendant or plaintiff, they were then paired with another participant and asked to negotiate a settlement with a scaled-down pot of money, with the threat that the court-imposed settlement would prevail if they failed to reach an agreement and both sides would face additional costs. In a first condition, participants learned their role in the negotiations before they read the court proceedings. In this case, plaintiffs believed the settlement would be about $18,555 larger than those who were assigned as defendants, and close to 30 percent failed to negotiate a settlement. Alternatively, those who learned about their role only after reading the proceedings differed by only $6,936, and only 6 percent failed to reach a settlement.

The second study was a field study. All school district presidents and teachers' union presidents in the state of Pennsylvania were surveyed. Both were asked to list school districts they considered comparable to their own for the purposes of salary negotiation. The responses displayed the hypothesized self-serving bias. The average salary for school districts listed by union presidents was $27,633. Alternatively, the average salary of school districts listed by the presidents of the school boards was $26,922. This is about a 2.4 percent difference between the two. The responses were then compared to the number and incidence of previous labor disputes. They found that a discrepancy of comparable income of $1,000 or more increases the probability of a strike by about 49 percent. Thus, teachers, students, and boards all feel the pinch of self-serving bias.

History and Notes

Sir Francis Bacon, in his 1620 treatise *Novum Organum*, laments that "The human understanding when it has once adopted an opinion . . . draws all things else to support and agree with it." Thus he was the first to articulate confirmation bias four centuries ago. Further, his reasoning on logic illustrates a relatively sophisticated notion of confirmation bias and the need to avoid it in engaging in scientific inquiry. His work was subsequently built upon in the 1740s by the philosopher David Hume, who questioned entirely our ability to use inductive reasoning to generalize the results of a hypothesis test from one context to another. This debate has led to the somewhat rigid rules of scientific argument and testing now employed. Wason was the first to test for the psychological bias directly, finding substantial support for Bacon's ancient assertion.

The modern notion of overconfidence was originally discovered by Stuart Oskamp when examining the accuracy of experienced and inexperienced psychologists in diagnosing or predicting behavior. His general result, that amateurs are about as accurate though more confident in their answers, has been generalized to many and various contexts, including economic forecasting.

Biographical Note

Colin F. Camerer (1959–)

B.A., Johns Hopkins University, 1977; M.B.A., University of Chicago, 1979; Ph. D., University of Chicago, 1981; held faculty positions at Northwestern University, University of Pennsylvania, University of Chicago, and California Institute of Technology

By the age of 22, Colin Camerer had already obtained an M.B.A. specializing in finance and his Ph.D. in behavioral decision theory from the University of Chicago Graduate School of Business and began his faculty appointment at Northwestern University. He is an accomplished and renowned scholar both in behavioral theory and in experimental economic methods. He is best known for his work on decision under risk and uncertainty and behavioral game theory. Camerer is the author of the premier book on behavioral game theory, as well as scores of articles and book chapters developing the theory of behavior in games. He has also contributed to the growing field of neuroeconomics, serving as the president for the Society of Neuroeconomics from 2005 to 2006. Camerer is a Fellow of the Econometric Society and a member of the American Academy of Arts and Sciences. In addition to his academic work, Camerer has taken an interest in punk music, founding and running his own punk recording label since 1983. His label, Fever Records, produced recordings for such underground Chicago bands as Bonemen of Baruma and Big Black.

THOUGHT QUESTIONS

1. Confirmation bias leads people to interpret the same information in very different ways. Given such a bias is pervasive, one must be careful in forming initial opinions. If confirmation bias is pervasive, what might this say about the quality of information sources that are available for controversial topics in which people often hold sharply diverging views? When people claim strong evidence for their opinion, should we believe them? Is there a way to obtain unbiased assessments?

2. Suppose you hold a stock and are considering whether to sell it or keep it. You initially believe that the probability the stock will rise in value in the long run is 0.7. You decide you will sell the stock when the probability of a long run drop in value reaches 0.5. Then, over the course of time you watch the changes in the value of the stock day to day, each day's outcome serving as a forecast of future value. Further, suppose that $P(RISE|rise) = 0.6$ where $RISE$ indicates a long-run future rise in value and $rise$ indicates an observed daily rise in value. Correspondingly, $P(FALL|fall) = 0.6$, where $FALL$ indicates a long-run decline in future values of the stock and $fall$ indicates a daily observed decline in value. Suppose the probability that you misperceive a signal given it contradicts your current belief is $q = 0.4$. How many daily declines would you need to observe before you would sell the stock according to Rabin and Schrag's model of confirmation bias? What would a Bayesian's beliefs be regarding the probability of a decline at that point? How many daily declines would you need to observe in order to sell if you had perfect perception $(q = 0)$?

3. In this chapter, we motivated the rational model of information search by showing that rational people should prefer information that is accurate no matter how it relates to their current hypothesis. People should continue to seek new information until they are certain enough of the answer that the cost of new information is not justified by the degree of uncertainty. Confirmation bias can lead to overconfidence, where people fail to recognize the level of uncertainty they face. What implications are there for information search by those displaying confirmation bias? When will they cease to search for information? What might this imply regarding people who have chosen to cease their education efforts at various phases? What education policy might be implied by this result?

4. Governments often require people to obtain insurance; for example, all drivers are required to carry auto insurance to cover damages to others in the event of a crash. Homeowners are often required by banks to carry insurance on their home. Why do these requirements exist? Would they be necessary if people truly recognized the risk they faced? One characteristic of an overconfident person is that she is continually surprised when what she thought was unlikely or impossible comes to pass. What would happen in these cases if people were not required to insure? What problems might arise if governments also prepared for emergencies in a way that displayed overconfidence? What mechanisms could prevent overconfidence in government action?

5. Suppose we consider producers in a competitive market. Hence all producers are price takers and earn profit $\pi = pq - c(q)$, where p is a random variable. Thus, the mean of profit is $E(\pi) = \mu_p q - c(q)$, and variance of profit is $VAR(\pi) = \sigma_p^2 q^2$. Further, suppose that each producer has an expected utility of wealth function that can be approximated as $E(u(\pi)) = E(\pi) - (R_A/2) \ VAR(\pi)$ and that each behaves so as to maximize expected utility of wealth. Consider that some producers are overconfident and others are not. Which will produce more (larger q)? Which will obtain a higher profit on average? Suppose that the mean price declines over time. What is the condition for shut down? Will rational or overconfident producers shut down first? What does this say about the rationality of firms in a competitive environment?

REFERENCES

Alpert, M., and H. Raiffa, "A Progress Report on the Training of Probability Assessors." In D. Kahneman, P. Slovic, and A. Tversky (eds.). *Judgment under Uncertainty: Heuristics and Biases.* New York: Cambridge University Press, 1982, pp. 294–305.

Babcock, L., and G. Loewenstein. "Explaining Bargaining Impasse: The Role of Self-Serving Biases." *Journal of Economic Perspectives* 11(1997): 109–126.

Barber, B.M., and T. Odean. "Boys will be Boys: Gender, Overconfidence and Common Stock Investment." *Quarterly Journal of Economics* 116(2001): 261–292.

Bogan, V., and D.R. Just. "What Drives Merger Decision Making Behavior? Don't Seek, Don't Find, and Don't Change Your Mind." *Journal of Economic Behavior and Organization* 72 (2009): 930–943.

Brockhaus, R.H. "Risk Taking Propensity of Entrepreneurs." *Academy of Management Journal* 23(1980): 509–520.

Busenitz, L.W., and J.B. Barney, "Differences Between Entrepreneurs and Managers in Large Organizations: Biases and Heuristics in Strategic Decision-Making." *Journal of Business Venturing* 12(1997): 9–30.

Compte, O., and A. Postlewaite, "Confidence-Enhanced Performance." *American Economic Review* 94(2004): 1536–1557.

Dahl, G.B., and M.R. Ransom. "Does Where You Stand Depend on Where You Sit? Tithing Donations and Self-Serving Beliefs." *American Economic Review* 89(1999): 703–727.

Darley, J.M., and P.H. Gross. "A Hypothesis-Confirming Bias in Labeling Effects." *Journal of Personality and Social Psychology* 44(1983): 20–33.

Malmendier, U., and G. Tate. "Who Makes Acquisitions? CEO Overconfidence and the Market's Reaction." *Journal of Financial Economics* 89(2007): 20–43.

Mynatt, C.R., M.E. Doherty, R.D. Tweney. "Confirmation Bias in a Simulated Research Environment: An Experimental Study of Scientific Inference." *Quarterly Journal of Experimental Psychology* 29(1977): 85–95.

Oskamp, S. "Overconfidence in Case-Study Judgments." *Journal of Consulting Psychology* 29(1965): 261–265.

Rabin, M., and J.L. Schrag. "First Impressions Matter: A Model of Confirmatory Bias." *Quarterly Journal of Economics* 114(1999): 37–82.

Ross, M., and F. Sicoly. "Egocentric Biases in Availability and Attribution." *Journal of Personality and Social Psychology* 37 (1979): 322–336.

Svenson, O. "Are We all Less Risky and More Skillful than our Fellow Drivers?" *Acta Psychologica* 47(1981): 143–148.

Wason, P.C. "Reasoning About a Rule." *Quarterly Journal of Experimental Psychology* 20(1968): 273–281.

9

Decision under Risk and Uncertainty

In many fields of occupation, there are regular and agreed-upon cycles to the job market. For example, because college students generally graduate in June, many employers focus their efforts for hiring entry-level positions to begin work soon thereafter. Some employers are very highly sought after for their level of pay and the future career opportunities of their employees. Consider a less-sought-after employer who has difficulty offering salaries that are similar to those commonly offered in the market. Very often, in such markets, less-sought-after employers start their process of seeking recruits earlier than their peers and make offers that expire before their competitors will make their initial offers. Such exploding offers are designed to put the recruit in a quandary. Consider a very qualified recruit with an exploding offer. He can take the offer and obtain the lower pay and a secure job with certainty. Alternatively, if he rejects the offer, he takes his chances and potentially fails to find a more-desirable job. If the salary offer is low enough, he might have a very high probability of obtaining a more-lucrative offer when the real cycle of offers begins. Nonetheless, it can be very difficult to turn down a job without another offer in hand.

People often face problems of decision under risk. In general, models of decision under risk consist of two-component models: a model of preferences over outcomes and a model of risk perception. Rational models of decision under risk depend heavily on the assumption that people understand the potential outcomes of any risky choice and the probability of each of those outcomes. In the previous chapters, we discussed several anomalies related to how people deal with probabilistic information. Behavioral models of risky choice generally base the component model of beliefs on behavior observed in experimental settings. For example, people seem to treat certainty in a very different way than probabilistic outcomes, an effect that might make exploding job offers more profitable for inferior firms. Or people may be reluctant to invest in the stock market despite higher average returns, opting for low-returning savings accounts. Interestingly, experimental observations of choice under risk sometimes contradict the common behaviors discussed in the previous chapters.

Examining the economics of decision under risk is a bit of a challenge. In a standard consumption context, we may observe whether someone chooses to purchase an apple or not. We know with relative certainty that the person understood the characteristics of either choice and we can also know with relative certainty what those characteristics are. In the context of risk, we may observe whether someone chooses to purchase a share of a particular stock, and we can observe subsequent changes in the value of that stock. However, we will never easily be able to observe what the purchaser thought the probability of each possible outcome was or the actual probability distribution. By basing choice models on experimental results, theorists have hoped to sidestep this measurement issue. In an experiment, the experimenter has the freedom to select the probabilities and outcomes and specify them exactly. This control is a substantial advantage relative to field observations, but it also creates a potential weakness. The experiments can present risky choices that do not represent the real-world choices that people face.

Many decisions are made without a clear understanding of what choices are available, what the possible outcomes of the choices are, or what the relative probability of those outcomes may be. For example, consider college freshmen considering their choice of major. Although it may be possible to determine all the possible majors available in a university, it may be difficult to know what sorts of knowledge and potential employment options would be available with each possible major. Such ambiguity about the possibilities leads nearly half of all students to change majors at least once as they discover new information that leads them in a different direction. Many students put off declaring a major until the last possible moment. Moreover, some students gain excessive credits in their search for the right major. This has led some universities (for example, the University of Wisconsin) to charge students who take too many credits, trying to encourage earlier decisions and earlier graduations. The latter portion of this chapter describes economic theories of how people deal with ambiguous choices such as these, as well as their impact on outcomes.

The ease with which people can introduce and test models of decision under risk has led to the introduction of dozens of competing models. In this chapter and the next I present the most important behavioral concepts arising from the behavioral risk literature, including only a small selection of the models that have been proposed. The interested reader who wishes to see a broader treatment of models of decision under risk is directed to the literature review compiled by Chris Starmer.

Rational Decision under Risk

Frank Knight, in his 1920s work on the importance of risk, distinguished between the terms **risk** and **uncertainty**. **Knightian risk** refers to a situation in which the outcome is not known with certainty but in which the decision maker knows all the possible outcomes and the probabilities associated with each (or at least has a subjective understanding of the probabilities). Gambles taken in a casino clearly fall into this category, as do most financial investments. Alternatively, **Knightian uncertainty** refers to situations in which either the set of possible outcomes or the probabilities associated with those outcomes are not known. Risk faced because of potential unforeseen and unknowable catastrophes may be classified as resulting in Knightian uncertainty. For example, before September 11, 2001, no one had experienced a calamitous terror attack on U.S. soil such as the attacks on New York and Washington, D.C. Having never experienced it, it would be difficult for people to know the range of possible financial implications for investors or the likelihood of any of those possible outcomes. People fearing a total collapse may be led to pull all of their money from stocks for fear of the unknown and unknowable. Knightian uncertainty is now more commonly referred to in the literature as **ambiguity** to avoid potential confusion with the term *risk*. As is common, I use the terms "risk" and "uncertainty" interchangeably, referring to Knightian uncertainty as ambiguity.

Expected utility theory is the most commonly accepted rational model of decision under risk. This model supposes that people select the choice that provides the highest expected utility of wealth. Expected utility theory was first proposed by Daniel Bernoulli in 1738 in an attempt to solve the St. Petersburg paradox. Suppose you had the possibility of playing a game. If you play the game, a coin would be tossed n times, where n was the number of tosses required before the first heads was tossed. Then, you would receive $\$2^n$. If such a game were available, how much would you be willing to pay in order to play? In the early 1700s, many had thought that the expected value of the payout of the gamble might be a good model of the value of such a game, but it seems implausible that anyone would be willing to pay the expected value for this particular game. In this particular game, the expected value is given by

$$E(x) = 0.5 \times 2 + 0.5 \times 0.5 \times 2^2 + 0.5 \times 0.5 \times 0.5 \times 2^3 \cdots + = \sum_{i=1}^{\infty} (0.5)^i \times 2^i = \sum_{i=1}^{\infty} 1 = \infty.$$
(9.1)

If someone maximized the expected payout, he would be willing to pay any finite price to play this game. Bernoulli believed that people must value money differently depending on how much they had accumulated. Thus, a dollar might not be worth as much to a billionaire as to one with only a couple hundred dollars to his name. This led Bernoulli to posit that people instead maximize their expected **utility of wealth**. For example, suppose the gambler's utility function were the natural log function (which displays a diminishing slope). In this case, the expected utility would be

$$E(U(x)) = \sum_{i=1}^{\infty} (0.5)^i \times \ln(2^i) = \ln(2) \sum_{i=1}^{\infty} i/2^i \approx 1.39,$$
(9.2)

which is equal to the utility that would be obtained by gaining $4. Thus, this person would be willing to pay at most $4 to play the game.

This model is considered rational because it is based on a series of three rational axioms. A rational axiom is a rule for making rational choices that the economist generally assumes all decision makers must adhere to. Let $\succ$ (read "preferred to") be a set of rational preferences. Then $\succ$ must satisfy the order, continuity, and independence axioms. We focus primarily on the order and independence axioms, because these are the central motivation for many behavioral models of risky choice.

The Order Axiom

Preference, $\succ$, must be complete and transitive. Completeness implies that if A and B are any two gambles, then either $A \succ B$ (meaning A would be chosen over B), $B \succ A$, or $A \sim B$ (meaning the gambler is indifferent between A and B). Additionally, transitivity implies that if A, B, and C are any three gambles, and $A \succ B$ and $B \succ C$, then $A \succ C$.

The order axiom imposes the same requirements on choice under uncertainty that rationality demands for choice under certainty (see the discussion of completeness and transitivity in Chapter 1). Thus, a gambler must be able to evaluate all possible gambles and must have preferences that do not cycle. Thus, any gamble that is better than a particular gamble must also be better than all gambles that are worse than that particular gamble.

The Continuity Axiom

If $A \succ B \succ C$, then there is exactly one value r such that neither B nor the compound gamble that yields the gamble A with probability r and the gamble C with probability $(1-r)$ are preferred; we write this as $rA + (1-r)C \sim B$. Further, for any $p > r$, the compound gamble that yields the gamble A with probability p and the gamble C with probability $(1-p)$ is preferred to B (we write this $pA + (1-p)C \succ B$), and for any $q < r$, B is preferred to the compound gamble that yields the gamble A with probability q and the gamble C with probability $(1-q)$, or $B \succ qA + (1-q)C$.

The continuity axiom requires that making small increases in the probability of a preferred gamble must increase the value of that gamble. For a full definition and discussion of the order and continuity axioms, see the Advanced Concept box at the end of the chapter. The independence axiom is described in detail later.

People who make decisions complying with the order, continuity, and independence axioms behave as if they are trying to maximize the expected utility of wealth resulting from the gamble. Thus, the utility of a probability p of obtaining \$100 and $(1-p)$ of obtaining \$0 can be represented as $p \cdot u(100) + (1-p) \cdot u(0)$, which is just the expected utility of the gamble. This provides the result that those who obey these three rational axioms will behave as if they are maximizing their expected utility when facing any choice involving risk.

Expected utility theory also implies that a **stochastically dominant** gamble is always chosen. For example, suppose you were presented a choice of

Gamble X:	Gamble Y:
0.4 probability of winning \$10	0.5 probability of winning \$11
0.6 probability of winning \$3	0.5 probability of winning \$3

In this case, Gamble Y always yields a higher probability of a larger amount of money. Let $P(X > k)$ be the probability that the result of Gamble X is larger than \$k. Formally, we say Gamble Y *stochastically dominates* Gamble X if $P(X > k) \leq P(Y > k)$ for all values of k. Thus, a gamble that has a higher probability of a larger prize for every prize level is stochastically dominant. For example, $P(X > 3) = 0.4 < P(Y > 3) = 0.5$. As well, $P(X > 10) = 0 < P(Y > 10) = 0.5$. This same relation would hold no matter what value k we choose.

Any time a Gamble Y stochastically dominates X, then $\sum_z P(Y = z) U(z) \geq \sum_z P(X = z) U(z)$, implying that the person will always choose Y. To see this, note that

$\sum_z P(Y=z)U(z) \geq \sum_z P(X=z)U(z)$ is equivalent to $\sum_z [P(Y=z) - P(X=z)]U(z) \geq 0$, which must be the case if Y stochastically dominates X and utility is positive valued. In this case, it seems like any reasonable decision maker would want to choose Y. In this example, Gamble Y dominates Gamble X. However, more generally it is not always possible to find a stochastically dominant gamble. For example, consider

Gamble X':	Gamble Y':
0.6 probability of winning $10	0.5 probability of winning $11
0.2 probability of winning $3	0.3 probability of winning $3
0.2 probability of winning $0	0.2 probability of winning $0

In this case, $P(X' > 3) = 0.6 > P(Y' > 3) = 0.5$, but $P(X' > 10) = 0 < P(Y' > 10) = 0.5$. Thus, neither gamble dominates.

EXAMPLE 9.1   Creating a Money Pump

Many have argued that people must display transitive preferences because anyone who did not have transitive preferences would be the subject of a **money pump**. For example, if Terry displayed preferences such that $A \succ B \succ C \succ A$, Robin, wishing to take advantage of Terry, could offer Terry the chance to play gamble A for free. Then, once Robin has guaranteed Terry a play of gamble A, Robin could offer Terry gamble C if Terry pays Robin some small amount of money. Once Terry is endowed with C, Robin could offer to trade Terry B if Terry pays Robin some small amount of money. Robin could then offer Terry A for some small amount of money and start the process all over again. If Terry's preferences were stable and intransitive, Robin could theoretically continue to do this until Terry was out of money. It seems unlikely that such a scheme would work in practice. Nonetheless, this might not doom the concept of intransitive preferences.

Suppose you were given a series of choices between possible gambles. Suppose you could first choose between

Gamble A:	Gamble B:
0.4 probability of winning $10	0.7 probability of winning $7.50
0.6 probability of winning $3	0.3 probability of winning $1

Graham Loomes, Chris Starmer, and Robert Sugden found that about 51 percent of participants in experiments would choose Gamble B over Gamble A. Suppose next you were asked to choose between

Gamble C:	Gamble D:
1.0 probability of winning $5	0.7 probability of winning $7.50
	0.3 probability of winning $1

Of participants in their experiment, about 88 percent chose Gamble C over Gamble D. Finally, consider a choice between

Gamble E:	Gamble F:
0.4 probability of winning $10	1.0 probability of winning $5
0.6 probability of winning $3	

Of participants in the experiment, about 70 percent chose Gamble E over Gamble F. Note however, that Gamble E and Gamble A are identical, as are Gambles B and D and Gambles C and F. Nearly 30 percent of participants chose A, C, and F, implying that $A \succ B \succ C \succ A$. Several similar sets of gambles were offered to 200 participants, with 64 percent displaying some preference cycle with at least one set of gambles. Thus, a majority of people appear to be subject to intransitive preferences, a violation of the order axiom.

In fact, experiments have found systematic intransitivities in individual preferences over gambles. These intransitivities are called **preference reversals**. This pattern of preference reversals was first discovered by Sarah Lichtenstein and Paul Slovic, who asked participants in their experiments to perform two distinct tasks. First, participants were asked to choose among pairs of gambles. Then, after some passage of time, people were asked to bid on each gamble individually, revealing their willingness to pay for each gamble. Each gamble consisted of some simple probability of winning some specified amount of money, and the remaining probability was assigned to the chance of losing some specified amount of money. In the choice experiment, gambles were paired so that one of the gambles had the possibility of winning a larger amount of money (called the **$-bet**, pronounced "dollar-bet"), while the other would have a larger probability of winning a positive amount of money (called the **P-bet**).

Lichtenstein and Slovic found that although people tended to choose P-bets over $-bets, they would often bid higher amounts for the $-bets. This is similar to the pattern of behavior above, where Gamble A represents the $-bet and Gamble B represents the P-bet. Here the P-bet is valued at less than $5 and the $-bet is valued at more than $5. However, many people tended to take the P-bet over the $-bet. Lichtenstein and Slovic's experiment was repeated on the floor of a Las Vegas casino, with patrons given the chance to switch gambles repeatedly without ever playing a gamble. Many actually fall into the money pump trap, though most eventually discovered their irrationality. If you go to Las Vegas, beware of experimental economists. In fact, economists' skepticism about the potential violation of the order axiom has made this one of the most tested and confirmed phenomena in behavioral economics.

EXAMPLE 9.2   Stochastic Inferiority

It might seem surprising to find violations of stochastic dominance, but in fact it is relatively easy to find examples in economic experiments. The most famous example was given by Daniel Kahneman and Amos Tversky, who asked 124 people to choose between two lotteries described by the percentage of marbles of different colors in a box and the amount of money that would result from a particular color marble being drawn at random.

Gamble A:		Gamble B:	
Marbles	**Money**	**Marbles**	**Money**
90% white	$0	90% white	$0
6% red	win $45	7% red	win $45
1% green	win $30	1% green	lose $10
3% yellow	lose $15	2% yellow	lose $15

Participants were told they would be chosen at random, with those selected facing real money outcomes from their choices. Clearly Gamble B stochastically dominates Gamble A. In B there is only a 2 percent chance of losing $15, with the remaining 1 percent chance now allocated to the possibility of losing $10. Gamble B has an additional 1 percent chance of winning $45, reallocated from the 1 percent chance of winning $30 in A. Nearly 60 percent of those participating chose gamble A, however. People were attracted to the choice with fewer negative outcomes and more positive outcomes, even though the choice with fewer negative outcomes was not as favorable.

Presenting the gambles in a way that makes the dominance clear leads to a much higher percentage identifying the dominant option. For example, when asked to choose between

Gamble C:		Gamble D:	
Marbles	**Money**	**Marbles**	**Money**
90% white	$0	90% white	$0
6% red	win $45	6% red	win $45
1% green	win $30	1% green	win $45
1% blue	lose $15	1% blue	lose $10
2% yellow	lose $15	2% yellow	lose $15

all respondents chose Gamble D. When gambles are presented in a convoluted fashion, people appear to resort to heuristics and rules of thumb to make their choices. We refer to the clarity of presentation as the **transparency**. When choices are presented in a transparent way, behavioral anomalies are often minimized. Michael Birnbaum and Juan Navarrete have found violations of dominance owing to lack of transparency to be a common phenomenon in economics experiments.

Modeling Intransitive Preferences: Regret and Similarity

Three primary explanations have been given for why we observe the violations of the order axiom. The first is based on the notion that preference reversals are simply evidence that people use different processes to perform the differing tasks (in this case choosing versus valuing). Thus, the probabilities and values enter into the decision process differently depending on which task the person is asked to perform. For example, when asked to formulate their willingness to pay, people may be drawn to anchor on the amount of money that can be won, and then adjust downward for the uncertainty. This likely leads to higher willingness to pay measures for bets involving larger amounts of potential winnings. Alternatively, when asked to choose between two gambles, the person might place more emphasis on the probabilities involved, opting for safer bets. Although this is probably the majority view of economists, Loomes, Starmer, and Sugden's experiment was designed primarily to combat the notion that response mode is the only source of preference reversals. In their experiment described in Example 9.1, they were careful not to ask for the person to formulate a willingness to pay but rather to ask which of two gambles the person preferred in each case, including several degenerate gambles.

Graham Loomes and Robert Sugden proposed **regret theory** as a procedurally rational explanation for why preference reversals occur. Regret theory supposes that someone's preference for a gamble depends upon the other possible options that may be chosen. Thus, we could not represent someone's valuation of a single gamble as we do when employing expected utility. Rather, we would need to know what options he is trading off. More specifically, regret theory supposes that a person has a utility function given by $U(x, y)$, where x represents the money or object the person obtains and y represents the outcome of the option forgone. We call this the *regret theory utility function*. Whereas increasing x leads to higher utility, increasing y decreases utility as people feel more and more disappointed that they did not choose the forgone gamble. For example, if one received \$5 when the alternative would have yielded \$1, one feels better than if the alternative yielded \$20. Regret theory supposes that people maximize the expectation of the regret theory utility function.

The regret theory utility function displays two important additional properties. First, for all outcomes x, y, $U(x, y) = -U(y, x)$ and $U(x, x) = 0$. A regret theory utility function meeting these conditions is called **skew symmetric**. The skew-symmetric property implies that the positive utility experienced from an outcome of \$10 when the alternative was \$5 is exactly the additive inverse of the negative utility experienced when the person received \$5 and could have received \$10. Thus, some symmetry of joy or disappointment is required. Second, for any outcomes $x > y > z$, it must be that $U(z, x) < U(y, x) + U(z, y)$. This property is called **regret aversion**. This implies that the regret felt when one obtains the lowest prize when the highest was the alternative is greater than the loss felt when obtaining the middle when the highest was the alternative plus the regret felt when obtaining the lowest when the middle was available. In other words, one would prefer two small disappointments to one large disappointment. An example of the regret utility function is displayed in Figure 9.1. You will quickly notice that this function is very similar to that of the prospect theory value function except that it is concave to the left of $x = y$ and convex to the right. Instead of a reference point, we now have an alternative outcome at the origin. Regret aversion implies that the slope of the utility function must be increasing as the difference between x and y increases. Holding y constant, this is displayed in the figure by an increasing slope as x increases above y and an increasing slope as x decreases below y.

Suppose Dominique could bet on one of two football teams that were playing each other: team A and team B. If Dominique bets on team A and team A wins, Dominique

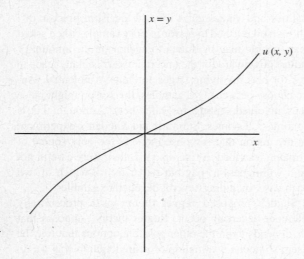

FIGURE 9.1
The Regret Theory
Utility Function Hold-
ing y Constant

receives $100. If Dominique bets on team A and team B wins, Dominique loses $100. Alternatively, suppose that if Dominique bets on team B and team B wins, Dominique will receive $50, but if team B loses, Dominique will lose $50. Finally suppose that the probability that team A wins is 0.3. Then the expected regret utility of choosing team A given B is available would be

$$EU(A|B) = 0.3U(100, -50) + 0.7U(-100, 50) \qquad (9.3)$$

and of choosing team B when A is available would be

$$EU(B|A) = 0.3U(-50, 100) + 0.7U(50, -100) = -EU(A|B) \qquad (9.4)$$

This last equality is a result of the skew-symmetric property. It must always be the case that the expected regret utility of one choice is exactly the negative of the expected regret utility of the other. Thus, we need only examine whether the expected regret utility of any one choice is positive to determine which will be chosen. Thus, bet A would be chosen if

$$0.3U(100, -50) + 0.7U(-100, 50) > 0. \qquad (9.5)$$

Consider the choices presented in Example 9.1, only now let us rewrite Gambles A, B, and C as in Table 9.1, which represents the gambles presented in the first example, only in terms of alternative states of the world with stable probabilities. In this case, a state of the world consists of a specified outcome for each of the possible gamble choices. This is truly how Loomes, Starmer, and Sugden presented the gambles in the experiments described in Example 9.1. Thus, the outcomes of the gambles were correlated (which does not alter the calculation of expected utility).

Table 9.1   Three Gambles (see Example 1)

	State		
	1	2	3
Probability	0.4	0.3	0.3
Gamble A	10.00	3.00	3.00
Gamble B	7.50	7.50	1.00
Gamble C	5.00	5.00	5.00

Given a choice of A and B, B will be chosen if

$$EU(B|A) = 0.4U(7.5, \ 10) + 0.3U(7.5, \ 3) + 0.3U(1, \ 3) > 0. \tag{9.6}$$

Further, given a choice of B and C, C will be chosen if

$$EU(C|B) = 0.4U(5, \ 7.5) + 0.3U(5, \ 7.5) + 0.3U(5, \ 1) > 0. \tag{9.7}$$

Finally, given a choice of A and C, A will be chosen if

$$EU(A|C) = 0.4U(10, \ 5) + 0.3U(3, \ 5) + 0.3U(3, \ 5) > 0. \tag{9.8}$$

Regret aversion can explain this behavior if equations 9.8, 9.9, and 9.10 can all hold simultaneously. For now, let us assume equations 9.8 and 9.9 hold, meaning that $A \succ B$, and $C \succ B$. These two are not, by themselves, a violation of order and could be reconciled with expected utility theory. However, given $A \succ B$, and $C \succ B$, expected utility theory could not allow $A \succ C$. Equation 9.9 implies that $A \succ C$ under regret theory. Let us examine if equation 9.10 could hold given that equations 9.8 and 9.9 both hold. The possible outcomes of the three gambles in state 1 are $10 > 7.5 > 5$. The property regret aversion tells us that $U(5, \ 10) < U(7.5, \ 10) + U(5, \ 7.5)$. Multiplying by -1 and noting that skew symmetry implies $U(10, \ 5) = -U(5, \ 10)$, we find

$$U(10, \ 5) > -U(5, \ 7.5) - U(7.5, \ 10). \tag{9.9}$$

The possible outcomes in state 2 are $7.5 > 5 > 3$. Regret aversion implies $U(3, 7.5) < U(5, \ 7.5) + U(3, \ 5)$. Subtracting $U(5, \ 7.5)$ from both sides and noting that skew symmetry implies $U(3, \ 7.5) = -U(7.5, \ 3)$, yields

$$U(3, \ 5) > -U(7.5, \ 3) - U(5, \ 7.5). \tag{9.10}$$

The possible outcomes in state 3 are $5 > 3 > 1$, with regret aversion implying $U(1, 5) < U(3, \ 5) + U(1, \ 3)$. Subtracting $U(1, \ 3)$ from both sides and noting that skew symmetry implies $-U(5, \ 1) = U(1, \ 5)$ yields

$$U(3, \ 5) > -U(1, \ 3) - U(5, \ 1). \tag{9.11}$$

The left side of inequalities 9.11, 9.12, and 9.13 are all the possible outcomes of choosing A when C was available (see equation 9.10). Thus, the restrictions implied by regret aversion and skew symmetry are that $EU(A|C) > -EU(B|A) - EU(C|B)$. Because the right side of this inequality is negative (by equations 9.8 and 9.9), any value of $EU(A|C)$ that is positive will satisfy both regret theory and equation 9.10. Thus, the theory permits the type of preference cycling implied by equations 9.8 to 9.10.

But not all types of preference cycling are permitted by regret theory. If A is chosen over B,

$$EU(B|A) = 0.4U(7.5, 10) + 0.3U(7.5, 3) + 0.3U(1, 3) < 0. \qquad (9.12)$$

And if B is chosen over C

$$EU(C|B) = 0.4U(5, 7.5) + 0.3U(5, 7.5) + 0.3U(5, 1) < 0. \qquad (9.13)$$

Now, equations 9.11, 9.12, and 9.13 imply that $EU(A|C) > -EU(B|A) - EU(C|B) > 0$, thus A must be chosen over C in this case. Thus, although $A \succ C \succ B \succ A$ is possible, $A \succ B \succ C \succ A$ is not. In fact, experiments have found a far greater percentage of those who violate the order axiom are of the nature predicted by regret aversion than of the nature that are excluded by regret aversion. In other words, if people evaluate individual gambles by considering the regret they will feel if unchosen options turn out to be best, then we should expect some sorts of intransitivity. In particular, the person will always cycle toward gambles that provide the lowest average regret. In this case, each gamble dominates at least one other choice in two of three states of the world, leading each to be preferred to one other option. Similarly, the person might violate stochastic dominance if the best outcomes of the inferior gamble are always paired with the worst outcomes of the dominant gamble (see the second thought question).

Notably, we have shown this result with distributions for each option that are statistically **dependent**. In other words, this result occurs because of the specific outcomes that occur in the same state. For a given set of preferences, the possibility of preference cycling might depend on whether the gambles were independent (so that the outcome of one does not provide us any information about the outcome of another). If the gambles are independent then these preference cycles would not occur. Regret theory still predicts preference cycling under independent gambling alternatives. It also predicts that some people will display preference cycling for dependent gambles but not for gambles with identical probabilities for each outcome that are statistically independent. Thus, some might choose $A \succ C \succ B \succ A$ when the gambles are presented as in Table 9.1 but not when presented as in Example 9.1.

Ariel Rubinstein proposed an alternative procedurally rational decision mechanism that can account for this particular pattern of preference cycling based on **similarity**. Rubinstein proposes a three-stage process for choosing between two gambles. First, the gambler inspects the gambles, determining if one stochastically dominates the other. If one is stochastically dominant, that gamble is chosen. If neither of the gambles is stochastically dominant, then the gambler compares the probabilities and the outcomes of the gambles. If the probabilities are similar, then one would make the decision based upon the outcomes. If the outcomes are similar, one would make the decision based upon the probabilities. If neither is similar, then the gambler would base the decision on some other mechanism. As an example, consider a pair of gambles

Gamble X:	Gamble Y:
p_x probability of winning $\$x$	p_y probability of winning $\$y$
$1 - p_x$ probability of winning $\$0$	$1 - p_y$ probability of winning $\$0$

Write $r \approx q$ if r and q are close enough that the gambler perceives them to be similar. Rubinstein's decision steps may be outlined as:

Step 1:   If both $x > y$ and $p_x > p_y$ then Gamble X is chosen. If both $y > x$ and $p_y > p_x$ then Gamble Y is chosen. If neither holds, then move to Step 2.

Step 2:   If $p_y \approx p_x$ but $x \not\approx y$ then choose the gamble with the greater payout. If $x \approx y$ but $p_x \not\approx p_y$ then choose the gamble with the larger probability of payout. If neither condition holds, then move to Step 3 (which is not specified).

Jonathan Leland modified Rubinstein's mechanism to consider more-complicated gambles. In essence, he proposes that Step 1 consider the expected utility of the gambles. If the expected utility of both gambles is similar (in other words, there is no clearly dominant gamble), then probabilities and outcomes would be compared to decide. Although Rubinstein's original formulation excludes the possibility that a gambler would choose a stochastically dominated gamble, this generalization allows it in the case that both gambles generate similar expected utility.

Consider again the choices outlined in Example 9.1. When comparing Gamble A to Gamble B, neither stochastically dominates the other. In comparing the gambles, $7.50 may be considered similar to $10, and $3 may be considered similar to $1. However, 0.7 (attached to $7.50) is much larger than 0.4 (attached to $10). Thus the gambler may be led to choose B. In comparing C and D, again neither stochastically dominates. If $5 and $7.50 are considered similar, then the gambler would clearly choose C, with a probability 1 of obtaining the payout. In comparing E and F, $3 may be similar to $5, and $10 is much larger. Thus, the gambler may be led to choose E, displaying the observed behavioral pattern. This explanation of preference cycling, however, does not appeal to the dependence or independence of the gambles involved. Thus, similarity predicts that preference reversals should occur about as often in independent and dependent gambles. In fact, Leland finds that preference reversals are as likely to occur with independent gambles as they are to occur with dependent gambles.

EXAMPLE 9.3   Lotteries, Litigation, and Regret

Those who run publicly sanctioned lotteries have long searched for innovative ways to induce potential customers to buy. This has led to a wide variety of scratch-off games and various other lottery mechanisms. Lottery players in the Netherlands are offered two variants of a lottery for their gaming pleasure. The first is a standard lottery in which one buys a ticket and selects a number, and if the number is drawn one wins. The second lottery is a postal code lottery. In this lottery, players either buy a ticket or not. The number is the postal code in which they reside. If their postal code is selected, they win. However, if they don't buy and their postal code is selected, many of their neighbors win and they don't. Such an outcome could induce regret for not having purchased a lottery ticket. Alternatively, not playing the standard lottery generally means you did not have a selected number in mind and thus would never know that you would have won had you simply bought a ticket.

Marcel Zeelenberg and Rik Pieters surveyed potential lottery players in the Netherlands regarding the two lotteries. A larger percentage associated feelings of regret with the postal code lottery than with the standard lottery. Moreover, these anticipated feelings of regret influenced people's intentions to buy lottery tickets. The more regret they anticipated due to knowing they had lost, the more likely they were to play the postal code lottery. Alternatively, regret had little to do with purchasing standard lottery tickets.

Chris Guthrie found similar sentiments when surveying law students about the potential to settle out of court rather than pursue trial. Going to trial is generally a risky proposition. Courts might decide in your favor and award you a substantial amount of money. Alternatively, they might decide against you, in which case you can incur significant court costs without compensation. In many cases, many plaintiffs sue for similar offenses. For example, several workers at a plant might sue for damages caused by unsafe working conditions. Each case should have the same chance of succeeding provided their lawyers have the same level of skill. In this case, a single worker might decide to settle out of court, but if others do not, they will likely learn of the potential outcome had they gone to court. Guthrie finds that law students believe litigants are more likely to settle out of court if they will likely never know what the outcome of the trial would be. This might mean that people in parallel cases are much less likely to settle, whereas combining their cases could lead them to avoid going to trial. Regret can push people to take much greater risk at substantial cost.

Independence and Rational Decision under Risk

Expected utility also requires that behavior conform to the independence axiom. This axiom provides a description of how people value compound gambles. A **compound gamble** is a gamble that consists of receiving some other set of gambles with fixed probabilities.

Independence Axiom

Let A, B, and C represent three gambles. If $A \succ B$, then the compound gamble that yields gamble A with probability p and gamble C with probability $(1-p)$ is preferred to the compound gamble that yields B with probability p and C with probability $(1-p)$, which can be written in shorthand form $pA + (1-p)C \succ pB + (1-p)C$.

The independence axiom imposes that preferences between two gambles should not be affected by common contingencies. Thus, if I prefer to bet \$5 on the red horse rather than the blue horse when they are the only two horses running, I should still prefer to bet on the red horse over the blue horse if a third (or even many more) horses are racing. Suppose that betting on the winning horse would double your money, but betting on any other horse would result in no payoff. Further, suppose there is 0.6 probability of the red horse beating the blue horse. Then betting on the red horse when they are the only two horses running (Gamble A) means taking a gamble that yields $10 with probability 0.6 and $0 with probability 0.4. Betting on the blue horse when only two horses are running (Gamble B) would yield $0 with 0.6 probability and $10 with 0.4 probability. Most would choose gamble A given it yields a higher probability of obtaining money. Now suppose a third horse (green horse) is also running. With all three, suppose that there is a 0.2 probability that the green horse will win, and the remaining 0.8 probability is distributed as before: $0.8 \times 0.6 = 0.48$ probability that red will win and $0.8 \times 0.4 = 0.32$ probability that blue will win. If given only the choice between betting on red or blue, the independence axiom requires that a bettor still prefers betting on red. In this case, Gamble C can be thought of as betting on either blue or red when green will win the race for certain. This results in a probability of 1 of receiving $0. Betting on red in the three-horse race is like taking the compound gamble that yields Gamble A with probability 0.8 and Gamble C with probability 0.2. Betting on blue in the three-horse race is like taking the compound gamble that yields Gamble B with probability 0.8 and Gamble C with probability 0.2.

One must be careful when applying the independence axiom to fully specify each gamble. For example, suppose we consider a man who has agreed to meet his spouse for an evening out. They had discussed on the phone either going to a movie or bowling, but the conversation was cut off before they had made a final decision. Thus, he must choose to go either to the bowling alley or to the movie theater with a chance that his spouse will choose to go to the other event. The man is indifferent between attending a movie or bowling by himself, but he would much prefer to be at an event with his spouse to attending alone. In this case, we might be tempted to say that if the husband is indifferent between going bowling with his spouse or to a movie with his spouse, $u(bowling, spouse) = u(movie, spouse)$, then the husband should also be indifferent among the following three gambles

Gamble A:	Gamble B:	Gamble C:
Spouse attends movie with certainty	Spouse attends bowling with certainty	0.5 probability spouse attends movie
		0.5 probability spouse attends bowling

However, this is not the case. In this case, we have not fully specified the gambles. If the man knows his spouse will be at the movie (Gamble A), he will choose to attend the movie and obtain a higher level of utility, $u(movie, spouse)$. If the man knows his spouse will be at the bowling alley (Gamble B), he will attend also and obtain a higher utility, $u(bowling, spouse)$. If instead, he believes Gamble C to be the case, whichever choice he takes (e.g., bowling) will result in a 0.5 probability of being there alone, yielding $U = 0.5u(bowling, spouse) + 0.5u(bowling, alone) < u(bowling, spouse)$. In this case, the specification of the gambles does not allow for the person's reaction. Suppose on the way to his car, the man runs into his spouse, who promptly blindfolds him and drives him to one of the events. Now he is guaranteed to be there with his spouse, and he is indifferent between the movie and bowling. If we consider Gambles A, B, and C in the context of the man's spouse choosing which event to go to, the independence axiom would now apply. Because he knows he will be there with his spouse, Gamble A will yield $u(movie, spouse)$ and Gamble B will yield $u(bowling, spouse)$. But in this case, if the spouse decides which event to attend by a simple coin flip (Gamble C), the husband will receive $U = 0.5u(bowling, spouse) + 0.5u(movie, spouse) = u(bowling, spouse)$. Thus, he doesn't care where the spouse decides to drive him.

The order axiom implies that we can represent the preferences of any degenerate gambles (gambles with only one possible outcome) using a utility function. Thus, we could define a function $u(x)$, where x represents an amount of money obtained with certainty. The continuity and independence axioms tell us how this utility function must relate to the preferences for gambles involving risk. From continuity and independence, we know we can represent the utility of the combination of any two gambles as the sum of the probability of each gamble multiplied by the utility derived from each gamble, thus yielding the expected utility model.

Economists have generally embraced expected utility since its reintroduction by John von Neuman and Oskar Morgenstern in the 1940s in their work creating the field of game theory. The axioms upon which expected utility rests make sense as behavioral rules. It would be hard to argue that people wishing to make themselves the best off they can be would violate such a clear and logical set of rules. Nonetheless, these rationality axioms make some strict predictions about behavior and preferences.

One simple way to think about expected utility theory is in terms of indifference curves over gambles involving the same outcomes but different probabilities of those outcomes. Figure 9.2 displays indifference curves over three outcomes in a display alternatively referred to as the unit simplex or the **Marschak–Machina triangle** (after

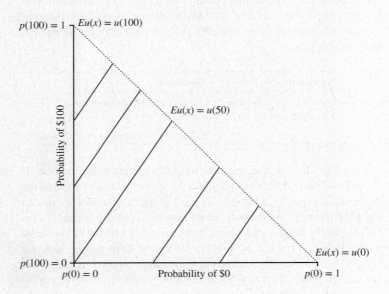

FIGURE 9.2
Indifference Curves over Compound Gambles involving $100, $50, and $0

Jacob Marschak and Mark Machina). The x-axis in the figure represents the probability of wining \$0, and the y-axis represents the probability of winning \$100. The probability of a third outcome, winning \$50, is not pictured on an axis. Thus, each point in the triangle represents a lottery with the probability of winning \$0 represented by the x-coordinate, the probability of winning \$100 represented by the y-coordinate, and the probability of winning \$50 equal to the remaining probability (one minus the x- and y-coordinates). The points along the x-axis represent gambles in which the probability of winning \$100 is 0. Thus all points on this line represent gambles that could result in winning either \$50 or \$0. The point (0,0) represents the gamble yielding \$50 with certainty. The point (1,0) represents winning \$0 with certainty. The points along the y-axis represent all gambles with a probability of 0 of winning \$0. The point (0,1) represents the gamble that yields \$100 with certainty. The dashed line running from the upper left to the lower right portion of the graph represents the boundary of the triangle. Along this boundary the sum of probabilities of \$100 and \$0 outcomes is 1, and thus the probability of winning \$50 is 0.

The parallel lines stretching from the lower left to the upper right represent indifference curves in the triangle. The indifference curve containing all points yielding utility identical to receiving \$50 with certainty is labeled. Because we have placed the probability of \$100 on the y-axis and \$0 on the x-axis, all indifference curves to the left of this curve represent a higher level of utility than \$50 and all to the right represent a lower level of utility. You will note that all indifference curves are parallel and straight lines. Let y be the probability of winning \$100 and x be the probability of winning \$0. In the triangle, an indifference curve is all probabilities y and x that satisfy

$$yu(100) + xu(0) + (1 - x - y)u(50) = k. \tag{9.14}$$

Solving equation 9.14 for y in terms of x yields

$$y = \frac{k - u(50)}{u(100) - u(50)} + x \frac{u(50) - u(0)}{u(100) - u(50)}. \tag{9.15}$$

Because the value k and the utilities are fixed, this always represents a line with slope given by

$$\frac{\Delta y}{\Delta x} = \frac{u(50) - u(0)}{u(100) - u(50)}. \tag{9.16}$$

Thus, expected utility theory implies that all indifference curves must be straight lines, with each having the identical slope. This property drives many of the tests of expected utility theory.

Note that the slope of the line in equation 9.15 is made up of the ratio of the difference in utility between \$50 and \$0 to the difference in utility between \$100 and \$50. Recall from Chapter 6, that a person's risk preferences are related to the curvature of the utility of wealth function. The greater the gambler's level of risk aversion, the more the slope of his utility function declines as wealth increases. If the gambler is risk averse, we should observe that the rise of the utility function from \$0 to \$50 is larger than the rise from \$50 to \$100 (both intervals have a run of \$50 needed to complete the standard formula for slope). More generally we can measure this decline in slope through the ratio of $u(50) - u(0)$ to $u(100) - u(50)$. Greater risk aversion means that $u(100) - u(50)$ is smaller relative to $u(50) - u(0)$, implying a larger value in the right side of equation 9.16. Thus, the more risk averse the preferences, the greater the slope of the indifference curves. This is always the case when the x and y axes contain the highest and lowest value outcomes, respectively.

EXAMPLE 9.4   Allais' Paradox

Maurice Allais was one of the earliest to criticize the expected utility model of decision under risk, believing it eliminated many of the important psychological factors involved in risky decisions. He made the argument using hypothetical choices between gambles that most readers would acknowledge seem to call expected utility theory into question. For example, suppose you had to choose between:

Gamble A:	Gamble B:
You receive \$100 with certainty	Probability 0.1 of receiving \$500
	Probability 0.89 of receiving \$100
	Probability 0.01 of receiving \$0

Now suppose you were deciding between

Gamble C:	Gamble D:
Probability 0.11 of receiving \$100	Probability 0.10 of receiving \$500
Probability 0.89 of receiving \$0	Probability 0.90 of receiving \$0

Many choose A rather than B because of the certainty of receiving something from the gamble. However, very few would choose C over D because the 1 percent additional probability of winning something in C does not feel as if it compensates for the reduction in payoff from \$500 to \$100.

But these two decisions contradict the rational axioms. Note, $A \succ B$ implies that

$$U(100) > 0.1U(500) + 0.89U(100) + 0.01U(0) \tag{9.17}$$

or

$$U(100) > \frac{0.1}{0.11}U(500) + \frac{0.01}{0.11}U(0). \tag{9.18}$$

Alternatively $D \succ C$ implies that

$$0.1U(500) + 0.90U(0) > 0.11U(100) + 0.89U(0) \tag{9.19}$$

or

$$U(100) < \frac{10}{11}U(500) + \frac{1}{11}U(0), \tag{9.20}$$

which clearly contradicts equation 9.17. This is often called the **Allais' paradox** or the **common outcome effect**.

The term *common outcome effect* refers to the structure of the gambles. Gambles A and C can be thought of as probability 0.11 of receiving $100 and probability 0.89 of receiving $X, where in A, X = 100 and in B, X = 0. Gambles B and D can be thought of as probability 0.1 of receiving $500, probability 0.89 of receiving $X, and probability 0.01 of receiving $0, where in B, X = 100, and in D X = 0. In all gambles, X is the common outcome (has the same value and probability in both choices). Expected utility theory implies that the value of X should not affect the gambler's choice. However, here we have observed that people change their preference depending on whether X is 100 or 0. Economics experiments have repeatedly found evidence of the common outcome effect in risky choice.

This is a violation of the independence axiom. This is relatively easy to see in the Marschak–Machina triangle, as seen in Figure 9.3. Gambles C and D are created by sliding gambles A and B to the right by 0.89 (increasing the probability of $0 by 0.89). The line segment AB is exactly as long and of the same slope as line segment CD. Recall that under the independence axiom, indifference curves in the Marschak–Machina triangle are straight parallel lines sloping upward. Further, preferred gambles should lie to the northwest of the indifference curves. If D is preferred to C, then indifference curves must be of a slope that could place D to the northwest and C to the southeast (as pictured). However, it is impossible to find a line of identical slope that would place A to the northwest and C to the southeast. Thus, the indifference curves must change slope in different parts of the triangle, with steeper indifference curves to the west. This is a common method for finding risky choices that violate the independence axiom.

Allais' choice problem is also an example of the **certainty effect**. The certainty effect is the name applied to choices in which decision makers display an irrational preference for outcomes with certainty. For example, in this case it might be that A is chosen

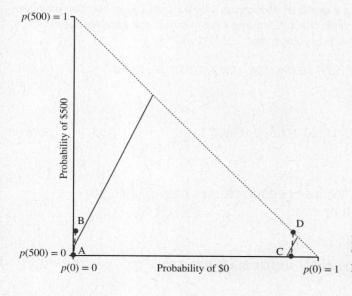

FIGURE 9.3

The Common Outcome Effect in the Marschak–Machina Triangle

because of the certainty effect, even though gambles that have the same relationship in the Marschak–Machina triangle that do not involve certainty (such as C and D) would display the opposite preferences. This observation that people tend to violate the independence axiom often in preference of a certain outcome has led to the hypothesis that people do not perceive probabilities as summing to 1. Rather, they perceive a probability p of outcome X as yielding $\pi(p)$ probability of receiving utility $U(X)$, where $\pi(p)$ is such that $\pi(p) + \pi(1-p) < 1$, called **subadditivity**. Thus, uncertain outcomes are discounted relative to certain outcomes. In this framework, called **probability weighting**, $A \succ B$ implies

$$U(100) > \pi(0.1)U(500) + \pi(0.89)U(100) + \pi(0.01)U(0), \tag{9.21}$$

or

$$U(100)[1 - \pi(0.89)] > \pi(0.1)U(500) + \pi(0.01)U(0) \tag{9.22}$$

And $D \succ C$ implies

$$\pi(0.1)u(500) + \pi(0.90)u(0) > \pi(0.11)u(100) + \pi(0.89)u(0) \tag{9.23}$$

or

$$\pi(0.11)U(100) < \pi(0.1)U(500) + [\pi(0.90) - \pi(0.89)]U(0). \tag{9.24}$$

Equations 9.24 and 9.22 could both hold if either $\pi(0.11) < [1 - \pi(0.89)]$ or $[\pi(0.90) - \pi(0.89)] > \pi(0.01)$, supposing the utility from \$0 is positive. Probability weighting is a way to represent systematic misperception of probabilities in choice preferences. Thus, subadditivity may be one explanation for the common outcome effect.

Chris Starmer is among a group of economists who suggest regret aversion may be behind the common outcome effect. Using the case above, if the gambles were independent, $A \succ B$ and regret theory imply that

$$0.1U(100, 500) + 0.89U(100, 100) + 0.01U(100, 0) > 0, \tag{9.25}$$

or

$$U(100, 500) + 0.1U(100, 0) > 0, \tag{9.26}$$

and $D \succ C$ implies

$$\begin{aligned} 0.11 \times 0.10U(100, 500) + 0.11 \times 0.90U(100, 0) + 0.89 \times 0.10U(0, 500) \\ + 0.89 \times 0.90U(0, 0) < 0 \end{aligned} \tag{9.26}$$

or

$$U(100, 500) + 9U(100, 0) + \frac{89}{11}U(0, 500) < 0. \tag{9.27}$$

Equations 9.27 and 9.26 are not contradictory so long as $U(0, 500)$ is sufficiently negative. In this case the person would feel so much regret from obtaining zero if 500 would have been drawn otherwise that their preferences reverse. Starmer and others have found some evidence that the common consequence effect and related behavior is due to the possibility of regret.

EXAMPLE 9.5   Common Ratio Effect

Allais also discovered the **common ratio effect**. Consider the following choices (from Kahneman and Tversky).

Gamble A:	Gamble B:
You receive $3,000 with certainty	Probability 0.80 of receiving $4,000
	Probability 0.20 of receiving $0

Now suppose you were deciding between

Gamble C:	Gamble D:
Probability 0.25 of receiving $3,000	Probability 0.20 of receiving $4,000
Probability 0.75 of receiving $0	Probability 0.80 of receiving $0

Kahneman and Tversky found that about 80 percent of those asked would choose Gamble A, and about 65 percent would choose Gamble D. However, choosing A and D is a violation of expected utility. To see this, note that $A \succ B$ implies

$$U(3000) > 0.8U(4000) + 0.2U(0) \tag{9.28}$$

and $D \succ C$ implies

$$0.25U(3000) + 0.75U(0) < 0.2U(4000) + 0.8U(0) \tag{9.29}$$

or

$$U(3000) < 0.8U(4000) + 0.2U(0). \tag{9.30}$$

Clearly, equations 9.30 and 9.28 cannot both hold. This is the common ratio effect again because of the structure of the gambles involved. Gamble C can be thought of as a 0.25 chance of playing gamble A and a 0.75 chance of receiving $0. Similarly, Gamble D can be thought of as a 0.25 chance of receiving gamble B (resulting in 0.20 probability of $4,000) and a 0.75 chance of receiving $0. Thus, the ratios of the probabilities of outcomes in gambles A and B remain the same in gambles C and D, with a common outcome added. This particular version of the common ratio effect may also be thought of as an example of the certainty effect given the involvement of Gamble A.

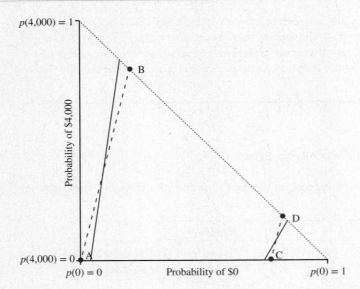

FIGURE 9.4
The Common Ratio
Effect in the
Marschak–Machina
Triangle

As with the common outcome effect, the common ratio effect is a violation of the independence axiom. This can be seen in Figure 9.4. The gambles A and B in the triangle form a line segment with the same slope as the line segment connecting C and D. Thus any indifference curve that places A to the northwest and B to the southeast would imply indifference curves that place C to the northwest and D to the southeast. Instead, the observed choice suggests that indifference curves are steeper in the western portion of the triangle than they are in the southeastern corner. As with the common outcome effect, probability weighting and regret provide two competing explanations for the violation of expected utility.

Allowing Violations of Independence

Both the common ratio and common consequence effects suggest that indifference curves are steeper in the western portion of the Marschak–Machina triangle than in the southeast portion. This led some to suppose that instead of parallel indifference curves, indifference curves fan out across the Marschak–Machina triangle. One way to salvage the axioms, or behavioral rules, that serve as the foundations for expected utility is to replace the independence axiom with the **betweenness axiom**.

Betweenness Axiom

If $A \succ B$, and C is a compound gamble that yields A with probability p and B with probability $(1 - p)$, then betweenness is satisfied if $A \succ C \succ B$.

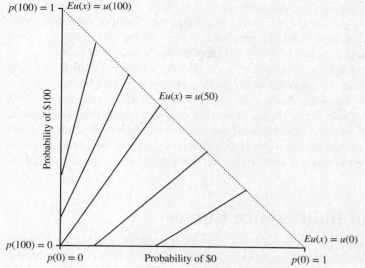

FIGURE 9.5

Indifference Curves under Betweenness

The betweenness axiom allows indifference curves to have different slopes, but it still requires indifference curves to be straight lines. Thus, the indifference curves may be like those displayed in Figure 9.5. To see that indifference curves must be straight lines, consider the gambles A and B that lie on a single indifference curve. Any gamble located directly between points A and B represents a gamble that is a combination of A and B (called C in the definition). Thus, betweenness requires that the gambler be indifferent between A, B, and C, and thus C must also lie on the indifference curve.

One of the first proposed theories to employ betweenness is called **weighted expected utility theory**. Let $p_1, .., p_n$ be the probabilities associated with outcomes $x_1, \ldots, x_n$. Then weighted expected utility preferences suppose that people act to maximize their weighted utility, which is given by

$$U = \frac{\sum_{i=1}^{n} p_i u(x_i)}{\sum_{i=1}^{n} p_i v(x_i)}. \tag{9.31}$$

Here, $u(x)$ is a standard utility of wealth function, and $v(x)$ constitutes some function used to weight the probabilities associated with particular outcomes. To derive indifference curves, consider all points (p_1, p_2) such that

$$\frac{p_1 u(x_1) + p_2 u(x_2) + (1 - p_1 - p_2) u(x_3)}{p_1 v(x_1) + p_2 v(x_2) + (1 - p_1 - p_2) v(x_3)} = k, \tag{9.32}$$

where the left side of equation 9.32 corresponds to the definition of weighted utility from equation 9.31, and the right side is just a constant. Rearranging obtains

$$p_1 [u(x_1) - u(x_3) - k(v(x_1) - v(x_3)] + p_2 [u(x_2) - u(x_3) - k(v(x_2) - v(x_3)]$$
$$+ [u(x_3) - kv(x_3)] = 0, \tag{9.33}$$

which, because outcomes and the functions u and v are fixed, yields an equation of the standard linear format $p_1 c_1 + p_2 c_2 + c_3 = 0$. To see that the slopes of the indifference curves may be different, note that k is a parameter of the constants c_1, c_2 and c_3. Thus, the slope depends upon the level of utility indicated by the indifference curve.

Several have noted that the weighted utility model does fit the data in the triangle significantly better than the expected utility model. However, others have noted that there is significant evidence that betweenness is violated. Colin Camerer and Tek-Hua Ho find that in laboratory settings, people show clear evidence of nonlinear indifference curves. Interestingly, however, the shape of the indifference curves depends substantially on the types of gambles presented. In particular, gambles that involve losses generate a very different pattern of indifference curves from those generated by gambles involving gains.

The Shape of Indifference Curves

By repeatedly asking people to choose between pairs of gambles representing different points in the Marschak–Machina triangle, experimental economists have discovered many regularities in the shapes of these indifference curves. Figure 9.6 provides an example of the general shapes of indifference curves found in laboratory experiments for gambles involving gains. In general, the curves are steeper than the 45-degree line in the northwest portion of the triangle, and they are flatter than the 45-degree line in the southeast portion of the triangle. The curves display significant fanning out around both the vertical and horizontal axes. However, the curves are close to parallel in the center of the triangle. There is some weak evidence that curves actually fan in around the hypotenuse of the triangle. Thus, the places where violations of expected utility are most likely to occur are near the edges of the triangle, where very large and very small probabilities are involved. Interestingly, when gambles with losses are examined, the indifference curves appear to be

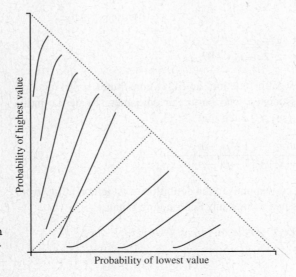

FIGURE 9.6
Indifference Curves in the Triangle for Gambles Involving Gains

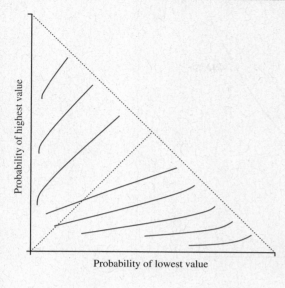

FIGURE 9.7
Indifference Curves in the Triangle for Gambles
Involving Losses

reflected around the 45-degree line (see Figure 9.7). This reflection results in many of the same properties but some distinct differences. In particular, people appear to be more risk loving (more shallow curves) in the center of the triangle.

Evidence on the Shape of Probability Weights

Malcolm G. Preston and Philip Baratta were the first to experiment with using probability weights to describe deviations from expected utility theory. They conducted several experiments in which they auctioned off various simple gambles (with some probability of winning an outcome and remaining probability of winning nothing). They discovered that willingness to pay for gambles was approximately linear in the amount of the reward but highly nonlinear in the probability associated with the outcome. This led them to suppose that people were misperceiving the probabilities in very systematic ways. In particular, people appeared to overweight small probabilities and underweight large probabilities. Similar work has confirmed their early findings with respect to the general shape of these perceived probabilities. Such systematic misperceptions would explain some of the violations of expected utility such as the common ratio and common consequence effects.

One prominent theory of decision under risk supposes that people seek to maximize their perceived expected utility, where their perception is described by **probability weights** (discussed earlier in examples 9.3 and 9.4). Probability weights are given by a function $\pi(p)$, which maps probabilities onto the unit interval. Generally $\pi(p)$ is thought to be an increasing function of the true probability, with $\pi(p) > p$ for all $p < \bar{p}$ and $\pi(p) < p$ for $p > \bar{p}$. Moreover, experimental evidence suggests that $\pi(\cdot)$ is a concave function when $p < \bar{p}$, and a convex function when $p > \bar{p}$. A typical probability weighting function is depicted in Figure 9.8. Generally, the fixed point (the point $\bar{p}$ such that

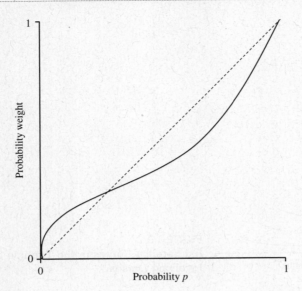

FIGURE 9.8
A Typical Probability
Weighting Function

$\overline{p} = \pi(\overline{p}))$ is believed to be smaller than 0.5. One commonly used functional form for a probability weighting function is given by

$$\pi(p) = \frac{p^{\gamma}}{(p^{\gamma} + (1 - p)^{\gamma})^{\frac{1}{\gamma}}}. \qquad (9.34)$$

This function has the same inverted s-shape as the function presented in Figure 9.8. Probability weights imply subadditivity under the right circumstances (for example, if all probabilities are larger than $\overline{p}$) and could thus explain the certainty effect. Alternatively, probability weighting would imply superadditivity (probabilities sum to greater than 1) if all outcomes had probability below $\overline{p}$, suggesting uncertain outcomes would be unduly preferred to certain outcomes in some cases.

Finally, probability weighting functions make preferences a nonlinear function of the probabilities. For example, using the probability weighting function above, the value of a gamble would be given by

$$V = \sum_{i=1}^{n} \frac{p_i^{\gamma}}{(p_i^{\gamma} + (1 - p_i)^{\gamma})^{\frac{1}{\gamma}}} U(x_i). \qquad (9.35)$$

Given the highly nonlinear nature of the function with respect to the probabilities, the indifference curves are also necessarily very nonlinear, potentially allowing the possibility of explaining some of the fanning out or fanning in of the indifference curves. In particular, if the slope of the probability weighting function only changes substantially for very high probabilities or very low probabilities, that might explain why the indifference curves in the triangle only display changes in slope near the edges of the triangle (or where some probability is necessarily low and another is necessarily high).

EXAMPLE 9.6   Performance Warranty

The evidence from laboratory experiments suggests that people are very poor at dealing with small probabilities. In particular, probability weighting suggests that people treat small-probability events as if they happen much more often than they do. This could potentially lead people to overvalue insurance against very low probability events. For example, many electronic devices come with an option to purchase an extended warranty. This warranty will replace the product should it fail over a particular period of time.

For example, a $400 media player is offered by one prominent retail chain with an optional two-year warranty for $50. The probability of failure for MP3 players is fairly low. Suppose that one in 20 fail in the first two years (the probability cited by the manufacturer of this product). Then the expected cost of replacement is $400 \times 0.05 = $20. In this case, the retailer is charging 250 percent of the expected replacement cost! What a profit margin. But why might people be willing to pay so much for such coverage? Suppose people were completely risk neutral, but they behaved according to probability weighting. If the perceived probability of failure $\pi(0.05) > 0.125$, then the buyer would be willing to purchase what is a very unfair insurance policy.

Some insurance and risk-related behaviors suggest other behavioral effects may be at work. For example, many homeowners are unwilling to purchase flood insurance despite relatively low prices and federal subsidies. In this case, people appear to undervalue the insurance offered to them. Similarly, consider individual behavior in purchasing lottery tickets. Lottery tickets sell for much more than their expected payout, yet people continue to buy these tickets on a regular basis. These behaviors appear to be inconsistent with probability weighting. Perhaps with such large rewards or penalties involved, other decision mechanisms take over, much like with the P- and $-bets discussed earlier.

Probability Weights without Preferences for the Inferior

Decisions based on probability weighting predict that people display a preference for stochastically dominated gambles. Suppose, for example, that the probability-weighting function is such that $\pi(0.9) = 0.89$ and $\pi(0.1) = 0.12$. Suppose further that the utility function is given by $U(x) = \ln x$. If the gambler's preferences are described by these functions, then clearly $20 is preferred to $19 (utility of 2.99 vs. 2.94). If instead we considered a gamble (Gamble A) that yields $20 with probability 0.9 and $19 with probability 0.1, we would find utility

$$U(A) = \pi(0.9)\ln 20 + \pi(0.1)\ln 19 \approx 0.89 \times 2.99 + 0.12 \times 2.94 \approx 3.02. \qquad (9.36)$$

But this suggests that the gambler would prefer a gamble A to receiving $20 with certainty. Of course this would be madness. No reasonable person would ever trade $20 for a gamble that would produce either $20 or $19. This is because the perceived probabilities are **superadditive**. In other words, the probability weights sum to more than 1 ($\pi(0.1) + \pi(0.9) = 0.12 + 0.89 = 1.01$). This superadditivity leads to a perception that the random outcome is better than certainty. Although it is possible to find dominated gambles that people will choose, this is generally thought to be due to a non-transparent presentation of the gamble rather than misperception of probabilities. Thus, this property of the weighted probability preferences seems implausible.

John Quiggin proposed a solution to this problem in which probability weights are a function of the rank of the outcome and not just the probability. Suppose that a gamble assigns probabilities $p_1, \ldots, p_n$ to outcomes $x_1, \ldots, x_n$, where $x_1 < x_2 < \ldots < x_n$ for $i = 2, \ldots, n$. Then Quiggin's rank-dependent expected utility is defined by

$$V = \sum_{i=1}^{n} U(x_i) \left[\pi \left(\sum_{j=1}^{i} p_j \right) - \pi \left(\sum_{j=1}^{i-1} p_j \right) \right]. \tag{9.37}$$

In our example, $x_1 = 19$ and $x_2 = 20$, $p_1 = 0.1$ and $p_2 = 0.9$. Thus, the rank-dependent utility would be given by

$$V = \ln(19)\pi(0.1) + \ln(20)[\pi(0.9 + 0.1) - \pi(0.1)]. \tag{9.38}$$

So long as the weighting function has $\pi(1) = 1$, the sum of the rank-dependent weights must be 1 (in this case, $\pi(0.1) + \pi(0.9 + 0.1) - \pi(0.1) = \pi(0.9 + 0.1) = \pi(1) = 1$). Thus, if $\pi(1) = 1$, then the rank-dependent expected utility given in equation 9.38 must be less than $U(20) = \ln(20)$. To see this, note that V is now identical to the expected utility of a gamble with similar outcomes and the probabilities $\pi(0.1)$ and $[\pi(0.9 + 0.1) - \pi(0.1)]$, which must be less than the utility of $20 with certainty. Because the weights sum to 1, they can now represent probabilities in some alternative perceived gamble. The same must hold no matter how many outcomes are possible. Rank-dependent expected utility thus allows nonlinear perception of probabilities but still preserves the preference for stochastically dominating gambles.

Practical Implications of Violations of Expected Utility

For a decision maker, the practical implications of the risky choice literature is clear. When left to their own devices, people have a difficult time dealing with risky choices. When choices become convoluted or otherwise complicated to deal with, people make significant mistakes. Further, people have difficulty in dealing with extreme probabilities. Thus, it is often a good idea for people dealing with risky choices to use more-rigorous decision processes. It would be difficult to fall prey to problems such as choosing a dominated gamble if one would use simple calculations of the mean and perhaps the variance of the gambles involved. The primary problem with implementing this advice is that people generally do not observe probabilities. When choosing investments, one may have historical data about previous returns but no credible information about future returns. Using rigorous statistical analysis can lead to much better estimates of probability distributions than simple feelings or perceptions, but they also have biases and statistical problems of their own. Nonetheless, in many situations simple calculations can make choices very clear. For example, when offered an extended warranty on a product, asking yourself the necessary probability of failure in order to make the price of the warranty equal to the expected replacement cost can save you substantial money. If the required probability exceeds reasonable expectations of performance, don't buy.

From the point of view of firms marketing risky products or risk-management products, it can be a simple matter to increase the demand for products by overemphasizing small-probability events, emphasizing the possibility of regret, or emphasizing the uniquely attractive properties of a risky choice. The overemphasis of small-probability events should allow substantial profit margins when selling insurance on low-probability risks or when people recognize the possibility of regret from passing up the opportunity to insure. Alternatively, drawing attention to extreme outcomes or extreme probabilities in a choice could appeal to those using a similarity heuristic decision mechanism. Thus, lotteries emphasize and advertise the big winners rather than the odds of winning or the smaller size prizes that may be available.

EXAMPLE 9.7 The Ellsberg Paradox

Suppose you were presented with two urns each containing 100 bingo balls that are either red or black. In the first urn you know that there are 100 balls, and you know that there are only red or black balls in the urn, but you do not know how many of each color. But you are allowed to inspect the second urn, and you find exactly 50 red balls and 50 black balls. You are told you will receive $100 if you draw a red ball and nothing if you draw a black ball. You are then given the choice to draw from either of the urns. Which urn would you choose, and why? Most people in this case decide to choose from the second urn, citing the knowledge of the probabilities of drawing a red ball. Suppose this was your choice. Now suppose that you had instead been given the opportunity to draw and told you would receive $100 if you drew a black ball. Which urn would you choose? Again, most decide to choose the second urn. But such a combination of choices defies the standard axioms of beliefs and probability.

Consider an expected-utility maximizer who chooses the first urn when hoping to draw a red ball. Let us set $U(0) = 0$, which we can do without losing general applicability of the result. Then choosing urn 2 implies that

$$0.50U(100) > p_r U(100) \tag{9.39}$$

which implies $0.50 > p_r$, where p_r is the person's belief regarding the probability of drawing a red ball from the first urn. Alternatively, choosing the second urn when hoping to draw a black ball implies

$$0.50U(100) > (1 - p_r)U(100) \tag{9.40}$$

where $(1 - p_r)$ is the person's belief regarding the probability of drawing a black ball from the first urn. Equation 9.42 implies that $0.50 < p_r$, contradicting equation 9.41.

There is no set of beliefs conforming to the laws of probability that would lead one to choose the second urn for both of these gambles. Rather, it appears that people make this choice to avoid the ambiguity associated with the first urn rather than forming any beliefs at all.

This paradox, proposed by Daniel Ellsberg in 1961, was designed to examine how people deal with situations where probabilities of the various outcomes are not known to the decision maker. Ten years later, Daniel Ellsberg himself faced a very important decision with high stakes and unknown probabilities of outcomes. His expertise on decision making was put to use in helping to study and advise U.S. strategy and decision making regarding the Vietnam War. While working with background documents he became convinced that each of three presidential administrations had deceived the public regarding the conduct of the war and the prospects to win. Without the electorate's having full information, the president was pressured to escalate a war that he believed was unwinnable. Ellsberg faced the choice to either make public the secret documents he had access to and lay bare the deceit or to keep these documents secret. Should he keep the documents secret, he would likely keep his job, and the war would escalate, resulting in continued loss of life. Should he go public with the documents, the war might stop, but he would likely lose his job and could be prosecuted for treason, resulting in a minimum of jail time and perhaps death.

In 1971, he contacted the *New York Times* and passed the documents to the paper for publication. The Pentagon Papers exposed several instances of deceit under several administrations—most notably the Johnson administration—and helped lead to a U.S. withdrawal from Vietnam under President Nixon. The Nixon administration brought several charges against Ellsberg, threatening up to 115 years in prison. The charges were later thrown out by the courts, partially owing to several extralegal methods employed by the Nixon administration in gathering evidence. In what may be seen as poetic justice, two of the charges against President Nixon in his impeachment proceedings stemmed from his treatment of Daniel Ellsberg.

What to Do When You Don't Know What Can Happen

The phenomenon on display in the Ellsberg paradox is often referred to as **ambiguity aversion**. Ambiguity aversion is displayed when a decision maker tends to choose options for which the information about probabilities and outcomes is explicit, over options for which either the probabilities or outcomes are unknown or ambiguous. For the purposes of this book, we explicitly examine cases in which the possible outcomes are known (or at least believed to be known) but the probability of each of those outcomes is unknown. We will refer to such a cases as displaying **ambiguity** or **uncertainty**. At the heart of ambiguity aversion is the necessity of holding (at least) two sets of inconsistent beliefs simultaneously. Rational theory (in this case called **subjective expected utility** theory) suggests we should hold one set of beliefs about the probability of drawing a red ball from the first urn, that these beliefs should satisfy standard laws of probability, and that all of our decisions should be based upon that set of beliefs. In the

Ellsberg paradox, people display ambiguity aversion because they behave as if $p_r < 0.5$ when they hope to draw a red ball and as if $p_r > 0.5$ when they hope to draw a black ball. A procedurally rational model of decision under uncertainty was proposed by Itzhak Gilboa and David Schmeidler, supposing that people choose the option that displays the best of the worst possible set of probabilities, called the **maxmin expected utility theory** of choice under ambiguity. Suppose that $P(x)$ represented the set of possible beliefs that one could hold regarding the outcomes of choosing action x. Further, let $\{p(y)\}$ represent one possible probability distribution of outcomes y when choosing action x. Then someone who behaves according to maxmin expected utility theory will choose

$$\max_x \left(\min_{\{p(y)\} \in P(x)} \sum_y p(y) U(y) \right). \tag{9.41}$$

Thus, people choose the action such that they will be the best off in the event that the worst possible set of probabilities prevail. An illustration may be helpful.

Suppose that Noor faces a choice between gamble A and gamble B. Gamble A would result in \$100 with probability p_A, with $p_0 \leq p_A \leq p_1$, and \$0 with the remaining probability. Gamble B would result in \$50 with probability p_B, with $p_2 \leq p_B \leq p_3$, and \$0 with the remaining probability. Then Noor will value gamble A according to

$$V(A) = \min_{p_A \in (p_0,\, p_1)} p_A U(100) + (1 - p_A) U(0) = p_0 U(100) + (1 - p_0) U(0). \tag{9.42}$$

In other words, the decision maker supposes that the worst set of possible probabilities are correct. Noor will evaluate gamble B according to

$$V(A) = \min_{p_B \in (p_2,\, p_3)} p_B U(50) + (1 - p_B) U(0) = p_2 U(50) + (1 - p_2) U(0). \tag{9.43}$$

Then Noor will choose A if $V(A) > V(B)$, or

$$p_0 U(100) + (1 - p_0) U(0) > p_2 U(50) + (1 - p_2) U(0). \tag{9.44}$$

Essentially, a maxmin expected utility maximizer assumes the worst of every gamble. Here, the worst possible beliefs regarding gamble A, or those producing the lowest utility, are $p_A = p_0$. Similarly, the worst beliefs for gamble B are $p_B = p_2$. The decision maker then chooses based upon these worst-case scenarios. Casting this into the framework of equation 9.41, the possible actions, x, are the choices of either A or B. The possible outcomes, y, are either \$100 or \$0 in the case of A, or \$50 and \$0 in the case of B. The set of probabilities, $P(x)$, are (p_0, p_1) for $x = A$, and (p_2, p_3) for $x = B$.

If we consider the case of the Ellsberg paradox, the choice of urn 2 corresponds to

$$V(Urn\ 2) = 0.50 U(100) + 0.5 U(0) \tag{9.45}$$

because we are told explicitly that half of the balls are red and half are black. We are not told the number of red and black balls in urn 1. There may be no red balls. Thus, the value of urn 1 is given by

$$V(Urn1) = \min_{p \in [0, 1]} pU(100) + (1-p)U(0) = U(0) \tag{9.46}$$

Clearly, urn 2 is superior to urn 1 in this case. If we then thought about making the same choice when a black ball will result in a reward, the calculation is the same. We haven't been told the probability, and for all we know there may be no black balls. Thus, equation 9.46 still holds.

A more general model of decision under ambiguity was proposed by Paolo Ghirardato, Fabio Maccheroni, and Massimo Marinacci, called **α-maxmin expected utility theory**. Their theory is based on the notion that the degree to which the decision maker gives weight to the worst possible beliefs represents just how averse to ambiguity the person may be. Let $\{\underline{p}(y)\}$ be the set of beliefs for a given action that results in the minimum expected utility, or the solution to arg $\min_{\{p(y)\} \in P(x)} \sum_y p(y)U(y)$ (the probabilities corresponding to the solution to the maxmin problem). Further, define $\{\overline{p}(y)\}$ as the set of beliefs that results in the maximum expected utility, or the solution to arg $\max_{\{p(y)\} \in P(x)} \sum_y p(y)U(y)$ (these are the probabilities that correspond to the best possible expected utility). Then an α-maxmin expected-utility maximizer will behave according to

$$\max_x \left(\sum_y \left(\alpha \underline{p}(y) + (1-\alpha)\overline{p}(y) \right) U(y) \right), \tag{9.47}$$

where $\alpha \in [0, 1]$. Here α can be considered an index of ambiguity aversion. The more ambiguity averse, the closer α is to 1. Someone with $\alpha > \frac{1}{2}$ is considered to be ambiguity averse, and someone with $\alpha < \frac{1}{2}$ is considered to be ambiguity loving. This model reduces to the maxmin expected-utility model when $\alpha = 1$, resulting in the person's reacting only to the worst possible beliefs for a given choice. If $\alpha = \frac{1}{2}$, the perceived probability of each event will be exactly 1/2 the probability from the maxmin solution plus 1/2 the probability from the maximum expected-utility solution. In the simple case of two possible outcomes, the subjective probabilities will be the same even if outcomes are swapped (as in rewarding the drawing of a black ball rather than a red ball). This means preferences will satisfy the subjective expected utility model. We will refer to α as the **coefficient of ambiguity aversion**.

To illustrate, consider again the Ellsberg paradox. The value of urn 2 will continue to be as given in equation 9.45 because the probabilities were explicitly given in this case. In the case of urn 1, the probability of obtaining \$100 can be anywhere between 0 and 1. The best-case beliefs—those that produce the highest expected utility—would be $p(100) = 1$, and the worst-case beliefs would be $p(100) = 0$. Thus, the decision maker would value urn 1 according to

$$V(Urn1) = (\alpha \times 0 + (1-\alpha) \times 1)U(100) + (\alpha \times 1 + (1-\alpha) \times 0)U(0)$$
$$= (1-\alpha)U(100) + \alpha U(0) \tag{9.48}$$

Comparing this to equation 9.45, the person will choose urn 1 if $\alpha < \frac{1}{2}$, implying ambiguity-loving behavior. In this case, the person assumes the outcome is closer to the more optimistic beliefs. The person will choose urn 2 if $\alpha > \frac{1}{2}$, implying ambiguity aversion. With $\alpha > \frac{1}{2}$, the person believes the outcomes will be closer to the more-pessimistic beliefs. Finally, if $\alpha = \frac{1}{2}$, the person is indifferent between the two urns—reflecting the lack of information about urn 1. Some of the experimental evidence suggests that people behave ambiguity loving over losses and ambiguity averse over gains. Such a possibility suggests a very close association between ambiguity aversion and risk aversion behavior.

EXAMPLE 9.8   Ambiguity in Policymaking

Ambiguity is relatively pervasive in many contexts where we may be considering a new technology, regulation, or change in strategy. Consider a deadly disease that has a 3/4 chance of killing anyone infected when given the accepted treatment. Alternatively, a new treatment has been proposed. The new treatment has not been fully tested through clinical trials, but researchers believe that it will result in probability of survival in the range of $p \in \left[\underline{p}, \overline{p} \right]$. The regulatory board that approves clinical trials is ambiguity averse, with a coefficient of ambiguity aversion equal to α. The regulatory board is considering approving a trial of the new treatment. Suppose that the board derives $U(Survive) = 100$ if a patient survives after treatment and $U(Death) = 0$ if a patient dies after treatment. Thus, the regulatory board values the current treatment according to expected utility theory

$$V(\text{Current Treatment}) = 0.25 \times U(Survive) + 0.75 \times U(Death) = 25. \qquad (9.49)$$

Alternatively, the new treatment results in ambiguity. In this case, if the regulatory council knew the probability of survival under the new treatment, they would value the new treatment as

$$V(\text{New Treatment}) = p \times U(Survive) + (1 - p) \times U(Death) = 100p, \qquad (9.50)$$

with $\max_p 100p = 100\overline{p}$, and $\min_p 100p = 100\underline{p}$. Thus, the regulatory board will value the ambiguous prospect of using the new treatment as

$$100 \left(\alpha \underline{p} + (1 - \alpha)\overline{p} \right). \qquad (9.51)$$

Thus, the new treatment will only be approved for trial if $25 < 100 \left(\alpha \underline{p} + (1 - \alpha)\overline{p} \right)$, or $.25 < \left(\alpha \underline{p} + (1 - \alpha)\overline{p} \right)$. If the board is fully ambiguity averse, then $\alpha = 1$, and they will only approve the new trial if $\underline{p} > 0.25$. In other words, it will only proceed to trial if it is guaranteed to reduce the probability of death. Alternatively, if the regulatory board is fully ambiguity loving, they will approve the trial if $\overline{p} > 0.25$. In other words it will be approved if there is *any* chance that the new treatment could reduce the probability of death. Finally, if we consider $\alpha = 0.5$, then the regulatory board will approve the trial if $.5 < \underline{p} + \overline{p}$. Thus, if the best possible probability is above 0.25 by at least as much as the worst possibility is below it, then the trial will be approved.

Ambiguity aversion in this case would lead the regulatory board to restrict new trials even if there is a substantial promise of better outcomes. Ambiguity aversion has also been used to describe government response to food safety scares and emissions regulation in the face of global climate change. In each of these cases, ambiguity aversion leads the government toward overregulation owing to the possibility of catastrophic outcomes.

History and Notes

Frank H. Knight was among the first economists to recognize the central role of risk in economic decision. In the 1920s he hypothesized that entrepreneurship resulted from a substantial tolerance for risk of the marketplace and the ambiguities of marketing new products. These early works by Knight led the way for later developments in the economics of risk by John von Neumann and Oskar Morgenstern, who proposed expected utility theory, and later Kenneth Arrow, who helped develop the theory. The behavioral work on risk owes much to this foundation. The overwhelming majority of behavioral models of decision under risk or uncertainty build directly on the foundation of expected utility. Many attempt to imitate the intuitive axiomatic definition proposed by von Neumann and Morgenstern, and others seek simple indices of risk behavior that closely resemble those proposed by Arrow in the expected utility context. Moreover, theories of ambiguity and ambiguity aversion were created in direct response to Knight's distinction between risk and uncertainty. Knight's own writings about risk and uncertainty clearly foreshadows the importance of psychology in economics.

Biographical Note

GABRIEL DUVAL/AFP/Getty Images

Maurice Felix Charles Allais (1911–2010)

École Polytechnique 1933; École Nationale Supérieure des Mines 1936; Ph.D Université de Paris, 1949; held faculty positions at École Nationale Supérieure des Mines, Université de Paris, Graduate Institute of International Studies in Geneva; held several positions at several national research centers

Maurice Allais obtained his college training in engineering and mathematics in the 1930s and began work in engineering examining issues common in mining. It was while working as an administrator in the Bureau of Mines Documentation and Statistics beginning in 1941 that Allais published his first academic research, a series of pieces examining, among other things, the foundational work of welfare economics. Paul Samuelson wrote that had these works been written in English "a whole generation of economic theory would have taken a different course." Allais' student Gerard Débreu won the Nobel prize for work extending the results derived by Allais. Allais' academic work in the field of economics ranged widely, creating the foundation for many of the most widely used macroeconomic models, and it also examined issues of energy use, mining, and other areas of applied economics. Some believe it is odd that he is best recognized for the Allais' paradox, because it was somewhat outside of the main body of his research. Nonetheless, his publication of the Allais' paradox in many ways marked the first true behavioral economics publication, inspiring later authors such as Daniel Kahneman and Amos Tversky. Though he would probably not consider himself a behavioral economist, the question he posed sparked widespread interest in alternative theories of decision under risk and eventually in alternative theories of decision making in all contexts. His contributions were not limited to economics. Allais also published papers in engineering, theoretical physics, and history. In 1988 he was awarded the Nobel Prize in economics for his contributions to the study of efficient markets.

THOUGHT QUESTIONS

1. Consider the utility function given by $U(x) = \ln(x)$ and the set of gambles with the possible outcomes \$10, \$20 and \$30. For each exercise, it may be useful to use a spreadsheet or other numerical tools.

   (a) Graph the indifference curves implied by expected utility in the Marschak–Machina triangle. What is the slope of the indifference curves?

   (b) Now suppose that the decision maker maximizes probability weighted utility, with the weights given by

   $$\pi(p) = \frac{p_i^{0.7}}{\left(p_i^{0.7} + (1 - p_i)^{0.7}\right)^{\frac{1}{0.7}}}.$$

   Graph a few examples of indifference curves. What does the probability weighting do to the shape of these curves relative to those in part a?

   (c) Repeat the exercise in b, now assuming the decision maker maximizes rank-dependent expected utility. Thus, now the probability weighting function is applied to cumulative probabilities.

   (d) Finally, consider the regret utility function given by

   $$U(x, y) = \begin{cases} (x - y)^2 & \text{if } x \geq y \\ -(x - y)^2 & \text{if } x < y \end{cases}$$

   Plot the implied indifference curves supposing the alternative choice would yield \$19 with certainty and compare the shape of these curves to those of the

   other models considered. How do these curves change when the foregone gamble is altered?

2. Suppose that there were three possible states of nature as represented in the table below:

States of Nature	1	2	3
Probability	0.35	0.4	0.25
Gamble 1	\$1,000	\$2,000	\$3,000
Gamble 2	\$1,800	\$1,800	\$1,800
Gamble 3	\$2,500	\$1,500	\$1,500

   (a) What conditions would be required for the regret theory utility function to predict preference cycling when choosing between pairs of the three possible gambles? Graph an example of a function that would satisfy these conditions.

   (b) Is it possible for preference cycling to occur given the same choices under expected utility maximization with probability weights? Show why or why not.

   (c) Would it be possible for preference cycling to occur given the same choices under rank-dependent expected-utility maximization? Show why or why not.

3. Confirm that the common ratio effect as found in Example 9.4 could be explained either by probability weighting or by regret theory. To do this, find utility

and weighting functions that satisfy the models and that lead to the choices found in Example 9.4.

4. Consider two gambles, each with outcomes \$10, \$20, \$30, and \$40. Gamble 1 has probabilities p_{10}, p_{20}, p_{30}, $1 - p_{10} - p_{20} - p_{30}$ for these outcomes and gamble 2 has probabilities q_{10}, q_{20}, q_{30}, and $1 - q_{10} - q_{20} - q_{30}$. Suppose that Gamble 2 stochastically dominates Gamble 1. Thus, $p_{10} > q_{10}$, $p_{10} + p_{20} > q_{10} + q_{20}$, and $p_{10} + p_{20} + p_{30} > q_{10} + q_{20} + q_{30}$. Show that anyone who maximizes rank-dependent expected utility must prefer Gamble 2 to Gamble 1.

5. Suppose that you are a policymaker considering instituting a tax to combat climate change. The current climate research is conflicting as to the probability that carbon emissions will lead to catastrophic climate change. Suppose that the probability of a catastrophic climate change is equal to $0.3 \times c^{\phi}$, where c represents carbon dioxide emissions and, depending on which scientists you listen to, ϕ can be as low as 0.1 or as high as 0.9. As a policymaker you wish to maximize expected social welfare. If a catastrophic climate change occurs, social welfare will be equal to 0, no matter how much other production occurs. If a catastrophic climate does not occur, then social welfare is given by the profit of the emitting industry, $\pi = (p - t) \quad y - k(y) = (3 - t)y - 0.15y^2$, where y is output, p is the output price, $k(.)$ is the cost of production, and t is the tax you impose. The firm chooses y to maximize profits, according to $y = (3 - t)/0.3$. Carbon dioxide emissions are given by $c = y$.

(a) Suppose you display α-maxmin expected-utility preferences, with $\alpha = 1$ (fully ambiguity averse). What tax will you choose? What level of social welfare will be realized if a catastrophic climate change is not realized? You may use a spreadsheet to determine the answer if needed.

(b) Suppose $\alpha = 0$ (fully ambiguity loving). What tax will you choose? What level of social welfare will be realized if a catastrophic climate change is not realized?

(c) Suppose that a definitive study shows that $\phi = 0.2$. What is the expected social welfare–maximizing tax? What is the resulting expected social welfare and the social welfare resulting if no catastrophic climate change is realized?

REFERENCES

Allais, P.M. "Le comportement de l'homme rationnel devant le risque: critique des postulats et axiomes de l'école Américaine." *Econometrica* 21(1953): 503–546.

Birnbaum, M., and J. Navarrete. "Testing Descriptive Utility Theories: Violations of Stochastic Dominance and Cumulative Independence." *Journal of Risk and Uncertainty* 17(1998): 49–78.

Camerer, C.F., and T.-H. Ho. "Violations of the Betweenness Axiom and Non-Linearity in Probability." *Journal of Risk and Uncertainty* 8(1994): 167–196.

Ellsberg, D. "Risk, Ambiguity, and the Savage Axioms." *Quarterly Journal of Economics* 75(1961): 643–669.

Ghirardato, P., F. Maccheroni, and M. Marinacci. "Differentiating Ambiguity and Ambiguity Attitude." *Journal of Economic Theory* 118(2004): 133–173.

Gilboa, I., and D. Schmeidler. "Maxmin Expected Utility with Non-Unique Prior." *Journal of Mathematical Economics* 18(1989): 141–153.

Guthrie, C. "Better Settle than Sorry: The Regret Aversion Theory of Litigation Behavior." *University of Illinois Law Review* 1999 (1999): 43–90.

Kahneman, D., and A. Tversky. "Prospect Theory: An Analysis of Decision under Risk." *Econometrica* 47(1979): 263–292.

Kahneman, D., and A. Tversky. "Rational Choice and the Framing of Decisions." *Journal of Business* 59(1986): S251–S278.

Leland, J. "Generalized Similarity Judgments: An Alternative Explanation for Choice Anomalies." *Journal of Risk and Uncertainty* 9(1994): 151–172.

Leland, J. "Similarity Judgments in Choice Under Uncertainty: A Reinterpretation of the Predictions of Regret Theory." *Management Science* 44(1998): 659–672.

Lichtenstein, S., and P. Slovic. "Reversals of Preference Between Bids and Choices in Gambling Decisions." *Journal of Experimental Psychology* 89(1971): 46–55.

Loomes, G., C. Starmer, and R. Sugden. "Observing Violations of Transitivity by Experimental Methods." *Econometrica* 59(1991): 425–439.

Machina, M.J. "'Expected Utility' Analysis Without the Independence Axiom." *Econometrica* 50(1982): 277–323.

Marschak, J. "Rational Behavior, Uncertain Prospects, and Measurable Utility." *Econometrica* 18(1950): 111–141.

Preston, M.G., and P. Baratta. "An Experimental Study of the Auction-Value of an Uncertain Outcome." *American Journal of Psychology* 61(1948): 183–193.

Quiggin, J. "A Theory of Anticipated Utility." *Journal of Economic Behavior and Organization* 3(1982): 323–343.

Rubinstein, A. "Similarity in Decision-Making Under Risk (Is There a Utility Theory Resolution to the Allais Paradox?)" *Journal of Economic Theory* 66(1995): 198–223.

Starmer, C. "Testing New Theories of Choice under Uncertainty using the Common Consequence Effect." *Review of Economic Studies* 59(1992): 813–830.

Von Neumann, J., and O. Morgenstern. *Theory of Games and Economic Behavior*. Princeton: Princeton University Press, 1944.

Zeelenberg, M., and Pieters, R. "Consequences of Regret Aversion in Real Life: The Case of the Dutch Postcode Lottery." *Organizational Behavior and Human Decision Process* 93(2004): 155–168.

Advanced Concept

The Continuity Axiom

Decision makers who adhere to the independence, order, and continuity axioms behave as if they maximize the expected (or mean) utility of wealth resulting from their choices. The order and independence axioms are defined in the text.

Continuity Axiom

If $A \succ B \succ C$ then there is exactly one value r such that neither B nor the compound gamble that yields the gamble A with probability r and the gamble C with probability $(1-r)$ are preferred (we write this as $rA + (1-r)C \sim B$). Further, for any $p > r$ the compound gamble that yields the gamble A with probability p and the gamble C with probability $(1-p)$ is preferred to B (we write this $pA + (1-p)C \succ B$), and for any $q < r$, B is preferred to the compound gamble that yields the gamble A with probability q and the gamble C with probability $(1-q)$, or $B \succ qA + (1-q)C$.

The continuity axiom imposes the notion that increasing the probability of a preferred gamble (and thus lowering the probability of inferior gambles) will increase one's preference for the gamble. Lowering the probability of the preferred gamble has the opposite effect. Suppose that A, B, and C are degenerate (in other words, there is probability 1 of receiving a particular outcome). For example, suppose A yields \$100 with certainty, B yields \$50 with certainty, and C yields \$0 with certainty. Then continuity implies that I can find only one probability r, maybe 0.6, such that I am indifferent between the gamble yielding 0.6 probability of \$100 and a 0.4 chance of \$0 and the gamble that yields \$50 with certainty. Raising the probability of getting \$100 and lowering the probability of getting \$0 will lead the gambler to take the compound gamble; lowering the probability of getting \$100 and raising the probability of getting \$0 will lead the gambler to choose the \$50 instead.

10 Prospect Theory and Decision under Risk or Uncertainty

On October 12, 2007, American investors celebrated a new high-water mark as the Dow Jones Industrial Average hit an all-time high of 14,093. Stocks were booming, and many people were buying. Home values had also increased substantially over the previous decade, producing substantial wealth for those who had invested in home ownership. Many had taken out large loans to buy up real estate as an investment, counting on continuing increases in home prices to produce value. With a large cohort of baby boomers preparing for retirement, many had built substantial wealth through stock and real estate investments and felt well prepared financially for a long and comfortable retirement. That's when things started to go sour.

Housing prices had begun to decline slightly between August and October, but by November the decline in home values had become too much for investors to ignore. Stock prices started a slow decline also. Although most prognosticators clearly predicted that further losses in real estate and stocks were ahead, optimistic investors began to reason among themselves, "I can't get out now, I will lose money." Sentiments such as "I don't want to sell at a loss. I will wait until the price goes back up to where I purchased, and then get out," were common. In January 2008, real estate prices started a steep decline. Many homes were now valued at less than the outstanding debt on the mortgage. Those who had counted on the money they could make upon selling their property to cover the mortgage would now be forced to default. Banks that had made these loans were in trouble. After a short period of stability, the housing market went into a steep decline, losing almost 30 percent between August 2008 and February 2009. The stock market took notice. By October 2008, stock prices began to crash, losing as much as 18 percent in a single day. Investors were finally ready to sell even at a loss. By March 2009, the Dow Jones Industrial Average was only 6,627. Stocks had shed nearly 53 percent of their value. Massive amounts of wealth had been destroyed, and baby boomers were left to come to grips with the fact that they might have to put off retirement for several years and perhaps cut back on their planned expenses.

Often the plan to buy low and sell high doesn't quite work out that way. Why are investors so willing to hold on to a losing investment when it becomes clear it will not perform? Although few would consider making new investments in what appears to be a losing investment, many are loath to shed losing investments if it means realizing a loss. Loss aversion has profound effects on the way decision makers deal with risky decisions. In many ways, the introduction of loss aversion to the economics of risky choice has been the

cornerstone of behavioral economics. In 1979, Daniel Kahneman and Amos Tversky introduced a model of risky choice based on loss aversion, which they called **prospect theory**. For
many economists, prospect theory was their first exposure to behavioral models. Prospect
theory makes powerful predictions regarding behavior under risk, providing some of the most
compelling evidence of behavioral biases in economic choice.

EXAMPLE 10.1   The Reflection Effect

Suppose you were given $1,000 in addition to whatever you own. Then choose between
the following two gambles:

Gamble A:	Gamble B:
$1,000 with probability 0.5	$500 with certainty
$0 with probability 0.5	

Daniel Kahneman and Amos Tversky asked 70 participants to decide between these
two options, and 84 percent chose option B. Choosing option B is not terribly surprising.
The expected value of Gamble A is $0.5 \times 1,000 + 0.5 \times 0 = 500$, the value of Gamble B.
Thus, anyone who is risk averse should choose Gamble B over Gamble A. A different set
of 68 participants were asked the following question:

*In addition to whatever you own, you have been given $2,000. You are now
asked to choose between*

Gamble C:	Gamble D:
− $1,000 with probability 0.5	− $500 with certainty
$0 with probability 0.5	

In every respect, this is the same choice as that between Gamble A and Gamble B.
Applying expected utility theory, the expected utility of Gamble A is given by
$0.5 \times U(w + 1000 + 1000) + 0.5 \times U(w + 1000)$, where w represents the amount of wealth
you currently possess. Alternatively, Gamble C is represented by $0.5 \times U(w + 2000 - 1000) + 0.5 \times U(w + 2000)$. These are clearly identical. Moreover, the expected
utility of Gamble B is $U(w + 1000 + 500)$, which is identical to the expected utility of
Gamble D, $U(w + 2000 - 500)$. Thus, anyone who behaves according to expected utility
theory and chooses Gamble B must also choose Gamble D. Yet, 69 percent of participants chose Gamble C when given the choice. On average, participants were risk loving
when choosing between C and D but risk averse when choosing between A and B. This is
a special case of the **reflection effect**, the observation that risk preferences over gains
tend to be exactly opposite of those over identical-magnitude losses.

Kahneman and Tversky discovered this effect by asking participants to choose
between a series of similar gambles with the money outcomes reflected around the
origin (i.e., positive values made negative), though without the wealth adjustment

presented in the previous problem. In each case, the majority of participants were risk averse when choosing between gains but risk loving when choosing between losses. The results of these choices are presented in Table 10.1. Without the wealth adjustment, these gambles do not truly demonstrate a violation of expected utility. For example, in the choice between the first two positive gambles in Table 10.1, choosing B implies that $0.8 \times U(w + 4,000) + 0.2 \times U(w) < U(w + 3,000)$. Choosing A in the corresponding negative gamble implies $0.8 \times U(w - 4,000) + 0.2 \times U(w) > U(w - 3,000)$. Because the utility function is evaluated at different points in the negative and positive gambles, no contradiction is implied. However, if this holds at every wealth level (as the results suggest), a contradiction is implied. Utility of wealth functions cannot be both concave and convex over the same range of outcomes (the violation noted in the first example in this section, which makes the wealth adjustment). Nonetheless, this is what the reflection effect implies.

Table 10.1   Reflected Gambles*

Gamble A		Gamble B		Percent Choosing A	
Probability	Outcome	Probability	Outcome	Positive Gamble	Negative Gamble
0.800	±$4,000	1.000	±$3,000	20	92
0.200	±$4,000	0.250	±$3,000	65	42
0.900	±$3,000	0.450	±$6,000	86	8
0.002	±$3,000	0.001	±$6,000	27	70

*See Example 10.1. For each gamble, the remaining probability is assigned to the outcome of $0. Gambles were originally denominated in shekels.

EXAMPLE 10.2   The Isolation Effect

Kahneman and Tversky also discovered another curious anomaly illustrated in the following choice problem.

> Consider the following two-stage game. In the first stage, there is a probability of 0.75 to end the game without winning anything and a probability of 0.25 to move into the second stage. If you reach the second stage you have a choice between

Gamble E:	Gamble F:
$4,000 with probability 0.8	$3,000 with certainty
$0 with probability 0.2	

> Your choice must be made before the game starts, that is, before the outcome of the first stage is known.

Of the 141 participants who faced this problem, 78 percent chose Gamble F. If we choose Gamble E, we have a 0.25 probability of moving to the second stage and then an

0.8 probability of receiving $4,000, or an overall probability of $0.25 \times 0.8 = 0.2$ to receive $4,000 and 0.8 of receiving nothing. Alternatively, if we choose Gamble F, we have a 0.25 chance of receiving $3,000, and a 0.75 of receiving $0. Thus we could rewrite this compound gamble as

Gamble E':	Gamble F':
$4,000 with probability 0.2	$3,000 with probability 0.25
$0 with probability 0.8	$0 with probability 0.75

Interestingly, when phrased this way, 65 percent of participants choose Gamble E' over F'. In this case, preferences seem to depend heavily upon how transparent the description of the gamble is. People apparently do not simplify compound lotteries the way expected utility would assume. Additionally, some participants were asked how they would choose between

Gamble E'':	Gamble F'':
$4,000 with probability 0.8	$3,000 with certainty
$0 with probability 0.2	

This gamble is identical to the second stage of the previous problem in isolation (gambles E and F). In this case, 80 percent of participants chose Gamble F'', very similar to the 78 percent in the original problem. It appears that decision makers ignore the first stages of such a compound lottery and focus only on the latter stages. In general, we might expect participants to eliminate common components of gambles in making decisions, such as the first-stage lottery in this example.

Risk Aversion, Risk Loving, and Loss Aversion

Recall from Chapter 6 that under the theory of expected utility maximization, risk aversion is represented by a concave utility function. As the payoff for the gamble increases, the utility of the marginal dollar (the slope of the utility function) declines. This leads participants to receive less expected utility from the gamble than they would from receiving a one-time payment equal to the expected value of the gamble. Figure 10.1 displays such a utility function when the participant faces a 0.5 probability of receiving x_2 dollars and a 0.5 probability of receiving x_1 dollars. Thus the expected value of the gambles is given by $E(x) = 0.5(x_1 + x_2)$, the point on the horizontal axis exactly halfway between x_1 and x_2. Alternatively, the expected utility of the gamble is given by $E(u(x)) = 0.5(u(x_1) + u(x_2))$, which is the point on the vertical axis that is exactly halfway between $u(x_1)$ and $u(x_2)$. This point will always be less than $U(0.5(x_1 + x_2))$ when the utility function is concave. The participant would be indifferent between taking $x_{CE} < E(x)$ and taking the gamble. Thus, concavity of the utility function is associated with risk-averse behavior.

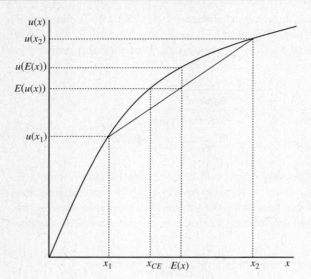

FIGURE 10.1
Risk Aversion and
Concavity

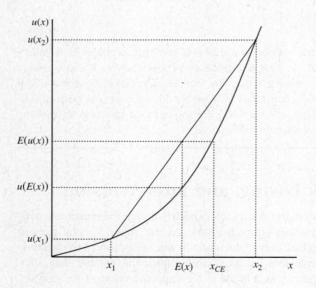

FIGURE 10.2
Risk Loving and
Convexity

The opposite is true when the decision maker has a convex utility of wealth function. In this case, displayed in Figure 10.2, the expected utility of the gamble $E(u(x)) = 0.5(u(x_1) + u(x_2))$ is always greater than $U(0.5(x_1 + x_2))$. Because the utility function is convex, the point on the utility function that corresponds to the point on the vertical axis that is halfway between $u(x_1)$ and $u(x_2)$ is always to the right of the expected value of the gamble. Decision makers would be indifferent between taking $x_{CE} > E(x)$ and taking the gamble. With a convex utility function, decision makers are made better off by taking the gamble than by taking an amount of money equal to the expected value of the gamble. In other words, they are risk loving. Thus, convexity of the utility function is associated with risk-loving behavior.

In previous chapters, "loss aversion" has been used to describe behavior in the context of consumer choices. For example, people tend to display the sunk cost fallacy when they classify sunk costs as a loss and future benefits from continuing an activity as a gain associated with that loss (see the section on "Theory and Reactions to Sunk Cost" in Chapter 2). Kahneman and Tversky proposed prospect theory based on the notion that people classify each event as either a gain or a loss and then evaluate gains and losses using separate utility functions. Gains are evaluated via a utility function over gains, which we have called $u_g(x)$, that is concave. Thus people display diminishing marginal utility over gains. In the context of gambles and lotteries, the argument of the utility function is wealth, or the money outcome of the gamble. Thus, the utility function over gains displays diminishing marginal utility of wealth, which is associated with risk-averse behavior. Losses are evaluated with respect to a utility function over losses, $u_l(x)$ where the utility function over losses is not only steeper than the utility function over gains but is also convex. Because the utility function over losses is generally steeper than the utility function over gains, the overall function is kinked at the reference point (see Figure 10.3). Thus losses are associated with risk-loving behavior.

Whether an outcome is considered a gain or a loss is measured with respect to a reference point. In the context of gambles, we generally consider the status quo level of wealth to be the reference point. Suppose I were to offer a gamble based upon a coin toss. If the coin lands on heads, I will give you $50. If the coin lands on tails, I will take $30 from you. In this case, you would classify heads as a $50 gain, and tails as a $30 loss. In more general circumstances, the reference point might not be current wealth (or zero payout) but some other salient reference level of payout k. For example, k may be $1 if considering the payouts of a casino slot machine requiring the player to deposit $1 to play. If we define our reference point as k, we can define the value function as

$$v(x|k) \equiv \begin{cases} u_g(x-k) & \text{if} \quad x \geq k \\ u_l(x-k) & \text{if} \quad x < k. \end{cases} \tag{10.1}$$

We often suppress the reference point in our notation by using the form $v(z) = v(x-k|0)$, in which case any negative value is a loss and any positive value is a gain.

Clearly, people who maximize the expectation of the value function behave risk averse if dealing only with possible gains and risk loving if dealing only with possible losses. Both of these cases would look identical to the cases presented in the figures above. However, because the value function is both convex and concave, the gambler might behave either risk averse or risk loving when both gains and losses are involved. The behavior depends heavily on the size of the risk and whether it is skewed toward gains or losses. Consider Figure 10.3, which displays a relatively small risk. In this case, the steeper slope of the loss function leads the function to behave like a concave function. The value function evaluated at x_1 is much farther below the reference value ($v(0)$) than the value function at x_2 is above the reference value, despite x_2 being slightly greater than $-x_1$. Thus, $E(v(x)) < v(E(x))$, and the gambler behaves risk averse.

Alternatively, consider the gamble presented in Figure 10.4, which involves relatively larger amounts. In this case, the steep loss function is not overwhelmed by the concavity

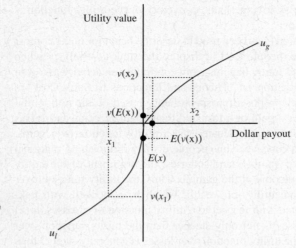

FIGURE 10.3
Risk Aversion and the
Prospect Theory
Value Function

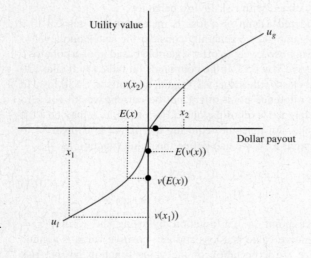

FIGURE 10.4
Risk Loving and the
Prospect Theory Val-
ue Function

of the gain function. Thus, $E(v(x)) > v(E(x))$. The larger the losses relative to gains, the more likely the behavior will display risk-loving properties. Moreover, the larger the amounts involved, the more likely the gambler will display risk-loving behavior. With either small amounts involved in the gamble or amounts that are skewed toward gains, the gambler is more likely to display risk-averse behavior. Thus, prospect theory predicts that people display both risk-loving and risk-averse behavior. Which of these behaviors prevails depends upon the size of the stakes involved and whether the gambler is dealing with potential gains or losses, or both. This observation forms the basis for prospect theory analysis of decision under risk.

Returning to Example 10.1, the prospect theory value function can resolve the reflection effect if we consider the reference point to be determined by whether the outcome is framed as a gain or a loss. The framing of the question as a gain or loss then determines whether the gambler behaves as if risk loving or risk averting. So whether you have been given \$1,000 or \$2,000 in addition to your current wealth, an outcome of −\$500 is a loss and an outcome of \$500 is a gain. In this case, choosing Gamble B over Gamble A implies that $0.5 \times v(1000) + 0.5 \times v(0) < v(500)$, implying risk-averse behavior. Alternatively, choosing Gamble C over Gamble D implies $0.5 \times v(-1000) + 0.5 \times v(0) > v(-500)$, implying risk-loving behavior. Though the monetary outcomes of the gamble are the same, framing the choice as a gain or a loss leads people to consider the outcomes in very different ways, leading to loss aversion.

Prospect Theory

Kahneman and Tversky proposed prospect theory as a potential solution to the reflection effect puzzle. The value function neatly explains how risk preferences could flip so dramatically over very similar gambles. However, simply using the value function does not address many of the other violations of expected utility theory we have observed in the previous chapter. To address each of these various effects, Kahneman and Tversky proposed a three-component version of prospect theory to deal with choice under risk. The three components are editing, probability weighting, and the value function.

   Editing refers to a phase of the decision-making process in which the decision maker prepares to evaluate the decision. In this phase, the decision maker seeks to simplify her decision, thus making the evaluation of the potential prospects easier. The decision maker reorganizes the information in each choice and sometimes alters the information slightly to make the decision easier. The editing phase is intended to represent the actual motivations and deliberative process of the decision maker. Because the need to edit is based on the limited cognitive ability of the decision maker, this can be thought of as a procedurally rational model. The editing phase consists of six types of activities:

i.   **Coding:** The decision maker determines a reference point (often her current level of wealth or some default outcome). Outcomes are then coded as either gains or losses with respect to the reference point.

ii. **Combination**: Probabilities associated with identical outcomes are combined. Thus, if a decision maker is told that a fair die will be rolled and \$300 will be given to her if an odd number results, she would combine the probability of rolling a 1, 3, and 5 (or $\frac{1}{6} + \frac{1}{6} + \frac{1}{6} = \frac{1}{2}$).

iii. **Segregation**: Certain outcomes are segregated from risky outcomes. Thus, a gamble that yields \$40 with probability 0.5 and yields \$65 with probability 0.5 is thought of as a sure gain of \$40, with a 0.5 probability of gaining \$25 and a 0.5 probability of gaining \$0.

iv. **Cancellation**: When the choices being considered all have common components, those components are eliminated when making the choice. Suppose someone were choosing between Choice A, 0.25 probability of gaining \$40, a 0.25 probability of gaining \$60, and a 0.50 probability of gaining \$0, and Choice B, 0.25 probability of gaining \$40 and 0.75 probability of gaining \$65. The first outcome is cancelled because they are similar, yielding Choice A, 0.25 probability of gaining $60 and 0.50 probability of gaining $0, and Choice B, 0.75 probability of gaining $65.

v. **Simplification**: Probabilities and outcomes are rounded. Thus a probability of 0.49 would be thought of as 0.50. As well, an amount equal to $1,001 would be thought of as $1,000.

vi. **Detection of dominance**: The gambles are inspected to determine if one of the gambles first-order stochastically dominates the other. If one clearly dominates the other, then that gamble is selected.

Activities i, iii, iv, and v lead to specific violations of expected utility theory. For example, i enables the reflection effect by allowing the value function to be employed. Activity iv creates the isolation effect described earlier. In Example 10.2, applying iv would mean the common first-stage lottery would be eliminated from consideration, leading to the observed preference reversal. Because these editing activities represent ways actual decision makers reason through risky decisions, they are a potentially powerful tool.

There are two strong drawbacks to this model of prospect editing. First, the order in which the different activities are applied will affect the edited gambles to be evaluated. Applying i through vi in order might imply a different decision than if one were to apply them in the reverse order or in some other random order. Thus, as a model, editing does not make very specific predictions. For example, consider the choice between

Gamble G:	Gamble H:
$1,000 with probability 0.49	$999 with probability 0.50
$0 with probability 0.51	$0 with probability 0.50

Notice that if we first applied v and just rounded the probabilities, we would replace the gambles with

Gamble G′:	Gamble H′:
$1,000 with probability 0.50	$999 with probability 0.50
$0 with probability 0.50	$0 with probability 0.50

At that point we might apply vi, and recognize that Gamble G′ dominates Gamble H′ and choose G. Alternatively, if we first rounded just the amounts, we would arrive at

Gamble G″:	Gamble H″:
$1,000 with probability 0.49	$1,000 with probability 0.50
$0 with probability 0.51	$0 with probability 0.50

In this case we might notice that H″ dominates G″ and choose H″. Similarly, applying each of the phases of editing in different orders can produce different outcomes. Moreover, it is clear from some of the anomalies in Chapter 9 that people do not always detect dominance. Hence it is possible to find convoluted gambles that can lead people to select dominated gambles.

A second drawback is that editing is difficult to apply to many real-world risky decisions. For example, if we were to consider stock investments, people are not told probabilities of specific outcomes, and the choices might not involve two or three potential gambles. Rather, outcomes could be anything in a continuous range of values, and the number of decisions could also be continuous (as in the number of shares to purchase). In this case, many of the editing activities become meaningless. Because of this, many economic applications of prospect theory have ignored all components of the editing phase aside from coding.

Once the editing phase has occurred, the decision maker then evaluates the gamble through the use of a probability-weighting function and a value function. Kahneman and Tversky originally proposed using a subadditive probability-weighting function as introduced in Chapter 9. Thus, the decision maker will maximize

$$V = \sum_i \pi(p_i)v(x_i), \tag{10.2}$$

where p_i is the probability of outcome i and x_i is outcome i. The use of the probability-weighting function allows many of the same anomalies described in Chapter 9, including the certainty effect, the common-outcome effect, and Allais' paradox. Alternatively, to eliminate the intransitive preferences implied by the subadditive probability-weighting function, it has become common to replace the probability-weighting function with a rank-dependent weighting function as described in Chapter 9. We refer to the use of prospect theory with rank-dependent weights as **cumulative prospect theory**.

Prospect Theory and Indifference Curves

Deriving indifference curves in the Marschak–Machina triangle is a little more difficult when dealing with probability weights. If we consider all possible gambles with outcomes of $100, $50, and $0, we are interested in all probability values that satisfy (see equation 9.3)

$$\pi(y)v(100) + \pi(x)v(0) + \pi(1-x-y)v(50) = k, \tag{10.3}$$

where x, y, and $1-x-y$ are the probabilities of receiving $100, $0, and $50, respectively. For the sake of example, let us set $v(0)=0$ (this assumption can be made without losing any generality). Without specifying the probability weighting function, we cannot determine the shape of the implied curve in the triangle. However, we can approximate the shape locally by totally differentiating equation 10.3 with respect to x and y to obtain

$$\frac{dy}{dx} = \frac{v(50)}{\frac{\pi'(y)}{\pi'(1-x-y)}v(100) - v(50)}. \tag{10.4}$$

where $\pi'(.)$ is the derivative (or slope) of the probability weighting function. Thus, the shape of the indifference curve depends on the probabilities of each of the outcomes.

Recall that a steeper slope of the indifference curve reflects greater risk aversion. In this case, the slope is steeper when $\pi'(y)$ is small relative to $\pi'(1-x-y)$. Recall from Chapter 9 that the probability-weighting function is believed to be steeper for small and large probabilities than for those closer to 0.5 (see Figure 9.8). Thus, equation 10.4 tells us that people tend to be more risk averse when probabilities for the largest outcome are near 0.5 relative to the probabilities for either the middle or lower outcome. Alternatively, when the probability of the largest outcome is extreme relative to that of the middle outcome, the person behaves more risk loving. This risk-loving behavior when the probabilities of gains are relatively small is the primary contribution of the probability-weighting function.

If we consider the shape of the indifference curves over losses of $100, $50, or $0, we must remember to reorder the axes. Now the y axis, which represents the probability of the superior outcome, is associated with a loss of $0, and the x axis, representing the probability of the most inferior outcome, is associated with a $100 loss. In this case, equation 10.4 can be rewritten as

$$\frac{dy}{dx} = \frac{\frac{\pi'(x)}{\pi'(1-x-y)} v(-100) - v(-50)}{v(-50)}. \tag{10.5}$$

In comparing equations 10.5 and 10.4, it is notable that the equations are almost exactly multiplicative inverses of one another (the difference being the negative values of the value function arguments). The gambler will display greater risk aversion if the probability of the lowest outcome is extreme relative to the probability of the middle outcome. Thus, the reference point of prospect theory implies that indifference curves over losses should be close to a reflection around the 45-degree line, as has been observed in laboratory experiments and as we displayed in figures 9.6 and 9.7. This provides some further evidence that people make decisions with respect to reference points and that they display loss-averse preferences.

EXAMPLE 10.3   Prospect Theory, Risk Aversion, Risk Loving, and Observed Behavior

Using data from laboratory experiments with 25 participants, Tversky and Kahneman attempted to find parameters for cumulative prospect theory that could explain the results of several risky choices. Each participant was asked to choose among several gambles, each with a pair of possible outcomes. Though the data are limited, they were able to find parameters that provide a relatively close fit to the observed behavior. The estimated model is of the form

$$v(x) = \begin{cases} x^\alpha & \text{if} \quad x \geq 0 \\ -\lambda(-x)^\beta & \text{if} \quad x < 0 \end{cases} \tag{10.6}$$

$$\pi(p|x) = \begin{cases} \dfrac{p^{\gamma}}{\left(p^{\gamma}+(1-p)^{\gamma}\right)^{\frac{1}{\gamma}}} & \text{if} \quad x \geq 0 \\[4mm] \dfrac{p^{\delta}}{\left(p^{\delta}+(1-p)^{\delta}\right)^{\frac{1}{\delta}}} & \text{if} \quad x < 0. \end{cases} \quad (10.7)$$

All parameter values are assumed to be positive. The rank-dependent weighting function in equation 10.7 allows the weighting to differ depending on whether the outcome associated with the probability is a gain or a loss. The parameters α and β in the value function (equation 10.6) determine the curvature of the value function (concavity or convexity). The parameter λ determines the degree to which the marginal utility of losses differs from that of gains at the reference point, with smaller positive values for λ corresponding to a wider difference in slopes. They find

$\alpha = 0.88$
$\beta = 0.88$
$\lambda = 2.25$
$\gamma = 0.61$
$\delta = 0.69$

Thus, the curvature of the value function for gains and losses is similar, though the difference in slope is severe (greater than a factor of 2).

Figure 10.5 pictures the estimated value function, having the familiar concave shape for gains, and convex for losses. The dominant feature, however, is the stark difference in slopes over gains and losses. Figure 10.6 displays the estimated probability-weighting

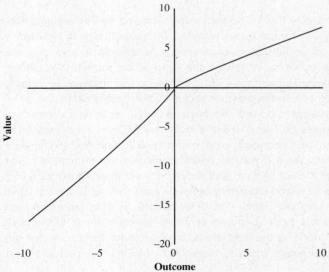

FIGURE 10.5
The Value Function under Cumulative
Prospect Theory

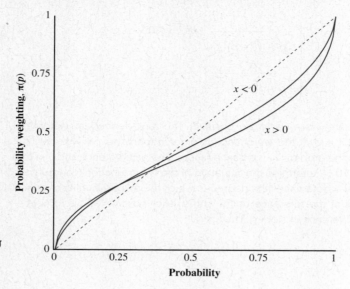

FIGURE 10.6
Probability Weighting
under Cumulative
Prospect Theory

function for gains and losses. Both display the familiar shape, overstating small probabilities and understating high probabilities. Despite the difference in the coefficients in these functions, the weighting functions are both very similar and might signal that there is little effect of coding gains or losses on probability weighting. Even though the curves are very close, there is a notable difference between the probabilities at the points where the curves cross the 45-degree line (0.33 for gains, and 0.37 for losses).

Figures 10.7 and 10.8 display the indifference curves implied by Tversky and Kahneman's estimates for gains and for losses, respectively. The resemblance to Figures 9.6 and 9.7, which were based on laboratory observations, is striking. In this case the indifference curves fan out as we move toward the hypotenuse. Further, the pattern of indifference curves is reflected around the 45-degree line, as was observed empirically and as was found mathematically in the previous section. One notable difference in the pattern of indifference curves has to do with the shape of the curves at their intersection with the hypotenuse. In Figures 10.7 and 10.8, the indifference curves are all parallel as they approach the hypotenuse. Laboratory experiments tend to find that indifference curves begin to fan in around the hypotenuse, and in particular near the center of the hypotenuse. Thus, although it is not perfect, cumulative prospect theory provides a very close approximation to the observed laboratory behavior under risk. In fact, cumulative prospect theory performs very well relative to other models in most laboratory and econometric tests. Though this model performs very well generally, much of the work examining which decision model is the best predictor of behavior concludes that different people conform to different models. Moreover, which model performs best

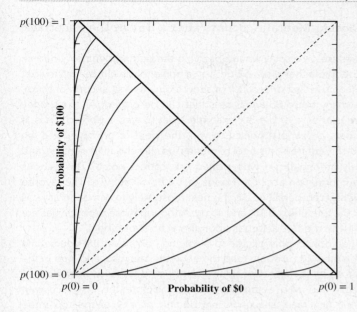

FIGURE 10.7
Cumulative Prospect Theory in the
Marschak–Machina Triangle: Gains

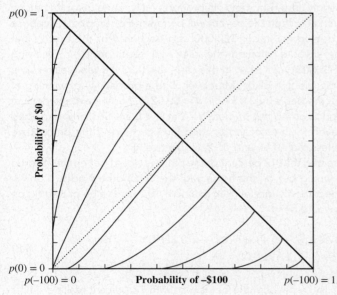

FIGURE 10.8
Cumulative Prospect Theory in the
Marschak–Machina Triangle: Losses

appears also to depend on the types of risky choices being presented. For example, when facing tradeoffs between gains and losses, prospect theory performs particularly well. Alternatively, when dealing with only gains and correlated gambles, regret theory appears to perform much better.

EXAMPLE 10.4 Closing Mental Accounts after a Day at the Racetrack

Many behavioral anomalies are on display when observing the betting behavior of horse race bettors. In general, people either place $2 bets on a horse to win a race, or they bet that the horse will place (come in first or second) or show (come in first, second or third), though there are usually many other potential bets that can be placed. All the money from those placing a particular type of bet, for example a bet to win, is pooled. Thus, if 1,000 people place $2 bets on various horses to win, the pool of money would be $2,000. The racetrack takes its cut from this pool of money, usually about 18 percent, and the rest is divided evenly among those who picked the correct horse. The patrons generally have access to information about the odds that a horse will win. The favorite generally wins with an average probability 0.32, the next most likely to win generally has an average probability of 0.21, the next 0.15, and so on. Although these probabilities are relatively stable, the payoff of the bet depends upon the actions of others.

Mukhtar M. Ali examined how people decide to place their bets over the course of a night. He finds that early in the night, people tend to bet on the favorites, and later in the night people tend to bet on long shots. Consider a bettor who behaves according to cumulative prospect theory and who enters the racetrack before the first race with $500 in her pocket. In the first race, she considers betting on any of the top three favorite horses, the seemingly less-risky bets. If proportionally more people bet on the favorite horse in the first race, then the payout will be lower. For simplicity, suppose there are 10,000 bettors betting a total of $20,000. If a fraction θ of the bettors bet on the favorite, then the favorite winning the race will result in their receiving $20,000 \times (1 - 0.18) \div (\theta \times 10,000) = \$1.64/\theta$. In this case, $\theta < 0.82$ if a win is to result in more money than was bet in the first place. Moreover, with a probability of winning of 0.32, the expected value of the bet is $0.32 \times \$1.64/\theta \approx \$0.52/\theta$. For the expected value to be higher than the $2 price of the bet, it must be that $\theta < 0.26$. Similarly, expected value only exceeds the payoff for the second or third favorite horse if the percentage betting on those horses is less than 0.17 and 0.12, respectively.

Suppose the bettor expected that 12 percent of the patrons would bet on the favored horse, but only 9 percent would bet on the horse with the second-best odds. Considering the cumulative prospect theory model from Example 10.2, the value of betting on the first horse in this case would be

$$V = \pi(0.32|13.67 - 2)v(13.67 - 2) + (\pi(1|-2) - \pi(0.32|13.67 - 2))v(-2)$$
$$\approx 0.33 \times 8.69 + 0.67 \times (-4.14) \approx 0.08 \tag{10.8}$$

where $\$1.64/0.12 = \$13.67$ is the payoff if the bet is won with 12 percent making similar bets. Alternatively, the valuation for betting on the second-favorite horse would be

$$V = \pi(0.21|18.22 - 2)v(18.22 - 2) + (\pi(1|-2) - \pi(0.21|18.22 - 2))v(-2)$$
$$\approx 0.27 \times 16.22 + 0.67 \times (-4.14) \approx 0.07 \tag{10.9}$$

where $\$1.64/0.09 = \$18.22$ is the payoff if the bet is won with 9 percent making similar bets. Note that this is a riskier prospect. The probability of success is lower, and the expected payoff is lower. However, there is a potentially higher payoff ($18.22 vs. $13.67) if the second-favored horse wins. The bettor, being risk averse over gains, would rather bet on the favored horse than on the second-favored horse.

Now suppose the bettor lost her first eight bets and was considering betting on the ninth and final race. Now instead of the $500 she arrived with, she only has $484. If she remembers her loss and does not adjust her reference point, she must win at least $16 more than she bet to return to her reference point of $500. A win of $11.67 results in a reduction of loss for a total loss of only $4.33. An additional loss of $2 results in a total loss of $18. The current valuation is $v(-16) = -25.81$, and the bettor will be willing to take any bet that puts her in a better position. Thus, calculating as before we find

$$V = \pi(0.32|-2.33-2)v(-2.33-2) + (\pi(1|-18) - \pi(0.32|-2.33-2))v(-18)$$
$$\approx 0.33 \times (-8.17) + 0.67 \times (-28.63) \approx -21.66. \tag{10.10}$$

And if we instead consider betting on the lower-rated horse,

$$V = \pi(0.21|2.22-2)v(2.22-2) + (\pi(1|-18) - \pi(0.21|2.22-2))v(-18)$$
$$\approx 0.27 \times 0.27 + 0.67 \times (-28.63) \approx -20.91. \tag{10.11}$$

Now the bettor prefers betting on the riskier horse because it might allow the larger return and the possibility of returning to her reference point of wealth despite the added risk. Because the bettor now codes all outcomes in the loss domain, she behaves risk loving. As losses rack up, people become more and more willing to risk lower-probability wins for higher potential payouts. This pattern of race track betting becoming more and more risky throughout the day appears to be a relatively robust phenomenon, and it often results in lower returns on risky horses in the last races each day as more patrons start betting down the ticket.

EXAMPLE 10.5 Loss-Averse Contract Labor

Labor contracts are often written in terms of a base level of pay plus some bonus for good performance and potentially minus some penalties for poor performance. Such contracts seem to be a natural application of prospect theory.

Consider a contract between a firm that sells pizza and a worker. The worker can either choose to put in high effort or low effort. With high effort the probability of producing a high-quality pizza is equal to 1. With low effort, the probability of producing a high-quality pizza is equal to 0.5. The firm can sell high-quality pizza for a higher price than it can sell low-quality pizza. But suppose the firm cannot observe the level of effort the laborer gives, only the quality of the pizza. Further, suppose high effort costs the laborer the equivalent of 2 utils in effort, and low effort costs the laborer only 1 util. The firm is trying to determine how to structure the contract.

Suppose they consider paying the worker r_h for a high-quality output but r_l for low-quality output. Suppose further that they frame the contract as a base level of pay of r_l with a bonus of $(r_h - r_l)$ if the quality of the output is high. If the worker signs the contract, the worker must choose what effort level to give. The worker will incorporate the base level of pay into her reference point, considering high pay a gain and low pay no gain or loss. Employing Tversky and Kahneman's value function and probability-weighting function, the value of choosing a high level of effort is

$$V_h = \pi(1|r_h)v(r_h - r_l) - 2 = (r_h - r_l)^{0.88} - 2. \tag{10.12}$$

where the cost of effort is segregated from the benefits guaranteed by the contract. Alternatively, giving low effort would yield

$$V_l = \pi(0.5|r_l)v(0) + (1 - \pi(0.5|r_l))v(r_h - r_l) - 1 = 0.58 \times (r_h - r_l)^{0.88} - 1. \tag{10.13}$$

The worker will choose the higher level of effort if $V_h > V_l$, or

$$r_h - r_l > 2.68. \tag{10.14}$$

If the firm states the contract as a base pay of r_h and a penalty of $(r_h - r_l)$ if the quality of the pizza is bad, the worker will consider the high rate of pay as no gain or loss and the low rate of pay as a loss. Then the value of high effort is given by

$$V_h = \pi(1|r_h)v(0) - 2 = -2. \tag{10.15}$$

Alternatively, giving low effort would yield

$$\begin{aligned} V_l &= \pi(0.5| - (r_h - r_l))v(-(r_h - r_l)) + (1 - \pi(0.5| - (r_h - r_l)))v(0) - 1 \\ &= 0.45 \times (-2.25) \times (r_h - r_l)^{0.88} - 1. \end{aligned} \tag{10.16}$$

The worker will thus choose the higher level of effort if

$$r_h - r_l > 0.99. \tag{10.17}$$

Note that the value in equation 10.17 is much lower than that in equation 10.14. Thus, it should take much less of a premium in pay to motivate workers if pay is framed as a loss rather than a gain. However, it is unclear what impact this would have on the workers' willingness to sign the contract in the first place. Notice that in both equations 10.15 and 10.16, we are comparing negative values of fulfilling the contract. It is unclear whether workers would be willing to take this contract unless there was a premium in the base level of pay to compensate for the potential losses. If this were the case, there may be a tradeoff in the cost of hiring workers and the cost of motivating them.

Does Prospect Theory Solve the Whole Problem?

Prospect theory is relatively effective in explaining the majority of decisions under risk observed in the laboratory and many behaviors observed in the field. However, most of these risks take on a very specialized form. The majority of risks presented in this chapter and in Chapter 9 are dichotomous choice problems. In other words, the decision maker can choose either to take the gamble or to reject it. Further, most of the gambles we have discussed can result in only a small set of discrete outcomes. In many cases there are only two or three possible outcomes. The majority of risky decisions that are studied by economists are not so simple. If we wished to study investment behavior, each investor has a nearly infinite choice of potential combinations of stocks, bonds, real assets, or commodities they can choose to invest their money in. Moreover, they may invest any amount of money they have access to. Thus, most interesting investment decisions are not dichotomous. Moreover, most investments have potential payoffs in a very wide range. One might lose all one's investment, might double it, or might fall anywhere in between. The lack of realism in the laboratory has caused many to question the veracity of prospect theory and other behavioral models of decision under risk. Perhaps these models only work when facing this very specialized set of decision problems.

Graham Loomes was one of the first researchers to explore continuous-choice investment in a laboratory setting. He designed a special experiment to mirror, in a limited way, the common investment problem. In Decision 1, he endowed his participants with $20 that they could allocate between two investments, A_1 and B_1. In the standard investment problem, investors must invest their money in a wide array of investments that might have different payoffs depending on the outcome. Typically, investors reduce the amount of risk they face by diversifying their portfolio of investments. Participants in Loomes' experiment had a probability of 0.6 of receiving the amount invested in A_1 and a probability of 0.4 of receiving the amount invested in B_1. An expected utility maximizer would solve

$$\max_{A_1 \leq 20} 0.6 U(A_1) + 0.4 U(20 - A_1). \tag{10.18}$$

The solution to equation 10.18 occurs where the expected marginal utility between the two investments is equal. This is depicted in Figure 10.9, where the vertical axis is the marginal utility weighted by the probability of a particular outcome, and the horizontal axis measures the allocation between investments A_1 and A_2. As you move to the right in the figure, the allocation to A_1 increases and the allocation to B_1 decreases. The curve labeled $0.6 U'(A_1)$ represents the probability of outcome A_1, which is 0.6, multiplied by the marginal utility of wealth given the allocation, $U'(A_1)$. One should continue to increase the allocation to A_1 until the weighted marginal utility from A_1 is equal to the weighted marginal utility from B_1, the curve labeled $0.4 U'(B_1)$. This point is depicted in the figure as $\left(A_1^*, B_1^*\right)$. This occurs where $0.6 U'(A_1) = 0.4 U'(20 - A_1)$, assuming that it is not optimal to put all of the money in one of the investments.

These first-order conditions can be written as

$$\frac{U'(20 - A_1)}{U'(A_1)} = \frac{0.6}{0.4} = 1.5. \tag{10.19}$$

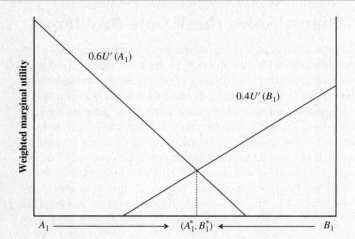

FIGURE 10.9
The Optimal Alloca-
tion in Loomes' Port-
folio Problem

For Decision 2, participants were then given another \$20 and asked to allocate it between A_2 and B_2. However, this time they were told that there was a probability of 0.3 of receiving A_2 and 0.2 of receiving B_2. They would receive nothing with the remaining probability, 0.5. In this case, an expected utility maximizer would solve

$$\max_{A_2 \le 20} 0.3U(A_2) + 0.2U(20 - A_2) + 0.5U(0), \tag{10.20}$$

where equating the expected marginal utility of the two investments yields $0.3U'(A_2) = 0.4U'(20 - A_2)$, which can be rewritten as

$$\frac{U'(20 - A_2)}{U'(A_2)} = \frac{0.3}{0.2} = 1.5. \tag{10.21}$$

Because the ratio of the marginal utilities in equations 10.19 and 10.20 are both equal to 1.5, any expected-utility maximizer must choose $A_1 = A_2$ and $B_1 = B_2$. This is because Decision 2 is proportional to Decision 1. It is equivalent to a two-stage problem in which the first stage results in playing Decision 1 with 0.5 probability, and a payoff of \$0 with 0.5 probability. Of 85 participants, 24 chose $A_1 = A_2$ and $B_1 = B_2$. Of the remaining, 1 chose $A_2 > A_1$, and 60 (the majority of participants) chose $A_1 > A_2$.

Notably, expected utility does not describe the behavior of the majority of participants. What about alternative theories? Consider any of the models that use probability weights (including prospect theory). In this case, the decision maker in Decision 1 would solve the problem

$$\max_{A_1 \le 20} \pi(0.6)U(A_1) + \pi(0.4)U(20 - A_1), \tag{10.22}$$

resulting in the solution described by

$$\frac{U'(20 - A_1)}{U'(A_1)} = \frac{\pi(0.6)}{\pi(0.4)}. \tag{10.23}$$

Decision 2 would have the decision maker solve

$$\max_{A_2 \leq 20} \pi(0.3)U(A_2) + \pi(0.2)U(20 - A_2) + \pi(0.5)U(0), \qquad (10.24)$$

with solution given by

$$\frac{U'(20 - A_2)}{U'(A_2)} = \frac{\pi(0.3)}{\pi(0.2)}. \qquad (10.25)$$

Equations 10.23 and 10.25 imply different allocations in the decision problems owing to the distortion of probabilities through the probability-weighting function. However, probability-weighting functions are believed to cross the 45-degree line at somewhere between 0.3 and 0.4. Above this, the probability weight should be lower than the probability, and below this it should be higher than the probability. Thus, $\frac{\pi(0.6)}{\pi(0.4)} < \frac{\pi(0.3)}{\pi(0.2)}$, implying that $\frac{U'(20-A_1)}{U'(A_1)} < \frac{U'(20-A_2)}{U'(A_2)}$. Given that all outcomes are coded as gains, people should display risk aversion, meaning that marginal utility is declining for larger rewards. Thus, $U'(20 - A)$ gets larger for larger values of A, and $U'(A)$ gets smaller for larger values of A, implying that $U'(20 - A)/U'(A)$ increases as A increases. Recall that probability weights lead us to believe that $\frac{U'(20-A_1)}{U'(A_1)} < \frac{U'(20-A_2)}{U'(A_2)}$, so that $A_1 < A_2$, the outcome observed in exactly 1 of 85 participants. The majority of participants behave in a way that is inconsistent with the probability-weighting model. Although no alternative theory has come to prominence to explain this anomaly, it may be a signal that continuous-choice problems result from very different behaviors than the simple dichotomous-choice problems that are so common in the laboratory.

Prospect Theory and Risk Aversion in Small Gambles

Further evidence that we might not fully understand how risky choices are made can be found by examining the small-risk problem identified by Matthew Rabin and discussed in Chapter 6. If we attempt to explain any risk-averse behavior using expected utility theory, the only tool with which we can explain it is diminishing marginal utility of wealth, or concavity of the utility function. The most fundamental principle of calculus is the observation that continuous functions are approximately linear over short intervals. Thus, when small amounts of money are at stake, a utility of wealth function should be approximately linear, implying local risk neutrality. If instead, we observe risk-averse behavior over very small gambles, this then implies that the utility function must be extremely concave, and unreasonably so. This led Rabin to derive the following theorem (see Chapter 6 for a full discussion and greater intuition).

Suppose that for all w, $U(w)$ is strictly increasing and weakly concave. Suppose there exists $g > l > 0$, such that for all w, the person would reject a 0.50 probability of receiving g and a 0.50 probability of losing l. Then the person would also turn down a bet with 0.50 probability of gaining mg and a 0.50 probability of losing $2kl$, where k is any positive integer and $m < m(k)$, where

$$
m(k) = \begin{cases} \dfrac{\ln\left(1 - \left(1 - \dfrac{l}{g}\right)2\sum_{i=0}^{k-1}\left(\dfrac{g}{l}\right)^i\right)}{\ln\left(l/g\right)} & \text{if} \quad 1 - \left(1 - \dfrac{l}{g}\right)2\sum_{i=0}^{k-1}\left(\dfrac{g}{l}\right)^i > 0 \\[4mm] \infty & \text{if} \quad 1 - \left(1 - \dfrac{l}{g}\right)2\sum_{i=0}^{k-1}\left(\dfrac{g}{l}\right)^i \leq 0. \end{cases}
$$

$$(10.26)$$

On its face, this is difficult to interpret without an example. Consider someone who would turn down an 0.50 probability of gaining $120 and 0.50 probability of losing $100. If this person were strictly risk averse and behaved according to expected utility theory, then the person would also turn down any bet that had a 0.50 probability of losing $600, no matter how large the possible gain. Although it seems reasonable that people might want to turn down the smaller gamble, it seems unreasonable that virtually anyone would turn down such a cheap bet for a 50 percent probability of winning an infinite amount of money. Several other examples are given in Table 10.2. Rabin takes this as further evidence that people are susceptible to loss aversion. Note that we relied on the smoothness and concavity of the utility function to obtain this result. Loss aversion does away with smoothness, allowing a kink in the function at the reference point. Thus, no matter how small the gamble, no line approximates the value function, and severely risk averse behavior is still possible in small gambles without implying ridiculous behavior in larger gambles. As demonstrated in Table 10.2, often what economists call a small amount is not very small at all. In general, when we talk about small risks, we mean that the risk is small in relation to some other gamble.

William Neilson notes that the problem is not exclusive to expected utility. If, for example, we use expected utility with rank-dependent weights, we can derive the following analogous theorem:

Suppose that for all w, $U(w)$ is strictly increasing and weakly concave. Let π be a probability-weighting function, with $\bar{p} = \pi^{-1}\left(\frac{1}{2}\right)$. Suppose there exists $g > l > 0$, such that for all w, a rank-dependent expected-utility maximizer would reject a $\bar{p}$ probability of receiving g and a $(1 - \bar{p})$ probability of losing l. Then the person would also turn down a bet with $\bar{p}$ probability of gaining mg and a $(1 - \bar{p})$ probability of losing $2kl$, where k is any positive integer, and $m < m(k)$, where $m(k)$ is defined in equation 10.26.

Thus, the previous example would hold if we simply adjust the probabilities to those that result in probability weights of 0.5. For example, using the estimates from Tversky

Table 10.2 Examples Applying Rabin's Theorem

If You Would Turn Down		Then You Should Also Turn Down	
Winning with 0.5 Probability	Losing with 0.5 Probability	Winning with 0.5 Probability	Losing with 0.5 Probability
$110	− $100	$555	− $400
		$1,062	− $600
		$∞	− $1,000
$550	− $500	$2,775	− $2000
		$5313	− $3000
		$∞	− $5000
$1,100	− $1,000	$5,551	− $4000
		$10,628	− $6000
		$∞	− $10,000

and Kahneman for the rank-dependent weighting function, a probability weight of 0.5 would correspond to a probability of 0.36 for the gain and 0.64 for the loss. Thus, anyone who would turn down a 0.36 probability chance of winning $120 and a 0.64 probability of losing $100 would also turn down any bet that had a 0.64 probability of losing $600 no matter how much they could win with the other 0.36 probability. Similar results would hold for all of the examples in Table 10.2.

By itself this might not seem damaging to prospect theory because we could still argue that this result is abolished by the kink at reference point. However, this only shifts the problem. Consider, for example, the case where the person has the choice between a gain of $600 or a gamble that would yield either $720 with probability 0.36 or $500 with probability 0.64. If they would choose the $600, and classify it as a $600 gain, then they would also rather have $600 than any gamble that would yield $0 with probability 0.64, no matter how much could be had with the other 0.36 probability. Note that this argument only holds if the $600 is considered a gain. If instead it is incorporated in the reference point, the problem goes away as it did before. One might therefore argue that the $600 would be treated as the new reference point. Nonetheless, it is possible to engineer clever gambles for which it would seem inappropriate for the $600 to be treated as the reference point and that produce similar results. One must remember that models are approximations and simplifications of how decisions are made. Thus, it is always possible to push the limits of the model beyond its reasonable application. This may be especially true of behavioral models that are not intended to provide a single unifying theory of behavior but rather a contextually appropriate description of regularly observed phenomena.

EXAMPLE 10.6 Sweating the Small Stuff

When purchasing a home, a buyer is most often required by the lending agency to purchase some form of homeowners insurance. However, the bank generally gives homeowners wide flexibility in the structure of the insurance they purchase, allowing applicants to choose what types of added coverage they would like as well as the deductible if a claim is filed. When purchasing insurance, a homeowner agrees to pay the insurance company an annual premium. In return, the insurance company agrees to write a check to the homeowner in the event of damage due to a specified list of events. This check will be enough to pay for repairs to the home or items in the home that are covered, minus the insurance deductible. For example, a homeowner who suffered $35,000 of damage from a tornado and who carried insurance with a $1,000 deductible would receive a check for $34,000. The deductible can also have an impact on whether a claim is filed. For example, a homeowner who suffered only $700 worth of damage would not likely file a claim if the deductible was $1,000 because the claim would not result in any payment by the insurance company.

The deductible allows the homeowner to share some of the risk with the insurance company in return for a lower annual premium. Also, because homeowners are offered a schedule of possible premiums and deductibles, the choice of deductible can offer a window into the homeowner's risk preferences. A homeowner who is risk loving might not want the insurance in the first place, only buying it because the lender requires it. In this case, she will likely opt for a very high deductible, sharing a greater portion of the risk in return for a much lower average cost. For example, a home valued at $181,700 would be covered for premiums of $504 with a $1,000 deductible. The same home could be insured for an annual premium of $773 with a $100 deductible. Standard policies specify a $1,000, $500, $250, or $100 deductible. Justin Snydor used data from 50,000 borrowers to examine how buyers choose the level of deductible and also to examine the risk tradeoffs involved. The plurality of buyers (48 percent) chose a policy with a $500 deductible. Another 35 percent chose a $250 deductible. A much smaller percentage (17 percent) chose the $1,000 deductible, and a vanishingly small 0.3 percent chose the $100 deductible.

Table 10.3 displays the average annual premium offered to homeowners by level of deductible. Consider a risk-neutral homeowner who is choosing between a $1,000 deductible and a $500 deductible. Choosing the $500 deductible means that the homeowner will pay about $100 more ($715 − $615) with certainty to lower the cost of repairs by $500 (the difference in the deductibles) in the event of damage greater than $500. We do not know the probability of filing a claim greater than $500. However, if we call the probability of filing a $500 claim p_{500}, then a risk-neutral buyer should prefer the $500 deductible to the $1,000 deductible if

$$p_{500}\$500 > \$100 \qquad (10.27)$$

This implies that $p_{500} > 0.20$. Although we don't know the actual probability of filing a claim, we know that only 0.043 claims were filed per household, meaning that a

Table 10.3   Homeowners Insurance Policies

Deductible	Average Annual Premium	Annual Number of Paid Claims per Household	Percentage Selecting
$1,000	$615.82	0.025	17
$500	$715.73	0.043	48
$250	$802.32	0.049	35
$100	$935.54	0.047	0.3

maximum of 4.3 percent of households filed a claim (some households might have filed multiple claims). Thus, it is likely that the probability of a claim is closer to 0.04—very small relative to 0.20. For the choice between the $500 deductible and the $250 deductible, the homeowner is paying an additional $85 ($801 – $716) a year for a $p_{\$250}$ probability of receiving $250 (the difference between the $500 deductible and the $250 deductible). In this case, a risk-neutral homeowner would prefer the $250 deductible if

$$p_{250}\$250 > \$85. \tag{10.28}$$

This implies that $p_{250} > 0.34$, yet only 0.049 claims are filed on average each year.

Anyone choosing the $500 or the $250 deductible is clearly paying more than the expected value of the added insurance, suggesting that the homeowners are severely risk averse. But just how risk averse are they? This is difficult to know with the limited information we have. An expected-utility maximizer should choose the deductible that solves

$$\max_i qU(w - D_i - r_i) + (1 - q)U(w - r_i), \tag{10.29}$$

where i can be $1,000, $500, $250, or $100, q is the probability of damage requiring a claim, D_i is the deductible i, r_i is the annual premium for the policy with deductible i, and U denotes the utility of wealth function. By specifying the utility function as[1]

$$U(w) = \frac{x^{(1-p)}}{(1-p)}, \tag{10.30}$$

and using the claim rate (column 3 of Table 10.3) as a probability of damage, Snydor is able to place some bounds on the parameter ρ for each person in the dataset. This parameter is a measure of risk aversion. The higher ρ, the more risk averse the homeowner. Using this lower bound, Snydor is able then to determine whether a buyer with the same level of ρ would be willing to take a gamble consisting of a 0.50 probability of gaining some amount of money G and an 0.50 probability of losing $1,000, much like Rabin's calibration theorem. In fact, he finds that in all cases, more than 92 percent of all homeowners should be unwilling to take a gamble that has a 0.50 probability of losing $1,000 no matter how much money could be had with the other 0.50 probability. This clearly suggests that the level of risk aversion homeowners display is beyond the level we might consider reasonable.

The alternative explanation, prospect theory, would not provide a solution to this problem under normal definitions because all of the outcomes deal in losses. Examining equation 10.29, note that all possible outcomes are smaller than current wealth. In the loss domain, homeowners should be risk loving, implying they should only buy the $1,000 deductible policy, and then only because the bank forces them to. Moreover, misperception of probabilities seems unlikely as an explanation because the homeowner would need to overestimate the probability of a loss by nearly 500 percent. Suppose, for example, that we consider the simplest form of the loss-averse value function consisting of just two line segments:

---

[1] Commonly called the constant relative risk aversion form.

$$V(x) = \begin{cases} x & \text{if} \quad x \geq 0 \\ \beta x & \text{if} \quad x < 0 \end{cases}, \tag{10.31}$$

where $\beta > 1$. If homeowners value money outcomes according to equation 10.31, and if they regard premiums as a loss, then the homeowner will prefer the $500 deductible to the $1,000 deductible if

$$\begin{aligned} &\pi(q)V(-500-715) + (1-\pi(q))V(-715) \\ &> \pi(q)V(-1000-615) + (1-\pi(q))V(-615) \end{aligned} \tag{10.32}$$

or, substituting equation 10.31 into equation 10.32

$$\begin{aligned} &\beta[\pi(q)(-1215) + (1-\pi(q))(-715)] \\ &> \beta[\pi(q)(-1615) + (1-\pi(q))(-615)]. \end{aligned} \tag{10.33}$$

Simplifying, the homeowner will prefer the smaller deductible if

$$\frac{\pi(q)}{1-\pi(q)} > 0.25. \tag{10.34}$$

But given that the probability of a loss is closer to 0.04, and given the parameters of the weighting function presented earlier in the chapter, $\pi(q)/[1-\pi(q)] \approx 0.11$. Thus probability weighting alone cannot account for the severely risk-averse behavior.

Segregation may be the key to this puzzle. If the homeowner did not perceive the premium as a loss (segregating the payment), prospect theory would suggest that she would then prefer the $500 deductible if the difference in the expected value of V between the two outcomes exceeds the change in price. Or,

$$\begin{aligned} &\pi(q)V(-500) + (1-\pi(q))V(0) - 715 \\ &> \pi(q)V(-1000) + (1-\pi(q))V(0) - 615. \end{aligned} \tag{10.35}$$

Note here that the value paid for the premium is not considered in the value function because it is segregated. Homeowners do not consider it a loss because it is a planned expense. Substituting equation 10.31 into equation 10.35 we obtain

$$-\pi(q)\beta 500 - 715 > -\pi(q)\beta 1000 - 615 \tag{10.36}$$

or

$$\beta\pi(q) > 0.2. \tag{10.37}$$

If we assume $q \approx 0.4$, then $\pi(q) \approx 0.1$. Additionally, the value of β is commonly thought to be just above 2, suggesting that prospect theory with segregation of the annual premium might explain some insurance behavior.

History and Notes

One complaint often lodged against research into the violations of expected utility theory is that they are based on somewhat contrived experiments. People seldom deal with the types of simple gambles presented in laboratory experiments. Laboratory experiments often involve small amounts of money that might not motivate well-reasoned responses. Further, most gambles presented in a laboratory setting involve a small number of possible outcomes with stated probabilities (such as those that can be represented in a Marschak–Machina triangle). Real-life risky choices are often not characterized by known probabilities but maybe by some general understanding of what might be possible. For example, one cannot know the probability that a certain stock will increase in value in the future. Instead, we are left to guess based upon previous experience and data from prior returns. Further, choices are often not between two possible gambles, but along a continuum. For example, I may purchase any number of shares (even fractions of shares) of a particular mutual fund. Thus it may not be a "this or that" type of question but a "how much" type of question. Finally, the choice experiments that have been used to examine nonexpected utility models are specifically designed to create choices that violate expected utility theory. In many real-world instances, the person is not presented with options that clearly violate expected utility theory. Thus, there may be some bounds to when behavioral models would be useful.

Nonetheless, several themes have developed from this stream of literature that have clear and practical applications. Among these are regret aversion, the systematic misperception of probabilities, and the use of choice heuristics when gambles are similar in some respect. Although these might not be applicable to every study of behavior under risky choice, they certainly make a substantive contribution in many circumstances. Kahneman and Tversky's prospect theory model of choice under risk has gained wide use because it embodies so many of the anomalies that are found most often in an experimental setting. In many ways, prospect theory has become the most visible face of behavioral economics in the general economics discipline.

Biographical Note

Peter P. Wakker (1956 –)

M.S., Nijmegen University, 1979; Ph.D., Tilburg University, 1986; held faculty positions at Leiden University, Tilburg University, University of Amsterdam, University of Maastricht, and Erasmus University

Peter Wakker obtained his first training in the fields of mathematics that focus on probability, statistics, and optimization. From there it was a very short hop to the study of economic decision making under risk. Wakker is one of the leading theorists in the world regarding decision under risk and uncertainty. He has written dozens of articles using mathematical theory to examine risky behavior, earning his position as one of the most highly cited economic theorists. His research has won several awards including the Career Achievement Award for the Society of Medical Decision Making. Among his most-cited articles are those examining the use of various probability or decision-weighting schemes, development of the cumulative prospect theory model and several other models of risky decision behavior, and explorations of cardinal measures of utility. Wakker has written two books, one providing a thorough treatment of the use of prospect theory for decisions under risk as well as uncertainty. He has an encyclopedic knowledge of the research literature on risk and uncertainty. As a service to the field, he publishes an annually updated annotated bibliography of risk research that is of vital use to anyone entering the field.

THOUGHT QUESTIONS

1. Consider that Kim has a choice among the following prospects

Gamble A:	Gamble B:
$60 with probability 0.24	$65 with probability 0.25
$33 with probability 0.24	$30 with probability 0.25
$0 with probability 0.52	$1 with probability 0.50

(a) Rewrite these gambles after applying each of the steps of the editing phase. Does the result depend upon the order in which you apply these steps?

(b) Calculate the value of both gambles using the cumulative prospect theory functions estimated by Tversky and Kahneman and appearing in equations 10.6 and 10.7, including their parameter estimates. Which gamble would the model predict would be chosen? Does this depend on the order of the steps applied in editing?

2. Stock market investments are inherently risky. Suppose that Sasha is heavily invested in a high-tech firm with a positive earnings outlook. Then reports come out that the firm's primary technology is under a legal challenge from a competitor. If they should successfully repel the legal challenge, they will make the spectacular profits that everyone had been expecting, creating the expected returns on investment. If they fail, their business model will be irreparably broken

and their stock will be worthless. Legal experts give the legal challenge a 60 percent chance of being successful. In the meantime, stock prices have plummeted in response to the news. Sasha previously had $1 million invested, and it is now worth only $400,000. What does prospect theory have to say about Sasha's likely reaction to the news and devaluation of the stock? What has happened to the level of risk? What is Sasha's likely reference point? Describe the change in risk aversion. Is Sasha likely to sell out now or hold the stock? Why? How might this explain behavior in a stock market crash?

3. You have a collection of valuable artwork worth $400,000. Suppose that you have preferences represented by the cumulative prospect theory model presented in Example 10.3. You are considering an insurance policy that will pay you the value of your collection should anything destroy it. Suppose that the probability of your artwork being damaged is 0.03.

   (a) Considering that the current value of your artwork is your reference point, what is the most you would be willing to pay for the coverage? Express this as a percentage of $400,000.

   (b) Now, suppose while you are filling out the paperwork, you are informed that a freak accident

has destroyed half of your collection, leaving you with only $200,000 worth of rare artwork. If we consider $400,000 to be the reference point, now what is the maximum percentage of $200,000 you would be willing to pay to buy insurance that will replace $200,000 should the remaining art be destroyed?

4. Consider the contract problem in Example 10.5. Suppose that when considering whether to take the contract or not, the worker tries to maximize the function $U(b) + \max_{i \in \{h, l\}} V_i$, where $U(b) = b^{0.88}$, the value b is the base level of pay in the contract, and V_i is as given in equations 10.12 through 10.17. Consider that if the worker takes no contract, she will receive $0.

   (a) What is the minimum level of base pay the worker will accept for a contract with a high base pay and penalties for poor performance (so $b = r_h$)? What are the resulting r_l, r_h?

   (b) What is the minimum level of base pay the worker will accept for a contract with low base pay and rewards for good performance (so $b = r_l$)? What are the resulting r_l, r_h?

   (c) Suppose the firm can sell high-quality pizza for $10 and low-quality pizza for $7. Which contract will the firm offer in order to maximize their profits?

REFERENCES

Ali, M.M. "Probability and Utility Estimates for Racetrack Bettors." *Journal of Political Economy* 85(1977): 803–815.

Kahneman, D., and A. Tversky. "Prospect Theory: An Analysis of Decision Under Risk." *Econometrica* 47(1979): 263–292.

Loomes, G. "Evidence of a New Violation of the Independence Axiom." *Journal of Risk and Uncertainty* 4(1991): 91–108.

Neilson, W. "Calibration Results for Rank-Dependent Expected Utility." *Economics Bulletin* 4(2001): 1–4.

Rabin, M. "Risk Aversion and Expected-Utility Theory: A Calibration Theorem." *Econometrica* 68(2000): 1281–92.

Snydor, J. "(Over)insuring Modest Risks." *American Economic Journal: Applied Economics* 2(2010): 177–199.

Tversky, A., and D. Kahneman. "Advances in Prospect Theory: Cumulative Representation of Uncertainty." *Journal of Risk and Uncertainty* 5(1992): 297–323.

TIME DISCOUNTING AND THE LONG AND SHORT RUN

Society often classifies certain actions as tempting, sinful, or indulgent. These are odd concepts within the standard economics framework. If rational decision makers decide to do something, it is because they feel it is the best for them when all things are considered. But then why does society look with disdain on the youth who has taken up smoking or drug use? Obesity has become a substantial policy issue, and many suppose we should take action to curb the ability of people to eat the food they would like to. Some externalities are associated with obesity, though these are primarily due to publicly funded medical care (e.g., Medicare and Medicaid). The public seems to be much more willing to ban or tax certain foods than to simply exclude care for complications resulting from obesity from publicly funded medical care.

Behavioral economists have developed a comprehensive theory of how people make decisions that might have short-term benefits but longer-term costs. In many cases, people appear to be willing to commit themselves to behavior that appears to hurt them in the short term in the hope of providing longer-term benefits. For example, people often prefer to receive monthly installments rather than a single lump sum, citing the possibility that they would waste the money or fail to save enough for future expenses. In each of these cases it seems that people are in conflict with themselves. One course of action provides a short-term benefit but could have disproportionately negative effects in the future, and the person would be better off to forgo the short-term benefit to retain the long-term welfare. In some situations the wise course of action seems so clear that we wish to restrict others' ability to take the wrong path. Even with all the information necessary to understand the tradeoffs, we might face difficulty in choosing the path that would appear to make us better off.

In this section, we discuss models of time discounting that give rise to time-inconsistent preferences. These models predict familiar behavior with respect to temptation and indulgence. Depending on how much people understand their own tendencies toward indulgence, discounting may might lead them to seek out commitment devices. Along with models of decision under risk, these models have become some of the most visible and widely used among all behavioral economics models.

Disagreeing with Ourselves: Projection and Hindsight Biases

11

On March 19, 2003, President George W. Bush announced that the United States was invading Iraq. This followed months of protracted arguments to the American people and to the world that Iraq had a chemical and biological weapons program that was in violation of their 1991 cease-fire agreement with the United States. Iraq had committed several other blatant violations of the cease-fire agreement, including firing on U.S. airmen. Nonetheless, the Bush administration had set as the centerpiece of its argument for invasion the existence of a thriving chemical and biological weapons program that presented a threat to the region.

Perhaps the most memorable of these arguments was given by the U.S. Secretary of State Colin Powell to the U.N. Security Council on February 5, 2003. Here he presented satellite photos of supposed mobile chemical weapons factories and bunkers for storage of chemical weapons, and he presented other intelligence that appeared to provide solid evidence that Iraq was building the capability to threaten stability in the Middle East. At one point he played tapes of Iraqi military communications in which the order is given to "remove the expression 'nerve agent' wherever it comes up in wireless communications" just before a U.N. inspection team arrived. The U.S. House of Representatives, several of the leading nations in the world, and the United Nations eventually took the intelligence argument as sufficient to warrant military action.

When the United States invaded, however, no such weapons were ever found. Moreover, the United States found no evidence to suggest that any such weapons had ever been there. Soon after it became clear that no chemical or biological weapons would be found, hundreds of blogs and much political commentary claimed, in fact, that the intelligence before the war conclusively showed that they did not exist. But if it were really so easy to see through the case that was made at the time, how could so many have been so blind? At one point before invasion the director of the Central Intelligence Agency had called the case a "slam-dunk." How could he have been so certain if the case was as weak as many claim it was?

Our circumstances often influence our judgment. Consider the purchase of a pool table. Those without such amenities in their homes might visit friends who possess one and find great pleasure in playing a few games of nine-ball. These tables can be a large investment, with new tables often costing between $3,000 and $10,000. After visiting friends and playing pool several times, you might convince yourself that the high price tag is worth it. Yet throughout basements in America, thousands of pool tables sit dormant.

After convincing themselves to spend such an amount on a table, many play several times within the first few months and then grow bored by the game. They still continue to pull out the cue sticks when friends are visiting who may be excited to play. But for the most part, the table just takes up a large amount of space and gathers dust. It is difficult to understand why someone would expend such money for so little use. Nonetheless, it appears to be common.

We have a difficult time determining how we will feel or think in other circumstances. This can lead us to make notoriously bad decisions, albeit with conviction. We purchase items we believe we will want in the future, only to abandon the items as useless at a later date. We might also claim that we should have known better. In this chapter we consider **projection bias** and **hindsight bias**. Projection bias deals with predicting how we will feel at some future date. Hindsight bias deals with remembering the information that was available for our judgment at some previous date. In both cases we discuss the evidence for such biases and how they may be modeled.

These biases create **time-inconsistent preferences**. That is, what we believe we will want at some other time disagrees with what we actually want at that time. We disagree with ourselves. The evidence for such disagreements is convincing. Moreover, we tend to display such disagreements about even the most deliberated and weighty issues—including decisions to go to college, get married, or even to go to war. Within the rational decision framework pervasive in economics, it is difficult to reconcile such systematic regret. Psychologists have shed much light on these internal conflicts and how they can occur. Behavioral economic work sheds further light on the potential impacts of such behavior and potentially how to avoid such impacts.

The Standard Models of Intertemporal Choice

When people make decisions that will affect available choices in the future, economists tend to make a series of simplifying assumptions. These assumptions are not necessary for a person to be rational, per se. Rather, these assumptions seem reasonable, and they allow us to make simple predictions from a complicated problem. Consider first a two-period decision-making model (we consider more periods in the following chapters). Originally the person has wealth given by w_1. In period 1 the person chooses what portion of w_1 to use to buy goods for current consumption, c_1, and then consumes these goods. The rest of the wealth is saved until the second period. In the second period, the person uses all remaining wealth, $w_2 = w_1 - c_1$, to buy goods for consumption, c_2, consumes these goods, and then dies. A general model of consumption might suppose that the person solves

$$\max_{c_1} U(c_1, w - c_1), \tag{11.1}$$

where $0 \le c_1 \le w_1$, and where $U(c_1, c_2)$ is the utility of consuming c_1 in period 1 and c_2 in period 2. This model allows consumption in period 1 to be either a complement or substitute for consumption in period 2. In other words, the marginal utility of consumption in period 1 can either increase or decrease when consumption in period 2 increases.

We could, of course, add a few bells and whistles, such as allowing the prices for consumption to change between periods (currently we assume a unit of consumption costs one unit of wealth), allowing savings to accrue interest, or allowing the person to receive additional wealth in the second period. However, with or without these bells and whistles, this model functions exactly like the two-commodity consumer problem presented in Chapter 1, where consumption in period 1 is one good and consumption in period 2 is another good. This general model of intertemporal consumption is presented graphically in Figure 11.1. The budget constraint is depicted by the line where $c_2 = w - c_1$. This budget constraint has a slope of negative 1. The convex curves represent indifference curves. Each indifference curve represents all points satisfying $U(c_1, c_2) = k$, for some constant k. Thus, the person is indifferent between each consumption bundle along the curve. Utility is assumed to increase as one moves from the origin, in the southwest of the figure, to the northeast portion of the figure. Thus, the problem is solved at the point(s) along the budget constraint that is contained in the northeastern-most indifference curve. In the figure, this occurs at $\left(c_1^*, c_2^*\right)$, where the slope of the indifference curve is also negative 1.

In this model, people who prefer current consumption over consumption in the next period would have more negatively sloped indifference curves, reflecting that losing one unit of current consumption must be compensated by greater period 2 consumption in order to maintain indifference. Having more negatively sloped indifference curves would also lead the optimal consumption bundle to lie farther to the southeast along the budget constraint. Alternatively, someone who preferred period 2 consumption over current consumption would have indifference curves with a very small negative slope, leading to optimal consumption bundles in the northwest portion of the budget constraint. The slope of the indifference curve could differ by location within the set of choices available. Thus, it could be that someone with relatively high w could have steep indifference curves and opt to consume more in period 1, whereas the same person would have

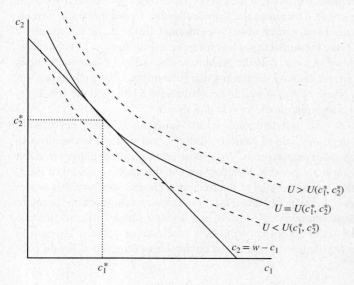

$U > U(c_1^*, c_2^*)$

$U = U(c_1^*, c_2^*)$

$U < U(c_1^*, c_2^*)$

$c_2 = w - c_1$

FIGURE 11.1
General Model of Intertemporal Choice

relatively shallow indifference curves with low wealth and consume more in period 2 (or vice versa). This model offers a lot of flexibility. For many purposes, economists feel this general model omits important information we have about individual preferences over current versus future consumption.

Economists commonly believe that people prefer current consumption to future consumption. Thus a hamburger today is more attractive than a hamburger tomorrow. Moreover, economists tend to believe that people's within-period preferences over consumption are relatively stable over time. Thus, if I begin to eat a bag of potato chips today, as I eat, my marginal utility declines at about the same rate per chip as it would if I were to instead eat identical chips tomorrow. Thus, in a majority of applications, the economic model of intertemporal choice modifies the model in equation 11.1, assuming

$$U(c_1, c_2) = u(c_1) + \delta u(c_2), \tag{11.2}$$

where $u(c)$ is the utility received within any time period from consumption within that time period (usually called the **instantaneous utility function**) and δ is a discount factor applied to future consumption. The utility function within each time period is identical except for the discount factor. Generally, $0 < \delta < 1$, indicating that future utility of consumption is worth less than current utility of consumption. This is commonly called an **additive model**, because utility of consumption is additively separable across periods. The slope of the indifference curves at any point (c_1, c_2) follows the form

$$\frac{dc_2}{dc_1} = -\frac{u'(c_1)}{\delta u'(c_2)}, \tag{11.3}$$

where $u'(c_i)$ represents marginal utility of consumption in period i.

Thus, increasing δ decreases the slope of the curves, reflecting a preference for period 2 consumption, and decreasing δ increases the slope, reflecting a preference for current-period consumption. Many have written about the discount factor, δ, as a measure of patience. If δ is equal to 1, the consumer considers future consumption just as valuable as current consumption. If we assume that the instantaneous utility of consumption is increasing in consumption and displays decreasing marginal utility of consumption, then the consumer optimizes where $c_1 = c_2 = w/2$. Alternatively, if $\delta = 0$, then the consumer only cares about current consumption and $c_1 = w$ and $c_2 = 0$.

This additive form of the intertemporal utility function is used pervasively in modeling investment decisions, use of natural resources, and strategic interactions in bargaining, among many other applications. It is most often used for longer-horizon problems—those involving $n > 2$ periods. Whether we use the additive model of intertemporal choice or the more general model of intertemporal choice, however, this model relies on the notion that people can predict their utility of consumption function for future time periods. Even if we use these models to consider decisions under risk, economists generally assume the risk is due to not knowing how much consumption will result in future periods, not from any degree of risk or uncertainty regarding the utility of consumption function.

EXAMPLE 11.1   Adapting to Chronic Kidney Disease

Kidney disease affects about one out of every nine adults in the United States and is always a life-altering disease. Milder forms of kidney disease result in reduced function of the kidneys. This generally requires the patient to follow a strict diet, cutting out many desirable foods, counting calories, and limiting liquid intake. Additionally, patients must engage in a strict exercise regimen. In the most serious cases, patients have to undergo kidney dialysis. This usually involves visiting a dialysis center three times a week and sitting in a chair for four hours while the patient's blood is processed outside the body through a dialyzer. Two needles are inserted into the patient, and tubes are connected to draw blood out and return blood back to the circulation. The dialyzer acts like an artificial kidney, cleaning the blood of foreign substances and reducing the amount of water in the blood. Dialysis patients must undergo this treatment several times a week, or else toxins quickly accumulate in the body, resulting in death. Dialysis patients are typically required to remain close to a home treatment center and cannot travel. Dialysis patients often report feeling weak or nauseated after a treatment. In short, dialysis is an unpleasant treatment, but it is necessary to prolong life. On the surface, one would expect the quality of life to decline substantially if the kidney disease is severe enough to warrant dialysis. Thus, it should be no surprise that when perfectly healthy people are asked, they in fact believe that going on dialysis would significantly reduce their quality of life.

David L. Sackett and George W. Torrance surveyed 189 people about the quality of life they would experience should they contract various diseases. Participants in the study were asked to rate each disease on a scale in which 1 means the respondent is indifferent between living with the disease and being perfectly healthy and 0 means the respondent is indifferent between living with the disease and dying. On average, people believed their quality of life would be 0.32 if they were required to visit a hospital to undergo dialysis for the rest of their life. Alternatively, when current dialysis patients were asked the same question, they rated the quality of life as 0.52 on average. Although 0.52 is a long way from 1, it is also a long way from 0.32. Why would dialysis patients feel so much better off than others might believe them to be? One potential explanation is that people with kidney disease use a different scale for their answers. Perhaps once you have such a reduced quality of life, you cannot remember how good "perfectly healthy" is, and thus your "1" is a healthy person's "0.6". This does not appear to be the case. Other studies have compared questions using a vague quality-of-life scale to one that uses a much more explicit scale and find that the more-explicit scale actually generates a wider divergence of values.

In another study, researchers found patients waiting for kidney transplants and asked about the quality of life they would experience if they did or did not receive the transplant within a year. They then tracked down the same patients after one year and found that they displayed similar bias in predicting their own quality of life. Those who had not received transplants were better off than they thought they would be. Those who had received the transplants were worse off than they thought they would be.

One reason people might perform so miserably at predicting their future well-being is that they give a knee-jerk judgment rather than reasoning through what life would really be like. Peter A. Ubel, George Loewenstein, and Christopher Jepson found that if healthy people were asked to think about the ways that they might be able to adapt their life to kidney disease and dialysis treatment, their predictions of quality of life improves to something that is somewhat closer to that reported by actual patients. Once people begin to consider their ability to adapt, they might realize that some of the things they enjoy most are still possible. People have a hard time predicting how they might adapt to future circumstances, which affects their ability to guess their future utility.

EXAMPLE 11.2   Choosing a College Based upon Weather

Many students are attracted to the warmer climates of Florida or southern California. It is a common theme for students to turn down better educational opportunities for climates that are more amenable to beachgoing or other outdoor sporting activities. One would thus expect that visiting a college in the northeastern United States, a region known for its bad weather, on a day with particularly bad weather, might lead students to question whether they could survive four years of such punishment. However, suppose the school had very little in the way of social or outdoor activities in the first place.

At one academically challenging school, Uri Simonsohn found that visiting on bad-weather days increases the probability that the potential student will actually enroll. He analyzed the decisions of 562 applicants who had been admitted to the school and who had visited the school before making a decision to enroll. Of the 562 visitors, 259 eventually decided to accept the offer of admission. He then used data from the National Oceanic and Atmospheric Administration collected from the weather station closest to the school on cloud cover for each day students visited the university. Cloud cover is measured on a scale of 0 to 10, with 0 being completely clear skies and 10 being completely overcast skies. Amazingly, he found that an increase in cloud cover by one point increases the probability of accepting the offer of admission by between 0.02 to 0.03, depending on what other control variables are used.

At first glance, one might think this suggests that prospective students are attracted to cloudy places, which seems counterintuitive. Rather, Simonsohn argues that this result occurs because the way people evaluate the options they will face in the future is biased by the options that are currently at hand. When it is sunny, one might wish to spend time outside engaging in recreational activities rather than hunkered down with a textbook. Being taken on a tour of a prestigious university on such a sunny day might underscore the lack of available recreation there. Thus, when students consider the prestigious school versus a school with more recreational options, they might opt for the school with more recreational opportunities, not wanting to be stuck indoors with their textbook when the sun is shining.

Visiting when there is significant cloud cover can make outdoor activities less attractive. In fact, about 78 percent of students polled report that they prefer studying on overcast days than on sunny days. Thus, students who visit the prestigious institution when there is significant cloud cover are in a state in which they prefer studying more than they would otherwise. This experience colors the projection of the utility they anticipate that they will experience in the future when attending the school. In this case, they suppose that they will not mind the lack of outdoor activities and decide to go to the prestigious school. Hence, college admissions officers at academically challenging, yet recreationally challenged, schools across the country regularly hope for rain.

Making Decisions for Our Future Self

The key to both the college admissions story and the example dealing with kidney disease is **projection bias**. Projection bias supposes that people believe they will value options in the future the way they value them today. They tend to ignore the impact of some factors that should change in the intervening time. In the case of weather and college admissions, the individual observation of weather (cloudy or sunny) has little to do with overall climate. At a university, any individual day a student chooses to engage in an activity will obtain utility $u(activity|university, w)$, where *activity* represents the chosen activity with possible values {*study recreate*}, *university* represents the chosen university, which can take on values {*prestige, party*}, and w represents weather, which can take on the values {*cloudy, sunny*}. Suppose that at the prestigious university, recreation options are very poor but still just slightly better than studying (only a slight abstraction). Thus, on a sunny day, a student decides to recreate, receiving utility $u(recreate|prestige, sunny)$, with $u(study|prestige, sunny) < u(recreate|prestige, sunny)$. But on a cloudy day, the student chooses to study, $u(recreate|prestige, cloudy) < u(study|prestige, cloudy)$.

Suppose that at another university under consideration (the party school), there are poor opportunities for studying. Thus studying at the party school yields $u(study|party, weather) < u(study|prestige, weather)$ for studying, which is strictly lower than the utility for studying at the prestigious university on either sunny or cloudy days. There are spectacular opportunities to recreate at the party school, thus $u(recreate|prestige, sunny) < u(recreate|party, sunny)$. Recreating when it is sunny is always chosen. However, when it is cloudy, despite the poor opportunities to study, studying is preferred to recreating. In fact, $u(study|party, sunny) < u(recreate|party, cloudy) < u(study|party, cloudy) < u(recreate|party, sunny)$.

Suppose every year, exactly half of the days are cloudy and half are sunny at both schools. Thus, if the student in question decided which college to attend based upon the additive utility model, with discount factor $\delta = 1$, we could write the utility of the prestigious university as

$$U(prestige) = \frac{N}{2}u(study|prestige, cloudy) + \frac{N}{2}u(recreate|prestige, sunny), \quad (11.4)$$

where N is the number of school days. Alternatively, at the party school the student would obtain

$$U(party) = \frac{N}{2}u(study|party, cloudy) + \frac{N}{2}u(recreate|party, sunny). \quad (11.5)$$

If $u(study|prestige, cloudy) - u(study|party, cloudy) < u(recreate|party, sunny) - u(recreate|prestige, sunny)$, then $U(party) > U(prestigioius)$, and the student should choose the party school no matter what the weather on the day of the visit. If instead $u(study|prestige, cloudy) - u(study|party, cloudy) > u(recreate|party, sunny) - u(recreate|prestige, sunny)$, then the student should choose the prestigious school no matter what the weather on the day of the visit.

Suppose, however, that students ignore the impact of weather on the utility of either recreation or studying, gauging their future utility based on the state of the weather that particular day. In this case, students visiting on a cloudy day might instead perceive

$$U(prestigious) = N \times u(study|prestige, cloudy) \tag{11.6}$$

but would perceive the utility of attending the party school as

$$U(party) = N \times u(study|party, cloudy). \tag{11.7}$$

In this case, they would be led to choose the prestigious university. Alternatively, if they visited on a sunny day, they would perceive

$$U(prestigious) = N \times u(recreate|prestige, sunny) \tag{11.8}$$

and

$$U(party) = N \times u(recreate|party, sunny), \tag{11.9}$$

in which case they would be led to choose the party school. Though when they actually arrive on either campus they will be subject to both sunny and rainy days, they might not consider this variation when comparing the two options. Such a process could explain why students visiting on cloudy days were more likely to choose to attend the prestigious university than those visiting on sunny days. It suggests that people bias their projection of the utility of an action in the future toward the utility they assign to that action at the moment.

Notably, if people are subject to projection bias, it can create situations in which they will regret their decisions, believing that they made a mistake. In the case of this example, if $u(study|prestige, cloudy) - u(study|party, cloudy) < u(recreate|party, sunny) - u(recreate|prestige, sunny)$, students would be better off at the party school, but if they visited the campus on a cloudy day, they choose the prestigious university. At the time of the decision, they consider the utility of studying because it seems that this will be what matters. After beginning to attend, students are exposed to sunny days (about half) and might realize that the party school would be a better option. When people at one period in time believe they will have one set of preferences in the future, but then later realize systematically inconsistent preferences, we call this **time-inconsistent preferences**.

George Loewenstein, Ted O'Donoghue, and Matthew Rabin proposed a model of projection bias based on the notion that people may be able to project the direction of the change in their future preferences but not the full extent of the change. In the language of the above example, they might recognize that on sunny days they will prefer to be at the party school recreating, but they might not recognize how much better off they would be at the party school on those days. Suppose that someone's preferences can be represented by a state-dependent utility function. A person receives utility $u(c, s)$ from consuming bundle c in state s. The state represents the external conditions that affect utility of consumption. This may be weather, as in Example 11.2, whether or not one has kidney disease, as in Example 11.1, or hunger, pain, or any other factor that could influence the utility of various consumption options. Suppose someone in state s' is placed in a situation where he needs to make decisions that will affect his consumption in some future state $s \neq s'$. In this case, the decision maker needs to predict the utility of consumption function he will face in this new state, $u(c, s)$. Let $\tilde{u}(c, s|s')$ represent the predicted utility of consumption under state s when the decision maker makes the prediction while in state s'. The decision maker displays **simple projection bias** if

$$\tilde{u}(c, s|s') = (1-\alpha)u(c, s) + \alpha u(c, s') \qquad (11.10)$$

and where $0 < \alpha \leq 1$. In this case, if $\alpha = 0$, the decision maker displays no projection bias and can perfectly predict the utility of consumption he will face in the future state s. Alternatively, if $\alpha = 1$, he perceives his utility in state s will be identical to his preferences in his current state s'. In general, the larger the α the greater the degree of simple projection bias. Thus, the decision maker's perception of the preferences he will realize in the future state lies somewhere between the preferences he will actually face and those that he currently holds.

People facing an intertemporal choice problem (see equation 11.1) in which the state affecting their preferences would change in the second period would thus solve

$$\max_{c_1} u(c_1, s') + \delta\tilde{u}(w - c_1, s|s') = u(c_1, s') + \delta[(1-\alpha)u(w - c_1, s) + \alpha u(w - c_1, s')],$$
$$(11.11)$$

where $0 \leq c_1 \leq w$. A pair of potential indifference curves representing this choice when $\delta = 1$ appear in Figure 11.2. Here, if $\alpha = 0$, then they do not display projection bias, and they perceive correctly that their future utility will be maximized at point B, where the indifference curve accounting for their true future utility is tangent to the budget

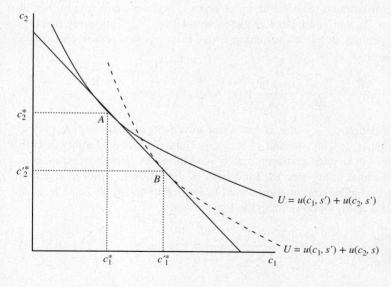

$U = u(c_1, s') + u(c_2, s')$

$U = u(c_1, s') + u(c_2, s)$

FIGURE 11.2

Intertemporal Choice with Projection Bias

constraint. This indifference curve, represented by the dashed curve in the figure, represents the highest level of utility it is possible to achieve. Alternatively, if $\alpha = 1$, then they will choose to consume at point A, where the indifference curve that assumes today's state persists for both periods is tangent to the budget curve. Point A lies closer to the origin than the dashed curve does, meaning that people are clearly worse off when choosing point A. The points between A and B represent the different possible bundles that people might choose given different values of α. The higher the level of projection bias, α, the closer the consumption bundle will be to point A and the lower the corresponding level of utility will be realized.

Projection bias unambiguously makes people worse off than if they could perceive the true preferences they would face in the new state. It is a relatively simple way to explain a multitude of behaviors we observe in which people tend toward actions they will later regret.

Projection Bias and Addiction

One commonly regretted action is that of acquiring an addictive habit. Suppose, for example, that we consider developing a habit of drinking coffee. One key feature of an addictive habit is that as one consumes the substance, one begins to require more of it, suggesting that marginal utility is increasing. A very simplified model of this considers a decision maker in two periods. In each period, suppose that the consumer decides how much coffee to consume and how much food to consume. The consumer has an initial endowment of wealth equal to w that can be used over the two periods and receives no further income.

Let's suppose that the consumer has an instantaneous utility function of the form

$$U\left(x_{c,\,t},\,x_{f,\,t}|x_{c,\,t-1}\right) = (\gamma_1 + x_{c,\,t-1})x_{c,\,t} - \frac{\gamma_2}{2}x_{c,\,t}^2 - \gamma_3 x_{c,\,t-1} + x_{f,\,t}, \qquad (11.12)$$

where $x_{c,\,t}$ is the consumption of coffee at time t, and $x_{f,\,t}$ is the consumption of food at time t, and where γ_1, γ_2 and γ_3 are positive parameters with $\gamma_1 > 2$. This utility function implies that the marginal utility of consuming coffee in any period (the instantaneous marginal utility) is given by

$$\frac{dU\left(x_{c,\,t},\,x_{f,\,t}|x_{c,\,t-1}\right)}{dx_{c,\,t}} = (\gamma_1 + x_{c,\,t-1}) - \gamma_2 x_{c,\,t}. \qquad (11.13)$$

Given prior consumption, $x_{c,\,t-1}$, this is just a downward-sloping line with respect to current consumption, $x_{c,\,t}$, with constant $\gamma_1 + x_{c,\,t-1}$. Thus, the marginal utility of consumption increases when prior consumption, $x_{c,\,t-1}$, increases. However, prior consumption decreases total utility (see the third term of the utility function in equation 11.12), indicating that more consumption would be needed to obtain the same level of utility. The marginal utility of consuming food is constant

$$\frac{dU\left(x_{c,\,t},\,x_{f,\,t}|x_{c,\,t-1}\right)}{dx_{f,\,t}} = 1. \qquad (11.14)$$

Let us suppose that before the first period, no coffee has been consumed, so that $x_{c,0} = 0$. A consumer displaying a simple coefficient of projection bias of α (and with discount factor $\delta = 1$) will solve

$$\max_{\{x_{c,1}, x_{f,1}, x_{c,2}, x_{f,2}\}} U(x_{c,1}, x_{f,1}|0) + \alpha U(x_{c,2}, x_{f,2}|0) + (1-\alpha)U(x_{c,2}, x_{f,2}|x_{c,1})$$

(11.15)

subject to the budget constraint (assuming a price of 1 for each unit of food and coffee)

$$w \geq x_{c,1} + x_{f,1} + x_{c,2} + x_{f,2}.$$

(11.16)

Projection bias in this case is associated with believing that the instantaneous utility function will not change no matter how much coffee is consumed in this period. The budget constraint must hold with equality given the positive marginal utility for drinking coffee and eating food. We can rewrite equation 11.15 as

$$\max_{\{x_{c,1}, x_{f,1}, x_{c,2}, x_{f,2}\}} V = \left\{ \begin{array}{l} \gamma_1 x_{c,1} - \dfrac{\gamma_2}{2} x_{c,1}^2 + x_{f,1} + \alpha\left(\gamma_1 x_{c,2} - \dfrac{\gamma_2}{2} x_{c,2}^2 + x_{f,2} \right) \\[2mm] + (1-\alpha)\left((\gamma_1 + x_{c,1})x_{c,2} - \dfrac{\gamma_2}{2} x_{c,2}^2 - \gamma_3 x_{c,1} + x_{f,2} \right) \end{array} \right\}$$

(11.17)

subject to equation 11.16. Because $\delta = 1$, food will offer the same marginal utility, one, whether consumed in the first or second period. Because units of food and coffee are assumed to have the same price, the solution to equation 11.15 will occur where the marginal utility of consumption for each good in each period is equal.

Intuitively, a consumer would always spend his next dollar on the item and period that yield the largest marginal utility. Marginal utility of coffee consumption in any period is declining with additional consumption, while the marginal utility of food consumption is constant at one. This is depicted in Figure 11.3, where the vertical axis measures marginal utility, the horizontal axis measures quantity of coffee consumption in period 1 as you move from the far left toward the right, coffee consumption in the second period is measured on the horizontal axis as you move from the far right toward the left, and food consumption is measured on the horizontal axis as the space between coffee consumption in period 1 and period 2. The consumer will choose to consume coffee in both periods until marginal perceived utility in that period declines to 1 or until the budget constraint is met. If the budget is large enough that enough coffee can be purchased in each period so that marginal utility of coffee consumption has declined to one for both periods, then the remaining money will all be spent on food.

We will assume that the budget is large enough for this to be the case. Given equation 11.15, the marginal simple projected utility of coffee consumption in the first period is given by

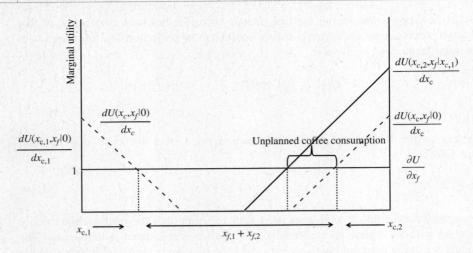

FIGURE 11.3
Addictive Behaviors
with Projection Bias

$$\frac{\partial V}{\partial x_{c,1}} = \gamma_1 - \gamma_2 x_{c,1} + (1-\alpha)(x_{c,2} - \gamma_3) = 1, \qquad (11.18)$$

where the right-hand equality is required for marginal utility of first-period coffee consumption to equal marginal utility of food consumption. The marginal simple projected utility of coffee consumption in the second period is given by

$$\frac{\partial V}{\partial x_{c,2}} = \alpha(\gamma_1 - \gamma_2 x_{c,2}) + (1-\alpha)((\gamma_1 + x_{c,1}) + \gamma_2 x_{c,2})$$

$$= \gamma_1 + (1-\alpha)x_{c,1} - \gamma_2 x_{c,2} = 1, \qquad (11.19)$$

where again the last equality is required for the optimal consumption bundle if marginal utility of consumption for coffee in the second period is equal to marginal utility of food consumption. Equation 11.19 can be rewritten as

$$x_{c,2} = \frac{\gamma_1 - 1}{\gamma_2} + \frac{(1-\alpha)}{\gamma_2} x_{c,1}. \qquad (11.20)$$

Substituting equation 11.20 into equation 11.18 and solving yields

$$x_{c,1}^* = \frac{(\gamma_1 - 1)\gamma_2 + (1-\alpha)(\gamma_1 - \gamma_2\gamma_3 - 1)}{\gamma_2^2 + (1-\alpha)^2}. \qquad (11.21)$$

Consider the case of complete projection bias, $\alpha = 1$. In this case, $x_{c,1} = (\gamma_1 - 1)/\gamma_2$, and planned consumption in period two will be $x_{c,2} = (\gamma_1 - 1)/\gamma_2$. Figure 11.3 depicts the perceived marginal utility curves for this case as the dashed curves. Because the consumer does not perceive how current consumption will affect future utility, he perceives the optimum to occur with identical coffee consumption in both periods—the points at which the perceived marginal utility curves intersect the marginal utility of food.

The consumer plans to consume the same amount of coffee in the future as he does in this period. However, when the next period comes, he instead is led to consume where instantaneous marginal utility, equation 11.13, is equal to 1, depicted in the figure as the solid marginal utility curve on the right side, or

$$\frac{dU\left(x_{c,\,2},\,x_{f,\,2}|x_{c,\,1}\right)}{dx_{c,\,2}} = (\gamma_1 + x_{c,\,1}) - \gamma_2 x_{c,\,2} = 1, \qquad (11.22)$$

which is satisfied if $x_{c,\,2} = (\gamma_1 - 1)/\gamma_2 + x_{c,\,1}/\gamma_2$. This results in an additional $x_{c,\,1}/\gamma_2 > 0$ of coffee he had not planned on purchasing or consuming. This requires him to cut planned food consumption by the same amount, substituting more of the addictive good for the nonaddictive good.

If instead, the consumer displays some lower degree of projection bias, equation 11.20 tells us that he will at least anticipate consuming some $(1-\alpha)x_{c,\,1}/\gamma_2$ of this additional amount. But again, when he finally arrives in the second period having consumed $x_{c,\,1}$, he is led to consume $x_{c,\,2} = (\gamma_1 - 1)/\gamma_2 + x_{c,\,1}/\gamma_2$ and is forced to cut back on planned food consumption in order to do it.

In general, the simple projection-bias model predicts that people will consume more of the addictive good than they plan in future periods because they did not realize exactly how addictive the substance was. This also means they eat less food in the second period. In general, addictive behaviors crowd other consumption activities out more than the consumer anticipates. Those who become compulsive viewers of pornography don't set out to lose their job when they become unable to resist viewing pornography at work. This misperception of the potency of addiction is the true contribution of the behavioral approach. This model of simple projection bias is procedurally rational in that it explains why people make decisions that are inconsistent with their initial plans. Rational approaches cannot explain this. Rather, models of rational addiction (proposed by Gary Becker) suppose that the preference for the addictive substance increases, but at a rate that is predictable and under the rational control of the decision maker. This appears to be inconsistent with individual experience. This is why addiction is thought of as such a pernicious trap.

Second, consider now the level of overall utility implied by consuming according to the simple projection bias model. Because consumers misperceive the level of utility they will obtain from consuming coffee in the second period, they fail to maximize their utility. The degree to which they fall short depends on α. People who can accurately project their future utility should be better off for this ability. These two results (both the reduction in utility and the tendency to increase consumption over the amount planned) are general results that should apply to all similar models of addiction with projection bias given positive instantaneous marginal utility of consumption for the addictive good.

EXAMPLE 11.3   Shopping while Hungry

Projection bias can affect consumers in profound ways. One of the clearest examples of this is found in the arena of supermarket shopping. You have probably been given the advice never to shop for food while you are hungry because you will buy more food than you need. Although this advice was originally based on folk wisdom, several behavioral experiments verify that people do indeed purchase more food when they are hungry, and they buy foods that are more indulgent. For example, Daniel Gilbert, Michael Gill, and Timothy Wilson ran a series of experiments in which shoppers at a grocery store were stopped on their way into the store and asked to participate in a food taste sample. They were then asked to list the things they planned to buy that day at the store. One set were then given a muffin to eat before they entered the store, and others were asked to return after they finished shopping and were given a muffin afterward. As you would expect, those who had the muffin before entering the store were on average less hungry than those who were not given the muffin. Those who had to wait until after shopping to receive the muffin had to shop hungry (or at least hungrier than their counterparts). After shopping, all receipts were collected to compare actual purchases to what the shoppers had planned to buy.

In total, 111 participants took part in the experiment. Those who had eaten a muffin before shopping made many purchases that were unplanned, about 34 percent. However, more than half (51 percent) of the items purchased by those who had not eaten a muffin were unplanned. Projection bias is a likely explanation for the difference. When you are hungry, food is attractive. Each item you pass in the store may be evaluated for how it would satisfy your current hunger and you might thus decide to pick up several items that would be particularly satisfying. Alternatively, when you are not hungry, you might not consider the impact on your enjoyment of consumption at some future date when you will be hungry. In this case, many of the items that would be particularly attractive to a hungry shopper are not as immediately attractive. Thus, they buy fewer of the items they had not planned on purchasing.

A potentially more convincing experiment was conducted by Daniel Read and Barbara van Leeuwen. People were asked in their place of work to choose a snack that they would receive in exactly one week. Some of the snacks were relatively healthy choices, and others would be considered indulgent. Some participants were told they would receive the snack in the late afternoon, and others were told they would receive the snack immediately after their lunch break. Those receiving the snack in the afternoon would anticipate that they would be hungry in the future. Those receiving the snack right after lunch would expect not to be hungry. Additionally, some participants were asked this question right after lunch, and others were asked late in the afternoon. Table 11.1 displays the percentage of participants who chose indulgent snacks in each of the four conditions. As can be seen, people who were hungry were more likely to choose indulgent snacks than those who were not hungry, and those who were choosing for a future hungry state were more likely to choose the indulgent snacks.

Table 11.1   Percentage Choosing Unhealthy Snacks by Current and Future Level of Hunger

Current Level of Hunger	Future Level of Hunger	
	Not Hungry (After Lunchtime)	Hungry (Late Afternoon)
Not hungry (after lunchtime)	26%	56%
Hungry (late afternoon)	42%	78%

Source: Read, D., and B. van Leeuwen. "Predicting Hunger: The Effects of Appetite and Delay on Choice." Organizational Behavior and Human Decision Processes 76(1998): 189–205.

Let c_h represent consumption of healthy snacks, and let c_i represent consumption of indulgent snacks. Further, let s_h represent a state of hunger, and s_n represent not being hungry. Let $u(c, s)$ be the utility of consuming c while experiencing hunger state s. Suppose first that people find indulgent treats more attractive when they are hungry, $u(c_i, s_h) > u(c_i, s_n)$ and that healthy snacks are less attractive, $u(c_h, s_h) < u(c_h, s_n)$. Finally, let us suppose that indulgent food is preferred when people are hungry, $u(c_h, s_h) < u(c_i, s_h)$, and healthy food is preferred when people are not hungry, $u(c_h, s_n) > u(c_i, s_n)$. Consider someone who suffers from simple projection bias. In a hungry state, considering his future consumption in a hungry state, he will consider

$$\tilde{u}(c_h, s_h | s_h) = u(c_h, s_h) < u(c_i, s_h) = \tilde{u}(c_i, s_h | s_h) \qquad (11.23)$$

and choose the indulgent snack. In this case he displays no projection bias and correctly chooses the indulgent snack in the future (78 percent chose this). Alternatively, if he is not hungry and is choosing his future consumption in a state in which he is not hungry, he will consider

$$\tilde{u}(c_h, s_n | s_n) = u(c_h, s_n) > u(c_i, s_n) = \tilde{u}(c_i, s_n | s_n) \qquad (11.24)$$

and choose the healthy snack. In this case, he again displays no projection bias and correctly chooses the healthy snack for his future self (74 percent chose this).

The problem only arises when one is choosing for a future hunger state that is different. A hungry person considering his consumption in a future state when he is not hungry will consider his projected utility of consuming the healthy snack

$$\tilde{u}(c_h, s_n | s_h) = \alpha u(c_h, s_h) + (1 - \alpha) u(c_h, s_n) \qquad (11.25)$$

versus the projected utility of consuming the indulgent snack

$$\tilde{u}(c_i, s_n | s_h) = \alpha u(c_i, s_h) + (1 - \alpha) u(c_i, s_n). \qquad (11.26)$$

Which is larger critically depends critically on the degree of projection bias, α. If $\alpha = 1$, perfect projection bias, then the person will choose the indulgent outcome, behaving as if he will be hungry in the future. Of the participants, 42 percent chose this option, much more than those who were not hungry. If $\alpha = 0$, the person would choose the healthy item. We observe that 38 percent of participants chose this option, many fewer than chose the healthy option when they are not hungry.

The data in Table 11.1 are consistent with the notion that at least some people display a high enough degree of projection bias that they will choose something for their future self that they would not want. The projection bias distorts their perception of the value of the tradeoffs involved in the choice. If this model of choice is right, people choosing for future states that are similar to today will be much better off than those choosing for different states. This brings us back to the question of whether to shop when you are hungry.

Certainly we have evidence that shopping for food while hungry will increase the number of purchases and likely decrease the nutritional content. However, if you intend to eat the food at some future time when you are hungry, this might make you better off in the end. The advice given by this behavioral model is to shop when in a hunger state that is similar to that in which you will choose to consume the food. The difficulty with this notion arises when the presence of indulgent food might affect how one assesses one's hunger, or if simply having the indulgent food leads one to eat whether it is the preferred food or not. The advice to only shop on a full stomach makes sense only if one is trying to impose some less-preferred behavior on one's future self. For example, a person might want to stay within a budget or be trying to lose weight. He knows if he shops in a hungry state he will purchase more or will purchase foods that when consumed will make him fat.

EXAMPLE 11.4   Impulse Buying and Catalogue Purchases

In the depths of winter, a vacation to the Caribbean may be very attractive. However, if you are planning for a vacation to be taken in August, it may be hard to remember that you will be leaving the August frying pan of your hometown for the August fire of the Caribbean. In the end it may be an unpleasant trip.

Simple projection bias suggests that weather might actually affect many of our decisions about future consumption. Consider ordering clothes out of a catalogue. When perusing a catalogue on a particularly cold day, your body's desire for warmth can color the projected enjoyment you will obtain from warmer clothing. On the other hand, when you receive the item, you might not be subject to the same projection bias any longer and simply decide to return it.

Michael Conlin, Ted O'Donoghue, and Timothy J. Vogelsang obtained records of more than 2 million catalogue sales of gloves, mittens, boots, hats, winter sports equipment, parkas, coats, vests, jackets, and rainwear. Each was an item that would be particularly useful in cold, snowy, or rainy weather—but not much use otherwise. Using regression analysis, they found that people are more likely to return the cold-weather items if the weather was particularly cold when they purchased them. In particular, if the temperature is 30 degrees cooler on the date of purchase, buyers are 4 percent more likely to return the item once they receive it. Similarly, more snowfall on the date of purchase leads to a higher probability of return. Both of these could also be explained potentially by people just being more inclined to purchase frivolously on cold or snowy days (i.e., I am stuck inside because of the weather so I buy clothes through a catalogue as entertainment). This led them to see if people would return more of the items they purchase during cold weather even if those items were not related to cold weather (e.g., windbreakers). When conducting similar analysis of nonwinter coats and gear they found no similar relationship, suggesting that projection bias, rather than boredom, is driving the frivolous purchases of later unwanted items.

If projection bias is driving the purchases of these cold-weather items, you would also expect that people would display some amount of projection bias at the time they decide whether or not to return the item. Once I have received my cold weather gear, if it is relatively cold over the period in which I can return the item, I may be less likely to return it. This relationship is not as easily seen in Conlin, O'Donoghue, and Vogelsang's analysis, partially because it is impossible to know the date the buyer makes this decision. The data are not inconsistent with this phenomenon, but the relationship is not particularly strong. Nonetheless, projection bias provides a cautionary note to all who may be out shopping in extreme weather. Apparently, current weather can unduly influence our purchases and can result in wasted money or the added hassle of returning unwanted items.

The Role of Emotions and Visceral Factors in Choice

A special class of projection biases are a result of what George Loewenstein calls **visceral factors**. Visceral factors include emotions and physical drives or feelings. Prominent examples of physical drives or feelings include hunger, pain, or feeling cold. Emotions include embarrassment, fear, anger, or jealousy. Visceral factors clearly affect preferences and decisions, though they have presented a challenge to economists historically because of their transient nature. For example, people generally become hungry several times a day, and each time their preferences change in response to the hunger. Weather can change very quickly and is often considered an entirely random process. Nonetheless, these visceral factors have predictable impacts on our preferences and cause some systematic behavior—for example, purchasing clothing we will later return.

We say that a person is in a **hot state** when a visceral factor is active. Thus, if we were studying decisions regarding food, one would be in a hot state when one is hungry. When the visceral factor is inactive, we say that the decision maker is in a **cold state**. Simple projection bias leads people to underestimate the impact of visceral factors on their preferences. People who are not hungry do not recognize how tempting more-indulgent food may be when they eventually find themselves in a hot state. This can lead dieters in a cold state to load the freezer with ice cream, believing that they can regulate their consumption. Later they regret their actions after a hot-state binge. Moreover, when in a hot state, one has a hard time remembering what it is like to be in a cold state. Thus, a particularly hungry shopper loads up on unplanned and less-healthy items that he might not really want when he is just mildly hungry. This inability to project utility across hot or cold states is called the **hot–cold empathy gap**.

It is extremely difficult to resist the urge to satisfy a visceral factor. Loewenstein goes so far as to question whether we can really talk about most responses to visceral factors as a choice. In some cases, humans are able to use cognitive reasoning or tricks to overcome such visceral factors. For example, children when told not to eat a marshmallow that is placed in front of them try to distract themselves by, for example, looking away or singing a song. Of course, resisting a visceral urge is difficult, and one is not always successful. Much of this failure may be attributed to the hot–cold empathy gap. By not recognizing how a change in visceral factors will affect preferences, decision makers can fail to give themselves the tools to deal with them when they arise. Loewenstein attributes three distinct types of behavior to the hot–cold empathy gap.

First, when negotiating a new contract or relationship, people fail to recognize how preferences will change should a situation arise that induces a visceral factor. For example, a new employee may be excited about his job and might not consider the possibility that he might one day become angry at management and decide to quit. The hot–cold empathy gap could lead this new employee to value some benefits more highly than he should. For example, a young worker taking his first job might consider benefits such as a guaranteed pension or college tuition for dependent children to be big selling points in taking the job. The worker might even have been willing to take a lower salary given the possibility of making use of the pension or tuition benefit. These benefits, however, are ineffective unless one stays in the employ of the company long enough for them to be effective. If the relationship with the employer turns sour before children begin college, the employee could find himself in a bind. College is a significant expense. Now this tuition benefit could force the decision maker to choose either to stay longer in a bad job or to cut back spending severely in order to quickly save for the expense.

Second, the hot–cold empathy gap can lead to self-control problems. Invariably, people who are trying to avoid some compulsive behavior must depend upon the decisions they make when they are in a cold state in order to withstand the hot state. Cold-state decisions can affect exposure to the visceral factor, access to the behavior that satisfies the visceral factor, and whether responding to the factor will be socially acceptable to the group in which the decision maker finds himself. For example, if you are trying to give up cigarettes, you might recognize that it is a bad idea to keep cigarettes around the house. However, in a cold state you might not recognize that being with a certain group of friends who continue to smoke could eventually trigger the desire to smoke. This group of friends might work to defeat your resolve and make cigarettes available to you when the craving eventually strikes. Moreover, after you have given in and you return to a cold state, you will not remember the intensity of the desire that led you to give in, asking yourself, "How could I have behaved this way?"

Finally, the hot–cold empathy gap can lead people to overrespond to certain risks owing to an overwhelming feeling of fear. In nearly every Jack Black movie, we find the main character with a crush on some relatively attractive woman who is entirely unaware of his feelings. He resolves several times to tell her his feelings and is presented the opportunity, but in the end cannot muster the courage to actually ask the woman out. This oft-repeated movie meme has real-world counterparts. When the person is not in the act of talking to the woman, the fear of rejection is not present. In this cold state it is easy to make plans to reveal one's feelings and expose oneself to the substantial risk of rejection. Thinking through the problem rationally, rejection is not such a bad outcome. In fact, rejection has much the same effect as never asking the woman out in the first place. In this case, why not ask her? When the time comes, though, fear takes hold, creating an irrational aversion to rejection. In this hot state, rejection is worse than a life of loneliness. Hence, the decision maker chickens out.

It is possible to model the hot–cold empathy gap in each of these behaviors using the simple projection-bias model already introduced. Thus, we could think of $u(x_1, x_2, s)$ as the utility of actions x_1 and x_2 in state s, where $s = \{s_h, s_c\}$. Here s_h represents a hot state, and s_c represents a cold state. If x_1 represents an action associated with the visceral factor, then changing the state has two effects on the utility function. Let $\bar{x}_1, \bar{x}_2$ be the level of consumption one would choose in the cold state; that is, the pair $(\bar{x}_1, \bar{x}_2)$ solve $\max_{x_1, x_2} u(x_1, x_2, s_c)$ subject to whatever budget constraints the decision maker might face. In many cases, $\bar{x}_1$ is 0. The first impact of state on the utility function is that being in

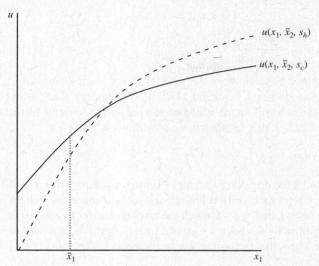

FIGURE 11.4
The Effect of Hot and Cold States on Utility

a hot state reduces the utility of consumption evaluated at $\bar{x}_1$, as depicted in Figure 11.4. Thus, a smoker who suddenly gets a craving for a cigarette finds himself feeling much worse off for not consuming a cigarette than he did before the craving. Second, the utility of action x_1 becomes steeper in a hot state than in a cold state. In general, this leads to choosing a much higher level of x_1 in the hot state than in the cold state.

In many cases we are interested in modeling people who are trying to quit some compulsive behavior. In this case, $u(x_1, x_2, s)$ represents the instantaneous preferences of the person, but it does not necessarily represent his well-being. Rather, in this case it would be common to think of $u(x_1, x_2, s_c)$, his preferences in a cold state, as representing his true well-being. Thus, in the hot state, one chooses to maximize $u(x_1, x_2, s_h)$ but ends up receiving $u(x_1, x_2, s_c)$. In this case, the visceral factor leads him to choose actions that leave him worse off than he could have been. Using this interpretation of, for example, the problem of shopping hungry leads to the clear conclusion that we should always shop on a full stomach. However, making such a statement requires us to know that $u(x_1, x_2, s_h)$ is a misperception—a controversial statement to say the least. In one state the person displays one set of preferences, and in the other he displays another set. It would be difficult to find some scientifically valid way to determine which was right and which was wrong (or even if there were a right and wrong). For this reason, many economists shy away from this type of language.

Modeling the Hot–Cold Empathy Gap

In many situations, we want to consider the visceral factor as a continuous variable. Then we can speak about the level of hunger (or anger, etc.) instead of just the possible states hungry or not hungry. In terms of calculus, the two requirements of a visceral factor can then be stated as

$$\frac{\partial u(\bar{x}_1, \bar{x}_2, s)}{\partial s} < 0, \qquad (11.27)$$

and

$$\frac{\partial^2 u(x_1, \bar{x}_2, s)}{\partial x_1 \partial s} > 0. \tag{11.28}$$

Equation 11.27 tells us that utility declines when the visceral factor, s, increases if one holds consumption of both goods constant. Equation 11.28 tells us that marginal utility of the good associated with the visceral factor becomes steeper as the visceral factor increases. One simple utility function that satisfies these conditions is given by

$$u(x_1, x_2, s) = -s + sx_1^{\gamma} + x_2^{\gamma}. \tag{11.29}$$

Let's use equation 11.29 to model the decision behavior of someone who is trying to cut back on smoking. In this case, s represents the level of craving, x_1 how much the smoker decides to smoke in that time period, and x_2 how much the smoker decides to engage in other activities. Consider that both activities have a price of \$1 per unit and that the smoker faces a budget constrain of w. Then, the decision maker must solve

$$\max_{x_1, x_2} u(x_1, x_2, s) \tag{11.30}$$

subject to

$$x_1 + x_2 \leq w. \tag{11.31}$$

Recognizing that the budget constraint will bind, we find that $x_2 = w - x_1$, and we can restate the consumer problem as

$$\max_{x_1} -s + sx_1^{\gamma} + (w - x_1)^{\gamma} \tag{11.32}$$

with a solution that is given by (assuming $s > 0$)

$$\frac{\partial u}{\partial x_1} = s\gamma x_1^{\gamma-1} - \gamma(w - x_1)^{\gamma-1} = 0. \tag{11.33}$$

This is solved where $x_1 = w / \left(1 + s^{-\frac{1}{1-\gamma}}\right)$ and $x_2 = w / \left(s^{\frac{1}{1-\gamma}} + 1\right)$. Note that if $s = 0$ then $x_1 = 0$, and $x_2 = w$. As s increases, $s^{-\frac{1}{1-\gamma}}$ decreases, leading to greater optimal x_1 and less-optimal x_2. Of course, here we have only modeled the difference in preferences between hot and cold states. Modeling the hot–cold empathy gap requires additionally implementing simple projection bias in an intertemporal choice problem. Thus, we may think about a first-period decision to either socialize with smoking friends or not socialize with smoking friends while experiencing a relatively low level of craving s. In addition, we must assume that deciding to socialize with smokers changes the utility function, either making smoking innately more attractive or potentially affecting s. Given a level of projection bias, α, we could then find a level of craving s that would lead to subsequently deciding to smoke. Such a model could easily account for self-defeating behavior in which the smoker places himself in a position where he is certain to give in to urges he wishes to control.

EXAMPLE 11.5	Raging Suburban Mothers

Shirley Henson, a 40-year-old secretary, set out on her way home from work one fateful day in Alabama. No doubt she was looking forward to returning home to her husband and son. She entered Interstate 65 and merged into traffic just behind Gena Foster, a 34-year-old mother of three children also on her way home from work. Neither had met before. Within hours, Gena was dead and Shirley was charged with her murder. Neither had had any previous history of legal problems or violence. Both had families who described them as generally kind people.

But, in a hurry to get home, Shirley was tailgating Gena. Gena became annoyed and angry and slammed on her brakes to scare Shirley. It didn't work. As they picked up speed again, Shirley was even more determined to ride the bumper of the car in front of her. Shirley describes Gena as making obscene gestures and even throwing small objects out of her car at her. Nonetheless, Shirley would not give Gena the satisfaction of slowing down. How could she capitulate to someone who had been so rude? Finally, Gena pulled off at an exit, perhaps trying to finally lose the tailgater. To Gena's astonishment, Shirley pulled off at the same exit and continued to tailgate.

That was it. Gena stopped her car, blocking Shirley's way. Gena got out and walked back to Shirley's car. Shirley rolled down her window. Exasperated, Gena began yelling at Shirley for tailgating. Shirley claims that Gena spat on her, and began to lunge at her. As Gena lunged, Shirley pointed a pistol squarely at Gena's face and pulled the trigger. Gena died instantly.

When one thinks of the passions that might drive a mother to take the life of another, one usually conjures up images of threats to her children or perhaps vile situations involving infidelity. One would be hard pressed to believe tailgating might be the cause. What would lead a seemingly calm and quiet person to shoot another at point-blank range? Shirley herself says she was not angry but fearful. She describes a situation in which she was full of adrenalin, and her survival instincts took over. She panicked. It would be hard to rationalize the actions that would eventually see her sentenced to 13 years in prison. Clearly, slowing down or even pulling off the road entirely would be preferable to 13 years in prison even if it meant she would be later in getting home. Even once Gena's actions had perhaps made her angry, escalating the event seems clearly to be a bad idea in retrospect.

Nonetheless, such visceral influences as anger can be difficult to control in the heat of the moment and can swamp out your longer-term—cold-state—preferences. It would seem like a better idea for Gena to simply pull of the road and let the other car go around than to risk injury by slamming on the brakes or initiating a roadside confrontation. No doubt, in a cold state Shirley would have made decisions to back off, pull off at a different exit, leave her window rolled up, and perhaps attempt to apologize when confronted. All else failing, even if the unarmed Gena would not have backed down, it seems preferable to take a measure of spittle, and even a substantial beating, rather than facing a charge of manslaughter or murder.

Everyone at some time or another is led to clearly self-destructive actions by anger, though perhaps not quite as destructive as this road-rage incident. A brother might have swiped a toy out of your hands when you were younger. Instead of finding another toy, you might have attempted to take the toy back, resulting in an escalation of hitting, kicking, scratching, and eventually calling for parents to intervene. It usually doesn't take more than a few minutes of retrospective thinking to come to the conclusion that some other course of action might have been better. If we believe in the hot–cold empathy gap, a cooling-off period could be key to avoiding substantially destructive behavior. Waiting for a visceral factor to dissipate allows one to make the choice while considering more-reasonable preferences. Suppose that after several miles of Shirley tailgating Gena, a traffic jam intervened and both were slowed to a dead stop for 20 minutes. The annoyance and anger might not have completely disappeared, but both women would likely have had the time to think of more productive responses to the situation.

Similarly, cooling-off periods can be helpful for consumers. One often receives the advice not to buy on impulse. Seeing a product demonstration or witnessing a particularly stirring sales pitch can lead us to a heightened sense of need for a product. In this visceral state, we may be led to make a purchase that we would regret in hindsight. Salespeople are skilled at creating a feeling of need and urgency to make the purchase. "This will be your last chance to get such a good deal," they might say. They clearly want to work on your emotions more than your sense of reason or rationality. For this reason, the government often requires those selling time-share vacation homes, and many other large and expensive investments, to allow consumers a period of 10 days in which to change their minds. Similarly, one must wait five days to obtain a handgun in many cases. Many states require a waiting period for obtaining a divorce. Under a rational decision-making model, such waiting periods would be superfluous. Why would anyone change their mind about buying a large investment in only 10 days' time? Similarly, how could five days reduce my desire to use a gun for some nefarious purpose? In fact, many people make use of the 10-day rule on time shares. Many couples decide to stay married after a term of separation—some even remarry their original spouse after a divorce. As a consumer (or a frustrated driver), taking your time to make a decision can help ensure that you are responding to long-term preferences and not a transitory visceral urge you might grow to regret.

EXAMPLE 11.6 An Obvious Pitch

To patent a new process, invention, or substance, one must demonstrate that it is new, it is beneficial to others, and it was not a trivial or obvious innovation at the time the innovation was made. The requirement that it be a nonobvious innovation excludes trivial innovations that more than likely were discovered by many people simultaneously. Of each of these requirements, the hardest to prove is that the innovation was nonobvious. In fact, most patents are challenged along these lines, and this patent requirement ends up in the courts more often than any other. Juries in these patent trials are first introduced to the innovation and then asked to determine whether it was obvious or not. This requires the jury members to consider whether the innovation was obvious, after they already have an understanding and knowledge of the innovation. In essence, they must attempt to consider the innovation as if they did not yet know what they have learned and determine if the knowledge is obvious or not. They must remember what knowledge was available to them at some prior point before the invention had been explained to them.

Gregory Mandel conducted a study using 247 new law students (none had taken any courses yet) who each got to play jury member in a patent law case. Participants were given background information based on jury instruction material from an actual case involving a new method for teaching how to throw different types of baseball pitches (e.g., a fast ball, curve ball, or slider). The materials described an inventor who had been asked to develop a method of teaching that allowed students to learn by holding a real baseball in their hand but did not require one-on-one instruction. Previous technologies included plastic replicas of baseballs with finger-shaped indentations where the fingers were to sit properly for each possible pitch, instructional videos, or cards illustrating the correct finger placement. The inventor proposed simply putting finger-shaped ink marks on real baseballs to illustrate the correct finger placement. In this way, the student could get his hands on a real baseball and make sure he had the proper hold for the pitch. This seems like a completely obvious idea. The technology required has existed as long as there have been baseballs and ink.

Students given this scenario were asked whether prior to the invention a solution to the problem (finding a method using real baseballs) would be obvious. In this case, the solution does seem fairly obvious. In fact, 76 percent of participants given the details of this patent case believed that the solution was entirely obvious. A second group of participants were given the same description of the request that was made of the inventor (produce a method to teach pitches with a real baseball), but were not told the solution. When asked if someone with average knowledge would see an obvious solution, only 24 percent believed they would. Why such a disparity? Once you know that there is such a simple and low-tech solution, it is hard to divorce yourself from that knowledge. In hindsight, the innovation is completely obvious. In foresight, it is a tricky puzzle that may be very difficult to solve. In this case, a jury given the entire case might throw out the patent even if it was not an obvious innovation simply because they are already familiar with the innovation.

Hindsight Bias and the Curse of Knowledge

People have extreme difficulty not letting recent information bias their assessment of prior decisions. This inability to disregard hindsight information is called **hindsight bias**. The phenomenon of believing one had more knowledge than one truly did can lead to dubious claims. After the fact, a surprising number claim that they knew their team should have prepared for the other team to call a trick play, though very few openly predict the trick play in advance. Economically, hindsight bias can play a significant role in staffing decisions. For example, an employee might propose a well-prepared and well-thought-out strategy that maximizes the expected returns of the strategy subject to some limit on the risks of negative returns given all the information that is available at the time. However, if the scenario that is subsequently realized involves substantial negative returns, a manager suffering from hindsight bias could claim that the outcome was obvious and he always knew that it was a bad idea. Such claims can be stifling in a work setting. Employees might begin to fear proposing anything innovative for fear they will be held responsible for information that is not available at the time a decision must be made. Similarly, courts often find accountants responsible for not anticipating poor outcomes that lead to businesses becoming insolvent. Much of the evidence suggests there is a heavy dose of hindsight bias in these court proceedings.

Hindsight bias is somewhat related to projection bias in that people are unable to project what their decision would be in a different state. However, hindsight bias does not deal with projecting preferences but beliefs. Thus, it should truly fall under the biases discussed in Chapter 7. However, projection bias may be a cause of hindsight bias. For example, a decision maker in a hot state might make decisions with bad consequences. If these consequences were foreseeable in the cold state, the decision maker might suppose the decision was poorly made. However, if the cold-state decision maker were placed in a hot state, he might readily make the decision again.

A close cousin of hindsight bias is the **curse of knowledge**. The curse of knowledge refers to the phenomenon of believing that others possess the same knowledge you do. The curse of knowledge is key to a whole class of economic problems often referred to as games of asymmetric information, in which one player has access to information that the other player or players cannot observe.

A classic example of asymmetric information is the purchase of a used car. The used-car seller usually has much better information about the condition and reliability of the car than does the buyer. In modeling such games, economists usually assume that the person with private information can accurately assess how much information the other players have. In the case of the used car, a rational seller should be able to recognize that consumers don't know the reliability of the car, and thus the consumer will not be willing to pay very much for the vehicle. Because there is no way to independently verify that the car is reliable, the buyer would necessarily offer less money owing to the risk involved. In this case, if the car is reliable, and therefore valuable, the seller will be better off not selling the car because he could not recover the value. Alternatively, if the car is unreliable, and therefore worthless, the seller will sell the car and receive a low, but fair, price for it.

Suppose instead that the seller suffered from the curse of knowledge. In this case, he would assume the buyer can tell a reliable car from an unreliable car, increasing the price of the reliable car and decreasing the price of the unreliable car. If the buyer continues to be so uncertain of the quality that he would not buy a high-priced car, then the seller will only sell low-quality cars but will sell at a lower price than if he did not suffer from the curse of knowledge.

Colin Camerer, George Loewenstein, and Martin Weber found experimental evidence of the hindsight bias in a series of stock-trading experiments. Some participants were asked to predict stock market performance for several companies. Later, others were shown the actual performance of the companies over the predicted time and allowed to study them. Then, while the information was available to them, these participants were given the opportunity to buy or sell shares that would pay dividends based on the predictions made previously by uninformed participants. Trades substantially favored those stocks that performed unusually well in actuality rather than those that had been predicted to perform well. Such problems can lead insiders with private information to conduct illegal trades based on private information. Believing that outsiders have access to the same information can lead them to ignore the potential consequences of trading on insider information—including substantial jail time.

EXAMPLE 11.7   War in Hindsight

War evokes strong feelings from all parties involved (and often those uninvolved). This is perhaps natural. Consider a British campaign in 1814 against a group of Nepalese. One text[1] describes the conflict this way:

> For some years after the arrival of Hastings as governor-general of India, the consolidation of British power involved serious war. The first of these wars took place on the northern frontier of Bengal where the British were faced by the plundering raids of the Gurkhas of Nepal. Attempts had been made to stop the raids by an exchange of lands, but the Gurkhas would not give up their claims to country under British control, and Hastings decided to deal with them once and for all. The campaign began in November, 1814. It was not glorious. The Gurkhas were only some 12,000 strong; but they were brave fighters, fighting in territory well-suited to their raiding tactics. The older British commanders were used to war in the plains where the enemy ran away from a resolute attack. In the mountains of Nepal it was not easy even to find the enemy. The troops and transport animals suffered from the extremes of heat and cold, and the officers learned caution only after sharp reverses. Major-General Sir D. Octerlony was the one commander to escape from these minor defeats.

Given this history, would you guess the conflict resulted in

a. British victory?
b. Gurkha victory?
c. Military stalemate with no peace settlement?
d. Military stalemate with a peace settlement?

Baruch Fischhoff used this historical example in a psychology experiment involving 100 students at Hebrew University in Jerusalem. After the students read the passage, they were asked to assess the probability of each of the four possible outcomes before the beginning of the campaign. One fifth of the subjects were given no information about the outcome of the conflict before the probability-assessment exercise. The others were randomly told that one of the four outcomes had in reality happened. Table 11.2 displays the results of Fischhoff's experiment. Note that without the simple statement as to what actually occurred, people assessed the probabilities of the events to be fairly even, with British victory and a stalemate with no peace settlement being slightly more probable. Alternatively, when participants were told one of the outcomes had actually occurred, they tended to assess that outcome to be more probable before the beginning of the conflict (this was the case for all but those told the outcome was a stalemate resulting in a peace settlement).

Military leaders fear setbacks in a war not only for the losses entailed directly; they also worry about public opinion. With substantial casualties or other setbacks comes the

---

[1] Woodward, E.L. *Age of Reform*. London: Oxford University Press, 1938, pp. 383–384.

Table 11.2   Assessments of the Probability of Outcomes of the British–Gurka Struggle

Potential Outcome	Average Assessed Probability Given Participant Told				
	No Information	British Victory	Gurkha Victory	Stalemate, No Settlement	Stalemate with Settlement
British victory	0.338	0.572	0.303	0.257	0.330
Gurkha victory	0.213	0.143	0.384	0.170	0.158
Stalemate, no settlement	0.323	0.153	0.204	0.480	0.243
Stalemate with settlement	0.123	0.134	0.105	0.099	0.270

Source: Fischhoff, B. "Hindsight ≠ Foresight: The Effect of Outcome Knowledge on Judgment Under Uncertainty." *Journal of Experimental Psychology: Human Perception and Performance* 1(1975): 288–299.

crowd that claims they should have known better. This has starkly been the case in nearly all modern conflicts. Even in the American Civil War, much of the antiwar movement in the North was galvanized by a string of Union losses in 1861 as Abraham Lincoln struggled to find a general he could work with.

History and Notes

The notion of utility originally had its foundation in the concept of emotion. Jeremy Bentham first proposed the concept of utility in the theory of decision making in the late 18th century. He classified emotions into 26 different categories: 12 that are painful and 14 that are pleasurable. He then considered that the best decision could be determined by calculating the net pleasure (pleasurable emotions minus painful emotions). This was the basis for his proposed cardinal measures of utility. By creating a cardinal (or intrinsic) measure of utility he hoped to find a way to make public policy decisions by a method of utility accounting. A cardinal measure of utility would allow us to know how many utils a particular policy would take from one person in order to make another person better off by so many utils. His particular method of accounting was problematic: People can value different emotions or objects differently. Thus, this emotion-based notion of utility was abandoned for the more-abstract notion of revealed preference. Revealed preference supposes that if a person chooses A when he could have chosen B, then he must obtain more utility from A than B. Revealed preference is an ordinal measure of utility and thus abandons the possibility of comparing utility tradeoffs across people. Revealed preference is the primary foundation for rational models of decision making. Ultimately, Bentham's notion of cardinal utility led to modern welfare economics. Modern welfare economics sometimes assumes a social welfare function or a function that represents the aggregate well-being of all actors in an economy. More often, welfare analysis is conducted using a revealed preference approach and theories such as Pareto efficiency that do not rely on finding a cardinal measure of utility.

Biographical Note

Bloomberg / Getty Images

Dan Ariely (1967–)

M.A. University of North Carolina, 1994; Ph.D., University of North Carolina, 1996; Ph.D., Duke University, 1998; held faculty positions at Massachusetts Institute of Technology and Duke University

Dan Ariely was born in New York, though he spent most of his time growing up in Israel. He studied philosophy as an undergraduate at Tel Aviv University and later obtained his master's and Ph.D. degrees in cognitive psychology, with an additional Ph.D. in business administration. He attributes his interest in irrational behavior to a horrifying experience in his senior year of high school. While volunteering with a youth group, he was engulfed in an explosion, suffering severe burns over 70 percent of his body. In recovering from this, he began to notice the behavioral strategies he used to deal with painful treatments and the general change in the course of his life. His research is wide ranging, including experiments that examine how people use arbitrary numbers from their environment (including their Social Security number) to formulate a response to questions about how much an item is worth to them and how people value beauty and cheating behavior. He is also well known for his popular books *Predictably Irrational: The Hidden Forces that Shape our Decisions* and *The Upside of Irrationality: The Unexpected Benefits of Defying Logic at Work and at Home.*

THOUGHT QUESTIONS

1. Projection bias causes people to suppose that dialysis patients have a much lower quality of life than actually prevails. However, when prompted by researchers to think about the ways they will adapt their lives to dialysis, people seem to make much more realistic assessments. Researchers also find that people several years after winning the lottery rate their quality of life about the same as those who through an accident had become quadriplegic (losing the use of their arms and legs) at about the same time. Relate this phenomenon to projection bias. How might projection bias affect people's choice to play the lottery? What might this say about get-rich-quick schemes in general? How might we think about correcting projection bias in this case?

2. To a large extent, one's lifestyle and the options available to one depend on choices made while relatively young: occupation, place of residence, and perhaps even long-term relationships. Suppose that for leisure, people can either choose quiet evenings with friends, c_q, or raucous parties, c_p. Suppose that when young, s_y, people strongly prefer raucous parties, $u(c_p|s_y) = 2$, $u(c_q|s_y) = 1$. Alternatively, when old, s_o, people strongly prefer quiet times with friends, $u(c_p|s_o) = 1$, $u(c_q|s_o) = 3$. Suppose that Chandra is choosing between majoring in business finance or recreation management. Both majors require just as much time and effort now and offer the same current opportunities for leisure. However, when old, those who majored in finance will only be able to engage in quiet time with friends (raucous parties could get you fired), whereas those in recreation management will only have access to raucous parties. Use the simple

projection bias model to discuss what Chandra will choose. What degree of bias is required before Chandra chooses to enter recreation management? What advice might this suggest to students in general?

3. Suppose that Marion is considering smoking the first cigarette. Marion's utility of consumption in the current period is given by equation 11.12, where good c is cigarettes, good f is all other consumption, $\gamma_1 = 4$, $\gamma_2 = 1$, and $\gamma_3 = 2$, and $x_{c,0} = 0$. Suppose the price of a unit of consumption for either good is $1 and that Marion has $10. Calculate Marion's optimal consumption given one future period of choice in which he has an additional $10. Now suppose that Marion suffers from simple projection bias. Calculate the consumption he will choose as a function of α. What impact will projection bias have on his realized utility? Formulas in equations 11.13 to 11.22 may be useful in making these calculations.

4. Researchers have found that people who are hungry tend to have greater craving for food that is more indulgent (i.e., high in sugar, fat, and salt). Consider that you are creating a line of convenience foods— either snack foods or frozen foods.

   (a) Describe the circumstances under which most people decide to eat convenience foods. What state are they likely to be in? Given this, what types of convenience foods are most likely to be eaten?

   (b) Consider now that most foods are purchased long before they are eaten, though most people only purchase items that they use. In what state are shoppers more likely to purchase convenience foods? Does this depend on whether convenience foods are healthy or indulgent?

   (c) Create a simple model of food choice based on simple projection bias. What food would a seller choose to sell to maximize profits, and how does this depend on α?

   (d) Describe your strategy for creating a line of convenience foods. Is there any way to create a successful line of healthy convenience foods?

5. Employers are constantly training new employees by using more-experienced employees as instructors.

   (a) What challenges might the curse of knowledge present in the training process? How might you suggest these challenges could be overcome?

   (b) Often new employees are given a short (but inadequate) training course and then afterward are given a mentor whom they follow for a brief period before being allowed to function fully on their own. Employers tend to use the same mentor repeatedly rather than using a different one each time. What might this suggest about the curse of knowledge and how it could be addressed?

REFERENCES

Camerer, C., G. Loewenstein, and M. Weber. "The Curse of Knowledge in Economic Settings: An Experimental Analysis." *Journal of Political Economy* 97(1989): 1232–1254.

Conlin, M., T. O'Donoghue, and T.J. Vogelsang. "Projection Bias in Catalog Orders." *American Economic Review* 97(2007): 1217–1249.

Fischhoff, B. "Hindsight ≠ Foresight: The Effect of Outcome Knowledge on Judgment Under Uncertainty." *Journal of Experimental Psychology: Human Perception and Performance* 1 (1975): 288–299.

Gilbert, D.T., M.J. Gill, and T.D. Wilson. "The Future is Now: Temporal Correction in Affective Forecasting." *Organizational Behavior and Human Decision Processes* 88(2002): 430–444.

Loewenstein, G. "Emotions in Economic Theory and Economic Behavior." *American Economic Review* 90(2000): 426–432.

Loewenstein, G., T. O'Donoghue, and M. Rabin. "Projection Bias in Predicting Future Utility." *Quarterly Journal of Economics* 118 (2003): 1209–1248.

Mandel, G.N. "Patently Non-Obvious: Empirical Demonstration that the Hindsight Bias Renders Patent Decisions Irrational." *Ohio State Law Journal* 67(2006): 1393–1461.

Read, D., and B. van Leeuwen. "Predicting Hunger: The Effects of Appetite and Delay on Choice." *Organizational Behavior and Human Decision Processes* 76(1998): 189–205.

Sacket, D.L., and G.W. Torrance. "The Utility of Different Health States as Perceived by the General Public." *Journal of Chronic Disease* 31(1978): 697–704.

Ubel, P.A., G. Loewenstein, and C. Jepson. "Disability and Sunshine: Can Hedonic Predictions be Improved by Drawing Attention to Focusing Illusions or Emotional Adaptation?" *Journal of Experimental Psychology: Applied* 11(2005): 111–123.

Naïve Procrastination

12

Except for a very select few, almost all federal taxpayers have the necessary materials in their hands to file their federal taxes by the middle of February. Nonetheless, every year, 40 million people in the United States wait until the week of April 15th (the federal deadline) to file their tax returns. This is just about a quarter of all tax returns filed in the United States. Most post offices remain open until midnight on April 15th just for this special class of procrastinators. Many of these procrastinators eventually receive tax refunds, and some refunds are substantial.

Waiting until the last minute can create a risk of missing the deadline. Those filing electronically might have their returns rejected for missing information or other errors. Sometimes communication lines go down in the waning hours of the 15th, overloaded by too many choosing to file at the same time. Those filing by mail often run into very long lines at the post office and risk missing the last opportunity to file. Moreover, putting off preparing taxes until the very last minute can create problems as taxpayers only realize that certain receipts or documents are missing once they have begun to fill out the forms. Ultimately, missing the deadline can result in financial penalties. So why do so many procrastinate until the last minute?

As teenagers and young adults we are bombarded with the advice to "never put off until tomorrow what you can do today." Nonetheless, procrastination seems to be engrained into human behavior from our earliest opportunities to make decisions. We put off studying until we are forced to cram all night for the big test. We put off cleaning, maintenance, or other work until we are forced into action. Then we must complete tremendous amounts of work in a very short time. Procrastination becomes a problem when we prioritize activities that are not particularly important over those that have real and if not immediate at least long-term consequences. After one has been burned time after time by failing to study early or after a steady stream of financial emergencies that could not be covered by a meager savings, it would seem like time to stop procrastinating. A quotation attributed to Abraham Lincoln is, "Things may come to those who wait, but only the things left by those who hustle." If that is so, why do we seem so apt to procrastinate? Some economists believe the answer lies in how we value today versus tomorrow versus the day after tomorrow.

Procrastination, like the hot–cold empathy gap described in Chapter 11, can result in time-inconsistent preferences. We might see others who went to work right away, look back on our actions, and consider that we have taken the wrong strategy. Firms interested in selling products can use customer procrastination to their own advantage through price discrimination or by charging customers for services or the option to take some action that they will never exercise. In some cases, finding last-minute tax preparation is more costly than early preparation. In others, people might pay in advance for flexible tickets that they never actually find the time to use. This chapter introduces the exponential model of time discounting, the most common in economic models, and the quasi-hyperbolic model of time discounting. The latter has become one of the primary workhorses of behavioral economics. This model is expanded on in Chapter 13, where we discuss the role of people's understanding and anticipation of their own propensity to procrastinate.

The Fully Additive Model

In Chapter 11, we introduced a general model of intertemporal choice when the consumer is deciding on consumption in two different time periods. In many cases that we are interested in, a consumer considers more than just two time periods. In some cases we are interested in planning into the distant future. This is often represented as a problem involving an infinite number of time periods, or an **infinite planning horizon**. We can generalize the model presented in equation 11.1 to the many-period decision task by supposing the consumer solves

$$\max_{c_1, c_2, \ldots} U(c_1, c_2, \ldots) \tag{12.1}$$

subject to some budget constraint, where c_i represents consumption in period i. This model is general in the behavior that it might explain because it allows every period's consumption to interact with preferences for every other period's consumption. Thus, consuming a lot in period 100 could increase the preference for consumption in period 47. This model is seldom used specifically because of its generality. We tend to believe people have somewhat similar preferences for consumption in each period. Moreover, we often deal with situations in which consumption in one period does not affect preferences in any other period. Thus, when dealing with intertemporal choice with many periods, economists tend to prefer the fully additive model, assuming exponential discounting. This model assumes that

$$U(c_1, c_2, \ldots) = u(c_1) + \delta u(c_2) + \delta^2 u(c_3) + \ldots + \delta^{i-1} u(c_i) + \ldots = \sum_{i=1}^{T} \delta^{i-1} u(c_i), \tag{12.2}$$

where δ represents how the person discounts consumption one period into the future and where T could be ∞.

The fully additive model is based upon two fundamental assumptions. First, the consumer has stable preferences over consumption in each period. Thus, $u(c_i)$ can be used to represent the benefit from consumption in each time period i, often referred to as the **instantaneous utility function**. This may be more important in the case where $u(.)$ has several arguments. For example, suppose that $u(c_i) = u(c_{1,i}, c_{2,i})$, where $c_{1,i}$ represents hours spent studying at time period i, and $c_{2,i}$ represents hours spent partying at time period i. Then the additive model assumes that the same function will describe the utility tradeoffs between partying and studying in every time period. Thus, whether you are three weeks from the test or one hour from the test, the student still has the same relative preference for studying and partying. Second, the consumer discounts each additional time period by a factor of δ, referred to as **exponential time discounting**. Consuming c next period will yield exactly δ times the utility of consuming c now. Moreover, consuming c two periods from now will yield exactly δ times the utility of consuming c next period, or δ^2 times the amount of utility of consuming c this period. This coefficient δ, often referred to as the **discount factor**, may be thought of as a measure of patience. The higher the discount factor, the more the consumer values future consumption relative to current consumption and the more willing the consumer will be to wait.

The solution to a problem such as that in equation 12.2 occurs where the discounted marginal utility of consumption in each period is equal, $\delta^{i-1}u'(c_i) = k$, where $u'(c)$ is the marginal utility of consumption (or the slope of the instantaneous utility function), and k is some constant. Intuitively, if one period allowed a higher discounted marginal utility than the others, consumers could be made better off by reducing consumption in all other periods in order to increase consumption in the higher marginal utility period. Similarly, if marginal utility of consumption in any period was lower than the others, consumers would benefit by reducing their consumption in that period in order to increase consumption in a higher marginal utility period. This would continue until marginal utility equalizes in all periods. Thus, given the instantaneous marginal utility of consumption function, you can solve for the optimal consumption profile by finding the values for c_i such that $\delta^{i-1}u'(c_i) = k$ for some k and such that all budget constraints are met. One way to picture this optimum is displayed in Figure 12.1. On each vertical axis is displayed the discounted marginal utility of consumption for one time period. Overall utility is optimized where consumption in each period yields the same level of discounted marginal utility (depicted by the horizontal line). The discount causes each successive curve to be less steep and to be scaled in toward the x axis by the discount factor. This results in declining consumption in each period.

Let us see how we can use this model to examine a simple choice. Suppose a decision maker is given a choice between consuming some extra now or a lot extra later. Suppose that to begin with a decision maker consumes c each period. Then, in addition to c, the decision maker is given the choice of consuming an additional x at time t or an additional $x' > x$ at time $t' > t$. The decision maker will choose x at time t if the additional utility of doing so, $\sum_{i \neq t}\delta^i u(c) + \delta^t u(c+x) > \sum_{i \neq t'}\delta^i u(c) + \delta^{t'} u(c+x')$, where the right side of

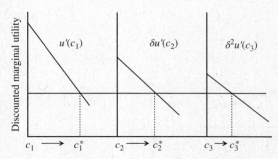

FIGURE 12.1
Optimal Consumption with More than Two Periods

the inequality is the additional utility of consuming x' at time t'. This will be the case if $\delta^{t'} u(c) + \delta^t u(c+x) > \delta^t u(c) + \delta^{t'} u(c+x')$, which can be written $u(c+x) - u(c) > \delta^{t'-t}[u(c+x') - u(c)]$. For example, suppose that the decision maker could choose x at time 0, or x' at time 7. She will choose to consume at time 0 if $\delta^7 < [u(c+x) - u(c)]/[u(c+x') - u(c)]$. If this is the case, then she would also choose x if given the choice of x at time period 257, or x' at time period $257 + 7 = 264$. However, she may choose x' if given the choice between x at 257 or x' at time period 260, because $\delta^{260-257}[u(c+x') - u(c)] = \delta^3[u(c+x') - u(c)] > \delta^{264-257}[u(c+x') - u(c)] = \delta^7[u(c+x') - u(c)]$. Thus, the choice between x or x' depends on the interval of time that passes between the two possible dates of consumption, $t' - t$, and not the point in time when x could be consumed (in this case, period 257). This property of the fully additive model is called **stationarity**. If preferences display stationarity, then the choice between two potential consumption bundles does not depend on the time they are offered, only upon the interval between possible consumption dates.

Discounting in Continuous Time

Sometimes we are interested in representing time as a continuous variable. In this case, the model is written as

$$\max_{\{c(t)\}} U(c(t)) = \int_0^\infty \delta^t u(c(t)) dt, \tag{12.3}$$

where t is a measure of the passage of time from the current point in time. In this case δ represents the discount applied to the passing of one unit of time, and the decision maker decides on a function $c(t)$ that indicates planned consumption at each point in time. Figure 12.2 displays the discount applied over time t for someone with $\delta = 0.9$. The blue circles mark the discount factors for discrete time periods 0 through 25, and

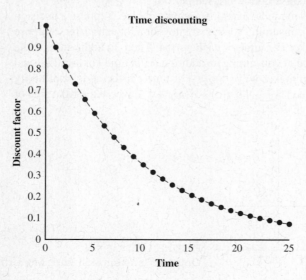

FIGURE 12.2
Exponential Time
Discounting of Utility

the dashed line displays the discount factor for a continuous-time model. The exponential discounting model discounts instantaneous utility according to the standard exponential function, creating the familiar function that slopes down and to the right. Asymptotically, as time stretches to infinity, the discount factor converges to zero. Thus, the model implies that people care less and less about the future the farther into the future we consider.

At first blush, it might seem arbitrary to assume that every period receives an identical discount, δ. There are two primary motivations for this assumption. First, it would be difficult to analyze models with discount factors that change over time. Manipulating models representing a general case where discounting can differ in every period would only be possible to analyze using sophisticated computer programs, and it would yield very few general or intuitive results. For this reason, assuming a stable discount factor from period to period became common early in economic work examining intertemporal choice. Additionally, Robert H. Strotz noted that a constant discount factor was required if people are to display time-consistent preferences.

Why Would Discounting Be Stable?

Because the mathematics of multiperiod intertemporal choice problems can get very complicated, it can often be useful to consider a very simplified version of the model. For example, suppose that a person had to choose between two consumption profiles. The first of the available consumption profiles would offer $c_1 = 20$ in the first period, $c_2 = 19$ in the second period and, $c_3 = 18$ in the third period, which we will write $c = \{20, 19, 18\}$. The second of these options offers $c' = \{20, 18, 19\}$. Once a consumption profile is chosen, the person is not allowed to change her choice in later periods even if she wishes to do so. We would not expect this restriction to be a problem to rational people if they can predict their own preferences in the future. Choosing one consumption profile in the first period and then wishing one had chosen the other once the second period is reached would result in time-inconsistent preferences. Notably, consumption in both profiles is equal in the first period, so it is really only consumption in later periods that matters when making the decision.

Suppose that the person discounts utility of consumption in the next period (tomorrow) by δ_2 and discounts utility two periods from now (the day after tomorrow) by δ_3. These discount factors allow the decision maker to discount at different rates depending on how far into the future the decision is, but she always treats tomorrow the same, and she always treats the day after tomorrow the same. Thus, in the first period the decision maker will choose c if

$$u(20) + \delta_2 u(19) + \delta_3 u(17) > u(20) + \delta_2 u(18) + \delta_3 u(19). \qquad (12.4)$$

Subtracting $u(20)$ from both sides of this inequality and collecting terms, this can be rewritten as

$$\delta_2 > \delta_3 \frac{[u(19) - u(17)]}{[u(19) - u(18)]}. \qquad (12.5)$$

Suppose that this is the case, and that the person chooses c. She will consume 20 in the first period and then enter the second period committed to the remainder of her consumption profile $c_R = \{19, 178\}$, having passed up the remainder of the consumption profile $c_R' = \{18, 19\}$. However, now the person judges period 2 as the current period and applies no discount to second-period consumption. As well, period 3 is now the next period and will be discounted by δ_2, rather than δ_3, as it was previously. If she had been able to choose which of these consumption profiles to pursue in period 2, she would have chosen c_R if

$$u(19) + \delta_2 u(17) > u(18) + \delta_2 u(19) \tag{12.6}$$

or

$$\delta_2 < \frac{[u(18) - u(19)]}{[u(17) - u(19)]}, \tag{12.7}$$

where the inequality flips because $u(17) - u(19) < 0$. If equation 12.7 holds, the person would regret having chosen c. Whether both equations 12.5 and 12.7 can be satisfied depends upon the values of δ_3, δ_2 and the instantaneous utility functional form.

For example, suppose that $u(c_i) = \sqrt{c_i}$, and let $\delta_2 = 0.45$, with $\delta_3 = 0.45\lambda$. If we evaluate the choice from the point of view of the consumer in the second period, equation 12.7 can be rewritten as

$$\delta_2 = 0.45 < \frac{[4.24 - 4.36]}{[4.12 - 4.36]} \approx 0.5, \tag{12.8}$$

meaning that because $\delta_2 < 0.5$, the person will always prefer consumption profile c_R once the second period is reached. However, if we evaluate the choice from the point of view of a first-period consumer, equation 12.5 can be rewritten as

$$\delta_3 \frac{[u(19) - u(17)]}{[u(19) - u(18)]} = 0.45\lambda \frac{[4.36 - 4.12]}{[4.36 - 4.24]} \approx \lambda 0.9 < 0.45 = \delta_2. \tag{12.9}$$

Thus, in the first period, the person would commit to the consumption profile c only if $\lambda < 0.5$. In the case of constant discounting, $\lambda = \delta_2 = 0.45$, in which case the person would prefer c in the first period and also once the second is reached. However, if $\lambda > 0.5$, then the person would commit to c' in the first period, but once the second period was reached she would regret her actions and wish she had chosen c. In this case, a value of $\lambda > 0.5$ generates time-inconsistent preferences.

Though consumption under both choices is identical in the first period, under $\lambda > 0.5$ the decision maker in the first period believes she will be patient enough once she enters the second period to be willing to trade off consumption of one unit in the second period to obtain two additional units in the third. However, once the person enters the second period she finds that her preferences are different from what she anticipated. Instead, she would prefer the additional unit of consumption now than to wait until the third period to consume two additional units.

Consider the general problem of choosing between $c = \{c_1, c_2, c_3\}$ or $c' = \{c_1, c_2', c_3'\}$, where again consumption in the first period is not affected by which profile is chosen. In the second period, the person would strictly prefer c if and only if

$$u(c_2) + \delta_2 u(c_3) > u(c_2') + \delta_2 u(c_3') \qquad (12.10)$$

or

$$\delta_2 [u(c_3) - u(c_3')] > u(c_2') - u(c_2). \qquad (12.11)$$

In the first period, the person would prefer c if and only if

$$u(c_1) + \delta_2 u(c_2) + \delta_3 u(c_3) > u(c_1) + \delta_2 u(c_2') + \delta_3 u(c_3') \qquad (12.12)$$

or

$$\delta_3 [u(c_3) - u(c_3')] > \delta_2 [u(c_2') - u(c_2)], \qquad (12.13)$$

which can be written as

$$\frac{\delta_3}{\delta_2} [u(c_3) - u(c_3')] > [u(c_2') - u(c_2)]. \qquad (12.14)$$

Note that equation 12.14 is always consistent with equation 12.11 if $\delta_3 = \delta_2^2$. In this case, equation 12.14 simplifies to equation 12.11. If utility in period 3 is discounted by the square of the discount factor applied to period 2, then preferences will always be consistent, and the decision maker will never regret the decisions she made in previous periods. Alternatively, if the discount factors follow any other pattern, there will be some set of choices that can produce time-inconsistent preferences. This can be shown to extend to any number of periods and to the more-general continuous consumption choices of the general additive model. Whenever the instantaneous utility of some future period i is always discounted by δ^i, preferences will be time consistent. Otherwise, regret may be rampant.

EXAMPLE 12.1   The End of the Month Effect on Food Stamps

The food stamp program was originally introduced in 1939 as a way to alleviate hunger in the United States. Now known as the Supplemental Nutrition Assistance Program (SNAP), the program provides each participant a card that can be used to purchase food, much like a debit card. Recipients receive a monthly transfer of money to their account generally on the first of the month. Thereafter, they can use that money for food. Close to 50 million Americans collect SNAP benefits to pay for at least part of the food budget, with a cost of over $75 billion per year. The average food stamp recipient does spend some of her other income in addition to the SNAP benefit each month on food. This finding was originally considered a sign of an effective program when discovered by economists.

Suppose that recipients receive some amount of money s in SNAP benefits that must be spent on food. If this then resulted in recipients spending exactly s on food, the restriction on spending of SNAP benefits is clearly binding, and the recipients would have been better off if they had just been given cash they could spend on anything. Alternatively, if they spend $k > s$ on food, the rational model implies that recipients could not be made better off by giving them cash instead. Suppose a rational person considering her consumption over the month would solve

$$\max_{\{x, c_0, \ldots c_{30}\}} v(x) + \sum_{t=0}^{30} \delta^t u(c_t), \tag{12.15}$$

where x represents all nonfood consumption, $v(x)$ represents the utility of nonfood consumption (irrespective of time within the month), c_t represents consumption of food at time t, and $u(c)$ is the instantaneous utility of consumption of food per day. The consumer given income of w and SNAP benefit of s must solve equation 12.15 subject to

$$\sum_{t=0}^{30} c_t \geq s \tag{12.16}$$

and

$$x + \sum_{t=0}^{30} c_t \leq s + w \tag{12.17}$$

in order to satisfy the constraints imposed by SNAP.

The constraint in equation 12.16 tells us that the recipient must consume at least her SNAP benefit in food. If she is spending more money than just the SNAP allotment on food, then equation 12.16 is not binding. The constraint in equation 12.17 tells us that she cannot spend more money than she has on hand for food. If instead the government simply gave the recipient s in cash that could be used for anything, the recipient must solve equation 12.15 subject to equation 12.17, eliminating the food restriction contained in equation 12.16. But if equation 12.16 wasn't binding under the SNAP program, then the cash transfer results in exactly the same optimization problem as the SNAP program. Thus, the recipient would consume the same amount of food and be just as well off as if she had received a cash transfer.

Alternatively, if the recipient spends no more than s on food under the SNAP program, then equation 12.16 is binding, and the recipient would behave differently if just given a cash transfer. In particular, if equation 12.16 is binding, the recipient is consuming more food than she would if equation 12.16 were eliminated. This added restriction on the solution must result in a lower level of utility than if the recipient were simply given cash.[1] If this were the case, the recipient could be made better off with a smaller cash transfer, and thus the policy is inefficient.

The U.S. government is concerned with the rising number of SNAP participants who are overweight or obese. Encouraging them to eat more than they would with a simple cash transfer could be viewed as counterproductive. Thus, economists viewed the news

---

[1] LeChatlier's principle tells us that maximizing $U(x)$ with constraints (1) through (n) must result in a value for $U(x)$ that is at least as large as if we maximized $U(x)$ subject to constraints (1) through (n) plus an additional constraint ($n + 1$).

that recipients spent some of their own money on food in addition to the SNAP benefit as good news: Recipients must be as well off as they would have been with a simple cash transfer, and we are not encouraging excess consumption.

The problems all started when someone decided to explore how recipients would react to a cash transfer equal in value to the SNAP benefits. In 1989, the U.S. Department of Agriculture conducted an experiment in which they randomly assigned households in Alabama and San Diego, California, to receive either the traditional SNAP benefit or an equivalent amount in cash. Although the differences were small, on average those receiving the SNAP benefits consumed about 100 to 200 more calories than those receiving cash—despite both groups spending in excess of the benefit on food. These two facts together contradict the standard economic model of choice.

Later work by Parke E. Wilde and Christine K. Ranney shed more light on the puzzle. They found that (for the period they studied) spending on food in the first two days after receiving the food stamp benefit spikes to about $5 per person per day. Spending the rest of the month hovers around $2 per person per day. Moreover, they find that for a large portion of those receiving food stamps, the calories consumed per day drops by more than 10 percent in the last week of the month relative to all other weeks. If we considered the model in equations 12.15 through 12.17, we should find a solution that satisfies

$$\delta^j u'(c_j) = \delta^k u'(c_k),\tag{12.18}$$

where $u'(c)$ is the instantaneous marginal utility, or slope of the instantaneous utility function, evaluated at c. People tend not to discount too much over short periods of time, like a single day, so δ should be close to 1. In this case, equation 12.18 says that for any two periods j and k, if they are relatively close together, c_j should be relatively close to c_k. Suppose $j < k$. The farther they are from each other in time, the greater will be the consumption in period j relative to period k. This is commonly referred to as **consumption smoothing**. We could see this in Figure 12.1, where each marginal utility function is slightly less negatively sloped than the last. If the discount factor by day is almost equal to one, the marginal utility function for one day should be almost identical to that of the previous day, leading to an optimal level of consumption that is almost identical.

Figure 12.3 displays another visualization of this optimization condition. Here, the curve $u(c)$ represents the instantaneous utility function with the familiar increasing but concave form. The solid line sloping upward has slope $\delta^{-j}K$, where K is some constant representing the slope at the optimal level of consumption in period 0. This line is tangent to the utility curve at one point, c_j, representing the optimal consumption at time period j. Optimal consumption in the next period occurs at the line with slope $\delta^{-j-1}K$, represented on the graph by c_{j+1}. Given the slight change in slope between these two lines, the amounts of consumption should be rather close together. Alternatively, n periods after period j, the optimal consumption will be given by $\delta^{-j-n}K$, which may be very different from consumption in period j. In any case, consumption from one period to the next should not change much. It should decline somewhat, but the rate of decline should create a smoothly declining function.

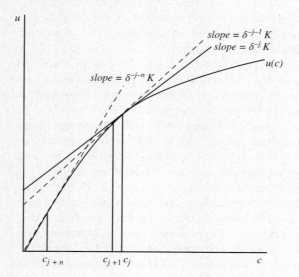

FIGURE 12.3
Consumption
Smoothing

Alternatively, in the SNAP data, we observe a sharp decline in food consumption in the last week. This signals yet again that the behavior is contradicting the standard economic model of choice. The rational model suggests that recipients will have the foresight to conserve their money to consume similar amounts every day rather than consume a lot up front and then run out of food and money in the last week of the month. A time-consistent model of decision making would not predict this behavior, nor can it be reconciled.

Naïve Hyperbolic Discounting

Robert H. Strotz first proposed a model of time-inconsistent preferences due to discounting that varies by the time horizon. Generally, he examined cases in which discount factors in the near term are relatively small, indicating that consumption now is much more valuable than in the near future. However, discount factors in the distant future are much closer to 1. His proposed model was used primarily as a method to explore the potential general-izations of the common exponential discounting model that might permit time-inconsistent preferences. Since his proposal, many have found empirical support for the notion of time-inconsistent preferences; George W. Ainsley proposed a model that, with some later modifications, is commonly called **hyperbolic discounting**. Hyperbolic discounting replaces the common exponential discount, δ^t, with the hyperbolic discount factor

$$h(t) = (1 + \alpha t)^{-(\beta/\alpha)}, \qquad (12.19)$$

where β, $\alpha > 0$ are parameters and t is the amount of time that will have passed by the instance of consumption. Thus, the consumer maximizes

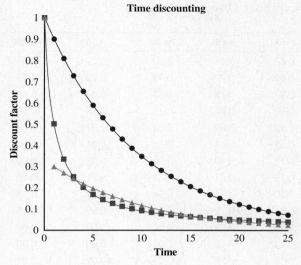

Time discounting

FIGURE 12.4
Hyperbolic (Squares) and Quasi-Hyperbolic
(Triangles) Time Discounting

$$\max_{\{c_1, c_2, \ldots\}} U(c_1, c_2, \ldots) = \sum_{i=1}^{T} (1 + \alpha i)^{-(\beta/\alpha)} u(c_i). \qquad (12.20)$$

Ainsley has found this form to be consistent with the behavior of animals in behavioral experiments introducing intertemporal choice, as well as with human behavior in similar experiments. Figure 12.4 displays the hyperbolic discount factor as well as the exponential discount factor for up to 25 time periods. The squares mark the hyperbolic discount factor and the circles mark the exponential discount factor. The hyperbolic discount factor declines very quickly over the first few time periods compared to the exponential discount function. Thus, a consumer behaving according to hyperbolic discounting will value near-term future consumption much less than someone who discounts according to exponential discounting. Alternatively, the hyperbolic discount function declines very slowly over the latter periods relative to the exponential discount function. Thus, a consumer who displays hyperbolic time discounting is much more willing to delay consumption in the distant future than in the near future. Values of the hyperbolic discount function for various parameter values and selected periods are displayed in Table 12.1. Note that the discount factor is increasing in α and decreasing in β and t.

Consider two questions posed by Richard Thaler. The first question is, "Would you rather have one apple today or two apples tomorrow?" Many people, when posed this question, consider that it is not worth it to wait a whole day just to obtain an additional apple. Thus, they elect to have the apple today. Let $u(1)$ be the instantaneous utility obtained from eating one apple, $u(2)$ be the instantaneous utility obtained from eating two apples, and δ the daily discount factor applied to decisions for consumption today versus tomorrow. Then choosing the apple today instead of two tomorrow implies $u(1) > \delta u(2)$. Now consider the second question: "Would you rather have one apple one year from now, or two apples one year and one day from now?" Many respond to this

Table 12.1   Values of the Hyperbolic Discount Function
for Various Parameters

$\alpha =$	$\beta =$	$t = 1$	$t = 2$	$t = 5$	$t = 20$	$t = 100$	$t = 200$
0.10	0.10	0.91	0.83	0.67	0.33	0.09	0.05
0.20	0.10	0.91	0.85	0.71	0.45	0.22	0.16
0.50	0.10	0.92	0.87	0.78	0.62	0.46	0.40
1.00	0.10	0.93	0.90	0.84	0.74	0.63	0.59
2.00	0.10	0.95	0.92	0.89	0.83	0.77	0.74
0.10	0.20	0.83	0.69	0.44	0.11	0.01	0.00
0.20	0.20	0.83	0.71	0.50	0.20	0.05	0.02
0.50	0.20	0.85	0.76	0.61	0.38	0.21	0.16
1.00	0.20	0.87	0.80	0.70	0.54	0.40	0.35
2.00	0.20	0.90	0.85	0.79	0.69	0.59	0.55
0.10	0.50	0.62	0.40	0.13	0.00	0.00	0.00
0.20	0.50	0.63	0.43	0.18	0.02	0.00	0.00
0.50	0.50	0.67	0.50	0.29	0.09	0.02	0.01
1.00	0.50	0.71	0.58	0.41	0.22	0.10	0.07
2.00	0.50	0.76	0.67	0.55	0.40	0.27	0.22

question by thinking one year and a day is not much different from waiting one year, and this small wait will result in twice the number of apples. Thus the majority select to wait the extra day. This is a clear violation of the stationarity property described earlier in this chapter.

Let ψ be the daily discount factor for decisions regarding consumption one year from now and γ the discount applied for waiting one year. This then implies that $\gamma u(1) < \gamma \psi u(2)$. Choosing one apple today and two apples a year and a day from now can only be reconciled if $\delta < \psi$—if the daily percentage discount decreases over time. The hyperbolic discount rate can accommodate this difference. For example, the hyperbolic discount rate for period 0 (today), and period 1(tomorrow) would be $(1)^{-(\beta/\alpha)} = 1$ and $(1 + \alpha)^{-(\beta/\alpha)}$. Thus $\delta = (1 + \alpha)^{-(\beta/\alpha)} < 1$. If α is large enough, δ is much smaller than 1. Alternatively, the discount applied to one year out and one year and one day are $(1 + \alpha 365)^{-(\beta/\alpha)}$ and $(1 + \alpha 366)^{-(\beta/\alpha)}$, respectively. Thus the daily discount one year out is

$$\psi = \left(\frac{1 + \alpha 366}{1 + \alpha 365} \right)^{-\left(\frac{\beta}{\alpha} \right)} \approx 1. \qquad (12.21)$$

This is a potential solution to the apple conundrum.

In general, the discount factor applied from one period to the next has the form

$$\psi(t) = \left(\frac{1 + \alpha(t + 1)}{1 + \alpha t} \right)^{-\left(\frac{\beta}{\alpha} \right)}, \qquad (12.22)$$

which converges to $\psi(t) = 1$ as t increases toward infinity. Thus, in the long run the period-by-period discount rate always goes to 1. Alternatively, the rate can be quite small for smaller values of t, particularly if α is large. If instead α is small, elementary calculus tells us that the value of the discount factor converges to

$$\lim_{\alpha \to 0} \psi(t) = e^{-\beta}, \tag{12.23}$$

which is a constant. Thus, when α is very small, the hyperbolic discount function behaves much like exponential discounting, with $\delta = e^{-\beta}$.

Let us revisit the behavior observed by food stamp (or SNAP) participants. If they display a sharply higher level of consumption in the first week of the month than in the last, it may be due to hyperbolic time discounting. If a SNAP recipient is a hyperbolic discounter, then on the first day of the month, she will solve

$$\max_{\{x, c_0, \dots c_{30}\}} v(x) + \sum_{t=0}^{30} (1 + \alpha t)^{-(\beta/\alpha)} u(c_t) \tag{12.24}$$

subject to the constraints equations 12.16 and 12.17. Now instead of equation 12.18, the consumption for any two periods j and k must conform to

$$(1 + \alpha j)^{-\left(\frac{\beta}{\alpha}\right)} u'(c_j) = (1 + \alpha k)^{-\left(\frac{\beta}{\alpha}\right)} u'(c_k), \tag{12.25}$$

where, as before, $u'(c)$ is the marginal instantaneous utility function evaluated at c, and let $j < k$. Equation 12.25 implies that the discount applied to the utility of consumption between any two periods j and k will be

$$\psi(j, k) = \left(\frac{1 + \alpha k}{1 + \alpha j}\right)^{-\left(\frac{\beta}{\alpha}\right)}. \tag{12.26}$$

Consider the case if we hold j constant and adjust k. Because of the hyperbolic shape of the function, in many cases $\psi(j, k)$ is substantially lower than one when j and k are relatively close together. Thus, as pictured in Figure 12.5, it may be that planned consumption changes by a relatively large and abrupt amount from one period to the next. In other words, consumption might not be so smooth in the near term. The recipient might convince herself that consumption now is extremely important relative to tomorrow but that it is not nearly so important to consume tomorrow rather than the next day. Thus, because $\psi(j, j + 1)$ converges to 1 as j gets large, planned consumption in the distant future will be smooth, though planned consumption in the near term is not. Thus a SNAP recipient who behaves according to hyperbolic discounting when receiving her benefits will plan to consume a lot today (or maybe in the first week) but then hope to smooth out her consumption over the rest of the month. Figure 12.6 offers another view of this behavior, where discounting between periods 1 and 2 is relatively steep, resulting in very different discounted marginal utility curves. Alternatively, discounting between periods 2 and 3 is very mild, resulting in nearly identical discounted marginal utility curves between periods 2 and 3 when planning from the point of view of period 1.

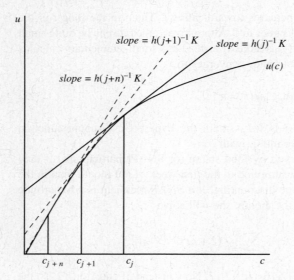

FIGURE 12.5
Hyperbolic
Discounting Increa-
ses Current Relative
to Future
Consumption

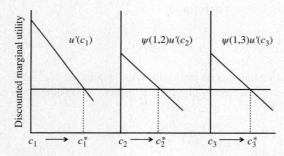

FIGURE 12.6
Consumption
Nonsmoothing
under Hyperbolic
Discounting

But then the rest of the month happens. Unfortunately with time-inconsistent preferences, the recipient does not live by her plan. Instead, when she arrives in the second
period, she solves

$$\max_{\{c_1, \ldots c_{30}\}} \sum_{t=1}^{30} \left(1 + \alpha(t-1)\right)^{-(\beta/\alpha)} u(c_t) \qquad (12.27)$$

subject to new constraints that reflect the consumption of the first day. The new time
index in the discount factor reflects that now the recipient is making her plans in period 1
rather than period 0. Thus, now consumption in period 1 enjoys a favored status relative
to period 2 and all future periods. The new solution must satisfy

$$\left(1 + \alpha(j-1)\right)^{-\left(\frac{\beta}{\alpha}\right)} u'\left(c_j\right) = \left(1 + \alpha(k-1)\right)^{-\left(\frac{\beta}{\alpha}\right)} u'\left(c_k\right). \qquad (12.28)$$

So, where before the difference in the slope of the utility function for consumption in
periods j and k could be represented by equation 12.26, now it is represented by

$$\hat{\psi}(j, k) = \left(\frac{1 + \alpha(k - 1)}{1 + \alpha(j - 1)} \right)^{-\left(\frac{\beta}{\alpha} \right)} < \psi(j, k). \qquad (12.29)$$

Previously, recipients had anticipated applying a discount of $\psi(1, 2)$ between the first and second periods. Now instead, they apply $\hat{\psi}(1, 2) = \psi(0, 1)$. Thus, despite the plans made previously, recipients now feel that they need to consume more now relative to the future. They thus consume more in period 1 than they had planned, leaving less for the future when they anticipated smoothing their consumption. In the following period, they again decide to consume more than they had planned to in either of the previous periods, again putting off consumption smoothing until a later date. Recipients continue to put off smoothing until they reach a point where they no longer have enough food to last the rest of the month, and their consumption is forced to drop off significantly.

Figure 12.7 displays the planned consumption on the first day of the month for the SNAP problem given a utility of food consumption function, $u(c) = c^{0.7}$ and a hyperbolic discounting function with $\alpha = 0.1$, $\beta = 1$. The planned consumption is much higher at the beginning of the month than at the end, but it allows some steady but low level of consumption from about day 20 of the monthly cycle onward. Alternatively, the actual level of consumption is obtained by solving the optimization again each period with a new discount function as given in equation 12.28. In this case, recipients decide once they are in the second period that they should consume more than they had planned. They continue to revise their consumption upward until the ninth period. After that, their budget does not allow them to continue to consume more than they had planned. Feast then turns to famine. At that point, they must begin consuming less and less. Consumption in the last 10 days is less than 1/10 of planned consumption and is nearly zero.

Hyperbolic discounting is a relatively simple way to represent the type of **present-biased preferences**, or an extreme discounting of the future, that seems the only explanation for such procrastination behavior. The model suggests that people plan to

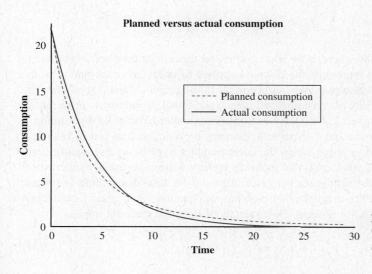

Planned versus actual consumption

- - - - Planned consumption
——— Actual consumption

Consumption (y-axis: 0, 5, 10, 15, 20)
Time (x-axis: 0, 5, 10, 15, 20, 25, 30)

FIGURE 12.7

The SNAP Problem with Hyperbolic Discounting

behave better in the future, but that future is never realized. In this case, food stamp recipients believe they will be able to restrain their appetites later in the month, but they never do. This eventually leads to severe shortages of food in the last week, as the data have documented. Often, hyperbolic discounting is misunderstood to simply embody heavy discounting of the future. Instead, it is a statement on how discounting of a pair of days in the future evolves as those days become closer to the present and how this causes recipients to change their consumption plans.

Naïve Quasi-Hyperbolic Discounting

One of the primary advantages of the exponential discounting function is the simplicity with which the exponential discount could be used in solving maximization problems. By contrast, the hyperbolic discounting model can be difficult to deal with mathematically given the functional form for the discount factor. This has led David Laibson to propose an approximation to the hyperbolic discounting function called **quasi-hyperbolic discounting**.

Quasi-hyperbolic discounting separates the hyperbolic profile of time discounting into two different discount factors. These two factors represent the discount applied to utility of consumption in the second period and the discount applied to the utility of consumption for each additional period, respectively. The discount factor applied to the second period is small relative to the other discount factor, representing the notion that people discount consumption tomorrow relative to today more heavily than the day after tomorrow relative to tomorrow. In other words, any consumption in the future receives some penalty in the mind of the consumer, but trading off consumption between two different periods in the future does not face such a steep penalty. Thus, instead of the model in equation 12.2, we write

$$U(c_1, c_2, \ldots) = u(c_1) + \beta u(c_2) + \beta \delta u(c_3) + \beta \delta^2 u(c_4) + \ldots + \beta \delta^{i-2} u(c_i) + \ldots$$
$$= \beta u(c_1) + \sum_{i=2}^{T} \beta \delta^{i-2} u(c_i), \tag{12.30}$$

where $0 < \beta < \delta < 1$, and where, if we want to consider the infinite time horizon problem, T may be ∞. Here β represents the discount applied to utility of consumption in the second period (which also multiplies utility in all future periods), and δ represents the discount applied to utility of consumption for each additional period as we move farther into the future. In general, if $\beta < \delta$ the function approximates hyberbolic discounting.

Figure 12.4 displays a quasi-hyperbolic discounting function (marked in triangles) that has been selected to approximate the corresponding hyperbolic discounting function. The advantage of this form is that it closely replicates the exponential mathematical form, thus restoring the simple mathematical formulas for time-discounting problems. The solution to the utility-maximization problem for equation 12.30 again requires that discounted marginal utility is equal. However, the differential discount implies

$$u'(c_1) = \beta \delta^{i-2} u'(c_i) \tag{12.31}$$

and for $i, j > 1$

$$u'(c_i) = \delta^{j-i} u'(c_j). \tag{12.32}$$

Both of these equations are reminiscent of equation 12.18. Thus, given a functional form for the instantaneous utility function, we can find a relationship between planned consumption in one period and the next.

For example, suppose that people must maximize their utility of consumption over an infinite time horizon, given an initial endowment of wealth w. Suppose further that $u(c) = c^\alpha$, so that the marginal utility (or slope of the utility function) of consumption is given by $u'(c) = \alpha c^{\alpha-1}$. Then equations 12.31 and 12.32 imply

$$\alpha c_1^{\alpha-1} = \alpha \beta c_2^{\alpha-1} = \alpha \beta \delta c_3^{\alpha-1} = \ldots = \alpha \beta \delta^{i-2} c_i^{\alpha-1} = \ldots \tag{12.33}$$

or

$$\alpha^{\frac{1}{\alpha-1}} c_1 = (\alpha\beta)^{\frac{1}{\alpha-1}} c_2 = \ldots = \left(\alpha\beta\delta^{i-2}\right)^{\frac{1}{\alpha-1}} c_i = \ldots. \tag{12.34}$$

This implies that $c_2 = c_1 \beta^{-\frac{1}{\alpha-1}}$, and that in general $c_i = c_1 \beta^{-\frac{1}{\alpha-1}} \delta^{-\frac{i-2}{\alpha-1}}$ when $i = 2, 3, \ldots$. The budget constraint implies

$$c_1 + c_2 + c_3 + \ldots = w, \tag{12.35}$$

or, substituting from above,

$$c_1\left(1 + \beta^{-\frac{1}{\alpha-1}} \sum_{i=0}^{\infty} \left[\delta^{-\frac{1}{\alpha-1}}\right]^i\right) = w. \tag{12.36}$$

By the properties of geometric series,[2] this can be rewritten as

$$c_1\left(1 + \frac{\beta^{-\frac{1}{\alpha-1}}}{1 - \delta^{-\frac{1}{\alpha-1}}}\right) = w, \tag{12.37}$$

leading to the closed-form solution

$$c_1 = \frac{w}{\left(1 + \frac{\beta^{-\frac{1}{\alpha-1}}}{1 - \delta^{-\frac{1}{\alpha-1}}}\right)}. \tag{12.38}$$

All other periods' consumption could then be calculated from the above formula via equation 12.34.

---

[2] Let $Y = k + kr + kr^2 + kr^3 + \ldots = \sum_{t=0}^{\infty} kr^t$, where $0 < r < 1$. Then, $Y = k/(1-r)$. To see this, note that $Y = k + kr + kr^2 + kr^3 + \ldots$. Also, $rY = kr + kr^2 + kr^3 + \ldots$. Thus, $Y - rY = k$, or $Y(1-r) = k$ implying the result. In this case, $k = \beta^{-\frac{1}{\alpha-1}}$, and $r = \delta^{-\frac{1}{\alpha-1}}$.

Table 12.2 Estimated Discount Factors for Different Amounts and Lengths of Time

	Time Delay			
Amount	6 Months	1 Year	2 Years	4 Years
$40	0.626	0.769	0.792	0.834
$200	0.700	0.797	0.819	0.850
$1,000	0.710	0.817	0.875	0.842
$5,000	0.845	0.855	0.865	0.907

Source: Benzion, U., A. Rapoport, and J. Yagil. "Discount Rates Inferred from Decisions: An Experimental Study." Management Science 35(1989): 270–284.

Alternatively, if we modeled the same decision using a hyperbolic discount function, equation 12.36 would be replaced by

$$c_1 \left[1 + \sum_{i=1}^{\infty} (1 + i\alpha) \right]^{-\frac{\beta}{\alpha}} = w, \qquad (12.39)$$

which cannot yield a closed-form solution. Thus, in many situations, economists use the quasi-hyperbolic approximation rather than the hyperbolic form. In fact, the quasi-hyperbolic form is much more common in practice than the hyperbolic form that it approximates.

Uri Benzion, Amnon Rapoport, and Joseph Yagil find evidence of changing discount rates over time. They asked 204 participants about their preferences between receiving bundles of money after various waiting periods. For example, one question asks participants to suppose they had just earned $200 for their labors, but after coming to pick up the money, they find their employer is temporarily out of funds. Instead, they are offered payment in six months. Participants were asked how much would need to be paid at the later time to be indifferent between receiving $200 now or the higher amount later. The amounts of money and the length of time were varied. Table 12.2 displays the estimated discount factors for each of the various scenarios similar to the scenario just described, assuming a money metric utility function.[3] For each, we see a relatively large discount factor for the first six months of delay. Discounts for longer periods are much smaller, reflecting the hyperbolic nature of discounting. If a person must delay a reward for some time, longer waits are no longer thought of as so costly. Similar experiments have been run with actual money payouts, finding additional evidence that discount factors climb over time, eventually becoming stable.

---

[3] They actually calculate average discount rate. This is the rate R such that $F = P(1+R)^t$, where P is the present amount, and F is the future amount. The discount factor that we have discussed in this chapter is equivalent to $\delta = 1/(1+R)$. The table displays the discount factor implied by the discount rate they report. The money metric utility function simply assumes that utility is linear in dollars.

EXAMPLE 12.2   Reading Days Are for Procrastination

It seems to have happened to all of us at one time or another. In fact, many of us have experienced it repeatedly. The big test is coming in two weeks, and we should be studying. But there is so much time before that. "I could put off studying one more day without hurting my grade," you may tell yourself. Each day you tell yourself this, until it is so late that you truly do not have as much time to study as you probably should have. Your grade is not what you wanted or what you could have achieved. Then the next semester, despite your previous experience, you procrastinate just as before.

Hyperbolic discounting might provide one explanation for why procrastination is so prevalent. Consider a student with the following (daily) instantaneous utility function

$$u(s) = -s^2, \tag{12.40}$$

where s is the portion of the day spent studying. Thus, one receives negative instantaneous utility from studying, with decreasing marginal pain from additional studying given by $u'(s) = -2s$. Moreover, suppose that the grade on a particular test is measured by an index g, as a function of time studying:

$$g(s) = s. \tag{12.41}$$

Of course it is more likely that grades show declining returns to studying, but this abstraction makes our example easier to calculate, and it ensures a solution will exist. Finally, suppose that the student's utility of receiving a grade of g is equal to $g/2$, discounted as if received on the day the results are announced. Finally, suppose that the student discounts future utility according to a quasi-hyperbolic discount function.

Suppose further that the exam will take place in four days, and the results will be announced seven days later. The student has set a goal of studying a total of 1.05 days. For simplicity, consider that the student is choosing between two different study plans. The first plan consists of $s_1 = \{0.21, 0.21, 0.21, 0.21, 0.21\}$, indicating that the student will study 0.21 of a day each day until the test. The second plan considers shirking today, but making up for it later, $s_1' = \{0.17, 0.22, 0.22, 0.22, 0.22\}$. These plans are not binding, meaning that the student could easily change her mind tomorrow. If s is chosen, the student obtains a negative instantaneous utility of $-(0.21)^2 = -0.0441$ today and each of the next four days. Then, seven days later, she will receive a grade of $0.21 \times 5 = 1.05$, yielding instantaneous utility 0.525. This can be written

$$U(s_1) = -0.0441 - \sum_{i=2}^{5} \beta \delta^{i-2} \times 0.0441 + \beta \delta^{10} \times 0.525. \tag{12.42}$$

So, for example, if $\beta = 0.75$ and $\delta = 0.99$, then $U(s_1) \approx 0.182$. Alternatively, if s' is chosen, then instantaneous utility in the first day will be $-(0.17)^2 = -0.0289$, and instantaneous utility on each succeeding day will be $-(0.22)^2 = 0.0484$. Moreover, the grade will be $0.17 + 4 \times 0.22 = 1.05$, yielding instantaneous utility 0.525:

$$U(s_1') = -0.0289 - \sum_{i=2}^{5} \beta \delta^{i-2} \times 0.0484 + \beta \delta^{10} \times 0.525. \tag{12.43}$$

Thus, if $\beta=0.75$ and $\delta=0.99$, then $U(s_1') \approx 0.184$, and the student will plan on s', shirking somewhat today and planning to make up the time with extra studying tomorrow.

The next day, however, the student needs to choose again how much to study. In this case, with only four days in which to study, suppose the choice is between sticking to the plan $s_2' = \{0.22, 0.22, 0.22, 0.22\}$ or shirking somewhat today and making it up with more time studying later $s_2'' = \{0.19, 0.23, 0.23, 0.23\}$, where again both plans yield the target amount of studying, 1.05. In this case, sticking to the plan would yield

$$U(s_2') = -0.0484 - \sum_{i=2}^{4} \beta\delta^{i-2} \times 0.0484 + \beta\delta^9 \times 0.525 \approx 0.145. \tag{12.44}$$

Choosing to procrastinate yields instantaneous utility of $-(0.19)^2 = 0.0361$ in the first period and $-(0.23)^2 = 0.0529$ in the three following periods. The grade obtained will be $0.17 + 0.19 + 3 \times 0.23 = 1.05$, yielding instantaneous utility of 0.525 when the grades are received, or

$$U(s_2'') = -0.0361 - \sum_{i=2}^{4} \beta\delta^{i-2} \times 0.0529 + \beta\delta^9 \times 0.525 \approx 0.147. \tag{12.45}$$

Thus, the student decides again to postpone the bulk of her studying.

Similar choices each day lead the student to postpone studying, planning to eventually make up the time and obtain the same grade. The next day, the student decides whether to continue with her new plan $s_3' = \{0.23, 0.23, 0.23\}$, yielding utility

$$U(s_3') = -0.0529 - \sum_{i=2}^{3} \beta\delta^{i-2} \times 0.0529 + \beta\delta^8 \times 0.525 \approx 0.107, \tag{12.46}$$

or to procrastinate again by planning on $s_3'' = \{0.21, 0.24, 0.24\}$ and yielding utility

$$U(s_3'') = -0.0441 - \sum_{i=2}^{3} \beta\delta^{i-2} \times 0.0576 + \beta\delta^8 \times 0.525 \approx 0.109, \tag{12.47}$$

where again the planned grade is 1.05. She again chooses to procrastinate and in the fourth day faces the choice of continuing with $s_4' = \{0.24, 0.24\}$, with $U(s_4') = -0.0576 - \beta 0.0576 + \beta\delta^7 \times 0.525 \approx 0.067$ or procrastinating with $s_4'' = \{0.23, 0.25\}$, yielding $U(s_4'') = -0.0529 - \beta 0.0625 + \beta\delta^7 \times 0.525 \approx 0.068$. In this fourth day she also chooses to procrastinate. In the final day, the student faces the choice to study according to plan $s_5''' = \{0.25\}$, yielding $U(s_5''') \approx 0.026$, or to just give up, $s_5'''' = \{0.16\}$, yielding $U(s_5'''') \approx 0.031$.

The student eventually has an actual study profile of $\{0.17, 0.19, 0.21, 0.25, 0.16\}$, yielding a grade of 1, less than the grade planned upon in each of the prior periods. The student's procrastination ends up costing her almost 20 percent of the anticipated grade on the test. This is the cost of not recognizing that as the test moves closer, she will change the way she discounts between the days of the study period. For the first four days of the study period, she believes she will trade off the disutility of studying between day 4 and day 5 by δ. By the time day 4 rolls around, she instead discounts day 5 disutility of studying by β. It is the constant shifting of the β discount through time that explains the procrastination behavior.

EXAMPLE 12.3 Going on a Diet

Obesity has become a major issue around the world, and particularly in the United States. Some economists have placed the annual economic cost of obesity and over-weight at around $500 billion. Almost 60 percent of Americans want to lose weight, but only about 15 percent are on a weight-loss diet at any time.

Put yourself in their shoes. Suppose you are overweight and want to go on a diet. Yet every day you face the choice to eat food you like, x^l, that will likely maintain your high weight, or to eat food that is healthy, x^h, which you do not like as much, and potentially lose weight. Let us suppose that people derive their utility from eating food and from their weight and that the instantaneous utility of each is additively separable. Thus, utility at time t, can be represented as $u(x_t, w_t) = u_x(x_t) + u_w(w_t)$, where x_t is food consumption at time t, $u_x(x)$ is utility of food consumption, w_t is weight at time t, and $u_w(w)$ is utility of weight. Suppose that eating what you like provides an instantaneous utility of $u_x(x_l) = u_l$, which is larger than the utility of eating food that is healthy, $u_x(x_h) = u_h$. Weight takes a long time to change. Let us suppose that weight is the result of a weighted sum of consumption over the last 180 days, $w_t = \sum_{i=t-180}^{t-1} \gamma_i x_i$, and that people receive instantaneous utility of weight according to $u(w) = -(\overline{w} - w)^2$, where $\overline{w}$ is the person's ideal weight. Thus, any deviation from this ideal induces a lower utility. At any point in time the potential dieter faces the decision (placing this in the framework of an infinite planning horizon problem)

$$\max_{\{x_t\}_{t=1}^{\infty}} u(x_1, w_1) + \beta \sum_{t=2}^{\infty} \delta^{t-2} u(x_t, w_t). \tag{12.48}$$

Let's begin by ignoring the current period and considering behavior in the *next* period. In that period, people could choose either to eat what they like or to eat healthy food. If they choose to eat healthy food in the next period, they will obtain

$$u(x_1, w_1) + \beta u_h - (\overline{w} - w_2)^2 + \beta \sum_{t=3}^{\infty} \delta^{t-2} u(x_t, w_t(x_2 = x_h)). \tag{12.49}$$

If instead they choose not to eat healthy food in the next period, they will obtain

$$u(x_1, w_1) + \beta u_l - (\overline{w} - w_2)^2 + \beta \sum_{t=3}^{\infty} \delta^{t-2} u(x_t, w_t(x_2 = x_l)). \tag{12.50}$$

They will thus plan to eat healthy food in the next period if

$$u_h - \sum_{t=3}^{\infty} \delta^{t-2} \left(\overline{w} - \sum_{i=t-180}^{t-1} \gamma_i x_i | x_2 = x_h \right)^2 > u_l$$

$$- \sum_{t=3}^{\infty} \delta^{t-2} \left(\overline{w} - \sum_{i=t-180}^{t-1} \gamma_i x_i | x_2 = x_l \right)^2 \tag{12.51}$$

or if the instantaneous difference in utility of consumption is smaller than the discounted difference in utility of weight:

$$\left\{ \begin{array}{l} \sum_{t=3}^{\infty} \delta^{t-2} \left(\overline{w} - \sum_{i=t-180}^{t-1} \gamma_i x_i | x_2 = x_l \right)^2 \\ - \sum_{t=3}^{\infty} \delta^{t-2} \left(\overline{w} - \sum_{i=t-180}^{t-1} \gamma_i x_i | x_2 = x_h \right)^2 \end{array} \right\} > u_l - u_h. \tag{12.52}$$

Although the impact of consumption on any one day probably has a very minimal impact on long-term weight, let us suppose that equation 12.51 holds. Moreover, because every period after period 2 can be described by the same discount factors and utility functions, if equation 12.51 holds, then every period thereafter people plan to eat healthy food.

Alternatively, consider period 1. If equation 12.51 holds, then in this period people choose to eat healthy food if

$$
\begin{aligned}
&u(x_h, w_1) + \beta \sum_{t=3}^{\infty} \delta^{t-2} u(x_h, w_t(x_i = x_h, i = 1 \ldots \infty)) \\
&> u(x_l, w_1) + \beta \sum_{t=3}^{\infty} \delta^{t-2} u(x_l, w_t(x_1 = x_l, x_i = x_h, i = 2 \ldots \infty))
\end{aligned}
\tag{12.53}
$$

or if the difference in instantaneous utility of consumption is less than the discounted utility of the difference in weight. However, now the discount includes the factor β

$$
\beta \left\{ \begin{aligned} &\sum_{t=3}^{\infty} \delta^{t-2} u(x_l, w_t(x_1 = x_l, x_i = x_h, i = 2 \ldots \infty)) \\ -&\sum_{t=3}^{\infty} \delta^{t-2} u(x_h, w_t(x_i = x_h, i = 1 \ldots \infty)) \end{aligned} \right\} > u_l - u_h.
\tag{12.54}
$$

The right-hand side of equation 12.54 must be identical to the right-hand side of equation 12.52. The left-hand side of equation 12.54 is equal to the left-hand side of equation 12.52 multiplied by β. If β is small enough, then the person will decide to indulge today and go on a diet tomorrow. The problem arises when tomorrow arrives. When tomorrow is finally here, then the β discount is now applied to period 3 and not to period 2. Thus, the person again decides to indulge but plans to go on a diet in period 3. A quasi-hyperbolic discounter will continue to plan to go on a diet tomorrow for the rest of eternity but never *actually* diet and never *actually* lose weight.

The Common Difference Effect

Decision makers are said to display the **common difference effect** if they violate the stationarity property. Recall that the stationarity property requires that if you choose x at time t over x' at time t', then you must also prefer x at time $t+k$ to x' at time $t'+k$ for all possible k. To find a violation of stationarity, we must be able to find a k such that decision makers reverse their preference despite the common difference in the passage of time when x and x' are offered.

Thaler's example of choosing between one apple today or two apples a day later is the classic example of violating stationarity. When offered one apple today or two tomorrow, many choose one today—a day is too long to wait to receive only one additional apple. However, if we ask the same question about one apple a year from now or two apples one year and one day from now, the preference often reverses. After waiting a year, a day doesn't seem like very long to wait to double consumption. Hyperbolic (or quasi-hyperbolic) discounting provides one explanation for why decision makers might display the common difference effect. The discount applied to the period 1 delay is different for different starting times. Thus, for the difference between today and tomorrow it may be β, but for the difference between one year from now and one year and one day from now it may be $\delta > \beta$. In fact, this would always lead one to be more patient in choices regarding distant future consumption but impulsive when considering near-term consumption. Thus, people often pass up far superior outcomes that require a small delay in the near term, potentially leading to regret.

One alternative procedural explanation is that people compare relative time intervals and make decisions based upon approximations and similarity. For example, a one-day wait might loom large when compared to immediate consumption. One looks large when compared to zero. However, one year might seem to be almost identical to waiting one year and one day. Some forms of the common difference effect may be the result of rounding errors, or comparison effects, used to reduce the problem into simpler terms.

The Absolute Magnitude Effect

People also appear to apply different discounts depending on the absolute size of money rewards involved. For example, recall the experiments of Benzion, Rapoport, and Yagil displayed in Table 12.2. Note that when the participants were asked about $5,000 outcomes, discount factors hovered between 0.85 and 0.90 and did not alter much over time. Alternatively, when the amounts were smaller, discount factors in the first six months were between 0.62 and 0.71, eventually rising to the 0.85 range for longer periods of time. It has generally been observed that when larger amounts are involved, people discount much less than for smaller amounts. These results are very similar to those found by Richard Thaler, displayed in Table 12.3. Participants expressed that they were on average indifferent between receiving $15 now or $60 in one year—four times as much. Alternatively, they were indifferent to receiving $3,000 now or $4,000 in one year—only 1.25 times as much. This is a substantial difference.

Some have suggested that the difference in discount factors by outcome size is due to the fact that researchers have not measured utility but only monetary value of outcomes. If people display diminishing marginal utility of money, then the discount factor calculated from questions about indifference between bundles of money in different time periods should not produce the discount factor used by the decision maker. Consider if one is indifferent between $15 now or $60 in 1 year. We would then calculate an **empirical discount factor**, the factor calculated in monetary terms, to satisfy $15 = \hat{\delta}60$, or $\hat{\delta} = 0.25$. Alternatively, the decision maker calculates by employing her utility function, according to

$$U(15) = \delta U(60). \tag{12.55}$$

Table 12.3   Estimated Discount Factors for Different Amounts and Lengths of Time

Amount	Time Delay		
	3 Months	1 Year	3 Years
$15	0.265	0.418	0.613
$250	0.578	0.746	0.813
$3,000	0.617	0.775	0.813

Source: Thaler, R.H. "Some Empirical Evidence on Dynamic Inconsistency." Economics Letters 8(1981): 201–207.

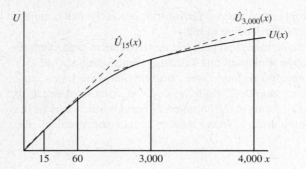

Let's approximate the utility function using a linear form, $\hat{U}_{15}(x) = U(15) + U'(15) \times (x - 15)$,[4] where $U'(15)$ is just the marginal utility (or slope of the utility function) if \$15 is received. Then using this approximation we can rewrite equation 12.55 as

$$U(15) \approx \delta_{15}[U(15) + 45U'(15)]. \tag{12.56}$$

Figure 12.8 displays such an approximation. The function $\hat{U}_{15}$ has the identical slope at the point $x = 15$ and represents the tangent line at that point. So long as we evaluate $\hat{U}_{15}$ close to the point where $x = 15$, this should provide a reasonable approximation to the value $U(x)$. Rearranging equation 12.56, we find

$$\delta_{15} \approx \frac{U(15)}{[U(15) + 45U'(15)]}. \tag{12.57}$$

Table 12.3 suggests that $\delta_{15} \approx 0.418$, implying that $U(15)/[U(15) + 45U'(15)] \approx 0.418$. Suppose $U(15) = 15$. Then, $U'(15) \approx 0.4641$, giving us an approximation of the marginal utility of wealth at $x = 15$. Alternatively, if one is indifferent between \$3,000 now or \$4,000 in one year, then

$$U(3000) = \delta U(4000). \tag{12.58}$$

Now let us consider a similar approximation $\hat{U}_{3000}(x) = U(3000) + U'(3000) \times (x - 3000)$, also displayed in Figure 12.8 (though clearly not to scale). Substituting into equation 12.58 and rearranging as before, we find

$$\delta_{3000} \approx \frac{U(3000)}{[U(3000) + 1000U'(3000)]}. \tag{12.59}$$

We want to determine if it is possible that we would observe the person being indifferent between \$3,000 now or \$4,000 in one year if the discount factor were stable over both this

---

[4] This is commonly referred to as a Taylor series approximation around the point $x = 15$. You might recognize this from introductory calculus coursework.

decision and the one involving \$15 now versus \$60 one year from now. Suppose that $\delta_{3000} = \delta_{15} = 0.418$. Then, $U(3000)/[U(3000) + 1000U'(3000)] \approx 0.418$, or $U'(3000) \approx 0.00139 \times U(3000)$. Moreover, because of diminishing marginal utility, $U(3000)$ must fall below $\hat{U}_{15}(3000)$, as depicted in Figure 12.8. Thus,

$$U(3000) < U(15) + U'(15) \times (3000 - 15) \approx 15 + 0.4641 \times 2985 = 1400.3385. \quad (12.60)$$

Thus,

$$U'(3000) \approx 0.00139 \times U(3000) < 1.949, \quad (12.61)$$

which would clearly be satisfied by any utility function displaying diminishing marginal utility given $U'(15) \approx 0.1935$. In other words, indifference between \$3,000 now and \$4,000 a year from now may be due to diminishing marginal utility (the extra \$1,000 is not as valuable to the recipient) instead of an inflated discount factor. Thus, although we have some evidence that larger amounts of money are discounted less heavily, it is unclear whether this result represents true underlying preferences or if it just the result of a shortcoming in our methods used to elicit discount factors.

The **absolute magnitude effect** implies that discounting is much closer to exponential with regard to larger amounts. This means that people are much less likely to display time-inconsistent preferences for large transactions than for small transactions. Similar experiments have been conducted by several different researchers, some using real and substantial money rewards.

EXAMPLE 12.4   Gains, Losses, and Addiction

Just as people appear to discount large and small rewards differently, they also appear to discount gains and losses differently. For example, Benzion, Rapoport, and Yagil also asked the 204 participants in their study about their preferences between being forced to pay a debt of money after various waiting periods. Participants were told they owed a debt of some amount of money (e.g., \$200), which was due immediately. Unfortunately they didn't have the means to pay it. Instead, they are offered the option to make a larger payment at some future date (e.g., in six months). Participants were asked how much the payment would need to be in order to be indifferent between paying the \$200 now or the higher amount later. As in the experiments over the gain domain, the amounts of money and the length of time were varied.

Table 12.4 displays the estimated discount factors for each of the various scenarios similar to the scenario just described, assuming a money metric utility function. In every case, the participant discounts future utility less when facing a loss than when facing a gain. When facing the prospect of a loss, suddenly future utility is more valuable. Again, we can see that larger amounts lead to larger discount factors, less discounting, and discounting that appears to be closer to the exponential model. In this case, however, it is more of a puzzle. The data suggest that people are indifferent between gaining

Table 12.4   Estimated Discount Factors for Different Amounts and Lengths of Time

Amount	6 Months	1 Year	2 Years	4 Years
		Time Delay		
Losses				
−$40	0.749	0.820	0.838	0.876
−$200	0.794	0.857	0.864	0.887
−$1,000	0.822	0.866	0.868	0.892
−$5,000	0.867	0.905	0.919	0.930
Gains				
$40	0.626	0.769	0.792	0.834
$200	0.700	0.797	0.819	0.850
$1,000	0.710	0.817	0.875	0.842
$5,000	0.845	0.855	0.865	0.907

Source: Benzion, U., A. Rapoport, and J. Yagil. "Discount Rates Inferred from Decisions: An Experimental Study." *Management Science* 35(1989): 270–284.

$40 now or $52 in one year. Using analysis similar to that in the previous section, this implies

$$U(40) = \delta U(52). \tag{12.62}$$

Substituting $\hat{U}_{40}(x)$ into (12.62) leads us to

$$\delta_{40} \approx \frac{U(40)}{[U(40) + 12U'(40)]}. \tag{12.63}$$

Table 12.4 suggests that $\delta_{40} \approx 0.769$, implying that $U(40)/[U(40) + 12U'(40)] \approx 0.769$. Suppose $U(40) = 40$. Then, $U'(40) \approx 1.00$. Table 12.3 also implies that people are indifferent to *paying* $40 now, or $49 one year from now. If one is indifferent between paying $40 now or $49 in one year, then

$$U(-40) = \delta U(-49). \tag{12.64}$$

Substituting $\hat{U}_{-40}(x)$ into (12.64) obtains

$$\frac{\delta_{-40}}{[U(-40) - 9U'(-40)]}. \tag{12.65}$$

We are again interested in determining if it is possible that the same discount factor could explain being indifferent between gaining $40 now or $52 in the future also explains being indifferent between losing $40 now or losing $49 in the future. Thus, suppose that $\delta_{-40} = \delta_{40} = 0.769$. Then, $U(-40)/[U(-40) - 9U'(-40)] \approx 0.769$, or $U'(-40) \approx -0.03338 \times U(-40)$. Diminishing marginal utility tells us that $U(-40) < \hat{U}_{40}(-40)$, or

$$U(-40) < U(40) + U'(40) \times (-40 - 40) \approx 40 - 1.00 \times 80 = -40, \tag{12.66}$$

which implies that

$$U'(-40) \approx -0.03338 \times U(-40) < 1.3351. \qquad (12.67)$$

Note that $1.3351 > 1.00 = U'(40)$. Thus, this difference in discount factors may be due to diminishing marginal utility, or due to some difference in discounting between gains and losses that will occur in the future.

The difference in discounting between gains and losses, called **gain–loss asymmetry**, has been observed in several settings. For example, Amy Odum, Gregory Madden, and Warren Bickel conducted several experiments asking people about either delaying treatment of an existing disease or delaying the onset of symptoms of a disease. Specifically, participants in their study are asked to consider the following hypothetical scenario:

> For the last 2 years, you have been ill because at some time in the past you had unprotected sex with someone you found very attractive, but whom you did not know. Thus, for the past 2 years you have felt tired and sometimes light-headed. Food has not tasted good. You have not found sex as desirable or enjoyable as you used to. For the past 2 years, you have come down with a lot of colds and other ailments, some of which have required hospitalization. You have lost a lot of weight and are getting increasingly thin. Some friends do not come to see you anymore because of your disorder and those who do feel uncomfortable being with you. Imagine that without treatment you will feel this way for the rest of your life and that you will not die during any of the time periods described here.[5]

Participants were then asked about their indifference between two treatments, one that would eliminate all symptoms immediately but last only for a limited time, or an alternative treatment that would eliminate all symptoms after some delay and last a longer period of time. Similar questions were asked regarding a different scenario in which a healthy person is told that there is a 100% chance they will begin to show symptoms of the same disease owing to a past experience with unprotected sex. They are then asked about treatments that will delay the symptoms for various lengths of time and that will be effective for various lengths of time. On average, people were willing to delay losses (in this case symptoms) more than gains (eliminating symptoms). People considering treatment for an existing disease were indifferent between 10 years of health beginning one year from now or 8.85 years of health now. When considering treatment for a newly acquired disease, 10 years of health delayed one year was equivalent to 8.25 years of health beginning immediately. Though similar to the effect found in the case of money outcomes, this is not a large difference.

The researchers conducted the same experiments on people who regularly smoke cigarettes, and they found a much wider disparity (7.75 years and 5 years, respectively). Interestingly, there is a substantial amount of research that finds greater discounting among those addicted to various substances, including cigarettes. This and other research seems to suggest a link between addiction and the onset of hyperbolic discounting. Much like the model of addiction in the previous chapter on projection bias, hyperbolic

[5] Odum, A.L., G.J. Madden, and W.K. Bickel. "Discounting of Delayed Health Gains and Losses by Current, Never- and Ex-Smokers of Cigarettes." *Nicotine & Tobacco Research* 4, Issue 3 (2002): 295–303, by permission of Oxford University Press.

discounting can offer an explanation for addictive behaviors through time-inconsistent preferences. Essentially, people might consider the benefit of the first cigarette to be high enough to overcome the negative utility derived from next period's stronger need for the substance. Moreover, smokers might believe that it will just be this once, because in the future they will discount in a manner that is closer to the exponential model. In that case, smokers don't think the cigarette will be worthwhile tomorrow, and they intend to quit. But as with all the models in this chapter, the planned actions do not come to pass.

Discounting with a Prospect-Theory Value Function

One explanation for gain–loss asymmetry may be that people do not display diminishing marginal utility of money over losses. George Loewenstein and Drazen Prelec propose that both gain–loss asymmetry and absolute magnitude effects may be reconciled by pairing the hyperbolic discount function with a prospect-theory value function displaying loss aversion in place of the standard utility function. Thus, people solve

$$\max_{\{c_1, c_2, \dots\}} V(c_1, c_2, \dots) = \sum_{i=1}^{T} (1+\alpha t)^{-\left(\frac{\beta}{a}\right)} v(c_i|k) \tag{12.68}$$

where

$$v(c|k) \equiv \begin{cases} u_g(c-k) & if \quad c \geq k \\ u_l(c-k) & if \quad c < k \end{cases} \tag{12.69}$$

as defined in previous chapters, where k is a reference point such that any level of consumption greater than k is considered a gain, and any amount less than k is considered a loss. It is common to suppress the reference point and write $v(z) = v(x-k|0)$. As defined in prior chapters, u_g is a concave function displaying diminishing marginal utility of gains, and u_l is a convex function representing diminishing marginal pain from losses. Moreover, the slope of u_l near the reference point is much steeper than the slope of u_g near the reference point, thus yielding the familiar shape in Figure 12.5. The hyperbolic discount factor is used to explain the common difference effect, as in previous examples. But note that the discount factor in equation 12.68 does not vary by the size of c or by whether c would be considered a gain or a loss. Rather, the asymmetry of gains and losses as well as the absolute magnitude effect are explained by the shape of the value function.

Previously, it was shown how a concave function could explain the absolute magnitude effect in the domain of gains. Alternatively, the asymmetry of gains and losses cannot be explained by the standard utility function that displays diminishing marginal utility (concavity) everywhere. Reconsider the example in the previous section. If the loss function is convex, then equations 12.66 and 12.67 need not hold, and thus no contradiction is created. Thus, it is possible that the person with a single and stable discount factor for utility realized one year from now could be indifferent between $40

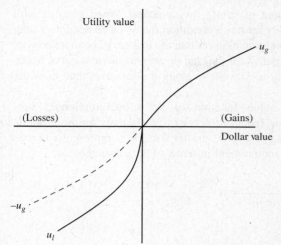

FIGURE 12.9
The Prospect Theoretic Value Function with
Intermediate Loss Aversion

now and \$52 a year from now and could also be indifferent between losing \$40 now and losing \$49 a year from now. Allowing u_l to be convex eliminates the contradiction created by discounting future losses less heavily than gains. To reconcile this model with each of the observed violations of the fully additive model, we must introduce three restrictions on the value function.

First, **intermediate loss aversion** requires that for any $c > 0$, $v(c) < -v(-c)$. Intermediate loss aversion requires that any loss of a particular size be experienced as a larger reduction in utility than the gain in utility that would result from a gain in consumption of the same size. This requires that the value function is steeper over the loss domain than over the gain domain. We call this *intermediate loss aversion* because it is a slightly weaker condition than strong loss aversion as defined in Chapter 3. Any value function that displays strong loss aversion also displays intermediate loss aversion. However, it is possible to find functions that are intermediate-loss averse but not strong-loss averse. Figure 12.9 displays a value function satisfying intermediate loss aversion. The function u_g is reflected around the origin, resulting in the dashed curve. It is apparent that u_l is everywhere below the reflected curve.

Second, the **asymmetric elasticity condition** requires that the utility of losses is more elastic than utility of gains. Let $z_2 > z_1 > 0$ be amounts of money. Then we can express this requirement in terms of arc elasticities

$$\varepsilon(-z_1, -z_2) = -\frac{(z_1 + z_2)[v(-z_1) - v(-z_2)]}{(z_2 - z_1)[v(-z_1) + v(-z_2)]} > \frac{(z_1 + z_2)[v(z_2) - v(z_1)]}{(z_2 - z_1)[v(z_1) + v(z_2)]} = \varepsilon(z_2, z_1)$$

$$(12.70)$$

or for any $z > 0$ in terms of exact elasticities as

$$\varepsilon(-z) = -\frac{zv'(-z)}{v(-z)} > \frac{zv'(z)}{v(z)} = \varepsilon(z),$$ $$(12.71)$$

where ε is the elasticity of the value of function with respect to outcomes.

This is very similar to the requirement of strong loss aversion. When coupled with intermediate loss aversion, this actually creates a condition that is more restrictive than strong loss aversion. The elasticity condition requires that the loss curve be more convex than the gain curve is concave. In Figure 12.9 this can be seen as the loss curve bends toward horizontal much more quickly as you move along the loss axis than does the reflection of the gain curve.

Finally, we must require the value function to be **subproportional**. Subproportionality requires that the value function increases in elasticity as the absolute value of consumption increases. Let $z_2 > z_1 > 0$, and let $0 < \Delta < z_1$ represent amounts of money. Then we can express this requirement in terms of arc elasticities as

$$\varepsilon(z_2, z_2 + \Delta) = \frac{(2z_2 + \Delta)[v(z_2 + \Delta) - v(z_2)]}{\Delta[v(z_2 + \Delta) + v(z_2)]} > \frac{(2z_1 + \Delta)[v(z_1 + \Delta) - v(z_1)]}{\Delta[v(z_1 + \Delta) + v(z_1)]} \quad (12.72)$$
$$= \varepsilon(z_1, z_1 + \Delta)$$

and

$$\varepsilon(-z_2, -z_2 + \Delta) = \frac{-(2z_2 + \Delta)[v(-z_2 + \Delta) - v(-z_2)]}{\Delta[v(-z_2 + \Delta) + v(-z_2)]}$$
$$> \frac{-(2z_1 + \Delta)[v(-z_1 + \Delta) - v(-z_1)]}{\Delta[v(-z_1 + \Delta) + v(-z_1)]} \quad (12.73)$$
$$= \varepsilon(-z_1, -z_1 + \Delta)$$

or in terms of exact elasticities as

$$\varepsilon(z_2) = \frac{z_2 v'(z_2)}{v(z_2)} > \frac{z_1 v'(z_1)}{v(z_1)} = \varepsilon(z_1) \quad (12.74)$$

and

$$\varepsilon(-z_2) = -\frac{z_2 v'(-z_2)}{v(-z_2)} > -\frac{z_1 v'(-z_1)}{v(-z_1)} = \varepsilon(-z_1). \quad (12.75)$$

This requirement imposes a minimum level of concavity (or convexity in the case of the loss domain) on the value function. Essentially, this requires that the difference in utility between relatively large outcomes must be minimal compared to the difference in utility of two relatively small outcomes of the same proportions. Another way to state this requirement is that whenever $z_2 > z_1 > 0$, and $\alpha > 1$, $v(z_2)/v(\alpha z_2) < v(z_1)/v(\alpha z_1)$, hence the name *subproportionality*.

If a person is indifferent between receiving $z_1 > 0$ now or $z_2 > z_1$ at some future specified date, then $v(z_1) = \psi(t)v(z_2)$, where $\psi(t)$ is the appropriate hyperbolic discount factor for a delay of t. If v displays intermediate loss aversion, then it will require more than z_2 at the future date to compensate the person for an immediate loss of

$z_1, -v(-z_1) < \psi(t)v(z_2)$. Thus, the person would not be willing to suffer a loss of z_1 now to obtain z_2 later. Moreover, $v(z_1) = \psi(t)v(z_2)$ can be rewritten as

$$v(z_2) - v(z_1) = (1/\psi(t) - 1)v(z_1) \qquad (12.76)$$

yielding an arc elasticity of preference

$$\varepsilon(z_1 z_2) = \frac{(z_1 + z_2)(1/\psi(t) - 1)v(z_1)}{(z_2 - z_1)(1/\psi(t) + 1)v(z_1)}. \qquad (12.77)$$

The arc elasticity over losses of z_1 and z_2 is given by

$$\varepsilon(-z_1, -z_2) = -\frac{(z_1 + z_2)[v(-z_1) - v(-z_2)]}{(z_2 - z_1)[v(-z_1) + v(-z_2)]}. \qquad (12.78)$$

If the person displays asymmetry of elasticity of preference, then

$$\varepsilon(-z_1, -z_2) = -\frac{(z_1 + z_2)[v(-z_1) - v(-z_2)]}{(z_2 - z_1)[v(-z_1) + v(-z_2)]} > \frac{(z_1 + z_2)(1/\psi(t) - 1)v(z_1)}{(z_2 - z_1)(1/\psi(t) + 1)v(z_1)} = \varepsilon(z_1 z_2), \qquad (12.79)$$

which, by cancelling terms, is equivalent to

$$v(-z_1) > \psi(t)v(-z_2), \qquad (12.80)$$

meaning that the person would prefer losing z_1 today to losing z_2 at time t. Thus, if z_3 is such that the person is indifferent between losing z_1 today and losing z_3 at time t, it must be that $z_3 < z_2$ (or that $-z_3 > -z_2$).

This is important considering the phenomenon of gain–loss asymmetry. Gain–loss asymmetry is observed by asking people for the amounts of money needed to compensate them for a forgone gain or a loss. Then discount factors are calculated from the dollar amounts rather than from the unobserved utility value. So if you were asked the amount of money at time t necessary to make you indifferent to gaining z_1 today you would respond z_2. This would lead an economist to calculate an empirical discount factor assuming a money metric utility function by finding the $\hat{\delta}$ satisfying $z_1 = \hat{\delta}_g z_2$, or $\hat{\delta}_g = z_1/z_2$. Asking for the amount you would need to lose at time t to make you indifferent to an immediate loss of z_1 would result in a response of $z_3 < z_2$. This would in turn lead to an empirical discount factor of $\hat{\delta}_l = z_1/z_3 > z_1/z_2 = \hat{\delta}_g$. Thus, the asymmetry of elasticity property implies behavior that is consistent with gain–loss asymmetry.

Finally, *subproportionality* is used to explain the absolute magnitude effect. Consider someone who is indifferent between obtaining $z_1 > 0$ now or αz_1 at some future date t, where $\alpha > 1$. Using her stated indifference to calculate an empirical discount factor results in $\hat{\delta} = z_1/\alpha z_1 = 1/\alpha$. Now suppose we were to ask about the amount necessary at time t to compensate for not receiving $z_2 > z_1$ immediately. Subproportionality requires that

$$\varepsilon(z_2, z_2 + \alpha z_2) = \frac{z_2(1+\alpha)[v(\alpha z_2) - v(z_2)]}{(\alpha - 1)z_2[v(\alpha z_2) + v(z_2)]} > \frac{z_1(1+\alpha)[v(\alpha z_1) - v(z_1)]}{(\alpha - 1)z_1[v(\alpha z_1) + v(z_1)]} = \varepsilon(z_1, z_1 + \alpha z_1),$$

$$(12.81)$$

where each side of the above inequality is the corresponding arc elasticity from equation 12.71. Cancelling terms yields

$$\frac{v(z_1)}{v(\alpha z_1)} > \frac{v(z_2)}{v(\alpha z_2)}. \tag{12.82}$$

Indifference between z_1 now or αz_1 at time t implies $v(z_1) = \psi(t)v(\alpha z_1)$, or that $\psi(t) = v(z_1)/v(\alpha z_1)$. Substituting into equation 12.82 implies that $\psi(t) > v(z_2)/v(\alpha z_2)$, and thus $v(z_2) < \psi(t)v(\alpha z_2)$, implying that the person would require less compensation than αz_2 at time t to compensate for the delay. Suppose instead that to be indifferent, the person would need to receive $z_3 < \alpha z_2$. Then the implied empirical discount factor would be $\hat{\delta} = z_2/z_3 > z_2/\alpha z_2 = 1/\alpha$. Thus the person would necessarily display the absolute magnitude effect if subproportionality is satisfied.

EXAMPLE 12.5　　Now or Later

Impatience can lead us to want good things to happen sooner rather than later. At the heart of many of the questions of intertemporal choice is how much we are willing to pay to speed up consumption, or how much we are willing to accept to slow down consumption. Suppose you purchased a $100 gift certificate to your favorite restaurant today and paid the maximum amount that you would be willing to pay. How much would you need to be compensated today not to use the gift certificate for six months?

George Loewenstein asked a group of M.B.A. students at Wharton Business School this question, receiving an average response of $23.85. Let $U(g, w)$ be instantaneous utility, where g represents the value of any gift certificates and w represents the value of any wealth one has in addition. The person must be indifferent between her current state, the state in which she has purchased the gift certificate for her maximum willingness to pay, and the state in which she has purchased the gift certificate and has been compensated for not using the certificate for six months. Before purchasing the gift certificate, her utility would be given by $U(0, w_1) + \psi(6)U(0, w_2)$. Let v_{now} be the maximum she would be willing to pay to receive a $100 gift certificate that could be used now. Then she must be indifferent between her current utility and the utility of purchasing that gift certificate for v_{now}, $U(100, w_1 - v_{now}) + \psi(6)U(0, w_2)$. Further, she must be indifferent between both of these values of utility and the utility obtained if she bought now and paid v_{now}, received an additional $23.85, and then could not use the certificate for an additional six months, $U(0, w_1 - v_{now} + 23.85) + \psi(6)U(100, w_2)$. These indifference relationships imply

$$\begin{aligned} U(0, w_1) + \psi(6)U(0, w_2) &= U(100, w_1 - v_{now}) + \psi(6)U(0, w_2) \\ &= U(0, w_1 - v_{now} + 23.85) + \psi(6)U(100, w_2). \end{aligned} \tag{12.83}$$

Alternatively, a second set of M.B.A. students was asked to consider a scenario in which they would purchase a $100 gift certificate in six months and pay the maximum amount they would be willing to pay. They were then asked how much they would pay to receive the gift certificate now. On average, they replied $10.17, about half as much as the compensation for waiting. These students must be indifferent between their current state, a state in which they pay today for a gift certificate in six months, $U(0, w_1 - v_{later}) + \psi(6)U(100, w_2)$, and the state in which they purchase the certificate and then pay $10.17 extra to use the certificate now, $U(100, w_1 - v_{later} - 10.17) + \psi(6)U(0, w_2)$. These indifference relationships imply

$$\begin{aligned} U(0, w_1) + \psi(6)U(0, w_2) &= U(0, w_1 - v_{later}) + \psi(6)U(100, w_2) \\ &= U(100, w_1 - v_{later} - 10.17) + \psi(6)U(0, w_2). \end{aligned} \quad (12.84)$$

Note that the first terms in equations 12.83 and 12.84 are identical, and thus all terms must be equal. This implies that

$$U(100, w_1 - v_{now}) + \psi(6)U(0, w_2) = (100, w_1 - v_{later} - 10.17) + \psi(6)U(0, w_2), \quad (12.85)$$

which requires that $v_{now} = v_{later} + 10.17$. Additionally,

$$U(0, w_1 - v_{now} + 23.85) + \psi(6)U(100, w_2) = U(0, w_1 - v_{later}) + \psi(6)U(100, w_2), \quad (12.86)$$

which requires that $v_{now} = v_{later} + 23.85$, which is of course a contradiction. In fact, the fully additive model always requires that the willingness to pay to speed up consumption should be identical to the willingness to accept to delay consumption.

This violation of the fully additive model, called **delay–speedup asymmetry**, is a common phenomenon that has been shown in many contexts. People are willing to pay between one fourth and one half as much to speed up consumption as they are willing to accept to slow down consumption.

The value function, given intermediate loss aversion, provides one explanation for this phenomenon. In this case, the framing of the question makes a difference. When using a value function to explain behavior, prior wealth is not incorporated into the reference point. The utility calculation before any transaction is now given by $v(0, 0) + \psi(6)v(0, 0)$, where $v(g, w)$ is the value of a change in gift certificates relative to the reference point of value g and a change in wealth relative to the reference point of w. When purchasing a $100 gift certificate to be used now at a price of v_{now}, the value is given by $v(100, -v_{now}) + \psi(6)v(0, 0)$. The person who first purchases the gift certificate for her maximum willingness to pay will satisfy

$$v(0, 0) + \psi(6)v(0, 0) = v(100, -v_{now}) + \psi(6)v(0, 0). \quad (12.87)$$

Then she is asked how much she would need to be compensated to put off consumption by six months. At this point, however, consumption has been incorporated in the reference point, as has the initial payment for the gift certificate. Thus, one considers having a gift certificate of $100 and initial wealth minus v_{now} to be the reference point, yielding $v(0, 0) + \psi(6)v(0, 0)$. Giving up the certificate for six months is considered a loss in this period but a gain in the future, and the payment of $23.85 received in order to wait is considered a current-period gain, $v(-100, 23.85) + \psi(6)v(100, 0)$. Thus, indifference now implies

$$v(0, 0) + \psi(6)v(0, 0) = v(-100, 23.85) + \psi(6)v(100, 0). \tag{12.88}$$

Alternatively, paying initially for a coupon to be received in six months results in the indifference relationship

$$v(0, 0) + \psi(6)v(0, 0) = v(0, -v_{later}) + \psi(6)v(100, 0). \tag{12.89}$$

Then, when the person is asked how much she is willing to consume immediately, she considers the purchase price already to be part of the reference point. Again she is finding the amount of money that would make her indifferent between $v(0, 0) + \psi(6)v(0, 0)$, her new current reference point, and a gain of a $100 certificate in this period and a loss of a $100 certificate in the future, $v(100, -10.17) + \psi(6)v(-100, 0)$. Thus, indifference now implies

$$v(0, 0) + \psi(6)v(0, 0) = v(100, -10.17) + \psi(6)v(-100, 0). \tag{12.90}$$

Because of the framing of the question, the $23.85 in compensation to slow down consumption enters as a gain, and the $10.17 payment to speed up compensation is recorded as a loss. Intermediate loss aversion requires that $v(x) < -v(-x)$ for any positive x. Thus, the gain of $23.85 has a smaller impact on utility than would a loss of $23.85.

Empirical evidence suggests losses are valued about twice the amount of an equivalent gain, offering one explanation for the delay–speedup asymmetry. Combining equations 12.88 and 12.90, we find

$$v(-100, 23.85) = v(0, -v_{later}), \tag{12.91}$$

or losing the maximum willingness to pay for consumption later is equivalent to losing the gift certificate and gaining $23.85. Other comparisons are not possible given the different state of the gift certificate in the latter period. No violations of this model can occur when comparing the delay–speedup problem because values are evaluated through different functions. When delaying, the gift certificate is evaluated as a loss now and a gain later. When speeding up, it is evaluated as a gain now and a loss later. Thus, not only is the discount factor involved but the difference in the shape of the gain and loss functions are involved also, allowing the asymmetric behavior.

It is noteworthy that the delay–speedup asymmetry is primarily observed for monetary outcomes or other items with mundane value. When we consider events that involve significant emotions, people can behave much differently. For example, George Loewenstein at one point asked several participants for their maximum willingness to pay to receive a kiss from the movie star of their choice immediately. He then asked them their maximum willingness to pay for the event at several future dates. Similarly, participants were asked the amount they would need to be paid to receive a 120-volt shock either immediately or at several intervals in the future. The results of this experiment are displayed in Figure 12.10.

One would think of receiving a kiss from the movie star of your choice as being a positive thing. Nevertheless, people are willing to pay *more* to delay the kiss by up to one year. Waiting ten years, however, results in a steep discount. Alternatively, receiving an electric shock, though it wouldn't kill you, would generally be considered an unpleasant experience, which generally means delay is preferred. Instead, participants had to be compensated much more if they were to receive the shock in the future rather

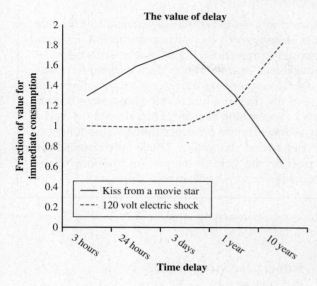

FIGURE 12.10
The Prospect-Theory Value Function with
Intermediate Loss Aversion

Source: Loewenstein, G. "Anticipation and the Valuation of
Delayed Consumption." *Economic Journal* 97(1987): 666–684,
John Wiley & Sons, Inc.

than immediately. In both cases, it appears the value of the event is not what has driven
the value of delaying, but rather the anticipation of the event. A kiss is a fleeting event.
Were you to kiss the movie star of your dreams this instant, you would have little time to
enjoy the event itself, and then it would be a memory. Alternatively, if it would take place
three days from now, you would be able to talk to your friends about it, fantasize about it,
and relish in the anticipation. Similarly, if you receive the 120-volt shock immediately, it
would be over in an instant. However, if you were told you would receive the shock in 10
years, you would spend the next 10 years dreading the moment when you would
experience the shock. Anticipation and dread are important factors in many intertemporal decisions and can lead to unintuitive behavior.

History and Notes

The hyperbolic discount function has its roots in classic psychology. The
function was proposed by George Ainslie, a psychologist, after examining
animal experiments with rewards. Many canonical experiments in psychology involve rewarding animals for performing some task. For example,
mice are given a pellet of food for pressing a lever or pigeons receive
some food after pecking on a button several times. Over time, experimenters had come to recognize that the strength of the incentive provided
to the animals was a hyperbolic function of the time between the action

and the time when the reward was received. Ainsley started to compare data examining people's preferences for delayed consumption. Examining decision makers' responses to questions about indifference between money or consumption now versus at some future date led him to notice the common-difference effect. Moreover, his training as a psychologist led him to recognize the shape of the discount function that was more convex than the exponential curve as something familiar. Thus was introduced a model of discounting that, along with the prospect-theory value function, has become ubiquitous in behavioral economics. These two models have thus far had a greater impact on the field of economics than any of the other modeling innovations arising from behavioral economics.

Biographical Note

Courtesy of University Relations
at Northwestern University

Robert H. Strotz (1922–1994)
Ph.D., University of Chicago, 1951
Held faculty positions at Northwestern University
and University of Illinois at Chicago–Navy Pier

Robert Strotz was born in Illinois and spent almost all of his career at Northwestern University. After completing his undergraduate work in economics in 1942, at the tender age of 20, he was drafted into military service during World War II. He spent much of his service in Europe, where he served in army intelligence. Part of his service included using econometric and statistical models to estimate the necessary supplies to support the occupied German population. His interest in econometric techniques led him to continue his training in Europe for several years following the war. Following this period of training he returned to the United States to earn his Ph.D. He was hired by Northwestern University four years before he finished his Ph.D. His contributions to economics include welfare theory, economic theories of behavior, and econometrics. Many of his works are concerned with foundational principles of welfare economics: Is utility measurable? How should income be distributed? Additionally, he made substantive contributions to the practice and interpretation of econometrics. His explorations of behavioral models of dynamic choice can truly be considered an offshoot of his interest in welfare economics. The general model he proposed has become a foundation point for modern behavioral economists examining time-inconsistent preferences. Strotz served on the editorial board for many of the most highly regarded journals in economics, including a 15-year stint as editor of *Econometrica*. He also served for a time as chairman of the Federal Reserve Bank of Chicago. In 1970 he was named president of Northwestern University, where he contributed substantially to the growth and vitality of that institution. Some see Strotz's leadership as key in attracting the faculty and endowment that made Northwestern one of the top research universities in the world.

THOUGHT QUESTIONS

1. Many have erroneously described hyperbolic discounting as an extreme bias toward current consumption. Describe why this is a false statement. Explain intuitively what hyperbolic discounting does to decisions involving intertemporal choice.

2. Naïve hyperbolic discounting leads people to make plans that are never executed. However, there are many reasons people might not execute plans. What other reasons might lead someone to abandon a plan for the future? What distinguishes plans that are not executed owing to hyperbolic discounting from alternative explanations for not executing plans? Do hyperbolic discounters regret not executing their plans?

3. Many people display something like hyperbolic discounting. Some businesses thrive on supporting this sort of short-term excess. For example, several establishments offer payday loans—short-term loans with ultrahigh interest rates designed to be paid off the next time the person is paid.

   (a) Suppose you were considering opening such a payday loan establishment. Given that hyperbolic discounters often fail to follow through on plans, how could you structure the loans to ensure payment? Use the quasi-hyperbolic model to make your argument.

   (b) The absolute-magnitude effect suggests that people are much closer to time consistency with regard to larger amounts. How might this explain the difference in the structure of consumer credit (or short-term loans) and banks that make larger loans?

   (c) Lotteries often offer winners an option of receiving either an annual payment of a relatively small amount that adds up to the full prize over a number of years or a one-time payment at a steep discount. Describe how time inconsistency might affect a lottery winner's decision. How might the lottery winner view her decision after the passage of time?

4. Harper is spending a three-day weekend at a beach property. Upon arrival, Harper bought a quart of ice cream and must divide consumption of the quart over each of the three days. Her instantaneous utility of ice cream consumption is given by $U(c) = c^{0.5}$, where c is measured in quarts, so that the instantaneous marginal utility is given by $0.5c^{-0.5}$.

   (a) Suppose Harper discounts future consumption according to the fully additive model, with the daily discount factor $\delta = 0.8$. Solve for the optimal consumption plan over the course of the three days by finding the amounts that equate the discounted marginal utility of consumption for each of the three days, with the amounts summing to 1.

   (b) Now suppose that Harper discounts future utility according to the quasi-hyperbolic discounting model, with $\beta = 0.5$, and $\delta = 0.8$. Describe the optimal consumption plan as of the first day of the weekend. How will the consumption plan change on day two and day three?

   (c) The model thus far eliminates the possibility that Harper will purchase more ice cream. In reality, if consumption on the last day is too low, Harper might begin to consider another ice cream purchase. Discuss the overall impact of hyperbolic discounting on food consumption or on the consumption of other limited resources.

5. Consider the diet problem of Example 12.3. Let $\delta = 0.99$, $u_l = 2$, $u_h = 1$, $\gamma_i = 1/180$ for all i, and $\overline{w} = 140$. Suppose that initial weight in the first period is 200. How high does β need to be before the person will actually go on a diet rather than just planning to in the future? Use geometric series to solve this analytically.

REFERENCES

Ainslie, G.W. *Picoeconomics.* Cambridge, UK: Cambridge University Press, 1992.

Benzion, U., A. Rapoport, and J. Yagil. "Discount Rates Inferred from Decisions: An Experimental Study." *Management Science* 35(1989): 270–284.

Bishop, J.A., J.P. Formby, and L.A. Zeager. "The Effect of Food Stamp Cashout on Undernutrition." *Economic Letters* 67(2000): 75–85.

Loewenstein, G. "Anticipation and the Valuation of Delayed Consumption." *Economic Journal* 97(1987): 666–684.

Loewenstein, G. "Frames of Mind in Intertemporal Choice." *Management Science* 34(1988): 200–214.

Loewenstein, G., and D. Prelec. "Anomalies in Intertemporal Choice: Evidence and an Interpretation." *Quarterly Journal of Economics* 107(1992): 573–597.

Odum, A.L., G.J. Madden, and W.K. Bickel. "Discounting of Delayed Health Gains and Losses by Current, Never- and Ex-Smokers of Cigarettes." *Nicotine & Tobacco Research* 4 (2002): 295–303.

Strotz, R.H. "Myopia and Inconsistency in Dynamic Utility Maximization." *Review of Economic Studies* 23(1955-56): 165–180.

Thaler, R.H. "Some Empirical Evidence on Dynamic Inconsistency." *Economics Letters* 8(1981): 201–207.

Wilde, P.E., and C.K. Ranney. "The Monthly Food Stamp Cycle: Shopping Frequency and Food Intake Decisions in an Endogenous Switching Regression Framework." *American Journal of Agricultural Economics* 82(2000): 200–213.

Committing and Uncommitting

13

The story of procrastination due to hyperbolic discounting is an intriguing one, but it seems to require the procrastinator to be rather dim—or in the words of economists, "naïve." Owing to hyperbolic discounting, people might realize that they should go on a diet but put off the diet until tomorrow given the steep discount they give to utility of consumption the next day. But when tomorrow arrives, that steep discount is applied to the next day, resulting in putting off the diet one more day. Exactly how many days in a row can people put off their diet before they realize their behavior is preventing them from achieving their goal? Similarly, how often can one put off studying until the last day before the exam without noticing how the behavior affects one's performance? And if the decision maker does start to recognize the problem of time inconsistency, what would his reaction be?

Consider first the would-be dieter. After several days of wanting to go on a diet, but putting it off "just this once," the dieter might realize "just this once" has become an eternal excuse. What he needs is some way to enforce his current preferences on his future self. The dieter might then race through the kitchen and decide to throw away all foods that would tempt him to break his diet tomorrow. Ice cream and cookies are thrown out, with maybe a few eaten along the way, so that tomorrow the dieter will not be able to break his diet except through extreme exertion—enough exertion that it would not be attractive even to a hyperbolic discounter. If the would-be dieter can make the cost of breaking his plan high enough, he will implement the plan, obtaining the long-term goal at the expense of the short-term splurge.

Commitment mechanisms are ubiquitous in our economic lives. Some might exist as a way to allow actors to assure others that they are negotiating in good faith, such as a contract for labor, but others seem incompatible with the rational model of decision making. Commitment mechanisms reduce the set of possible choices available in the future. In all cases, a rational decision maker would consider a reduction in the choice set to be something that at best leaves the decision maker no better off. But then, no rational decision maker would ever consider paying to engage in a commitment mechanism. Consider the familiar story of Odysseus, who with his crew must sail past the Sirens. He is warned by Circe that the Sirens' song is irresistible and that all who hear it are led unwittingly to an ignominious death as their boat is wrecked on the jagged rocks near the island. No sailor has ever escaped their temptation, even though he might have known of the legend.

Odysseus commands his men to fill their ears with wax so that they cannot hear the song and thus cannot be tempted, though they would still have the choice of where to steer the ship.

Odysseus further commands his men to tie him to the mast so that he cannot escape. While thus tied to the mast, he could be exposed to the temptation but would not have the choice to steer the ship toward the Sirens' song. He could thus become the only man to have heard their song and lived. By restricting his choice set, he could indulge in the song without giving in to the temptation that accompanied it. In this case, he could consider himself better off for making the commitment because he expected to do something that would harm him if he was not thus committed. In other words, Odysseus must have believed he would make the wrong choice in order for being tied to the mast to make sense. In a similar sense, commitment mechanisms can be used by those who recognize their own time inconsistency to tie themselves to the mast.

Rationality and the Possibility of Committing

The fully additive exponential model of discounting predicts that people will display time-consistent preferences. In this case, people would have no desire to precommit to a specific path because they know they would eventually take that preferred path anyway. There is no temptation to do anything else in the rational model. Consider again the fully additive model presented in Chapter 12, in which the decision maker solves

$$\max_{\{c_1, c_2, \dots\}} U(c_1, c_2, \dots) = \max_{\{c_1, c_2, \dots\}} \sum_{i=1}^{T} \delta^{i-1} u(c_i) \qquad (13.1)$$

subject to whatever budget constraint he faces. This model assumes that consumers determine their entire consumption path, the consumption quantity for each individual time period, all at the initial time period. Thus, this model in reality assumes that the consumer can commit to the consumption path that solves equation 13.1. If instead we are attempting to model the case in which consumers cannot commit to a consumption path, then the model must reflect that consumers decide on the level of consumption in this period based upon what they believe they will decide to do in the future. Thus, in period t, the consumer solves the **recursive optimization problem**:

$$\max_{c_t < w_t} \left\{ u(c_t) + \delta \max_{c_{t+1} < w_{t+1}} \left\{ u(c_{t+1}) + \delta^2 \max_{c_{t+2} < w_{t+2}} \left\{ u(c_{t+2}) + \dots \right\} \right\} \right\}, \qquad (13.2)$$

where w_t is the budget constraint in period t that depends on consumption in all prior periods.

Equation 13.2 can be a little difficult to interpret at first. Consumers maximize their utility of consumption in this period given that they will behave so as to maximize their utility of consumption again in each future period as well. This may be easiest to see in a finite horizon problem. Consider consumers who have initial wealth w and must allocate it to consumption over three periods. After the third period, they will die, and no further consumption will be possible. Further suppose that the cost of one unit of consumption is one unit of wealth. Then, when consumers are deciding on consumption in the first period, they anticipate the maximization problem they will face in the second and third periods.

A fully continuous problem for the general consumption case is presented in the Advanced Concept box at the end of the chapter. For a simple example, consider the discrete-choice problem where, in the first and the second period, laborers can either decide to work, receiving instantaneous utility of w, or shirk, receiving instantaneous utility of s, where $s > w$. In the third period, the laborers receive \$10 for each day they worked, yielding instantaneous utility $u(10x) = 10x$, where x is the number of days worked. In the third period, the laborers have no actions they can take, and thus they simply receive instantaneous utility of the payment. If we consider the choice the laborers face in the second period, given their action in the first period, they must solve

$$\max_{z_2 = \{w,s\}} z_2 + \delta \times 10x, \tag{13.3}$$

where z_i is the action chosen in period i, and

$$x = \begin{cases} 2 & \text{if} & z_1 = w, z_2 = w \\ 1 & \text{if} & z_1 = w, z_2 = s \\ 1 & \text{if} & z_1 = s, z_2 = w \\ 0 & \text{if} & z_1 = s, z_2 = s \end{cases}. \tag{13.4}$$

They will choose to work so long as

$$w + \delta(x_1 + 10) > s + \delta x_1, \tag{13.5}$$

where x_1 is the reward resulting from the action chosen in the first period. This can be rewritten as

$$10\delta > s - w. \tag{13.6}$$

Let us suppose that this is the case, so that no matter what was chosen in the first period, laborers will choose to work in the second period. Then, in the first period, laborers face the problem

$$\max_{z_1 = \{w,s\}} \{z_1 + \delta \max_{z_2 = \{w,s\}} (z_2 + \delta \times 10x)\} = \max_{z_1 = \{w,s\}} z_1 + \delta w + \delta^2(x_1 + 10), \tag{13.7}$$

where the second and third terms result from the laborer choosing to work in the second period regardless of the first-period decision. The laborer will decide to work in the first period if

$$w + \delta w + \delta^2 20 > s + \delta w + \delta^2 10 \tag{13.8}$$

or, rewriting,

$$10\delta^2 > s - w. \tag{13.9}$$

Let us suppose that this is not the case, but that the laborer decides to shirk because $10\delta^2$, the discounted reward for working in the first period, is less than the immediate difference in utility between working and shirking, $s-w$. For example, suppose $s=3$, $w=-2$, $\delta=0.7$. Then, from equation 13.6, $10\delta=7$, which is greater than $s-w=5$, implying the laborer will decide to work in the second period. However, $10\delta^2=4.9$, which is less than $s-w=5$. Thus, according to equation 13.9, the laborer would choose to shirk in the first period. Thus, the recursive optimization problem results in the laborer choosing to shirk in the first period, working in the second period and receiving \$10 in pay in the third period.

This method of solving for the optimal sequence of decisions is called **backward induction**, and it is commonly used by economists to model decision makers' anticipation of behavior (either their own or others') in future periods. This model essentially assumes that the laborer will optimize in each period, conditional on assuming he will reoptimize in each subsequent period. Backward induction is most often used by economists to model games involving sequential decisions by multiple players. In the case of a potentially time-inconsistent decision maker, it may be thought of as a game involving decisions by several different selves, one for each period of the optimization. Backward induction yields the optimal plan, taking account of the potential for time-inconsistent preferences. In the case of exponential discounting, however, the decision maker should not display time-inconsistent preferences.

To see this last point, consider the standard fully additive model from equation 13.1. In the framework of our laborer, in the first period he would simply solve

$$\max_{z_1,z_2\in\{w,s\}} z_1 + \delta z_2 + \delta^2 10x. \tag{13.10}$$

In this problem there are several possibilities, and the utility of all possible choices can be written as

$$U(z_1, z_2) = \begin{cases} w+\delta w+\delta^2 20 & \text{if} \quad z_1=w, z_2=w \\ w+\delta s+\delta^2 10 & \text{if} \quad z_1=w, z_2=s \\ s+\delta w+\delta^2 10 & \text{if} \quad z_1=s, z_2=w \\ s+\delta s & \text{if} \quad z_1=s, z_2=s \end{cases}. \tag{13.11}$$

Note from equation 13.11 that the possible choices $(z_1=w, z_2=w)$ and $(z_1=s, z_2=w)$ are identical to the choices from the recursive problem in equation 13.7. Among these two options, the laborer would again choose $(z_1=s, z_2=w)$, indicating no time-inconsistent preferences. If there is any chance for time-inconsistent preferences, it must come from one of the other options. But each of the other options is clearly dominated by one of the two choices from equation 13.7. Choosing $(z_1=s, z_2=s)$ could only happen if

$$s+\delta s > s+\delta w+\delta^2 10, \tag{13.12}$$

the utility resulting from $(z_1=s, z_2=w)$, which implies that $10\delta < s-w$. But this contradicts our assumption from equation 13.6. Choosing $(z_1=w, z_2=w)$ could only occur if

$$w + \delta w + \delta^2 20 > s + \delta w + \delta^2 10, \qquad (13.13)$$

the utility resulting from ($z_1 = s$, $z_2 = w$), which implies that $\delta^2 10 > s - w$. But we also already assumed that this was not the case. Thus, there is no possibility for time-inconsistent preferences.

In general, with exponential discounting, the decision problem of the decision maker in the nth period from the point of view of the decision maker in the nth period always has the same solution as the optimization problem from the point of view of the first period given the first $n - 1$ choices. Backward induction can only eliminate choices that would be dominated from the point of view of a first-period decision maker. This is because every period after the nth period is discounted by δ relative to the nth period, just as it would be from the point of view of the first period. The property of stationarity guarantees that backward induction never results in a conflict with the standard optimization. Stationarity tells us that exponential discounting results in preferences that remain the same when trading off consumption in period t and $t + \Delta$, no matter the value of t. Thus, the fact that the second period is one period removed from the third drives the decision to work in period 2 regardless of how far distant period 2 may be from the decision maker's point of view.

Thus, in the case of exponential discounting, decision makers need not worry about enforcing their current will on their future self. Decision makers do not display time-inconsistent preferences; their preferences today about future consumption will be realized whether they can commit to a consumption path today (as in equation 13.1) or can only commit to today's level of consumption (as in the recursive optimization problem in equation 13.2). Choosing the consumption path implied by the recursive optimization problem implies exactly the same level of utility as committing to the consumption path that solves the standard optimization problem. Committing to a consumption path now would yield the utility stream described by ($z_1 = s$, $z_2 = w$). Not committing would also yield the utility stream described by ($z_1 = s$, $z_2 = w$). In fact these are identical, and thus decision makers should not be willing to give up anything to obtain a commitment mechanism.

Commitment under Time Inconsistency

Now consider a sophisticated person who faces the same three-period consumption problem but who discounts the utility of future consumption according to the quasi-hyperbolic discounting model. If a decision maker could commit to a consumption path now, he would choose

$$\max_{\{c_1, c_2, \dots\}} u(c_1) + \sum_{i=2}^{T} \beta \delta^{i-2} u(c_i) \qquad (13.14)$$

subject to whatever budget constraint might apply. Thus, decision makers would choose the consumption path that maximizes their current perception of utility and impose this consumption stream on future (potentially unwilling) versions of themselves.

People without access to a credible way to commit to future acts must then anticipate their future actions by solving the recursive optimization problem. Only now, because of the quasi-hyperbolic discount function, the problem becomes somewhat more complicated than that written in equation 13.2. Instead, the decision maker must solve

$$\max_{c_1} u(c_1) + \sum_{i=2}^{T} \beta \delta^{i-2} u\left(c_i^*\right),$$ (13.15)

where c_i^* is defined recursively as solving

$$\max_{c_i} u(c_i) + \sum_{j=i+1}^{T} \beta \delta^{j-2} u\left(c_j^*\right),$$ (13.16)

where the budget set in each period is conditioned on the consumption decisions from previous periods. We refer to decision makers who behave as if they solve the recursive optimization problem as **sophisticated**, and we refer to those who solve the standard maximization problem (as in equation 13.1) as **naïve** or **committed**, depending on the context. Sophisticated decision makers anticipate their future behavior, and naïve decision makers do not consider how their future plans will change based upon changes in how they discount a particular period relative to other periods. Alternatively, those who can commit to a particular consumption path will also solve equation 13.1 because they need not worry about their future behavior. The commitment mechanism ensures that behavior conforms to their current preferences.

To develop some intuition about what this model means, consider the three-period model from the previous section, only now suppose that the laborer discounts according to the quasi-hyperbolic model, with parameters β and δ. We can solve this problem by backward induction as before. In the third period, laborers face no choices but just receive the reward for their prior actions. Thus we begin by considering the choice from the point of view of second-period laborers. In this case, laborers will solve

$$\max_{z_2 = \{w,s\}} z_2 + \beta \times 10x.$$ (13.17)

They will choose to shirk so long as

$$w + \beta(x_1 + 10) < s + \beta x_1,$$ (13.18)

where x_1 is the reward resulting from the action chosen in the first period. This can be rewritten as

$$10\beta < s - w.$$ (13.19)

Let us suppose that this is the case. Then the laborer chooses to shirk in the second period no matter what happens in the first period. Then, in the first period, the laborer would solve

$$\max_{z_1 = \{w,s\}} \{z_1 + \beta \max_{z_2 = \{w,s\}} (z_2 + \delta \times 10x)\} = \max_{z_1 = \{w,s\}} z_1 + \beta s + \beta \delta x_1,$$ (13.20)

where the second and third terms result from the laborer choosing to shirk in the second period regardless of the first-period decision. The laborer will decide to work in the first period if

$$w + \beta s + \beta \delta 10 > s + \beta s \qquad (13.21)$$

or, rewriting,

$$10\beta\delta > s - w. \qquad (13.22)$$

But if equation 13.19 holds, clearly equation 13.22 cannot. Thus, the laborer would choose to shirk in both periods and earn no reward.

We can contrast this solution with the choice made if the laborer could commit to his work plan in the second period without the possibility of changing his mind. Then, the laborer in the first period would solve

$$\max_{z_1, z_2 \in \{w, s\}} z_1 + \beta z_2 + \beta \delta 10 x. \qquad (13.23)$$

Proceeding as in the previous section, this is equivalent to maximizing the function

$$U(z_1, z_2) = \begin{cases} w + \beta w + \beta \delta 20 & \text{if} \quad z_1 = w, z_2 = w \\ w + \beta s + \beta \delta 10 & \text{if} \quad z_1 = w, z_2 = s \\ s + \beta w + \beta \delta 10 & \text{if} \quad z_1 = s, z_2 = w \\ s + \beta s & \text{if} \quad z_1 = s, z_2 = s \end{cases}. \qquad (13.24)$$

In this case, the choices $(z_1 = w, z_2 = s)$ and $(z_1 = s, z_2 = s)$ are identical to the choices that were available to the first-period decision maker using backward induction in equation 13.20, and thus clearly $(z_1 = s, z_2 = s)$ would dominate between these two options. But the other two options were not available. The option $(z_1 = w, z_2 = w)$ would be chosen if $w + \beta w + \beta \delta 20 > s + \beta s$, or, rewriting,

$$20 \times \frac{\beta\delta}{1 + \beta} > s - w. \qquad (13.25)$$

Given that equation 13.22 holds, this could only be the case if $2/(1 + \beta)$ is much greater than 1.

Let us suppose that this is not the case. For example, suppose $s = 3$, $w = -2$, $\delta = 0.7$, $\beta = 0.5$. Then,

$$20 \times \frac{\beta\delta}{1 + \beta} \approx 4.67 < s - w = 5, \qquad (13.26)$$

implying that the laborer would prefer to shirk in both periods than to work in both periods. The remaining choice, $(z_1 = s, z_2 = w)$, would be chosen over the other options if $s + \beta w + \beta \delta 10 > s + \beta s$, or, rewriting, if $\delta 10 > s - w$. Using the numerical example, this would hold because $\delta 10 = 7 > s - w = 5$. Thus, given the option to bind himself to a work plan in the future, the laborer will choose to shirk today and work tomorrow. Of course, he will not really want to work when tomorrow comes, but his commitment eliminates the choice. He is a slave to his prior preferences.

We have examined a simple example with only four possible decision paths. A more general example of the exponential, quasi-hyperbolic discounting, naïve, committed, and sophisticated decision makers is presented in the Advanced Concept box at the end of the chapter, though the discussion requires substantial use of calculus. In general, the decision path for the recursive optimization problem always lies between the planned consumption path of the naïve quasi-hyperbolic discounter (which is identical to the optimal consumption path for a committed decision maker) and the consumption path of the rational exponential discounter with discount factor of δ.

Without the ability to commit, the decision maker will choose to shirk in the first period, just as the naïve quasi-hyperbolic discounter would. However, naïve discounters do this thinking they will be able to make up for their shirking in the next period. Committed decision makers could force themselves to work in the next period and potentially obtain a higher level of utility. The lack of ability to commit leads to a loss in utility to decision makers. Using the numerical example, the utility of the committed decision maker is

$$U_{committed} = s + \beta w + \beta \delta 10 = 5.5. \qquad (13.27)$$

Instead, the sophisticated, but uncommitted decision maker will obtain

$$U_{sophisticated} = s + \beta s = 4.5. \qquad (13.28)$$

Sophisticated decision makers obtain a lower utility knowing that they cannot count on their second-period self to save them. It is always the case that the sophisticated decision maker will be made no worse off, but could be made better off, by the option of committing.

Finally, consider the naïve decision maker explored in Chapter 12. People who are naïve regarding their time inconsistency will solve equation 13.23 to determine this period's work plan. But, if they are not committed to their work plan, they will reoptimize every period and execute a different plan in the future. In this particular case, naïve decision makers will reoptimize in period 2 and determine to shirk again, obtaining the same utility as the sophisticate. In general, a naïve decision maker's utility (evaluated from the point of view of the first-period decision maker) will be as low as, or lower than, the sophisticate's. Naïve decision makers would not be willing to pay for a commitment device because they don't foresee that they will deviate from their planned consumption path. Thus, they are worse off for their inability to predict their own behavior in the future. In each case, this would lead to indulgence and greater consumption (or shirking) in early periods, leaving little for consumption in later periods.

EXAMPLE 13.1   Savings Clubs and Federal Tax Refunds

Though they are not particularly popular anymore, at one time many people belonged to a Christmas club. To join a Christmas club, you would stop by your bank and sign an agreement that would commit you to transferring a certain amount of money out of your checking account every week to place it in an account that could only be accessed in December as Christmas approached. The idea was to allow bank patrons to save up for their Christmas shopping without having to remember or to make the decision each month to put some aside. The person was committed to save for Christmas, and the bank would pay the customer *lower* interest than would accrue in a regular savings account in return. The idea caught fire during the Great Depression, as more families had difficulty providing for a traditional Christmas. So why would families give up the added interest to commit to something they could very easily accomplish without the commitment?

Christmas clubs are mostly a thing of the past, but many people persist in using federal income tax withholding as a form of saving. More than three fourths of those filing a federal income tax form receive some income tax refund, with the average refund totaling about $3,000. Each paycheck, the government withholds a certain amount from each wage-earner's pay to cover anticipated income tax. The amount withheld is based upon how much the worker earns and on the number of exemptions he claims. If, on average, workers are receiving a substantial refund, they could simply claim a greater number of exemptions and reduce the withholding. Instead, many intentionally have excess amounts withheld, worried that they would not be able to save the amount if they were left to their own willpower. The federal withholding creates a commitment device that allows them to save for a new TV or other products. However, the federal government does not pay interest on these excess withholdings. Thus, people who receive refunds are forgoing all interest on the money they have saved over that year.

In modeling committed saving, let us suppose that Guadalupe earns $30 each week. On the first of the year, Guadalupe has 48 weeks to save before the money becomes available. Suppose that he is a quasi-hyperbolic discounter, with $\beta = 0.5$ and $\delta = 0.97$. Moreover, suppose that he has an instantaneous utility of consumption (for a week of consumption) given by $u(c) = \sqrt{c}$, but that in week 49, Guadalupe has utility given by $u_{49}(c_{49}, \chi) = 0.371 \times \sqrt{\chi c_{49}}$, where χ is the amount spent on Christmas gifts. Let us suppose that there is no other reason to save, and so there is no additional utility of saving in week 49. Finally, suppose that the regular savings account offers an annual interest rate of 5 percent, compounded weekly. Thus, if Guadalupe has s in his savings account at week t, he earns $(0.05 \div 52) \times s \approx 0.001s$ in interest. In each period, savers can choose to spend any savings, and thus their budget constraint is given by $30 + (1.001)s_{t-1}$, where s_{t-1} is the savings from last period. Initial savings is equal to 0.

Further, let us suppose that Guadalupe is sophisticated, and thus anticipates his savings behavior in the future. We can solve this problem using backward induction. In the 49th week, Guadalupe will have savings s_{49}, and thus will solve

$$\max_{c_{49}, \chi} 0.371 \times \sqrt{\chi c_{49}} \qquad (13.29)$$

subject to the constraint $\chi + c_{49} \leq 1.001 s_{48} + 30$. Because marginal utility is always positive, Guadalupe will continue to consume in each period until the budget constraint is met with equality:

$$\chi + c_{49} = 1.001 s_{48} + 30. \tag{13.30}$$

This problem is identical to the single-period consumption problem with two possible goods presented in the early chapters of this book. Thus, the solution can be found where the marginal utility of c_{49} and χ are equal (noting that both have the same price, $p = 1$). The marginal utility of c_{49} implied by equation 13.29 is

$$u_{c_{49}}(c_{49}, \chi) = 0.371 \times 0.5 \chi^2 c_{49} \tag{13.31}$$

and the marginal utility with respect to χ is

$$u_{\chi}(c_{49}, \chi) = 0.371 \times 0.5 \chi c_{49}^2. \tag{13.32}$$

Setting equation 13.31 equal to equation 13.32 implies that

$$\chi = c_{49} \tag{13.33}$$

Substituting equation 13.33 into the budget constraint for period 49, equation 13.30, yields

$$c_{49}^{\star} = \frac{1.001 s_{48} + 30}{2} = 0.5005 s_{48} + 15 \tag{13.34}$$

$$\chi^{\star} = \frac{1.001 s_{48} + 30}{2} = 0.5005 s_{48} + 15. \tag{13.35}$$

Given this solution to the last week, we can solve the 48th week's problem, which is now given by

$$\begin{aligned} \max_{c_{48}, s_{48}} V(c_{48}, s_{48}) &= \sqrt{c_{48}} + \beta \left\{ 0.371 \sqrt{c_{49}^{\star} \chi^{\star}} \right\} \\ &= \sqrt{c_{48}} + \beta \{ 0.371 (0.5005 s_{48} + 15) \} \end{aligned} \tag{13.36}$$

subject to the constraint $c_{48} + s_{48} \leq 1.001 s_{47} + 30$. Again, the budget constraint must hold with equality

$$c_{48} + s_{48} = 1.001 s_{47} + 30. \tag{13.37}$$

This problem is now identical to a single-period consumption problem with two goods: c_{48} and s_{48}. The solution is given where the marginal utility of each good is equal. The marginal utility of consumption, c_{48} is given by

$$V_{c_{48}}(c_{48}, s_{48}) = \frac{1}{2} c_{48}^{-\frac{1}{2}} \qquad (13.38)$$

and the marginal utility with respect to savings, s_{48}, is given by

$$V_{s_{48}}(c_{48}, s_{48}) = \beta \times 0.371 \times 0.5005 \approx 0.1857\beta. \qquad (13.39)$$

Setting equation 13.38 equal to equation 13.39 yields

$$c_{48}^{*} \approx \frac{1}{0.1379\beta^2} \approx 29. \qquad (13.40)$$

Substituting equation 13.40 into the budget constraint 13.37 yields

$$s_{48}^{*} \approx 1.001 s_{47} + 1. \qquad (13.41)$$

Note that because income is \$30, we are assured that c_{48}^{*} is feasible. We can then solve the problem for week 47 as a function of s_{46} using similar methods, and so on until we reach week 1.

Following the same procedure to solve for consumption and savings in week 47 obtains

$$\begin{aligned} \max_{c_{47}, s_{47}} V(c_{48}, s_{48}) &= \sqrt{c_{47}} + \beta\left[\sqrt{c_{48}} + \delta\{0.371(0.5005 s_{48} + 15)\}\right] \\ &= \sqrt{c_{47}} + \beta\left[\sqrt{29} + \delta\{0.371(0.5005(1.001 s_{47} + 1) + 15)\}\right] \end{aligned} \qquad (13.42)$$

subject to the budget constraint $c_{47} + s_{47} \leq 1.001 s_{46} + 30$, which will again hold with equality. The marginal utility of consumption, c_{47}, is now given by

$$V_{c_{47}}(c_{47}, s_{47}) = \frac{1}{2} c_{47}^{-\frac{1}{2}} \qquad (13.43)$$

and the marginal utility of savings, s_{47}, is now given by

$$V_{s_{47}}(c_{47}, s_{47}) = \beta\delta 0.371 \times 0.5005 \times 1.001 \approx 0.09. \qquad (13.44)$$

Setting the marginal utilities equal yields

$$c_{47} = 30.76. \qquad (13.45)$$

But note that this is only feasible if Guadalupe has saved enough from prior periods to produce \$0.76 in addition to the \$30 in income earned for the period. Otherwise, he will simply decide to consume the entire budget, $c_{49} = 1.001 s_{46} + 30$. Thus, we obtain $c_{47} \approx \min(1.001 s_{46} + 30, 30.76)$. In fact, in all weeks 47 and before, we obtain a solution such that Guadalupe will consume all budget up to some constant k_t, where in period 47 $k_{47} = 30.76$. Thus in any week 47 and before with $k_t > 1.001 s_{t-1} + 30$, Guadalupe will decide to consume all of his wealth. If we solve all of the periods using backward induction until week 1, we find that $k_1 > 30$. Moreover, each period's constant k_t until week 47 exceeds the implied budget constraint. Thus, sophisticates consume all of their income each week until the week before Christmas, in which they will decide to save \$1. Then the next week they cut their consumption in half in order to spend half of their income (and half of the \$1 in savings) on Christmas presents. This results in overall utility (evaluated in week 1) of $U = \sqrt{c_1} + \beta \sum_{i=2}^{48} \delta^{i-2} \sqrt{c_i} + 0.371 \times \beta \delta^{47} \sqrt{\chi c_{49}} \approx 82$.

Now suppose Guadalupe is faced with the choice of making a binding commitment to take the same amount each week and put it in a savings account that would earn interest rate $r \in (0, 1)$ until December. For simplicity, suppose that if you choose to participate in this Christmas club, you cannot participate in the standard savings account, so that all income not placed in the Christmas account will be consumed each period. Moreover, suppose that all savings will begin in period 2. Now Guadalupe solves

$$\max_s \sqrt{30} + \beta \sum_{i=2}^{48} \delta^{i-2} \sqrt{30-s} + 0.371 \times \beta \delta^{47} \sqrt{\chi c_{49}} \qquad (13.46)$$

where

$$\chi + c_{49} \leq 30 + \sum_{i=2}^{48} s\left(1 + \frac{r}{52}\right)^{49-i}, \qquad (13.47)$$

the budget constraint that results from saving s each period at annual interest rate r, compounded weekly. This constraint will hold with equality.

Just as before, Guadalupe decides to divide all wealth in the last period evenly between Christmas presents and consumption to find the level of consumption and spending that equates marginal utility across the two activities. Thus, the budget constraint equation 13.47 implies that

$$\chi \times c_{49} = \frac{\left(30 + \sum_{i=2}^{48} s\left(1 + \frac{r}{52}\right)^{49-i}\right)}{2} \times \frac{\left(30 + \sum_{i=2}^{48} s\left(1 + \frac{r}{52}\right)^{49-i}\right)}{2}. \qquad (13.48)$$

Thus, by substituting equation 13.48 into equation 13.46 the problem can be rewritten as

$$\max_s V(s) = \sqrt{30} + \sqrt{30-s}\,\beta \sum_{i=2}^{48} \delta^{i-2} + 0.371$$
$$\times \beta \delta^{47} \left\{ 30 + s \sum_{i=2}^{48} \left(1 + \frac{r}{52}\right)^{49-i} \right\}. \qquad (13.49)$$

This is similar to the problem of utility maximization in one good, in this case s. The solution occurs where the marginal utility of s is equal to zero. Saving less than this results in positive marginal utility of savings, meaning Guadalupe could increase his utility simply by increasing savings. Above this point, Guadalupe has negative marginal utility from savings, meaning he could increase utility simply by decreasing savings. This solution is depicted in Figure 13.1, where the top panel displays the discounted utility function $V(s)$, the bottom panel displays the corresponding marginal utility function $V_S(s)$, and the horizontal axis measures per-period savings.

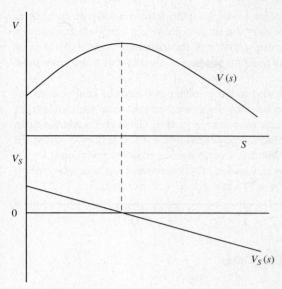

FIGURE 13.1
Optimal Savings with a Christmas Club

The marginal utility of s in this case can be written as

$$V_s(s) = -\frac{1}{2}(30-s)^{-\frac{1}{2}}\beta\sum_{i=2}^{48}\delta^{i-2} + 0.371 \times \beta\delta^{47}\left\{\sum_{i=2}^{48}\left(1+\frac{r}{52}\right)^{49-i}\right\}. \tag{13.50}$$

Setting equation 13.59 equal to zero yields the solution

$$s = 30 - \left(\frac{\sum_{i=2}^{48}\delta^{i-2}}{0.742 \times \delta^{47}\left\{\sum_{i=1}^{48}\left(1+\frac{r}{52}\right)^{49-i}\right\}}\right)^2. \tag{13.51}$$

If $r=0$, so Guadalupe earns no interest, $s=21.11$, and he thus commits to save almost two thirds of his income in every period after the first. This leads to utility of $U = \sqrt{30} + \beta\sum_{i=2}^{48}\delta^{i-2}\sqrt{8.89} + 0.371 \times \beta\delta^{47}1015.41 \approx 87$, which is greater than that obtained from not enrolling in the Christmas club and following the uncommitted strategy discussed earlier when interest is available. Thus Guadalupe would give up all interest in order to force himself to save up for Christmas.

Instead, suppose we solved for the r that would make Guadalupe indifferent between committing to the Christmas club and not. The interest rate that leads to indifference is around $r \approx -0.3$, leading to a savings per week of $s \approx 18$ and ultimate utility of $U \approx 82$. In other words, people who display quasi-hyperbolic discounting according to the parameters we have specified and who are sophisticated enough to recognize the time inconsistency in their behavior would be willing to give up about a third of their savings every year just to have the commitment device that ensures that they will save. Although this is an extreme example, it illustrates how knowing that you will procrastinate in the future as well as in the present does not eliminate the welfare loss from time inconsistency. Recognizing the time inconsistency can increase your immediate well-being if commitment mechanisms are available, but there may be a heavy cost to pay for such a device.

Commitment devices have also proved to be an effective means to spur savings for retirement. Richard Thaler and Shlomo Benartzi demonstrated this when such a plan was offered to the employees of a particular manufacturing firm. Given the opportunity to commit themselves to put a fraction of future pay raises into a retirement investment, 78 percent opted to join the program, with the overwhelming majority continuing in the program through several subsequent pay raises. The retirement savings rate among participants increased from an average of 3.5 percent to 13.6 percent.

EXAMPLE 13.2   Homework Due Dates

If people recognize that they have a problem with procrastination, one result is that they may be willing to set binding deadlines for themselves. This is a form of commitment mechanism. In fact, Dan Ariely and Klaus Wertenbroch used a class of M.B.A. students to explore this possibility.

Of the students in their class, 51 were assigned three papers and told that they could be turned in at any time during the semester. The students were given the option to set whatever deadlines they wished for each of the papers. The papers would be graded such that students would lose 1 percent of their grade for every day after the deadline in which the paper had not yet been turned in. There would be no penalty for setting the deadlines later rather than earlier. In this case, time-consistent decision makers would simply decide to set the deadline at the last day of class for all three papers and turn in the papers whenever they decided to finish them. Similarly, naïve decision makers would do the same, not anticipating that they would procrastinate completing the papers. Alternatively, sophisticated decision makers may be willing to risk the penalties and set early deadlines simply to commit themselves to finish them.

In fact, the majority of students set binding deadlines: 44 days before the end of the semester for the first paper, 26 days before the end of the semester for the second paper, and 10 days before the end of the semester for the third paper. This suggests that the students understood their tendency to procrastinate and decided to use the commitment mechanism, as Odysseus did, to bind themselves to the mast. However, the authors also found that the students did not set the deadlines in a way that maximized their performance on the papers.

Another group of 48 students were given deadlines specified by the instructor. The students who did not have control over their deadlines did significantly better on the assignments, earning about 3 percentage points more than those who could choose. Perhaps we know we will be behave badly but we do not recognize the full extent of the problem.

Choosing When to Do It

With many activities, such as studying for an exam or taking a vacation, comes the decision of when it should be done. Pleasurable activities, like taking a vacation, can lead us to an immediate reward but a long-term cost. Other activities, like cleaning a bathroom, give us an upfront cost but a longer-term reward. As experience informs us, people might want to postpone costs and speed up rewards. Thus, we might tend to do pleasurable things with long-term costs earlier than those with near-term costs and long-term benefits.

Ted O'Donoghue and Matthew Rabin propose a very simple model of such decisions of when to complete an activity. Suppose the activity can only be performed once, and the decision maker must decide on the period in which to do it. The activity can be completed in any period $t = 1, \ldots, T$. The rewards and costs depend on when the task is completed. The rewards, in terms of accrued utility, are given by $v \equiv (v_1, \ldots, v_T)$, where $v_t \geq 0$ is the reward that is realized if the task is completed in period t. Thus, if the task is completed in period 3, the decision maker will receive v_3. Similarly, the costs, in terms of utility lost, are given by $c \equiv (c_1, \ldots, c_T)$, where $c_t \geq 0$ is the cost of the task if completed in period t. However, the rewards and costs are not necessarily realized in the same period in which the project is completed. We will consider the decision maker to be a quasi-hyperbolic discounter.

Now let us compare the behavior of those who are naïve (**naïfs**) and those who are sophisticated (**sophisticates**) regarding their time inconsistency, with those who display no time inconsistency. We assume that time-consistent preferences in this case are represented by $\beta = \delta$, and that in other cases, β takes on some smaller value representing a misperception (an underestimate) of the discounting of future utility. This makes a very specific assumption about the nature of the irrationality of both naïfs and sophisticates. In particular, it assumes that irrationality derives from a discount factor of the first future period being too low. Because we cannot observe preferences, but only actions, this is truly a philosophical assumption. Alternatively, for example, it could be the case that people do not discount all future periods heavily enough (δ could be lowered until it equals β). Intuitively, this makes less sense, but there is no behavioral evidence that could point us to one conclusion versus the other (or any of the other possibilities that could be compared to a case of $\beta = \delta$).

Given this assumption about the true realized utility, O'Donoghue and Rabin note two requirements for behavior stemming from the time-consistent model. No rational decision maker should violate either of these properties given these assumptions about underlying preferences.

PROPERTY 13.1: DOMINANCE A decision maker obeys dominance if whenever there exists some period t with $v_t > 0$ and $c_t = 0$, the person will not choose to complete the task in any period t' with $c_{t'} > 0$ and $v_{t'} = 0$.

Dominance simply says that if decision makers can complete a task in some period t for some positive benefit and no cost, then they will never choose to complete the same task in another period for which there is no benefit but some cost.

PROPERTY 13.2: INDEPENDENCE OF IRRELEVANT ALTERNATIVES A decision maker obeys independence of irrelevant alternatives if whenever the decision maker chooses $t' \neq t$, when given the choices embodied in $v = (v_1, v_2, \ldots, v_{t-1}, v_t, v_{t+1} \ldots, v_T)$ and $c = (c_1, c_2, \ldots, c_{t-1}, c_t, c_{t+1}, \ldots, c_T)$, the decision maker will also choose t' when given the choices embodied in $v = (v_1, v_2, \ldots, v_{t-1}, v_{t+1} \ldots, v_T)$, $c = (c_1, c_2, \ldots, c_{t-1}, c_{t+1}, \ldots, c_T)$.

Independence of irrelevant alternatives simply says that if completing the task at time t' is the optimum when it could have been completed at time t or some other time period, then it will also be the optimum if time t is removed from the set of possible choices. If I am planning to wash the car on Friday, when Wednesday, Thursday, and Friday are the only possible days, then I should not decide to wash the car on Thursday if suddenly Wednesday is not available.

Let k_v be the number of periods the person must wait after completing the task to realize the reward, and let k_c be the number of periods before the cost comes due. Either of these values could be zero, in which case the cost or reward occurs when the task is completed. Note that time-consistent decision makers will not violate dominance, because they always choose when to complete the task according to

$$\max_{t \in \{1, \ldots, T\}} \delta^{t+k_v-1} v_t - \delta^{t+k_c-1} c_t = \max \left\{ \delta^{k_v} v_1 - \delta^{k_c} c_1, \ldots, \delta^{T+k_v} v_T - \delta^{T+k_c} cT \right\}. \tag{13.52}$$

Clearly if $c_t = 0$ and $c_{t'} > 0$, then $\delta^{t+k_v-1} v_t > -\delta^{t'+k_c-1} c_{t'}$, implying that time-consistent decision makers would always choose to complete the task at time t rather than t'. Time-consistent decision makers will also avoid violating independence of irrelevant alternatives. In equation 13.61, note that if $\delta^{k_v} v_t - \delta^{k_c} c_t > \delta^{k_v} v_{t'} - \delta^{k_c} c_{t'}$ for all $t' \neq t$, then t will also be the greatest outcome if any inferior option is removed. However, naïfs and sophisticates may both violate dominance and independence of irrelevant alternatives.

Naïfs may violate dominance because they misperceive the way they will discount the future. Suppose that $v = (8, 20, 0)$, and $c = (0, 9, 1)$, and that $k_v = 1$, and $k_c = 0$. Then, in the first period the naïf will solve

$$\max \left\{ 8\beta, \beta(20\delta - 11), -\beta\delta^2 \right\}. \tag{13.53}$$

Let us suppose that $\beta = 1/2$, but that $\delta = 1$. Then in the first period the naïf will postpone because $8\beta = 4 < \beta(20\delta - 11) = 4.5$. But then the second period the naïf will solve

$$\max \{ 20\beta - 11, -\beta\delta \}. \tag{13.54}$$

But $20\beta - 11 = -1 < -\beta\delta = -1/2$. Thus, the naïf will decide to postpone until the last period even though the outcome in the last period is clearly dominated by the outcome obtained by completing the task in the first period. Thus the naïf violates dominance.

Now, suppose we remove the option of completing the task in the second period. In this case, the naïf in the first period must choose between doing it now and receiving

$u = 8\beta$ or doing it in period 3 and receiving $-\beta\delta^2$. In this case, the naïf would always choose to complete the task now and obtain positive utility. Removing the unselected second-period option creates a preference reversal and thus a violation of the independence of irrelevant alternatives.

Sophisticates may also violate dominance if they fear that their future self will choose the dominated option. Suppose that the sophisticate faces $v = (0, 9, 1)$, and $c = (6, 16, 0)$, with $k_v = 0$, and $k_c = 1$. We can solve for the sophisticate's decision using backward induction. In the second period, the sophisticate either chooses to complete the task at that point and receive $u = 9 - 16\beta = 2$, or chooses to postpone the task to the last period and receive $u = \beta = 1/2$. In this case, the sophisticate would prefer to complete the task in the second period than in the last. In the first period, the sophisticate must then decide whether to complete the task then and receive $u = -\beta 6 = -3$, or postpone until the second period and receive $u = \beta(9 - \delta 16) = -3.5$. In this case, the sophisticate will choose to complete the task in the first period, despite this outcome being dominated by completing the task in the last period. Sophisticates do this because they are afraid they will choose to complete the task in the second period given the chance, which is perceived in the first period to be much worse than completing the task in the first period. Now suppose we again remove the option of completing the task in the second period. In this case, the sophisticate in the first period must choose between doing it now and receiving $u = -6\beta = -3$, or completing it in the last period and receiving $u = \delta\beta = 1/2$. In this case, the sophisticate would choose to complete the task in the last period. Again, removing an unselected option changed the decision, which is a violation of the independence of irrelevant alternatives.

From this point on, we will assume $\delta = 1$. Because the decision maker does not discount tradeoffs in utility between two future periods, we can treat utility changes in future periods as if they all occur in the same period. For example, if someone is deciding whether to complete the activity in period t, which would produce a reward in period $t + 3$, then the decision maker values this reward as $u = \beta\delta^2 v_t = \beta v_t$. Alternatively, if the reward would be given in period $t + 27$, the decision maker would value this reward as $u = \beta\delta^{26} v_t = \beta v_t$. This simple form of discounting allows us to more easily illustrate the intuition of the quasi-hyperbolic discounting model.

Suppose there are two types of activities: **immediate cost** and **immediate reward**. In immediate-cost activities, costs are realized in the period in which the activity is completed, but the rewards are received in future periods, $k_v > 0$, $k_c = 0$. Alternatively, in immediate-reward activities the rewards are received in the period in which the activity is completed, and the costs are paid in future periods, $k_v = 0$, $k_c > 0$.

Consider a task with immediate costs. In this case, in any period t in which a time-consistent decision maker completes the task, the utility of doing so will be $v_t - c_t$ (recall that for time-consistent decision makers $\beta = \delta = 1$). For example, consider someone who must go in for a thorough (and uncomfortable) medical exam sometime in the next four days. Completing this medical exam will allow him to take part in a high-adventure activity that should be enormous fun several weeks later. The next four days, however, might each provide different costs in terms of opportunities forgone. For example, a close friend has invited the decision maker to an amusement park on day 4, and a get-together with family is planned for day 2. We may represent the costs of these four days by $c = (7, 8, 9, 10)$. However, no matter when the decision maker completes the medical exam, the benefit will be the same, $v = (\bar{v}, \bar{v}, \bar{v}, \bar{v})$, realized one week from now. A time-consistent person will thus choose when to have the medical exam, t, so as to maximize the net benefit of the action. The problem becomes

$$\max_{t \in 1, \ldots, 4} v_t - c_t = \max\{\bar{v} - 7, \bar{v} - 8, \bar{v} - 9, \bar{v} - 10\}. \tag{13.55}$$

Thus, in this example, the time-consistent person will choose to complete the medical examination on the first day. If he were only allowed to choose from the last three days, he would choose the first day in which he was allowed to undergo the exam.

Now suppose that the decision maker is a naïf. Then all future utility would be discounted by β. In this case, the person considering when to go in for the exam from the perspective of the first day solves

$$\max\{\beta\bar{v} - 7, \beta(\bar{v} - 8), \beta(\bar{v} - 9), \beta(\bar{v} - 10)\}. \tag{13.56}$$

In this case, the benefit always arrives in the future and is thus discounted. However, taking the exam on the first day will not be discounted, but it will be on all other possible days. Thus, on the first day, the naïve person puts off the exam until the second day, so long as $8\beta < 7$. However, he will plan to complete the task on the second day because $8\beta < 9\beta < 10\beta$. The next day, he would decide to postpone again as long as $9\beta < 8$. The naïve decision maker would procrastinate again on the third day if $10\beta < 9$ but would then be forced to complete the exam on the fourth day. Procrastinating to the very last day requires only that $\beta < 0.875$.

PROPOSITION 13.1   A naïf always completes an immediate-cost task either at the same time as or later than a time-consistent decision maker does.

Proof
A time-consistent decision maker will choose t such that $v_t - c_t > v_{t'} - c_{t'}$ for any $t' \neq t$. Consider some time $t' < t$. At t' naïfs perceive the utility of completing the task at time t' to be $\beta v_{t'} - c_{t'}$, and their perception of completing the task at time t would be $\beta(v_t - c_t)$. Because $v_t - c_t > v_{t'} - c_{t'}$, and $0 < \beta < 1$, it must be that $\beta v_{t'} - c_{t'} < \beta(v_t - c_t)$. Thus, naïfs at least put off the activity until the same time as the time-consistent decision maker.   ■

Consider alternatively a time $t' > t$. At time t, the naïf must now decide whether to complete the task at time t with perceived utility $\beta v_t - c_t$, or to complete it at t' with perceived utility $\beta(v_{t'} - c_{t'})$. If it is the case that $\beta c_{t'} < c_t$, then the naïf will decide to postpone the activity beyond t and thus choose to complete the task later than the time-consistent decision maker would.

Consider instead how a sophisticate would respond to an immediate-cost problem. Consider again the immediate-cost example above with $c = (7, 8, 9, 10)$, and $v = (\bar{v}, \bar{v}, \bar{v}, \bar{v})$. In this case, we can solve for the sophisticate's decision using backward induction. On the fourth day, given he had not yet gone for the exam, the sophisticate would be forced to go for the examination, receiving $u = \beta\bar{v} - 10$. On the third day, given he had not yet gone for the exam, he must decide between going now and receiving $u = \beta\bar{v} - 9$, or going the following day and receiving $u = \beta(\bar{v} - 10)$. If $10\beta < 9$, then the sophisticate would in this case choose to go on the last day rather than the third. Let us suppose this is the case. Now consider the decision on the second day. The sophisticate now decides between doing it on the second day and receiving $u = \beta \bar{v} - 8$, or doing it on the last day (because the third day has been eliminated) and receiving $u = \beta(\bar{v} - 10)$. The sophisticate will choose the last day only if $10\beta < 8$. If this were the case, the sophisticate in the first day would choose between doing it the first day and receiving $u = \beta \bar{v} - 7$, or doing it on the last day and receiving $u = \beta(\bar{v} - 10)$. Again, the sophisticate would only postpone the exam if $10\beta < 7$. Thus, while the naïf puts off the exam to the last day if $\beta < 0.875$, the sophisticate would only ever procrastinate to the last day if $\beta < 0.7$.

PROPOSITION 13.2 A sophisticate always completes an immediate-cost task either at the same time as or before a naïf would.

Proof

Suppose a naïf eventually performs an immediate-cost task at time t. Then $\beta v_t - c_t > \beta(v_{t'} - c_{t'})$ for all $t' > t$. If this is the case, a sophisticate would also never choose to postpone beyond time t. ∎

Note that the sophisticate might do it sooner than the naïf. Suppose the naïf completes the task at time t, then the sophisticate will complete the task sooner if for some t', t'' with $t' < t'' < t$

$$\beta(v_{t''} - c_{t''}) > \beta v_{t'} - c_{t'}, \tag{13.57}$$

$$\beta(v_t - c_t) > \beta v_{t''} - c_{t''}, \tag{13.58}$$

and

$$\beta v_{t'} - c_{t'} > \beta(v_t - c_t). \tag{13.59}$$

The first inequality, equation 13.57, implies that at time t' the naïf will postpone, potentially believing he will take action at time t'' (or some better time). The second inequality tells us that at time t'' the naïf would prefer to postpone to time t. The last inequality tells us that at time t' the sophisticate will recognize that postponing to time t will make him worse off. In this case, the sophisticate would not postpone past t' because he recognizes that he would never choose to engage in the activity at time t'', even though it looks attractive at time t'.

Now consider an immediate-reward activity in which costs will accrue at some later date. For example, consider a young man who has agreed to take a young woman out for an expensive date involving dinner and a show sometime in the next four days. The young man doesn't have on hand the money to pay for the entertainment and must therefore charge it to a credit card. The particular show they go to will determine how much of a reward the young man receives. On day 1, the only show available is a rather tired musical that neither of them will enjoy much. The second through the fourth day, various newer shows are playing with varying interest. The time profile of the rewards is given by $v = (7, 8, 9, 13)$; however, the costs for each show is the same, $c = (\bar{c}, \bar{c}, \bar{c}, \bar{c})$. As in the previous example, the time-consistent decision maker would solve

$$\max\{7 - \bar{c}, 8 - \bar{c}, 9 - \bar{c}, 13 - \bar{c}\}. \qquad (13.60)$$

In this case, $13 - \bar{c}$ clearly dominates all other choices. Thus, the time-consistent decision maker will choose to go out on the fourth night.

On the other hand, on the first day the naïf will solve

$$\max\{7 - \beta\bar{c}, \beta(8 - \bar{c}), \beta(9 - \bar{c}), \beta(13 - \bar{c})\}. \qquad (13.61)$$

In this case, $\beta(13 - \bar{c}) > \beta(9 - \bar{c}) > \beta(8 - \bar{c})$. Thus, the naïf must decide between going the first night and receiving $7 - \beta\bar{c}$ or going on the fourth night and receiving $\beta(13 - \bar{c})$. The naïf will plan to go out on the fourth night unless $7 > 13\beta$, or $7/13 > \beta$. Let us suppose that this is the case, so that the naïf decides to go out on the first day.

PROPOSITION 13.3   A naïf always completes an immediate-reward task either at the same time as or earlier than a time-consistent decision maker.

Proof
A time-consistent decision maker will choose t such that $v_t - c_t > v_{t'} - c_{t'}$ for any $t' \neq t$. Consider some time $t' > t$. At t the naïf perceives the utility of completing the task at time t' to be $\beta(v_{t'} - c_{t'})$, and his perception of completing the task at time t would be $v_t - \beta c_t$. Because $v_t - c_t > v_{t'} - c_{t'}$, and $0 < \beta < 1$, it must be that $\beta(v_{t'} - c_{t'}) < v_t - c_t$. Thus, the naïf will at least execute the activity at the same time as the time-consistent decision maker. ∎

The naïf will conduct the activity earlier than the time-consistent decision maker if for some t' with $t' < t$

$$v_t - c_t > v_{t'} - \beta c_{t'} > v_{t'} - c_{t'} \qquad (13.62)$$

and

$$v_{t'} - \beta c_{t'} > \beta(v_t - c_t). \qquad (13.63)$$

Inequality 13.62 tells us that the time-consistent decision maker would prefer to complete the task at time t than at time t'. Inequality 13.63 tells us that the naïf at time t' would prefer to complete the task at time t' than to wait until time t. In this case, the time-consistent decision maker will wait until t, and the naïf will perceive a greater net benefit to conducting the activity earlier.

Now consider the sophisticate facing the same problem of deciding when to go out on a previously agreed-upon date, with rewards and costs described by $v = (7, 8, 9, 13)$ and $c = (\bar{c}, \bar{c}, \bar{c}, \bar{c})$, and where rewards are received today but costs are delayed. Recall we had already assumed that $\beta < 7/13$. As before, we can solve the recursive optimization problem using backward induction. On day 4, the young man would be forced to go on the date to meet his agreement and would receive $u = 13 - \beta \bar{c}$. Thus, on the third day, the young man can either choose to go out on the date then and receive $u = 9 - \beta \bar{c}$, or he can wait until the fourth day and receive $u = \beta(13 - \bar{c})$. So long as $9/13 > \beta$, the sophisticate would choose to go out on the third day rather than the fourth day. Then, on the second day, the sophisticate can either go out that day and receive $u = 8 - \beta \bar{c}$ or postpone the date until the third day and receive $u = \beta(9 - \bar{c})$. The sophisticate would rather go out on day two than day three if $8/9 > \beta$. On the first day, the sophisticate must choose to go out that day and receive $u = 7 - \beta \bar{c}$ or postpone until the second day and receive $u = \beta(8 - \bar{c})$. The sophisticate will choose to go out on the first day if $7/8 > \beta$. Thus, with $\beta > 7/8$, the sophisticate will also choose to go out on the first day, much earlier than the time-consistent decision maker. Note that in each round, the required β gets higher and higher for the young man to postpone rather than complete the task earlier.

PROPOSITION 13.4 A sophisticate always completes an immediate-reward task either at the same time as or earlier than a naïf does.

Proof
Suppose a naïf performs an immediate-reward task at time t. Then $v_t - \beta c_t > \beta(v_{t'} - c_{t'})$ for all $t' > t$. If this is the case, then a sophisticate would also never choose to postpone beyond time t. ∎

The sophisticate may complete the task earlier than the naïf if for some t' and t'' with $t' < t'' < t$, where the naïf completes the task at time t,

$$\beta(v_{t''} - c_{t''}) > v_{t'} - \beta c_{t'}, \tag{13.64}$$

$$\beta(v_t - c_t) > v_{t''} - \beta c_{t''}, \tag{13.65}$$

and

$$v_{t'} - \beta c_{t'} > \beta(v_t - c_t). \tag{13.66}$$

In this case, inequality 13.64 implies that the naïf will always postpone beyond t', potentially hoping to complete the task at t''. Inequality 13.65 shows that the naïf will postpone beyond t''. Inequality 13.66 implies that the sophisticate will never choose to complete the task at t if he could choose to complete the task at t', recognizing that he would never actually complete the task at time t'' if given the opportunity.

If we consider the utility function of the time-consistent decision maker to be the true utility of all decision makers and the quasi-hyperbolic discount function to arise solely by misperception, then we can make some normative statements about how decision makers should behave and assess their welfare under different scenarios. For example, proposition 13.1 tells us that the naïf always postpones an immediate-cost task later than he should, leading to a reduction in realized utility. Alternatively, proposition 13.3 tells us that the naïf completes immediate-reward tasks too soon, again leading to a loss in utility. According to proposition 13.2, the sophisticate completes an immediate-cost task earlier than the naïf but after the time-consistent decision maker. Thus, the sophisticate does not realize the utility he could if he completed the task earlier, but he is better off than the naïf in this case. Alternatively, proposition 13.4 tells us with an immediate reward, the sophisticate completes the task even earlier than the naïf, leading potentially to an even severer loss of welfare. Thus, the sophisticate may be worse off owing to his misperception of how he will discount utility in the future and his awareness of how this perception of discounting will lead him to behave in future periods. Sophisticates might correctly perceive how they will behave in the future, but they still misperceive the value of future rewards and costs. The welfare penalty to being a sophisticate in immediate-reward activities depends heavily on the assumption that sophisticates undervalue future rewards, because $\beta < \delta$, though they anticipate the decisions they will make in the future.

Of Sophisticates and Naïfs

Although the dichotomy of sophisticates and naïfs is appealing, it seems unrealistic. In our own personal experience with the world, we can find examples where we anticipate that we will procrastinate, but might not realize the extent to which we will procrastinate. When undesirable outcomes occur, instead of saying, "I knew I would do this," we might instead say "I knew I would procrastinate, but I never imagined it would go so far."

O'Donoghue and Rabin propose modeling a form of partial naïfs. A **partial naïf** anticipates that he will make decisions in the future based upon quasi-hyperbolic discounting with a parameter $\hat{\beta}$, but he actually behaves as a quasi-hyperbolic discounter with parameter β for any current-period decision. The parameter $\hat{\beta}$ represents the person's perception of future discounting and is such that $\beta \leq \hat{\beta} \leq \delta$. Thus, the decision maker always perceives that he is closer to having time-consistent preferences than he truly is. This model allows people to be trapped by temptation owing to their misperception of future discounting, at the same time still taking precautions to avoid such traps.

Consider the student who must choose when to study for a test that will take place in three days. Let us suppose that the cost of studying will be the same no matter which of the three days he studies, but studying earlier will provide a greater benefit. Specifically, suppose that $v = (15, 12, 7)$ and $c = (8, 8, 8)$, and that studying is an immediate-cost activity. For simplicity, suppose that $\delta = 1$. Then, the partial naïf believes he will behave like a sophisticate with parameter $\hat{\beta}$ but will actually behave according to β. Let us suppose that $\beta = 1/2$.

To solve for how partial naïfs behave in the first period, we can solve by backward induction. In the second period, partial naïfs believe that they will either study in that period and obtain $u = 12\hat{\beta} - 8$ or postpone to the last period and receive $u = \hat{\beta}(7 - 8) = -\hat{\beta}$. Thus partial naïfs would anticipate choosing period 2 over period 3 if $\hat{\beta} > 8/13$. Suppose this is the case. Then the partial naïfs believe they will choose to study in period 2 rather than 3. In evaluating the decision in the first period, however, they employ their actual parameter β. Thus, they choose between studying now and obtaining $u = 15\beta - 8 = -0.5$, or studying the next day and obtaining $u = \beta(12 - 8) = 2$.

Thus, partial naïfs decide to postpone studying until the second day, believing that they will have the willpower to study on the second day. But when they actually arrive at the second day, they now decide between the second and third day using the actual parameter $\beta = 1/2$. Thus, they choose either to study in that period and obtain $u = \beta 12 - 8 = -2$, or study on the third day and obtain $u = \beta(7-8) = -1/2$. Thus, partial naïfs decide to postpone until the last day even though they had planned to complete the studying in the second day. You can use backward induction to confirm that in this case, if $\hat{\beta} = \beta = 1/2$, the sophisticate would have studied the first day instead.

EXAMPLE 13.3 Gym Membership and Incentives

Gyms often offer several membership plans, including automatic monthly fees that allow you to visit the gym as often as you like, or a fee for each visit. Usually the monthly fees equal the cost of going to the gym several times at the individual visit price. Obviously, those who anticipate going to the gym often will benefit from a monthly fee relative to the fee-for-visit plan. Alternatively, those who anticipate not going very often could save money by just paying for the few times they do visit. As mentioned in Chapter 2, gym patrons in many cases behave in ways that do not make much sense. Stefano DellaVigna and Ulrike Malmendier found that at a group of three gyms, monthly membership fees of $70 allow members to visit as often as they like, whereas members without the monthly membership can buy a 10-visit pass for $100. Thus, members should only buy the monthly membership if they anticipate attending the gym more than seven times per month on average. Otherwise, they could buy the 10-visit pass for an average cost of $10 per visit. But instead of more than seven visits per month, the average member who pays the monthly fee attends only 4.3 times a month. This is clearly not consistent with rational preferences. But what could explain it?

Several other findings might help shed light on the behavior. Through a survey administered at a local mall, DellaVigna and Malmandier found that people attend the gym about half as often as they plan to. Survey respondents were asked how many times they planned to attend the gym in a particular month. These responses were then compared to actual attendance frequencies. This is consistent with naïve decision making, because people are not able to carry out the plans that they anticipate. Second, they found that people who stop going to the gym altogether tend to wait an average of 2.3 months (a cost of $187) before cancelling the gym membership. Whereas sophisticates would know to cancel their gym membership when they would no longer attend, a naïf would not necessarily cancel the gym membership, believing they would attend in the future. In fact, the evidence points to gym members who are at least partial naïfs. The authors calibrate a model of naïve gym membership that closely predicts all of the observed behavior, with daily discount factors of $\delta = 0.9995$, and $\beta = 0.7$. Thus, although it is possible to find examples of commitment mechanisms suggesting sophistication, there is also substantial evidence of naïve behavior.

EXAMPLE 13.4   Choosing What and When

Jess has just come into $11,000, and wants to find a good strategy for investing the money. In perusing the investment options, he discovers that the number and types of investments available are overwhelming. He knows it will take significant work to determine the best investment strategy. Thus, he decides to put $10,000 in a savings account that earns nearly zero interest for now and put $1,000 in a simple mutual fund designed to mirror a general stock index. The stock index fund returns about 5 percent per year but can be risky. He resolves to invest the necessary time to determine the best place to put his money in the future. In the future, however, he never seems to find the time, and after three years he has not yet invested the $10,000. The $1,000 however, increases in value in the same time to about $1,160. Had he invested the rest at the same time, he could have made a substantially greater return. Often people put off doing what is best in favor of doing what is good. Ted O'Donoghue and Matthew Rabin point to the role of time-inconsistent preferences in these seemingly misplaced priorities.

Consider an infinite-horizon decision problem in which Kerry has two actions available to him, x_1 and x_2. These actions might represent investment options or other tasks that induce an immediate cost but accrue benefits into futurity—forever. Each action can only be completed at one point in time, and if you complete one of these tasks you cannot complete the other task at any point in time. For example, you cannot invest all of your money in the stock market *and* invest all of your money in a bank account. Suppose that taking any action x_i, $i = 1$, 2 will result in an immediate cost of $c_i \geq 0$ and then a benefit of $v_i \geq 0$ that is given to Kerry each period thereafter. Let x_0 represent the action of not completing any task, with $c_0 = 0$, $v_0 = 0$. A time-consistent decision maker will decide on which activity to complete by maximizing his discounted utility. Thus, in any period in which Kerry has not yet completed the task, $\bar{t}$, he must choose a time period ($\bar{t}$) and an activity (i), solving

$$\max_{\substack{i \in \{0,1,2\} \\ \bar{t} \geq 0}} -\delta^{\bar{t}} c_i + \sum_{t=\bar{t}+1}^{\infty} \delta^t v_i = \delta^{\bar{t}} \left(\frac{\delta}{1-\delta} v_i - c_i \right), \tag{13.67}$$

where the last equality follows from the properties of geometric series.[1] Note that for any i such that $\delta v_i/(1-\delta) - c_i > 0$, Kerry would decide to complete the task now (at $\bar{t} = 0$), because $\delta^0 = 1 > \delta^t$ for any $t > 0$, deriving greater benefit from doing it now. Thus time-consistent decision makers always choose the task that maximizes $\delta v_i/(1-\delta) - c_i$ and perform the task immediately.

Now, suppose instead that Kerry is partially naïve, with parameter $\beta < \hat{\beta} \leq 1$. The decision maker always faces exactly the same decision in any time period that is reached. The payouts to different activities only depend on what period an action is taken, and these payouts are fixed. Thus, if Kerry's preferences and perceptions lead him to postpone until period 2, he would also decide to postpone until period 3, and so on, forever.

---

[1] Let $Y = kr^{\bar{j}} + kr^{\bar{j}+1} + \ldots = \sum_{i=0}^{\infty} kr^i$, where $0 < r < 1$. Then $Y = kr^{\bar{j}}/(1-r)$. To see this, note that $Y = kr^{\bar{j}} + kr^{\bar{j}+1} + kr^{\bar{j}+2} + \ldots$. Also, $rY = kr^{\bar{j}+1} + kr^{\bar{j}+2} + kr^{\bar{j}+3} + \ldots$. Thus, $Y - rY = kr^{\bar{j}}$, or $Y(1-r) = kr^{\bar{j}}$, implying the result. In this case, $k = v_i$, and $r = \delta$.

However, if Kerry recognizes that such procrastination will occur, he will instead decide to act now.

Let $u(i, \bar{t}|t')$ be the utility function Kerry in period 1 believes he will face when entering period t' from taking action i at time $\bar{t}$. In period t', if the action is taken at $\bar{t} = t'$ Kerry will perceive a utility function

$$u(i, \ t'|t') = -c_i + \sum_{t=0}^{\infty} \hat{\beta}\delta^t v_i = \frac{\hat{\beta}}{1-\delta} v_i - c_i. \qquad (13.68)$$

If the action is taken later, Kerry at period 1 believes he will perceive in period t'

$$u(i, \ \bar{t}|t') = \hat{\beta}\delta^{\bar{t}-t'-1}\left(-c_i + \sum_{t=1}^{\infty} \delta^t v_i\right) = \hat{\beta}\delta^{\bar{t}-t'-1}\left(\frac{\delta}{1-\delta} v_i - c_i\right). \qquad (13.69)$$

Note that in both cases, if $\delta v_i/(1-\delta) - c_i > 0$, Kerry would never choose to postpone the activity more than 1 period beyond t'. This is because $\hat{\beta}\delta^{\bar{t}-t'-1}(\delta v_i/(1-\delta) - c_i)$ is greatest when $\bar{t} = t'$. Note that this is Kerry's perception in period 1 considering a generic period in the future, t'. Because Kerry would never delay more than one period beyond the next, if he considers what he would do if he postponed executing an activity until period 2, he believes only one of five things could happen: execute x_1 in period 2, execute x_2 in period 2, execute x_1 in period 3, execute x_2 in period 3, do nothing in either.

Kerry anticipates that he will compare the discounted utility from the point of view of a period 2 decision maker for each of these options, choosing the option that yields the greatest utility:

Execute x_1 in period 2:	$u(1, 2|2) = \dfrac{\hat{\beta}}{1-\delta} v_1 - c_1$
Execute x_2 in period 2:	$u(2, 2|2) = \dfrac{\hat{\beta}}{1-\delta} v_2 - c_2$
Execute x_1 in period 3:	$u(1, 3|2) = \hat{\beta}\left(\dfrac{\delta}{1-\delta} v_1 - c_1\right)$
Execute x_2 in period 3:	$u(2, 3|2) = \hat{\beta}\left(\dfrac{\delta}{1-\delta} v_2 - c_2\right)$
Do nothing	$u(0, \ -|-) = 0$

If either $u(1, 2|2)$ or $u(2, 2|2)$ is the greatest of these five options, then in the first period Kerry decides on whether executing either x_1 or x_2 in period 1 would yield more utility (as perceived in period 1) than the corresponding action in period 2.

Suppose action x_i in period 2 is the greatest of the five, and thus Kerry anticipates completing action x_i. Then in period 1, he contemplates the utility (from the perspective of the period 1 decision maker) of the three options: execute x_1 in period 1, execute x_2 in period 1, execute x_i in period 2. The corresponding utilities are given by

Execute x_1 in period 1:	$u(1, 1\|1) = \dfrac{\beta}{1-\delta} v_1 - c_1$
Execute x_2 in period 1:	$u(2, 1\|1) = \dfrac{\beta}{1-\delta} v_2 - c_2$
Execute x_i in period 2:	$u(i, 2\|1) = \beta\left(\dfrac{\delta}{1-\delta} v_i - c_i\right)$

Kerry would then choose the best of these options. However, if choosing to perform x_i in period 2 is the best option, Kerry will put off the decision until period 2. But, once entering period 2, he faces a decision problem identical to that faced in period 1. Now Kerry discounts period 3 according to β but believes once entering period 3 he will discount period 4 according to $\hat{\beta}$. In this case, equations 13.68 and 13.69 represent from the point of view of period 2 the utility that will be perceived by a period 3 decision maker contemplating executing in period 3 or later. In this case Kerry would then make the same decision to procrastinate. Similarly, Kerry would procrastinate endlessly—always planning to perform x_i in the next period but never actually executing.

Alternatively, if $u(1, 3|2)$ or $u(2, 3|2)$ yields the greatest utility of the five options available when evaluating the anticipated second-period decision (thus either executing x_1 in period 3 or x_2 in period 3 are anticipated to be perceived the best choices in period 2), then the anticipated third-period decision maker would also decide to postpone or procrastinate. To see this, consider the third-period decision from the point of view of the first-period decision maker. The possible choices are again execute x_1 in period 3, execute x_2 in period 3, execute x_1 in period 4, execute x_2 in period 4, do nothing in either. The decision maker in period 1 believes that he will perceive the following utilities in period 3:

Execute x_1 in period 3:	$u(1, 3\|3) = \dfrac{\hat{\beta}}{1-\delta} v_1 - c_1$
Execute x_2 in period 3:	$u(2, 3\|3) = \dfrac{\hat{\beta}}{1-\delta} v_2 - c_2$
Execute x_1 in period 4:	$u(1, 4\|3) = \hat{\beta}\left(\dfrac{\delta}{1-\delta} v_1 - c_1\right)$
Execute x_2 in period 4:	$u(2, 4\|3) = \hat{\beta}\left(\dfrac{\delta}{1-\delta} v_2 - c_2\right)$
Do nothing	$u(0, -\|-) = 0$

These are identical to the options thought to be perceived by a second-period decision maker. Thus Kerry will again choose to postpone to period 4. Because the first-period decision maker recognizes this infinite procrastination will take place, he will recognize that postponing to period 3 means never doing anything and will instead choose either to execute an action in period 1 or do nothing ever. In this case he must choose between $u(1, 1|1)$, $u(2, 1|1)$ and $u(0, -|-)$ in the first period.

Given the complexity of varying perceptions and anticipated beliefs, an example might make this clearer. Suppose that $\beta = 0.6$, and $\hat{\beta} = 1$. Thus Kerry will discount the next period according to $\beta = 0.6$, but believes that when the next period arrives, he will discount the following period according to $\hat{\beta} = 1$ (no discounting). Consider an example where $v_1 = 11$, $c_1 = 0$, and $v_2 = 20$, $c_2 = 40$. In considering the options Kerry thinks he will perceive upon entering period 2 from the perspective of period 1, the five options are

Execute x_1 in period 2:	$u(1, 2\mid 2) = \dfrac{1}{1-\delta}11$
Execute x_2 in period 2:	$u(2, 2\mid 2) = \dfrac{1}{1-\delta}20 - 40$
Execute x_1 in period 3:	$u(1, 3\mid 2) = \dfrac{\delta}{1-\delta}11$
Execute x_2 in period 3:	$u(2, 3\mid 2) = \dfrac{\delta}{1-\delta}20 - 40$
Do nothing	$u(0, -\mid -) = 0$

Kerry doesn't believe he will discount quasi-hyperbolically after the first period, so he thinks all future decisions will be time consistent. Of these options, $u(1, 3\mid 2) < u(1, 2\mid 2)$, $u(2, 3\mid 2) < u(2, 2\mid 2)$, and $u(0, -\mid -) < u(1, 2\mid 2)$, and thus postponing action until the third period or doing nothing would be eliminated from consideration. Kerry will anticipate completing task 1 in the second period, given nothing is done in the first period, if $u(1, 2\mid 2) > u(2, 2\mid 2)$ or $\delta < 31/40 = 0.775$. Otherwise, he will anticipate completing action 2. In the first period he discounts all future outcomes by $\beta = 0.6$ and thus chooses among

Execute x_1 in period 1:	$u(1, 1\mid 1) = \dfrac{0.6}{1-\delta}11$
Execute x_2 in period 1:	$u(2, 1\mid 1) = \dfrac{0.6}{1-\delta}20 - 40$
Execute x_i in period 2:	$u(i, 2\mid 1) = 0.6\left(\dfrac{\delta}{1-\delta}v_i - c_i\right)$
Do nothing	$u(0, -\mid -) = 0$

Again, doing nothing is dominated by the option to do x_1 in period 1. Also, $u(1, 1\mid 1) > u(2, 1\mid 1)$ if $\delta < 173/200 = 0.865$, implying x_2 in period 1 would never be chosen if δ were below this number, and x_1 in period 1 would never be chosen if δ were above this number. If $\delta < 0.775$, then Kerry will always choose to complete action x_1 immediately because $u(1, 1\mid 1) > u(1, 2\mid 1)$. If $0.775 < \delta < 0.865$, then Kerry must choose between x_1 in period 1 and x_2 in period 2. In this case, $u(1, 1\mid 1) > u(2, 2\mid 1)$ implies that $\delta < 153/180 = 0.850$. Thus, Kerry chooses to complete task x_1 immediately if $\delta < 0.850$. However, if $0.850 < \delta < 0.865$, Kerry plans to postpone and perform x_2 in the next period, though in each period thereafter he will actually decide to continue to postpone because the same decision process is repeated. If $\delta > 0.865$, then Kerry must decide between performing x_2 immediately, or performing x_2 in the next period. In this case, $u(2, 1\mid 1) > u(2, 2\mid 1)$ implies $\delta > 1$. Thus, Kerry always chooses to procrastinate eternally if $\delta > 0.850$.

Over the range of $\delta \in (0.850, 0.865)$ Kerry continually postpones, hoping he will eventually perform task x_2. By always procrastinating, he obtains utility 0. The high-reward task has a large upfront cost but a much larger potential reward $20/(1-\delta) > 133$. The immediate cost and his time-inconsistent preferences lead him not to do the smaller-reward activity now but to continually postpone the larger-reward activity. If the larger-reward activity were not available (i.e., x_1 did not exist), Kerry would anticipate performing x_1 in the second period. In this case, the choice in the first period would be between $u(1, 1|1)$ and $u(1, 2|1)$. Kerry would always choose to perform x_1 immediately because $u(1, 2|1) = \delta u(1, 1|1)$. In this case, having a high-reward option available that is not immediately attractive can induce infinite procrastination, leading Kerry to be much worse off. Partial naïfs are not always better off when given more choices.

Uncommitting

Sophistication when possessing time-inconsistent preferences can be a double-edged sword. Although a person always wants to commit to a future consumption path to maximize his current perception of utility, when the future finally arrives, he will be willing to pay a premium to break that commitment. Consider Robin, a sophisticate who has trouble making it to the gym.

Let us consider an infinite-horizon decision problem in which each period represents a week. Exercising in any period yields an immediate cost of c and a reward in all subsequent periods of v. Moreover, suppose that Robin must pay k_0 each week as part of his gym membership, and that he cannot easily rescind his membership. In the first period, Robin anticipates that in any period t he will solve

$$\max_{x_t, x_{t+1}, \dots} -k_0 - x_t c + \beta \sum_{i=0}^{\infty} \delta^i \left(-k_0 - x_{t+i+1}c + \sum_{j=1}^{t+i} x_j v \right), \tag{13.70}$$

where x_t are dummy variables taking a value of 1 if Robin chooses to exercise in period t and a value of 0 otherwise. Robin will decide not to exercise in period t if the additional discounted utility of doing so is less than that of not exercising, or (using the properties of geometric series again; see footnote 2)

$$\frac{\beta}{1-\delta} v - c < 0. \tag{13.71}$$

Let us suppose that this is the case. Thus, without commitment, Robin would always choose not to exercise. The would-be athlete in period t will instead wish he will exercise in the next period (and each period thereafter) if the utility of doing so is greater than not doing so, or if

$$\beta \left(\frac{\delta}{1-\delta} v - c \right) > 0. \tag{13.72}$$

If this is the case, then the sophisticate in the first period must decide whether to exercise then, (and never again), or not to. Equation 13.71 implies that he will forgo exercising forevermore.

Now suppose that the gym offers two gym memberships, one that results in a weekly cost of k_0, and another that adds k_1 to the weekly cost (thus charging the member $k_0 + k_1 > k_0$ for the membership). For this additional fee, the gym agrees to fine gym members $k_2 > 0$ after any week in which they do not use the gym. Under this system, equation 13.70 becomes

$$\max_{x_t, x_{t+1}, \cdots} \begin{aligned} &-k_0 - k_1 - x_t c - (1 - x_t)k_2 \\ &+ \beta \sum_{i=0}^{\infty} \delta^i \left(-k_0 - k_1 - x_{t+i+1}c - (1 - x_{t+i+1})k_2 + \sum_{j=1}^{t+i} x_j v \right) \end{aligned} \qquad (13.73)$$

so that the athlete now forgoes the gym in period t only if

$$\frac{\beta}{1-\delta} v - c < -k_2. \qquad (13.74)$$

If k_2 is large enough, the threat of the penalty will act as a commitment mechanism, and Robin will plan to exercise in period t and not procrastinate. By participating in the commitment mechanism, Robin pays k_1 every week into the infinite future. This results, by the properties of geometric series, in a net present value of the cost given by $k_1 / (1 - \delta)$. The additional utility of exercising *every* week is given by

$$-c + \beta \sum_{i=0}^{\infty} \delta^i \left(-c + \sum_{j=1}^{t+i} v \right) = \beta \sum_{i=0}^{\infty} \delta^i (iv) - c \left(1 + \frac{\beta}{1-\delta} \right). \qquad (13.75)$$

Robin will buy the commitment mechanism and begin to exercise every week if

$$\beta \sum_{i=0}^{\infty} \delta^i (iv) - c \left(1 + \frac{\beta}{1-\delta} \right) > \frac{k_1}{1-\delta}. \qquad (13.76)$$

By offering the commitment mechanism, the gym is able to make more money from the sophisticated gym user, potentially increasing their profits (given that the cost of maintaining gym equipment does not increase too much). But this also creates another opportunity. Suppose Alex, an enterprising person who loves to exercise, sees that he can now make some money from the would-be athlete. In any period, while Robin would like to make a commitment for future gym use, he would also be willing to pay some amount to break his commitment. So Alex offers to pose as Robin, exercising for Robin and signing in at the gym under Robin's name. In return, Alex asks that Robin pay him $k_3 < k_2$. In this case, equation 13.74 now becomes

$$\max_{x_t, x_{t+1}, \cdots} \left\{ \begin{aligned} &-k_0 - k_1 - x_t c - (1 - x_t)k_3 \\ &+ \beta \sum_{i=0}^{\infty} \delta^i \left(-k_0 - k_1 - x_{t+i+1}c - (1 - x_{t+i+1})k_3 + \sum_{j=1}^{t+i} x_j v \right) \end{aligned} \right\} \qquad (13.77)$$

and Robin will decide not to exercise if

$$\frac{\beta}{1-\delta} v - c - k_1 < -k_3. \qquad (13.78)$$

So long as k_3 is small enough that equation 13.78 is satisfied, Robin will break his commitment and Alex will be paid to go to the gym.

In fact, any time time-inconsistent decision makers are willing to pay to enter a commitment mechanism, they will also be willing to pay to break the commitment at some future when it binds. This preference reversal leads to a money pump of the sort described in the first section of this book. We can pump all of the money out of sophisticates by first charging them to commit, then charging them to uncommit, and repeating. Some companies actually use such models. For example, time-share vacations allow users to commit themselves to vacations in advance by offering very low prices. Then, when the users cannot bring themselves to meet the commitment (work or other more important responsibilities encroach), they allow the members to pay a fee to cancel. Of course, such a money pump only works so long as sophisticates are not aware of the possibility to uncommit at the time they enter the commitment device. Once they get wise to this option, the pump is dead. Alternatively, partial naïfs might enter and sustain a money pump even with this knowledge. This happens because they do not fully recognize how likely they will be to pay to opt out of the commitment.

EXAMPLE 13.5   Quitters, Inc.

A short story by Stephen King, dramatized as one part of the movie *The Cat's Eye*, illustrates our willingness to enter into commitment devices and our lack of ability to control our own future behavior. The main character, Dick Morrison, finally wants to quit smoking, and, based on the testimonial of an old college friend, decides to try Quitters, Inc. Upon visiting Quitters, Inc., he finds that the company was originally founded by a mob boss who was losing the fight with lung cancer due to his own habit. The counselor he meets with openly tells him that the company had served as a front for the Mafia but that they still care very deeply about getting people to quit. In fact, his counselor guarantees that by the completion of their program, Dick will never smoke again.

Their plan illustrates a severe commitment device. Those who enroll will be under surveillance constantly. Those caught smoking will face severe and increasingly horrid penalties. For the first cigarette, associates of the program will kidnap Dick's wife and torture her in front of Dick. If he gives in to temptation again, Dick will be captured and tortured. Other family members would follow and suffer more-severe versions of torture. If Dick gives in to temptation a tenth time, a Quitters, Inc., associate will be sent to kill him, guaranteeing he will never smoke again. At once, knowing that such steep penalties face us, we would almost certainly find it much easier to keep the commitment to abstain from such indulgent but destructive activities as smoking.

In fact, many programs to help people quit addictions rely on addicts having friends or others who check up on them regularly. Although most of these do not include threats to personal well-being, they certainly include threats of embarrassment, but they also include support for those who are facing temptation. Such mechanisms seek to alter the cost and benefit associated with the behavior. If we truly had full control of our actions, no one fully intending to quit would be the least bit reluctant to join a Quitters, Inc.–style program. Our reluctance reveals quite a lot about the amount of control we truly feel we have over ourselves and the strength of our resolve. Thankfully for Dick, he was able to kick the habit with very few slip-ups. Now if he can only maintain his weight.

EXAMPLE 13.6 Illiquid Assets, Liquid Assets, and the U.S. Savings Rate

U.S. consumers hold the lion's share of their assets in illiquid assets, such as a 401k retirement account, or other assets that are difficult at best to access in the short term. Households keep an average of two thirds of their wealth in accounts that cannot be accessed immediately. We tend to hold very small amounts of money in savings accounts, CDs, or even mutual funds or stocks that could be sold in the short run. When our assets are in illiquid investments, we effectively limit our own ability to access and use our money.

Although holding such illiquid assets seems unintuitive generally, David Laibson notes that people with time-inconsistent preferences might seek such illiquid assets to prevent themselves from spending the money they should really be saving. Thus, illiquid assets function as a commitment mechanism for sophisticated (or at least partial naïf) savers. Given the opportunity to place their money either in an account that can be easily accessed or one that requires notifying the bank at least one period ahead of when they will need the money, a sophisticate might prefer the illiquid account even if the expected return on investment is lower than with the liquid account.

This is a simple application of the sophisticate model to savings decisions, but it is one that has some impressive implications. From 1947 to 1983 the average American had saved between 8 percent and 12 percent of every dollar he or she received. Then the savings rate began a long and rapid decline, bottoming out close to 1 percent in 2007. Several competing theories have tried to explain America's long trend toward living paycheck to paycheck. One potential explanation lies in the increasing amount of innovation within the financial sector.

Over the years since 1983, potential savers have increased their access to money through the wider distribution of credit cards, the introduction of automated teller machines (ATMs), and the introduction of assets that had properties of long-term investment accounts but that could be accessed more quickly and easily. For example, home equity lines of credit became much more prevalent, with people charging items to the increasing value of their home. Once approved for the line of credit, homeowners could simply start borrowing up to their limit, often using checks or a plastic card. Internet banking has further liquefied what would have been illiquid assets.

Without ATMs and Internet banking, one would almost certainly have to go to the bank to conduct almost any transaction. Such travel time and waiting in line creates a certain cost to access your money. Now money may be accessed at anytime from anywhere. Perhaps this introduction of additional liquidity contributed the eroding of the U.S. savings rate. After the recession of 2008, the savings rate started to rebound, at the same time that stock returns plummeted and consumer credit began to evaporate. One alternative explanation for the decline in savings is the expectation that stock returns would allow people to increase wealth without the hard work of saving. This expectation disappeared in 2008. The simultaneous evaporation of U.S. credit might make it difficult for economists to completely disentangle these competing explanations for wide swings in U.S. savings behavior.

History and Notes

When Robert Strotz introduced time-inconsistent discounting, he proposed a model that assumed sophistication. The model was originally introduced as a way to explain the wide use of commitment mechanisms. David Laibson, George Akerlof, and others then used extensions of this model in highly influential applications. As complicated as the sophisticated model might seem, it was the model that was originally proposed. The naïve model was proposed as an alternative when it was noted that people often forgo commitment when it could help them. This pair of models explaining time inconsistency has been widely used to explain investment and savings behavior, macroeconomic activity, and procrastination by workers. The implications for marketers are important. Often, less is more. Food distributers could charge more to dieters for smaller portions if purchased in advance (like a frozen meal). Selling commitment mechanisms can be big business. Often the commitment mechanism costs little for the seller to implement, but it can be sold for a substantial price. Credit cards themselves are an interesting example of a commitment mechanism. Someone who has not been able to save for a high-priced consumer item can commit to save for the item ex post. Similar payday loan systems exist for the intertemporally challenged among us. These firms charge ultrahigh interest rates (annualized rates are often in excess of 400 percent) for very small and short-term loans. The ubiquity of such evidence of time inconsistency has helped quasi-hyperbolic discounting models make their way into the mainstream of economic modeling and thought.

Biographical Note

Photo Courtesy of David Laibson

David Laibson (1966–)

A.B., Harvard University, 1988; M.S., London School of Economics, 1990; Ph.D., Massachusetts Institute of Technology, 1994
Held faculty positions at Harvard University

David Laibson's work on savings rates, retirement portfolios, and other macroeconomic issues has become some of the most widely read and cited work in recent economics history. The application of the quasi-hyperbolic model to savings revitalized the original work of Robert Strotz, bringing it into the mainstream of economics research. Particularly intriguing is the ability of such time-inconsistent preferences to explain how savers could at once hold long-term illiquid savings devices, yet demonstrate incredible impatience in their savings and consumption patterns. Without behavioral models, these behaviors would appear to be irreconcilable. Some of his other work has highlighted the impact of limits on rational decision making in other macroeconomics contexts, as well as the impact of default mechanisms on savings. In contrast to the theoretical work described in this chapter, much of his work relies heavily on sophisticated econometric analysis of investment data. By using field data generated by natural decisions, Laibson is able to provide clear examples of how behavioral effects are important in a general economics setting. Laibson has won high praise for his work, including election to the National Academy of Sciences.

THOUGHT QUESTIONS

1. In this chapter and the last, we have presented three models of intertemporal decision making: naïve, sophisticated, and partially naïve. As presented here and in the literature, naïve decision makers seem doomed to repeat their mistakes over and over. This seems unrealistic. Alternatively, sophisticates anticipate their procrastination problem perfectly and avoid procrastinating wherever possible. Thus, sophisticates would never procrastinate unless they anticipated that they would. This, too, seems unrealistic. Finally, the third model allows misperception of how one might act in the future, allowing unexpected procrastination. But this model also allows people to procrastinate forever, never learning from their mistakes.

   (a) Write about an experience you have had with procrastination and how the behavior may be explained by one of these models. (Write a mathematical model if you can.)

   (b) Write also about what parts of your behavior could not be explained by any of these three models. Is there a way to modify one of these models to include a description of this behavior?

2. Consider the savings club problem from Example 13.1. Suppose again that Guadalupe earns $30 each week but that the time period is only three weeks. In weeks 1 and 2, instantaneous utility of consumption (for a week of consumption) is given by $u(c) = \sqrt{c}$, so that marginal utility of instantaneous consumption is given by $0.5c^{-05}$. In week 3, Guadalupe has utility given by $u_3(\chi) = 0.371\chi$, where χ is the amount spent on Christmas gifts (there is no other consumption in week 3). The instantaneous marginal utility of Christmas is given by 0.371. Savings beyond the third period leads to no additional utility. The regular savings account offers an annual interest rate of 5 percent, compounded weekly, whereas placing money in a savings club offers an annual interest rate of r. For the following, it may be useful to use the formulas derived in Example 13.1.

   (a) Suppose that $\delta = 0.97$. Solve for the optimal consumption and savings decision in each period, supposing that the decision maker has time-consistent preferences. To do this, solve for the amount of consumption in weeks 1 and 2 and the amount of gifts in week 3 that yield equal discounted marginal utilities.

   (b) Suppose that $\beta = 0.5$. Solve for the optimal savings and consumption decision supposing the decision maker is a naïf.

   (c) Now suppose that the decision maker is a sophisticate. Solve for the optimal savings and consumption decisions.

   (d) Finally, suppose that the decision maker is a partial naïf, with $\hat{\beta} = 0.8$. Now solve for the optimal savings and consumption decisions.

   (e) Solve for the r that would be necessary to induce the time-consistent decision maker, the naïf, the sophisticate, and the partial naïf to commit to the Christmas club. What is the optimal savings and consumption profile in this case?

3. Consider O'Donoghue and Rabin's model of choosing when to complete a one-time task. Let $\delta = 1$, $\beta = 0.5$ and $\hat{\beta} = 1$. For each of the following profiles, solve for the time-consistent, naïve, sophisticated, and partially naïve optimal strategy. In each case, suppose that the task must be completed by the end of the fourth period.

   (a) $v = (12, 11, 10, 9)$, $c = (7, 8, 9, 10)$

   (b) $v = (7, 8, 9, 10)$, $c = (12, 11, 10, 9)$

   (c) $v = (10, 9, 12, 11)$, $c = (9, 10, 7, 8)$

   (d) $v = (9, 10, 7, 8)$, $c = (10, 9, 12, 11)$

   (e) Describe how the above illustrate propositions 13.1 through 13.4.

4. Consider the problem of the sophisticate who has a membership at the gym. Let us limit the problem to four periods. Exercising in any period yields an immediate cost of c and a reward in all subsequent periods of v. Suppose that the member must pay k_0 each week as part of the gym membership and that he cannot easily rescind his membership.

   (a) Suppose that the gym offers two potential gym memberships, one that results in a weekly cost of k_0, and another that adds k_1 to the weekly cost. However, for this additional fee, the gym agrees to fine the gym member k_2 after any week in which he does not use the gym. Solve for the maximum amount k_1 and minimum amount k_2 such that the sophisticate will commit for periods 2 and 3.

   (b) Now consider the problem of the entrepreneur who, for a small fee, will pose as the gym member, allowing him to shirk his commitment without penalty. Solve for the maximum fee k_3 that entrepreneur can charge given the amounts k_1 and k_2 in part a.

5. Consider O'Donoghue and Rabin's model of choosing when and which activity to do. In each case, suppose that $\beta = 0.6$ and $\hat{\beta} = 1$

   (a) Suppose $v_1 = 22$, $c_1 = 0$, $v_2 = 40$, $c_2 = 40$. Solve for the behavior that would result from a sophisticate as a function of δ.

   (b) Suppose $v_1 = 44$, $c_1 = 0$, $v_2 = 40$, $c_2 = 80$. Solve for the behavior that would result from a sophisticate as a function of δ.

   (c) For parts a and b, solve for the behavior that would occur if action 2 was not available.

   (d) Compare these answers to the examples in the text. What might this imply about the size of the rewards available and the tendency to procrastinate?

REFERENCES

Ariely, D., and K. Wertenbroch. "Procrastination, Deadlines, and Performance: Self-Control by Precommitment." *Psychological Science* 13(2002): 219–224.

DellaVigna, S., and U. Malmendier. "Paying Not to Go to the Gym." *American Economic Review* 96(2006): 694–719.

King, S. "*Quitters Inc.*" In *The Night Shift*. New York: Doubleday, 1978.

Laibson, D. "Golden Eggs and Hyperbolic Discounting." *Quarterly Journal of Economics* 112(1997): 443–477.

O'Donoghue, T. and M. Rabin. "Doing it Now or Later." *American Economic Review* 89(1999): 103–124.

O'Donoghue, T., and M. Rabin. "Choice and Procrastination." *Quarterly Journal of Economics* 116(2001): 121–160.

Thaler, R. H., and S. Benartzi. "Save More Tomorrow: Using Behavioral Economics to Increase Employee Saving." *Journal of Political Economy* 112(2004): S164–S187.

Advanced Concept

The Continuous Choice Problem with Backward Induction

Consider the choice problem presented in equation 13.1 for an individual who lives for three periods. Given consumption of c_1 and c_2 in the first two periods, the individual in the third period must solve

$$\max_{c_3} u(c_3) \tag{13.A}$$

subject to the budget constraint $c_3 \le w - c_1 - c_2$. As long as utility is strictly increasing in consumption, then equation 13.A is solved by $c_3^* = w - c_1 - c_2$. Given this solution to the third-period problem, the second-period problem is given by

$$\max_{c_2 < w - c_1} \{ u(c_2) + \delta \max_{c_3 < w - c_1 - c_2} u(c_3) \}$$
$$- \max_{c_2 < w - c_1} u(c_2) + \delta u(w - c_1 - c_2) \tag{13.B}$$

This is exactly the two-period consumption problem presented in Chapter 11, and it is solved where the marginal utility of consumption in period 2 is equal to the marginal utility in period 3 weighted by the discount factor

$$u'(c_2) = \delta u'(w - c_1 - c_2) \tag{13.C}$$

Recall from Chapter 12 that this is also the condition for the solution in the last two periods when solving the standard (and not the recursive) optimization problem. Let $c_2^*(c_1)$ be the solution to equation 13.C, given the level of consumption in period 1. Then, in the first period, the decision maker must solve

$$\max_{c_1} u(c_1) + \delta u(c_2^*(c_1)) + \delta^2 u(w - c_1 - c_2^*(c_1)) \tag{13.D}$$

This problem now behaves as the two-period problem, only now in the second period the decision maker receives $u(c_2^*(c_1)) + \delta u(w - c_1 - c_2^*(c_1))$. Now the condition for optimization is the first order condition given by

$$u'(c_1) + \delta u'(c_2^*(c_1)) \frac{dc_2^*}{dc_1} - \delta^2 u'(w - c_1 - c_2^*(c_1)) \left(1 + \frac{dc_2^*}{sc_1} \right) = 0 \tag{13.E}$$

owing to application of the chain rule. Cancelling like terms in equation 13.E and combining with equation 13.C yields

$$u'(c_1) - \delta^2 u'(w - c_1 - c_2^*(c_1)) = 0 \tag{13.F}$$

Combining the optimization conditions in equations 13.F and 13.C, we find that the solution to the three-period recursive optimization problem must solve

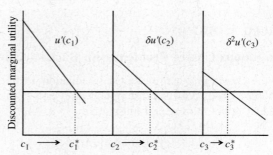

FIGURE 13.2
Optimal Consumption
in the Fully Additive
Model

$$u'(c_1^*) = \delta u'(c_2^*(c_1^*)) = \delta^2 u'(w - c_1^* - c_2^*(c_1^*)) \qquad (13.\text{G})$$

This solution is depicted in Figure 13.2, where the weighted marginal utilities of consumption are equal in all periods. This same visual was used in Chapter 12 to depict the solution to the nonrecursive problem.

If we considered the standard fully additive model from equation 13.1, the decision maker would simply solve

$$\max_{\{c_1,c_2,c_3\}} u(c_1) + \delta u(c_2) + \delta^2 u(c_3) \qquad (13.\text{H})$$

subject to $w \geq c_1 + c_2 + c_3$. This is solved where the discounted marginal utility of consumption from each period is equal, or

$$u'(c_1^*) = \delta u'(c_2^*) = \delta^2 u'(c_3^*), \qquad (13.\text{I})$$

which, when combined with the budget constraint $c_3 = w - c_1 - c_2$, is identical to the solution found for the recursive optimization problem.

If instead the consumer discounts the future according to the quasi-hyperbolic discount function, the problem becomes somewhat more complicated than that written in equation 13.2. Instead, the consumer must solve

$$\max_{c_1} u(c_1) + \sum_{i=2}^{T} \beta \delta^{i-2} u(c_i^*) \qquad (13.\text{J})$$

where c_i^* is defined recursively as solving

$$\max_{c_i} u(c_i) + \sum_{j=i+1}^{T} \beta \delta^{j-2} u(c_j^*) \qquad (13.\text{K})$$

where the budget set in each period is conditioned on the consumption decisions from previous periods.

We can solve this problem by backward induction as before. In the third period, given consumption of c_1 and c_2 in the first two periods, the decision maker must solve

$$\max_{c_3} u(c_3) \tag{13.L}$$

subject to the budget constraint $c_3 \leq w - c_1 - c_2$, which under the condition that utility is increasing in consumption will yield the solution $c_3^* = w - c_1 - c_2$. Next, we consider the second-period consumption decision. In this case, the decision maker will solve

$$\max_{c_2} u(c_2) + \beta u(w - c_1 - c_2) \tag{13.M}$$

which is solved where discounted marginal utilities are equal:

$$u'(c_2) = \beta u'(w - c_1 - c_2) \tag{13.N}$$

which is solved by some $c_2^*(c_1)$, similar to the second period of the three stage problem with exponential discounting. In the first stage, the decision maker now solves

$$\max_{c_1} u(c_1) + \beta u\big(c_2^*(c_1)\big) + \beta \delta u\big(w - c_1 - c_2^*(c_1)\big) \tag{13.O}$$

with first-order conditions

$$u'(c_1) + \beta u'\big(c_2^*(c_1)\big)\frac{dc_2^*}{dc_1} - \beta \delta u'\big(w - c_1 - c_2^*(c_1)\big)\left(1 + \frac{dc_2^*}{dc_1}\right) = 0 \tag{13.P}$$

Combining equation 13.N with equation 13.P, we can rewrite the relationship in terms of consumption in the first and second period:

$$u'(c_1) = \delta u'\big(c_2^*(c_1)\big) + (\delta - \beta)u'\big(c_2^*(c_1)\big)\frac{dc_2^*}{dc_1} \tag{13.Q}$$

Note that we can calculate dc_2^*/dc_1 by totally differentiating equation 13.N with respect to c_2 and c_1 to obtain

$$\{u''(c_2) + \beta u''(w - c_1 - c_2)\}dc_2^* + \beta u''(w - c_1 - c_2)dc_1 = 0 \tag{13.R}$$

or

$$\frac{dc_2}{dc_1} = -\frac{\beta u''(w - c_1 - c_2)}{\{u''(c_2) + \beta u''(w - c_1 - c_2)\}} \tag{13.S}$$

Diminishing marginal utility of consumption implies $u'' < 0$, so $-1 < dc_2^*/dc_1 < 0$.

We can contrast this solution with the choice made if the decision maker could commit to a consumption path

$$\max_{\{c_1,c_2,c_3\}} u(c_1) + \beta u(c_2) + \beta \delta u(c_3) \qquad (13.\text{T})$$

subject to $w \geq c_1 + c_2 + c_3$. Proceeding as in the previous section (replacing $c_3 = w - c_1 - c_2$), we obtain the first-order conditions

$$u'(c_1) - \beta \delta u'(w - c_1 - c_2) = 0 \qquad (13.\text{U})$$

$$\beta u'(c_2) - \beta \delta u'(w - c_1 - c_2) = 0 \qquad (13.\text{V})$$

implying

$$u'(c_1) = \beta u'(c_2) \qquad (13.\text{W})$$

If we compare this condition to equation 13.Q, the two consumption paths would be identical if $dc_2^*/dc_1 = -1$. But as we showed earlier, $dc_2^*/dc_1 > -1$. Moreover, if $dc_2^*/dc_1 = 0$, then equation 13.Q would be identical to the condition in equation 13.C, representing the exponential discounting case with a discount factor of δ. But we also know that $dc_2^*/dc_1 < 0$. In fact, the consumption path for the recursive optimization problem will always lie between the planned consumption path of the naïve quasi-hyperbolic discounter (which is identical to the optimal consumption path for a committed decision maker) and the consumption path of the rational exponential discounter with discount factor of δ.

Without the ability to commit, decision makers will choose consumption in the first period that is lower than consumption of the naïve quasi-hyperbolic discounter, because they know they will not be able to commit to the low level of consumption in the second period that would be necessary to preserve consumption possibilities in the third period. Moreover, decision makers will consume more in the first period than they would if they discounted all periods by δ because they still suffer from present-biased preferences—discounting all future consumption utility by $\beta < \delta$. In the second period, the sophisticated decision maker will choose to consume more than the committed decision maker. This occurs because the decision maker first anticipates that owing to present biased preferences, the decision maker will value utility of consumption in the third period at only β that of consumption in the second period at the time the decision maker makes this decision. Secondly, the decision maker consumes more because more wealth is left (consumption was lower in period 1). The sophisticated decision maker still consumes more in the second period than would the rational decision maker with discount factor δ. Finally, in the third period, the sophisticated decision maker consumes less than the committed decision maker.

To see this, note that equation 13.Q and equation 13.N can be combined to find

$$u'(c_1) = \beta \delta u'\big(w - c_1 - c_2^*(c_1)\big) + \beta(\delta - \beta) u'\big(w - c_1 - c_2^*(c_1)\big) \frac{dc_2^*}{dc_1} \qquad (13.\text{X})$$

First, consider what would happen if $dc_2^*/dc_1 = 0$. In this case, equation 13.X is similar to the condition for the committed consumer in equation 13.U, except that the sophisticated decision maker consumes less in the first period than the committed consumer does. This means that consumption in the third period would also be smaller given the utility functions are increasing and concave. However, the second term on the right side of equation 13.X is negative because $dc_2^*/dc_1 < 0$. This means that the first term is actually greater than $u'(c_1)$. Because of diminishing marginal utility of consumption, the only way $u'(w - c_1 - c_2^*(c_1))$ can be made larger is by further decreasing the argument—c_3. Thus, the sophisticated consumer ends up consuming less in the third period.

The lack of ability to commit leads to a loss in utility to the decision maker (which is illustrated in Example 13.1). Because the decision maker must put off consumption today to make sure his period 2 self will not leave his period three self with too little, the decision maker in period one feels worse off. He would thus be willing to pay some amount to allow greater consumption now, without endangering his third-period consumption. Thus arises the desire for a commitment mechanism: Let me consume more now, but make sure I don't indulge tomorrow. In longer-period problems, the commitment mechanism can allow indulgence today while ensuring that the consumer will consume at more-reasonable levels for long periods (potentially infinite) of time. Thus, the would-be dieter can eat with confidence knowing that tomorrow the diet will kick in whether he likes it or not.

SOCIAL PREFERENCES

Thus far, we have focused on how people deviate from standard models of economics owing to misperceptions or miscalculations or by using heuristics in their decision framework. A vibrant branch of behavioral economics examines how people deviate from standard models because of the way they incorporate others' actions or well-being into their own preferences. We commonly experience the kindness of others, often in cases where others appear to receive no reward for their behavior. At other times, we might feel that an colleague or teacher has it in for us and seem to be willing to damage us even if it means they must damage themselves in the process. Moreover, we may be motivated to treat someone differently depending not just on their actions but also on the motives we believe they possess. Thus, we might appreciate a heartfelt and sincerely given gift. However, if the same gift is given by someone trying to win our favor for some selfish purpose, we might just as soon decide to return the gift.

So much of our behavior is shaped by our social interactions with others, it would be hard to ignore the impact. For this reason, studies examining the impact of social preferences have a long history in economics. Behavioral economists have added to this literature by examining how these social preferences are formed and manifested and the effect they have on economic transactions. From the impact on savings rates to the rate of recovery from disasters, social preferences have major effects not only within the family but also in business management and public policy.

The next three chapters provide an introduction to social preferences. We begin by examining the nature of altruistic behavior, or kindness shown to others. Although altruism is not necessarily irrational, the majority of economic models assume purely selfish motives. Chapter 15 examines the desire people have for fairness; this leads them to seek evenly divided rewards. Additionally, people seek to reward those who are perceived to be fair and to punish those who are not. Finally, we examine the propensity of people to trust one another and to reward the trust they are given.

Selfishness and Altruism

14

One of the key features of *Homo economicus* is an utter disregard for anyone else. Generally, economic models feature actors who choose to maximize their own well-being, be it utility or profit, while ignoring the well-being of others. Such behavior is not required for rationality, but it is often assumed because it makes mathematical models of behavior much simpler. Some of the basic concepts in welfare economics, a study of how economic policies can affect the overall well-being of all actors in an economy, rest upon the assumption of selfish actors. The first fundamental welfare theorem states that under a set of strict conditions, including the condition that all actors in the economy do not consider others in their preferences, a competitive equilibrium is a Pareto optimum. Unless there is interference in the market through taxes or other actions, this result does not hold with actors who are not utterly selfish. In this case, actors in the market who care about the outcomes of others lead to a market equilibrium in which someone could be made better off without making others worse off. If only everyone could be a little more selfish.

The first welfare theorem was first proved by Gerard Debreu. Debreu won a Nobel Prize for, among other things, his proof of the first welfare theorem. When Debreu received his prize he was extolled by the press as the man who had proved that free markets get things right. One (possibly apocryphal) story relates that when he was asked to comment on his proof that markets "get it right," he replied that the number of questionable conditions and caveats necessary to prove that markets are Pareto optimal was so great that he almost wondered if in fact he hadn't proven that markets almost certainly get things wrong.

Economists generally refer to people who are willing to pay to make others better off as **altruistic**. Altruism is a subclass of **other-regarding preferences**, also called **social preferences**, or preferences that take into account the well-being or actions of others. Being altruistic does not imply irrationality. It is certainly possible to have complete and transitive preferences and still care about others. However, many of our theories conveniently assume that people only care about their own outcomes so as to simplify the theory or to make measurement of important outcomes using statistical data more straightforward. In fact, many economists who would not classify themselves as behavioral economists study altruistic behavior and use economic theories that assume some form of altruism. Nonetheless, the assumption of a purely selfish actor is so ubiquitous in economics that behavioral economists have focused substantial resources on determining the extent to which people care about others and how the welfare of others figures into one's decisions.

Exactly how selfish would one need to be to satisfy the conditions of the first welfare theorem? A well-known parable in Christian scripture refers to a man who was beaten and robbed and left naked by the side of the road. Suppose that *Homo economicus* happens to be walking on that road carrying three extra changes of clothes, bandages, and plenty of money. The unfortunate man asks *Homo economicus* how much he would take in exchange for a coat. *Homo economicus* replies, "This coat is worth $120 to me, I would not be willing to part with it for less." The bleeding man tells him that he has just been robbed and beaten, but that when he is able to return to his house, he could give him $119 (all he has). "Sorry, that is just too little for this coat." What about other clothing or bandages? "Well, I could sell you bandages for $5, and a set of clothes for $40. But that would be if you gave me the money now. If you cannot pay me until tomorrow, I would need to receive somewhat more. Moreover, if you only have $119 total, you sound like a bit of a credit risk to me. Do you have anything you can give me as collateral?" The bleeding man asks if *Homo economicus* could at least help the bleeding man up to his feet. "How much would you be willing to pay me to stand you upright? You don't have any blood-transmitted diseases do you?"

Our abhorrence of anyone who would act in such a way reflects just how foreign *Homo economicus* is to our notions of common, acceptable, and reasonable behavior. Nonetheless, this assumption is critical to much of economic thought. Clearly the feelings of others, our regard for cultural norms, and our concern for those in dire circumstances matter in our decisions and thus should matter in economics. Though many who have studied such matters would not classify themselves as behavioral economists, the assumption of selfish actors is ubiquitous enough in economics that behavioral economists consider other-regarding preferences as part of their jurisdiction. Altruistic behavior might not be irrational, but it demonstrates a deviation from the most commonly made assumptions of economic models.

On the surface it might seem simple to delineate purely selfish behavior from behavior that is motivated by a desire to help others. It turns out, however, that it is difficult to determine which behaviors are actually altruistic and which are based on self-interest. In this chapter we examine the empirical evidence of altruism and some of the applications. Of course, altruism is not the only form in which others' well-being can enter in to one's decisions. We also explore important theories of how we regard others and base our own preferences on how we perceive our neighbors.

EXAMPLE 14.1   Spoiling the Child

A commonly cited example of altruistic behavior is that of parents' willingness to sacrifice their own pleasure and consumption for the well-being of their child. It is estimated that including food and clothing costs, childcare, and other regular expenses, parents in the United States spend an average of $227,000 rearing their child. Beyond this, parents spend countless hours teaching, training, consoling, and nurturing children, all with the seeming goal of making them into independent and responsible adults capable of providing for their own happiness. Introspection might lead us to believe that this is truly altruistic behavior. Nonetheless, some point out that this behavior might all be self-interested.

Historically, many farmers had large families to provide labor for the farm. This provided plenty of incentive to keep a family well fed and in good health. One piece of evidence for work being a motivation to have children comes from 19th-century Sweden, where orphans were auctioned off to would-be parents. Sofia Lundberg found that parents were willing to bid much more for orphans who were healthy and able to provide substantial labor. Moreover, the parents were also willing to bid more if more work was needed in their farm or other operation. More recently, children might not be desired for the work they provide around the house while they are children but for the support and care they will provide when parents become too old to care for themselves. Even a bequest to children upon death may potentially be viewed as a reward in exchange for good behavior. In fact it is difficult to separate any single act a parent performs for a child from a potential reward that the parent might receive in return, thus making it difficult to detect any pure altruism on the behalf of the parent.

If parents truly desire to provide the child utility without receiving *anything* in return, they might end up encouraging (or at least failing to discourage) bad behavior. Consider, for argument's sake, parents with a child whom they do not care for except for what they will receive in return from that child in the form of elderly care. The parent might know that the child's ability to provide elderly care for them will depend on the level of bequest they promise the child as a reward, as well as on the child's eventual financial success. Thus, this parent decides to implement a schedule of penalties and rewards for grades, work, and other outcomes and habits that will prepare the child for financial success. These penalties and rewards might not be malicious, but they reflect the optimal incentive they can provide the child. Now, alternatively, consider altruistic parents who, in addition to caring about the level of elderly care they will receive, also care directly about how much fun, enjoyment, and utility their child obtains. In this case, the altruistic parent might not be willing to impose some of the same penalties because it would cause them some disutility. Thus, the child might not perform as well with respect to school, work, or other training because she does not face the same incentives. In this case, altruism could lead to an inefficient set of incentives for the child and also a reduction in the total resources available to the parent and child. Similar arguments suppose that charitable giving to those falling on hard luck could induce less effort on the part of those facing the hard luck.

Some evidence suggests that such inefficiency exists in some circumstances. Many firms (e.g., Walmart) are operated as part of a family organization. William Schulze, Michael Lubatkin, and Richard Dino theorize that if a family with altruistic preferences controls a firm, the same problem can arise in trying to provide the proper incentives for family workers to provide thoughtful, skilled, and timely labor and to prepare family members for the management task of taking over the business once the current CEO resigns, retires, or passes on. In fact the fraction of successful family businesses that manage the transition to the second generation is only about one third. Only about half of those that mange to pass the management of their family firm to the second generation are able to pass the business on to the third. In other words, people appear to be promoted to management positions because the current CEO cares about the family members rather than about their qualifications or ability to perform. Some have found, for example, that family firms are less effective at using strategic planning to obtain sales growth than firms not controlled by a family. This provides at least some weak evidence that family members may be held to a lower standard than others.

Rationality and Altruism

In Chapter 1, we defined *rational* in a broad sense as being embodied by preferences that are complete and transitive. *Completeness* simply means that given the choice between any two states of the world, s_1 or s_2, one either prefers s_1, written $s_2 \prec s_1$, or prefers s_2, $s_1 \prec s_2$, or one is indifferent between the two, written $s_1 \sim s_2$. Transitivity requires that for any three options s_1, s_2, and s_3, preferences must be such that if $s_1 \prec s_2$ and $s_2 \prec s_3$ then $s_1 \prec s_3$. If transitivity is violated, then we could devise a money pump by asking a person to pay to cycle among each of the three choices. If a person satisfies these two requirements, we can represent her preferences as a utility function, $u(s)$, that assigns a real value number to each state of the world s, where the person behaves so as to maximize the utility function over the set of available choices.

Altruism does not imply any violation of either of these rules. Define $v(s)$ as the utility function representing the well-being of some other person (not the decision maker) contingent on the state of the world. We may then represent an altruistic decision maker as having preferences embodied in a utility function of the form $u(s, v(s))$, where $u(\cdot, \cdot)$ is increasing in $v(\cdot)$. Here the impact of the first argument of the utility function may be thought of as the decision maker's utility of own consumption, and the impact of the second argument as the utility derived from the other person's well-being. For this to satisfy rationality would require that both people have complete and transitive preferences.

This approach might become clearer if instead of defining utility in terms of states of the world, we define utility based on consumption of some aggregate good x. First, let utility of the other person be given by $v(x)$, where $v(\cdot)$ is increasing in x. Then, where x_1 represents the amount of own consumption of good x, and x_2 represents the amount of the other person's consumption, we can represent the state of the world as $\boldsymbol{x} = (x_1, x_2)$, and define $U(x_1, x_2) \equiv u(\boldsymbol{x}, v(\boldsymbol{x}))$. Thus, we may denominate the decision maker's utility of the second person's preferences in terms of x_2, simplifying the model. Let $\bar{x}_2$ be the amount the second person would consume without any transfer of wealth from the first person. Thus, the decision maker would solve

$$\max_{x_1, T} U(x_1, \bar{x}_2 + T) \tag{14.1}$$

subject to the budget constraint

$$p(x_1 + T) \leq w_1, \tag{14.2}$$

where p is the price of good x, w_1 is the amount of wealth available to the first person, and T is the amount of consumption transferred to the second person from the decision maker. Note that this problem is identical to the simple two-good consumer problem introduced in the first chapter, except that both goods have the same price. The solution to this problem occurs where the marginal utility of own consumption is equal to the marginal utility to the first person of the second person's consumption. In other words, when consuming the optimal bundle, the first person should be indifferent between an additional unit of own consumption and an additional unit of the other person's consumption. Figure 14.1 displays the solution as the tangent point·between an indifference

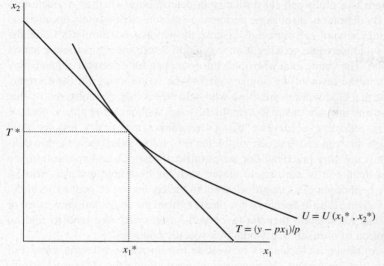

x_2

T^*

x_1^* x_1

$U = U(x_1^*, x_2^*)$

$T = (y - px_1)/p$

FIGURE 14.1
Utility Maximization with Altruistic
Preferences

curve and the budget constraint. Note that the budget constraint necessarily has a slope of -1 because both goods have the same price. It is this slope that ensures that the marginal utility of both goods is equal (see equation 1.6).

Now consider the second person. For clarity in this discussion, let's refer to the original decision maker as a parent and the second person as the child. Suppose the child has only selfish interests and derives utility only from own consumption, $v(x_2)$, where $x_2 = \bar{x}_2 + T$ and $\bar{x}_2 = w_2/p$, and where w_2 is the wealth of the child. However, suppose this child has a choice that could affect the wealth of the child and the of parent (e.g., how diligent the child is in the family business). The child could either choose option 1, which will result in $w_1 = 10$, $w_2 = 10$, or option 2, in which $w_1 = 12$, $w_2 = 9$. Which option would the child choose? If both parent and child were selfish, the child would always choose option 1, because it gives the child more wealth and thus more consumption.

If the parent is altruistic, the child might choose option 2 if the selfish child is given more than 1 unit of consumption in return. For example, if the parent's utility is given by $U(x_1, x_2) = x_1 x_2$, then marginal utility of the parent's own consumption is $U_1(x_1, x_2) = x_2$, and the parent's marginal utility of the child's consumption is $U_2(x_1, x_2) = x_1$. Thus, the parent will always choose to consume where $x_1 = x_2$. Suppose that $p = 1$. In this case, option 1 would result in a total of 20 units being purchased, with $x_1 = 10$ and $x_2 = 10$. The parent decides not to make any transfer to the child because the marginal utility of consumption is already equal for x_1 and x_2. Alternatively, option 2 would result in a total of 21 units being purchased, with $x_1 = 10.5$ and $x_2 = 10.5$. The parent decides to transfer 1.5 units of consumption to the child in order to equalize marginal utility of own and child consumption. Thus, the selfish child is better off choosing a lower personal wealth if it creates greater wealth for both the parent and child. Thus, the child might appear to behave altruistically, though the true motive for the child's generosity is pure self-interest.

In general, there is a philosophical difficulty in determining whether any action is purely altruistic. By definition, if someone performs a generous action solely because she believes the eventual reward will outweigh the cost, the action is not altruistic. Often the awaited reward is unobservable, making it impossible to determine if a particular action was altruistic or not. The young man who holds the door open for a decrepit old man may be expecting to win the favor of the young woman who is observing. In the extreme, those who believe that God will reward those who help others may be motivated by that reward rather than any intrinsic desire to help. In this case, without being able to observe someone's beliefs regarding a supreme being, we cannot technically test for pure altruism. Although this can cause severe problems for philosophical purists, this definition of altruism is not very practical. For the purpose of research and application, we often modify our definition of altruism to ignore such unobservable rewards. Thus, a birthday gift may be thought of as an altruistic act in the context of an economic study, even if the person giving the gift derives some pleasure from the appreciation received or if she harbors some expectation that the favor will be returned. We tend to find an operational definition of altruism that works in a specific context.

Altruism can introduce inefficiencies or welfare loss in many different ways. For example, suppose that the parents are considering either giving the child a Christmas present worth $40 or just giving the child $40. If the parents give the child the $40, then the child will choose consumer goods so as to maximize her utility subject to the budget constraint. However, if the parents buy a gift, they try to maximize their own utility function, which includes the utility of the child, $U(s, v(s))$. But what if the parents have some misconceptions about the child's preferences? The child might then obtain a utility $v(s)$ that is strictly less than what she would achieve by making a $40 purchase on her own. In turn, the parents then do not derive the amount of utility they anticipated because $v(s)$ is lower than they believed it would be. Joel Waldfogel refers to the resulting loss of utility as "the deadweight loss of Christmas." In fact, Waldfogel shows that more-distant relatives (uncles, aunts, and grandparents) are much more likely to give cash than in-kind gifts, theorizing that they do so to avoid this deadweight loss.

EXAMPLE 14.2   The Games Dictators Play

Given the difficulty in observing whether actions are truly altruistic in everyday transactions, it is common to use experimental economics to determine if people have other-regarding preferences. The most common experiments used to detect altruism are based upon the **dictator game**. The dictator game is actually not a game by formal definition, though it involves two players. In the dictator game, the first player, the dictator, is given some amount of money and asked to divide it between Player 1 and Player 2. The dictator may choose to keep as much of the money as she likes, and then Player 2 receives her share of the money. Thus, economic theory suggests that Player 1 will solve

$$\max_{w_1, w_2} U(w_1, w_2) \tag{14.3}$$

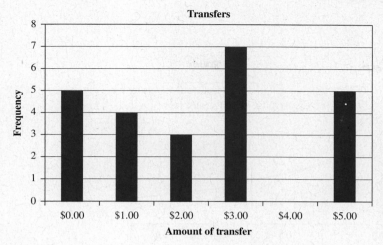

Transfers

FIGURE 14.2
**The Frequency of Transfers in the
Dictator Game**

Source: Reprinted from Games and Economic
Behavior Vol. 6(3), Forsythe, R., J.L. Horowitz, N.E.
Savin, and M. Sefton. "Fairness in Simple Bargaining
Experiments," pp. 347–369, Copyright (1994),
with permission from Elsevier.

subject to $w_1 + w_2 = w$, where w is the total endowment of money, w_1 is the amount allocated to Player 1, and w_2 is the amount allocated to Player 2. If Player 1 does not regard Player 2's well-being in her own preferences, then $U(w_1, w_2) = u(w_1)$. In this case, the solution is $w_1 = w$. But if Player 1 divides the money with $w_2 > 0$, then it must be that she receives some positive utility from giving Player 2 money. In fact, it must be that it provides her more utility to give Player 2 that money than to take it herself.

Robert Forsythe led a team of researchers who explored how people would react to such a decision. In one iteration, 24 different pairs of players played the game, with Player 1 being asked to divide $10 between the two. Player 1 was given instructions on how the game was played and was informed that Player 2 was in another room. Player 2 waited in the other room and then received her money. Neither of the players could determine with whom they were paired. Figure 14.2 displays the frequency of the resulting transfers. Of the 24 dictators, only five chose to take the whole $10, even though they could not be identified by their counterpart. This is the same number of dictators who decided to split the money evenly (valuing consumption by the other roughly as much as their own consumption). Almost three quarters of participants decided to allocate at least some of the money to an anonymous stranger. This at least provides some evidence that in rather clean conditions, people tend to regard others' preferences. Despite the clean conditions, the results have been heavily debated. Does this really indicate that the people regard others' well-being?

James Andreoni and Lise Vesterlund modified the dictator game by making it costly to transfer money to the other participant. Participants in their experiment were given a set of tokens that could be used to buy money either for themselves or for the other player, who was again anonymous. Thus we can think of the player solving equation 14.3 subject to a budget constraint $p_1 w_1 + p_2 w_2 = E$, where E is the endowment of tokens, p_1 is the price of own consumption, and p_2 is the price of other consumption. The relative prices (ratio of the price of other consumption to own consumption) ranged from 3/1 to 1/3. They again confirm that many people consider others' preferences in their own

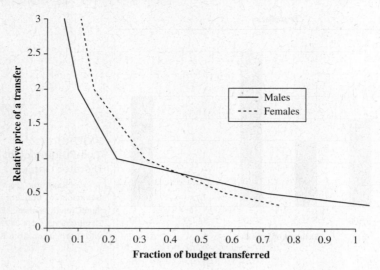

FIGURE 14.3
Gender Differences in
Response to the Price
of Altruistic Transfers
Source: Andreoni, J., and
L. Vesterlund. "Which is
the Fair Sex? Gender
Differences in Altruism."
*Quarterly Journal of
Economics* 116, Issue 1
(2001): 293–312, by
permission of Oxford
University Press.

decisions, but they find substantial differences in the response to price changes for the transfers depending on whether the dictator was a man or a woman. Figure 14.3 shows how the fraction of wealth transferred to the other responded to changes in the relative price of the transfer. Both men and women shared with their counterparts, but men tended to give more to their counterparts when the price of the transfer was low. This is most pronounced when the price is low enough that the total size of the pie to be shared is larger when some is given to the counterpart. Women, on the other hand, transfer more of their wealth when the transfers are costly. In other words, they are more willing to destroy part of the pie in order to share.

Andreoni and Vesterlund used the results from their experiment to examine how the responses of the participants resembled the behavior predicted by three well-known utility functions. If people don't regard others' preferences at all, their preferences could be represented by a selfish utility function, $U(w_1, w_2) = w_1$. This is the assumption most often employed in economic models. If instead participants prefer that both people have an equal wealth allocation, their preferences could be represented by a Leontief utility function, $U(w_1, w_2) = \min(w_1, w_2)$. This utility function essentially suggests that the person is only as well off as the worse off of the two of them. The marginal utility of money given to the one with less is 1, and the marginal utility of money given to the one with more (even if it is the dictator herself) is 0. Thus the best possible outcomes would be an equal division. This is an extreme form of other-regarding preferences, where the pain of anyone is everyone's pain.

Finally, if a person considers others' consumption to be a perfect substitute for her own consumption, her preferences could be represented by a linear utility function $U(w_1, w_2) = w_1 + w_2$. This utility function supposes that one is indifferent between own consumption and the consumption of others. In this case, the decision maker doesn't care who consumes so much as she cares that somebody consumes. Table 14.1 displays

Table 14.1   Other-Regarding Preferences by Sex

Utility Function	Male	Female
Selfish	47.4%	37.0%
Leontief	25.3%	54.3%
Perfect substitutes	27.4%	8.7%

Source: Andreoni, J., and L. Vesterlund. "Which is the Fair Sex? Gender Differences in Altruism." *Quarterly Journal of Economics* 116(2001): 293–312.

the percentages of each sex whose preferences most resemble each of these utility functions. A plurality of male participants are selfish in their preferences, and the majority of female participants display Leontief preferences. Female participants in this experiment tend to derive the most utility when consumption is evenly divided between themselves and others. Interestingly, a larger percentage of male participants consider consumption by others to be a perfect substitute with their own consumption. In all, female participants were 10 percent more likely to regard others' preferences. Similar results have been found by other researchers in variations on the dictator game, suggesting that while women on average are just slightly more altruistic, the nature of their altruism is very different from that seen commonly among men.

Rationally Selfless?

Although altruistic behavior is clearly outside the realm of the majority of economic models, it is unclear whether the altruistic behavior commonly observed in the laboratory or the field is irrational. Using the same data set already described, James Andreoni and John Miller created a series of tests for rational behavior. To test for rationality, we must define some notion of rationality. Each of the tests used by Andreoni and Miller essentially looks for violations of various forms of transitivity using **revealed preference**. People reveal their preferences when they make a choice among some set of choices. The chosen bundle of goods must yield at least as much utility as any of the forgone options. Economists can then use the revealed preferences from several choices to see if transitivity is violated. Several definitions are helpful. **Directly revealed preferred** and **indirectly revealed preferred** states are defined as follows:

Directly revealed preferred: The state s_1 is directly revealed preferred to s_2 if s_1 is chosen when s_2 is in the set of available choices.

Indirectly revealed preferred: If s_1 is directly revealed preferred to s_2, and s_2 is directly revealed preferred to s_3, and s_3 . . . to s_{T-1}, and s_{T-1} is directly revealed preferred to s_T, then s_1 is indirectly revealed preferred to s_T.

The available choices discussed here are the possible divisions of money between the dictator and her counterpart. In this case, people were allotted tokens that could be used to buy points. Each point was worth $0.10. The price of a point ranged from one to four tokens in the experiment, with relative prices for own and other consumption ranging from 1/3 to 3. The participants were also given various endowments of tokens. The endowment of tokens for a single decision ranged from 40 tokens to 100 tokens. This resulted in widely varied budget sets from which the dictators must choose the alloca-tion. For each budget set, the dictator chose one allocation, which was then considered to be directly revealed preferred to all other potential allocations in that available budget set. Then the dictator was faced with a new budget set that excluded some of the previous options and potentially included other options. The choices from various budget con-straints could then be compared to determine if the dictator had violated the constraints of rationality.

The definitions of the two preference concepts allow us to define several gradations of rationality tests. Each of these tests is based upon some application of the requirement of transitivity, as seen in the **weak axiom of revealed preference** (WARP).

Weak Axiom of Revealed Preference

If s_1 is directly revealed preferred to s_2 then s_2 is not directly revealed preferred to s_1.

WARP is the most basic requirement for transitive preferences. It simply states that if two budget sets both contain two possible allocations, w and w', the decision maker will not choose w in one of the budget sets and then choose w' in the other.

However, it is possible for a rational person to violate WARP. For example, consider the preferences represented in Figure 14.4, in which the indifference curves have flat portions. In this case a budget constraint like the one pictured can result in any choice along the flat portion without violating rationality. None of these choices is strictly preferred. Rather, they all lie along the same indifference curve, and the decision maker is indifferent to each possible division of money along these curves. In this case, someone presented with the budget set once may choose w, making w directly revealed preferred (and thus indirectly revealed preferred) to w'. Presented the next time with the same budget set, the person may choose w', thus violating WARP. If, instead, the indifference

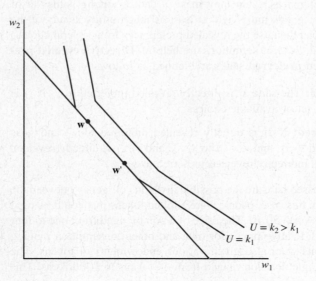

FIGURE 14.4
Violating the Weak Axiom of Revealed Preference with Rational Choices

curves have the familiar convex shape, a unique bundle represents the maximum utility that can be gained given a budget constraint, and this issue will not arise.

It is also possible to violate transitivity and satisfy WARP. For example, suppose the decision maker had to first choose between the two allocations $\{w, w'\}$ and chose w', so that w' is directly preferred to w. Then when faced with a choice between the two allocations $\{w', w''\}$ the individual chose w'', so now w'' is directly revealed preferred to w'. Finally, suppose that given the possible choices $\{w, w''\}$, the dictator chose allocation w. This is clearly a violation of transitivity, but it does not violate WARP. At no time in these three choices does she face the same pair of choices, eliminating the possibility of violating WARP. Instead, this violates a stronger condition on revealed preference, defined in the **strong axiom of revealed preference** (SARP).

Strong Axiom of Revealed Preference

If s_1 is indirectly revealed preferred to s_2, then s_2 is not directly revealed preferred to s_1.

SARP eliminates this violation of transitivity. In the example just discussed, w'' is indirectly preferred to w because it was chosen when w' was available, and w' is directly preferred to w. In fact, if a decision maker satisfies SARP on all possible budget sets, then she must satisfy transitivity, and her preferences can be represented using a standard utility function.

As with WARP, a rational person may violate SARP. Consider the preferences represented in Figure 14.5, in which the indifference curves have flat portions. In this case, a budget constraint like B_1 can result in any choice along the flat portion without violating rationality. None of these choices is strictly preferred. Rather, they all lie along the same indifference curve, and the decision maker is thus indifferent to each possible division of money along these curves. In this case, someone presented with the budget

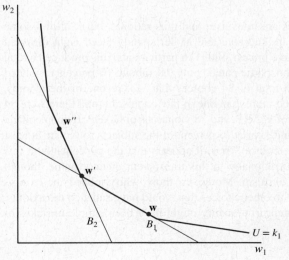

FIGURE 14.5
Violating the Strong Axiom of Revealed Preference
with Rational Choices

set B_1 may choose w, making w directly revealed preferred to w'. The same person presented with budget set B_2 may choose w', making w' revealed preferred to w'', and making w indirectly revealed preferred to w''. However, if the person is given the choice between just the two allocations w and w'', she may choose w'' because they yield the same utility, violating SARP. This leads us to an additional definition of preference relative to a budget constraint, **strictly revealed preferred**.

> **Strictly revealed preferred:** An allocation $w = (w_1, w_2)$ is strictly revealed preferred to $w' = (w'_1, w'_2)$ if it is directly revealed preferred and if $p_1 w'_1 + p_2 w'_2 < p_1 w_1 + p_2 w_2$.

Thus, a bundle is only strictly revealed preferred to other items that were available, but it did not lie on the boundary of the same budget set.

For example, in Figure 14.4, if chosen, w would not be strictly revealed preferred to w', but it would be strictly revealed preferred to w'', which is interior to the budget constraint. In this case, a rational person for whom greater amounts of both goods results in higher utility could never choose w'' when w was available. If w'' somehow happened to lie along the same indifference curve as w, then there must be some other indifference curve that yields higher utility that lies to the right of w'' and that meets the budget restriction. This is the case if indifference curves are not fat—in other words, if increasing the amount of both w_1 and w_2 always results in a higher utility. Indifference curves can only have width (and thus be fat) if increasing the amount allocated to both w_1 and w_2 results in no change in utility for at least some allocation in the set of possible allocations, a situation covered by the **generalized axiom of revealed preference** (GARP).

Generalized Axiom of Revealed Preference

If s_1 is indirectly revealed preferred to s_2, then s_2 is not strictly directly revealed preferred to s_1.

GARP implies that preferences are transitive, and thus rational, but it allows some violations of SARP. Participants in Andreoni and Miller's study faced eight different combinations of budgets and relative prices. With 176 participants, this produced a total of 1,408 choices. Of the 176 who participated, only 18 (about 10 percent) violated GARP, SARP, or WARP, with a total of 34 choices that violate one of the axioms, though some of the choices violated more than one of the axioms. In total there were 34 violations of SARP, 16 violations of WARP, and 28 violations of GARP. If people made choices totally at random, we would expect 76 percent of the subjects to violate at least one of the axioms of revealed preference. Thus, it appears that the participants in this experiment behaved very close to rationally in this transparent dictator game, though they displayed characteristics of altruism. Moreover, those who violated the axioms made choices that were very close to other choices that would have satisfied the axioms. In other words, some of the apparent irrationality might have been simple mistakes or approximation error.

Thus, while altruistic behavior may be outside the purview of *Homo economicus*, it does not fall outside the realm of rational decision making. This is not to say that all altruistic behavior is rational. Certainly under the conditions that would create preference cycling, altruistic behavior is also likely to display violations of rational preference axioms. However, under transparent choice decisions, we are as likely to see rational altruistic behavior as we are to see rational behavior in situations where altruism is not an option. More generally, GARP, SARP, and WARP have been used to look for rationality of consumers using data from real-world purchases (e.g., grocery store purchases). In many instances, it appears that consumers violate these notions of transitivity. However, when we apply transitivity to field data, we must recognize that we often cannot observe changes to the budget constraints or other shifting factors that make true comparison of available options and chosen bundles possible. Controlled laboratory experiments such as those conducted by Andreoni and Miller provide a much cleaner test of rational preferences.

EXAMPLE 14.3 Unraveling and Not Unraveling

One of the primary reasons economists generally suppose people are purely selfish is because it leads us to such simple predictions. In the field of game theory, we typically describe each possible outcome of the game in terms of payoffs, which are meant to be actual measures of utility rather than dollar rewards that one might derive utility from. Unfortunately, when we go to the laboratory or the field to test the predictions of our theory, we cannot easily assign or observe someone's utility.

Consider for example, the two-player take-it-or-leave-it (TIOLI) game (also called the centipede game) displayed in Figure 14.6. This is a sequential move game, in which each node (where two branches of the game intersect, represented by a black circle in the figure) represents a decision to be made by the player, indicated by the number above the node. Thus, in the first period, Player 1 can either decide to take it (labeled "T" on the diagram) and end the game, or leave it ("L") and continue the game. If Player 1 chooses T, then Player 1 receives a payoff of 0.40 and Player 2 receives a payoff of 0.10, and the game is over. If Player 1 chooses L, then in the next period, Player 2 can choose either T or L. If Player 2 chooses T, then Player 1 receives a payoff of 0.20 and Player 2 receives a payoff of 0.80, and the game ends. If instead Player 2 chooses L, then the game continues, and Player 1 gets to make the next decision, and so on until the last node.

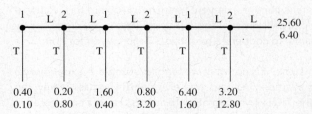

FIGURE 14.6
Take-It-or-Leave-It Game

In searching for behavioral predictions in games, we generally use the concept of the **subgame-perfect Nash equilibrium** (SPNE). Let us first review the definition of a strategy. A strategy for player i, s_i, is a list of choices player i plans to make—one for each node in which she has a decision to make. A simple decision for one node (e.g., in period 1 choose T) does not constitute a strategy. For example, a strategy for player 1 in this case might be $s_1 = (T, T, L)$ because it lists a choice to be taken at each possible node she might be found in. Note that this strategy indicates that in the first period Player 1 will choose T, in the third period (should the game get that far) she will choose T, and in the fifth period (should the game get that far) she will choose L. Clearly, if Player 1 chooses T in the first period, the game will never get to period 3 or 5. However, a strategy must specify what the player plans to do at each node in which she has a choice, even if she does not expect to arrive at that node. Let $\pi_i(s_i|\mathbf{S}_{-i})$ be the payoff received by player i for playing strategy s_i, when all other players are playing strategies represented by the symbol $\mathbf{S}_{-i}$. The Nash equilibrium is a collection of strategies $\mathbf{S} = \{s_1, \ldots, s_n\}$, such that for each player i, $\pi_i(s_i|\mathbf{S}_{-i}) \geq \pi_i(s_i'|\mathbf{S}_{-i})$, where $\mathbf{S} = s_i \cup \mathbf{S}_{-i}$. Intuitively, the Nash equilibrium is a set of strategies, one for each player, such that each player is maximizing her payoff given the strategies of all others involved. Thus, given the strategies of all others, any single player should not be better off for choosing a different strategy.

An SPNE is a set of strategies that constitutes a Nash equilibrium in every subgame of the original game. A subgame is any set of consecutive nodes containing the last node of the game. For example, the last three nodes constitute a subgame, but the first three nodes do not. The most common way to solve for an SPNE is to use the tool of backward induction introduced in Chapter 13. If we examine the subgame that consists of the last node (period 6), Player 2 can either choose T, resulting in $\pi_1 = 3.20$ and $\pi_2 = 12.80$, or L, resulting in $\pi_1 = 25.60$ and $\pi_2 = 6.40$. Player 2 does better by choosing T. Player 1 has no choices in this subgame. Hence $s_1 = \{\varnothing\}$, $s_2 = \{T\}$ is the Nash equilibrium for this subgame. Thus any SPNE must include a strategy for Player 2 that chooses T in the last period.

Now let us consider the subgame consisting of the nodes for periods 5 and 6. In this period Player 1 can either choose T, resulting in $\pi_1 = 6.40$, $\pi_2 = 1.60$, or L, resulting in the subgame consisting of the node for period 6. Because there is only one Nash equilibrium for the node 6 subgame, Player 1 must choose as if L will result in Player 2 choosing T, with $\pi_1 = 3.20$ and $\pi_2 = 12.80$. In this case, Player 1 would do better by choosing T. Thus, the SPNE for the subgame beginning with node 5 is $s_1 = \{T\}$, $s_2 = \{T\}$. Continuing with node 4, and so on to node 1, the SPNE for the game is $s_1 = \{T, T, T\}$, and $s_2 = \{T, T, T\}$. At each node, the player realizes that she can receive a higher payoff by taking now than by leaving, which would result in the other player taking in the next period. Thus, both players would be better off if they chose L for at least a couple periods before choosing T, but their immediate incentives prevent them from doing this. Rational players shrink the pie in the name of selfishly strategic behavior. There is no credible way (given just the structure of the game) to cooperate to obtain a larger payoff for both. This is called the **unraveling effect**.

As dismal as this prediction may be, it is not what we tend to observe in experimental games of the same form. For example, Richard McKelvey and Thomas Palfrey ran experiments using this form of the TIOLI involving 58 participants drawn from classes at Pasadena Community College and California Institute of Technology. Participants received the specified payoffs in cash. In all, McKelvey and Palfrey observed the game being played 281 times. Of those 281 plays, in only two plays did Player 1 choose T in the first round. In fact, the most likely outcome by far was for the game to end in period 4; about 38 percent of all games observed ended this way. Similar experiments have shown that when pairs play several TIOLI games in a row, alternating roles, substantial numbers never play T. This happens even though no matter how many finite periods it might alternate, SPNE predicts unraveling should reduce us to the same T in period 1 result.

Selfishly Selfless

There are many possible explanations for players choosing L in the early phases of the TIOLI game. One explanation is that people are somewhat altruistic. Recall that although SPNE is based upon the idea that the payoffs are measured in utility, in actuality the experimental payouts are in dollars. It could be that people derive utility not just from their own payment but also from the payment given to their opponent in the game. Thus, perhaps player 1 when facing node 1 would be willing to give up $0.20 in order to give the other player an extra $0.70. In fact, if each player is willing to cut her own payoff by 50 percent in order to increase the other person's payoff by 700 percent, the implied SPNE would now be $s_1 = \{L, L, L\}$, $s_2 = \{L, L, L\}$. Thus altruism in this case could help grow the pie to be split between the two players. Consider for an instant a Player 2, who is selfish and believes her opponent to be selfish (and that selfishness is common knowledge). In this case, if the game makes it to node 2, Player 2 must reconsider the behavior of her opponent. Her opponent is clearly not behaving like the rational and selfish person Player 2 anticipated. In this case, Player 2 might consider that playing L would lead to similarly irrational behavior by Player 1 in the future.

Both players do not have to be altruistic in order to reach the later nodes of the game. Consider the possibility that some players are altruistic and some players are not. Let us define an altruistic player as one who evaluates her utility according to $u(\pi_i, \pi_{-i}) = \pi_i + 0.5\pi_{-i}$, where i is the altruistic player and $-i$ represents the other player. Selfish players value only their own payoff, $u(\pi_i, \pi_{-i}) = \pi_i$. Suppose that both players may be altruistic, but that neither knows whether the other player is in fact selfish or altruistic. Let us consider how we might solve for the SPNE. Consider again the last node, in which Player 2 can choose either T or L. If Player 2 is selfish, she will certainly choose T, because it gives a payoff that is twice what she would receive otherwise. However, if Player 2 is altruistic, the, payoff for T is $u = 12.80 + 0.5 \times 3.20 = 14.40$, and the payoff for L is $u = 6.40 + 0.5 \times 25.60 = 19.20$. Thus, an altruist would choose L. This seems straightforward.

Now consider node 5. Let us suppose that Player 1 is selfish. In this case, if Player 2 is selfish, Player 1 would want to play T. Alternatively, if Player 2 is altruistic, Player 1 would want to play L, because it would result in a much higher payoff. Unfortunately, Player 1 cannot observe whether Player 2 is an altruist. Player 1 might have some guess as to the probability that Player 2 is an altruist, but Player 1 cannot know for certain. One way to think about the payoff is to suppose that ρ is the probability that Player 2 is an altruist. Then, choosing T at node 5 results in a payoff to Player 1 of 6.40. Alternatively, playing L results in probability ρ of receiving 25.60, and $1 - \rho$ of receiving 3.20. If Player 1 maximizes expected utility, then she will choose L if $\rho 25.60 + (1 - \rho)3.20 > 6.40$, or if $\rho > 0.14$. In fact, if both players believe that there is something around a 15 percent chance the other is altruistic, it is in their best interest to play L *even if they are both selfish* until the later stage of the game.

In this case, it is difficult for anyone to discern whether their opponent is selfish or altruistic by their actions. Rather, they can only rule out the possibility that the other is selfish and believes that all others are selfish. Such a player would always take in the first round. Thus, the very fact that there are *any* altruists can lead selfish players to cooperate and behave as if they were altruistic. In general, behavior that appears to be altruistic may be a result of some unobserved reward anticipated by one or more of the players in the game.

EXAMPLE 14.4   Someone Is Watching You

At first blush, the dictator game seems to be a very powerful test of altruistic preferences. Nonetheless, even in a laboratory, it is nearly impossible to control for all potentially important factors. As previously mentioned, it could be that players in the game are motivated by a belief that they are being observed by a deity and will be rewarded later for their actions. This would be very difficult to control for experimentally. Nonetheless, it is possible to approach some unobserved motivations in the common dictator game. For example, it may be that people are motivated to please the experimenter, whom they might believe will punish them for bad behavior at some point in the future. Many of these experiments are conducted by professors with students as participants. These students might anticipate that professors will form long-range opinions of them based on their behavior in this very short-run experiment. Moreover, it may be that people have simply become accustomed to situations in which their behavior is observed and rewarded. This was part of the motivation behind the experiments run by Elizabeth Hoffman, Kevin McCabe, and Vernon Smith examining the experimenter effect on dictator games.

Hoffman, McCabe, and Smith conducted experiments placing participants in several different versions of the dictator game. In some of their experiments, the experimenter was not in the room with the dictators and could not observe which decisions were made by which participants. In others, the experimenter made a point of receiving the money resulting from the decisions and recording it next to the names of the participants who made the decisions. In each of the conditions, the dictator was asked to allocate $10 between her and her counterpart. When the experimenter could observe the actions of the dictators, more than 20 percent of the participants gave more than $4 to the other player. More than half gave at least $2. Alternatively, when the experimenter was not able to determine who gave how much to whom, around 60 percent gave nothing to their anonymous counterpart, around 20 percent gave more than $1, and only about 10 percent gave more than $4. Clearly, many of the participants were motivated to act as if they were altruistic because the experimenter was observing rather than because they cared directly about the player who would receive the money.

Terence Burnham explored how anonymity of the dictator could influence decisions. He included a picture of the corresponding dictator with the money that was delivered to the other player. This, of course, creates the possibility that the other player could enforce some sort of social cost on the dictator in the future. Imagine what you might do if you ran into the dictator who gave you nothing in an experiment a few weeks ago. Knowing that their picture would be revealed to their counterparts increased the percentage giving $5 to the counterpart from 3.8 percent without the picture to 25 percent with the picture. This clearly suggests a certain amount of self-interest in the dictators' actions. This is perhaps to be expected.

Alternatively, when Burnham gave a picture of the recipient to the dictator (when no picture would be provided to the recipient), 25 percent of the dictators gave $5. In this case, there was no threat of reprisal. Burnham attributes this increase in generosity to the notion that people have an easier time showing empathy when they know about the beneficiary. In fact, this notion is on display in the advertisements and marketing materials for charitable organizations. Many of these organizations go out of their way to share the specific stories of people touched by the generosity of their charity organization. Some, such as Save the Children, go so far as to promise to connect a specific donor with a specific beneficiary so that the donor may learn about the beneficiary. The donor receives a picture and a description of the beneficiary's life situation and what makes the beneficiary deserving of help. Such details tug at the heartstrings and bring out the altruist in otherwise selfish donors.

EXAMPLE 14.5 Using Others as a Reference Point

We might often display altruistic feelings, but it is clear that we are not always motivated by a desire to make others better off at our own expense. In fact, it seems clear that in many cases, we consider our own feelings of well-being to be related directly to our status relative to our peers. Robert Frank argues that much of our behavior is driven by a desire to "keep up with the Joneses." Thus, when we observe our neighbor has bought a new luxury sport-utility vehicle, we now feel worse about our five-year-old midrange sedan.

Consider the following thought experiment designed by Frank. Suppose you were forced to choose between A and B.

Option A:	Option B:
You save enough to support a comfortable standard of living in retirement, but your children attend a school whose students score in the 20th percentile on standardized tests in reading and math.	You save too little to support a comfortable standard of living in retirement, but your children attend a school whose students score in the 50th percentile on standardized tests in reading and math.

This choice that might represent the economic choices so common among middle-class America. School districts tend to be supported by taxes in the district. Thus, districts that can afford higher levels of taxation are often able to fund much better instruction.

Moreover, if wealthier families use their excess wealth to buy homes in districts with better-performing schools, they drive up the price of housing in these districts. This means that to place children in better schools, a family must pay more in terms of taxes and housing. Many, given the choices above, choose Option B, considering it too much of a sacrifice to place their children in the lowest 20 percent of students. This problem states school performance relative to performance in other schools. Option A sounds particularly bad because children in these schools perform worse than about 80 percent of students in the country. But even if all schools in the country were spectacular in terms of their achievements, at least 20 percent of schools would necessarily fall below the 20th percentile.

Such framing of goods relative to what others receive creates what Frank calls **positional externalities**, which results from a very different set of other-regarding preferences. My owning a 3,000-square-foot house might make me much happier in a community of 1,500-square-foot houses than it would in a community of 5,000-square-foot houses. Suppose one lived in a community in which everyone owned a 1,500-square-foot house. This was about the median size of a home in the United States in 1973. If offered the opportunity to build a 1,600-square-foot house in this community, many in the community would be willing to pay a high premium. Owning the largest house on the block could be a great symbol of status and thus provide satisfaction beyond just the simple consumption of goods. But then a neighbor might realize she could add 100 square feet to her house without too much problem. Before long, anyone who has the resources is building a 1,600-square-foot home, and owning such a home begins to lose its distinction and status. By 1977, the median home in the United States was larger than 1,600 square feet. The median home is now almost 2,200 square feet. Eventually people build larger and larger homes to maintain this utility of status relative to their neighbors in addition to the utility of consuming. The marginal utility of house size declines as the houses get larger. It would not be worth it to purchase the larger house simply for the additional space. Rather, it only becomes worth it in the eyes of the buyer to purchase a larger home because of the status in conveys. Thus, the fact that others have larger homes reduces the utility I gain from a particular size home—an externality.

Consider a simple example of Lindsay, whose utility given by $u(x, r, c) = \sqrt{x} - 10r + c$, where x is the size of a home, r is the rank of the size of home compared to others in the town (equal to 1 if Lindsay has the largest house), and c is the amount of other goods consumed. Suppose that all homes in the town are 1,500 square feet. Lindsay is contemplating building either a 3,000-square-foot home or a 5,000-square-foot home. Further, suppose that a unit of consumption costs 1 unit of wealth (denominated in $1,000 units). Then, given that Lindsay maximizes her utility subject to a constraint on wealth, $p + c < w$, where p is the price of the home, we can determine Lindsay's willingness to pay to upgrade to the larger home by comparing utility with and without each house. Willingness to pay for the larger house should solve

$$\sqrt{3000} - 10 + (w - WTP_{3000}) = \sqrt{5000} - 10 + (w - WTP_{5000}), \qquad (14.4)$$

where the left side of equation 14.4 represents the utility obtained if Lindsay purchases the 3,000-square-foot house, thus becoming the owner of the largest house, and pays WTP_{3000} for it. The right side is the utility obtained if Lindsay purchases the 5,000-square-foot house, becoming the owner of the largest house in the community, and WTP_{5000} is paid. This implies that the additional willingness to pay would be given by $WTP_{5000} - WTP_{3000} = \sqrt{5000} - \sqrt{3000} \approx 15.9$. Thus Lindsay would only be willing to upgrade to the larger house if it cost less than $15,900.

Suppose instead that other homes in the town were all 4,500 square feet, and suppose that there are nine other homes in the town. Then, the maximum willingness to pay to upgrade to the 5,000-square-foot home from the 3,000-square-foot home would be given by

$$\sqrt{3000} - 100 + (w - WTP_{3000}) = \sqrt{5000} - 10 + (w - WTP_{5000}) \qquad (14.5)$$

because having a 3,000-square-foot home would yield the 10th largest house, but having a 5,000-square-foot home would yield the largest house. equation 14.5 implies $WTP_{5000} - WTP_{3000} = \sqrt{5000} - \sqrt{3000} + 90 \approx 105.9$. Now Lindsay would be willing to pay substantially more ($90,000, to be exact) to upgrade because of the status. The additional utility of having 2,000 extra square feet is only worth $15,900, but the added utility of being the biggest and best leads Lindsay to be willing to spend much, much more.

Suppose it cost $40,000 to increase the size of the planned house from 3,000 to 5,000 square feet. In this case, Lindsay would buy the larger house and take a large cut in consumption. However, this large cut in consumption is not in order to obtain utility of space but to obtain utility of status. Note that if everyone in town had similar preferences, everyone in town could be made better off if *all* choose smaller houses so long as the rank ordering was maintained. In this case, all residents could maintain their status while reducing their expenditures on housing until marginal expense is closer to marginal utility of use.

Psychologists have used simple questions about personal well-being to find very telling relationships between wealth and well-being. You might expect that peoples' tendency to compare themselves to their neighbors might lead to a situation such that if one person experiences an increase in income she will believe her well-being has increased, but if everyone's income increases she will consider herself no better off. Richard A. Easterlin compared surveys of individual well-being in countries experiencing massive growth in the 1960s and 1970s, finding a high correlation between income and well-being in any given country but a relatively low correlation across countries. For decades, this was described as the Easterlin paradox. However, cross-country data in that era were spotty and of relatively low quality, especially for developing countries that could experience such growth. More recently, Betsey Stevenson and Justin Wolfers have examined broader multinational datasets that have been collected much more systematically and have found extremely high correlations between income and well-being at both the individual and national levels. This result does not tell us that relative income doesn't matter so much as it tells us that absolute income matters a lot in determining individual well-being.

More-definitive evidence regarding the importance of relative income comes from women's labor-market decisions. Here, economists have found that a woman's decision to work is highly correlated with the difference between her brother-in-law's (sister's husband's) income and her own husband's income. Controlling for other factors, if a brother-in-law earns more money than her own husband, the woman is more likely to decide to work outside the home, perhaps to keep up with her sister's consumption. This effect might also play a role in the low rate of savings observed among Americans relative to the rest of the world. Americans face a much more unequal distribution of income and thus it is very difficult for even middle class people to keep up with their richer peers.

EXAMPLE 14.6   Growing Up Selfish

Economists have often argued that we learn to be rational as we gain experience in the marketplace. Thus, it would seem, adults should behave more rationally considering the additional exposure they have gained in making transactions and bargaining in the real world. William Harbaugh, Kate Krause, and Steven Liday set out to see if children truly develop into something resembling *Homo economicus* as they mature. Such studies of how decision making changes as children mature is common among developmental psychologists, but it is a true novelty among economists.

They enlisted 310 children in second, fourth, fifth, ninth, and twelfth grades to play the standard dictator game. The game was played with tokens that were worth $0.25 each. Each dictator was given 10 tokens to allot between herself and another child of her age. Both the dictator and her counterpart were anonymous, though children knew that they were playing the game with another child in their class. Recall that adults tend to give their counterpart an average of around $2 in the $10 dictator game. This is similar to the behavior observed in the twelfth-grade participants: They allocated an average of 2.1 tokens to their counterpart. This contrasts sharply with children in grades four, five, and nine, in which the average is less than 1.5 tokens being allocated to the other player. It appears that preteens and adolescents are more selfish than adults. Most selfish of all were those in second grade, who gave an average of 0.35 tokens to their counterpart. In fact, the youngest among those tested appeared to behave more like the predictions common in economic theory—ultraselfish—than the more-mature participants.

Given the structure of their experiments, it is difficult to draw any clear conclusions about how a child's development relates to the development of altruistic behavior. However, the authors argue that their data suggest that altruistic behavior is ingrained in us culturally in our childhood and that many of the differences in how we behave may be a product of our social relationships in these formative years. The fact that children are more selfish than adults is probably not surprising to anyone outside the field of economics. In fact, we commonly call selfish people childish, and parents work hard to teach their children to think of others. Outside the field of economics, many probably take comfort in the notion that people attaining the age of majority have come to display altruistic attributes. For economists, however, this means more-complicated models are needed to describe those we are most often interested in studying.

Public Goods Provision and Altruistic Behavior

One of the primary applications of economics to public policy is in the study of how one can efficiently provide public goods. A **public good** is defined as a good that is nonrival and nonexcludable. **Nonrival** means that one person consuming the good does not prevent others from consuming the good also and does not diminish others' utility of consumption. **Nonexcludable** means that it is not possible to bar someone from consuming the good. One example of a public good is national defense. It would not be possible to provide a defense from foreign invasion only to people in the country who paid for the defense. We must either defend our borders and government functions to preserve them for all or let the invading power take over for all. This makes it a nonexcludable good. Moreover, my deriving utility from the national defense does not diminish your utility from that same national defense. The problem with providing public goods is that a free market cannot generate the revenues necessary to provide the level of the good that would make all consumers best off.

Consider the issue of flood control on the Mississippi river. Suppose each farmer in the floodplain of the Mississippi is asked to contribute to the flood control system. There are thousands of farmers in the floodplain. Suppose each one has a utility function $u(c, x) = c + x^{0.5}$, where c is consumption denominated in dollars and x is the level of flood control provided, also denominated in dollars. Suppose further that each farmer has an endowment of wealth, w, that can be allocated to consumption or given to the flood-control effort. Although consumption is private, and thus dollars spent on c are consumed only by the farmer spending the dollars, flood control is public. If any farmer contributes to flood control, every farmer is able to benefit from that contribution.

If flood control were excludable, a firm could charge each farmer her willingness to pay for the level of flood control provided. The profits to this firm would be given by willingness to pay for the level of flood control multiplied by the number of farmers, minus the cost of flood control. This can be written as

$$\max_x nx^{0.5} - x, \tag{14.6}$$

where n is the number of farmers. Note, $x^{0.5}$ is willingness to pay for flood control because $x^{0.5}$ would be required to purchase consumer goods yielding the same utility as this x amount of flood control. Marginal revenue of this flood-control firm is given by $MR = 0.5 \times nx^{-0.5}$ and marginal cost is given by $MC = 1$. Hence, profit would be maximized where

$$x = \frac{n^2}{4}. \tag{14.7}$$

Thus, if we could charge the farmers for their flood protection and exclude those who did not pay, we could charge $n/2$ and provide $n^2/4$ to all who paid. Suppose there were 4,000 farmers. This would result in $x = 4,000,000$ in flood protection. Summing up the utility from each of the farmers, this results in total utility to all farmers from flood protection of $nx^{0.5} = 4,000 \times 2,000 = 8,000,000$.

But recognize that because x is a public good it is thus nonexcludable. All farmers will benefit from flood protection whether they contribute their own money to additional flood protection or not. In this case, no one will be willing to pay for additional units of x unless their personal benefit directly from the increase in x exceeds their own cost. Note that, $x = \sum_i x_i$, where x_i indicates the contribution of farmer i to flood control. The individual farmer decides how much to contribute by setting her own marginal utility of consumption equal to her private marginal utility of flood protection. Marginal utility of consumption is given by $\partial u / \partial c = 1$, and marginal utility of flood protection is given by $\partial u / \partial x_i = 0.5x^{-0.5}$, where $x = \sum_i x_i$. Recognizing that the budget constraint requires that $c = w - x_i$, the optimal allocation occurs where

$$\frac{\partial u \left(w - x_i, \, x_i + \sum_{j \neq i} x_j \right)}{\partial c} = 1 = 0.5(x_i + \sum_{j \neq i} x_j)^{-0.5} = \frac{\partial u \left(w - x_i, \, x_i + \sum_{j \neq i} x_j \right)}{\partial x_i}, \quad (14.8)$$

which implies that

$$x_i = \begin{cases} 0.25 - \sum_{j \neq i} x_j & \text{if} \quad \sum_{j \neq i} x_j \leq 0.25 \\ 0 & \text{if} \quad \sum_{j \neq i} x_j > 0.25 \end{cases}, \quad (14.9)$$

where the farmer will choose to contribute nothing if all other farmers combined have already contributed 0.25 or more. If all farmers are identical and make identical contributions in equilibrium, the solution is for each to contribute $x_i = 0.25/n$, which if there are 4,000 farmers, is only 0.0000625. This results in exactly $x = 0.25$, a much lower level of flood control than if we could exclude farmers from flood protection they did not pay for. This results in total utility of all farmers from flood protection of only $nx^{0.5} = 4,000 \times 0.5 - 2,000$, much less than the 8,000,000 that would result if we could exclude people from consuming flood protection they did not pay for. This is an example of the **free-rider problem**.

One way that governments and policy makers have tried to deal with the free-rider problem is by providing government grants for public goods. For simplicity, let us suppose that the government now taxes each individual farmer T and then contributes the total to the public good—in this case flood protection. The question is how this public funding affects the private giving by each farmer. Under the tax-and-grant plan, $x = \sum_i x_i + nT$, because now each farmer must pay T. The condition for the optimal level of individual contribution is again solved where the marginal utility of consumption equals the marginal utility of contributing to flood control, where now equation 14.8 becomes

$$\frac{\partial u \left(w - T - x_i, \, x_i + \sum_{j \neq i} x_j \right)}{\partial c} = 1 = 0.5(x_i + nT + \sum_{j \neq i} x_j)^{-0.5}$$

$$= \frac{\partial u \left(w - T - x_i, \, x_i + \sum_{j \neq i} x_j \right)}{\partial x},$$

(14.10)

which results in the solution

$$x_i = \begin{cases} 0.25 - nT - \sum_{j\neq i} x_j & \text{if} \quad nT + \sum_{j\neq i} x_j \leq 0.25 \\ 0 & \text{if} \quad nT + \sum_{j\neq i} x_j > 0.25 \end{cases}. \qquad (14.11)$$

So long as the tax is not so much that the individual farmer does not give at all, every dollar that is given in the grant (represented by nT) results in a completely equivalent reduction in the giving of the farmers. So long as there is still private contribution in addition to the grant, $x = 0.25$ no matter how much is given through the tax. Thus public contributions crowd out private contributions and should only result in an efficient allocation if private contributions are crowded out entirely. This general result is called the **crowding-out effect** and holds for almost any public goods problem in which the individual farmer cares about the provision of the public good.

| EXAMPLE 14.7 | Warm Glow Giving |

Several studies have tried to test for the crowding-out effect. For example, Kenneth Chan led a team of researchers who ran experiments in a laboratory simulating the public goods problem as described in the previous section. Participants were placed in small groups and were given an apportionment of tokens that could be allocated either to a private good or a public good. The private good would yield a money payoff just for them. The public good would yield a payoff for all in the group. The experiment was run several times, with some treatments involving a mandatory tax to provide a public good. Participants were given 20 tokens to allocate in each round. With no tax, people voluntarily contributed an average of 4.9 tokens to the public good. A second round taxed each participant 3 tokens and allocated it toward the public good. Notice that 3 tokens is less than the average contribution, and thus we would expect the tax to reduce voluntary contributions by exactly 3 tokens to 1.9. Instead people voluntarily gave 2.9 tokens in addition to the 3-token tax. A third round of the experiment required a 5-token tax. In this round, people voluntarily contributed 1.5 tokens. In other words, there was some degree of crowding out, but not to the extent economic theory would predict.

This result mirrors results observed in the real world. For example, increases in federal or state contributions to higher education do not lead to a dollar-for-dollar decrease in voluntary giving to higher education. Neither did the rise of public welfare programs eradicate private contributions to welfare. Why do people continue to give their private contributions to these public goods even when the government increases their contributions? One theory is that people are motivated to give by the **warm glow** of knowing that they have contributed. Thus, people might have a utility function described by $u(c, x, x_i)$, so that they derive some utility from the provision of the public good, x, but also derive some utility from contributing to that public good. Preferences of this nature are referred to as reflecting **impure altruism**, because they display a selfish (or private) value of giving to the public good.

Suppose, for example that $u(c, x, x_i) = c + (x + x_i)^{0.5}$. Under this new utility function, marginal utility of consumption is still $\partial u / \partial c = 1$. But now, marginal utility of contributing to flood protection is given by $\frac{\partial u}{\partial x_i} = (x + x_i)^{-0.5}$ where again $x = \sum_i x_i + nT$, so that now own giving is valued twice in the utility of flood protection potentially owing to a warm-glow feeling. Now we can modify equation 14.10 to accommodate the new utility function. Equating the marginal utility of giving and the marginal utility of consumption requires

$$1 = (2x_i + nT + \sum_{j \neq i} x_j)^{-0.5} \tag{14.12}$$

which is solved where

$$x_i = \begin{cases} \dfrac{1 - nT - \sum_{j \neq i} x_j}{2} & \text{if} \quad nT + \sum_{j \neq i} x_j \leq 1 \\ 0 & \text{if} \quad nT + \sum_{j \neq i} x_j > 1 \end{cases} \tag{14.13}$$

Note that raising the tax by 1 unit per person increases provision of the good by n units but decreases private giving only by $n/2$. Increasing the government contribution to the public good reduces the amount of the personal contribution to the public good, but by less than the amount of the tax on the individual, so long as $\partial u(c, x, x_i)/\partial x_i > 0$. Because the decision maker derives utility directly from giving and not just from the public good itself, government contributions will not directly crowd out private giving.

Although the theory of warm-glow giving has found much support in both field and laboratory tests, it is not the only possible explanation for incomplete crowding out. For example, one alternative explanation for why people might continue to give even when government has forced some contribution through a tax is that they believe their gift will lead others to decide to give also. For example, placing money in a plate passed at a church service provides some information to others and might induce them to decide to give as well. If the individual contributor believes that a contribution will result in contributions from others, she will believe her donations matter more than just the value of a dollar. If the primary motivation to give is to induce such donations from others, the government contribution might not be fully crowded out. The experimental evidence is quite consistent with the notion that people truly behave as if they receive some private satisfaction from contributing to others, and this has become the most commonly accepted theory among public goods economists.

EXAMPLE 14.8   Disaster Recovery

Several times each year, pictures from some wasteland of a developing country grace our television and computer screens. Whether from hurricanes, earthquakes, tsunamis, or human-made causes, widespread disaster can have a devastating impact on the lives of poor people throughout the world. The call goes out to donate for the relief efforts, and international organizations send in money, food, and other supplies to help. Despite the best efforts of all, recovery is often a long and difficult path. Many continue to feel the effects of the disaster decades after the initial event.

Such was the case with hurricane Mitch, which hit Honduras in October 1998. Mitch had a measurable and durable impact on the lives and livelihoods of Honduran citizens. Immediately upon impact, one third of the value of that year's crop was destroyed, and homes, infrastructure, and farming structures were also destroyed. Farm land was eroded to the point that farms would be unproductive without significant investments in soil and landscape improvement. Farmers' investments were wiped away, leaving them with less-productive farms and with incomes that would be permanently lower without further investment. It is estimated that 5 percent of the population was immediately reduced to poverty, increasing the poverty rate to 75 percent.

In developing countries such as Honduras, where financial markets and formal insurance might be unavailable to most, the speed of recovery depends very heavily on the ability of informal mechanisms to function. Thus, the ability of the rural poor to care for one another, often without monetary or material reward, can help speed the recovery. Michael Carter and Marco Castillo set out to determine the extent to which altruism can help speed the recovery from a disaster. They collected experimental data from 389 farm households in Honduras a few years after hurricane Mitch.

Each household, in addition to answering several questions about the damage they suffered and their recovery from Mitch, also participated in a dictator game with other households. The dictator game asked them to divide money between themselves and another household. Any money passed to the other household would be tripled. On average, households passed 42 percent to others. More impressively, how much people shared with others was directly related to the speed of the recovery. Increasing the amount of altruistic giving by 10 percent was associated with a 1 percent increase in the rate of recovery (rate at which they returned to their previous level of assets). This suggests that in communities for which altruism is the norm, recovery from natural disasters may be much more effective for all. Perhaps such observations provide us some clues as to how altruism became so prevalent in modern societies.

History and Notes

Altruism is not only a topic of interest for economists or other social scientists. Evolutionary biologists have also taken an interest in altruistic behavior. Much like economics, the study of evolution often assumes that people maximize not their utility function but their own fitness, most often defined as one's ability to pass on one's genes to the next generation. At first blush, it would seem that risking your own life or reducing your own sustenance would reduce fitness. However, many examples of seemingly altruistic behavior can be found in nature. For example, Gary Becker notes that baboons often risk substantial harm to protect other baboons. Nonetheless, such acts of seeming altruism can help promote fitness for the group, increasing the probability that genes are passed on for any one individual. More prominently, sociobiologists argue that altruistic motives toward children may be directly motivated by fitness. Similarly, altruistic behavior can lead to outcomes that are superior to purely selfish behavior under a wide set of circumstances.

Among humans, evolutionary psychologists have theorized about the attraction of females to males who are kind, and reciprocally males' tendency to display kindness to females but to act aggressively at other times. Clearly no female would want a mate who would threaten their children. But with every such theory we find counterexamples. For example, male grizzly bears often attack grizzly cubs under the protection of their mother. The female praying mantis eats her mate after fertilization. The female of some species of spiders eats a potential mate that is deemed not attractive enough. In a true oddity of evolution, a persistent and relatively stable percentage of fishing spiders engage in **excess sexual cannibalism**. That is, some set such a high bar for a mate that they kill and eat every potential mate, thus never passing their genes along. It would seem such a practice should be weeded out in short order, though it persists. In general, although altruism might have its roots in evolution, this is not to the exclusion of malicious behavior. Malicious behavior is to be found among humans as well, as we discuss in the following two chapters.

Biographical Note

Courtesy of Robert H. Frank

Robert H. Frank (1945–)

B.S., Georgia Institute of Technology, 1966; M. A., University of California at Berkeley, 1971; Ph. D., University of California at Berkeley, 1972 Held faculty or visiting positions at Cornell University, École des Hautes Études et Sciences Sociales (Paris), Stanford University, International Institute of Management (West Berlin)

When Robert Frank had completed his undergraduate studies in mathematics, he immediately joined the Peace Corps. As a Peace Corps volunteer he taught science and mathematics in Nepal. After his return to the United States, he earned an M.A. degree in statistics on his way to a Ph.D. in economics. Frank is well known for his contributions to economics in examining the role of emotions and status. In addition to his studies of how positional externalities and inequality can undermine the middle class, Frank has also examined how such seemingly irrational emotions like romance and rage may be beneficial and functional when considered in longer-term relationships. Frank has been a prolific author of highly respected and widely cited academic papers and of best-selling books written for a lay audience. Books such as *Falling Behind*, *Choosing the Right Pond*, and *Passions in Reason* have had an influence well beyond the field of economics. Frank regularly writes a column of economic issues for the *New York Times*, providing insights on how economists think about current policy debates. He has also authored and coauthored several introductory-level economics textbooks. His work on inequality has led him to advocate for progressive consumption taxes, which would discourage excess consumption. Such a tax could help alleviate the "keeping up with the Joneses" effect.

THOUGHT QUESTIONS

1. Economists often model businesses as strictly maximizing profits. However, we also observe many firms giving money to charity or providing some of their products to disadvantaged consumers for free or at a reduced price. Are these acts altruistic? What other motives might firms have? Use real-world examples to argue your case.

2. Consider Hong, who is endowed with a number of tokens. The tokens can be allocated between Hong and another person. Each unit of Hong's own consumption, x_1, can be purchased for p_1 tokens. Each unit of the other person's consumption, x_2, can be purchased for p_2 tokens. Consider each of the following sets of choices. Determine if each violates WARP, SARP, or GARP.

   (a) When endowed with 20 tokens, with $p_1 = 1$ and $p_2 = 1$ Hong chooses $x_1 = 17$, $x_2 = 2.05$. When endowed with 30 tokens, with $p_1 = 0.5$, $p_2 = 10.5$, Hong chooses $x_1 = 18$, $x_2 = 2$. When endowed with 100 tokens, with $p_1 = 1.72$, $p_2 = 2.9$, Hong chooses $x_1 = 20$, $x_2 = 1.9$.

   (b) When endowed with 20 tokens, with $p_1 = 1$ and $p_2 = 1$ Hong chooses $x_1 = 18$, $x_2 = 2$. When endowed with 30 tokens, with $p_1 = 0.5$, $p_2 = 10.5$, Hong chooses $x_1 = 17$, $x_2 = 2.05$.

   (c) When endowed with 20 tokens, with $p_1 = 1$ and $p_2 = 1$ Hong chooses $x_1 = 17$, $x_2 = 3$. When endowed with 30 tokens, with $p_1 = 1$, $p_2 = 2$, Hong chooses $x_1 = 10$, $x_2 = 10$. When endowed with 100 tokens, with $p_1 = 5$, $p_2 = 5$, Hong chooses $x_1 = 18$, $x_2 = 2$.

   (d) When endowed with 20 tokens, with $p_1 = 1$ and $p_2 = 1$ Hong chooses $x_1 = 17$, $x_2 = 3$. When endowed with 30 tokens, with $p_1 = 1$, $p_2 = 2$, Hong chooses $x_1 = 20$, $x_2 = 5$. When endowed with 100 tokens, with $p_1 = 10$, $p_2 = 5$, Hong chooses $x_1 = 5$, $x_2 = 10$.

3. Consider the prisoner's dilemma game, in which two prisoners are accused of a crime. Both are isolated in the prison. Without a confession, there is not enough evidence to convict either. Any prisoner who confesses will be looked upon with lenience. If one prisoner confesses and the other does not, that prisoner not confessing will be put away for a much longer sentence. The payoffs can be represented as pictured in Figure 14.7 (Player 1's payoffs are in the upper right, and Player 2's are in the lower left).

FIGURE 14.7
The Prisoner's Dilemma

(a) Determine the Nash equilibrium strategy for each player. What would be the result of the game if both players chose this strategy?

(b) In most experiments involving the prisoner's dilemma, we observe that players tend to choose not to defect a reasonable proportion of the time. How might this be motivated by altruism?

(c) If a selfish player is playing the prisoner's dilemma against an opponent she believes to be altruistic,

what would her strategy be? Is this similar to the observation in the TIOLI game? Why or why not?

(d) Now suppose that the prisoner's dilemma is played three times in sequence by the same two players. How might a belief that the other player is altruistic affect the play of a selfish player? Is this different from your answer to c? What has changed?

REFERENCES

Andreoni, J., and J. Miller. "Giving According to GARP: An Experimental Test of the Consistency of Preferences for Altruism." *Econometrica* 70(2002): 737–753.

Andreoni, J., and L. Vesterlund. "Which is the Fair Sex? Gender Differences in Altruism." *Quarterly Journal of Economics* 116 (2001): 293–312.

Burnham, T.C. "Engineering Altruism: A Theoretical and Experimental Investigation of Anonymity and Gift Giving." *Journal of Economic Behavior and Organization* 50(2003): 133–144.

Chan, K.S., R. Godby, S. Mestelman, and R.A. Muller. "Crowding-out Voluntary Contributions to Public Goods." *Journal of Economic Behavior and Organization* 48(2002): 305–317.

Carter, M.R., and M. Castillo. "Morals, Markets and Mutual Insurance: using Economic Experiments to Study Recovery from Hurricane Mitch." In C.B. Barrett (ed.). *Exploring the Moral Dimensions of Economic Behavior*. London: Routledge, 2004, 268–287.

Easterlin, R.A. "Does Money Buy Happiness?" *The Public Interest* 30(1973): 3–10.

Forsythe, R., J.L. Horowitz, N.E. Savin, and M. Sefton. "Fairness in Simple Bargaining Experiments." *Games and Economic Behavior* 6(1994): 347–369.

Frank, R.H. "The Frame of Reference as a Public Good." *Economic Journal* 107(1997): 1832–1847.

Frank, R.H. "Progressive Consumption Taxation as a Remedy for the U.S. Savings Shortfall." *The Economists' Voice* 2(2005): Article 2.

Harbaugh, W.T., K. Krause, and S.J. Liday. "Bargaining by Children." *University of Oregon Economics Working Paper* No. 2002–4.

Hoffman, E., K. McCabe, and V.L. Smith. "Social Distance and Other-Regarding Behavior in Dictator Games." *American Economic Review* 86(1996): 653–660.

Lundberg, S. "Child Auctions in Nineteenth Century Sweden: An Analysis of Price Differences." *Journal of Human Resources* 35 (2000): 279–298.

McKelvey, R.D., and T.R. Palfrey. "An Experimental Study of the Centipede Game." *Econometrica* 60(1992): 803–836.

Schulze, W.S., M.H. Lubatkin, and R.N. Dino. "Altruism, Agency, and the Competitiveness of Family Firms." *Managerial and Decision Economics* 23(2002): 247–259.

Stevenson, B., and J. Wolfers. "Economic Growth and Subjective Well-Being: Reassessing the Easterlin Paradox." Working Paper 14282. Cambridge, MA: National Bureau of Economic Research, 2008.

Waldfogel, J. "The Deadweight Loss of Christmas." *American Economic Review* 83(1993): 1328–1336.

Fairness and Psychological Games

15

One of the most fascinating reads is the classic tale of Edmond Dantes found in Alexandre Dumas' *The Count of Monte Cristo*. As a young sailor, Dantes has a promising future ahead. He appears to be in line for promotion to captain, he is engaged to a beautiful and loving woman, and he appears to be very near achieving the goals that will make him happy. But just as he is about to realize his dreams, three jealous competitors conspire to have him falsely arrested and imprisoned for high treason. After spending years in prison, Dantes gives up hope and decides to starve himself to death. At this point, an older prisoner, Abbe Faria, accidently tunnels into Dantes' cell in a failed attempt to escape. They become fast friends, and Faria uses their time not only to instruct Dantes in high culture, science, and languages but also to share with him the location of an enormous fortune that awaits Dantes should he ever successfully escape.

After Faria dies, Dantes succeeds in escaping, and he finds the seemingly inexhaustible fortune Faria had told him of. At this point, a perfectly selfish person would take the money and live the most opulent life imaginable. Someone motivated by altruism might take his fortune and use some for his own enjoyment and also use a substantial amount to enrich the lives of his lost love or other unfortunate friends from his prior life. In fact, Dantes does give an anonymous gift of cash to the Morrel family, who had stood by him throughout his troubles. However, he uses the remainder of his fortune to exact the slowest and most painful revenge he can on each of the conspirators who had put him in prison—one of whom is now married to his former fiancée. At each turn of the knife, the reader feels somehow victorious and happy that the conspirators receive their just reward for vile villainy against the innocent, though Dantes seems to become less and less the hero.

The notion of altruism provides a very simplistic view of how people deal with one another. In truth, we do not always have others' best interest at heart. In some cases, we even seek to harm others at our own expense. Among the most extreme examples of this are suicide bombers who give their lives in the hope that they can injure or kill others. These actions are clearly incongruous with either the selfish decision maker or the altruistic decision maker. Moreover, it seems unlikely that we could find people who behave in such a cruel or vindictive manner generally to everyone they meet. In this chapter we introduce a more-nuanced set of theories about other-regarding preferences. The majority of these theories have developed out of the notion that people seek a fair distribution of consequences. This may be one of the reasons we see nearly even splits in many of the versions of the dictator game discussed in Chapter 14. The notion of fairness has had many different definitions in the literature, and we will cover the most important of these.

One branch of the research on fairness concerns how people react not only to the distribution of outcomes but also to the motivations and perceptions of others. Such conceptions of psychological motivations in games can provide powerful explanations of the behavior commonly observed in laboratory games. These models of behavior also have implications for the real world. Much of work and business is conducted in teams or other groups in which the actions of each individual involved will affect the payouts of all. How teams perceive the diligence of each of their individual members can have a substantial impact on how any one individual will decide on how much effort to put forth. Similarly, firms can use the way they are perceived in the community (e.g., socially conscious vs. greedy) to market their products and services. In each case, how actions are perceived can have a big impact on the behavior of others and ultimately on the profits of firms and well-being of consumers and workers.

EXAMPLE 15.1　Giving Ultimatums

The notion that people desire outcomes in which the payoffs are evenly divided has been a common explanation for the behavior observed in the dictator game. However, as you recall, these results tended to erode once the dictators knew that their choices would be completely anonymous. Thus, the dictators seemed to be partially motivated by what others might think of their actions. One wonders how the second player in the dictator game felt about his portion of the money and the dictator who gave it to him. If the second player had the option of expensive retaliation, we would be allowed to see explicitly how others react to the dictator's actions. This is the motivation behind the **ultimatum game**. In the ultimatum game, two players are to divide an amount of money, say $10. Player 1 proposes a split of the money between the two players. For example, Player 1 could propose that Player 1 will receive $7 and Player 2 will receive $3. Then, Player 2 can accept the proposal, and then both players receive the amounts Player 1 proposed, or Player 2 can reject the offer and both players receive nothing.

We can solve for the subgame perfect Nash equilibrium (SPNE) of this simple game by using backward induction. Given any split proposed by Player 1, a selfish Player 2 will prefer to receive any positive amount to $0. Thus, so long as Player 1 proposes that Player 2 receive at least $0.01, then Player 2 should accept. Given this strategy by Player 2, a selfish Player 1 should always choose to take all the money aside from $0.01. If Player 1 is altruistic, he might decide to allot more to Player 2. Whether Player 2 is selfish or altruistic, he should not reject an offer that provides him at least a penny. The selfish player will take the money because it makes him better off. The altruistic player will accept it because rejecting it would make both players worse off. Rejecting any positive offer of money would hurt Player 2 in order to hurt Player 1. It is an extreme and purely destructive move.

Werner Güth, Rold Schmittberger, and Bernd Schwarze engaged 42 participants in a laboratory experiment in which each pair played the ultimatum game. Each player participated twice, once exactly one week after the first game. However, players were not aware that the second game would take place until after they had already completed the first game, thus eliminating the chance for strategic behavior. In the first game, two of the 21 players delivering the ultimatum chose a split in which they would receive all of the money, seven decided on an even split, and only five chose a split in which Player 1 would receive more than 67 percent of the money. On average, Player 1 offered a split giving Player 1 64.9 percent of the money. Clearly, this is out of line with the SPNE. On the other side of the table, nearly all of those playing the role of Player 2 chose to accept the split; two did not. One had been offered 20 percent of the money, and one had been offered none. Aside from the Player 2 who rejected 20 percent of the money, all of those playing the role of Player 2 behaved according to the rational selfish model: accepting a positive offer and either accepting or rejecting an offer of zero. These results are consistent with the results from other experiments involving the ultimatum game, where the majority of participants tend to offer a nearly even split, with Player 2 receiving 40 percent to 50 percent.

Given one week to consider the game, players returned and were paired with different participants for a second round. This time, 11 of those playing the role of Player 1 offered a split giving themselves more than 67 percent, and one participant offered the partner a single penny. Every player offered their partner at least a penny. Again, only one player behaved according to the SPNE, though the offers were much closer to the selfish and rational offer. On average, Player 1 offered a split resulting in Player 1 receiving 69.0 percent of the money. Those playing the role of Player 2 were incensed by the relatively unfavorable offers they received. Of the 21 participants playing the role of Player 2, six decided to reject the offer, even though all offers included a positive payout for Player 2. These players received offers in which they would receive 0.200 percent, 0.167 percent, 0.200 percent, 0.250 percent, 0.250 percent or 0.429 percent. Offers of more than 43 percent of the money were all accepted. In this case, about 25 percent were willing to pay money (by giving up the amount offered to them) to keep Player 1 from receiving any money. This behavior appears to be in retaliation for offers that gave Player 2 too little money. In similar experiments we find that 40 percent to 50 percent of offers in which Player 2 would receive less than 20 percent of the money are rejected.

This game provides an interesting illustration of the puzzle of other-regarding preferences. The offers by those in the role of Player 1 clearly deviate from the selfish rule of offering only one penny. In fact, they tend to gravitate toward offering about half (or almost half) to their opponent. This, and the behavior in the dictator game discussed in Chapter 14 suggest that people are willing to give up money in order to make others better off, which is consistent with altruism. Alternatively, many playing the role of Player 2 were willing to forgo money to keep their partner from receiving money; this behavior seems diametrically opposed to altruism. Moreover, the behavior seems to be contingent on the offer Player 2 received. Players wished to punish those who had given them an unfavorable split and were willing to pay in order to administer that punishment. If the game would be played only once, there was no plausible future monetary reward for punishing Player 1.

Inequity Aversion

One might have several potential motivations for rejecting a low offer. However, the correct explanation seems likely to involve other-regarding preferences in some way. One proposal put forward by Ernst Fehr and Klaus Schmidt is that people tend to want outcomes to be equitable. In this case, people might try to behave so as to equalize the payoffs between themselves and others. Thus, if Player 1's monetary payout is lower than others' in the game, Player 2 will behave altruistically toward Player 1. Alternatively, if Player 1's monetary payout is larger than others' in the game, Player 2 will behave spitefully. Players are **spiteful** if they behave so as to damage another player even if it requires a reduction in their own payout. We refer to preferences that display this dichotomy of behaviors (altruistic to the poor, spiteful to the rich) as being **inequity averse**. A simple example of inequity-averse preferences is represented where player i maximizes utility given by

$$U(x_1, x_2, \ldots, x_n) = x_i - \frac{\alpha}{n-1}\sum_{j \neq i}\max\{x_j - x_i, 0\} - \frac{\beta_i}{n-1}\sum_{j \neq i}\max\{x_i - x_j, 0\}$$

(15.1)

and where x_i is the monetary payoff to player i, n is the total number of players, and α and β_i are positive-valued parameters. Here α represents the disutility felt by the decision maker whenever others receive a higher payout than he does (perhaps due to jealousy), and β_i represents the disutility felt by the decision maker whenever he receives a higher payout than some other player does (perhaps due to sympathy). In this case, players decide whether they will be spiteful or altruistic toward any one player based upon whether that player receives more or less from their payout. Thus, behavior motivated by inequity aversion is much like the notion of positional externalities discussed in Chapter 14.

Preferences such as those represented in equation 15.1 are easily applied to two-player games such as the dictator and ultimatum games we have used as examples. For example, consider the dictator game in which a dictator is called upon to divide \$10 between himself and a peer. In this case, the problem can be represented as

$$\max_{x \in [0,10]} x - \alpha \max\{10 - 2x, 0\} - \beta \max\{2x - 10, 0\},$$

(15.2)

where x is the amount the dictator receives and $10 - x$ is the amount the other player receives. Thus, the difference between the payout to the dictator and the other player is $x - (10 - x) = 2x - 10$. One example of this utility function is displayed in Figure 15.1 (with $\alpha = 0.7$ and $\beta = 0.6$). If the dictator takes \$5, then the value of the second two terms in equation 15.2 are zero, and the dictator receives utility of 5. If, instead, the dictator takes any more than \$5, the utility function has a slope of $1 - 2\beta$. If the dictator takes less than \$5, then the utility function has a slope of $1 + 2\alpha$. If $\beta < 0.5$, then the utility function will be positively sloped everywhere, and the dictator will choose to take all the money. If $\beta > 0.5$, then the utility function will be negatively sloped above \$5, and the dictator would only ever take \$5.

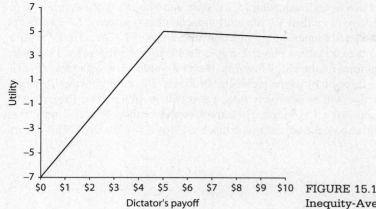

FIGURE 15.1
Inequity-Averse Preferences in the Dictator Game

Inequity-averse preferences are also instructive in considering the ultimatum game. To find the SPNE, let us first consider the second player's decision. Given that Player 1 chooses to allocate x to himself and $10 - x$ to Player 2, Player 2 then faces the choice of whether to accept or reject the offer. Player 2 thus solves

$$\max_{h \in \{0,1\}} [h \times (10 - x - \alpha_2 \max\{2x - 10,\, 0\} - \beta_2 \max\{10 - 2x,\, 0\}) + (1 - h) \times (0)],$$

$$(15.3)$$

where h is the choice variable, equal to 1 if Player 2 accepts the offer and equal to 0 if Player 2 rejects it, and subscript 2 indicates the parameters of Player 2's utility function. The first term in the braces represents the utility gained from accepting the offer, and the second term (which is always 0) is the utility of rejecting the offer. Player 2 will thus reject the offer if the utility of accepting is less than 0, or if

$$10 - x < \alpha_2 \max\{2x - 10,\, 0\} + \beta_2 \max\{10 - 2x,\, 0\}. \qquad (15.4)$$

In other words, Player 2 should reject the offer if the offer falls below some threshold level defined by Player 2's preferences. If, for example, we only consider offers that give Player 2 less than Player 1, Player 2 will reject if the offer $10 - x < 10 - 10(\alpha_2 + 1)/(1 + 2\alpha_2)$. This corresponds to Player 1's receiving $x > 10(\alpha_2 + 1)/(1 + 2\alpha_2)$. Falling below this threshold would represent a split that was so unequal that Player 2 would prefer everyone to receive nothing. Thus, an inequity-averse person might decide to reject an offer from Player 1, even if the offer would provide Player 2 more money than rejecting the offer.

To find the SPNE strategy for Player 1, consider the choice of Player 1 in the first stage of the game. If Player 1 is inequity averse, then his decision will be much like that in the dictator game. So long as Player 1 offers an amount to Player 2 that is greater than $10 - 10(\alpha_2 + 1)/(1 + 2\alpha_2)$, Player 2 will accept. Player 1 must thus solve equation 15.2 subject to the constraint $x < 10(\alpha_2 + 1)/(1 + 2\alpha_2)$. If Player 1 takes $5, then the value of the second two terms in equation 15.2 is zero, and Player 1 receives utility of 5. If the dictator takes any more than \$5, the utility function has a slope of $1 - 2\beta_1$. If the dictator takes less than \$5, then the utility function has a slope of $1 + 2\alpha_1$. Thus, Player 1 will never take less than \$5 unless Player 2 would decide to reject this offer. However, given the functional form for the utility function, Player 2 would never reject this offer (it yields utility of $5 > 0$ for both). If the parameter of Player 1's utility function $\beta_1 < 0.5$, then the utility function will be positively sloped everywhere. In this case, Player 1 will choose the allocation that gives Player 1 the most money without Player 2 rejecting. Thus Player 1 would choose the largest x such that $x < 10(\alpha_2 + 1)/(1 + 2\alpha_2)$. This occurs where

$$x = 10\frac{(\alpha_2 + 1)}{(1 + 2\alpha_2)}. \tag{15.5}$$

Thus, the more-averse Player 2 is to obtaining less than Player 1, the greater the offer to Player 2, with a maximum value of 5 as α_2 goes to infinity. If $\beta_1 > 0.5$, then the utility function is negatively sloped above \$5, and Player 1 would only ever take \$5 in the first stage.

Clearly, this is a very restrictive theory, and it cannot fully explain all of the various behaviors we observe, particularly in the dictator game. Many of the outcomes of the dictator game have the dictator taking something between \$5 and \$10—an outcome excluded by this model. However, this simple model clearly communicates the idea that people might have an aversion to unequal distributions of payouts. More-general models have been built on the same ideal (e.g., by allowing increasing marginal disutility of inequality) that would potentially explain more of the various outcomes observed in the dictator game.

EXAMPLE 15.2　Millionaires and Billionaires

Inequity aversion often finds its way into political discourse. In 2011, facing mounting deficits, the United States faced the possibility of a downgrade in its credit rating. If reduction of a budget deficit is the primary goal, there are only two ways to reach it: raise revenues (primarily through taxes) or reduce spending (primarily by cutting social programs). Major disagreements formed over whether to focus more on raising taxes or on lowering expenditures. President Barack Obama argued that raising taxes on the rich would be a reasonable way to proceed. In a speech, he argued that the wealthy receive much of their income through capital gains, which are taxed at a low 15 percent relative to income. Income could be taxed up to 35 percent for higher income earners. This leads to a situation where those making the most money might actually pay a lower tax on overall income than those who obtain most or all of their income through salaried employment. Referring to the iconic billionaire investor, he protested, "Warren Buffett's secretary should not pay a higher tax rate than Warren Buffett." The president continually argued for increases in taxes on millionaires and billionaires. "It's only right that we should ask everyone to pay their fair share." Moreover, he pointed out that cutting spending would hurt the poor, who have the least to give.

On the other side of the aisle, many members of Congress argued that the rich were paying more than their fair share relative to the poor. They argued that a majority of overall tax revenues were taken from the relatively tiny percentage of people in the United States who could be considered wealthy. The top 10 percent of earners accounted for 46 percent of income but paid more than 70 percent of total income taxes. This group included those earning $104,000 and above, far short of the "millionaire and billionaire" image the President portrayed. By many measures, it is the group of earners in a range from $250,000 to $400,000 who face the highest tax burden of any in the country—a group that the President was targeting with tax increases. Instead, others prefer cutting spending that, among other things, goes to the poor, who often face no income tax burden but who benefit from these social programs.

It is perhaps not surprising that both sides could look at the same statistics and come to far different conclusions. Of note, however, is how both sides cloak their arguments in terms of inequity. One side claims that increasing tax rates for the wealthy is necessary to make outcomes equal. The other claims that taxes on the wealthy are already too high and that equity requires that spending on the poor be cut. Neither seems to question the desirability of equity in their arguments, perhaps because they are pandering to an inequity-averse electorate. Often the perception of what is an equitable division of the spoils depends upon how the spoils are framed.

Consider the experiments conducted by Alvin Roth and Keith Murnighan examining how information can influence bargaining. In their experiment, two players were given a number of lottery tickets and were given a certain amount of time to come to an agreement about how to divide the tickets. The proportion of lottery tickets held by a player determined their chance of winning a prize. So having 50 percent of the tickets would result in a 50 percent chance of winning a prize. If no agreement was reached before time ran out, no one would receive lottery tickets. One player would win $5 if one of his lottery tickets paid off, and the other player would win $20 if one of his tickets paid off. Players were always informed of what their own payoff would be should they win, but players were not always informed of their opponents' payoff. Interestingly, when the $5 player was unaware of the payoff to the other player, players often agreed to a division of lottery tickets that was very close to 50/50. If instead the $5 player knew the other player would receive $20 for a win, the division of lottery tickets was much closer to 80/20 in favor of the $5 player. In this case, without the information about unequal payoffs, equal probabilities looks like a fair deal. However, once one knows that payoffs are unequal, probabilities that are unequal now look more attractive. The sharing rule is influenced by how inequality is framed.

One possible explanation of the difference between the two sides of our tax and spend debate is **self-serving bias**. Thus comparing income tax and capital gains taxes and comparing those in the middle class to those who make billions a year makes perfect sense if your goal is to increase the consumption of the poor relative to the ultrawealthy. Alternatively, comparing income tax rates of the mid-upper income ranges to income taxes by those in poverty—and particularly those on welfare rolls—might make sense if your goal is to maintain consumption of the upper-middle class.

In essence, people tend to bias their opinion of what is fair or equitable to favor their own consumption. For example, Linda Babcock, George Loewenstein, Samuel Issacharoff, and Colin Camerer gave a series of participants a description based on court testimony from an automobile accident. Participants were then assigned roles in the case and given the opportunity to try to negotiate a settlement, with participants receiving $1 for every thousand dollars of the settlement. They were given 30 minutes to negotiate a settlement in which a fixed amount of money would be divided among them. If they could not reach an agreement, then the actual judgment made in court would be enforced. Some, however, were assigned roles before they read the court testimony, and others were assigned roles only after they had read the court testimony. Those who did not know their roles were able to reach a settlement 22 percent more often than those who knew their roles while reading. This suggests that those who did not know their roles took a more-objective approach to understanding the details of the case than those who had been assigned a role to argue. Once we have a stake in the game, our perceptions of fairness are skewed toward our own self-interest in a way that can affect our judgment in all business transactions.

EXAMPLE 15.3   Unsettled Settlements

In 2003, American Airlines ended a years-long negotiation with the flight attendants' union. The flight attendants had been working without a contact for most of a decade. They had been unwilling to yield to American Airlines in the negotiations due to their demand for a large increase in pay. In fact, American Airlines had conceded an increase in pay over the period while negotiations took place, but the increase was much lower than the flight attendants had demanded. Interestingly, the contract the flight attendants finally accepted actually reduced their pay. Why did they finally accept? After the tragic attacks of September 11, the airline industry had been hard hit, and American Airlines was bleeding money. Eventually the flight attendants (and pilots also) made concessions because they wanted to be fair. When American Airlines started to lose money, suddenly the flight attendants believed that American Airlines was being honest when they claimed that pushing the salaries any higher would lead to bankruptcy. The flight attendants' negotiators felt they were making a sacrifice to help save the company and to make room for a more fair and equitable distribution of the dwindling profits.

Two days after an agreement was reached, news broke that top executives at American Airlines were going to receive large bonus checks and other retention incentives. Immediately the deal was off. The flight attendants were again up in arms. Had this changed the monetary offer to the flight attendants? No. But it led them to feel the executives had been dishonest and greedy. If they were going to be greedy, then the flight attendants would too. Eventually, under extreme pressure, the executives gave back their bonuses. This pacified the flight attendants and other workers who had been irked by the bonuses paid to executives. In the end, the flight attendants were not angry over the $10 billion in concessions and lower salary they had been forced to accept. Instead, they were angry about the tens of millions of dollars given to about 10 executives. Redistributing this money would have made a negligible difference in the salaries of the flight attendants—a couple hundred dollars at most. Nonetheless, they were not about to accept the lower salary unless the executives had to do without their bonuses. Even though the bonuses had made no real difference directly in the profitability of the company, the perception that executives had been greedy and callous nearly bankrupted the company by stirring another costly labor dispute.

In fact, simple inequality aversion has a difficult time explaining many of the behaviors we observe. Armin Falk, Ernst Fehr, and Urs Fischbacher demonstrated this using a simple version of the ultimatum game in which Player 1 could only select one of two possible splits between the two players. In one game (call this game 1), the first player could propose that both would walk away with $5 or that the Player 1 would receive $8 and Player 2 would receive $2. In this game, 44 percent of those playing the role of Player 2 rejected the offer if the proposed split was $8 and $2. But in another game (call this game 2), Player 1 could only choose between a split in which Player 1 receives $8 and Player 2 receives $2, or a split in which Player 1 receives $2 and Player 2 receives $8. Only 27 percent of those playing the role of Player 2 rejected an offer that gave them only $2 in this game, though it was exactly the offer that induced 44 percent to reject in game 1. Note that if Player 2's preferences display inequality aversion as presented in equation 15.1, then rejecting the offer in game 1 means $U(2, 8) = 2 - \alpha(8 - 2) < 0 = U(0, 0)$. But accepting the split in game 2 implies $U(2, 8) = 2 - \alpha(8 - 2) > 0 = U(0, 0)$. Here, it appears that the particular options that were available to Player 1 changed the calculation of what was fair in the eyes of Player 2. In other words, the motives of Player 1 matters as well as the particular split of the money that is realized.

Holding Firms Accountable in a Competitive Marketplace

Customers and employees hold firms to a standard of fairness that has sore implications. For example, in 2011 Netflix Inc., a firm that provided streaming movies and DVD rentals through the mail, chose to nearly double the prices for subscriptions at the same time that they limited their customers to either receive DVDs through the mail or to download—but not both. The customer backlash was strong, leading the CEO to apologize several times and provide explanations about how the profit model was changing, and eventually capitulating to incensed customers by allowing both DVD rentals and downloads.

Daniel Kahneman, Jack L. Knetsch, and Richard Thaler used surveys of around 100 people to study how we evaluate such actions by firms. For example, 82 percent of participants considered it unfair for a firm to raise the price of snow shovels the day after a major snow storm. Similarly, 83 percent considered it unfair to reduce an employee's wages even if the market wage for that occupation has declined. It is acceptable, according to 63 percent, however, to reduce the wages of a worker if the firm abandons one activity (e.g., software design) for another in which the going market wages are lower (e.g., software support). Thus, it is okay to cut salary if it is associated with a change in duties.

In general, economists have found that consumers consider it fair for a firm to raise its price to maintain profits when costs are on the rise. However, it is considered unfair to raise prices simply to profit from an increase in demand or to take advantage of market power (e.g., due to a shortage). In other words, raising prices is considered unfair if it will result in a higher profit than some baseline or reference level. This principle is described as **dual entitlement**. Under dual entitlement, both the consumer and the seller are entitled to a level of benefit given by some **reference transaction**. This reference transaction is generally given by the status quo. Hence, if costs rise, the seller is allowed to increase prices to maintain the reference profit. However, the seller is not allowed to increase his profit on the transaction if costs do not rise, even if there are shortages of the item. To do so would threaten the consumer. Similar effects can be found in the labor market considering the transaction between an employer and employee. This leads to three notable effects in both consumer and labor markets.

Markets Might Not Clear When Demand Shifts

When increases in demand for a consumer product occur and producer costs do not increase, shortages will occur. This leads to waiting lists or other market-rationing measures because the price is not allowed to rise enough to reduce the quantity demanded. In labor markets, a reduction in demand for outputs generally does not lead to a reduction in wages. Rather, firms maintain wages but reduce the number of employees. Maintaining the same wages but reducing the number of employees generally leads to labor markets that do not clear, resulting in unemployment.

Prices and Wages Might Not Fully Reflect Quality Differences

If a firm offers two variations of an item that cost identical amounts to manufacture but that differ substantially in value to the consumer, consumers will consider it unfair to charge prices that differ by too much. For example, a majority of football fans might value tickets to the big rivalry game more than when their home team faces other opponents. This should lead to much higher ticket prices for the big game. But fans' opinions about fairness can limit the increase in price, leading to more fans being willing to purchase tickets for this game at the listed price than there are seats in the stadium. For example, the University of California charged $51 for most of their home games in 2010. However, they charged $66 for a seat at the game against Stanford, their primary rival. This game was sold out, as is the case every year when the two play. Clearly they could charge a much higher price and still fill the stadium. Similar effects are found with peak and offseason prices for hotel rooms.

With regard to wages, this leads to a case where more-productive workers are not paid quite as much as they are worth relative to other workers in the same firm and occupation. For example, many universities pay professors of the same rank similar salaries regardless of their field and level of productivity. This commonly leads to a situation where the most productive faculty are also the most undervalued and thus the most likely to leave for more lucrative work elsewhere. Universities often cannot increase the pay of the most productive faculty to the market rate because it would be perceived as unfair by others who are less productive or less valuable in similar positions.

Prices Are More Responsive to Cost Increases than Decreases

Because consumers are willing to allow producers to increase prices to maintain a reference level of profit, producers are likely to take advantage of this quickly. Alternatively, they may be slow to advertise when costs decline, leading to higher profits. They would only lower prices in response to the potential impact it could have on their competitive position in the market. Producers also have incentives to use temporary discounts to consumers rather than actual price decreases. Price decreases can alter the reference transaction in favor of the consumer, whereas discounts will be viewed as a temporary gain by the consumer. Although there is some evidence that prices respond asymmetrically, there is also some substantial counterevidence.

On the other hand, there is substantial evidence the wages are slow to decline and quick to increase. This is often referred to as wages being "sticky downward." The slow decline can lead to prolonged periods of unemployment when market wages decline. This happens when many are willing to work at the going (lower) wages but cannot find employment. Employers will not hire, preferring to keep a smaller workforce at higher salaries rather than being perceived as unfair by cutting salaries of the currently employed. Additionally, employers may be inclined to give workers a portion of their pay in the form of a bonus in order to allow flexibility to reduce pay without being perceived as unfair.

Fairness

Important to note in the case of American Airlines executives and flight attendants is how key the perception of deception was to the flight attendants' union. Even without the bonuses, it is clear that the outcome would be lopsided. The 10 executives would still be receiving salaries that could not be dreamed of by even the most senior flight attendants. The motive for dropping the agreement wasn't to create a more-equal sharing of the rewards. The motive was to punish executives who were now perceived to be greedy and deceptive. The perception was that the executives had not negotiated in good faith. The perception of their duplicity drove the flight attendants to drop an otherwise acceptable labor agreement.

Matthew Rabin proposes that people are motivated to help those who are being kind and hurt those who are being unkind. Thus, he suggests that people are not motivated simply to find equal divisions (and sacrifice well-being in order to find them) but that they are also motivated by the intent and motivations of others. When people are willing to sacrifice in order to reward the kindness of others, or to punish the unkindness of others, we refer to them as being motivated by **fairness**. Rabin proposes that people maximize their utility, which is a sum of their monetary payout, and a factor that represents their preferences for fairness.

Formally, consider any two-player game in which Player 1 chooses among a set of strategies, with his choice represented by the variable a_1. Player 2 also chooses among a set of strategies, with his choice represented by a_2. As with all games, a strategy represents a planned action in response to each possible decision point in the game. The payoff to each player is completely determined by the strategies of both players, and thus the payout to Player 1 can be represented by a function $\pi_1(a_1, a_2)$, and the payout to Player 2 can be represented as $\pi_2(a_1, a_2)$. The Nash equilibrium is thus described as (a_1, a_2) where Player 1 selects a_1 so as to maximize $\pi_1(a_1, a_2)$ for the given a_2 and Player 2 maximizes $\pi_2(a_1, a_2)$ for the given a_1. Let us suppose that these payout functions represent **material outcomes**, such as the money rewards generally employed in economic experiments like the ultimatum game. If players are motivated by fairness, their total utility of a particular outcome will depend not only on the material outcome but also on the perception of whether the other player has been kind and whether the decision maker has justly rewarded the other player for his kindness or lack thereof. To specify this part of the utility of the decision maker, we thus need to define a function representing the perceived kindness of the other player and the kindness of the decision maker.

Let b_1 represent Player 2's beliefs about the strategy that Player 1 will employ, and let b_2 represent Player 1's beliefs about the strategy of Player 2. These perceived strategies will help define whether, for example, Player 1 believes Player 2 is being kind or **cruel**. We can then define a function $f_1(a_1, b_2)$, called a **kindness function**, that represents how **kind** Player 1 is intending to be toward Player 2. This kindness function can take on negative values, representing the notion that Player 1 is being cruel to Player 2, or positive values, representing the notion that Player 1 is being kind to Player 2. Note that how kind Player 1 is intending to behave is a function of his own strategy, a_1, and the strategy he believes the other player is employing, b_2. Rabin's model also assumes that both players agree on the definition of kindness, and thus this kindness function also represents how kind Player 2 would perceive the strategy of a_1 by Player 1 to be in response to the strategy $a_2 = b_2$ by Player 2. Similarly, Player 2 has a kindness function given by $f_2(a_2, b_1)$ defined analogously.

Finally, let c_1 represent what Player 1 believes Player 2 believes Player 1's strategy is and let c_2 represent what Player 2 believes Player 1 believes Player 2's strategy is. This can begin to sound a little tedious. These values are used to help determine if, for example, Player 1 believes that Player 2 believes that Player 1 is being kind or cruel. We can then define the function $\tilde{f}_2(b_2, c_1)$, which represents Player 1's belief about how kind Player 2 is being. Note that this perception is a function both of Player 1's belief regarding Player 2's strategy, b_2, and Player 1's belief about what Player 2 believes Player 1's strategy is, c_1. Again, this function takes on negative values if Player 2 is perceived to be cruel, and it takes on positive values if Player 2 is perceived to be kind. Similarly, we can define payer 2's belief about how kind Player 1 is, $\tilde{f}_1(b_1, c_2)$. With these functions in hand, we can now define Player 1's utility function as

$$U_1(a_1, b_2, c_1) = \pi_1(a_1, b_2) + \tilde{f}_2(b_2, c_1) \times f_1(a_1, b_2). \quad (15.6)$$

The first term represents Player 1's perception of his material payout for playing strategy a_1 given that Player 2 employs strategy b_2. The second term represents the utility of fairness. If Player 2 is perceived to be cruel, $\tilde{f}_2(b_2, c_1)$ will be negative, and Player 1 will be motivated to make $f_1(a_1, b_2)$ more negative by choosing a strategy that is also cruel. Alternatively, if Player 2 is perceived as being kind, $\tilde{f}_2(b_2, c_1)$ will be positive, leading Player 1 to choose a strategy that will make $f_1(a_1, b_2)$ more positive by being more kind. Player 2's utility function is defined reciprocally as

$$U_2(a_2, b_1, c_2) = \pi_2(b_1, a_2) + \tilde{f}_1(b_1, c_2) \times f_2(a_2, b_1). \quad (15.7)$$

We can then define a *fairness equilibrium* as the set of strategies (a_1, a_2) such that a_1 solves

$$\max_{a_1} U_1(a_1, a_2, a_1) \quad (15.8)$$

and a_2 solves

$$\max_{a_2} U_2(a_2, a_1, a_2), \quad (15.9)$$

where $a_1 = b_1 = c_1$, $a_2 = b_2 = c_2$. Equations 15.8 and 15.9 imply that the fairness equilibrium is equivalent to the notion of a Nash equilibrium, taking into account the utility from fairness, and requiring that all have correct beliefs regarding the intent of the other player. In other words, players are choosing the strategy that makes them the best off they can be given the strategy the other player chooses. Additionally, the equilibrium requires that each player correctly perceives what strategy the opponent will play and that each player correctly perceives that the opponent correctly perceives the strategy the player will play. Given that this is a complicated concept, a few examples with a specific kindness function may be useful.

First, consider the classic game often titled "Battle of the Sexes." This game is intended to represent a husband and wife who wish to go out on a date and can choose between attending the opera or a boxing match. The husband and wife both left the house for work in the morning agreeing to meet each other for a night out but did not have time to agree on which event to attend. Assume the husband and wife have no chance to communicate during the day and are forced to guess about the actions of the other. The material payoffs to the players can be represented as in Figure 15.2. Both would prefer to attend an event together rather than to go to different events. However, the wife would prefer the opera and the husband would prefer boxing. There are two pure strategy Nash equilibria for this game based upon the material payoffs: (boxing, boxing) and (opera, opera). If the wife chooses boxing, the husband is clearly better off choosing boxing and receiving 1 than choosing opera and receiving nothing. Alternatively, given the husband chooses boxing, the wife is clearly better off choosing boxing and receiving 0.5 than choosing opera and receiving nothing. A similar argument can be made for (opera, opera).

Now let us define a kindness function. Rabin suggests one key to defining fairness is whether the other person is hurting himself in order to hurt his opponent. Many different candidates may exist, but for now let's use

$$f_{Wife}(a_{Wife}, b_{Husband}) = \begin{cases} 0 & if & a_{Wife} = Opera, \ b_{Husband} = Opera \\ -1 & if & a_{Wife} = Boxing, \ b_{Husband} = Opera \\ -1 & if & a_{Wife} = Opera, \ b_{Husband} = Boxing \\ 0 & if & a_{Wife} = Boxing, \ b_{Husband} = Boxing \end{cases} \qquad (15.10)$$

FIGURE 15.2
The Battle of the Sexes

as the kindness function describing how kind the wife is attempting to be toward her husband. If she believes the husband is going to choose opera, the wife must be trying to be cruel if she decides to choose boxing. To do so costs her one unit of payout to reduce the husband's payout by 0.5. Hence, we assign this a -1. Similarly, if she believes her husband is going to choose boxing, she must be cruel if she decides to choose opera. In this case she gives up 0.5 in payout to reduce the payout she believes her husband will receive by 1. Thus we assign a -1 to this outcomes also.

The value 0 is assigned to the outcome of (opera, opera) because in this case, the wife is maximizing her payout given that she believes the husband will choose opera. Maximizing your own payout is considered neither kind nor cruel, because the wife is not sacrificing her own well-being to hurt or help her husband. Similarly, we assign a 0 in the case she believes the husband will choose boxing and she chooses boxing, because again she is maximizing her own payout. The husband's kindness function is defined reciprocally as

$$f_{Husband}\left(a_{Husband},\ b_{Wife}\right) = \begin{cases} 0 & if \quad a_{Husband} = Opera,\ b_{Wife} = Opera \\ -1 & if \quad a_{Husband} = Boxing,\ b_{Wife} = Opera \\ -1 & if \quad a_{Husband} = Opera,\ b_{Wife} = Boxing \\ 0 & if \quad a_{Husband} = Boxing,\ b_{Wife} = Boxing \end{cases}, \quad (15.11)$$

which represents how kind the husband is intending to be toward his wife.

We can also define the set of functions that yield each player's perception of whether the other player is kind or cruel. We will define $\tilde{f}_2(b_1,\ c_2) = f_2(c_2,\ b_1)$, or in this case, $\tilde{f}_{Husband}\left(b_{Wife},\ c_{Husband}\right) = f_{Husband}\left(c_{Husband},\ b_{wife}\right)$, where the latter function is as defined in equation 15.11. Thus, the wife perceives the husband to be kind or cruel using the same measure as the husband himself uses to measure his own kindness or cruelty. Similarly, $\tilde{f}_1(b_1,\ c_2) = f_1(c_2,\ b_1)$, or in this case, $\tilde{f}_{Wife}\left(b_{Husband},\ c_{Wife}\right) = f_{Wife}\left(c_{Wife},\ b_{Husband}\right)$, where the latter function is as defined in equation 15.10. Thus, the husband uses the same functions to assess his wife's fairness as does the wife to assess her own fairness. In this case, all players agree on the definition of fairness. The fairness equilibrium requires that all perceptions of strategy align with actual strategy, $a_{Wife} = b_{Wife} = c_{Wife}$ and $a_{Husband} = b_{Husband} = c_{Husband}$. Given this restriction, we can rewrite the game in terms of total utility rather than just material rewards, where substituting into equation 15.7

$$U_{Wife}\left(a_{Wife},\ b_{Husband},\ c_{Wife}\right) = \pi_{Wife}\left(a_{Wife},\ a_{Husband}\right) + \tilde{f}_{Husband}\left(a_{Wife},\ a_{Husband}\right)$$
$$\times f_{Wife}\left(a_{Wife},\ a_{Husband}\right). \quad (15.12)$$

For example, consider the potential strategy pair in which the wife decides to play the strategy $a_{Wife} = Boxing$ and the husband decides to play the strategy $a_{Husband} = Opera$. To see if this pair of strategies can be a fairness equilibrium, we must see if it is a Nash equilibrium given $b_{Wife} = c_{Wife} = Boxing$ and $b_{Husband} = c_{Husband} = Opera$—in other words, where both believe that the wife will choose boxing and the wife believes the husband believes she will choose boxing, and where both believe that the husband will choose opera and the husband believes that the wife believes he will choose opera. In this case, the wife will obtain total utility

$$\begin{aligned} U_{Wife}(Boxing,\ Opera,\ Boxing) &= \pi_{Wife}(Boxing,\ Opera) + \tilde{f}_{Husband}(Boxing,\ Opera) \\ &\quad \times f_{Wife}(Boxing,\ Opera) \\ &= 0 + (-1) \times (-1) = 1. \end{aligned} \tag{15.13}$$

Thus, the wife receives a utility of 1 by choosing to go to boxing when she believes her husband has chosen opera even though he knew she would be going to the opera. In this case, the utility results not from a material payoff (which is zero in this case) but from being cruel to a husband who is treating her poorly. He is making himself worse off in order to hurt her materially, which then gives her the desire to hurt him even at her own expense.

We can make similar calculations for each of the players in each of the outcomes, yielding the final utilities displayed in Figure 15.3. With the utilities defined this way, the fairness equilibria are now given by (boxing, opera) and (opera, boxing). For example, if the wife chooses opera, the husband will be better off choosing boxing and receiving a utility of 1 by intentionally hurting her rather than cooperating with her, going to the opera, and receiving 0.5. Alternatively, given that the husband is choosing boxing, the wife is better off choosing opera and receiving a utility of 1 by intentionally hurting her noncooperative husband than by cooperating with him, going to boxing, and receiving only 0.5.

Similar analysis tells us that (boxing, opera) is a fairness equilibrium, though each player would be just as well off to choose the other event given the other player's strategy. In this case, the motivation for fairness leads both to choose to punish the spouse rather than cooperate because the rewards for punishing each other are larger than the material rewards for the basic game. This is an extreme example. However, if the original material payoffs had been large relative to the possible values of the kindness functions, the fairness equilibria would have been identical to the Nash equilibria (e.g., if the material rewards had been 160 and 80 rather than 1 and 0.5).

Husband \ Wife	Opera	Boxing
Boxing	1 / 1	0.5 / 1
Opera	1 / 0.5	1 / 1

FIGURE 15.3
Fairness Utilities in the Battle of the Sexes

Kindness Functions

In this case we have defined kindness functions following a recipe suggested by Matthew Rabin—a rather complicated recipe. One way to index the fairness of a strategy is to compare it to the set of **Pareto optimal** outcomes. Recall that an outcome is Pareto optimal if no one can be made better off without making someone else worse off. In any non-Pareto optimum, someone can be made better off without making other players worse off. If this occurs it may be because someone has given up some of their own reward to give more to another (kindness) or because someone has given up some of their reward in order to hurt another (cruelty).

In the case of the Battle of the Sexes, there are two Pareto optimal allocations: (boxing, boxing) and (opera, opera). All other allocations strictly make everyone worse off. Examining the outcome (boxing, boxing), it would only be possible to make the wife better off by switching to the equilibrium (opera, opera), but this would result in making the husband worse off. When examining (opera, opera), it is possible to make the husband better off, but only by making the wife worse off. Thus, these are the two Pareto optimal outcomes. If the outcome is not a Pareto optimum, then it is possible to make one player better off without making either player worse off. In this case, one (or both) player(s) must be intentionally making the other worse off at the first player's expense. For example, if we observe the outcome (boxing, opera), either player could make both players better off by switching their strategy.

Suppose Player 2 decides to play strategy b_2. Then, the lowest amount the player would expect to obtain given Player 1 is being kind is the smallest possible Pareto optimal outcome given Player 2 employs b_2. So, for example, if the wife decided to choose opera, then the lowest Pareto optimal payoff is 1. If the husband knows the wife will go to the opera, any payoff lower than 1 could only occur if the husband were being cruel and lowering his own payout by 0.5 in order to reduce her payout by 1. Let $\underline{\pi}_2^P(b_2)$ be the smallest Pareto optimal payoff that can be received by Player 2 given Player 2 employs strategy b_2. Then, any result yielding a payout to Player 2 below $\underline{\pi}_2^P(b_2)$, given Player 2 follows b_2, must result from Player 1 being cruel, leading to a negative value of the kindness function $f_1(a_1, b_2)$.

Alternatively, Player 2 will never receive more than the largest Pareto optimal payoff that can be received by Player 2 given Player 2 plays strategy b_2 unless Player 1 is being kind. A higher payout could only be achieved by Player 1 intentionally giving up some of his payout in order for Player 1 to receive more. Let $\overline{\pi}_2^P(b_2)$ be the largest Pareto optimal outcome that can be received by Player 2 given Player 2 employs strategy b_2. This must result from Player 1 giving up some material payoff in order to allow Player 2 a higher payout, resulting in a positive value of the kindness function, $f_1(a_1, b_2)$. Thus, Rabin proposes the kindness function

$$f_1(a_1, b_2) = \frac{\pi_2(a_1, b_2) - \frac{\overline{\pi}_2^P(b_2) + \underline{\pi}_2^P(b_2)}{2}}{\overline{\pi}_2^P(b_2) - \underline{\pi}_2(b_2)}, \quad (15.14)$$

where $\underline{\pi}_2(b_2)$ is the minimum possible payout (whether Pareto optimal or not) among all outcomes with Player 2 playing strategy b_2. This function is negative if Player 2 receives less than the midpoint between the highest and lowest Pareto optimal amounts, and it is positive if Player 2 receives more than this amount.

This function leads directly to the kindness functions specified in equations 15.10 and 15.11. Consider the Battle of the Sexes from the wife's point of view. The lowest Pareto optimal amount the husband can receive if he chooses opera is $\underline{\pi}^P_{Husband}(Opera) = 0.5$. The maximum Pareto optimal material payout given he chooses opera is $\overline{\pi}^P_{Husband}(Opera) = 0.5$. The minimum amount overall that he can receive when choosing Opera is $\underline{\pi}_{Husband}(Opera) = 0$. Alternatively, if the husband chooses boxing, these values are $\underline{\pi}^P_{husband}(Boxing) = \overline{\pi}^P_{Husband}(Boxing) = 1$, $\underline{\pi}_{Husband}(Boxing) = 0$. Thus, the wife's kindness function is given by

$$f_{Wife}\left(a_{Wife},\, b_{Husband}\right) = \begin{cases} \dfrac{0.5 - \frac{0.5+0.5}{2}}{0.5 - 0} = 0 & if \quad a_{Wife} = Opera,\, b_{Husband} = Opera \\[2ex] \dfrac{0 - \frac{0.5+0.5}{2}}{0.5 - 0} = -1 & if \quad a_{Wife} = Boxing,\, b_{Husband} = Opera \\[2ex] \dfrac{0 - \frac{1+1}{2}}{1 - 0} = -1 & if \quad a_{Wife} = Opera,\, b_{Husband} = Boxing \\[2ex] \dfrac{1 - \frac{1+1}{2}}{1 - 0} = 0 & if \quad a_{Wife} = Boxing,\, b_{Husband} = Boxing \end{cases}$$

$$(15.15)$$

Clearly, if the wife believes the husband is going to choose boxing and decides to choose opera in response, she is trying to be cruel, resulting in a value of −1. Similarly, if she believes he will choose opera and she decides to choose boxing in response, she is being cruel. Otherwise, she is giving him the best outcome he can achieve given his strategy—moreover she is doing so without any sacrifice of her own well-being. Thus, in either of the Pareto optimal outcomes, the kindness function value is 0.

Reciprocally, we can find the wife's perceived kindness function, defining how kind she perceives her husband is being toward her. We define Player 1's perception of the kindness of Player 2 as

$$\tilde{f}_2(b_2,\, c_1) = \frac{\pi_1(c_1,\, b_2) - \frac{\overline{\pi}^P_1(c_1) + \underline{\pi}^P_1(c_1)}{2}}{\overline{\pi}^P_1(c_1) - \underline{\pi}_1(c_1)}, \tag{15.16}$$

where the values $\overline{\pi}^P_1(c_1)$, $\underline{\pi}^P_1(c_1)$, and $\underline{\pi}_1(c_1)$ are defined as before, only now they represent the reward to Player 1 given Player 1 employs strategy c_1. Recall that c_1 is the strategy Player 1 believes that Player 2 believes Player 1 will employ. The lowest Pareto optimal amount the Wife can receive if she plays Opera is $\underline{\pi}^P_{Wife}(Opera) = 1$. The maximum Pareto optimal material payout given she plays Opera is $\overline{\pi}^P_{Wife}(Opera) = 1$.

The minimum amount overall that she can receive when playing Opera is $\underline{\pi}_{Wife}(Opera) = 0$. Alternatively, if the Wife plays Boxing, these values are $\pi^P_{Wife}(Boxing) = \overline{\pi}^P_{Wife}(Boxing) = 0.5$, $\underline{\pi}_{Wife}(Boxing) = 0$. Thus, the Wife's perception of the kindness of the husband is

$$\tilde{f}_{Husband}(b_{Husband}, c_{Wife}) = \begin{cases} \dfrac{1 - \frac{1+1}{2}}{1-0} = 0 & \text{if} \quad c_{Wife} = Opera, b_{Husband} = Opera \\[2ex] \dfrac{0 - \frac{1+1}{2}}{1-0} = -1 & \text{if} \quad c_{Wife} = Boxing, b_{Husband} = Opera \\[2ex] \dfrac{0 - \frac{0.5+0.5}{2}}{0.5-0} = -1 & \text{if} \quad c_{Wife} = Opera, b_{Husband} = Boxing \\[2ex] \dfrac{0.5 - \frac{0.5+0.5}{2}}{0.5-0} = 0 & \text{if} \quad c_{Wife} = Boxing, b_{Husband} = Boxing \end{cases},$$

$$(15.17)$$

which is identical to the kindness function assumed in equation 15.11. As before, if the wife believes the husband thinks she will play opera, and he decides to play boxing in response, she believes he is behaving cruelly—hurting himself in order to hurt her. Alternatively, if the wife thinks the husband believes she will play boxing and he plays opera in response, she believes he is behaving cruelly. Both of these result in a value of -1. Alternatively, if she believes he is intending to coordinate with her to be at the same event, she believes he is not acting maliciously but maximizing both of their payouts. This results in a fairness value of 0.

There are many other candidate kindness functions that could be employed. The primary contribution of the fairness equilibrium is that people can behave very differently if they seek to reward the intent of their opponents rather than responding solely to the actions themselves. If intent is rewarded, cooperation can break down, leading to lower material payoffs for all. However, because the fairness equilibrium requires that all players have correct perceptions, it will always be the case that if any player is behaving kindly, both players behave kindly. Alternatively if any player is behaving cruelly, both players must behave cruelly or at best neutrally.

EXAMPLE 15.4   Rewarding Intent

Fairness provides one explanation for behavior in the ultimatum game. Consider an ultimatum game played between two players with kindness functions as proposed in the previous section. Suppose that the first player is given $10 to split between the two players, and the second player can either accept or reject. Given that this is a sequential game (Player 2 knows what Player 1's strategy is by the time he makes any decisions), let us generalize the notion of a fairness equilibrium to a subgame perfect fairness equilibrium (which must constitute a fairness equilibrium in all subgames). In this case, a strategy by Player 1 will specify a proposed split of the cash between the two players. A strategy by Player 2 will specify which values will be accepted and which will not. For example, one reasonable strategy might specify that Player 2 would accept if he will receive more than \$2.50 by doing so. Suppose that the first player offers a split in which Player 1 receives a_1 and Player 2 receives $10 - a_1$. All possible splits are Pareto optimal. The only outcomes that are not Pareto optimal are those in which Player 2 rejects and both players receive \$0.

Suppose that a_2 is of the form reject if $10 - a_1 < k$ and accept otherwise, where k is some constant between 0 and 10. The maximum Pareto optimal reward for Player 2 is thus $\bar{\pi}_2^P(a_2) = 10$. The minimum Pareto optimal amount that could result from this strategy would be $\underline{\pi}_2^P(a_2) = k$. Any offer that results in less than k would yield an outcome that is Pareto inefficient. The overall minimum reward is $\underline{\pi}_2(a_2) = 0$. Thus, if $a_2 = b_2 = c_2$, $a_1 = b_1 = c_1$,

$$f_1(a_1, b_2) = \tilde{f}_1(b_1, c_2) = \begin{cases} \dfrac{10 - a_1 - \frac{10+k}{2}}{10 - 0} = \dfrac{1}{2} - \dfrac{a_1}{10} - \dfrac{k}{20} & \text{if} \quad 10 - a_1 \geq k \\[4mm] \dfrac{0 - \frac{10+k}{2}}{10 - 0} = -\dfrac{1}{2} - \dfrac{k}{20} & \text{if} \quad 10 - a_1 < k \end{cases}$$

(15.18)

Similarly, the maximum Pareto optimal reward for Player 1 given the proposed split of a_1 is $\bar{\pi}_1^P(a_1) = a_1$. This is the amount Player 1 would receive if Player 2 accepted the offer no matter what it was. The minimum Pareto optimal amount that Player 1 could receive given a proposed split of a_1 is also $\underline{\pi}_1^P(a_1) = a_1$, because anything less must result from a rejection of the offer. The overall minimum reward is $\underline{\pi}_1(a_1) = 0$. Thus, if $a_2 = b_2 = c_2$, $a_1 = b_1 = c_1$,

$$f_2(a_2, b_1) = \tilde{f}_2(b_2, c_1) = \begin{cases} \dfrac{a_1 - \frac{a_1 + a_1}{2}}{a_1 - 0} = 0 & \text{if} \quad 10 - a_1 \geq k \\[4mm] \dfrac{0 - \frac{a_1 + a_1}{2}}{a_1 - 0} = -1 & \text{if} \quad 10 - a_1 < k \end{cases}$$

(15.19)

Thus, Player 2 must find the minimum amount he will accept, k, that solves

$$\max_k \pi_2(a_1, a_2) + \tilde{f}_1(a_1, a_2) f_2(a_2, a_1)$$

$$= \begin{cases} 10 - a_1 + \left(\dfrac{1}{2} - \dfrac{a_1}{10} - \dfrac{k}{20}\right) \times 0 = 10 - a_1 & \text{if} \quad 10 - a_1 \geq k \\[4mm] 0 - \left(\dfrac{1}{2} + \dfrac{k}{20}\right)(-1) = \dfrac{1}{2} + \dfrac{k}{20} & \text{if} \quad 10 - a_1 < k \end{cases}$$

(15.20)

The value of this function is $10 - a_1$ for any value of $k \leq 10 - a_1$, and he will receive $1/2 + k/20$ otherwise. The maximum value Player 2 can receive if he rejects is $1/2 + (10 - a_1)/20$, which will be received if the rejection point is set just above the anticipated offer $10 - a_1$. Thus Player 2 will set k to some value lower than $10 - a_1$ if $10 - a_1 > 1/2 + (10 - a_1)/20$, which means the reward from accepting would be larger than the maximum possible reward from rejecting. Player 2 will be indifferent between accepting and rejecting if

$$10 - a_1 = \frac{1}{2} + \frac{(10 - a_1)}{20}, \tag{15.21}$$

which implies that $10 - a_1 = 10/19$. For any value below this, Player 2 would be better off rejecting. But for any value above this, Player 2 would be better off accepting. Therefore, $k = 10/19$.

We can now examine Player 1's decision. In this case, $f_1(a_1, b_2) = \tilde{f}_1(a_1, b_2)$, and $\tilde{f}_2(b_2, c_1) = f_2(b_2, c_1)$. Again, given that $a_2 = b_2 = c_2$, $a_1 = b_1 = c_1$, we can thus write Player 1's strategy as solving

$$\max_{a_1} \pi_1(a_1, a_2) + \tilde{f}_2(a_2, a_1) f_1(a_1, a_2)$$

$$= \begin{cases} a_1 + (0) \times \left(\frac{1}{2} - \frac{a_1}{10} - \frac{1}{38} \right) = a_1 & \text{if} \quad 10 - a_1 \geq \frac{10}{19} \Leftrightarrow a_1 \leq \frac{180}{19} \\ 0 - (-1) \times \left(\frac{1}{2} + \frac{1}{38} \right) = \frac{20}{38} & \text{if} \quad 10 - a_1 < \frac{10}{19} \Leftrightarrow a_1 > \frac{180}{19} \end{cases} \tag{15.22}$$

Given this set of possible outcomes, and noting that $180/19 > 10/19$, Player 1 will choose the strategy in which Player 1 receives $a_1 = 180/19 \approx 9.47$ and Player 2 receives approximately 0.53. This split seems unfair, particularly for a fairness equilibrium. If the kindness function were scaled up by multiplying each kindness function by some factor greater than 1, the fairness equilibrium would display more evenly split proposals in equilibrium. This could be achieved, for example, by writing the utility functions in the form $U_1(a_1, b_2, c_1) = \pi_1(a_1, b_2) + \phi \tilde{f}_2(b_2, c_1) \times f_1(a_1, b_2)$, where ϕ is some number greater than 1. This implies that Player 2 will reject if $k < \phi/(2 - \phi/10)$. Thus, if $\phi = 4$, then Player 2 will reject if the offer yields less than \$2.50 for Player 2, and Player 1 will choose a split of \$7.50 for Player 1 and \$2.50 for Player 2, much like the observed outcomes.

The key notion of fairness is a desire to punish those who are cruel and reward those who are kind. Kahneman, Knetsch, and Thaler conducted a series of experiments that tested directly whether people wished to reward those who behave kindly and punish those who behave cruelly. Their experiments were based on a variation of the dictator game. The experiment took place in two phases. In the first phase, each player was made a dictator and could choose between two possible allocations of money between themselves and another anonymous player. In one allocation, the dictator would receive \$18 and the other player would receive \$2. In the other allocation, both would receive \$10. A total of 161 participants took part in this experiment, with 76 percent choosing an even split.

Next, in phase 2, players were randomly and anonymously paired with two other participants. They were told that one of the participants, whom we will call U for uneven, had played the role of dictator in the first round and taken \$18, and the other participant, whom we will call E, had made an even split. The participant could then choose to share \$12 with U, with both receiving \$6, or to share \$10 with E, with both receiving \$5. The player in this second round did not know who either U or E were. Moreover, neither U nor E had made any decision that involved the decision maker. The uneven and even splits of money were all made with some other player who was now uninvolved in the game. Thus, strictly speaking, the definition of fairness given in the previous section should not apply. Any cruelty by U was directed elsewhere and should not affect the decision maker. We might thus expect people to take the larger reward by sharing with U. However, 74 percent decided to take the smaller reward and share with E.

Thus, it appears that decision makers are motivated not just to reward those who are kind to them and punish those who are cruel to them but also to reward those who are kind to others and punish those who are cruel to others. To consider this in the framework of the fairness model of utility, we could extend the basic model to include beliefs about how others have been treated by an opponent. Thus, a player in the second round could take U's treatment of some other player as an indication that this player is cruel and E's treatment of some other player as indicating that E is kind. In this case, the decision maker's problem could be represented through a utility function that includes the fairness coefficients for both opponents involved:

$$U_2(i) = \begin{cases} 6 + \tilde{f}_1(U)f_2(6) + \tilde{f}_1(E)f_2(0) & \text{if} \quad i = U \\ 5 + \tilde{f}_1(U)f_2(0) + \tilde{f}_1(E)f_2(5) & \text{if} \quad i = E \end{cases}, \qquad (15.23)$$

where $\tilde{f}_1(i)$ is negative if the opponent chose U in the first round, reflecting that the player was cruel, and $\tilde{f}_1(i)$ is positive if the opponent chose E in the first round, reflecting that the player was kind. Alternatively, $f_2(0) \leq 0$ represents cruel (or at least neutral) treatment of the player who receives no material reward, and $f_2(6) > f_2(5) > 0$ represents kind treatment of the player who receives a positive material reward. Thus, the player will choose E if

$$5 + \tilde{f}_1(U)f_2(0) + \tilde{f}_1(E)f_2(5) > 6 + \tilde{f}_1(U)f_2(6) + \tilde{f}_1(E)f_2(0) \qquad (15.24)$$

or

$$\tilde{f}_1(U)[f_2(0) - f_2(6)] + \tilde{f}_1(E)[f_2(5) - f_2(0)] > 1. \qquad (15.25)$$

This would be the case if $\tilde{f}_1(U)$ was negative enough relative to $\tilde{f}_1(E)$, reflecting a severe aversion to rewarding cruel behavior. The observed behavior in the experiment suggests that in the general population we would find such a strong aversion to helping out cruel people.

EXAMPLE 15.5   For a Good Cause

Firms often advertise that they donate a portion of their profits for a specific cause. For example, several firms (ranging from beer bottling companies to Walmart) made a point of advertising their help in providing food and water to victims of Hurricane Katrina, which devastated the Gulf Coast in 2008. Such charitable giving might seem on the surface to be counterproductive to the goals of a profit-maximizing firm. If we assume, as economists do, that the firm's only goal is to maximize profits, they should not be giving product or profit away. But, in reality, firm giving is pervasive.

One example may be instructive. A prominent yogurt brand, Yoplait, has an ongoing campaign in which they cap their yogurt containers in pink lids. They encourage their customers to collect the lids and redeem them online by typing in codes found on the lids. In return, for every lid redeemed, Yoplait promises to donate $0.10 toward breast cancer research and programs for those suffering or recovering from the disease. The lids are colored pink to draw attention to them and state that you can help fight breast cancer by visiting Yoplait's website. If enough lids are redeemed, they promise to donate up to $2 million. This truly sounds like a firm being kind and helping others at a significant sacrifice of profits.

But then why would they ask customers to redeem the lids? It requires some effort and time to redeem the lids, which produces at least some cost. Moreover, it requires expenditure of money to administer the website and manage the dissemination and collection of lid codes. Previous incarnations of this program actually required customers to send the lids to the company through the mail. This required the customers to pay postage every time they sent in lids. In fact you would need to send in four lids before the donation to the cause would exceed the postage. If the company had set a goal to donate money out of their profits for the cause of breast cancer, they would not require such effort on the part of the customer because it reduces the amount donated. Rather, they could simply donate their $2 million plus whatever such efforts cost and possibly do more good. But doing so would eliminate the ability of the company to play upon the feelings of fairness their customers possess.

A large portion of yogurt consumers are women, and it is quite likely that a large portion of these customers feel strongly about breast cancer. Thus, donating some of the proceeds might help to win the loyalty of this customer base. However, to do so, you must find a powerful way to inform the customer base of your good deeds. In fact, Yoplait has made their donation directly proportional to the purchases of customers who are not only aware of the program but also feel strongly enough about breast cancer to take the time to redeem the lids. Not a single dime will go to breast cancer without first someone buying Yoplait yogurt and then, knowing about the good that Yoplait does, taking time to visit their website and enter in the codes on the lids. No money is wasted in building this reputation for kindness. In 1999 Yoplait promised to donate $0.50 per lid up to a maximum donation of only $100,000. But they received 9.4 million lids, which, but for the cap, would have resulted in a donation of $4.7 million. This nearly resulted in a lawsuit when the state of Georgia began to investigate the program. Make no mistake, corporate philanthropy is very carefully calculated and limited.

Kindness has many applications in the business world, from human resources to customer relations. For example, one much-publicized study has found that doctors who are at fault for a medical error face fewer lawsuits and lower costs if they simply apologize. In the context of the kindness model, doctors who appear to be at fault but are unwilling to admit it look as if they will not admit the error simply to avoid paying for damages. This type of treatment can be interpreted as cruel by the harmed patient, who might then wish to inflict financial pain on the doctor, even at the patient's own expense, by filing a lawsuit. The doctor who apologizes legally admits fault and thus would be responsible for any damages should the case go to court. But seeing that the doctor opened himself up to such a possibility of legal claims might remove the patient's desire to sue. At that point, the patient no longer wants to inflict pain on the errant doctor. Kindness pays.

EXAMPLE 15.6 Fairness, Wages, and Teams

One puzzle that has perplexed economists is the lack of detail in most labor contracts. Often a contract states nothing more than a per-hour wage and the possibility of being fired for any reason. Economic theory suggests that if possible, the employer and the laborer would both like to specify a contract that outlined the circumstances that would result in bonuses or raises as well as deductions to wages for poor performance. An employer should like to be able to go so far as to specify the attitude of the employees, presumably instructing them to be cooperative, compliant, and upbeat. Without more included in the contract, what prevents workers from shirking their duty substantially or even making themselves something of a nuisance to others in the workplace so long as they continue to provide some positive value? Employers really don't have the ability to observe everything the worker does, or their attitude toward their work, which should lead to substantial shirking. In this case, however, it may be effective to rely on the worker's sense of fairness to incline the worker toward a better attitude and a higher level of effort.

Ernst Fehr, Simon Gächter, and Georg Kirchsteiger used a series of experiments to see if someone in the employer's position could use fairness to elicit higher effort from their employees. This laboratory experiment paired people in the role of employee and employer. Employers could select a wage, w, and a desired effort level, $\hat{e}$, where $1 \leq \hat{e} \leq 10$, for their employees. There were six employers who made such decisions and eight workers who could decide to accept any of the contracts. However, only one worker could be employed by any employer, and thus there was an excess of labor in this market. The employee who accepted the contract could decide on any level of effort he desired, e, where $1 \leq e \leq 10$, even if that level were below that desired by their employer, and would receive w irrespective of their effort level. The employer would then earn $\pi = 10e - w$, and the worker would receive $u = w - c(e)$, where $c(e)$ was a positive and increasing function of effort.

In this case, a purely selfish employee should behave so as to solve

$$\max_e w - c(e) \tag{15.26}$$

and because w does not depend on e, and because the cost of e is positive, the worker should choose the minimum possible effort, $e = 1$, no matter what the wage. Knowing this, the selfish employer should offer the lowest wage possible that ensures that a worker will take the contract:

$$\max_w \pi = 10e - w = 10 \times 1 - w \tag{15.27}$$

subject to

$$w > c(1). \tag{15.28}$$

This will be solved where $w = c(1)$. Note that the desired level of effort doesn't play any role in either decision and is thus irrelevant in the standard SPNE. Instead, no matter what desired effort level is specified, the result should be low wages and low-effort employees.

Instead, suppose that the employee displayed fairness preferences. In this case, the employee's problem would be given by

$$\max_e w - c(e) + \tilde{f}_{employer}\big(w, \hat{e}|e^*(w, \hat{e})\big) \times f_{employee}(e|w, \hat{e}) \tag{15.29}$$

where $e^*(w, \hat{e})$ is what the employee believes the employer will believe the optimal fairness strategy of the employee is, and $\hat{e}$ is the employer's desired level of effort. If the wage offered relative to the desired effort level is high, then employees would expect to reap a large profit even if they didn't put in the effort requested. This could lead to employees assigning positive value to $\tilde{f}_{employer}$, because the employer is subjecting himself to possible losses in order to benefit the employee.

Suppose for example that $\tilde{f}_{employer} = k_1 \times (w - c(\hat{e}))$. In turn, employees might then feel bad if they deliver less than the level of effort desired, reflected in a negative value for $f_{employee}$ if $e < \hat{e}$, with the value becoming more negative the less effort is put in. For example, suppose that $f_{employee} = k_2 \times (e - \hat{e})$. This turns the last term of equation 15.29 to be increasing in effort, potentially leading the employee to provide much more effort than the minimum requested. Given the two example functions we have specified, the employee would solve

$$\max_e w - c(e) + k_1 k_2(w - c(\hat{e}))(e - \hat{e}). \tag{15.30}$$

Now the marginal cost of effort remains the slope of the $c(e)$ curve, represented by $c'(e)$, but there is now also a benefit to effort if $w > c(\hat{e})$ given by the third term. The marginal benefit in this case is $k_1 k_2(w - c(\hat{e}))$. Thus, the worker would provide effort such that marginal benefit of effort equals marginal cost of effort, $c'(e) = k_1 k_2(w - c(\hat{e}))$, as depicted in Figure 15.4. If the marginal cost of effort is increasing in the level of effort, this suggests that the level of effort would be increasing in wage and decreasing in desired effort level. The employers should respond to this by offering a wage that is high relative to the level of effort desired.

In fact, the average effort level observed was 4.4, well above the level of 1 that would be predicted by the selfish model. Additionally, employers offered relatively generous wages. If employees had worked the average desired effort level stated in the contract, which was $\hat{e} = 7$, they would have taken just under half of the surplus, only a little less than the employers. Their actual take was more than half, however, because employees gave somewhat less effort than the contract had requested. While employees shirked, they did

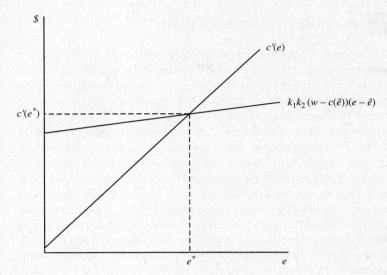

FIGURE 15.4
Fairness and Effort Level in Labor Contracts

perform better than they would have had they been selfish, and employers received more profit than if they had offered the minimum wage for a minimum level of effort.

Fairness might not only be a reason for relatively high wages in the marketplace; it might also be a reason for the use of teams in contract labor. Standard economic theory suggests that teams may be a particularly bad idea for managing work. If people are purely selfish, then working in a team can offer an opportunity to hide the fact that they are putting in a very low effort. We have all had experience with group assignments in a class in which one of the members does very little work but receives the same grade as the rest of the team. This is an illustration of what happens when people are selfish. If all people are selfish, managers should avoid teams. However, if they must use teams, then the manager would need to impose severe team-wide penalties for low performance to align the individual member's incentives with the manager's own desires. In this case, all would be punished for the sins of any one shirker.

Instead, if team members act according to fairness, such steep incentives might not be necessary. In fact, in some circumstances, fairness can lead teams to be more efficient than each employee is in individual labor assignments. If team members observe others in the team making sacrifices for the good of the team, feelings of fairness can drive the rest to similar behavior. This could lead to strong motivations for each individual employee to perform well above the level that could be enforced by an individual labor contract. Alternatively, team members who observe others shirking could go into punishment mode, with efforts devolving into a cutthroat and unproductive mess.

Firms use teams for many functions: product design, implementation, and marketing. The firms that design and create some of the most successful products in the world are designed in teams. Firms like Apple seem to elicit from their employees work that goes well beyond the response to the basic incentives their job would provide. Workers describe being involved in something extraordinary and transcendent. When people feel this way they tend to cooperate and act in a way that rewards the efforts of others around them. Understanding fairness and the basics of human relationships is essential to effectively managing workers.

EXAMPLE 15.7   Punishing for the Greater Good

The provision of public goods is of central interest to many economists. As discussed in prior chapters, if everyone benefits from the provision of a good, people will not want to contribute their private funds for the benefit of all and may instead decide to rely on others to contribute. Across the United States, on July 4 thousands of small communities put on a public fireworks display to celebrate the anniversary of the signing of the Declaration of Independence. These displays are often very costly, yet they often rely on voluntary contributions of the townspeople. A fireworks display usually can be seen for miles around, making it impossible to charge everyone who enjoys the display an admission fee. Instead, the plea goes out for contributions to the annual fireworks fund.

Consider a small town with just one truly wealthy family and many with much more modest means. Each year the wealthy family could foot the bill, but it likes to see the other families contribute. The wealthy family behaves so as to reward kindness and to punish cruelty. When they see others contributing to the effort, even if it is a relatively small amount, they consider this a kind gesture and like to reward this effort by making up the difference necessary to provide a satisfying show. When many of the townsfolk don't contribute, but rather decide to take a free ride off the contributions of others, the wealthy family perceives this as a cruel act and wishes to punish it. But therein lies the problem. There is no direct way to punish a single free rider. Instead, the only punishment available is to eliminate their contribution to the fireworks display, eliminating the possibility of a display for that year. Such a punishment would punish not only the free riders but also everyone else in the town. In this case, if there are enough selfish people in the town who decide to free ride, the wealthy family—though behaving only so as to reward others for their behavior—could end up behaving as if they were selfish by eliminating their own contribution.

In general, those who desire fairness may decide to free ride if they want to punish other free riders. This could lead to underprovision of public goods even if there are only a relatively small number of selfish actors. Ernst Fehr and Simon Gächter found this behavior in a simple experiment where four people were each given 20 tokens. They could keep these tokens or contribute some amount of them to a public good yielding each member of the group 0.4 tokens. By keeping all of their tokens, they would be strictly better off, but if all gave all of their tokens to the public good, each would walk away with a total of 32 tokens, much better than the 20 they would otherwise walk away with. However, if people are given the option to provide punishment to an individual rather than the group, suddenly one can induce the selfish players to behave as if they are kind. In the case of their experiment, any player could strip one other player of tokens by paying 1/3 of a token for each token eliminated from the other player's purse. When players are given the option to punish a single bad apple, selfish individuals realize they stand to lose if they are singled out for punishment by the rest. In this case, it is now in their self-interest to give for the public good. In this case, the way punishment is administered can play a big role in whether or not a public good will be provided.

Game theorists have noted the importance of being able to punish other players in obtaining better outcomes for all. One of the most important theorems in all of game theory deals with games that are repeated over and over again for an infinite number of periods (or at least players don't know when the game will end, so it is treated as an

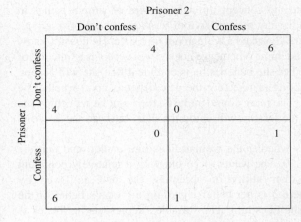

Prisoner 2

FIGURE 15.5
The Prisoner's Dilemma

infinitely repeated game). The folk theorem tells us that in repeated games, players can enforce nearly any outcome if each player employs a strategy in which they punish any player who deviates from that outcome in every period after a deviation forever. The only outcomes that could not be enforced in this way are outcomes for which eternal punishment by all others in the game does not erase the gains from deviating from the outcome being enforced. For example, two players playing the common prisoner's dilemma repeatedly for eternity could (if payouts are designed right) sustain collusion for eternity if both players employ a strategy in which they defect in every period after the other player has defected. One example of such a prisoner's dilemma is presented in Figure 15.5. Collusion in this case means both players would choose not to confess, though each would be better off in any single period by confessing no matter what the other player's strategy that period is. The long-term threat of punishment can lead to a condition in which players behave as if they are seeking their mutual benefit. However, truly, this is just self-serving behavior.

Psychological Games

Rabin's fairness model and equilibrium is a special case of a more-general class of games known as **psychological games**. Psychological games have been suggested as a way to include higher-order beliefs in simple games. These higher-order beliefs can include how people believe they will be perceived or how players will perceive the other players who receive various rewards. For example, fairness relies on the perception of whether others are being cruel or kind. More generally, psychological games can be used to model other emotions such as guilt, anger, surprise, confidence, or sympathy. In general, the payoff of one player can depend upon the motivations and emotions of others. In other words, each player's payoffs depend at least partially on what everyone in the game thinks the others are doing. These higher-order beliefs become part of the utility function, much like the fairness coefficients were incorporated into the payoff functions of players. Psychological games were originally proposed by John Geanakoplos, David Pearce, and

Ennio Stacchetti, who demonstrate the concept through a series of simple games in which one of the players do not have any moves. Two of these games are instructive.

Consider first a man who has already asked a woman out on a date. He doesn't know if the woman likes him or doesn't like him. Whether or not she will accept is a function of whether she likes him and of whether she believes he is confident that she will accept. His own utility of her either accepting or rejecting the date depends upon whether he expects that she will accept or not. The more confident he is, the more he will enjoy the date. The more pessimistic he is, the less he will enjoy the date, but also the less disappointed he will be if she says no.

Suppose that nature determines whether the woman likes him or not, and that the probability of her liking him is 0.50. She wants to go out with a relatively confident man. If the woman likes him, her utility of accepting the date is given by $u_{woman}(accept|like) = 3(\tilde{q} + \tilde{s})$, where $\tilde{q}$ is her belief regarding the man's belief of the probability she would say yes if she likes him. The variable $\tilde{s}$ represents her belief as to his belief of the probability she would say yes if she did not like him. Thus, she receives a higher utility from going on the date if she thinks he believes she will say yes whether she likes him or not. Her utility of saying no is given by $u_{woman}(reject|like) = 1$. Alternatively, if she does not like him, her utility of accepting is $u_{woman}(accept| doesn't\ like) = 0$ and the utility of rejecting is $u_{woman}(reject|doesn't\ like) = 1$.

His utility is given by $u_{man}(accept) = 1 + q + s$, whether she likes him or not, where q is his belief regarding her probability of accepting if she likes him and s is his belief regarding her probability of accepting if she does not. Thus, his utility of her accepting is higher if it is a high-probability event—he doesn't like the risk of being rejected even if he is not rejected. Alternatively, if she rejects, he will receive $u_{man}(reject) = -4(q + s)$ whether or not she likes him. If he is rejected, he would rather rejection to have been a high-probability event—he wouldn't have had high expectations.

The solution concept for a psychological game requires that all beliefs reflect reality, just as in the fairness equilibrium. In this case, this means $s = \tilde{s} = r$, where r is the actual probability of her accepting his offer if she doesn't like him determined by her employed strategy, and $q = \tilde{q} = p$, where p is the actual probability of her accepting his offer if she likes him determined by her strategy. Clearly, if she does not like him, she will always reject in any equilibrium obtaining a utility of 1 rather than 0. Thus, $s = \tilde{s} = r = 0$. If we examine only pure strategies (where actions are taken with certainty) then her accepting with probability 1 given she likes him would imply $q = \tilde{q} = p = 1$, and thus she would receive $u_{woman}(accept|like) = 3$ which is greater than $u_{woman}(reject|like) = 1$. This would constitute one equilibrium. In this case, because she is so likely to accept, he is very confident and is thus a much more enjoyable date.

Alternatively, if she rejects with probability 1 given she likes him, then $q = \tilde{q} = p = 0$, and thus she would receive $u_{woman}(reject|like) = 1$, which is greater than $u_{woman}(accept|like) = 0$. This also constitutes an equilibrium. In this case, because she is so discerning, he lacks confidence, which means he wouldn't have been much of a date anyway.

If all players have realistic beliefs and the solution is a Nash equilibrium given those beliefs, we call it a **psychological equilibrium**. The key to finding the psychological equilibrium is noting that the payoffs to each strategy change depending on the beliefs of each player. Thus, in equilibrium, the beliefs must be consistent with reality, and the players must still have the incentive to play the strategies implied by their beliefs.

In general, we look for a psychological equilibrium as the solution to any game in which beliefs are incorporated into the payoff functions of the participants. It is possible to incorporate higher-order beliefs (e.g., Player 1's belief about Player 2's belief about Player 1 and so on) of any order into the psychological game. Such games have been key to interpreting the odd behavior often observed in practice when examining games in an experimental lab.

EXAMPLE 15.8 Guilt and Grit

The game that virtually all students of economics are familiar with is the prisoner's dilemma, pictured in Figure 15.5. The story, as you recall, is that two men have committed a crime. The police have arrested the men but have insufficient evidence. They place the prisoners in separate rooms for interrogation. If both prisoners keep their mouths shut, both get short sentences. If one confesses, implicating the other, the one who confesses goes free and the betrayed prisoner gets a long sentence. If both confess, both get moderate sentences.

The Nash equilibrium for this game is given by (confess, confess). Given Prisoner 1 chooses to confess (and implicate Prisoner 2), Prisoner 2 does strictly worse by choosing not to confess (and implicate Prisoner 1). If Prisoner 1 chooses not to confess, Prisoner 2 does strictly better by confessing and vice versa.

But suppose that, in addition to the time in jail, we considered the prisoner's feelings of guilt or vindication in their payoffs. For example, suppose that Prisoner 1 is the dominant thief and the mastermind of their heist. He feels Prisoner 2 is somewhat spineless and dimwitted. Thus, Prisoner 1 would take some satisfaction in demonstrating his grit by not confessing if he believes Prisoner 2 is going to waffle under pressure and confess. Thus, Prisoner 1's perception of the probability that Prisoner 2 will confess will increase the payoff to not confessing and decrease the payoff to confessing whether Prisoner 2 actually confesses. Prisoner 1 would feel this satisfaction in addition to the disutility resulting from the substantial jail sentence he will serve. Prisoner 1 will feel like a wimp if he decides to confess and Prisoner 2 does not even though this would result in Prisoner 1 going free. Thus, Prisoner 1's perception of the probability of Prisoner 2 confessing enhances the payoff to confessing and decreases the payoff to not confessing if Prisoner 2 doesn't confess. Alternatively, Prisoner 2 is rather timid and also very worried about how Prisoner 1 perceives him. Thus, he would feel embarrassed and guilty if he is found to have confessed while Prisoner 1 did not. Thus, his utility of confessing if Player 1 does not confess is enhanced if it was highly probable Prisoner 1 was going to confess. Let $\tilde{p}$ represent the beliefs of Prisoner 2 regarding Prisoner 1's probability of confessing. Further, let $\tilde{q}$ represent Prisoner 1's beliefs regarding Prisoner 2's probability of confessing. Then, we could represent the prisoners' payoffs as in Figure 15.6.

In this case, the Nash equilibrium of the standard game could not be the Nash equilibrium of the psychological game. In that outcome, both choose to confess, so $p = \tilde{p} = q = \tilde{q} = 1$. In this case, Prisoner 1 obtains 0 and would clearly prefer not to confess. Alternatively, consider the outcome in which neither prisoner confesses. In this case, $p = \tilde{p} = q = \tilde{q} = 0$. Prisoner 1 is indifferent between confessing and not confessing, receiving a utility of 5 in either case. Alternatively, Prisoner 2 strongly prefers to not

Prisoner 2

	Don't confess	Confess
Don't confess	4 4+(1−$\tilde{q}$)	6−3(1−$\tilde{p}$) 0+$\tilde{q}$
Confess	0 6−(1−$\tilde{q}$)	1 1−$\tilde{q}$

Prisoner 1

FIGURE 15.6
The Prisoner's
Dilemma with Guilt
and Grit

confess, receiving a utility of 4 rather than 3. Thus, in this case, both players could enforce collusion owing to the emotional responses they have to how they might be perceived by the other player. Although this might not be an accurate description of the emotions or beliefs involved, the prediction is closer to observed behavior in an experimental prisoner's dilemma. Results in the laboratory suggest that people are much more likely to try to collude than to confess. However, it is difficult to observe or discern the emotional responses and higher-order beliefs they are employing. Thus, although we have some evidence higher-order beliefs are involved, we do not really know what form they take.

History and Notes

The behavioral economists who research the concepts of fairness, altruism, equity, and related concepts have been very slow to arrive at a common vocabulary. Some authors refer to fairness as defined in this chapter as *reciprocity*. Others use the word *fairness* to describe what we have defined as *equity*. Each of these terms has been used commonly to mean very different things. This has led to a condition in which most academic papers must define every term they use to avoid confusion with other common uses. I have chosen the definitions and terminology primarily because they are the terms used in the papers I first came to read in the literature as a student and not necessarily because they are the most common definitions.

Part of the confusion in definition goes beyond the standard problems that always arise at the onset of a new literature. Most of the concepts of fairness and equity are based upon historical arguments among philosophers about the most desirable distribution of wealth among people. These philosophers (who helped define the field of welfare economics) also had difficulty agreeing on what was fair and just. For example, John

Rawls argued that we are best off with the policies that yield the best outcome for the worst-off person. Others have suggested we should maximize the sum of all incomes in the economy or perhaps use some weighting of the average income. Pareto's notion was that we are better off as a society when someone is made batter off with no one being made worse off. Fairness to some has meant that all achieve the same income. Others use fairness to describe an outcome where all are rewarded equally for equal innovation and work. These are not likely to be concepts that we can come to a true philosophical agreement on. In any case, it can be useful to have a common language to describe the different concepts that can be used in modeling behavior.

Biographical Note

© Andreas Teichmann/laif/Redux

Ernst Fehr (1956–)

Undergraduate degree, Bregenz, Austria, 1975; M.S., University of Vienna 1980; Ph.D., University of Vienna, 1986; held faculty positions at University of Technology in Vienna, University of Zurich, Massachusetts Institute of Technology, and New York University

Ernst Fehr completed his undergraduate studies in business and continued on to obtain both his master's and Ph.D. degrees in economics. Fehr has made major contributions to the theory of social preferences, and in particular how people choose to cooperate with one another or how they fail to cooperate. He is one of the best-known experimental economists in the world, with several of his experimental pieces being among the most highly cited economics papers. His work ranges from tightly designed experiments in a laboratory to wide-ranging field experiments. His experimental work has been extremely influential in developing and refining theories of social preferences. Several of his contributions are highly theoretical, addressing some of the most fundamental and long-standing economics questions (e.g., regarding the existence of money illusion). His work is at the forefront of behavioral economics, incorporating theories from evolution, sociology, and psychology, including some major contributions in neuroeconomics. He often claims that standard economics has tried too hard to strip humans of all of their recognizably human traits: their emotions, compassion, and social awareness. Fehr has won several prizes and awards for his work, including the distinguished Marcel Benoist Prize, given to researchers for outstanding achievements in science and the humanities, and four honorary doctoral degrees. He is a fellow of the American Academy of Political and Social Sciences and the American Academy of Arts and Sciences.

THOUGHT QUESTIONS

1. Inequity aversion has been used to explain why outcomes in the ultimatum and dictator games deviate so distinctly from the selfish outcomes generally predicted in economic theory.

    (a) Derive the predictions of the inequity aversion utility function found in equation 15.1 for Kahneman, Knetsch, and Thaler's experiment in Example 15.4. Assume $\alpha = \beta = 0.5$. Remember that utility is now a function of each player's monetary outcome.

    (b) Derive the predictions of inequity aversion in the prisoner's dilemma.

    (c) Often, political arguments are made in terms of inequity aversion. For example, in September 2011, thousands of protesters occupied Wall Street and other venues, protesting what they claimed was an unfair economy. Their targets were clearly those making mass amounts of money in investing. Which theories of social preferences would best describe the actions of such protesters? What might these theories say about the response by investors, investment firms, or the government?

2. Consumers often impose rules of fairness on the firms that sell them goods, leading to the failure of markets to clear. Several theories suggest that when markets clear, we achieve a desirable outcome in terms of market welfare (the sum of consumer and producer surplus). Suppose a disaster occurs, causing a severe decline in the amount of gasoline on hand in the affected region. Standard economic theory would suggest the price of gasoline should rise to eliminate shortages. Suppose that because of the perception of consumers, firms do not let prices rise. What is the impact on consumer and producer surplus? Who wins and who loses? Why might firms comply with this rule?

3. Consider again the prisoner's dilemma. Use the kindness functions defined in equations 15.14 and 15.16 to determine a fairness equilibrium for the game. Describe how the motivation for fairness could lead to such an equilibrium. Use the same functions to derive the fairness equilibrium for the dictator game. Does fairness appear to explain the outcomes commonly found in experimental implementations of either of these games?

4. Consider the game represented in Figure 15.7, often referred to as Chicken. This game is intended to represent the decisions in a game of chicken where two drivers drive their cars directly at each other on a narrow road. The drivers can either dare to continue driving straight, or chicken out and turn off the road. Daring to stay on the road while the other chickens out will yield a big reward. However, if both dare to stay on the road they will both almost certainly die. Solve this game for the fairness equilibria using the kindness functions defined in equations 15.14 and 15.16. How do the equilibria depend upon the value of x? Provide an interpretation of this result.

FIGURE 15.7
Chicken

5. Consider the extensive form psychological game described by Figure 15.8 in which Player 1 first can choose either Down, resulting in a reward of 0 for both players, or Up, resulting in a node in which Player 2 can choose either Up or Down. If Player 2 chooses Up, Player 1 receives a reward of $-\tilde{p}$, where $\tilde{p}$ is Player 1's belief regarding Player 2's belief of the probability that Player 1 will choose Up. Solve for all the psychological equilibria. Which of these equilibria are subgame perfect?

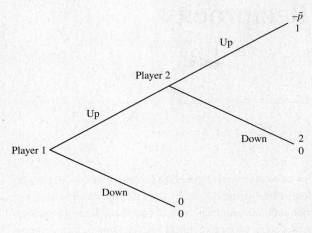

FIGURE 15.8
An Extensive Psychological Game

REFERENCES

Falk, A., E. Fehr, and U. Fischbacher. "On the Nature of Fair Behavior." *Economic Inquiry* 41(2003): 20–26.

Fehr, E., and S. Gächter. "Fairness and Retaliation: The Economics of Reciprocity." *Journal of Economic Perspectives* 14(2000): 159–181.

Fehr, E., S. Gächter, and G. Kirschsteiger. "Reciprocity as a Contract Enforcement Device." *Econometrica* 65(1997): 833–860.

Fehr, E., and K.M. Schmidt. "A Theory of Fairness, Competition and Cooperation." *Quarterly Journal of Economics* 114(1999): 817–868.

Geanakoplos, J., D. Pearce, and E. Stacchetti. "Psychological Games and Sequential Rationality." *Games and Economic Behavior* 1 (1989): 60–79.

Güth, W., R. Schmittberger, and B. Schwarze. "An Experimental Analysis of Ultimatum Bargaining." *Journal of Economic Behavior and Organization* 3(1982): 367–388.

Kahneman, D., J.L. Knetsch, and R. Thaler. "Fairness as a Constraint on Profit Seeking: Entitlements in the Market." *American Economic Review* 76(1986): 728–741.

Kahneman, D., J.L. Knetsch, and R. Thaler. "Fairness and the Assumptions of Economics." *Journal of Business* 59(1986): S285–S300.

Rabin, M. "Incorporating Fairness into Game Theory and Economics." *American Economic Review* 83(1993): 1281–1302.

Roth, A.E., and J.K. Murnighan. "The Role of Information in Bargaining: An Experimental Study." *Econometrica* 50(1982): 1123–1142.

16 Trust and Reciprocity

We often hear the repeated warning to be on constant guard for identity thieves—those who would use our personal information to steal money or credit from us. We should check our credit records regularly, not give out important numbers such as our Social Security number, and use only wired and secure Internet connections to conduct financial transactions. Almost 60 percent of Americans describe identity theft as a major worry. This is almost identical to the percentage who actually bank online. Some people go to great lengths to ensure that they are not exposed to identity theft: Some buy a special computer for online transactions, some use temporary credit account numbers for online transactions, some go so far as to not transact online at all. More than 50 million Americans use some form of credit-monitoring service to alert them in the case of identity theft. Such steps are sometimes taken at great cost, reflecting a real suspicion that someone is scheming to obtain their information.

Millions of people fall prey to identity theft every year, and the overall level of distrust for all things Internet may seem justified. Yet only about 10 percent of identity theft occurs through some form of Internet-based transaction. Overwhelmingly, identity theft occurs through misplaced or erroneously delivered paperwork or lost wallets. Almost half of those victimized by identity theft have a prior personal relationship with the person who victimized them. In many cases, a family member has successfully stolen their identity using their access to confidential financial records. Children have stolen parent's identities, and parents have stolen children's identities. However, without trusting our own family, family life would be transformed into something quite foreign and unpleasant. Few could imagine locking up wallets, keys, and other valuable items to prevent parents or siblings from stealing. For most, these relationships define trust, and they constitute some of the only people with whom we can be completely candid.

Even beyond our own family, a majority of our economic decisions depend on trust. In many cases, we must rely on others to provide us with information that may be tainted by their own motive. For example, given our lack of training in the medical field, we must rely on physicians to diagnose our illnesses. But some diagnoses may be more profitable for the physician (e.g., if they require regular follow-up visits). Similarly, a mechanic might lead us to believe some unnecessary work should be done on our car in order to maintain proper functioning if we are not as knowledgeable as the mechanic is. How we respond to a doctor's diagnosis or a mechanic's recommendation often hinges on whether we trust that they are being honest with us. Whenever we go to a restaurant, we must trust that the server will only use our credit card to charge the meal we have just eaten and will not steal the numbers for unauthorized uses. Without full trust in these situations, life would become more costly and less convenient. But why do we feel we can trust some mechanics?

Certainly there may be some motive for a mechanic to generate a reputation as being trustworthy. However, we must also acknowledge that a mechanic acting strictly as a selfish and rational actor would seek to take advantage of our lack of knowledge to some extent. Moreover, we must consider how easy it would be for the server to steal credit card numbers on a regular basis and take small amounts from customers with little chance of detection. Beyond this, the restaurant must trust that we not only have the means to pay when they first serve us the food but that we also intend to pay. Without a basic level of trust, economic transactions become costly, and some transactions will not take place.

In this chapter, we examine human behavior related to trust from a behavioral economics perspective. Trust is inherent in economic transactions. Yet in many cases, trust is a public good, and one for which private motives to be trustworthy should be minimal. Yet because both trust and trustworthiness exist and are widespread, we are all better off. This trust allows us substantial savings and increases our ability to conduct economic transactions as well as to conduct rewarding social interactions. Much of the literature on trust is closely related to the literature on fairness and altruism. We will emphasize this relationship.

EXAMPLE 16.1   Trust Relationships

Given the prominence of trust in our observed relationships, it is fair to question whether trust is a natural trait in human behavior, and if so how it came to be so. Observing trust, however, is not as easily accomplished as observing some of the other social preferences we have discussed. Fairness and altruism can be observed in a single choice or a set of choices that all occur at one point in time. However, to observe trust requires observing different players making a set of decisions that occur at different points in time. For example, we need to observe first the decision of the restaurant patron to be willing to give the server the credit card, then the server having the opportunity to either be honest or to steal the card number. For our purposes, we define **trust** as referring to a person's willingness to place others in a position to make decisions that could either help or harm the person.

The canonical experiment used to measure trust was originally proposed and conducted by Joyce Berg, John Dickhaut, and Kevin McCabe. They designed an experiment in which participants were randomly assigned to one of two rooms. All the subjects were given $10. Those in Room A were told they could take any portion of their $10 and send it to a random and anonymous recipient in Room B; we refer to a person in Room A as a *sender*. Whatever money is sent to Room B is tripled. The people they were paired with, the *receivers,* could then decide to send back whatever portion of that money they wished. We refer to this as a **trust game**.

Let us first examine the Nash equilibrium of this game assuming selfish actors. Suppose that the sender sends $x to the receiver. The receiver must then find the split of $3x that maximizes their own utility. A selfish receiver will choose to take $3x, leaving nothing for the sender. A selfish sender will choose to send $0 no matter how much is

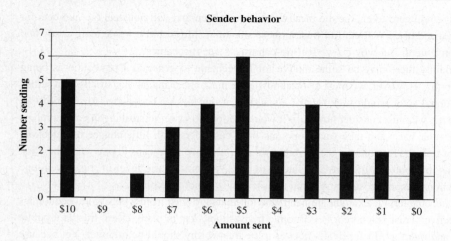

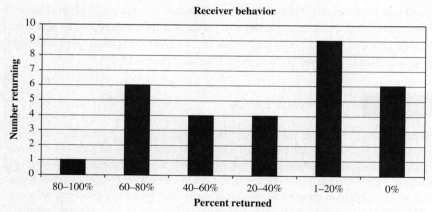

FIGURE 16.1
Behavior in the Trust Game

Source: Berg, J., J. Dickhaut, and K. McCabe. "Trust, Reciprocity and Social History." *Games and Economic Behavior* 10(1995): 122–142.

sent back to the sender. Thus, in the Nash equilibrium, each player goes home with $10, and no money is sent. Because there are only two stages in this game, it is not possible for trust to develop as a result of repeated interactions and reputation (as in the Take-It-Or-Leave-It game presented in Chapter 14).

The results are pictured in Figure 16.1. Of 32 senders, 30 sent some amount of their $10 to Room B. On average, they sent $5.16, with the modal choice (six chose it) being $5. Nearly as many (five) chose to send the entire $10 to Room B.

In the terminology of this chapter, almost all of the senders trusted the receivers. All but two decided it was worthwhile to send some of their money to their counterpart even though the receiver could decide to just take all of the money sent. The sender's trust was not always justified. In fact, 17 of the receivers who received some positive amount of money decided to send back less than the sender had originally sent. Eleven decided to send back more than they received. Six decided to send back nothing. On average, receivers returned only $4.66, somewhat less than the $5.16 that was sent to them. Thus, although senders were inclined to trust their anonymous counterparts, those counterparts were not particularly trustworthy on average.

This suggests first that people who are trusting might have incorrect beliefs about how trustworthy people are in general. This result causes some problems for the inequity aversion and fairness models. If receivers sent back less than was originally sent, this means they decided to take more than two thirds of what they received, in addition to the $10 they were given for participating, leaving the sender with less than $10. Moreover, the fact that the sender had sent a positive amount in the first place enabled the receiver to take at least some of the surplus. Thus, it seems that the sender should interpret the amount sent as a signal that the sender is being kind.

For example, suppose that the receiver employed the strategy in which she would return $y = \alpha x$, where x is the amount sent by the sender. All Pareto optima in this game involve the sender sending the full $10, and in fact every allocation in this case results in a Pareto optimum. Thus, the only Pareto optimum with the receiver employing a strategy of returning αx, yields $\overline{\pi}_2^P(b_2) = \underline{\pi}_2^P(b_2) = 40 - 30\alpha$. The worst possible outcome for the receiver is that in which the sender sends nothing, yielding $\underline{\pi}_2(b_2) = 10$. The kindness function proposed in equation 15.14 would have a value

$$f_{sender}(x, y) = \frac{10 + 3x - \alpha x - 40 + 30\alpha}{40 - 30\alpha - 10} = \frac{3x - \alpha x - 30 + 30\alpha}{30 - 30\alpha} = \frac{3 - \alpha}{30(1 - \alpha)} x - 1. \quad (16.1)$$

Senders sent an average of $x \approx \$5.16$, with receivers returning $\alpha \approx 0.90$ of this. But if this is the case, equation 16.1 is positive. Thus, both the sender and the receiver should believe that the sender is being kind. Because this is positive, it should induce kind behavior by the receiver under the fairness-equilibrium hypothesis. But this does not occur on average. Instead, the split in the surplus return highly favors the receiver. Equation 16.1 also implies that the more the sender sends, the more the receiver should be willing to send back. In fact, there is no relationship between the amount sent and the amount returned.

Interestingly, the subgame in which the receiver decides how much money to send back to the sender is identical to the dictator game in which the receiver is the dictator. In this case, the results are fairly different from those in the dictator game. In general, the results of the dictator game did favor the dictator, but a large minority of the responses clustered very close to an even split between the dictator and the dictator's counterpart. In this game, that would have meant a large number of receivers sending back about 1.5 times as much as was originally sent by the sender. This occurred in only a small number of cases. Thus, in response to the apparently kind behavior by the sender, the receiver appears to be less kind on average. This is a surprising result.

In an alternative treatment at a later point with different participants, senders and receivers were given a summary of the behavior from this first trust experiment. You would think that senders, given the chance to see how the game had been played by others, would send less in order to minimize their losses. This was not the case, with senders now sending an average of $5.36, more than in the previous experiments. In fact, although a larger fraction sent $0 (3/28), a larger fraction also sent the entire $10 (7/28). Seven of the 28 sent $5.

One potential explanation for this unintuitive behavior is that the information on the behavior in prior experiments created a **social norm**. Thus, for example, it may be that we don't think twice about giving a waiter or waitress our credit card because we see

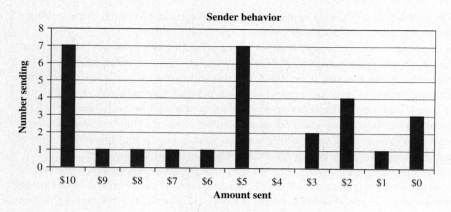

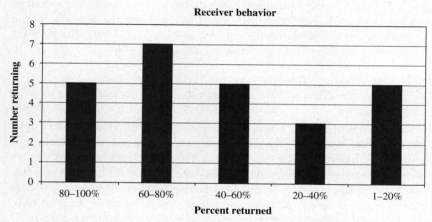

FIGURE 16.2
Behavior in the Trust Game with Information on History

Source: Berg, J., J. Dickhaut, and K. McCabe. "Trust, Reciprocity and Social History." *Games and Economic Behavior* 10(1995): 122–142.

others do the same so often. We behave this way because we believe that it is expected and that there may be some negative social consequence to violating the norm. However, it seems unlikely that such a social norm could be established if those who adhered to the social norm would be punished for it.

Interestingly, although sender behavior did not change much with information on others' behavior, receiver behavior changed substantially. The results of this game are displayed in Figure 16.2. Of the 25 receivers who were sent money, 17 returned at least as much as the sender sent. A majority, 13, sent back more than the sender had sent, resulting in an average amount returned of $6.46. With common information on others' behavior in similar situations, suddenly trust pays. Moreover, with the information on others' behavior, suddenly the amount returned increases with the amount sent, as predicted by Rabin's fairness model. This again may be the result of the social norm established by the information. In this case, the social norm seemed to signal to receivers what amounts indicated that they had been trusted and what amounts indicated that they were not trusted.

Of Trust and Trustworthiness

Social scientists have long studied the importance of trust in economic as well as other relationships. These studies began in earnest with large-scale surveys administered by the National Opinion Research Center beginning in 1972. This survey asks participants the simple question, "Generally speaking, would you say that most people can be trusted or that you can't be too careful in dealing with people?" Early work using these data shows a stark relationship between the number of organizations to which a person belongs and the degree to which the person trusts people in general. By itself it might seem that this result occurs from reverse causality. In other words, it could be that belonging to a group causes one to trust others, or it could be that trusting others leads one to join groups. Another possibility is that some other factor influences both trust of others and joining groups. For example, the prevalence of the Lutheran Church within communities throughout the United States in the early part of the 20th century strongly predicts both the degree of trust indicated by responses to the survey question and the prevalence of participation in social groups. It could be that the teachings and culture of the Lutheran Church caused both trusting behavior and a tendency toward social connections.

These early survey results on trust led many to suppose that trust, and perhaps trustworthiness, is related to social capital. **Social capital** is a term originating in sociology; it refers to the durable social relationships one has and can draw upon as resources for goods—tangible, emotional, or informational. This leads to a few predictions about who should and should not be trusting of others. For example, those who are older might have built up more social capital than those who are younger, leading older people to be more trusting. College students spend valuable time not only building skills for the workplace but also building social capital, thus leading college graduates to be more trusting than others. Older people and more-educated people do belong to more groups and organizations. In fact, these college-educated and older people also appear to be more trusting according to the results of the survey. But it is difficult for economists to take survey results blindly. In this case, the survey question is so vague that it is difficult to know whether it is really measuring how people behave.

Edward Glaeser led a team of researchers in examining how social capital relates to trust and trustworthiness using experimental methods. Participants in their experiments were first asked a series of questions regarding their relationships with others and how often they trust others. A few weeks later they were asked to play a modified trust game. At the beginning of this game, students were paired with other subjects and asked to fill out a survey together. This survey asks questions about how well the two participants know each other, along with other questions about friendships, to the point of requesting a list of all friends they have in common. The pairs were then split into separate rooms and roles were assigned. Senders were given $15 and could decide to send whatever portion of that $15 they wished. Receivers would then receive double the amount that was sent and could decide how much of the money they received they wished to return to the sender. But before the sender decided how much to send, some receivers could send one of two messages to the sender. They could send a message promising to return at least as much as was sent or a message that they made no promise. These promises were not binding, and they constitute what economists refer to as **cheap talk**. Cheap talk is essentially any nonbinding communication. In other words, one could say one promised to return at least as much as was sent, and then decide to keep all of the money. Of the receivers, 48 percent of those who could send messages chose not to promise to return at least as much as was sent. Of those who received money, 68 percent of the receivers chose to send back exactly the amount that had been sent, keeping the excess returns for themselves. Alternatively, when promises were not allowed, only 48 percent returned as much as had been sent. Thus, it appears that the ability to promise to return at least as much as was sent set up a sort of social norm of returning exactly as much as had been sent.

The amount that participants sent and returned depended heavily on the number of social connections the participants had in general and more specifically on how socially connected the sender and receiver were. For example, for every month the sender and receiver had known each other before the experiment, the sender decided to send $0.10 more on average. Thus, once a sender had known the receiver a year, she would be willing to trust the receiver with approximately $1.20 more than she would send a complete stranger. On the other hand, receivers sent back 0.6 percent more for each month they had known the receiver. Apparently social capital accumulates slowly.

Having friends in common increased the amount one was willing to return, but it had no real impact on the amount sent. Individual measures of social capital were largely unrelated to the amount the sender decided to send. The only question that had a substantive relationship to the amount sent was whether the participant was involved in a sexual relationship with any partner. On the other hand, the sender's number of close friends, hours spent volunteering, consumption of beer, and whether the sender was involved in a sexual relationship all increased the amount the receiver decided to send back. Oddly, the sender's social capital appears to influence the trustworthiness of the receiver. Because senders in most cases were randomly assigned, this suggests a causal relationship between a person's social connectedness and how trustworthy others behave toward that person. This provides a plausible explanation for the survey data. Social capital might not directly influence how trusting a person is. Rather, social capital may be correlated with how trustworthy a person believes others are given that social capital is associated with trustworthiness generally.

This view of trust suggests that our observation of trust, say in a trust game, must be very related to one's aversion to risk. Trusting another person inherently involves some degree of risk. Clearly if one is less risk averse, one may be willing to send more money given the same assessment of the probability it will be paid back. Is trust just an artifact of risk preferences and beliefs, or is it an independent behavior all on its own?

Ernst Fehr has devoted substantial effort to answering this question. He points to evidence from a wide array of trust games. In one set, participants were randomly given drugs that affect psychosocial functioning before they participated in the trust games. Those given the drugs were much more trusting, but the drug did not affect their behavior in other experiments involving only risk and not trust. Although risk aversion is related to trust in survey work, trust is not entirely a function of risk preferences. Fehr finds that trust is a result of both risk preferences and social preferences. In his view, trust and trustworthiness develop as a result of the actions of all actors involved. In this case, both trust and trustworthiness can result from a structure much like, though clearly distinct from, Rabin's fairness preferences, where beliefs regarding others' motives can switch on (or switch off) trust-related behavior.

Mathematical models of trust behavior have been elusive, and none have come into wide use or acceptance. Thus, this chapter is focused primarily on the basic behaviors that have been observed and the relationships that have been identified rather than a theoretical exploration.

EXAMPLE 16.2   Keep on Smiling

Have you ever noticed how spokesmen and spokeswomen in commercials talk through a wide and often exaggerated smile? We are advised to keep a smile on our face in job interviews, in social situations, or even when we are teaching a class. The thought is that by smiling, we can connect with those we are speaking to, win their sympathy, and be more persuasive. In other words, a smile can allow us to leverage our social capital. Just how much is a smile worth?

This was the object of a series of psychological experiments by Jörn Scharlemann and a team of researchers. Within these experiments, participants were led to believe they were playing a game with a randomly paired partner. The game was structured as pictured in Figure 16.3. This game is much like the take-it-or-leave-it game presented in Chapter 14. The SPNE of this game has each player choosing T at any node in which he or she controls the game. In the last period, Player 1 would prefer 1.20 to 1.00, and would thus choose T. In the second node, Player 2 would rather have 1.25 than the 1.20 that would result from choosing L, and thus chooses T. Given that Player 2 will choose T, Player 1 then would decide to choose T at the first node in order to obtain 1.00 rather than 0.80. However, a trusting person might decide to choose L if she believes Player 2 is trustworthy and thus is willing to forgo the extra 0.05 in order to be true to the trust Player 1 has placed in her.

Before making her decision, Player 1 is given a picture of the player she is said to be paired with. This being a psychology experiment, the participants were deceived regarding these partners. In fact, they were playing against predetermined strategies programmed into a computer. Nonetheless, each player believed she was playing against the player pictured. The experimenters threw in one added twist. There were actually two pictures of each hypothetical Player 2. One of the pictures depicted the player smiling, and the other depicted the player with a straight face. Participants were randomly assigned to see either a smiling partner or a straight-faced partner. Overall, participants were about 13 percent more likely to choose L in the first node

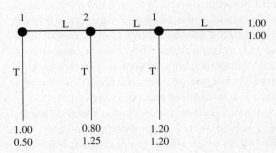

FIGURE 16.3
Take-It-or-Leave-It Trust Game

if their supposed opponent was smiling. Thus, they took the smile as a signal of being trustworthy.

The difference between those seeing smiling and straight-faced opponents was much larger for male participants than female participants. Male participants trusted a smiling opponent nearly 80 percent of the time, compared to 59 percent of the time with an opponent who was not smiling. On the other hand, the corresponding percentages choosing to trust were 58 percent and 52 percent for female participants. Apparently girls and women are not as easily taken in by a smile. Further experiments by the same team found that the assessed sincerity of the smile or other facial expressions also had an impact on the willingness of Player 1 to trust Player 2.

So why might it be so important to smile? With nothing to go on but a snapshot of a person's facial expressions, people somehow act as if they can judge the very character of an individual. Some research has shown that such snap judgments tend to persist even in very long-term relationships. Such a snap judgment could play a role in long-term payoffs for both the judge and the subject of the judgment.

EXAMPLE 16.3   Economic Consequences of Trust

As with most experiments, one must question whether the behavior we observe in trust games is really representative of how people behave in the real world. Given that trust is so important in reducing transaction costs, one would naturally hypothesize that societies with higher levels of trust might reap some dividends from that trust. With higher levels of trust, less needs to be spent in monitoring business dealings or other activities, perhaps lowering the taxes necessary to support enforcement. Moreover, the greater the level of trust, the less effort one needs to exert to determine if one's business partners are dealing fairly with one. In fact, using an international survey of 21 countries including measures of trust and data on national income, Stephen Knack and Philip Keefer find some evidence that increased levels of trust are associated with accelerated growth in gross domestic product. Other measures of social capital in a country behaved similarly. Several others have found similar results, confirming that trust and social capital can play an important role in macroeconomic performance of the national economy.

The next natural question one may ask is whether trust, as measured by a trust game, is also important in an economy? Survey measures of trust are not motivated by economic outcomes. It may be that many are willing to say they are trusting but not to act that way. Issues of trust can be of supreme importance in trying to help bring those living in developing nations out of poverty. To examine the impact of trust on economic growth and performance in a community, Michael Carter and Marco Castillo conducted a series of trust experiments in 14 communities in South Africa. Half of these communities were urban, and the other half were rural. The participants were relatively poor by U.S. standards, and the average participant had only six total years of education. The amounts of money involved in the trust game were on the order of two days' wages.

On average, senders trusted their anonymous partners with 53 percent of their purse, remarkably close to the percentages observed in U.S. experiments. However, the amounts sent varied substantially depending on which village the participant was from.

Table 16.1   Trust and Reciprocity in South Africa

Village	Median Share Sent (percent)	Median Share Returned (percent)
Umlazi	40	33
Mpumalanga	40	33
Imbali	40	33
Mpakama	60	42
Kwamashu	60	33
Madadeni	50	33
Umzumbe	40	33
Kwabrush	60	50
Emkimdini	60	33
Buxeden	40	33
Chatsworth	60	39
Dundee	60	42
Okhlahlamba	40	33
Nkandla	60	42

Source: Carter, M.R., and M. Castillo. "Trustworthiness and Social Capital in South Africa: Analysis of Actual Living Standards Data and Artifactual Field Experiments." *Economic Development and Cultural Change* 59, Issue 4 (2011): 695–722, University of Chicago Press.

Table 16.1 displays the median amount given by those from each of the 14 villages. Note that senders tended to choose amounts that were around 10 percent increments of their purse to send to the receiver, resulting in the tidy 40 percent, 50 percent, and 60 percent results. When the money was sent, it was tripled before the receiver got it. Thus, receivers who decided to send back 33 percent would be returning to the sender just what was sent and keeping the rest of the pot for themselves. This was the median response in most of the villages, suggesting that participants could be trusted to return the amount they were entrusted with but would not share the profits. The average receiver returned 38 percent of the pot, suggesting a small premium for trusting. Only 20 percent of receivers returned less than was received, suggesting a relatively high level of trustworthiness.

More interesting is that villages with higher levels of trust also tend toward higher levels of trustworthiness and reciprocity. Reciprocity refers to participants' intention to reward senders for trusting them by returning more than was sent. This is an effect similar to the rewarding of kindness in a fairness equilibrium. In fact, many use the term **reciprocity** to represent behavior embodied in the addition of kindness functions to the standard utility function. As the sender increased the amount sent by about 6 percent of the original purse the sender was endowed with, the average amount returned by the receiver increased by 12.5 percent, demonstrating reciprocity. The correlation coefficient between the percentage of budget sent and the percent of budget returned is 0.66, suggesting a significant positive relationship. This should not be too surprising. It is unlikely people would develop trust for others if those in the community around them are untrustworthy.

The notion that trust and trustworthiness may be a shared community characteristic leads one to wonder exactly what the overall consequences might be of living in a trusting community rather than a less-trusting community. Carter and Castillo found that there are rather robust relationships among trust, trustworthiness, and the per-capita expenditures of a typical household (a measure of household well-being). Surprisingly, however, trust and trustworthiness have different impacts on household expenditures, depending on whether the household is located in a rural or urban village. In an urban setting, a 10 percent increase in trust (measured by the average share of budget sent by the senders in that village) is associated with a 2.4 percent increase in expenditures. Alternatively, in a rural setting, a 10 percent increase in trust is associated with a 2 percent decrease in household expenditures. Similarly, reciprocity has different impacts on household expenditures in urban and rural settings. In an urban setting, increasing reciprocity (as measured by the share of the pot that is returned) by 10 percent is associated with a 7 percent increase in household expenditures, whereas in a rural setting it has virtually no effect.

It is difficult to understand how trust or reciprocity could be a bad thing in rural villages. One potential explanation is that in rural villages, one is related to many of those one comes in contact with and is closely socially connected to a large percentage of those in the village. Being trusting in this case has little return because of the limited number of social connections one might have. Beyond this, it may be that the level of trust allows substantial **moral hazard**. Moral hazard occurs when a person can take actions that are not fully observed by others but that affect the welfare of both the actor and others. A trusting rural village might mean that people generally assume that everyone will perform their civic and economic duties and not need to monitor others closely. A less-trusting village will monitor more closely whether villagers are actually performing their work—potentially leading to higher returns for all. Alternatively, in an urban area very few are related. This means that trusting others might allow you to gain a wider social network, potentially creating some substantial individual returns. Other similar studies have found that societies that engage in market-style production are relatively more trusting societies. It may be that this also depends upon whether the society is more isolated and rural or more integrated and urban.

Trust in the Marketplace

Much has been hypothesized and written about the impact of trust and trustworthiness on the functioning of the markets. Consider, for example, one of the simplest business transactions: hiring a kid down the street to paint your living room. First off, although painting is a relatively simple task, it does require some skill and preparation to do it right. One must be careful to cover surfaces that will not be painted. Spreading drop-cloths over the floor and furniture is relatively easy, but if the painter isn't careful, the drop cloth can slide and expose the wrong surface. Borders and trim must be taped, and the painter must make sure that paint is applied evenly without drips. Each of these requirements could be explained to an average teen with little difficulty.

At that point, if the homeowners trusts the teen, they could leave her with the necessary materials believing she will do a good job, returning to pay her when the job is completed. But if the homeowner doesn't trust the teen to take the proper care in following instructions or to put in the relatively low effort but high attention to detail required, then the homeowner will need to monitor the work. Thus, instead of leaving to complete their own work for the day, the homeowner will need to stop in every half hour or so and see that the painter is complying with the instructions. In this case, the homeowner is paying not only with money for the work but also with time and hassle. Note, though, that the time spent in monitoring is not directly beneficial to either the homeowner or the painter.

This time spent monitoring constitutes what economists call **transactions costs**. The potential exists for trust to reduce transactions costs, allowing a larger benefit to both the painter and the homeowner. In this case, if the transactions costs of employing the kid down the street are high enough, the homeowner might instead hire a professional painter. This professional painter may be more expensive but should require less monitoring or instruction. Websites like Angie's List provide customer feedback about various service firms specifically to reduce the transactions cost for firms by identifying those that are untrustworthy and those that are trustworthy.

Of course, transactions costs and trust are not limited to service industries. Consider the more-complicated transaction of purchasing a used car from a dealership. If the dealer and the buyer both trusted each other fully, the buyer could walk into a used car dealership, identify the cars she was interested in, ask the dealer about their condition, and agree to make payments on the car she wished to buy. Instead, the lack of trust has made buying a used car much more of a hassle. First, a typical used car buyer will do substantial research about the value of various used cars to determine what reasonable prices are available. This might involve buying access to reports on the quality or value of cars such as the *Kelley Blue Book* or *Consumer Reports*. Then, once selecting a potential candidate vehicle and determining that the used car dealership is willing to sell at a reasonable price, the buyer often pays to have an independent mechanic inspect the vehicle to determine whether the dealer is giving an accurate report of the condition of the vehicle. Finally, once the vehicle is determined to be in working order and the dealer has accepted the buyer's offer, the dealer pays a credit agency to determine if the buyer can be trusted to fulfill the obligation to make payments on a car loan. Consider the amazing amount of time and resources consumed by a lack of trust in this transaction. Indeed, some researchers have found that real estate transactions between family members occur at substantially lower costs than those occurring generally, often saving the buyer up to 30 percent of the cost.

Trust is perhaps one of the reasons people place such high value on brand-name goods. A brand name is tied to a reputation for quality. A firm faced with a customer complaint is motivated to satisfy the customer in order to maintain the reputation for trustworthiness they have developed with their customer base. Firms that fail to deliver on customer service or fail in delivering the promised quality quickly lose that reputation and their customers. This can also explain why people tend to develop longer-term business relationships with a mechanic or a physician. Both of these services require a substantial amount of trust. A mechanic may be hesitant to sell you unneeded repairs if there is the possibility of losing years of future business. Customers who just randomly choose whatever mechanic they happen on might not be so lucky. To this end, many economists expect that developed economies and well-functioning markets are predicated on a certain level of trust existing between generic actors in that economy. Without that trust, economic transactions are burdened by unnecessary transactions costs that can diminish everyone's well-being.

EXAMPLE 16.4   Whom Do We Trust?

Often we have just a few seconds to determine whether we will trust someone or not. Whether it be asking a stranger for directions, determining whether to help a stranded motorist, or determining whether to patronize a street vendor, we have a need to assess a person's trustworthiness almost instantaneously. In fact, in a typical day walking through a city we can come into contact with hundreds of people to whom we must quickly decide whether we can trust our personal safety and well-being. How can we make so many decisions so fast? In the absence of more-accurate information, people often retreat to the superficial: what we can see. Thus, we look to see if the person smiles and looks generally friendly. We also, unfortunately, look to classify the person by categories: class, sex, race, or external clues of religion.

One example of this can be found in the research of Damian Stanley, Peter Sokol Hessner, Mahzarin R. Banaji, and Elizabeth Phelps. As part of their work, they engaged 43 participants in a psychological experiment in which they would play a modified version of the trust game. Participants were to play the sender role and were shown a picture of their receiver (because the experiment was conducted by psychologists, no receivers actually participated). Senders were told that receivers would receive four times as much as they sent. Receivers then either returned half of the amount they received or returned nothing. The sender could then choose how much of their original endowment to send. The pictures of the receivers were varied by race, so that sometimes senders believed they were playing with a black receiver, and sometimes they believed they were playing with a white receiver.

Interestingly, there was no real difference in the amounts sent on average to white and black receivers ($3.75 versus $3.74). Even if we looked just at white senders, or just at black senders, there was no difference in the amounts sent on average. Other measures of trust based on survey responses to questions of how trustworthy a person appeared were also similar across race. Additionally, participants were asked to play a word-association game designed to test whether they associate more negative or positive feelings with those of white or black races. This measure of racial bias was associated with racial bias in both offers in the trust game and with assessments of trustworthiness. This provides us some evidence that race can be taken (at least by some) as an indicator of trustworthiness and thus can affect transactions costs and economic well-being.

Olof Johansen-Stenman, Minhaj Mahmud, and Peter Martinsson ran several experiments along the same vein using the trust game in Bangladesh, where nearly 90 percent of the population is Muslim, though there is a substantial Hindu minority. They examined the impact of pairing Muslims with Muslims, Hindus with Hindus, and Hindus with Muslims in the trust game to see the impact both on trust and trustworthiness, finding some weak evidence of differences between religions, displayed in Table 16.2. Although some patterns appear to emerge, the samples were small enough that none of these differences in trust could be considered to be outside the margin of error.

Edward Glaeser and a team of researchers also examined the impact of race on trust and trustworthiness in the United States. Although differences in gender had little impact on either trust or reciprocity, they find that if the sender and receiver are of different races, the receiver is likely to return less money to the sender. In their analysis they

Table 16.2   Trust and Trustworthiness in Bangladesh

Average Portion	Muslim Sender Muslim Receiver	Muslim Sender Hindu Receiver	Hindu Sender Muslim Receiver	Hindu Sender Hindu Receiver
Sent	0.46	0.46	0.43	0.50
Returned	0.46	0.51	0.42	0.44

Source: Johansson-Stenman, O., M. Mahmud, and P. Martinsson. "Trust and Religion: Experimental Evidence from Rural Bangladesh." Economica 76(2009): 462–485, John Wiley & Sons, Inc.

examined pairs where the sender was white and the receiver was of another race, as well as those where the sender was not white and the receiver was white. In both cases, they observed a 10 percent reduction in the amount returned relative to when a white sender was paired with a white receiver. Others have studied the impact of gender, finding that women display more reciprocity than men and that men are generally more trusting.

Biologists have long thought of trust as evolutionary behavior. In this line of thought, trust develops as a way to promote evolutionary fitness. This line of thought suggests that people over generations should become hardwired to promote the well-being and survival of others to whom they are related. Lisa DeBruine examined this in a set of trust game experiments. These psychology experiments[1] involved participants playing the trust game and being shown photos of people whom they were told were their partner in the game. Before playing the game, participants were photographed. Then, participants were shown pictures of their supposed partner that in actuality were randomly selected photos of other people that had been altered to contain some characteristics of the participant's own features. This same photo was also used in another trust game played by another participant as a control. In fact, participants were much more trusting of the partners whose photos had been manipulated to look like themselves than they were of partners whose photos had not been altered.

This might explain a potential tendency toward racial bias in trust games as well as some of the human need to dress and look like we fit in with those around us. Moreover, it can explain the real importance of providing advertisements and promotional materials that represent a broad set of demographics. Narrowly focusing advertising around a small demographic might fail to generate the trust and familiarity desired with any other group; customers might think "They simply don't look like me."

EXAMPLE 16.5   The Benefits of Blame

Contractual relationships necessarily involve trust. In fact, contracts themselves are designed to increase the level of trust between the two parties for the mutual benefit of both. To increase this trust, the contract often specifies penalties that will occur if a contracting party chooses not to fulfill their part of the contract. In such cases, they are said to be at fault, generally releasing the other party from their agreement and assessing a penalty to the party who is at fault. The entire point of the contract is to enhance the certainty that both parties can be trusted to complete their promised actions. But if

---

[1] Economic experiments do not permit deception such as that which occurred in the experiment described. However, deception such as this is common in psychology experiments.

the penalties for breaking the contract are too small, one party might decide to betray the trust of their partner. Moreover, if a contract can be broken without assigning fault, it becomes much less useful in creating trust.

The opposite of reciprocity is **opportunism**, defined by some as self-interest unconstrained by moral considerations. An opportunistic receiver when playing the trust game immediately takes the whole pot, not considering the impact on or expectations of the sender. In a contract, one signer often has the opportunity to take substantial gains at the expense of the other signer. Consider what would happen in the trust game if the parties could agree beforehand to split the additional returns evenly. Thus, if no contract is signed, the game is played as described previously. If the contract is signed, senders agree to send all of their money, facing a penalty y that will be given to their receiver if they break their promise. The receiver, who then plans on receiving three times the amount sent, agrees to return two times the amount sent or face a penalty of z that will be given to the receiver. Then, after signing the contract, the parties play the trust game, with the added threat of penalties.

We already know that without the penalties, the Nash equilibrium strategies result in no money being sent and no money returned. Suppose x is the amount sent by the sender. If a contract is signed, the receiver then chooses either to return $r \geq 2x$ and receive $3x - r$, or return $r < 2x$ and receive $3x - r - z$. In this case, opportunistic receivers would maximize their payout by selecting either $r = 2x$, if $3x - 2x = x \geq 3x - z$, or $r = 0$ otherwise. So long as $z > 2x$, the opportunistic receiver would choose to comply with the contract. In this case senders would choose to send as much as possible and would double their money. In this case, the possibility of the receiver being found at fault can reduce the risk from trusting the receiver and can lead to a mutually beneficial outcome. Even in the absence of the contract, we observe that senders trust receivers and often earn a return. However, the contract can make trust less of an issue given the threat of legal action.

One form of contract in which the ability to seek a finding of fault has eroded over time is marriage. In marriage, spouses have traditionally contracted to abstain from outside sexual relationships and to divide labor for the welfare of their family. Though not explicit in law, this traditionally involved a man providing material support through labor or employment and a woman providing domestic labor and rearing of children (the most precious investment of the venture). Although it is ideally built on love and trust, until the last several decades marriage also had the force of law to encourage trust. Marriage could only be ended by an injured party suing the spouse for divorce and proving that the spouse was at fault. Fault could be found for abandonment, adultery, or abuse. Unless you could show that your spouse was guilty of one of these violations of the marriage covenant, you were required to continue in the marriage agreement. Moreover, if the spouse was found at fault, he or she would face a severe penalty in the divorce— either monetary or due to the impacts on long-term social reputation. Such a threat could lead one who is on the fence with regard to the marriage to consider deeper investments in the marriage relationship. Alternatively, the threat of penalties resulting from divorce could lead one to feel more secure or apt to enter a marriage with someone who otherwise might behave opportunistically.

In all states, it is now possible to file for a no-fault divorce. In this case, the marriage is dissolved, and property is divided for the most part without respect to how much effort the spouse put into maintaining the marriage. Instead, the no-fault divorce option protects people entering marriage from the potential negative effects of a marriage breaking up as a result of their own actions. By offering this option, a spouse discouraged in a marriage could easily dissolve the contract without facing the financial or other penalties. This offers an easy way out.

The introduction and wide acceptance of no-fault divorce has affected the rates of marriage and divorce and the distribution of outcomes after a divorce. Robert Rowthorn has written about many of the observed changes. For example, women with children have experienced a decline in their standard of living following a divorce. Some estimate the decline to be as much as 36.6 percent. An econometric study finds that eliminating fault also led to an increase in spousal abuse, effectively reducing the penalty for such abuse. It also led to greater number of total working hours (both domestic and outside the home) for women, who now had greater need to insure against the possibility of abandonment and the reduced payout from such a dissolution of their marriage.

In every case, the partner who initiates the divorce is better off under no-fault divorce laws because the initiating spouse minimizes his or her initial investment in the marriage he or she is reluctant to continue, and more importantly because the initiating spouse faces no penalty after the end of the marriage for the reduced investment of time, effort, or money that led to the eventual breakup. Moreover, marriage rates have declined and divorce rates have increased. Over time, it is apparent that perceptions of marriage and the ability one has to trust one's spouse have changed substantially. Thus, it is clear that whereas trust and reciprocity have some behavioral foundations, they can also be substantively affected by social norms, incentives, and institutions. In this case, although trust may be a naturally occurring behavior, having the ability to punish fault can create substantial benefits for both parties.

Trust and Distrust

It has often been observed that trust is difficult to build but very easy to destroy. Years and years of good-faith behavior can all be overshadowed by a single visible indiscretion. This is true in many contexts. Paul Slovic, in discussing the public trust of scientists and scientific research, outlined several principles that characterize the creation and destruction of trust. His principles focus on how media reporting on scientific findings can lead to trust or distrust of science in general, but they can be applied more widely. The principles Slovic outlines are based on empirical research, but the principles may rightly be called working hypotheses, because none has been proved in a general setting. There are four principles.

Trust-destroying events are more visible or more noticeable than trust-building events. In the case of scientific misconduct, media seldom report on incidents of well-executed and valid methods. Alternatively, if the media discover a scientist has fabricated data or altered results of an experiment, the event quickly becomes a front-page news story. The same is true more generally. Seldom does a friend bring up in casual conversation the integrity of a faithful spouse. However, a spouse who has been caught cheating becomes a topic of nearly all conversations for those in the know. This can work to make the trust-destroying event more prominent in decision making, much like availability bias.

Trust-destroying events carry more weight than trust-building events. In general, humans tend to believe that trust-destroying events are more representative of unobservable behavior than trust-building events. Thus people often respond to a visible breach of trust by assuming it is consistent with a broader and more-common set of behaviors.

People tend to believe sources of negative or trust-destroying news more than those that are trust-building. Sensational stories of politicians engaging in sexual harassment, betrayal of a spouse, or other ethical violations have a life of their own. These stories, once published, can plague a candidate throughout his or her career. Stories explaining the context of the behavior are often looked upon with skepticism. In other contexts, we might have a tendency to believe the rumormongers more than those sharing legitimate information.

Distrust is self-reinforcing. Once we have experienced a trust-destroying event, we often reduce contact with the person we no longer trust. For example, a spouse caught cheating might be expelled from the house. In this case, the opportunity to rebuild trust is diminished, much like confirmation bias. With fewer interactions, it is difficult to have the opportunity to create any trust-building experience.

Given this bias toward distrust, it is easy to see how public feuds or deep divisions between social or demographic groups can arise. Within the context of business, it is easy to lose customers after very minor customer-service issues. Customers who believe their trust has been betrayed might simply abandon their relationship with the company. Because trust is fragile, it is also extremely valuable both to the trustee and the truster.

Reciprocity

Notably, it is impossible to measure trust without also inducing some measure of reciprocity. Recall that to measure trust, one person must give another person a decision that will affect both persons' outcomes. Much like the trust game, to observe trust by the sender we must offer the second player an opportunity to behave opportunistically or reciprocally. If the trustee does not have an incentive to behave opportunistically, then the first player need not rely on trust. For example, if the receiver is given a greater reward for returning more of the pot to the sender, then the sender need only rely on self-interest and not trust. Reciprocity functions much like Rabin's notion of fairness, the difference being that reciprocity is defined much more broadly as an in-kind response to the actions of others. Thus, if others are behaving in a way that appears kind, kindness is returned, whereas those behaving in a way that appears cruel are treated cruelly.

The subtle difference is that beliefs are not necessary to define kindness or cruelty, as in the definition of fairness. Ernst Fehr and Simon Gächter cite several examples that illustrate the point. A waitress who smiles at her customers receives more in tips than a waitress who does not smile. The smile does not necessarily make the customer better off, but it gives some subtle signal that the waitress is happy to be serving the customer. They also point to samples given out in supermarkets. Customers feel some social pressure to buy the product once they have tried a sample, *even if they did not like it*. These behaviors are based not on the notion that the supermarket or the manufacturer was being kind to them so much as the fact that they were given something and feel the need to reciprocate. Similarly, we have the urge to insult anyone who takes a dig at us. Discussions in the next section illustrate more clearly how reciprocity can differ from the notion of fairness.

In the trust game, a receiver might feel compelled to provide some return to the sender simply because the receiver has been given the opportunity for a larger return by the sender. Because trust cannot be measured without also eliciting the presence of reciprocity, it is difficult to define trust without appealing to reciprocity. If reciprocity is an innate behavior, it could be that trust is simply self-interest given the presence of reciprocity. In this case, trust is really just an expression of risk preferences given the probability of reciprocal actions. Neurological and biological research into trust behavior suggests that this is not the case. For example, some drugs affect trust behavior in the trust game but not risk behavior in risk games. The fact that this risk is based in social interactions with others appears to lead us to use different decision-making mechanisms than we would to judge, say, risks from weather damage. Scientists have even found systematic differences in trust behavior between people who have physiological differences in how certain chemicals are processed in the brain. Thus there is strong evidence that trust is its own behavior with its own decision mechanism.

As mentioned in Chapter 15, many use the terms **fairness** and **reciprocity** interchangeably. However, the definitions of each differ substantially among authors. In this book I have drawn a distinction between the two common concepts that are often referred to as either fairness or reciprocity and selected the names I felt were most appropriate. Students should take care to understand the terminology used by a particular author when proceeding further with their studies in this area.

EXAMPLE 16.6   Reciprocity as Distinct from Fairness

Reciprocity, as I have defined it, need not be equivalent to fairness. Fairness dictates that one rewards intentions to be kind and punishes intentions to be cruel. Alternatively, reciprocity rewards actions that are kind and punishes actions that are cruel. Consider that you are in a hurry and fall in traffic behind a car going 15 miles per hour under the speed limit. To make matters worse, you are driving in a no-passing zone. When passing is finally allowed, you zoom past the slow car and might have the urge to put the proverbial exclamation point on your action by yelling, staring, or gesturing at the driver. This is true even if it is clear the driver was completely oblivious to your time pressure. But if the driver were truly oblivious to your plight, fairness would not predict any particular punishment should be desired. However, a negative reciprocal act does not require malice on the part of the one being reciprocated. Certainly malice likely induces further reciprocal action. However, we often feel a desire to punish someone even for behavior that unintentionally damages us.

One good example of this comes from an upstate New York high school, where the school, in an effort to encourage better nutrition, decided to limit those purchasing a school lunch to only one ketchup packet. The senior class was so incensed that they put together a protest on graduation day. As each senior crossed the stage to shake the hand of the principal, the student placed a ketchup packet in his hand, leaving him with a pocket full of ketchup by the end of the ceremony. Clearly the principal was not seeking the destruction or harm of the class. Nonetheless, they felt compelled to reciprocate the actions of the school's cafeteria staff by sending him a clear negative message. In this case, the school administrators most likely felt that they were helping the students by limiting their ketchup consumption. Nonetheless, the students believed punishment was in order.

The notion of punishing negligent or unintentional behavior is canonized in our legal system. For example, one who kills a person intentionally is charged with murder and potentially faces life in prison or even death. Alternatively, someone who kills another through negligence faces charges of manslaughter and could face a long prison sentence. Note that the unintentional acts are punished, but less severely. Moreover, penalties are often made explicitly contingent on not only how cruel the crime is but also on extenuating circumstances. Thus, one committing murder when the victim was engaged in aggravating the perpetrator might face a much easier sentence than one committing murder unprovoked. Although research into reciprocity and fairness is still developing rapidly, it appears that people may be motivated by both in the course of events.

EXAMPLE 16.7   Reciprocity as a Business Model

In the last half of the 1990s, a new business model emerged for the software industry: open source. Open source software is available free to all, which might seem to limit the ability of a firm to capitalize on the distribution of their software. Many open-source projects rely on programmers to contribute code or applications that will also be made available freely. These applications require substantial time to program and are given ostensibly on a volunteer basis. One might thus question how this could be a sustainable model of business, or even a good idea for programmers to give away their services. A more-recent example is the existence of crowdsourcing efforts. In this realm, a firm or individual invites volunteers to provide some particular service generally for free. For example, Wikipedia invites people to contribute articles for their online encyclopedia without remuneration. The articles are then edited, modified, and revised by members of the crowd. Again, what would motivate a skilled writer or one with specialized knowledge to contribute for free? Nonetheless, Wikipedia has become the most comprehensive source for general information available, and it is often the first place one visits to learn about a topic. Clearly, people with the necessary knowledge have been sufficiently motivated.

People contributing to unpaid efforts such as crowdsourcing or open-source coding do have the possibility of direct personal rewards. For example, an open-source programmer may be creating an application or improving the functionality in some way that is directly applicable to his or her own work. In other words, programmers might use the program themselves and thus benefit from it. Still, it would be possible to use the program and not distribute it to others for free. Additionally, people may be able to use such visible projects to signal their own skill, essentially advertising for future jobs. This certainly explains some of the most breathtaking contributions to open-source projects. Nonetheless, a large group of contributors cite the feeling of contributing to a community that likes to give back as their primary reason for contributing to open-source projects. According to Boston Consulting Group, around 29 percent of contributors consider the need to reciprocate as a primary reason for contributing open-source code. This is about as many as contribute to improve their status or for their own private benefit. Interestingly, software developers and programmers are some of the biggest users of open-source software.

Firms involved in open-source software are able to make money through the distribution of support, licenses, training, and other benefits. Additionally, you often find attached to the software license a plea for donations. Donations make up a key part of the industry, allowing firms to purchase hardware and equipment and compensating the time of administrators. Popularity and visibility can have a big impact on the amount of donations received. A popular application often generates much more in donations than the distributors ask for.

Surprisingly, the most commonly cited reason for using open-source software is to reduce the dependence on privately licensed software providers. Thus, one might decide to use an open-source word-processing program to free oneself from Microsoft or other vendors who they feel overcharge or use barriers (like lack of backward compatibility) to force paid upgrades. A survey by Computer Economics suggests that only 20 percent of firms using open-source software cite the cost savings as the primary reason for their decision. Though the software is directly free, often converting to the new software and maintaining and supporting it are not at all free. Though other explanations exist, it appears that reciprocity plays a major role in the existence, use of, and donations to support open-source efforts.

History and Notes

In the seminal work of economics, Adam Smith's *An Inquiry into the Nature and Causes of the Wealth of Nations*, Smith wrote extensively about the importance of trust in economic behavior. For example, Smith supposes that those engaged in commerce would be much more willing to engage in domestic trades given that they are more familiar with the people with whom they are dealing and can thus trust them. Alternatively, when dealing with foreign entities the person might need to charge a premium to overcome the distrust she might have for the foreign entity because she is unfamiliar with it. Moreover, Smith acknowledges the role of institutions, such as governments, in encouraging and establishing an environment in which trust can flourish. When people deal domestically, they are also familiar with the legal system and might know what recourse is available should they be dealt with deceitfully. This is not always clear when dealing in foreign markets, where governments might have different standards or practices in distributing justice.

Smith also wrote about the impact of charity in securing the good feelings and devotion of others. Specifically, he documents how providing food to the poor or others who were needy had led monasteries to a position of prominence. People felt obliged to protect the church at great expense, often because they had been supported at some time by the church's charitable efforts. The clergy's respected place made it difficult even for a sovereign king to threaten or diminish the clergy in any respect. Truly, trust and reciprocity have played a central role in history and in the creation of the institutions, governments, and societies of which we are a part.

Biographical Note

Courtesy of Paul Slovic

Paul Slovic (1938–)

B.A., Stanford University, 1959; M.A., University of Michigan, 1962; Ph.D., University of Michigan, 1964

Held faculty positions at the University of Oregon and visiting positions at Hebrew University (Jerusalem) and the University of Padova (Italy)

Born in Chicago, Paul Slovic completed both his undergraduate and graduate studies in the field of psychology and soon after began work as a research associate at the University of Oregon. Slovic has made seminal contributions to the psychology of risk perception and communication. His contributions center on how emotion plays into perceptions of risk and risk response. For example, risks can loom larger than they would otherwise if they are associated with some emotion-laden event such as a terrorist attack. He has collaborated often with Daniel Kahneman and Amos Tversky, among many others. Slovic has served on the editorial board of dozens of academic journals and received honorary doctoral degrees from the Stockholm School of Economics and the University of East Anglia. He is also an associate of the National Academy of Sciences. The American Psychological Association has recognized him with its exclusive Distinguished Scientific Contribution Award. He is still very active in his research and is well known for riveting seminars given far and wide. Slovic gave Cornell University's Center for Behavioral Economic and Decision Research 25th Anniversary Lecture, celebrating the long-standing vibrant behavioral research community.

THOUGHT QUESTIONS

1. Trust is not easily observed in isolation. Rather, it must be measured simultaneously with reciprocity. Describe why these two must coexist, and what this could mean for interpreting our measures of trust. What other behaviors might trust be related to?

2. Find an example of how trust can reduce the costs of a transaction. What institutions may help to facilitate this trust?

3. Consider that you are a bank manager. You know that if depositors trust your bank, they will be willing to take a smaller interest rate.

   (a) Given the what we know of how people develop trust, what might you do to enhance their trust?

   (b) Given what we know of the potential biases in our judgment of trust, what steps might you take to ensure that your loan officers can avoid potential pitfalls?

4. Find an example of how an advertising campaign tries to enhance trust. What is the motivation of the firm? What principles do they use to enhance trust?

5. How can you use the principles of this chapter to improve your performance in job interviews? In what other settings could you apply these principles?

REFERENCES

Berg, J., J. Dickhaut, and K. McCabe. "Trust, Reciprocity and Social History." *Games and Economic Behavior* 10(1995): 122–142.

Brinig, M.F., and S.M. Crafton. "Marriage and opportunism." *Journal of Legal Studies* 23(1994): 869–894.

Carter, M.R., and M. Castillo. "Trustworthiness and Social Capital in South Africa: Analysis of Actual Living Standards Data and Artifactual Field Experiments." *Economic Development and Cultural Change* 59(2011): 695–722.

DeBruine, L.M. "Facial Resemblance Enhances Trust." *Proceedings of the Royal Society of London B* 269(2002): 1307–1312.

Fehr, E. "On the Economics and Biology of Trust." *Journal of the European Economic Association* 7(2009): 235–266.

Fehr, E., and S. Gächter. "Fairness and Retaliation: The Economics of Reciprocity." *Journal of Economic Perspectives* 14(2000): 159–181.

Glaeser, E.L., D.I. Laibson, J.A. Scheinkman, and C.L. Soutter. "Measuring Trust." *Quarterly Journal of Economics* 115(2000): 811–846.

Johansson-Stenman, O., M. Mahmud, and P. Martinsson. "Trust and Religion: Experimental Evidence from Rural Bangladesh." *Economica* 76(2009): 462–485.

Knack, S., and P. Keefer. "Does Social Capital Have an Economic Payoff? A Cross-Country Investigation." *Quarterly Journal of Economics* 112(1997): 1251–1288.

Rowthorn, R. "Marriage and Trust: Some Lessons from Economics." *Cambridge Journal of Economics* 23(1999): 661–691.

Scharlemann, J.P.W., C.C. Eckel, A. Kalcelnik, and R.K. Wilson. "The Value of a Smile: Game Theory with a Human Face." *Journal of Economic Psychology* 22(2001): 617–640.

Slovic, P. "Trust, Emotion, Sex, Politics, and Science: Surveying the Risk-Assessment Battlefield." *Risk Analysis* 19(1999): 689–701.

Stanley, D.A., P. Sokol-Hessner, M.R. Banaji, and E.A. Phelps. "Implicit Race Attitudes Predict Trustworthiness Judgments and Economic Trust Decisions." *Proceedings of the National Academies of Science* 108(2011): 7710–7715.

GLOSSARY

A

absolute magnitude effect is the observation that people tend to require proportionally less compensation to delay larger amounts of consumption. This leads to an observation of higher empirical discount factors when larger amounts are in play and behavior that is much closer to rational exponential discounting. One explanation for this effect is found in asymmetric elasticity condition employing a prospect-theory value function.

absolute risk aversion is a measure, based on expected utility theory, of how willing someone is to take on a dollar of risk. Absolute risk aversion measures the relative curvature of the utility function and can be written as $R_A = -u''/u'$, where u is the utility of wealth function. The larger the value, the less willing one is to take on a given risk.

acquisition utility is the utility obtained from consumption of the good minus the utility lost from giving away an amount of wealth equal to the cost of consumption. In this book this is often referred to as the utility of consumption.

additive model of intertemporal choice supposes that one's utility function of consumption in this period, c_1, and consumption next period, c_2, can be represented by $U(c_1, c_2) = u(c_1) + \delta u(c_2)$, where δ represents a discount factor.

Allais' paradox is a violation of the independence axiom generated by manipulating a common outcome between two gamble choices. Independence implies that any two gambles that include probability p of outcome x should lead to the same choice no matter what x is chosen. Typically this paradox is observed when the choice between a pair of gambles where $x = 0$ is compared to the choice between a pair in which $x > 0$.

α-maxmin expected utility theory is a model of ambiguity aversion. Let $\{p\}$ be the set of possible probability distributions over outcomes. Further, let $\underline{p} \in \{p\}$ be such that $\max_x E(U(x)|p = \underline{p}) \leq \max_x E(U(x)|p \neq \underline{p})$, for all $p \in \{p\}$. Also, let $\overline{p} \in \{p\}$ be such that $\max_x E(U(x)|p = \overline{p}) \geq \max_x E(U(x)|p \neq \overline{p})$, for all $p \in \{p\}$. Then a person behaving according to α-maxmin expected utility theory will behave so as to solve $\max_x \alpha E(U(x)|p = \underline{p}) + \alpha E(U(x)|p = \overline{p})$. The coefficient α is a measure of ambiguity aversion. A person is considered ambiguity averse if $\alpha > \frac{1}{2}$ and ambiguity loving if $\alpha < \frac{1}{2}$.

altruistic refers to preferences such that decision makers are willing to reduce their own consumption in order to increase to consumption of at least one other person.

ambiguity is a situation in which either decision makers face unknown probabilities associated with outcomes resulting from their choices, or they are not aware of the possible outcomes.

ambiguity aversion is a tendency to choose gambles with explicitly stated probabilities over those that involve ambiguity (probabilities are not known) even if this could result in loss of utility.

anchoring and adjusting is a heuristic process for forming beliefs in which the decision maker takes some convenient value as an anchor and then makes adjustments from this value to determine the final answer. Often the anchor is some unrelated number that happens to be presented at the time of decision. Generally this anchor then affects the outcome belief despite being unrelated to the decision at hand.

asymmetric elasticity condition requires that the utility of losses is more elastic than utility of gains. Let $z_2 > z_1 > 0$. Then we can express this requirement in terms of arc elasticities as $-\frac{(z_1 + z_2)[v(-z_1) - v(-z_2)]}{(z_2 - z_1)[v(-z_1) + v(-z_2)]} > \frac{(z_1 + z_2)[v(z_2) - v(z_1)]}{(z_2 - z_1)[v(z_1) + v(z_2)]}$, or for any $z > 0$ in terms of exact elasticities as $-\frac{zv'(-z)}{v(-z)} > \frac{zv'(z)}{v(z)}$. This is closely related to the notion of strong loss aversion. Asymmetric elasticity is one explanation for the gain–loss asymmetry in intertemporal choice.

availability heuristic leads one to estimate the probability of an event by how easily one can recall or construct an event in one's mind. Thus, events that might have been more publicized or more extreme can be judged to be more probable than they truly are.

B

backward induction is method of solving for the optimal behavior of an intertemporal decision maker with sophisticated preferences. To employ this method, you begin by solving for the optimal behavior in the last period of the decision problem, then solve for behavior in the second-to-last period assuming optimal behavior in the last, and so on. This method is also often used in game theory to solve for subgame perfect Nash equilibrium (SPNE).

base rate neglect is the tendency to ignore or severely discount prior information about the frequency of an event when judging the probability of that event. In the terms of Bayes' rule, the prior information is underemphasized and the likelihood information is overemphasized.

Bayesian Nash equilibrium is the Nash equilibrium concept employed in games involving uncertain payoffs. This is in reference to the requirement that each player must have beliefs regarding the strategies and playoffs of all other players that is consistent with their strategies in the equilibrium. In this game we require that each player has the same prior beliefs regarding the distribution of valuations and that each anticipates the correct strategy of others given their valuation. At each information set, beliefs are updated according to Bayes' rule, a statistical tool for updating probabilities based on information available.

behavioral anomaly is defined as behavior that differs from the predictions of the rational choice model. The term *anomaly* generally suggests that the behavior is rare, though still potentially important.

behavioral choice model is a model designed to describe observed choices without necessarily explaining the motivations or considerations of the decision maker when making the decision.

behavioral economics is the study of how observed human behavior affects the allocation of scarce resources. This field of economics incorporates the tools from psychology and sociology into more traditional economic theory.

behavioral model *see* behavioral choice model.

betweenness is an axiom often used in place of the independence axiom. If $A \succ B$, and C is a compound gamble that yields A with probability p and some gamble B with probability $(1-p)$, then betweenness implies that $A \succ C \succ B$. Betweenness implies that all indifference curves must be straight lines, though they may differ in slope.

bliss point is the lowest amount of consumption above which the consumer no longer desires to consume no matter what the price. This is the maximum point on the utility of consumption curve considering the consumption of all other goods to be fixed.

bounded rationality is the notion that people behave rationally given the constraints on information, cognitive resources, and time.

bracketing refers to how choices are grouped in the process of decision making. Broadly bracketed decisions take many simultaneous choices into account at once. Narrowly bracketed decisions may ignore the effect of one decision on the other choices facing the consumer.

C

calibration refers to one's ability to accurately relate probabilistic information. One is well calibrated if, when one forecasts that an event will happen with probability x, the event happens about x *percent* of the time.

cancellation is one component of the editing phase of prospect theory. In cancellation, components that are common to the gambles being considered are eliminated before the choice is made.

certainty effect is the general tendency of decision makers to prefer outcomes with certainty beyond what is implied by expected utility theory. Uncertain outcomes face an additional penalty beyond the loss of probability associated with them.

certainty equivalent is the amount of money with certainty that players would receive in place of a gamble that would leave them with the same level of utility.

cheap talk refers to nonbinding discussions or commitments between players in a game.

coding is one activity engaged in by decision makers in the editing phase of prospect theory decision making under risk. The decision maker codes each outcome as a gain or a loss.

coefficient of ambiguity aversion is a measure of ambiguity aversion resulting from the α-maximin expected utility model of decision under ambiguity. The higher the value of α, the more ambiguity averse the person. The person is considered ambiguity averse if $\alpha > \frac{1}{2}$, and ambiguity loving if $\alpha < \frac{1}{2}$. The coefficient of ambiguity aversion must be contained in the unit interval.

cold state refers to a state in which visceral factors (such as hunger, anger, or arousal) are latent. In this state, people might have a difficult time anticipating their preferences at some future date when these visceral factors become active.

combination is one activity in the editing phase of prospect theory. In combination, probabilities associated with identical outcomes are combined before the decision is made.

commitment mechanisms allow decision makers to impose penalties on their future self if they deviate from their planned activities.

committed decision maker is one who can enforce her consumption plans on her future self no matter what her future preferences.

common difference effect is the observation that period-by-period discount factors applied to future consumption appear to change depending upon how far in the future the events will take place. Let δ be the period by period discount factor. The fully additive model of time discounting imposes that people will be indifferent between consuming c at time t and c' at time t' if $U(c) = \delta^{t'-t} U(c')$, where the discount only depends on the interval between t and t' and not the starting time. However, research has found that empirical discounts tend to be much deeper in the near future than in the distant future.

common outcome effect is a violation of the independence axiom. See Allais' paradox for a description.

common ratio effect is a violation of the independence axiom generated by offering a choice between a pair of gambles, and then a choice between two compound lotteries in which the decision maker has a fixed probability of obtaining the original gambles, and a remaining probability of obtaining a payoff of \$0. The violation typically occurs when the probability of \$0 added to each gamble is relatively high and the gambles are of a \$-bet and P-bet form.

common-value auction is an auction for an item that has the same value to each bidder bidding in the auction, though this value is unknown and uncertain.

complete preferences implies that for any two potential choices people either prefer the first, prefer the second, or are indifferent between the two. This is a general requirement for rational decision theory.

compound gamble is a gamble that consists of the combination of two separate gambles.

conditional probability function is a function $p(A|B)$ that measures the probability of event A given that event B has occurred or will occur.

confidence interval is an interval that represents the most probable location of an unknown parameter. Let θ be an unknown parameter and $\hat{\theta}$ be an estimate of the unknown parameter. Then, the x percent confidence interval is a confidence interval $[\hat{\theta} - l, \hat{\theta} + u]$, such that $P(\hat{\theta} - l < \theta) = (100 - x)/200$, and $P(\hat{\theta} + u > \theta) = (100 - x)/200$.

confirmation bias is a general tendency commonly displayed either to seek information that is likely to confirm one's currently held beliefs or to interpret vague information as being generally supportive of one's currently held beliefs.

confirmatory information is information that could potentially conform to one's currently held belief but that cannot possibly (or is at least unlikely to) contradict one's currently held belief.

confirming forecast is an information forecast that almost always results in information that is congruent with current beliefs.

conjunction effect is the tendency to judge the probability of two events A and B occurring jointly to be larger than the probability of event A, where B is a representative event and A is an unrepresentative event.

conservatism is the tendency to discount or ignore new information and continue to hold on to prior beliefs. This is the opposite of base rate neglect.

constant additive loss aversion describes a set of reference structures that satisfy constant loss aversion and for which $v_r(x) = \sum_{i=1}^{n} R_i(x_i)$.

constant loss aversion describes a set of reference structures that assume that the utility of gains and losses differs by a multiplicative constant. A reference structure is displaying constant loss aversion if the preferences can be represented as a utility function of the form $v_r(x) = U(R_1(x_1), \ldots, R_n(x_n))$, with

$$R_i(x_i) = \begin{cases} u_i(x_i) - u_i(r_i) & \text{if} \quad x_i \geq r_i \\ (u_i(x_i) - u_i(r_i))\lambda_i & \text{if} \quad x_i < r_i. \end{cases}$$

Here $u(\cdot)$ is an increasing function, and λ_i is a positive constant representing the degree of loss aversion.

constant sensitivity is an assumption under loss aversion that people display constant marginal utility for gains and constant marginal pain from losses.

consumption smoothing refers to the behavior of rational consumers facing an intertemporal choice problem. Because discounting from period to period has small effects, rational decision makers will consume nearly equal, though declining, amounts each period. Plotting the consumption profile over time should result in a relatively smooth curve with no spikes or jumps.

consumption utility *see* acquisition utility

continuity axiom is one of the foundational axioms of expected utility theory. Continuity requires that if $A \succ B \succ C$ then there is exactly one value r such that $rA + (1-r)C \sim B$. Further, for any $p > r$, $pA + (1-p)C \succ B$, and for any $q < r$, $B \succ qA + (1-q)C$.

contrapositive statements are logical statements implied by a proposition. For example, the proposition "if P then Q" results in the contrapositive statement, "if not Q then not P."

crowding-out effect occurs when a government subsidy of a public good results in a dollar-for-dollar decrease in private contributions to the provision of that public good.

cruel refers to a motivation to harm another person at the expense of the actor.

cumulative prospect theory is a version of prospect theory of decision making in which the probability weighting function is a rank-dependent probability weighting function. This eliminates the possibility of intransitive preferences over gambles.

curse of knowledge occurs when people possess some unique knowledge and cannot fully anticipate how others without this knowledge will behave. The person acts as if others also possess this same knowledge.

cursed equilibrium is a generalization of the Bayesian Nash equilibrium where people believe with positive probability that others randomly select their actions from a distribution irrespective of any private information they might have and with the remaining probability that actions are strategic. The equilibrium requires that each person is maximizing his expected payout of the game given the distribution of actions by others and the strategies employed by others. In this case, people fail to take others' actions as a signal of any private information held by other players.

D

default option is the option that is automatically selected when the decision maker expresses no explicit choice.

default option bias is a decision maker's tendency to select the default option.

delay–speedup asymmetry is the observation that people must be compensated much more to undergo a delay in consumption than they would be willing to pay to speed up consumption by the same amount of time. This framing effect clearly violates the fully additive model of intertemporal choice.

dependent refers to random variables for which the outcomes are related. Knowing the outcome of one will provide you information about the outcome of the other.

detection of dominance is one activity in the editing phase of prospect theory. In this activity the decision maker examines the gambles available to determine whether one of the options is first-order stochastically dominated by another gamble. If a gamble is determined to be dominated, it is eliminated from consideration.

dictator game is a game with two players in which one player, the dictator, is given money to be shared between both players. The dictator decides how the money is to be divided, and then the second player receives her portion.

diminishing sensitivity is an assumption under loss aversion that people display diminishing marginal utility from gains and diminishing marginal pain from losses. Thus, one becomes less sensitive to changes in wealth or consumption as one moves farther from the reference point.

directly revealed preferred is the relationship of the state s_1 to s_2 if s_1 is chosen when s_2 is in the set of available choices.

disconfirmatory information is information that is likely to (or at least that could possibly) contradict currently held beliefs.

discount factor is the coefficient applied in each time period to utility of consumption to represent the consumer's preference for current over future consumption. Thus, if $U(c)$ is the instantaneous utility of consumption, consuming c in the future, t periods from now, would yield $\delta^t U(c)$ in present calculated utility.

disposition effect is the tendency of investors to sell gaining investments rather than losing investments in order to avoid realizing losses.

diversification bias is the tendency to choose a consumption bundle for the future that includes a wide variety of items and then to wish one had less variety when the time arrives for consumption.

$-bet is a bet that in comparison to other choices has a larger potential payoff but a smaller probability of obtaining that payoff.

dominance is the state in which, if whenever there exists some period t with benefits of performing and action $v_t > 0$ and costs $c_t = 0$, the person will not choose to complete the task in any period t' with $c_{t'} > 0$ and $v_{t'} = 0$.

dominant strategy is a strategy that results in a superior payout no matter what the actions of other players.

double-entry accounting is a system of accounting whereby every transaction is entered as a gain in one ledger and a loss in another ledger. For example, purchasing an item is listed as a loss of money in the acquisitions ledger, and the value of the good acquired is listed as a gain in the inventory ledger.

dual entitlement refers to the rules of fairness that consumers and employees enforce on firms regarding fair prices and wages. For example, consumers consider it tolerable to increase prices when the cost to the firms has increased, allowing the firms to maintain profits. It is not acceptable to increase prices simply owing to a shift in demand.

Dutch auction is an auction mechanism that begins by the auctioneer calling out a high price, and then decreasing the price by small increments until one bidder is willing to buy.

E

editing is a component of prospect theory decision making in which people simplify their decision. This can include rounding probabilities and outcomes, eliminating similar components of each choice, and coding outcomes as either gains or losses.

Ellsberg paradox results when people are asked to choose between two urns filled with red and black balls from which to draw a ball. Urn 1 contains only red and black balls in an unknown ratio. Urn 2 contains 50 percent red balls and 50 percent black balls. When asked which to draw from when a red ball will result in a prize, people tend to choose urn 2. When asked to choose when a black ball will result in a prize, they also choose urn 2. In both cases, people tend to choose the urn with specified probabilities rather than the ambiguous outcome, violating subjective expected utility theory. This paradox results from ambiguity aversion.

empirical discount factor is the discount factor calculated by asking a person to name an amount of money in one time period and another amount of money in another time period such that the person is indifferent between the two. Let z_1 be the amount in time t_1, and z_2 the amount in time t_2. Then the empirical discount factor can be calculated as $\hat{\delta}$, such that $z_1 = \hat{\delta}^{t_2 - t_1} z_2$. This differs from the discount factor that would represent the person's preferences because it omits the utility function, instead assuming each dollar is valued equally.

endowment effect is the phenomenon whereby people are willing to pay substantially less money to obtain an item than they are willing to accept to give the item up if given to them.

English auction is an auction in which the auctioneer begins by calling out a small price and continues to raise the price by increments until only one bidder continues to be willing to pay the called price.

excess sexual cannibalism refers to the practice among some female fishing spiders of killing and eating all potential mates, thus ensuring they never pass their genes on to the next generation.

expectation is the mean of a random variable. If the distribution of a random variable x can be represented as $p(x)$, the expectation is given by $E(x) = \sum_x p(x)x$. Alternatively, if the variable is continuously distributed with probability density $f(x)$, the expectation is given by $E(x) = \int_x x f(x)dx$.

expected utility theory is a theory of decision under risk that supposes people behave so as to maximize the expected utility of wealth. Expected utility theory is a rational model, built on three rational axioms of behavior under risk. These axioms include independence, continuity, and transitivity.

exponential time discounting is a model that assumes that people maximize $U(c_1, c_2, \ldots) = \sum_{i=1}^{T} \delta^{i-1} u(c_i)$, where c_i is consumption in period i, $u(c)$ is the instantaneous utility of consumption, and δ is the discount factor applied to each period. This model is considered the only rational model of intertemporal choice because it is necessary to imply time-consistent preferences. In continuous time, the utility function can be stated as $\max_{\{c(t)\}} U(c(t)) = \int_0^{\infty} \delta^t u(c(t)) dt$, where t represents time measured continuously.

external validity is the ability to use a study to predict behavior in a broader setting. Secondary data analysis generally results in more external validity than an experimental study.

F

fairness refers to a motivation to help those who are intending to be kind and to hurt those who are intending to be cruel.

false consensus is a tendency to believe that others hold beliefs and preferences that are similar to their own.

first-price auction is an auction in which the highest bidder wins the auction and pays his bid for the item.

fixed cost is the fixed investment required by a firm to produce. In general economic decisions, fixed costs are the portion of costs that do not depend on the amount produced or consumed.

flat-rate bias is a behavioral preference that people display to buy services based on flat-rate pricing rather than linear pricing even when they can obtain the same level of use more cheaply using linear pricing.

flat-rate pricing is a pricing scheme that charges a fixed rate for access to a good and no additional fees no matter how much is consumed.

framing refers to the external cues surrounding the description of a decision. Often the wording of a decision problem influences the decision that is made by signaling the decision maker to classify outcomes as gains or losses.

framing effect refers to the impact of wording on a decision. Often identical choices can be worded to focus decision makers on losses associated with choices or to focus them on gains associated with choices. The framing effect is the change in decision-making behavior that results from this shift in focus.

free-rider problem refers to the problem that in a free market, people are unwilling to contribute an amount equal to the value they obtain from a public good. This leads to underprovision of the public goods.

fully cursed equilibrium is an alternative to the Bayesian Nash equilibrium where people believe that others randomly select their actions from a distribution irrespective of any private information they have. The equilibrium requires that each person is maximizing her expected payout of the game given the distribution of actions by others and the strategies employed by others. In this case, people fail to take others' actions as a signal of any private information held by other players.

fungible means that an item can be transferred easily between uses. A dollar in an account is fungible if it can be easily transferred to other accounts or spent as any other dollar might be spent.

G

gain–loss asymmetry is the observation that people tend to discount the utility of future losses less than the utility of future gains. Thus, delayed gains require much greater compensation to induce indifference than equivalently delayed losses. This phenomenon can be modeled by using a prospect theoretic value function that satisfies the asymmetric elasticity condition.

gambler's fallacy is the tendency to believe, after observing a series of realizations of a random variable of the same value, that the probability of realizations of other values of the random variable becomes more probable.

game is a collection of available actions for all players, and a set of payoffs, with one potentially random value of payoff corresponding to each possible collection of actions by all players. A game generally involves situations in which one player's actions can affect the payouts of other players.

generalized axiom of revealed preference states that if s_1 is indirectly revealed preferred to s_2, then s_2 is not strictly directly revealed preferred to s_1.

H

hedonic editing refers to a process of integrating loss events and segregating gain events to maximize the enjoyment of a series of events. There is some evidence that decision makers do not engage in hedonic editing.

hedonic framing refers to the wording of decision options to integrate or segregate events so as to make one or a set of options more or less attractive. For example, a marketer can integrate a series of losses while segregating a series of gains to make a purchase more attractive.

heuristic is a simple decision rule or rule of thumb that may be used to approximate rational optimization when decision resources are limited.

hindsight bias occurs when people evaluate past decisions as if they possessed a foreknowledge of the results of the various decisions. People act as if it were obvious which decision would produce the best result.

hot–cold empathy gap refers to projection bias by people in either hot or cold states (e.g., states in which visceral factors such as hunger are either active or latent).

hot hand is the illusion that a series of realizations of independent random variables of the same value constitutes a streak indicating that the realizations are positively correlated.

hot state refers to a state in which visceral factors (such as hunger, anger, or arousal) are active. In this state, people have difficulty anticipating their preferences at some future date when these visceral factors will be satisfied and thus latent.

hyperbolic discounting replaces the discount factor δ^t in the exponential utility model with the hyperbolic discount factor, $h(t) = (1 + \alpha t)^{-(\beta/\alpha)}$, where β, $\alpha > 0$ are parameters and t is the amount of time that will have passed by the instance of consumption.

The function generally represents deep discounting of near-future events relative to distant future events. The hyperbolic discount factor induces time-inconsistent preferences. Thus, people who display hyperbolic discounting often do not execute the consumption plans that they use to calculate current optimal consumption.

hypothesis-based filtering is actively seeking information that is likely to confirm a currently held belief while scrutinizing information that disconfirms a currently held belief.

I

illusion of control is the tendency to believe that one has some control over the outcome of completely random events.

immediate cost actions are actions that incur a cost in the period in which they are completed and rewards that accrue in future periods.

immediate reward actions are actions that induce an immediate reward in the period in which the action is completed and costs that accrue in future periods.

impure altruism in considering contributions to a public good refers to the private motive to contribute to a public good in order feel the satisfaction of having contributed.

income expansion path is the set of points that represent the optimal consumption bundle as the budget is varied.

incremental bidding behavior occurs when a bidder in an auction initially bids below their valuation of a good and increases their bid in increments in response to other bidders.

independence implies that two random variables are not related to one another. Thus knowing the outcome of one does not provide further information about the outcome of the other. If two events are independent, then the probability of both occurring is the product of the probabilities of each event, or if events A and B are independent, then $P(A \cup B) = P(A)P(B)$.

independence axiom is one of the foundational axioms of expected utility theory. Independence requires that if $A \succ B$, then $pA + (1-p)C \succ pB + (1-p)C$. This axiom implies that indifference curves are straight and parallel lines in the Marschak–Machina triangle.

independence of irrelevant alternatives A decision maker obeys independence of irrelevant alternatives if whenever the decision maker chooses $t' \neq t$, when given the choice of when to complete a task embodied by the potential rewards $\mathbf{v} = (v_1, v_2, \ldots, v_{t-1}, v_t, v_{t+1} \ldots, v_T)$, and costs $\mathbf{c} = (c_1, c_2, \ldots, c_{t-1}, c_t, c_{t+1}, \ldots, c_T)$, the decision maker also chooses t' when given the choices embodied in $\mathbf{v} = (v_1, v_2, \ldots, v_{t-1}, v_{t+1} \ldots, v_T)$, $\mathbf{c} = (c_1, c_2, \ldots, c_{t-1}, c_{t+1}, \ldots, c_T)$.

indirect utility function is the maximized value of the utility function as a function of wealth and prices.

indirectly revealed preferred If s_1 is directly revealed preferred to s_2, and s_2 is directly revealed preferred to $s_3, \ldots$ to s_{T-1}, and s_{T-1} is directly revealed preferred to s_T, then s_1 is indirectly revealed preferred to s_T.

induced value refers to the amount a bidder may win in an experimental auction. This amount is assigned by the researcher and may differ between participants in the auction.

inequality averse refers to a person's motivation to avoid outcomes in which some people receive lower payouts than others.

inference refers to the information we discern from the data we are able to observe.

infinite planning horizon refers to intertemporal-choice problems involving an unending planning horizon. In discrete time problems, consumption must be planned for time periods $t = \{0, \ldots \infty\}$. In continuous time problems, the consumption must be planned over $t = [0, \infty)$.

instantaneous utility function in a multiperiod consumption problem refers to a function that represents the current utility of consumption in a particular time period. Most models of intertemporal choice suppose that the instantaneous utility function is identical for each time period, but that utility of future consumption is multiplied by a discount factor to represent the fact that current consumption is preferred to future consumption.

integrated events are considered together when evaluating their joint utility. Thus, if two integrated events resulted in monetary outcomes x and y, they would result in a value of $v(x + y)$. See also segregated events.

intermediate loss aversion requires that for any $c > 0$ the prospect theoretic value function satisfies $v(c) < -v(-c)$.

internal validity is the ability to show causality in a study. Generally, experimental design is necessary to obtain internal validity.

K

kind refers to an actor's motivation to help another person at the expense of the actor.

kindness function measures how cruel or kind someone is intending to be as a function of her beliefs about other players' strategies and her own chosen strategy. A positive value indicates kindness and a negative value indicates cruelty. This function becomes part of the utility function together with material payoffs in a kindness equilibrium.

Knightian risk refers to a situation in which the outcome is not known with certainty but in which the decision maker knows all the possible outcomes and the probabilities associated with each.

Knightian uncertainty is a situation in which decision makers know all possible outcomes and the probabilities associated with each outcome given each possible decision they may make.

L

law of large numbers can be stated as follows: let $\{x_i\}_{i=1}^{n}$ be a sequence of independent random variable, each identically distributed with mean μ and variance σ^2. Then, for any $\varepsilon > 0$, $\lim_{n \to \infty} P(|\hat{\mu} - \mu| < \varepsilon) = 1$, where P represents the probability function.

law of small numbers is a tendency to wrongly believe that small samples of data have very similar properties to the population from which the sample is drawn. Belief in the law of small numbers leads people to jump to conclusions.

likelihood is a conditional probability function $P(A|B)$ in Bayes' rule, where we are interested in learning about $P(B|A)$. The likelihood function represents the new information in the Bayes' learning problem.

linear pricing is a pricing scheme that charges a fixed marginal price for consumption of a good.

loss aversion is the notion that people experience significantly greater marginal pain from losses than marginal benefit from gains of the same size.

loss aversion in consumption space is typified by indifference curves that discontinuously change slope as they cross a reference point, requiring greater amounts of any item considered a gain to compensate a unit of loss in another item. Formally, let x and y be any two consumption bundles, with $x_i > y_i$ and $y_j > x_j$. Further, let r and s be any two reference points, with $x_i \geq r_i > s_i$, $s_i = y_i$, and $r_j = s_j$. A reference structure displays loss aversion if for any consumption bundles and reference points satisfying these conditions, $x \succ_r y$ whenever $x \sim_s y$

M

Marschak–Machina triangle is a graphic representation of gambles with three possible outcomes. The triangle is a right triangle, with the right angle placed in the southwestern corner. Probabilities of the lowest possible outcome are represented along the horizontal axis of the triangle, and probabilities of the highest possible outcome are represented along the vertical axis. This graph is generally used to plot gambles and indifference curves representing risk preferences.

material outcomes refer to the standard payoffs from a game, often thought of in dollar or utility terms.

maxmin expected utility theory is a model of ambiguity aversion. Let $\{p\}$ be the set of possible probability distributions over outcomes. Then someone behaving according to maxmin expected utility theory will behave as if the value of each choice is given by $\min_{p \in \{p\}}\{\max_x\{E(U(x)|p)\}\}$. In essence, the person assumes the worst possible probabilities that could describe each choice are the true probabilities.

melioration is the tendency of people to make decisions that maximize current utility and to ignore the future consequences of these actions.

mental accounting is a model of consumer decision making whereby the person evaluates all events as gains or losses in a prospect theory value function, uses a mental double-entry accounting ledger to keep track of transactions, and creates separate mental budgets for various categories of purchases. Although this heuristic bars the possibility of maximizing overall utility, it can result from decision makers' attempts to simplify the cognitive effort of optimization.

money pump is created when one displays intransitive preferences among three or more gambles. In this case, the person would be willing to pay to trade gamble A for B, B for C, and C for A. You could infinitely cycle the person between gambles, taking more money from him for each trade.

moral hazard occurs when someone can take actions that are not fully observed by others but that affect the welfare of both the actor and others.

N

naïfs are decision makers who have preferences embodied in the quasi-hyperbolic discounting model and who do not recognize that their preferences are time inconsistent. They thus plan to behave so as to maximize their discounted utility in the first period; however, they do not necessarily execute this plan in future periods.

naïve decision maker *see* naïf.

Nash equilibrium, intuitively, is a set of strategies, one for each player, such that each player is maximizing their payoff given the strategies of all others involved. Let $\pi_i(s_i|\mathbf{S}_{-i})$ be the payoff received by player i for playing strategy s_i, when all other players are playing strategies represented by the symbol $\mathbf{S}_{-i}$. The Nash equilibrium is a collection of strategies $\mathbf{S} = \{s_1, \ldots, s_n\}$, such that for each player i, $\pi_i(s_i|\mathbf{S}_{-i}) \geq \pi_i(s_i'|\mathbf{S}_{-i})$, where $\mathbf{S} = s_i \cup \mathbf{S}_{-i}$.

negatively correlated random variables are two variables x and y such that observing higher values of x increases the probability of observing lower values of y. More formally, $E(x - E(x))E(y - E(y)) < 0$.

node is a decision faced by a player in a game. A node is characterized by the information available to the player as well as the actions available to the player.

nonexcludable means that it is not possible to bar someone from consuming the good. One good example of a nonexcludable good is national defense.

nonrival means one person consuming the good does not prevent others from consuming the good also and does not diminish his utility of consumption.

normal distribution is a common distribution commonly referred to as a bell curve. The normal distribution is completely determined by its mean and variance. The probability density of the normal distribution is given by $f(x) = \exp\left\{-(x-\mu)^2/2\sigma^2\right\}/\sqrt{2\pi\sigma^2}$, where μ is the mean of x and σ^2 is the variance of x. Generally the probability that x falls in the interval $(\mu - 2\sigma, \mu + 2\sigma)$ is approximately 0.95.

O

one-tailed test is a statistical test of an initial hypothesis that can be represented as an inequality. Thus, if one were to test the hypothesis that $\theta < \theta_0$, where θ is the unknown parameter and θ_0 is the hypothesized value, one would use a one-tailed test.

opportunism is self-interest unconstrained by moral considerations.

optimistic overconfidence is displayed when one holds beliefs that the state of the world is more favorable for one than it truly is.

order axiom is one of the foundational axioms of expected utility theory. Order is satisfied if $\succ$ is complete and transitive. Completeness implies that if A and B are any two gambles, then either $A \succ B$, $B \succ A$, or $A \sim B$. Additionally, transitivity implies that if A, B, and C are any three gambles, and $A \succ B$ and $B \succ C$ then $A \succ C$.

other-regarding preferences refers to preferences such that one's own utility depends on the utility or actions of others.

overconfidence of one's own knowledge is displayed when she assesses the probability she is correct as x, when in fact she is correct less than x percent of the time.

overconfident is a general underestimation of the amount of risk faced in a specific context. This can arise because of overconfidence in one's own knowledge regarding the context or because one holds beliefs that fail to acknowledge the possibility of unfavorable states of the world.

P

P-bet is a bet that in comparison to other choices has a smaller potential payoff but a larger probability of obtaining that payoff.

Pareto optimal refers to an outcome in which no player can be made better off without making at least one player worse off.

partial naïf is a decision maker who anticipates the behavior of a sophisticate with parameter $\hat{\beta}$. However, in any period he actually makes decisions discounting the future according to $\beta < \hat{\beta}$. Thus the partial naïf might not execute plans in the future but might still engage commitment devices.

payment decoupling occurs when the consumer ceases to consider the purchase price in the cost of consumption because the purchase and use of a good are separated by substantial passage of time.

payment depreciation is the phenomenon of consumers gradually discounting the memory of payment over time when considering future consumption or investment.

peanuts effect is the tendency people have to treat decisions involving small amounts of money as inconsequential in aggregate because they are inconsequential individually.

positional externalities refers to a reduction in utility that occurs for others when one decision maker consumes goods that increase her status or position in the group.

positively correlated random variables are two variables x and y such that observing higher values of x increases the probability of observing higher values of y. More formally, $E(x - E(x))E(y - E(y)) > 0$.

precision is the ability to predict events using probabilities that are close to either 1 or 0. A weather forecast with 98 percent chance of rain is precise.

preference reversal is set of observed choices that violates either transitivity or order. One may choose a when a and b are available, b when b and c are available, and c when a and c are available—a violation of transitivity. More simply, one may choose x when x and y are available and in another choice, select y when x and y are available—a violation of the order axiom.

present-biased preferences refers to a condition in which when someone considers a trade-off in consumption between two future periods, the individual gives increasingly more weight to utility in the earlier period as those periods draw closer to the present.

primacy is displayed when initial information is more prominent in beliefs than subsequent information.

prior refers to the unconditional probability density in the Bayes' learning problem. This represents the initial beliefs about how likely event B is when learning about $P(B|A)$.

probability of an event is the relative proportion of times that the event would occur if an experiment could be repeated under identical conditions an infinite number of times.

probability density function is a function describing the relative likelihood of outcomes of a random variable. Thus, if $f(x)$ is a probability density, the function will be higher where the random variable x is more likely to be realized. The probability of x falling in any interval $[\underline{x}, \bar{x}]$ is given by $\int_{\underline{x}}^{\bar{x}} f(x)dx$.

probability weighting supposes that people maximize $\sum_{i=1}^{n} \pi(p_i)U(x_i)$, where p_i is the probability of outcome x_i occurring. The function $\pi(\cdot)$ is a probability weighting function that is everywhere increasing. Evidence from laboratory experiments suggest that $\pi(p) > p$ for small values of p, while $\pi(p) < p$ for large values of p. Thus people overweight small probabilities and underweight large probabilities. This function might explain some behaviors that violate the independence axiom.

procedurally rational model is a model that describes a rational procedure that is used to arrive at a decision given potential misperception or a lack of cognitive resources. The decision is not necessarily rational given the human limitations implied, though it is reasoned. A procedurally rational model tries to explain why someone makes a particular choice given his perception of the decision structure.

projection bias refers to peoples' inability to predict their own preferences when a different state of the world prevails. People tend to believe that their current preferences will persist even when very different circumstances prevail.

prorating refers to the tendency of people to consider future payments for a good in relation to the number and value of future uses of the good. Payments on a good with no future use episodes will feel more painful than those with some expected future use.

prospect theory is a theory of behavior that explains loss-averse behavior using a concave utility function over gains and a convex utility function over losses. In particular, prospect theory supposes that people classify outcomes as either gains or losses and evaluate gains and losses using different utility functions, experience a greater marginal pain for a given monetary loss than pleasure for the same monetary gain so long as the given monetary amount is relatively small, and experience diminishing marginal pain from losses. When used as a model of risky choice, prospect theory dictates that decision makers engage in three distinct tasks: prospect editing, probability weighting, and evaluating outcomes via the loss-averse value function. People displaying loss aversion take severe risks or other steps to avoid losses.

psychological equilibrium is a set of strategies and beliefs, one strategy and one set of beliefs for each player, such that all beliefs are accurate representations of the actual strategies employed, and each player is maximizing her payout given the strategies of all other players.

psychological games are games in which the payouts to one or more players depend on the higher-order beliefs of players regarding the strategies of the players involved. Higher-order beliefs refer to, for example, player 1's belief regarding player 2's beliefs regarding player 1's strategy, and so on.

public goods are goods that are nonrival and nonexcludable in consumption.

Q

quasi-hyperbolic discounting is a model of intertemporal choice in which the decision maker maximizes $U(c_1, c_2, \ldots) = \beta u(c_1) + \sum_{i=2}^{T} \beta \delta^{i-2} u(c_i)$, where $\beta < \delta$, where c_i is consumption in period i, $u(c)$ is the instantaneous utility of consumption, and β and δ are discount factors. This is an approximation of the hyperbolic discount function that produces time-inconsistent preferences.

R

rational choice model supposes that people find the best possible choice for their well-being. Often rational choice models impose full information, a well-defined set of preferences, and infinite ability to reason. Behavioral economics builds on the rational choice model with an aim of incorporating more human decision qualities.

recency is displayed when recent information is more prominent in beliefs than initial information.

reciprocity is an in-kind response to the actions of others. Much like fairness, reciprocity leads people to reward kind behavior or punish mean behavior. In this book, reciprocity is defined so that intent to be kind or malicious is not as important as impact of the action taken by another when considering how to reciprocate.

recursive optimization problem is a way to represent an intertemporal choice problem as a recursive series of maximization problems. Thus the standard intertemporal choice problem can be written recursively as $\max_{c_t < w_t}\{u(c_t) + \delta \max_{c_{t+1} < w_{t+1}}\{u(c_{t+1}) + \delta^2 \max_{c_{t+2} < w_{t+2}}\{u(c_{t+2}) + \ldots\}\}$ where the consumer maximizes utility of consumption in each period assuming they will also maximize their utility in each subsequent period.

reference point is a comparison point used in making decisions. Often outcomes above a reference point are considered a gain, and an outcome below a reference point is considered a loss. Alternatively, facing a cost above the reference point can result in a loss of transaction utility, and paying less that the reference cost results in positive transaction utility.

reference point in consumption space is a consumption bundle to which all other bundles are compared. If a bundle contains more of good i than the reference point, then that bundle is considered a gain in dimension i. If a bundle contains less of good i than the reference point, then that bundle is considered a loss in dimension i.

reference state is an externally determined factor (or set of factors) that results in a rational preference relation. Thus, when the reference state is held constant, the decision maker makes decisions that satisfy completeness and transitivity. However, if the reference state is allowed to change, preferences can violate transitivity.

reference structure is a set preference relations that each satisfy rationality, indexed by a reference state.

reference transactions refers to a transaction price and quantity that is used as a reference to determine the fair division of surplus between a buyer and a seller. A seller may raise prices and still be considered fair if the rise in price results from a corresponding rise in costs.

reflection effect is observed when a decision maker presented two gambles with only positive outcomes chooses one gamble, and when facing the same gambles, only with outcomes replaced with the same magnitude, but negative values, chooses the other gamble. Risk preferences for gains are exactly opposite of those over losses.

regret aversion is satisfied if for any outcomes $x > y > z$, it must be that $U(z, x) < U(y, x) + U(z, y)$, where $U(a, b)$ is the utility of obtaining a when an alternative choice would have resulted in b. This property represents the negative feelings of regret when obtaining a lower outcome than what would have been possible with a different choice.

regret theory is a procedurally rational model of choice under uncertainty in which the person obtains utility $U(a, b)$, where a is the object obtained and an alternative choice would have resulted in b. This theory embodies feelings of regret resulting from outcomes that are worse than would have obtained with different choices.

relative risk aversion is a measure, based on expected utility theory, of how willing someone is to take on a gamble putting a given fraction of her wealth at risk. Relative risk aversion measures the relative curvature of the utility function and can be written as $R_R = -u''w/u'$, where u is the utility of wealth function, and w is a measure of wealth. The larger the value of relative risk aversion, the less willing one is to put her wealth at risk.

representativeness heuristic is the tendency to judge the probability of an event based on how representative the observable data are of the event in question.

revealed preference refers to people revealing their preferences when a choice is made among some set of choices.

reversion to mean is displayed by random variables whereby after a particularly high (or low) realization of the random variable x, there is high probability that the next independent realization will be lower (or higher). For example, the child of a tall parent, given the family history, is likely to have a shorter child.

risk is a situation in which decision must be made before one can know the payoffs of the alternative choices with certainty. However, the decision maker does know the options available, the possible outcomes associated with each choice, and the probabilities associated with each outcome given each possible choice.

risk averse means that people would prefer the expected value of a gamble with certainty to taking the said gamble.

risk aversion refers to a person's preference to avoid risk. In general a person is risk averse if he is willing to forgo a risk with expected payout x for some amount of money less than x.

risk loving means that an person would prefer to take a gamble than to receive the expected value of the gamble with certainty.

risk neutral refers to a person's indifference to risk. A risk-neutral decision maker behaves so as to maximize the expected value of her payout. The person is indifferent between taking a gamble and receiving the expected value of the gamble with certainty.

risk premium is the amount one is willing to give up in expected value to obtain a payoff with certainty. This is the difference between the expected value of a gamble and the certainty equivalent of that gamble.

S

salience is a state of prominence in decision making.

second-price auction is an auction in which the highest bidder wins the auction and pays a price equal to the second-highest bid.

segmentation independence is the rational decision-making property that decisions made sequentially are identical to decisions made simultaneously if the choices available are otherwise identical and if the decision maker is aware of all available choices in each case.

segregated events are considered separately when evaluating their joint utility. Thus, if two segregated events resulted in monetary outcomes x and y, they would result in a value of $v(x) + v(y)$. See also integrated events.

segregation is one activity in the editing phase of prospect theory. In segregation, outcomes that occur with certainty are segregated from risky outcomes for the purpose of evaluation.

self-serving bias is a general tendency of people to overestimate their ability to perform a specific task or to overestimate their ex post contribution to a task. In some circumstances it can also refer to people's tendency to evaluate what is fair or equitable in a way that favors their own position.

significantly different at the α level means that the probability that an unknown parameter is different from an observed value given the observed data is smaller than α.

similarity is a theory of decision under risk that supposes that people rely on rules of thumb to make risky choices when the choices are reasonably similar. If the gambles have similar outcomes, then the decision maker relies on the probabilities associated with those outcomes. If the probabilities are similar, then the decision maker makes the choice based upon the outcomes associated with the probabilities. Such general rules could explain the types of preference cycling observed in laboratory experiments.

simple projection bias is a model of projection bias that supposes people making a current decision for consumption to be realized in a future state s maximize $\sim u(c, s|s') = (1 - \alpha)u(c, s) + \alpha u(c, s')$, where $u(c, s)$ is the utility of consuming c in the future state s, $u(c, s')$ is the utility of consuming s in the current state s', and $\alpha \in [0, 1]$ is a simple weighting of the two utility functions.

simplification is one activity in the editing phase of prospect theory. In simplification, the decision maker rounds dollar amounts and probabilities to round numbers. Similar outcomes will be combined.

skew symmetric is satisfied by the function $U(\cdot, \cdot)$ if for all outcomes x, y, $U(x, y) = -U(y, x)$ and $U(x, x) = 0$. This is a general property of regret-theory utility functions.

social capital is a term originating in sociology that refers to the durable social relationships one has and can draw upon as resources for goods—tangible, emotional, or informational.

social norm a behavior one engages in because one wishes to comply with the behavior of others. This social norm might or might not be enforced by the threat of punishment or penalty.

social preferences are preferences that depend on the well-being or actions of others.

sophisticated decision maker *see* sophisticates.

sophisticates are decision makers with preferences embodied in the quasi-hyperbolic discounting model, who recognize that their time preferences are inconsistent. They thus anticipate how their future self will behave and respond accordingly. This can lead sophisticates to seek a commitment device to impose their current preferences on their future self. Their future self might seek to defeat such a commitment device.

spiteful is behaving in a way that makes others worse off at the expense of the actor.

standard normal distribution is a normal distribution with a mean of 0 and variance of 1. Thus, the probability that a standard normal variable falls between -2 and 2 is approximately 0.95.

stationarity requires that the magnitude of discounting utility between time periods depends only the amount of time between the two periods considered. The fully additive model of time discounting imposes that decision maker is indifferent between consuming c at time t and c' at time t' if $U(c) = \delta^{t'-t}U(c')$, where the discount only depends on the interval between t and t' and not the starting time.

status quo bias is a tendency by a consumer to continue with current consumption decisions even when new attractive opportunities arise.

stochastic dominance rank orders two gambles. Let gambles A and B have possible outcomes $x_1, \ldots, x_n$, such that $x_i < x_{i+1}$. Further, let gamble A have associated probabilities $p_1, \ldots, p_n$ and gamble B have associate probabilities $q_1, \ldots, q_n$. Gamble A stochastically dominates gamble B if for all $i = 1, \ldots, n, \sum_{j=1}^{i} p_i \leq \sum_{j=1}^{i} q_i$. If gamble A stochastically dominates gamble B, then A is always preferred under expected utility theory.

strategy is a collection of the actions a player will take at each possible node of a game should that node be reached.

strictly revealed preferred An allocation $w = (w_1, w_2)$ is strictly revealed preferred to $w' = (w'_1, w'_2)$ if it is directly revealed preferred and if $p_1 w'_1 + p_2 w'_2 < p_1 w_1 + p_2 w_2$.

strong axiom of revealed preference If s_1 is indirectly revealed preferred to s_2, then s_2 is not directly revealed preferred to s_1.

strong loss aversion is displayed by a value function if for any two positive numbers z_1 and z_2 with $z_1 < z_2$ it is always the case that $v_g(z_2) - v_g(z_1) < v_l(z_2) - v_l(z_1)$. This requires that a loss function always has a greater slope than the gain function a given distance from the reference point.

subadditivity occurs when the sum of probability weights over all possible outcomes is less than 1. This has been used as one explanation for the certainty effect, because it implies a penalty associated with uncertain outcomes relative to outcomes with certainty (which always have perceived probability 1).

subgame-perfect Nash equilibrium of a game is a set of strategies that constitute a Nash equilibrium in every subgame.

subjective expected utility theory is a theory of how people make decisions under ambiguity. In subjective expected utility theory, the decision maker hypothesizes a single probability distribution of outcomes associated with each action and then maximizes expected utility theory based upon this probability distribution.

subproportional requires that the value function increases in elasticity as the absolute value of consumption increases. Let $z_2 > z_1 > 0$, and let $0 < \Delta < z_1$. Then we can express this requirement in terms of arc elasticities as $\frac{(2z_2 + \Delta)[v(z_2 + \Delta) - v(z_2)]}{\Delta[v(z_2 + \Delta) + v(z_2)]} > \frac{(2z_1 + \Delta)[v(z_1 + \Delta) - v(z_1)]}{\Delta[v(z_1 + \Delta) + v(z_1)]}$ and $\frac{-(2z_2 + \Delta)[v(-z_2 + \Delta) - v(-z_2)]}{\Delta[v(-z_2 + \Delta) + v(-z_2)]} > \frac{-(2z_1 + \Delta)[v(-z_1 + \Delta) - v(-z_1)]}{\Delta[v(-z_1 + \Delta) + v(-z_1)]}$ or in terms of exact elasticities as $\frac{z_2 v'(z_2)}{v(z_2)} > \frac{z_1 v'(z_1)}{v(z_1)}$ and $-\frac{z_2 v'(-z_2)}{v(-z_2)} > -\frac{z_1 v'(-z_1)}{v(-z_1)}$. A subproportional value function displays smaller relative differences in utility between relatively large outcomes compared to the difference in utility of two relatively small outcomes of the same proportions. Another way to state this requirement is that whenever $z_2 > z_1 > 0$, and $\alpha > 1$, $v(z_2)/v(\alpha z_2) < v(z_1)/v(\alpha z_1)$, hence the name subproportionality.

sunk cost is investment in a project that cannot be avoided nor recovered.

sunk cost fallacy is displayed when sunk costs influence decisions to continue a project. Here people might try to recover sunk costs by engaging in a losing project.

superadditivity occurs when the sum of probability weights over all possible outcomes is greater than 1. This can lead to preferences for stochastically dominated outcomes.

support is a range of possible values for a random variable.

T

time-inconsistent preferences occur when people make decisions for their future selves that they later regret. This is generally due to people not being able to anticipate their preferences in some future state.

transaction utility is enjoyment or pleasure consumers derive from feeling they have received a good deal on a purchase or paid a relatively low price for the level of consumption.

transactions costs are time or resources that must be spent to effect a transaction. These costs benefit neither of the primary parties of the transaction directly.

transitive preferences imply that if bundle a is preferred to bundle b, and bundle b is preferred to bundle c, then bundle c cannot be preferred to bundle a. Transitivity is a general requirement of rational decision theory.

transparency refers to the clarity with which a gamble is presented. People violate expected utility much more often when gambles are presented in a way that obscures stochastic dominance or other relationships between gambles. Transparent gambles tend to lead to more consistently rational behavior.

transparent means that people can easily discern their payout from each possible action without making complicated calculations or guesses.

trust refers to a person's willingness to place others in a position to make decisions that could either help or harm the person.

trust game refers to a game in which a sender is endowed with money that she may send to a second player, called a receiver. Any money sent is tripled. The receiver then decides how much of this money to return to the sender. The sender must trust the receiver in order to send money. The receiver is said to reciprocate if she returns more money than was sent.

two-part tariff is a pricing scheme that charges a fixed access fee for consumption in addition to a fixed marginal price for consumption.

two-tailed test is a statistical test of an initial hypothesis that can be represented as an equality. Thus, if one were to test the hypothesis that $\theta = \theta_0$, where θ is the unknown parameter and θ_0 is the hypothesized value, one would use a two tailed test.

U

ultimatum game is a game in which player 1 proposes a division of a money reward between both players. Player 2 can then either accept the split, resulting in that split being realized, or reject the proposal, resulting in a zero payout to both players.

uncertainty is a situation in which the decision maker faces either unknown probabilities associated with outcomes resulting from her choices or is not aware of the possible outcomes. This is often referred to as ambiguity.

unraveling effect refers to the inability of rational agents to cooperate in a sequential move game such as the take-it-or-leave-it game in order to obtain larger payoffs for both players. In each stage of the game, players choose larger immediate payoffs rather than turning control of the game to the other player.

utility of wealth is a function describing the consumer's preferences over levels of wealth. This function is used in expected utility theory to describe risk preferences. People who display diminishing marginal utility of wealth (a concave function of wealth) behave risk averse, and those with increasing marginal utility of wealth (a convex function of wealth) behave risk loving.

V

variance is a measure of the dispersion of a random variable. The variance is larger if there is a greater probability of the random variable falling farther away from the mean. Variance can be defined as $\sigma^2 = E[(x - E(x))^2]$.

Vickrey auction is a second-price sealed-bid auction. No bidders may know what others will bid before submitting their own bid. The highest bidder wins the auction and pays a price equal to the second-highest bid.

visceral factors are emotions, physical appetites, or other physical factors that can be aroused. Visceral factors (such as hunger or anger) can fluctuate, but they influence individual preferences.

W

warm glow refers to a feeling of satisfaction obtained from knowing one has contributed to a public good.

weak axiom of revealed preference If s_1 is directly revealed preferred to s_2 then s_2 is not directly revealed preferred to s_1.

weighted expected utility theory supposes that one's preferences can be represented by maximizing the function $U = \dfrac{\sum_{i=1}^{n} p_i u(x_i)}{\sum_{i=1}^{n} p_i v(x_i)}$. This function allows for indifference curves that are straight lines but that fan out across the Marschak–Machina triangle.

windfall gain is any unexpected income, though usually referring to large income events.

winner's curse is the tendency for the highest bidder in a common-value auction to have bid more than he anticipated relative to the actual value of the item. The highest bidder is the most likely to have bid more than the value of the item, leading to an unanticipated lower expected payout or even a negative expected payout.

X

χ-cursed equilibrium of a game is given by the set of strategies such that each player maximizes their own expected payout assuming probability χ that all other players' actions are not related to their underlying estimate of valuation, and $(1 - \chi)$ probability is assigned to the event that all other players are fully strategic in responding to their estimate of valuation.

INDEX